D1179105

Great
World War II
Air Stories

Great World War II Air Stories

Enemy Coast Ahead
Guy Gibson
VC DSO DFC

The Last Enemy
Richard Hillary

Reach for the Sky
Paul Brickhill

Enemy Coast Ahead first published in Great Britain
in 1946 by Michael Joseph Ltd

The Last Enemy first published in Great Britain
in 1942 by Macmillan London Ltd

Reach for the Sky first published in Great Britain
in 1954 by William Collins Sons & Co Ltd

This edition first published in Great Britain in 1985 by

Octopus Books Limited
59 Grosvenor Street
London W1

in collaboration with

William Heinemann Limited
10 Upper Grosvenor Street
London W1

and

Martin Secker & Warburg Limited
54 Poland Street
London W1

ISBN 0 7064 2317 8

Printed and Bound in Great Britain by Collins, Glasgow

Contents

Enemy Coast Ahead

Guy Gibson
VC DSO DFC

INTRODUCTION

This is a magnificent story, well and simply told by as great a warrior as these Islands ever bred. It is also History.

Guy Gibson was not a professional airman; he joined the service in peace time 'because he wanted to learn to fly'. War supervened and he remained an airman until his death in action.

His natural aptitude for Leadership, his outstanding skill and his extraordinary valour marked him early for command; for Great Attempts and Great Achievements. His personal contribution towards victory was beyond doubt unsurpassed.

In every facet of his character he was a thoroughbred. He was not only admired but loved by all who knew him.

In this book he tells of the Bomber's work as he saw it from the necessarily somewhat circumscribed viewpoint of an individual cog in a vast machine, as Commander of a Flight and later of a Squadron.

Guy Gibson fought from the first days of the 'phoney' war (phoney because we had nothing to keep fighting with) until his death. He lived to see the dawn of certain victory; and no one man did more to bring it about. He would not stop fighting. He resisted or avoided all efforts to rest him from operations. For his first 'rest' he asked to be transferred to night fighting, and as a highly skilled night pilot he was of great value to Fighter Command in raising and training the night-fighting force which eventually defeated the 'blitz'. To enforce a second 'rest' on him I had to make a personal appeal to another warrior of similar calibre – Winston Spencer Churchill – who there and then ordered Gibson down to Chequers and took him with him to the United States. There he arranged for Gibson to be detained for a short period of travelling round air bases to talk to American airmen. In a third and final effort to force him to rest from operations, he was put on his Group's staff. A few days later he was found in his office with – literally – tears in his eyes at being separated from his beloved crews and unable to go on operations.

It was in fact breaking his heart.

He always had direct access to me, and on further pressure from him and his AOC I quite wrongly allowed him to return to operations.

He appointed himself 'Master Bomber' – the most dangerous and most vital task of all – on his last operation, which was of course, a complete success. He was heard to give his crews a pat on the back over the radio and start them homeward. He never returned.

Throughout the story something is indicated of the difficulties of obtaining the means and the equipment which during the last eighteen months of the war enabled us to find and hit ever smaller objectives, under more and more difficult conditions. That is another story, of the wonderful achievements of our scientists, which will some day I hope be written. The difficulties were immense, but they were overcome. No one did more than Guy Gibson to overcome them.

It may well be that the references to 'parties' and 'drunks' in this book will give rise to criticism, and even to outbursts of unctuous rectitude. I do not attempt to excuse them, if only because I entirely approve of them. In any case, the 'drunks' were mainly on near-beer and high rather than potent spirits.

Remember that these crews, shining youth on the threshold of life, lived under circumstances of intolerable strain. They were in fact – and they knew it – faced with the virtual certainty of death, probably in one of its least pleasant forms. They knew, well enough, that they owed their circumstances to the stupidity, negligence and selfishness of the older generations who since 1918 had done little to avert another war and even less to prepare for it.

If, therefore, something of cynicism was occasionally manifest in their attitude to whatever might remain to them of life, and if on occasion the anticipation of an event, or the celebration of a success and an unexpected survival, called for a party, for the letting off of steam in an atmosphere of eat, drink and be merry, for next time we shall most certainly die – who amongst the older generations who sent them and tens of thousands like them to their deaths, will dare criticize?

If there is a Valhalla, Guy Gibson and his band of brothers will be found there at all the parties, seated far above the salt.

ARTHUR HARRIS

FOREWORD AND DEDICATION

In writing this book on the past four years of war, I have had to work without notes, and without help from diaries. I have never kept a diary because I never even dreamt that the lot would fall to me, in 1944, to try to describe the work of aircrews in Bomber and Fighter Squadrons. The fact that I have been extremely lucky to have survived must go without saying. Only a few will disagree, and they don't know. But I hope that living people who have served with me will forgive me if I have left them out, or worse, put words into their mouths which they never said. A memory is a short thing, and flak never does it much good. However, the aim of this book is to illustrate the growth of a small baby in 1939 to the awesome colossus that it has become today – the growth of Bomber Command.

Not only in size and bomb capacity, but also in accuracy it has achieved immense proportions, and has now reached the stage, perhaps the ultimate stage, when whole industrial areas or single factories can be wiped off the face of the earth in a single night, despite weather conditions and despite opposition over the target itself.

In admiring the air crews who are now engaged in completing the destruction of the Third Reich, we must remember that their lot, side by side with the American daylight crews, is to wage the toughest war of all. The losses in percentage in any one air raid are not unduly high – rarely above ten per cent – but remember this used to go on for some sixty missions, and the bare fact remains that out of a squadron of twenty-five crews, not many are left at the end of three months. Well, these boys know all this, and yet not in the slightest degree does it deter them from pressing home their attack with the highest possible sense of duty; in fact, they are proud to be members of the only offensive team bringing the war home to the Germans, inside Germany itself. These boys have got guts; and they must have or they never would be able to do the job.

Nor must we forget the ground crews, who make these raids possible by their untiring efforts under very tiring conditions. Nor the Squadrons and the Groups, and the WAAF and the clerks, the Ministry of Economic Warfare, the Directors of Bombing Operations in the Air Ministry, and Air Chief Marshal Harris himself and his staff. And perhaps, above all, the scientists and MAP backroom boys who have made such progress.

It will happen that by the time this book is published new events will be taking place in Europe. New place-names may be appearing in the headlines of our daily papers, and the role of the heavy bombers may even be changed to that of tactical necessity rather than strategical. If that is the case, then let no one forget the work done by home-based bombers during the dark years of 1940, 1941, 1942 and 1943, who alone fought the enemy on his own ground, and alone stand as one of the mighty factors that have brought about the changed war situation. All-powerful in the war, let the bombing forces be all-powerful in peace over Europe . . . Then, when one task has been done, the yellow skies of Japan will hear the same dreaded hum of thousands of aircraft, American and British, the same crump of bigger and better block-busters and the rattle of cannons. And the Japs won't like it.

To dedicate a book of this nature is not easy. Many different people are involved. Above all, I should like to mention the wives, the sweethearts and the mothers of all crews operating from this country against Germany.

Peace and war are vastly different. But the atmosphere our crews live in is shared by their next of kin. One moment they are together living their own lives and happy; a man and wife walking hand in hand down a country lane may in a few hours be separated, perhaps for ever. True, sailors leave home for the countless dangers of the Seven Seas, but their people have not got a television set which can see them every few days dive-bombed, torpedoed, undergoing the hardships of war on the sea. Those at home worry, but they don't know, and they don't want to know. A soldier in the front line, it is true, lives in the turmoil of battle; but his girlfriend does not see him every week grimy, unshaven, stepping over the dead bodies of his comrades to advance another few yards. His people cannot see him doing his job.

But picture peaceful England on a cool spring evening; the flowers are blooming, the hum of serenity is in the air. Suddenly there is a snarl of four motors, and a few hours later your airman is fighting the hell of flak and destruction over the target.

At home they wait, brave and patient, asking the same questions, again and again: I hope he gets back all right; when are they due? It is grim for them, grim and terrible. For this reason I should like to dedicate this book to 'Those at Home': my wife – your sister – his brother – the girlfriends – and the mothers. But I know they would say no. They are brave people, and like all brave people they would have it no other way but to turn their heads aside and say: Give this book to Them.

I therefore dedicate this book to the boys who have not been so lucky; who have given all they can give to their country for Freedom's sake. Let us never, never forget Them.

To the following Pilots and their Crews who fought with me against our enemy:

83 Squadron

P/O Keith Brooke-Taylor	Killed	April	7, 1940
P/O Wilfred Roberts	Killed	April	7, 1940
F/O Kenneth Sylvester	Missing – Presumed killed	April	15, 1940
F/O Neville Johnson	Killed	May	15, 1940
P/O Alan Vagg	Killed	May	15, 1940
Sgt Stanley Jenkins	Killed	May	23, 1940
Sgt Peter Josse	Killed	May	23, 1940
P/O Charles Greenwell	Missing – Presumed killed	June	4, 1940
F/O Ian Haydon	Missing – Presumed killed	June	4, 1940
S/Ldr Denys Field	Missing – Presumed killed	June	6, 1940
Sgt George Little	Missing – Presumed killed	July	2, 1940
P/O Douglas Redmayne	Missing – Presumed killed	July	2, 1940
Sgt Cyril Hallet	Killed	July	8, 1940
Sgt Leonard Howard	Killed	July	8, 1940
P/O Oliver Launders	Killed	July	8, 1940
F/Lt John Bowman	Missing – Prisoner of war	July	21, 1940
Sgt Geoffrey Jones	Missing – Presumed killed	July	26, 1940
P/O Bill Tweddell, DFC	Missing – Presumed killed	July	26, 1940
T/W/O Walter Barber	Missing – Prisoner of war	Aug	9, 1940
P/O Ian Muir	Missing – Prisoner of war	Aug	9, 1940
F/O Ellis Ross, DFC	Missing – Presumed killed	Aug	13, 1940
F/Lt Allen Mulligan	Missing – Prisoner of war	Aug	13, 1940
Sgt Douglas Hayhurst	Missing – Prisoner of war	Sept	16, 1940
A/S/Ldr James Pitcairn-Hill DSO, DFC	Missing – Presumed killed	Sept	19, 1940
S/Ldr Anthony Bridgman, DFC	Missing – Prisoner of war	Sept	24, 1940
Sgt James Loveluck	Missing – Presumed killed	Oct	26, 1940

29 Squadron

P/O L. G. H. Kells	Missing from 'Battle Climb' in Blenheim	Mar	1941
Sgt Skillen	Missing		1943
P/O Graham-Little	On leaving 29 Squadron joined one of the first Mosquito NF Squadrons. Killed in an air accident	May	1942
Sgt Freer	Killed at West Malling on the night of London's last Blitz	May	10, 1941
P/O D. Parker	Killed in action	Jan	1943
P/O D. Humphreys	Killed while on an intruder flight in a Hurricane; was S/Ldr DFC		
Sgt J. French	Posted to a Havoc Squadron, afterwards killed in a Hudson		
P/O D. I. Buchanan	Killed at Digby in a Beaufighter	Feb	1941
P/O R. Miles	Killed at Bluebell Hill, Wrotham	July	1941
P/O A. Grout	Destroyed 2 E/As on his 1st Op. Killed at Staplehurst	July	1941

106 Squadron

F/Sgt Appleyard, DFM	Killed on operational flight	July	26, 1942
P/O Worswick, DFC	Missing – Reported killed	June	2, 1942
W/O Young, R. F. H.	Missing – Reported killed	Aug	25, 1942
F/O Loftus	Posted	May	4, 1942
F/Sgt Bussell, H. C.	Missing – Presumed killed	Mar	30, 1942
W/O Merrals, DFC	Missing – Reported killed	Aug	1, 1942
F/Sgt Picken, W. J., DFC	Missing – Reported killed	Mar	5, 1943
P/O Dunlop-Mackenzie	Missing – Presumed killed	Mar	26, 1942
P/O Cann	Missing – Reported killed	Mar	26, 1942
P/O Duff, DFC	Posted	June	9, 1942
P/O Stoffer	Missing – Reported killed	April	24, 1942
P/O Prescot-Decie	Missing – Prisoner of war	April	24, 1942
F/Sgt Dimond	Missing – Presumed killed	Mar	30, 1942
Sgt Fixter	Missing – Prisoner of war	May	3, 1942
Sgt Power	Missing – Reported killed	April	17, 1942
F/Sgt Hard	Missing – Prisoner of war	May	3, 1942
S/Ldr Robertson, DFC	Missing – Reported killed	July	27, 1942
P/O Scratchard	Missing – Reported killed	April	17, 1942
P/O Grein	Missing – Reported killed	Aug	12, 1942
Sgt Wale	Missing – Reported killed	May	19, 1942
Sgt McHardy	Missing – Presumed killed	May	19, 1942
Sgt Brinkhurst	Missing – Reported killed	Dec	22, 1942
P/O Williams	Missing – Reported killed	Sept	14, 1942
P/O Coates	Missing – Reported killed	Aug	16, 1942
P/O Butterworth	Missing – Reported killed	Oct	3, 1942
P/O Crowfoot, DFC	Missing – Reported killed	Oct	16, 1942
P/O Broderick	Missing – Presumed killed	July	9, 1942
F/Lt Healey, DFM, DFC	Missing – Reported killed	Jan	13, 1943
Sgt Gaskell	Missing – Reported killed	Aug	1, 1942
Sgt Hart	Missing – Reported killed	June	2, 1942
P/O Carlile	Killed	July	21, 1942
Sgt Stamp	Missing – Prisoner of war	Sept	19, 1942
Sgt Butler	Missing – Reported killed	July	26, 1942
Sgt Marshman	Killed	July	21, 1942
P/O Downer	Missing – Presumed killed	Sept	14, 1942
S/Ldr Howell	Missing – Reported killed	Sept	14, 1942
Sgt Smith	Missing – Reported killed	Sept	8, 1942
Sgt Anderson	Missing – Reported killed	Dec	14, 1942
Sgt Abel	Missing – Reported killed	April	27, 1943

F/Lt Broderick, L. C. J.	Missing – Prisoner of war	April	13, 1943
F/Lt Curtin, Bar to DFC	Missing – Reported killed	Feb	21, 1943
F/Sgt Cronk	Missing – Reported killed	Jan	11, 1943
F/Sgt Hayward, VC	Missing – Reported killed	Feb	11, 1943
S/Ldr Hill	Missing – Reported killed	Oct	15, 1943
S/Ldr Hayward, E. L., DFC	Missing – Reported killed	Mar	29, 1943
Sgt Irvine	Missing – Presumed killed	April	8, 1943
F/Sgt McDonald	Missing – Reported killed	Mar	12, 1943
Sgt Markland	Missing – Reported killed	Feb	18, 1943
P/O McGregor	Posted	July	24, 1943
F/Sgt Phair	Missing – Reported killed	Jan	13, 1943
Sgt Piercy	Missing – Prisoner of war	Oct	15, 1942
P/O Page	Missing – Reported killed	June	24, 1943
Sgt Reed	Missing – Reported killed	Feb	3, 1943
Sgt Thompson	Missing – Prisoner of war	Feb	4, 1943
P/O White	Missing – Prisoner of war	Oct	13, 1942
F/O Wesley	Missing – Presumed killed	Feb	23, 1943
F/O Windsor	Missing – Reported killed	Feb	25, 1943

617 Squadron

S/Ldr Melvyn Young	Missing – Believed killed	May	17, 1943
S/Ldr Henry Maudslay	Missing – Believed killed	May	17, 1943
F/Lt David Astell	Missing – Believed killed	May	17, 1943
F/Lt John Hopgood	Missing – Believed killed	May	17, 1943
P/O Burpee (Canada)	Missing – Believed killed	May	17, 1943
P/O Byers (Australia)	Missing – Believed killed	May	17, 1943
F/Lt Barlow (Australia)	Missing – Believed killed	May	17, 1943
P/O Ottley	Missing – Believed killed	May	17, 1943
F/Lt H. S. Wilson	Missing – Believed killed	Sept	14, 1943
S/Ldr David Maltby	Missing – Believed killed	Sept	14, 1943
F/Lt Ralph Allsebrook	Missing – Believed killed	Sept	15, 1943
F/Lt L. E. S. Knight (Australia)	Missing – Believed killed	Sept	15, 1943
P/O Dival	Missing – Believed killed	Sept	15, 1943
S/Ldr George Holden	Missing – Believed killed	Sept	15, 1943
F/O Allan Rice	Missing – Believed killed	Dec	20, 1943
F/Lt Youseman	Missing – Believed killed	Nov	18, 1943

AND MY CREW

Missing, night September 15, 1943

F/O Spafford	'Spam'
F/O Taerum	'Terry'
F/Lt Hutchison	'Hutch'
P/O Deering	'Tony'
F/Lt Trevor-Roper	'Trev'

CHAPTER ONE

FLIGHT OUT

The moon was full; everywhere its pleasant, watery haze spread over the peaceful English countryside, rendering it colourless. But there is not much colour in Lincolnshire, anyway. The city of Lincoln was silent – that city which so many bomber boys know so well, a city full of homely people – people who have got so used to the Air Force that they have begun almost to forget them. Lincoln with its great cathedral sticking up on a hill, a landmark for miles around. Little villages in the flat Fenland slept peacefully. Here nice simple folk live in their bastions on the East Anglian coast. The last farmer had long since gone to bed; the fire in the village pub had died down to an ember; the bar, which a few hours ago was full of noisy chattering people, was silent. There were no enemy aircraft about and the scene was peaceful. In fact, this sort of scene might not have changed for a hundred years or so. But this night was different – at least different for 133 men: 133 young fliers, and I was one of those men. This was the big thing. This was it.

We were flying not very high, about 100 feet, and not very far apart. I suppose to a layman it was a wonderful sight, these great powerful Lancasters in formation, flown by boys who knew their job. Below us, and also practically beside us, at 200 miles an hour flashed past trees, fields, church spires and England.

We were off on a journey for which we had long waited, a journey that had been carefully planned, carefully trained for, a mission which was going to do a lot of good if it succeeded; and everything had been worked out so that it should succeed. We were off to the Dams.

Those who have seen a Lancaster cockpit in the light of the moon, flying just above the earth, will know what I mean when I say it is very hard to describe. The pilot sits on the left of a raised, comfortably padded seat fitted with arm-rests. He usually flies the thing with his left hand, resetting the gyro and other instruments with his right, but most pilots use both hands when over enemy territory or when the going is tough. You have to be quite strong to fly a Lancaster.

In front of him the instruments sit winking. On the sperry panel, or the blind-flying panel as bomber pilots call it, now and then a red light, indicating that some mechanism needs adjusting, will suddenly flash on. The pilot of a bomber must know everything. He must know the duties of the rest of the crew inside out, and should be able to take any one of them over should the occasion arise. The flight-engineer is the pilot's mate and sits beside him watching the engine instruments. Most flight-engineers were ground mechanics of Bomber Command who have volunteered to fly on operations, and a grand job of work they do too.

It is warm inside and both pilot and flight-engineer are very lightly clad, their oxygen masks hanging on one strap from the corner of the face. These masks are necessary evils. When over enemy territory they are worn continuously, not only because oxygen is required but because the pilot has no time to take his hand off the wheel and put the microphone up to his face. The result is that one gets quite chapped after six hours with the thing on. Many times the question is asked, 'Why can't we have throat microphones like the Americans?'

Between the two front windows is a large instrument, perhaps the most important of all: the repeating compass, worked by a master unit at the back. The pilot's eyes constantly perform a non-stop circle from the repeater to the ASI,* from the ASI to the horizon, from the horizon to the moon, from the moon to what he can see on the ground and then back to the repeater. No wonder they are red-rimmed when he returns.

Such is the scene. The glass house. Soft moonlight. Two silent figures, young, unbearded, new to the world yet full of skill, full of pride in their squadron, determined to do a good job and bring the ship home. A silent scene, whose only incidental music is provided by the background hiss of air and the hearty roar of four Merlin engines.

In my Lancaster it was pretty warm even though Hutch had turned off the heat. I was in my shirtsleeves and my Mae West. Incidentally, my Mae West was a German one, pinched off some fellow shot down back in 1940, and the envy of the whole squadron. The windows were open and a jet of cool air was blowing in, making a tremendous screeching noice. I yelled to Pulford, the flight-engineer, at the top of my voice, 'Close that window, for Christ's sake.'

Pulford, a Londoner, and a sincere and plodding type, was pushing and struggling and at last got the thing closed; like the silence at the end of a crash the noise snapped off and we were in comparative silence. Then I spoke to Terry. 'Where are we now, Nav?'

'I think we are about a mile to port. I'll just check. What do you think, Spam?'

Spam was the bomb-aimer, and it was some time before he answered because he had been taking off his parachute harness and was now picking up his position from a roller map. It looked like a roll of lavatory paper. But no matter what it looked like, it had to do a pretty important job: the job of that roll and Spam and Terry was to get us to the target.

* Airspeed Indicator.

'Yeah, you're right, Terry, we are a little over a mile to port; there's the railway going to King's Lynn.'

Spam, the Australian, was the best bomb-aimer there is, but he was not too hot at map-reading, and Terry looked over my shoulder to check him up. Later he popped back into his cabin to make a quick calculation. Then I was told to alter course three degrees to starboard, and by the slightest pressure of the rudder the great Lancaster almost imperceptibly pointed her grim blunt nose a little farther south, and the boys on either side did the same.

After a while Terry spoke again:

'Ten minutes to the coast. We will be able to get a pretty good check there – we go slap over Yarmouth.'

Good boys these, Terry and Spam. F/O Taerum came from Calgary, Canada. He had a soft Canadian accent, was well educated and in love with a very nice girl, a WAAF from Ireland called Pat. Probably the most efficient navigator in the squadron, he had done about thirty-five trips and knew what he was doing. I never knew Terry to lose his temper over anything, but sometimes he and Spam would argue the point over where they were. Spam, or F/O Spafford, DFM, as his real name was, came from Melbourne, Australia. He was a grand guy and many were the parties we had together; in his bombing he held the squadron record. Just before, he had asked me if he could take off his parachute harness because we were flying so low, anyway, that we would not have been able to bale out even if we had the chance. But that just illustrates what he thought of flying. It was just one big gamble and he had put his counter on the right mark. Spam had done a little more than Terry, about forty trips, and used to fly with one of the crack pilots in 50 Squadron. When he came to our squadron I think he was a bit nervous of my flying, but he seemed to recover after his first few trips. Both had pretty good accents deriving from their respective Dominions. I have, if anything, a southern English accent which in the air sounds rather a drawl, with the result that when we, as the offensive team in the bomber, got annoyed with one another, no one, particularly ourselves, knew what the hell we were talking about, which was a pretty good thing anyway.

In the back sat Trev – in the rear-turret in Air Force parlance – and of all places in the bomber I think it is the most uncomfortable. He was in his shirtsleeves, too, but later on pulled on his old teddy-bear flying-suit, not because it kept him warm but because of its smell. All clothes which have been on a lot of raids have a smell, a peculiar but not unpleasant smell which shouts aloud to all bomber crews who are in the know that the wearer, or owner, whichever the case may be, is pretty experienced; a Gen-man. A wife or loving mother would send the thing to the laundry if she had her way, but you try to do that with the boys. As far as I can see, the stronger the smell the better it is liked!

F/Lt Algernon Trevor-Roper, DFM, rear gunner, came of a pretty good family, and all that sort of thing, was twenty-eight, English, Eton, Oxford and sixty-five trips. He was one of the real Squadron characters. At night he might go out with the boys, get completely plastered, but would be always up dead on time in the morning to do his job. He got his DFM for shooting down two fighters which tried to down him one night last year. Now his wife was living in Skegness and was about to produce a baby within the next few days. I guessed he was thinking of this. Anyway, he was pretty silent, because he hadn't said a word up to now. He was probably thinking exactly what I was thinking: was this the last time we would see England?

Farther forward Hutch was in his place at the wireless. He had flown with me on about forty raids and had never turned a hair. He was one of those grand little Englishmen who have the guts of a horse. On most trips he invariably got airsick, but after he had done his stuff just carried on as if nothing had happened. He was in love, too, with a girl in Boston. In the front turret was Jim Deering of Toronto, Canada, and he was on his first bombing raid. He was pretty green, but one of our crack gunners had suddenly gone ill and there was nobody else for me to take.

As I sat back in my comfortable seat I could not help thinking that there were seven men in a bomber bound for somewhere in Germany. Seven men with wives and sweethearts, for all we knew sleeping in one of the houses we had just roared over. England virtually was at peace, but we were at war, the toughest, hardest war there is, the bomber war. I had been in the racket for some time and it had become practically part of me, but when I thought of all the friends I knew who had come and gone, to be mere memories, a name on the casualty sheets in the Air Ministry, or the scroll of honour in a Squadron Mess, then I shuddered. After a while I just sat back in my comfortable seat and relaxed and dismissed these thoughts from my mind and concentrated on steering my course. Suddenly in the distance, like a great arc drawn across the land by silver paper, came the North Sea – the sea which now seemed unfriendly because we were going the wrong way. I hoped it would look different a few hours later.

And then Terry was saying, 'Yes, there's Yarmouth coming up in front.'

'That's right.'

'Yeah, there's the harbour.'

'Sure it's Yarmouth?'

'That's it all right.'

'OK, alter course 110.'

'110 OK.'

'OK.'

And our noses were then going straight for the point at which we had to cross the Dutch coast. The sea was as flat as a mill-pond, there was hardly a ripple. Once we were over we dropped lower and lower down to about fifty feet, so as to avoid radio detection. I tried to put in George the automatic pilot, but unfortunately it was US, and as I engaged it the nose plunged forward and I just disengaged it in time. One of the aircraft on my left flashed me a red light, as if to say, 'What the hell are you doing?' Then I settled down again, but after a time tried to light a cigarette. In doing so we again nearly hit the drink, and the boys must have thought I was mad. In the end I handed the thing to Pulford to light for me. The night was so bright that it was possible to see the boys flying on each side quite clearly. On the right was John Hopgood, in M Mother, that grand Englishman whom we called 'Hoppy'; one of the greatest guys in the world. He was devoted to his mother and devoted to flying; used to go out with us a lot, get drunk – used to go out a lot to Germany and do a wonderful job. He had no nerves, he loved flying, which he looked upon rather as a highly skilled art in which one can only become proficient after a lot of experience. He was one of the boys who firmly refused to be given a rest and had done about fifty raids with me in my last squadron. Perfect at formation was Hoppy, too. There he was, his great Lancaster only a few feet from mine, flying perfectly steady, never varying position. Once when training for this raid we had gone down to Manston in Kent and shot up the field with wings inside tail-planes, and even the fighter boys had to admit it was the best they had ever seen. I should say Hoppy was probably the best pilot in the squadron.

On my other side, flashing him a message with his Aldis lamp, rather as ships do in a convoy at sea, was Micky Martin. Micky Martin came from Australia and he too had done a lot of flying. He was slightly more split-arse than Hoppy, and flying to him was nothing unless it was dangerous. In fact, many times after a raid on Berlin or Hamburg, instead of coming back with the boys at 22,000 feet, he would scream down to the deck and fly home via Holland, Belgium and France, shooting up anything he could see. That, to him, was a bit of fun and something that he and his crew liked. However, tonight he had to be good and stick to the plan because if he didn't things would go wrong, and so there he was flying dead level with Hoppy on the other side. Now and again he would drop down even lower than I was, and I was a bit frightened in case he hit the drink. But apparently he knew what he was doing because he never came closer than thirty feet to the water. Farther back were the rest of them – Melvyn Young from America, leading Bill Astell and David Maltby – followed by Henry Maudslay leading Dave Shannon and Les Knight, who were both Australian. This was my formation, and a great team they were.

The sea was calm as I had never seen it before, and as Micky got lower and lower on the water I could see his reflection quite clearly coming up to meet him. In the north there is that bomber boys' bad dream – the glow. Some scientists call it the Aurora Borealis, but you ought to hear what we call it when there are fighters about! That glow never disappears in the summer; and this was summer. The hours of darkness were limited; we had to go fast to get there and back in time.

There were no other aircraft operating in the whole of the home-based Air Forces. No one even knew that we were operating except for a few, and even they did not know where we were going.

But deep down in the ground two hundred-odd miles away were the Germans. In their plotting-rooms they sat watching their cathode-ray tubes, waiting for some indication that would set all their defences alert. The lower we flew the closer we could get before they picked us up, but I knew that at a range of about thirty miles they would get us even if our bomb-doors clove a furrow through the water. Then their guns would be ready. Then the fighters would take the air. Then there would be a chattering and a babbling in the Observer Corps plotting-rooms. And so, Huns and Quislings would set up late at night in sandbagged emplacements waiting for the roar of the Lancaster.

Hutch was reading the message.

'What is it, Hutch?'

'He says we are going to get damn drunk tomorrow night.'

'Send him back this: You're darn right we are. It's going to be the biggest binge of all time.' And then Hutch was busy flashing this message.

Soon we passed over a little convoy who engaged us with the challenge signal. We quickly fired the correct Very light before they opened up on us, and as usual they flashed us 'Good Hunting.' Hutch, who was as good with his Aldis lamp as he was with his key, and who did not drink, replied: 'We are going to get damn drunk tomorrow night.'

The skipper of the ship, whoever he was, did not reply because he must have been wondering whether this was a code message, or else we – the boys on board – were nuts.

As England receded far behind our tails, Terry, who had been quiet, had been working out our ground speed on the G Box, a special navigation instrument which shows the aircraft's position relative to the ground. He suddenly said: 'There's no wind tonight, Skip, so we shouldn't have any drift – but we'll just check, so I'll throw out a flame-float.'

Then he yelled to Trev behind: 'Will you get a drift, Trev?'

A little later Trev's voice was heard from the back. 'OK. There's no drift, the flame-float is about ten miles behind; it's still straight behind my guns.'

So Terry was very pleased and was able to get down to his calculations. Later he came up again and said unemotionally: 'Our ground speed is 203½ miles an hour; we will be there in exactly one hour and ten minutes, thirty seconds. We ought to cross the coast dead on track, so everything's fine. Incidentally, you're one degree off your couse.'

Navigators are funny chaps. They always think a fellow can steer a course to an absolute degree, and I smiled to myself as I swung myself back. Navigators have a union called 'The Navigators' Union', which is about the most powerful thing there is. Now they are even taking over squadrons, let alone being captains of aeroplanes, and, anyway, I think they deserve it. Navigation is a tricky job, and after four years of war they really know what they are doing. Probably for sheer precision the night navigators of Bomber Command are the best in the world, because they have to be for their very own sakes, for the laws of survival.

One hour to go, and one hour left before Germany, one hour of peace before flak. I thought to myself: here are 133 boys who have got an hour to live before going through hell. Some of them won't get back. It won't be me – you never think you are not coming back. We won't all get back, but who is it will be unlucky out of these 133 men? What are they thinking about?

Are they just thinking about their job, or steering their couse? What is the rear-gunner in Melvyn Young's ship thinking? Because he won't be coming back. What's the bomb-aimer in Henry Maudslay's ship thinking? Because he won't be coming back. What is the rear-gunner in Hoppy's plane thinking? What are his ideas on life? Because he is going to bale out at about eighty feet, survive by a miracle and be put in a prison camp. He and the bomb-aimer are going to be the only boys in this raid to be taken prisoner. The rest are going to be killed – those who don't get back. One hour to go, one hour to think of these things, one hour to fly on a straight course and then it will be weaving and sinking to escape the light flak and the fury of the enemy defence. And as I thought of these things, and many other things, of my wife, who thought I was instructing; my dog, who was killed last night; of the scientists who made this raid possible. I wondered, what am I doing here, anyway? How am I here? Why have I been so lucky? And I began to think of those first few days when the war became a reality and we became changed from peacetime Air Force playboys to fellows faced with death many days in a year, every year, for four years.

CHAPTER TWO

PEACE AND WAR

August 31, 1939, was a pretty hot day. I was sitting on the centre-board of a little sailing dinghy, clad in swimming-trunks, trying to get a tan from the early autumn sun. At the same time I was trying to splice a broken sheet, a job which I found very difficult even though I had been a Scout some years back. The sun was terrific. The sea had taken on a deep hazy blue colour.

In the back of the boat, surrounded by cushions, sat Ann, blonde and pretty. She was asleep. Windy, my all-swimming and all-flying cat, who had put in more flying hours than most cats, lay purring on her lap. I gazed at her reflectively, thinking of many things. A few hundred yards off lay the shore. I could faintly hear the murmur of the surf, but it was not rough today, and so we, anchored a little way out, were only slightly moving. This suited Ann, who, though glamourous, was apt to get seasick.

From Monkstone Beach came the noisy chatter of children building castles, playing leapfrog and generally making the beach one vast happy playground. One group, I remember, were hurriedly building a small sea wall to protect their elaborate sandcastle. As the tide came in, wave after wave would lap against the wall, crumbling it. Now and then a larger wave would cause a small breach and some water would go into the moat. This would quickly become a weak spot in the defences, but instantly willing spades dug in sand, fast and furiously, to repair the breach; but at last it was all over and an extra big wave washed the whole lot away, amidst shrieks and yells, and also amidst the wetting of many small pairs of pants! Then they packed up for lunch.

I could not help thinking that the little scene was significant. Although war seemed very distant, I was fully up with the news, and there was no doubt that this was pretty grim. Germany had delivered an ultimatum to Poland; this had been rejected. Berlin had said 'Unless . . .' and then there was that Russo-German Pact.

I never thought that Poland would fight for her Corridor. She had cavalry, Germany had tanks. She had only a few ancient aircraft, Goering had long been telling the world the strength of his pet baby, the Luftwaffe. And if Germany invaded Poland we would be in it too. Then what?

We were unprepared; only last week I had been flying in our summer home defence exercises. Twice we had 'raided' London from the direction of Holland. On neither occasion had we seen any 'enemy' fighters, and flown on another 150 miles to 'flatten' the English Air Force Headquarters at Abingdon. When we landed we had boasted about this to all and sundry, but later on the Army told us that we had been 'shot down' by anti-aircraft fire when we crossed the English coast on the way in. This tickled us a lot because, although this was just sheer wishful thinking on the part of the ack-ack boys, we had, in fact, been fired at by the Hook of Holland. The formation leader of our wing had swung rather wide when making his turn there, with the result that the squadron on the left infringed neutral territory. This was my baptism of fire, and it looked to me very cissy, just a few black puffs in the sky; but how lovely it was to be ignorant, and anyway, they were shells fired by friendly guns and were some way away, although accurate for height.

But bad though the situation was today, it had been much worse last year. Then we did not even possess Hampden bombers, but operated in Hawker Hinds, top speed 185, load 500 pounds, range 200 miles. Yes, this crisis was better than the last. It was a standing joke in Lincolnshire last year that we bomber boys did everything in the way of preparation for war, while Chamberlain and Hitler were conceiving a world safe for Democracy. We had loaded our guns, we had filled our tanks, we had even camouflaged our aeroplanes in war-paint. The only snag was there had been no bombs on the station. These turned up three weeks later!

Anyway, it was no use thinking of these things; it would not do any good. Besides, this was my holiday, and I began to go to sleep, conscious only of the hot sun on my back and the ripple of the waves on the free-board of the boat. War for me just did not exist.

Suddenly a boat slipped by and a voice woke me up. 'Hey, Guy, there is a telegram for you on the beach.'

This was the son of the local doctor, a keen sailing enthusiast himself. So what? A month or two back I had taken a long navigation course. Maybe the telegram came from the Adj to say that I had failed, or passed. 'Thanks, John – you woke me up,' I yelled after him, but John was already some distance away trying to get the best out of a calm day.

On the beach there was a boy, the apple of the eye of his proud parents, whom I knew slightly. For good or for bad, this boy could swim a few strokes, and here was his opportunity to show his young girl friend that he was much better than Bill, his ten-year-old rival. And so, telegram in mouth, he had jumped into the warm water and was approaching. I watched him with indifferent interest with Ann, who had by now come to. He was swimming rather like a crab, a mixture of side and breast stroke, and making a noise like a hyena, and my telegram was getting wet. As he got closer I could see that it was not a greetings telegram. At last he reached the side, but we could not get him aboard because before I could grab his hand he had turned and begun his struggling journey back to the beach.

I looked at the telegram. The ink had run, but I could see it had been addressed to the village post-office. This was because I had not known my address when I came away and actually I was staying at Mrs. Thompson's for the modest sum of 4s. 6d. a day – a price which suited my flying-officer's pay very well. The telegram was marked 'Urgent'. The daughter of the village postman, who knew me slightly (I think I met her at a village hop), had seen this and had jumped on her bike and brought it down to the beach. Ann's voice broke the silence.

'Hadn't you better open it?'

Still thinking of Exams I read it aloud. It was pretty straightforward. All it said was, 'Return to Unit immediately'.

Two hours later I had packed. I had given Windy to Mrs. Thompson to look after for the duration, but I knew that she would never recognize me again. Then came a lot of goodbyes. Goodbyes to the Crawfords, at whose house I had stayed last summer; there were a few tears, and I felt like a film war hero about to return to the front. Goodbye to Ann. Goodbye to Ruth Windsor Bowen, with whom I had quarrelled earlier in the season and had just made it up. I'd had a date with her the night before, but she had gone off with another chap. There was Desmond, who had just joined the Army. There were many others, but I cannot remember their names.

Then Freddy Bilbey drove up in his Alvis. Freddy had just come down from Oxford, where he had been reading biology. He was twenty-three, fair-haired, good-looking and a great friend of mine. His Alvis was 1928 vintage, and as we set off down the village, receiving a friendly wave from odd fishermen and yokels whom we knew so well, that raucous exhaust blared out its tune for the last time.

As we snorted down the road, overtaking anything going our way in a most alarming manner, we kept silent. At Carmarthen we stopped for an early supper and mine host of the 'Boar's Head' gave us two most beautiful steaks and some good beer to wash them down. Then, on our way again, past Brecon through the valley to Hereford. Then on the broad highway to Stratford-on-Avon. Several times we lost our way.

Already signs of coming war were apparent, particularly in the great queues for petrol outside filling-up stations; I suppose everyone thought that petrol would be rationed on the first day of war. Many times we passed cars packed with luggage and families on the way back to their own homes, probably to find when they got there that most of the children, anyway, would have to be evacuated back to the country again.

As we whirled along, my thoughts were mixed. I had a feeling of dull, pent-up excitement, a funny empty feeling, because this time it might be the real thing. It was Freddy who broke the silence.

'You know, Guy, it is a queer feeling, this – we don't know, either of us, what we are going to do in the next few days, do we? Yesterday we were looking forward to a cocktail party. Now what are we going to do? I don't suppose you have any idea.'

'I certainly don't. If there is a war – and I'm afraid it looks mighty like it – my squadron will be used for close support in France, and I don't suppose we will live long enough to know much about it, or care.' I was convinced of this; that is why I said it. 'But, surely, you'll have to use your medical experience in some way?'

'Yes, I'm OK. I have finished with Oxford and passed my MD. I think I'm going down to Kent to an advance dressing-station which will move into France as soon as things get hot. I think it's going to be pretty bloody.'

I smiled to myself. Freddy, the idealist, the doctor. He was going to save lives, and I, a realist, was going to take them. Two jobs of war both very different, both very necessary, and as I watched the countryside roll by I wondered what would happen, what this time next year would hold for me.

How I loathed the Nazis. How could the common people of Germany allow such a world-conquering crowd of gangsters to get into power and stay in power? Ruthlessness and swaggering, domineering brutality, that was their creed. The Rhineland, Austria, Czechoslovakia, Abyssinia and Albania, the beginning of a long list. I thought of the children playing on the beach with the sand-wall and their magnificent sand-castle. How that little scene was like the world situation. The oncoming tide was Nazism. The sandcastle was freedom and the children were the Democracies. Their own weak wall was no protection against the massing, encircling rush of the water. But if only they had built it in time, before the tide had begun to come in, with sand and stone and cement and with the aid of all the other children who were sitting idly on the beach. Then the tide could have been held until it had receded again. If only nations would stick together when international freedom was in danger, whatever their ideals, whatever their language, then they could muster such armed forces that the aggressor would be unable to break the vital barrier.

America was saying this was a European war. 'Let's stay out.' Russia had made her pact. The rest of the friendly neutrals were strictly non-belligerent, and it looked as if France and England would have to carry the baby.

I was no serviceman; I joined the Air Force in 1936 purely to learn to fly. Last April I was due to leave the RAF to become a test-pilot – a good job with plenty of money in it – but Mussolini had put paid to that when he invaded Albania. Now Hitler had ruined my summer leave and was likely to do the same thing for many more summers to come.

That England was unprepared there was no doubt. Although the Navy talked about the big blockade which would bring Germany to her knees in six months, although the lion had its wings, what were the facts? We had very few bombers, mostly Wellingtons, Hampdens and, perhaps best of all, the good old Whitleys. None of these could carry many bombs and only a few could even find their targets. Navigation was at a very low ebb. Our fighters were mostly Gladiators and Mark I Hurricanes and a squadron of Spitfires. Typhoons and Lancasters were but twinkles in their designers' eyes.

Of flying training-schools there were few and those were in easy range of German bombers. The Empire Air Training Plan had not even been put into operation. What would happen after the initial wastage? Would we go on fighting, getting smaller and smaller until there was nothing left? The last few war pilots serving in the RAF today told us that the life of the average bomber boy was only about ten hours in the air. There's no future in that. What would happen to the towns and factories when the Germans started bombing them on the first day? We had no anti-aircraft defence of any strength. Only this summer I had been invited by a Brigadier to attend the standard Army summer game of shooting at a pilotless aeroplane, the 'Queen Bee', down at Manorbier. I went, and for two hours watched the Army gunners fire hundreds of shells at the little biplane as it flew forward and backwards over their heads at 5,000 feet. It was pretty poor shooting and it wasn't even touched. However, when it glided down to make its pilotless landing, 'George' held off too high and it crashed on one wing into the sea. I remember an Army officer saying, 'Well, we got it in the end, didn't we?' and the look on the face of the RAF officer who had to repair it for the shoot next day!

Look at the state of the Army – few tanks, few modern weapons, few trained personnel, although it certainly wasn't their fault. Look at our own civilians; they even complained that we were keeping them awake when we flew over London trying to find out how to intercept the night bomber. They called us the playboys of Mayfair! Dull apathy and smug complacency seemed to be about to bring the British Empire tottering to its knees, if it didn't knock it out altogether.

In 1936 the Air Force had begun to expand, but the process had been painfully slow and even now we were not much bigger than we were in 1938.

Munich. What a show! But perhaps Chamberlain had done the right thing, who knows? All I knew was that, thank God, we did not make war in 1938.

As for France, our ally, what of her? In July we had flown down to Marseilles and back, over Paris and Lyons, to show the flag. On the way we passed over many airfields, but not once did we see a single French aircraft. Where were they all? Where was her Air Force? No one seemed to know. She, too, had had her fair share of 'finger trouble' in her Governments.

Why had two great nations come so low? Perhaps it was the old story.

The cream of their youth had fought the last war, and were either killed or too brassed off to try to pull their countries together afterwards. This left those other people to carry on. If, by any chance, we had a hope of winning this war – and it seemed very remote – then in order to protect our children let the young men who have done the fighting have a say in the affairs of State.

I had read books on the last war and knew that apart from the many lives lost and the chaos, misery and devastation it caused, new, evil and unknown things blighted the country, such as inflation, racketeers and industrial money-grabbers. I hoped that this would not happen in this war, and, if it did, that there would be the severest punishment for such criminals.

My thoughts were interrupted as we rumbled down Woodstock Road, past my old school, St Edward's, into Oxford. Freddy drew the old Alvis up in front of a pub and we went in to have a quick one. After a couple of beers, in walked some boys he knew. They were all in the same boat. Some were going to the Oxford University Squadron, others were going back to their army units, others were waiting for the Navy to call them up. We left after the twelfth can, feeling much better, and went to have dinner. It was fairly late and we were pretty hungry, and fed like kings with some excellent 1928 burgundy.

Then, after a few more drinks, I was almost literally poured into the train.

'Goodbye, Freddy; good luck.'

'Goodbye, Guy. God knows when I will see you again. All the best.'

And the train started north.

What a journey! The train had been blacked out. It was completely packed with soldiers and civilians, all going somewhere. After many stops, during which there was shouting and yelling and clinking of milk-cans, and with my hangover getting steadily worse, we arrived at Lincoln at 4 a.m. After much trouble and the signing of a couple of forms, I was taken by transport to Scampton. Sunny Scampton we call it because it is in Lincolnshire and one doesn't see much sun up there. It's a fine old Bomber Base dating from the last war, but as we drove in through the gates I saw that the windows had been blacked out and that the street-lighting had been switched off.

In the Officers' Mess there was a dim sinister blue light. You couldn't possibly see to read, but then there were not enough blackout curtains for every building. As I was having my breakfast and about to go to bed, all the boys came in. Normally there is no one about in an R.A.F. Officers' Mess at six o'clock in the morning, but this was different. They had been standing by since dawn. They had not changed; they were cheerful in their greetings.

'Wotcha, Gibbo!'

'Good leave, old boy?'

'Hullo, you old so-and-so; so you've come back for the war, have you?'

But a little later there was a silence when we heard that at dawn that morning Germany had invaded Poland, and I went to bed.

The next two days moved very quickly with tremendous activity on all sides. Complete bedlam reigned all over bomber stations in the north and ours was typical. There were tractors driving round the perimeter roads in the sweltering heat, some with long bomb trailers bouncing behind; others pulling our Hampdens along cinder tracks far into the country to dispersal points fairly safe from enemy bombs. All round the airfield sand-banked gun emplacements were being put up by aerodrome defence squads, but there were not many guns. Gas officers were running round placing yellow detectors in the right places. These detectors were of two kinds and always amused me. The yellow ones were supposed to turn red in the presence of gas, but they failed to do so on many an occasion. Then there was another which resembled a piece of cheese hanging on a hook. What these were meant to do I never found out, but the cheese was always disappearing – perhaps the birds in the district liked the stuff!

All the station transport was spread out over the whole area of the camp, so it was nothing out of the ordinary for the C.O. to find a petrol bowzer in his back garden. No one was allowed to leave the camp.

Deep down in the ground below station headquarters lived the denizens of the operations room. This was strictly out of bounds to everyone. At the door, a great half-inch steel structure, sat a couple of airmen armed with rifles. Many an identity card was examined here, and the two lads had the time of their lives turning away such ogres as the station warrant officer. Inside the gloom of the blue lights, moved WAAFs and clerks, preparing maps in many shapes, cutting them, clipping them, rolling them, folding them. There were maps of Holland, maps of France, the Siegfried Line; there was even a map of Berlin.

In another corner two officers were sorting out target maps. I noticed as I passed by that there was a photograph of Wilhelmshaven clipped to each. In the middle, surrounded by a huge desk, was the Station-Commander, looking very harassed. He had cause to be, for in front of him was a great pile of files marked 'War Plan: phase 1, phase 2', etc. All these were directives to be used only in time of war, or in case of mobilization. His round face was a puzzle, frowning at all this extraordinary activity. The frown would develop into a very black look now and then, especially when some WAAF giggled at something whispered to her by the pimply young airman who spent most of his time standing on a ladder pushing pins into a map on the wall.

In the hangars there was the ringing of metal against metal as cowlings were being beaten out and dents knocked in. There was that empty noise which all hangars have, drowned occasionally by the raucous voice of some fitter singing his weary love-song. And then the Flight-Sergeant, or 'Chiefy', would come rushing in and the song would stop.

Taking things all round there was, as the saying is, a tremendous flap going on.

Not so the air crews. We were sitting or lying on the grass in front of the Squadron Mess most of the day. The sun was beating down and most of us had taken off our flying kit, which was lying strewn around untidily and scattered in all directions. We were officially 'standing by'. For what, we did not know, but we thought it was sure to be a bombing raid somewhere, sometimes. Conversation was carefree – of girls, of parties, but strictly limited about the war. We had all heard that our ambassador in Berlin had presented Hitler with an ultimatum asking for the withdrawal of German troops from Poland. There was still some hope. I was holding forth to my crew that we all had been recalled from leave too early and that it was a damn shame because Hitler would never bomb Great Britain until after the Nuremburg Rally on September 13.

As no one had been allowed to leave the camp, there had been some pretty heavy drinking going on at nights. As usual on these occasions, the squadrons concerned – our own and 49th, our deadly rivals in the camp – had had a pretty good beat up, and all the boys were quite content to sleep off their hangovers. At such a time as this I can only remember kaleidoscopic scenes: the C.O. roaring someone up for not having his parachute handy; anxious faces crowding round the radio for their hourly news bulletins, snatching hurried meals, then back to the hanger in an overcrowded truck. One poor chap fell off when the back dropped and broke his leg – he was our first war casualty. Those gramophone records, the heat. Extra large headlines in the newspapers every day, including a memorable 'No war this year'. My old batman, Crosby, coming in to wake me every morning at four o'clock saying in his doleful bass voice: 'Here's your cup of tea, Sir. The news is much worse today, Sir. Shall I run your bath, Sir?'

A world about to go mad. For us a funny feeling that the next day we might not be in this world.

And so September 3 found the boys of A Flight sitting in the Flight-Commander's office. We had just finished our morning tea, which a Naafi girl had brought in, and the room was full of smoke. Oscar Bridgman, the Flight-Commander, sat with his hat at the back of his head, his feet on the table and his chair liable to fall over backwards at any minute. He was a tremendous character, was Oscar. He had a quick temper, but could fly as well as any man. I could never wish for a better Flight-Commander and we were all right behind him. Then there were the rest of them. Jack Kynoch, tall, swimming champion, not too much sense of humour. There were Mulligan and Ross (we used to call them Mull and Rossy), two Australian boys who joined us back in 1937. They did nearly every thing together. Sometimes they would have long heated arguments which were the amusement of the whole Flight. There was Ian Haydon, English, married to a very pretty girl called Dell. Very wrapped up in Dell, Ian always shot off to Lincoln, where they lived, as quickly as possible every night. He was a bit morose because he hadn't been able to get home for a few nights. There was Silvo. What a chap! A tall fellow, who got into most amazing scrapes. There was Pitcairn-Hill, a permanent, and in fact the only permanent, commissioned officer in our Flight. He had been a boy at Halton. A straightlaced and true Scot. An excellent sportsman, Pit used to play rugger for the RAF. Then there were others whose names I need not mention but who were just as much a part of A Flight as any. We were proud of ourselves, we boys of A Flight, because we were always putting it across B both in flying and drunken parties.

Suddenly the door opened and in came Chiefy. 'All kites ready for testing.' 'OK, Flight,' said Oscar, as he took his feet off the desk, and F/Sgt Langford went out again. Great fellow was F/Sgt Langford. He was the NCO in charge of Maintenance in our Flight. For years he had been coming in saying that all aircraft were ready for testing, and no doubt he is still doing it to this very day.

I could write a lot about the ground crews. They are wonderful men and do a really hard job of work for very little pay; only their pride in their squadrons keeping them going.

Oscar had just been reciting a limerick about the Bishop of Belgrave when suddenly the door burst open and Crappy came in. Crappy Kitson looked as though he was about to have a baby. There was something wrong. He did not say much but just went over to the window and turned on the radio. In silence we listened to Chamberlain's solemn words telling the world that a state of war existed between Britain and Germany. So the balloon had gone up. This was war. No one knew quite what to say. Oscar inhaled slowly, then blew the smoke out though his nose. Then he said quietly and rather strangely: 'Well, boys, this is it. You had better all pop out and test your aeroplanes. Be back in half an hour's time. There will probably be a job for you do.'

I went off out to look over C Charlie and found her sitting on her usual dispersal point. She was my own aeroplane, and a lousy one at that. On take-off she swung like hell to the right and flew in the air with her left wing low. Sometimes an engine died out, but that was nothing. We loved her because she was ours. At that time I did not have a full crew, but my second pilot was a Somersetshire man called Jack Warner, and there was old MacCormick, Mac for short, who was my scruffy radio operator. It did not take long to check the old faithful over. The ground crew had done a good job of work and she was quite all right.

When we came to the Mess those terrible gramophone records pushed out by the BBC were grating on. We had a quick lunch, which was interrupted by the Tannoy: 'All crews to the lecture room immediately. That is all.'

We expected to be told to take off immediately for Germany, or to be told that the Germans were taking off immediately for us, but instead Group Captain Emmett, the Station-Commander, was there to give us an address. He did not say much. He was a big, kind-hearted South African, with fingers like a bunch of bananas, fond of food and drink. He said nothing much, just a few words – that we were now in the war, that he expected the full support of all officers and men on the Station to back him up and to back Bomber Command up in whatever operations we had to carry out. He told us that we would probably be operating according to the standard plan; that is, two weeks of maximum effort (which means raiding as often as possible), one week of sustained effort (which is approximately half the maximum), then one week of rest. He told us that the German Air Force was not very good, anyway, and was pretty sure to have suffered losses in Poland. Then we went back to finish our lunch. We waited all day but the dreaded order never came. That night the bar was empty. The boys were writing letters.

Next day Rossy and I went down to A Flight Office alone. I do not know where the other boys were – I think they were playing cricket out on the tarmac. Suddenly Leonard Snaith walked in. He was the Squadron-Commander; well known in the Air Force. One of the high-speed Schneider trophy pilots and a great fellow, he was a small man with a sad, mousy face. He, too, used to play rugger for the RAF and also held the quarter-mile record. In fact, he was an excellent type all round. But he had a slow temper and it was best not to get on the wrong side of Leonard. But he was not there to talk of rugger today.

He said in a strange voice, 'We are off on a raid.'

Rossy and I said nothing.

'We have got to provide six aircraft – three from A Flight and three from B Flight. I don't know where the target is. I think it is against shipping – probably German battleships. We are carrying four 500 pounders each; they have all got a delay of 11½ seconds, so we can go in pretty low. F/Lt. Collier is leading the three from B Flight. You two had better come with me. Take-off will be at 15.30.'

As I saw him write my name on a small scrap of paper my feelings were completely indescribable. A few days ago I was sunbathing, having the time of my life, carefree, looking forward to simple things, and now

I was going to war, probably never to come back. Rossy felt the same. Although he didn't say anything, his face was as good as a loudspeaker.

Soon everything was fixed. The crews had all been got together, the bombs had been put on our aeroplane, and we went to the briefing. Actually, to call it a briefing would be absurd. We all gathered round a table while the Station-Commander told us where we were going. 'You are going to attack the German pocket battleships which are lying in the Schillig Roads at the entrance to the Kiel Canal. If by any chance there are no warships there, you may bomb the ammunition depot at Marienhof, but on no account, and I must warn you that serious repercussions will follow, must you bomb civilian establishments, either houses or dockyards. The weather will be bad. You will have to attack very low. There have been some reports of balloons in this area, but you will not see them; they will be flying in the clouds. Do not stay in the area long. Return if you think that an attack cannot be carried through according to plan.'

After these words of wisdom, Snaith quickly outlined his plan. We were to take off in formation. I was to be on the right. Rossy on the left. When we approached the *Von Scheer* we were to spread out to about 500 yards on either side and attack from three directions. Someone asked what would happen if the bombs bounced off the armoured decks. The reply came from the Station Armament Officer, who said that the idea was to lodge the bomb in the superstructure, where it would go off after the aircraft had passed safely over it. Then spoke Pitt, a Flight-Lieutenant, who used to be a schoolmaster. He was now Station Intelligence Officer. He told us that ships of the pocket-battleship class were armed with machine guns, and read us a long paragraph from Air Publication 3,000, in which it is stated that the best height to attack in order to avoid flak is about 3,000 feet – that is, above the machine-gun fire and below the heavy flak fire. He again repeated that on no account were we to bomb Germany.

After that another man got up and told us how to take off with a bomb load on. None of us had ever done it before and we did not even know whether our Hampdens would unstick with 2,000 pounds of bombs. The advice we got was to ease them off by working the tail trimming tabs afer the tail had come up. If we were still on the ground when the hedge came along we were to yank back the stick as hard as we could and pull the emergency boost control. All this sounded good gen to us because nobody knew anything about it, but on looking back I sometimes think how absurdly little we did know at that time, bearing in mind that since then thousands of Hampdens have taken off with heavier bomb loads.

There was not much time to waste as we dashed down to the crew room, our plan of action ready. As we went out to the bus little Willie gave us one final word of advice. On no account were we to break formation unless he gave the signal. We were to stick together and act as an element, not as individuals. This was about two-thirty.

Just as we were climbing aboard the lorries to take us out to our aircraft a message came from Ops: Take-off delayed to 16.00.' This was a bit tough on the boys because they were now all fairly het up and most of them would have preferred to get into the air rather than hang around for another hour. So we lay in the sun, smoking, saying very little but thinking what an extraordinary thing it was that in a few hours' time we would know what aerial warfare was like.

At 15.30 another message came through to say that the takeoff was delayed until 17.00. This time a roar of four-letter words went up to greet the messenger. By now we were very nervous; in fact my hands were shaking so much that I could not hold them still. All the time we wanted to rush off to the lavatory; most of us went about four times an hour.

At last the time came to climb aboard the lorry and we moved off to our aircraft. The boys who were to be left behind stood round self-consciously; they did not know quite what to say because no one knew anything about this sort of thing. In the end they gave a quick wave of goodbye and someone said, 'Have a good time. See you tonight.'

As I climbed up into my pilot seat. Taffy, one of the ground crews, bent over my ear and said. 'Good luck, Sir; give those bastards a real hiding.' I don't think I replied, but smiled up at him with that sort of sickly smile which one gives when one does not quite hear what another fellow says. But Taffy, the rigger, was one of the old school. He knew what was wrong. and as he put my safety harness over my shoulders he made a funny remark. 'Now don't you worry,' he said. 'You will be OK. You will always come back.' Up to now he has been right.

At about five minutes to five we ran up our engines and then taxied out one after another, waiting for 49 boys to take off led by George Lerwill. It is still George's doubtful boast that he was the first aircraft in 5 Group to take-off for Germany.

One after another we watched them go. Some swung very badly, but apart from that did not seem to have much trouble for the take-off. And then off went Willie, followed by Rossy, a stream of dust blowing back making them completely disappear from view for a few minutes.

By now I was calm and quite ready for what was to come. I grasped the brake lever firmly and pushed both throttles to full, then I let off the brakes and the old Hampden slowly got its tail up, and after about thirty seconds lumbered into the air and we were off to Germany.

The aeroplane felt very heavy, there was no doubt about that. It was some time before we picked up any speed at all, her turns were sluggish and she tended to slip inwards. After a while I managed to catch Willie Snaith up and we set course over Lincoln Cathedral. Dimly I heard Jack

Warner say, 'OK. Course 080° magnetic, speed 160,' but my thoughts were far away as I saw the fields pass underneath.

I could not believe that I was leaving England to go to Germany to carry out an act of war. It was unbelievable. Many times we had flown off like this on mock raids, but there was always a certainty of coming back; we could always be sure of that first can of beer in the Mess afterwards. Now it was different. The fields looked very beautiful – even Lincolnshire looked beautiful. I didn't want to leave, I wanted to turn back. I even wished that old C Charlie would develop some trouble so that we'd have to return, but no such luck. She hummed along like a sewing-machine, blast her. Then, far ahead, the coast came up and soon we were over Butlin's holiday camp near Skegness. Only two months ago I had spent two days there with a crowd of other boys in the Flight, and what fun we had had. But the camp had disappeared far behind and Germany was two hours ahead.

Slowly the time passed. We were flying low, about 1,000 feet, and the waves down below looked grimmer than I had ever seen them before, but maybe this was my imagination.

Little Willie was looking straight ahead. I think he was concentrating on the course he was steering. My own head was on a swivel because I had heard from one or two chaps who had fought in the last war that this was the only way to survive. Perhaps this looking straight ahead business was why Willie missed seeing a German flying-boat which passed about 500 feet below us. It was a Dornier 18 and was merely doing a steady rate I, turning to the left. Quite clearly I could see the two German pilots with their white, anxious faces looking up at me through their windscreen. Probably they thought we would attack them. The thought crossed my mind to go and have a bang myself, but it is written way back in the code of bomber rules that the bomber's job is to get to the target and get back again, not to go doing any fancy stuff, and so we kept straight on, watching Willie's straight head.

About forty miles from Wilhelmshaven the cloud suddenly descended to about 300 feet in rain and we closed formation. I had to open the window, getting very wet, in order to see Willie at all. The sea was now very rough down below, and to put it mildly the weather was stinking. About ten miles from our objective we could see gun-fire ahead; that must have been the first boys doing their stuff. The cloud was now about 100 feet from the deck. To my mind this was fine for bombing warships because we would have been able to attack in bad visibility and climb up into the cloud to avoid the flak. But to my astonishment Snaith suddenly began to turn to the left. Not quite knowing what he was doing, I followed. I saw poor old Rossy on the other side looking left and right, watching his wingtip, which seemed to be about to go into the drink at any minute. Then the leader straightened up, and I suddenly realized that he had turned back. Of course, he was dead right, there was no doubt about that. For all we knew we were miles off our course: the gun-flashes ahead might have been the Dutch islands or they might have been Heligoland, and he was not going to risk three aircraft in order to make an abortive attack; but now our blood was up, we were young and keen and we wanted to go on alone. The temptation was very great, but discipline held; we had been told not to break formation and that was what we must not do.

On the way back we saw the same flying-boat which we saw on the way out. I think it must have been put there to spot aircraft coming in. We had jettisoned our bombs in the sea and now we were not bombers, but fighters. I saw no reason why we should not shoot this thing down, and called up the leader and told him so, but there was no answer and so we missed a wonderful opportunity to shoot down the first aircraft of the war.

When we re-crossed the coast at Boston it was dark. All the beacons had been moved to code positions and Willie's navigator got hopelessly lost. We floated around Lincolnshire for about two hours finding our position. It was only when the moon came up that we were able to follow the canal right up to Lincoln and turned north to our base. And so at last we landed. It was my first landing in a Hampden at night, and I think that went for all. What an abortive show, what a complete mess up! In fact, for all the danger we went through it couldn't be called a raid, but, nevertheless, we went through all the feelings, even worse perhaps.

The first thing I saw when I went into the Mess was a look of surprise on the boys' faces as they drank their cans of beer. 'We thought you had been shot down,' they said. 'A wireless operator in Z for Zebra saw you go down vertically towards the sea. What happened?' I told them I didn't know what the hell they were talking about and went to bed. Looking back it is funny to think that out of the those boys there, with one exception, I was the only one who never was to go vertically down towards the sea or land.

Such was the first raid. True, it was abortive. True, we did not press home our attack, but in those days we knew so little about the whole thing that it is a wonder that we flew through such weather and got back at all. We had seen flak fired by the enemy; only on the horizon, but it had been fired at us. There it was, and I thought that if they are all like that they won't be too bad.

But although we had not done so well, a few Blenheims of No. 2 Group had done some good work and managed to damage the *Von Scheer*. They had flown in low, about two hours earlier, had seen the 'washing on the line', and one 500-pound bomb had lodged in her superstructure, blowing the aircraft and catapult gear out of the ship when it went off. Next day the papers were full of it. Much was made of the crews who had managed to press home this attack, and S/L Doran, who is now a prisoner of war, was given the DFC, an award well deserved.

In America and other neutral countries this raid was good propaganda. It showed that no matter how decrepit the old lion had become, it was still capable of kicking off hard and on the right foot.

The Germans, too, were not slow in their propaganda to claim that we had bombed civilians and that reprisals would follow a hundredfold. Goering and Hitler were said to be fuming; the fat Luft-Marshal wanted to send 100 bombers over London, but Hitler made him stay his hand. Goebbels, that nasty little man, was quick to introduce a brand-new method of enemy showmanship by making one of the airmen who was shot down broadcast to England on the Haw-Haw wavelength. The conversation, as far as I can remember, ran something like this:

Announcer: 'Now tell me, Sergeant, are you well?'
Sgt-Pilot (hesitatingly): 'Yes, very well.'
Announcer: 'Are you being treated well?'
    Pause, then:
Sgt-Pilot: 'Everyone is very kind to me.'
Announcer: 'How is the food you are getting?'
    A longer pause,
Sgt-Pilot: 'Wonderful, just like home.'

What a ham effort! you could practically see the revolver sticking in the poor lad's back.

Next day I became the second war casualty. I had just been down to move my kit from C Charlie after the night before. When I entered the Mess I noticed a large black Labrador sitting in the hall. Being fond of dogs I went up to him and gave him a friendly pat to show that he was welcome to the Mess, but the dog did not agree. In a flash his great jaws had clamped down on my hand and then I was running into the washroom, hand streaming with blood and with half the seat of my pants missing. They were new ones, too. As the monster chased me, jaws dripping for another bite, Pitcairn happened to come out of the bar with his flying-boots on. A hefty man was Pit, and one kick lifted the brute into the air and it ran away howling. Then I was free, but the damage was already done. I could practically see daylight through the great holes in my hand, and even if I say it myself, it was extremely painful. The boys and I wanted the dog court-martialled on the spot, but it happened to belong to the Group-Captain, so he was given a free pardon and told not to do it again. The Group-Captain came to see me while I was having the fifth stitch put in. He was breathing heavily because he had just had his lunch. 'I hear you had some trouble with Zimba,' he said 'Pity. You want to watch him.' Watch him! I nearly blew up on the spot. Of all the things to say. But then I wasn't feeling too good at the time. Poor old Zimba had to pay later for his crimes though. After running up the unenviable score of 2 certs, 4 probables and many damaged, he was finally posted elsewhere. Maybe his score is even greater today.

Wing-Commander Jordan, who had taken the squadron over, gave me thirty-six hours' sick leave for this incident. Jordan was a fine type, and in the few days he was in the squadron everyone got to know and like him well. He spent most of his time shouting. I remember one day I went into his office and he had two telephones, one on either ear. To the Group-Commander he was explaining that he only had nineteen aeroplanes and the nineteenth would not be serviceable for some ddays. On the other phone he was speaking to the Mess about the bad condition of the roast potatoes he had had for lunch. After a while I think he got mixed up between the two phones and the Adjutant had to close the door before he burst his sides. He was never afraid of taking decisions and the thirty-six hours' leave he gave me was entirely off his own bat, as at that time there was definitely no leave for anybody in the Services.

My brother was getting married on the 5th and I was to be his best man, so the thirty-six hours came in handy. The journey to Rugby was most eventful in a browning-off sort of way. It was still boiling hot and the blood from my hand had begun to soak through the bandage and on to the sling. As I stood waiting for my train at Nottingham station an old woman came up. 'Bad luck, you poor young boy,' she said. 'Kiel, I suppose?'

Then a young man – 'My brother was on your do. Simpson's his name. He wasn't wounded too, was he?'

At the wedding an old man put the cap on it. He sidled up with the air of a man about to give away a great secret. 'I was in the last lot, my boy,' he whispered. 'I admire you for that.'

I nearly shot a cat. Can't a chap walk around with a bloody arm in a sling (and I mean bloody) without everyone presupposing he had had it shot off or something? Dogs bite sometimes. One bit me. But it was no good, and I reached for the bottle.

I arrived back in Scampton with an aching arm and a bad hangover. All the boys had left and the aeroplanes had gone too. Someone had learned that in Poland the Hun was wiping out scores of aeroplanes on the ground, and so War Plan, Phase 10, was in action. They had flown all their aeroplanes over to Ringway, near Manchester, where they would be safe from enemy bombers. I had heard by jungle telegraph that the boys were having a very good time in Manchester, and it was not surprising, therefore, that as soon as the doc had pulled out my stitches I was on my way.

It was a dull, cloudy day when I arrived there and taxied up to the clubhouse. Then Rossy told me the news. The boys had certainly tucked themselves well in. Oscar had taken over a pub where there were bags of beer, a jukebox and some very pretty barmaids. One of the boys claimed already to have made the grade with one, but he was a bit of a lineshooter about these things. This pub was in a pretty good strategical position, halfway between Manchester and the airport. Thus, service transport could be used to get to Manchester, which saved time and money, which in turn could be used for other things, such as drinking.

For a few days we lived rather primitively; about forty of us slept on palliasses on the floor of a large committee room upstairs. There were no washing facilities and the pub had only one bathroom. But whoever chose Ringway chose well, because this was the recruiting centre for the Manchester WAAFs. They were all in civilian clothes and some were extremely nice girls. These were the type who volunteered to come in right at the beginning when things looked bad, and not because they were forced to by the grim alternatives offered by Ernest Bevin.

Of work at Ringway there was little. Each day all we had to do was to test our aeroplanes. This usually took about half an hour and involved some pretty good beat-ups of the clubhouse. The rest of the day we spent having baths and shaving and making ourselves generally presentable until the bus took us to the pub at five o'clock. Now and again there were flaps. Once a German battleship was reported in the Irish Sea, but flaps were not alarming and generally we had a very easy time.

There were many parties. Needless to say, the sight of a boy in blue drew much attention in all the bars. We for our part were out to have a pretty good time. The war occupied our minds and we all thought that we would be fighting for our skins within a month. So why not make merry while the sun shone? And the sun did shine in Manchester. The hospitality was almost embarrassing. People just could not do enough. Houses were thrown open, girls were plentiful, theatre tickets were booked and we lived like kings.

At that time some poor long-suffering souls were nightly droning over the Third Reich for their sins but not dropping bombs. They were either on reconnaissance or dropping leaflets advising the Germans to surrender or to throw Hilter out or both. In Manchester the word got around that we were the boys doing this job, although it was the last thing that we would claim to do. And so, one Sunday when Oscar took off for Scampton with the sole purpose of getting some money and some clean clothes. I was rather shaken when one of the waitresses in the aerodrome café came up to me while I was watching him go. She spoke softly, as though she had something on her mind. 'I hope he comes back all right,' she whispered. 'I hope he comes back, too.' I answered, thinking of the five quid he owed me and which I should see the next day.

Gradually we began to know all the local people, and from then on our time was not our own. Every night there were parties and girls and everything else. We were fond of Manchester and it seemed that they were fond of us. One day when Bruce Harrison and I were having coffee in a café a couple of WAAFs under training came and sat at our table. That night we took them out. There wasn't much to do, but we sat in the Midland Hotel until midnight, drinking Haigs and listening to the salon orchestra. I had never really thought much about women up to now; they were things that just came and went in parties. Sometimes they were dumb, sometimes they were too intelligent, rarely had I been impressed by any one. I think it was the war or else whose eyes, but to cut it fairly short I fell in love, that awful boyish love which hurts. From then on there was a not a moment in the day when I did not think of her. She could fly, her handicap was 12 at golf, she had driven in the Monte Carlo Rally. She was pretty. She was wonderful, and so it went on. But although Barbara was very sweet, one day she told me quite firmly that her heart was with someone in the Fleet Air Arm. So that was that. I saw her quite a bit afterwards, but it wasn't the same. But it struck me as funny that it should take a war to make a chap even think of falling in love.

One misty day at Ringway, Sam Threapleton, the second in command of the squadron, rolled in from the east. He had come over to reorganize. He had heard that we were having too good a time. Someone has sent him to see what we were up to. In the afternoon he requisitioned a temperance hotel and de-requisitioned our pub. Naturally there were many downcast faces in the squadron, especially as some of the boys were beginning to have a pretty good time in that locality. The temperance hotel was miles away, and although I should not say this, we had one of the most drunken parties I have ever had in my life the only night we ever slept there.

By now some weeks had passed. There had been rumours that we were going to stay at Ringway for the duration. But someone in Bomber Command decided otherwise.

It looked as though the enemy was too preoccupied over in Poland to do any bombing in England for quite a while. But next day, when I was sitting in the crew room waiting for the fog to lift, Mac, my wireless operator, came to me suddenly. 'There is a message coming through from Group,' he said. There was a pause, then we went to the wireless room. In order to defeat the remarkable delays of up to ten hours on the long-distance GPO line, we had rigged up a little wireless set in direct communication with Scampton. This was strictly against orders, but it served it purpose. When Mac had taken it all down he handed the slip of paper to Rossy, who was the code king. Of all things that take a long time to do, decoding a message is one of the worst, and so there was much impatience as we crowded round looking over his shoulder. The first sentence he wrote slowly. This cypher started off on a particularly difficult letter: 'From Base to 83rd detachment, Ringway.'

We waited.

We were going to France?

We were going to Iceland?

This was war. This was the real thing.

Maybe this was from Oscar to tell us that he was coming back tonight and to tell us to provide a girl friend for him.

Then Rossy read the rest. 'Return Base PM for concentrated night-flying training.' As Rossy read the last sentence there were yells of disappointment.

'Night flying. What a bind!'

'Leaflets. O Christ!'

But Bruce was thinking of the party that night. Mull was thinking, I imagined, of a girl he was going to meet at the Café Royal. Silvo was probably thinking of nothing. I thought of Barbara and cursed.

When we got back to Scampton I found myself well behind the rest of the aircraft because I had not been able to catch up in my slow old C Charlie. Just to show them what was what, we beat up the place in no mean manner. When we whipped over the Control Tower in a split-arse turn, I thought I saw a little figure standing on top, waving. I was not sure who, but the very sight of that little figure sent a sinking feeling down my spine. I therefore pulled off a sneaky landing right on the far side of the field where I thought I could not be seen. When I got to the Flight Office I found I was right. It was little Willie. He was back. For three years I had known that if anyone didn't like beat-ups it was Snaith, and this time I had buzzed the field properly, as they say. And this time I paid the price. The next few nights found me office i/c night flying. But after Ringway I was pretty broke, anyway, so I didn't care.

The days passed slowly, September petered away and brought the fogs of October. Night-flying training had been cancelled. Why we did not know, but it had been. We were now standing by for shipping strikes. Every day they wanted nine aircraft from each squadron bombed up, ready to start at half an hour's notice. It was a question of being up at 7 a.m. all day in the crew rooms, smoking, reading, sometimes listening to lectures. Then as soon as it got dark we were released. Not a happy life. Not a life good for a bomber-pilot's soul, and we soon began to get browned off. The only spot of enjoyment we had was our Ringway clipper, an old Anson which used to take us to Ringway on our twenty-four hours off, so that we could renew some old dates there. Even this got stopped when some brass hat got to know of it.

And so the days dragged on through October in the same dreary routine. It seemed that the whole war had begun to go through thick oil. It was moving at a snail's pace. Standing by. Standing to. Standing down. A dull procession. Gradually we began to realize that our parties of the month before were a waste of money, a waste of time, a waste of everything. We were not going to be flying in the front line in France; we were not going to die. This was a static war. It made me smile a bit because at last I could go to the dentist. In the early days of September I had had an appointment with the dentist but didn't turn up. He had seen me in the Mess afterwards. 'I did not come along,' I explained, 'because I didn't see any point in having my teeth fixed and going through agony in the process, when I was likely to die within the next few days.' That was what I honestly thought at the time, and it was typical of the feelings of all the boys up there.

Now it was different. It seemed that Germany was now licking her wounds. What she would do next was one big question mark. What we would do next was pretty easy to guess – nothing. Poland had been overrun. Two great armies were now facing each other across the Maginot Line, yelling through loudspeakers all sorts of threats, insults and invitations to the Frenchmen to turn against their British allies.

There was a story which got around that even the Germans had a rather peculiar sense of humour. One day during the heat of a battle a Messerschmitt 110, then brand-new and secret, was forced to land on a flat space between the Maginot Line and the Siegfried Line. All day long both sides watched carefully for any move by the other. For their part the British and the French organized a very special patrol to creep out when it got dark and to try to tow the secret aeroplane into the French lines. Night came; it was cloudy and pitch dark. On their hands and knees, the patrol slunk out, hardly daring to breathe in case they were heard by the Germans. At last they reached the Messerschmitt. After minutes of suspense they managed to get a rope round the tail, but they were greatly hampered by the fact that they could not use any light at all. But after an hour they had at last done their job and began to crawl back. Suddenly two German searchlights flashed straight on them. There they were, silhouetted brightly, feeling like thieves caught in the act. Then one of those great loudspeakers roared out with a voice that could be heard ten miles all round 'IF YOU WANT LIGHT WHY THE HELL DIDN'T YOU SAY SO?' Then they opened up with machine guns.

Next day the French guns opened up a barrage on the Germans as a reprisal. And the world waited and said, as in a game of consequences, 'What a funny war!'

Not so funny for some air crews though. We were lucky – we weren't the guinea-pigs – but one or two squadrons at Hemswell, up the road, had to pay the price. We did not know a thing about aerial warfare and it was up to us to learn. Someone had to be unlucky. One squadron of twelve aircraft was sent to attack three destroyers off Heligoland. Only six came back and they had the queerest story to tell. They had found that a destroyer does not possess machine guns, as they had been told, but very strong AA fire in the shape of light flak guns which make a single low-level attack practically suicidal unless backed up by waves by of aircraft. They found that a destroyer could manoeuvre too quickly for single attacks, and they found that German fighters were up to meet them even though they were not within sight of land.

Another squadron went to attack shipping in the Bight; one Flight was separated from the other, but no shipping was found, anyway. On the way home it appears fighters were sighted and the flight-Commander decided to jettison his bombs in order to gain a few more miles an hour. The bomb doors opened, the pilot pressed the button. It was the last thing he ever did; they were only 500 feet and all were blown sky high. Nothing was ever found. Many stories like this can be told, probably from the German side as well. This was a new war in the air and this was ourselves learning it.

A raid on Wilhelmshaven by Wellingtons without fighter cover was a good example of not knowing, but I am not blaming the planners at that time. Then it may have seemed sound that a close formation of Wellington bombers could have protected themselves against repeated attacks of Me. 109's but the proof of the pudding lies in the fact that a raid of that nature was never repeated. Why? Because it was hell for the crews and uneconomical for the country. At the same time that raid gave a very good clue to the German claims. In all they claimed to have destroyed fifty-four aircraft, a figure well above the number of Wellingtons actually operating at the time.

The Germans, too, were having their fling. They began at Scapa Flow. This was unsuccessful because of extremely poor bombing. According to the BBC only a rabbit was killed, and I think this was true. But later a submarine, closely following the film script of a current motion picture, stealthily stole through the boom defences of the great naval base and sank the *Royal Oak* and slipped out again. 'There appears to have been some laxity in the boom defences,' said someone in the Admiralty. 'This has now been remedied.'

A few days later the Hun airmen made their next sortie. Across the misty waters of the Firth of Forth they came, about twelve of them, to attack shipping lying off Edinburgh. Our fighters, first Gladiators, then Spitfires, were up in a flash, and a few Heinkels failed to return. Remarkable though it may seem, some of the pilots who carried out this raid were of the better German types, men who used to fly for Luft-Hansa. There is a story that one of our more ardent auxiliary Squadron-Leaders had quite a party with one. He had already shot down a Heinkel, then chased another past Drem, on to the green fields of

Berwick, where he saw it land safely. After having put up a good show, and anxious to be the first airman to capture his own personal victims, the Squadron-Leader made a plan. After circling the field twice, his only audience being the crew of the Heinkel, who sat outside their wrecked aircraft watching him with interest, he decided to land. In he came, motor well on, flaps right down. No sooner had the wheels touched muddy earth than crash! and over the Spit went on to its back. The Squadron-Leader did his best to get out, but it was no use. He was trapped, and so he hung there upside down, listening to the unpleasant sound of dripping petrol and waiting for help from outside. The Germans, having watched all this with a certain amount of amazement, at last decided to do something about it. Running over, they had him free in a second. As he emerged from the wreck the Squadron-Leader quickly pulled out his pistol. 'You are all under arrest,' he said. 'Do any of you speak English?' In a casual Oxford accent the Nazi Captain answered quietly, 'I usually do, I was educated at Malvern and Trinity. By the way, Squadron-Leader, that was a pretty lousy landing of yours!'

Such tales got around. Whether they are true or not is unknown, but there must be some basis for such a story, and this was a stock one for many moons around the pubs in Lincoln.

Here I must say that the auxiliary boys at that time had not quite been able to get the full hang of operational flying. It was true that a year later they were to distinguish themselves in the most glorious fashion possible, but in the dark days of 1939 they were very light on the trigger. But more of this later.

November brought rain. The squadron began rapidly to fill up. New faces appeared from training units. One day we were sitting around in the Flight Office doing nothing in particular when five new types walked in – Jackie Withers, Tony Mills, Bill Tweddell, Dickie Bunker and Greenie Greenwell. All were English except Greenie, who came from South Africa. They came in nervously, not quite knowing what to expect. Except for Jackie Withers they were all pretty young. Oscar looked them over. I do not think they expected to see such a young Flight-Commander, and I don't think they expected to see their Flight-Commander with his tunic undone and his hat on the back of his head, his feet on the table and behaving so casually.

'All you fellows have very good records,' he said, taking out his pipe; 'that is why you have come to my Flight. All the stooges go to B Flight! All I want from you while you are here is loyalty and good flying discipline. You may have been taught to fly Hampdens well, you may even think yourself aces, but I am afraid you are in for a shock. You are going to be second pilots. This means that you have got to learn to navigate, and this means you will hardly ever fly as pilots except on night-flying tests.'

Quickly he allocated each a pilot. Tony Mills went to Jack Kynoch, Greenie went to Ian. 'You, Gibbo' – he looked at me with that funny smile of his – 'because you've got the scruffiest wireless operator and worst aeroplane, and because you are just a little fellow yourself, you can have *him*.' He pointed to Jackie Withers. I knew Oscar was joking, but I know Jackie didn't.

'OK, Oscar, thanks very much,' I said, and then turned to Jackie. 'You're a lucky devil; you have come to the best pilot in the squadron.' I just got out of the door in time, followed by yells of 'You bloody old line-shooter.' 'He's awful, he'll kill you,' and a hail of flying-boots thudded on the door as I banged it behind me.

Then I had a look at Jackie. Jackie was an amusing character. His mother was an opera singer. He himself had been trained as a ballet dancer. He could play jazz on the piano as well as any man. He could even sing like Harry Roy. But the main thing about Jack was that he had a heart of gold and the guts of a lion, and some time later I was to find out that he could fly very well, too.

One day late in November someone said that someone had reported that three German destroyers were within two miles of Newcastle. We were detailed to carry out a recco. If this was true and if the destroyers were there, both squadrons were to take off as quickly as possible and carry out a medium-level attack. Needless to say there was nothing about, and we were about to return to base when we got another message which told us to sweep the North Sea within twenty miles of Sylt. Jackie, sitting in front, said, 'Oh, hell, I haven't got any maps.' But it didn't matter because we followed Oscar all the way and didn't see a thing, not even a fishing-boat. When we got to Sylt there was nothing about except a long layer of cloud, over the mainland. I suppose that was why there were no fighters about. When we got back we knocked back a few cans in the Mess on the strength of being the first crews in our Group to see Germany in daylight – another doubtful boast.

All this time the German pocket battleship *Deutschland* was making a nuisance of herself in the Atlantic. Her sister ship the *Graf Spee* had already been disposed of. And so the Bomber chief looked to the Air Force to dispose of her with equal skill. One day it was reported that the *Deutschland* had left Kiel and was on her way out to attack shipping in the North Atlantic. She had been reported steaming north up the Norwegian coast, south of Stavanger. At dawn there was a tremendous flap at Scampton. First of all, all crews were wanted. In the end only nine aircraft from each squadron.

The briefing did not take long; there was not time. Aircraft were to attack in Flights of three. The total number of aircraft in the formation was about fifty. In case of fighter attack we were to bunch together and get as much mutual protection as possible. At the last moment Joe Collier took my place and left me fuming on the ground. But he was to regret his keenness a few hours later.

And so they set off. The raid was led by W/Com. Sheen, who commanded 49th Squadron. In one aircraft was an observer, and his job was to look for the *Deutschland* through binoculars. If he recognized it as such he was to fire a coloured light so that all bomb-aimers in the formation would attack the ship with a clear conscience, knowing that they had not attacked a British cruiser hurrying to the battle.

Across the windy waters of the North Sea they went, flying at about 10,000 feet, and at last they came to Norway. It had only taken them about two hours to get there because there had been a terrific tail wind behind them, so Sheen, in the leading aircraft, enthusiastically decided to fly farther up the Norwegian coast than necessary. Keeping well outside the three-mile limit and in wonderfully clear weather, watching all the fjords and little towns pass by, the formation went up far north to a point where it was hopeless to go on any farther. Then it turned west for England. By now the tail wind had developed into a head wind which had developed into a gale. Our Hampdens were not very fast, and by looking down on the sea you could seen see that the ground speed was very, very low. After about four hours on this course the observer on board developed the startling theory that the whole formation had overshot the north tip of Scotland and were now over the Atlantic. He therefore promptly advised that they should all turn south-east. This was done. There was no inter-aircraft radio communication in those days and if there had been the ether would have been very thick with rather unattractive words. After a while the resident navigator on board the leading aircraft managed to convince the observer that he was talking through his hat, and again the formation turned west.

By now they were beginning to get short of petrol. They had all been flying for ten hours and many eyes were glancing at the gauges, which were registering round the 100 gallons mark. Land was not in sight. It looked as though the whole formation would have to land in the sea.

Suddenly out of the mist ahead appeared a small fishing-smack. It was about five o'clock in the evening; it was just getting dark, and an old man with his hand on the tiller had done his day's work and was about to go home. He was somewhat surprised when about fifty Hampdens suddenly began circling his little boat flashing urgent secret messages; but as he had no wireless or lights on board all he could do was to wave at them, thinking they were merely having some fun. Another squadron, meanwhile, commanded by a Scot called Willie Watt, in gaining altitude during the turn happened to see land in the distance and broke off quickly, and another fifteen minutes found them safely landed at Montrose. One after another the other squadrons did the same thing. One

Sergeant-Pilot was coming in to land when one engine stopped for lack of petrol. He quickly opened the other to full power, but this also stopped within a few seconds. He crashed into a graveyard near the aerodrome, but managed to walk out of it.

December 1st was an uneventful day except for the fact that the Russians invaded Finland. Why they did this will not be known until after the war, but I myself have the greatest faith in the Russians, and I am sure that whatever the reason they planned this invasion, it was a pretty sound one. I didn't think this at the time, though.

December 1st was also the day I went on three days' leave – my first few days off since my dog-bite. We were not allowed to go very far because we had to be within twelve hours' recall, so I drove down to Coventry to stay with my brother. He was in the Warwickshires and his headquarters were in the centre of the town. The leave was uneventful except for the usual amount of beer and a game of rugger. But one night at a party I met a girl called Eve Moore, whom I liked very much the moment I met her. She was small and very fair and, above all, could talk. In those days of hectic parties and boring war news, it was nice to meet someone who could discuss books, music and places. Most people who discuss these things well don't look so good, but this girl was really attractive. Her parents were in shipping in Cardiff.

I was still smarting after my broken heart (so I thought) with Barbara, and as most of the boys in the squadron claimed to have regular girls, I saw no reason why I should not have one myself, and Eve looked all right to me. It was pleasant being able to live normally, going round with a nice girl for a couple of days, but it was soon over.

On the last night we had a party in the King's Head Hotel which packed up about three next morning. It was a pretty ordinary sort of party – the usual chattering sort with bags of hooch around. The only thing I can remember particularly outstanding about it was that I mixed rum with whisky; a thing a connoisseur or an old hand would never do even in his worst moments. After saying goodbye to my brother and the rest of the boys and girls, I got into my car to drive the hundred-odd miles back to Scampton. One never feels very good at three o'clock in the morning and the rum and whisky didn't help: besides, the blackout was terrible. My headlights were the standard mask type, which, as everyone knows, give no light whatsoever. After an hour of losing my way and nearly hitting hedges I gave up and I went to sleep to wait for the dawn. An hour or two later I woke up with a splitting head and the vilest taste in my mouth. Rum, they say, always does that.

As soon as I got to Scampton I drove straight to the hangars and went to sleep in the pilots' rest room. I was a few hours overdue and I did not want Willie to catch me with my breath smelling of rum. It was quite and peaceful in this warm room and I had a lot of sleep to catch up. Just as I was dozing off some of the boys came in. 'Hello! Gibbo's back,' I heard someone say, through a haze. Then another voice, 'God, look at those bags under his eyes; he must have had a wizard time!'

There was a snigger of dirty laughter and that was enough for me. I jumped to my feet. 'Get out, you dirty-minded devils,' I yelled at the two sprogs who had been doing the talking. 'I have just driven a hundred miles in the blackout with a hell of a hangover. Now scram.' The two went out sympathetically. They knew exactly how I felt.

December brought dirty weather. Although we spent our time standing by, always waiting for the order to take off, although we even took off on two occasions to hunt for the elusive *Deutschland* and were recalled within an hour of being airborne, we couldn't claim to be earning our pay. Life was very boring. Every day fog clamped down on the aerodrome, and it was quite an event if we could see the farmhouse on the far side, about a mile away.

One day someone in the Air Ministry decided that Scampton's flying field was too small. That farmhouse was in the way of the proposed expansion. It would have to be knocked down. Johnnie Chick, the Wing-Commander, who had taken over from Sheen in the other squadron, had a brainwave. Why not knock it down ourselves with 500-pound bombs? We would get some low-level practice, and it would be interesting to see the behaviour of these bombs when dropped at low altitude. A competition between squadrons was quickly organized and everyone waited for the great day.

At last a suitable occasion arrived. And at the last moment the Air Ministry had stepped in and said that we could use only dummy bombs, but these could have a live smoke charge fitted to the tail to make the thing look realistic.

Off the boys went one by one. They were bombing at about 100 feet, and although they tried hard, no one was much good; some over-shot, some dropped short and bounced clean over the building to explode about a quarter of a mile beyond. We learned a lot that day. We learned that low-level bombing was harder than we had thought; and, most important of all, that bombs bounce for a long distance when fitted with the tail action fuse. Someone suggested that it would be better if these bombs were fitted with spikes so that they should stick in the ground, rather like a dart. Funnily enough, Johnnie Chick swept the field by placing his bomb into the top bedroom window – funny because he was lousy at darts.

And so December passed by. Once or twice we organized competitions. There were landing competitions; there were bombing competitions. All this to try to keep ourselves busy. But taking things all round, everybody was getting browned off. We ourselves began to think that this was a phoney war.

One day Oscar, Ian and I flew down to St. Athan in South Wales, to have some secret equipment fitted to our Hampdens. It was a dirty trip; low cloud all the way. Just when we were breaking cloud in the Bristol Channel at about 500 feet a convoy opened up on us and we all missed being shot down, thanks to the inaccuracy of the gunners concerned. We must have been sitters. The weather closed in more and more, so we decided to stay the night and go back next day. This suited me down to the ground, as I was able to go to Eve's house and meet her parents. Then back to beat-up Cardiff with the boys.

On Christmas Day, the first wartime Christmas, we stood by from dawn onwards for a large enemy shipping strike. As we stood around at lunchtime, eating oranges and other rations to be used only for the flight, we thought of other more fortunate souls who were drinking and making merry. But later someone heard our prayer and the whole thing was cancelled. Then the party started. First, to the Airmen's Mess to serve them their dinners, accompanied by the howls of delight from our erks. Yells of 'Up 49th', then a louder, deafening noise from the 83rd supports: 'It's not 81, it's not 82; It's 83'. Then an equal crack back from the 49th boys until the dining-hall resembled a vast smoky, howling bedlam.

This is an old tradition of the RAF. On Christmas Day all officers must serve the airmen with their Christmas fare and all airmen can call the officers whatever names they like, and so many rude words were flying around. As the beer flowed faster and faster, so the party got rougher and rougher and the words even more rude. In the end it is another age-old tradition that all officers must leave the dining-room when plates begin to sail through the air, otherwise they might get hurt.

Then to the Sergeants' Mess, where for twenty-five years the NCOs have had the privilege of slipping a gin into some unsuspecting officer's beer. I have had it done to me and I didn't remember getting home that night. This time no punches were pulled. This was a wartime Christmas; there might not be another one, not in our lifetime.

After we had seen that all the other ranks on the Station were enjoying themselves and were fully stocked with beer, we all went up to the Officers' Mess to have our own dinner. This was a complete shambles. There were no women in the Mess, none were invited. This was a stag party, and what a party! I remember that as the evening drew on one squadron got to one side of the room and the other to the other, and suddenly someone shouted: 'Come on, boys – free for all!' I remember being pulled out from underneath a mass of writhing bodies to be told I was wanted on the phone. It was Eve wishing me a happy Christmas. Then back into the fray. It was amazing that no one got hurt.

At last I thought I had better go to bed. I had had my fill and found it rather difficult to walk straight. As I was trundling along the corridor there happened to be four fire extinguishers in the way. These I did not see, partly for the obvious reason and partly because the corridor was dark. Anyway, I had the misfortune to trip over them and one by one they went off. I did not know what to do. First I tried to sit on them to keep the liquid foam from going on the corridors; that was no good. The stuff seeped through my trousers and then began to spray out again. There was no way for it. Nearby was a large and ornamental door covered with glass. One by one I threw the fire extinguishers out, making a most horrible noise of tinkling glass and squirting extinguishers. Then I went to bed, feeling that I had done my best in difficult circumstances.

Next day the Mess Secretary impolitely informed me that I had been taken off drinking for a month in the Mess because of the wilful damage I had caused the night before. I was furious and went to see Willie Snaith, but he put it another way which made me satisfied. 'Look, Gibbo,' he said, 'they have done you a good turn. Think of the money you will save so that you can spend it on your girlfriend.' That remark meant a lot to me and for the next month I didn't touch a drop.

And so 1939 ended. It ended on the wrong note – a note of a party and not a note of war, but if we had known what we were in for in the next three years that party would have been even bigger.

CHAPTER THREE

LEARN BY MISTAKES

Everyone will remember those early days of January 1940. Snow came in all its fury. There was snow everywhere; it blocked the runways, blocked the hangar doors, it got into the aroplanes, it made life unbearable. The road to Lincoln was blocked for a week. The Mess ran out of beer. A long-range Wellesley bomber on the other side of England, in response to urgent requests, came over low one day and dropped us a few crates by parachute, but the boys soon drank it all up.

Mull and I decided one night to go to a cinema in Lincoln. We set off in my car down the road in the blinding snow. It was quite impossible to see through the windscreen, and he had to walk beside the car with a light, while I drove as slowly as possible. Suddenly we arrived back at the main gates again; somehow or other *en route* we had turned right round and had gone back the way we had come. We saw no cinema that night.

Meanwhile, a few officers on the camp who had seen service in the last war told us that the thing to do when the weather was bad was to get round a piano and sing songs. We had no ideas of our own, we could only copy them. So there we were, Jackie Withers hammering away at the keys while the boys sat around with their beers and me with my orange juice, singing at the top of our voices. Many songs were sung – some good, some bad; mostly bad.

One night Oscar came howling with laughter into the Mess. It was unlike Oscar to howl with laughter, so we asked him what was wrong. He could hardly speak. 'Go into the billiard-room,' he said, 'and see what I have seen.' Quickly we went along, and there a sight met our eyes which made us almost collapse. Three padres were sitting solemnly around a piano, each with a glass of beer in his hand, each one looking very serious. They were singing: 'Here's to the next one to die'.

As is usual in any Service when operational air crews, or whatever they are, cannot risk their necks, out of the pigeon-holes and office crevices of Higher Authority comes red tape. So to us came the order to transform our squadron into a school. Every morning we had to attend three-hour lectures. We began to call ourselves the 83rd OTU.* There were lectures on navigation, lectures on armament, lectures on meteorology – all stuff we knew years ago. There was a parade every morning at 8.30 and a roll call taken so that Flight-Commanders could be sure that all were present. Life was miserable, broken only by quick forty-eight-hour leaves in which I managed to get over to Sheffield to see Eve, who was appearing there in her show.

About the end of January, when the snow was beginning to thaw and the waters had run down the side of the aerodrome and had swamped the WAAF quarters, came a series of conflicting rumours. Both squadrons were to move north to Kinloss and Lossiemouth to hunt for submarines and to stand by in case of a chance to bomb German warships. At last the rumour became a fact and much preparation was made to go. I wangled with Willie Snaith to let Jackie Withers take the aeroplane up there, so that I could take a train to Glasgow and pay another quick visit to Eve, whose show had moved up there.

It was a rotten journey, and most people who have done a wartime night journey in a third-class compartment to Glasgow have nothing to boast about. The trains were not running to time by any means and I was forced on my way to Lossiemouth to stay the night in Perth.

At last I arrived at Lossiemouth. The boys met me in the golf club and told me that they had had a good trip up, but that all the aircraft were unserviceable because when they had taken off the slushy surface the ice

* Operational Training Unit.

had punctured all their flaps and they were now being repaired. It was a few days before we did anything.

Life at Lossiemouth was very pleasant. The Gulf Stream plays around the Moray Firth and it is warm and springlike up there even in February. Day after day we would spend our time walking on the beaches, watching the fish come in the harbour and the queer gesticulations of the salesmen. Sometimes we would do a little flying. The Station-Commander and the Squadron-Leader Administrative Officer, whom we called the Brains Trust, had come up too, why I did not know, probably to do a bit of shooting.

As usual, rumours began to set in after we had been there a while, and the favourite one was that we were going to be there for the duration. Again the prospect seemed pleasant, for Scotland is certainly a very lovely place.

Day after day we practised formation flying and I am told that in the end the whole squadron got very good at it. But we nearly had some very serious accidents. One day we had to take off on the short run in a squadron take-off, and Willie Snaith told us to use full flap. This, of course, means full take-off flap, which is about thirty degrees. Old Pitcairn-Hill, my section leader, however, took Willie at his word and slammed his flaps right down. As it is the right thing to do to keep very close to the leader on take-off, Pit and I nearly came to grief. With his full flap he became airborne just over the hedge at about sixty miles an hour. As I was not airborne my wheels hit the hedge and we very nearly went for a burton. But the crowning achievement of all was our great anti-submarine patrol, led by Sam Threapleton. It was an unfortunate affair and was really no one's fault, but in the squadron records it is still written in as a black mark.

We were all standing by one day in the crew room when we were told to take off and fly to a point near Norway where a German ocean-going submarine was returning from an Atlantic cruise. We were told not to bomb any other submarines in the vicinity because they might be British submarines hunting the Nazi. Loaded up with special bombs, we were away. After a few hours a Very light shot up from Sam's aircraft and we knew that he had sighted something. Instantly Jackie Withers took up the cry. 'Yes, there it is, there he is,' he cried. 'There's the submarine. It's a German all right.' Instantly all aircraft with bomb doors wide open sailed into the attack. We were all bad shots and our bombs missed by a few feet and the submarine hurriedly crash-dived. Then we resumed our patrol. A little farther on we came across another submarine, but this time we gave it a wide berth; our orders had been not to bomb submarines in the vicinity because they might be British. Then we returned to base.

An Admiral was waiting for us when we landed and he was not in a good mood. In the operations room he told us in scathing terms that we had attacked His Majesty's submarine – and that it was only just our bad bomb aiming that had saved her crew. Then Sam began to go red in the face and we all realized that the second submarine which we had carefully avoided was the Atlantic raider. This sort of thing happens in all forms of aerial warfare and we all thanked God that we hadn't killed any of our own sailors.

There were many parties up at Lossiemouth and the local people were very kind in initiating us into such lovely Scotch drinks as Glen Grant Cream and Glenfiddich, but again we were getting bored. Often we would take off, go far into the North Sea to try to find something, but nothing was found. I have never seen so much sea in my life with so little in it. However, we were thankful for the good weather and at least we did get some hours in.

Fortunately an order came for us to return to Scampton just before we really got browned off, and it was a happy day for the whole crowd when our wheels finally touched good old Scampton mud on March 19, 1940.

When we went into the Saracen's Head that night none of the usual crowd was around. This was unusual, but we soon learned the reason. Next day the papers were full of the great raid made on Sylt by squadrons of Hampdens as a reprisal for the German raids on Scapa Flow and the Firth of Forth. This was not exactly a *débâcle*, but it was not a successful attack. The Germans said that no damage was done at all; they even took American journalists round to show them, but they did not show them the northern aeroplane base at Hornum, where most of the bombing took place. One fellow had the misfortune to drop two bombs on the Danish island of Bornholm, but this was just sheer bad luck, as they were attacking from 2,000 feet, and the searchlights from Hornum two miles away were blinding. Most of the pilots who took part in this raid, like ourselves, had never carried out an act of war, and their reports were highly illuminating. They found the flak very interesting and 'pretty' and the searchlights very bright and everything very new. But they didn't hit the target . . .

The next weeks were spent in concentrated night-flying training. Off we would go over the snow-covered fields of England, map-reading our way from here to there at 2,000 feet; sometimes we would lose our way, but with each practice we got better and better. It seemed now that Hampden squadrons were going to be used for night raiding only; they were too vulnerable in daylight.

At this time the Germans suddenly launched on England their new secret weapon, the magnetic mine. At first everyone was puzzled as to how this thing was laid so close into our channels and estuaries. The navy was on guard well outside to prevent any high-speed launches carrying out their evil work, so it was presumed that the whole thing was done by seaplanes.

As most seaplanes took off from bases between Sylt and Borkum on the north-west coast of Germany, the Commander-in-Chief of Bomber Command instituted secret patrols whose job was to fly between these two islands all night long and drop a bomb on any flare-path light in the sea to keep these mine-laying seaplanes from taking off and landing. Strange as it may seem, these security patrols were very successful, and they did succeed in curtailing the work of seaplanes for the job. But by then the Hun had already modified his Heinkel 111 for the job and these aeroplanes were taking off from bases well inside Germany, and so nothing much could be done after the first few days.

When we had got fairly proficient at night flying we were despatched on a form of armed reconnaissance over Germany so that we could learn our way about over the Third Reich. I never carried out a leaflet raid myself, but many of our pilots were lucky enough to do so. I say lucky enough because I mean it. The first raid over enemy territory is always the worst, and a leaflet raid was a pretty good way of breaking the ice to show the type of procedure to be carried out on these raids. But everyone will always admit they were always a complete bind.

Meanwhile in the squadron Sam Threapleton had gone. We were sorry because he was a grand type; a good-living Yorkshireman who had a great sense of humour. But he was replaced by an even better type, S/L Dennis Field. Field was golf champion of the Air Force. He immediately got down to organizing his Flight in order to bring it into rivalry with our own. Spring was in the air, the squadron was fully trained, we had plenty of crews. It looked as though the war would soon get moving, and there was nothing for us to do but sit and wait. We were thankful for the respite we had had since September 3 because then we were not ready, now in our limited way we were. We could fly at night; we could navigate fairly accurately; we could drop a bomb within half a mile from 12,000 feet; we could even land on the beam. Yes, that respite had been very welcome and in a way we had made full use of it.

As the spring days passed we watched with pride the flowers we had planted in our garden grow up and bloom; we knew we had a few weeks to wait but we were ready.

CHAPTER FOUR

THE FUN BEGINS

April 9 dawned cold and clear. For some reason I was awake, and as I lay in bed, warm and comfortable, I listened to Bruce snoring in the next bed and pitied the girl he was to marry. I tried to look at my watch, but it was too dark and I cursed, remembering we had forgotten to pull up the anti-gas curtain the night before; that's the worst of having a late night. I had no idea of the time and settled myself down for a restful doze. Suddenly with a thump on the door and with a crash of tinkling teacups rattling in his shaky hand Crosby, my batman, came in to do his stuff.

'Good mornin', Sir; nice mornin'; but 'itler's on the move again. 'E's invaded Norway.'

In a flash I was out of bed and shaking Bruce.

'They have done it, Bruce,' I yelled. 'Wake up, you old stooge.'

Bruce was in a bad way and it took him some time to recover from his coma, but at last he came to. Then we got moving. In half an hour we had breakfasted and were saluting Oscar smartly in the Flight Office.

Much speculation went on to find out what we were going to do. Oscar as usual thought it was all a bluff.

'I can't see how he can get away with it.' He seemed to be talking to himself, rather than to the other boys in the room. 'The Navy have said they will sink every ship in the Skagerrak, both by submarine and surface craft. I cannot see Hitler's idea in provoking an action with far superior naval forces. After all, what have they got? At Kiel there's the *Scharnhorst* – that's in floating dock – and a few cruisers, then there's the *Gneisenau* and a pocket battleship at Hamburg. They haven't got a chance.'

I am afraid I completely failed to see his point. I was thinking of his E-boats.

'I would have attacked France first,' someone said.

'Me too.'

We were all puzzled. Then the telephone rang. It was Willie. Impatiently we sat around listening to Oscar.

'Yes, Sir.' 'OK, Sir.' 'We are all ready, Sir.' 'How many, Sir?' 'All right, I'll come up.'

As he put down the phone there was a clamour of voices.

'Good show, chaps.'

'Put me down, Oscar.'

'You have got to include me.'

'How many do they want?'

'Do you want a crack crew? If so, I'm all ready.' This was Bruce shooting his line.

'Shut up, you crowd of beggars,' cried Oscar. 'If anyone's going it's me. After that Gibbo and Rossy. Hang on the phone, Ian; I am going up to see the CO.'

To say that we were all keen would be a masterpiece of understatement. For months we had hung around; for months we had waited for this. We had waited so long that we were all completely brassed off.

It was not unnatural, therefore, that the chance to fly on operations seemed, that day, to be the sweetest thing in the world. Quite a change from those bad nervous days in September.

For two days we waited, then we got the gen. Because we had done more night flying than other squadrons we were detailed, ours and 49, to carry out some very special missions. We were to drop *our* first magnetic mines in German coastal waters. While the winter months had dragged on, our scientists, the backroom boys, had not been idle. They had developed a special weapon, weighing about 1,700 pounds, which was virtually sweep-proof. This weapon was to be known as a vegetable and was to be planted with great accuracy in special spots somewhere in the Skagerrak and Kattergat.

The plan was simple – and at the time seemed good. Germany was trying to invade a country by sea. The ships and supplies she had collected together for the job were extremely hard to attack. They moved at night, and our Navy was unable to operate in the Baltic waters. Although the port of Kiel was packed with ships laden with tanks, guns and troops, no bombing attack had yet been made which might harm civilian establishments. To get from Kiel to Oslo (which had already fallen) these ships had to pass through one of three well-marked channels. In the middle there was the Great Belt, over in the east there was a channel between Copenhagen and Malmö, and in the west there was the bottleneck channel at Middelfart. It was our job to mine these channels so thoroughly that we would, in the conventional tabled form:

(1) sink a large ship, thus blocking the channel;
(2) damage a great number, forcing them to return or go aground;
(3) drown a few thousand German troops (we hoped).

These mines, which contain a lot of explosives, could be dropped in fairly deep water, and even if the ship was some distance away the force of the explosive was such that it would always practically lift it out of the water.

The Norwegian Expeditionary Force was already in existence. By preventing German reinforcements from getting to southern Norway we hoped that our mines would play a large part in winning the Norwegian war.

Everyone was very optimistic. Many blatant articles appeared in newspapers, written by armchair warriors; bold statements were made by leading men, among them the famous 'Hitler has missed the bus'. And in America it was said that 'the fox was now out of his lair and can now be caught'. I do not blame anyone; we all thought the same. After all, we were a seafaring nation and our sea power was being challenged. Someone had dared to put to sea under our Navy's nose – a blue nose, it is true – but a long one at that. Now we were going to show them who actually ruled the waves.

And so business did well in London bars and many a glass was raised to Hitler's great blunder. In the City stock prices were on the up and up.

On the 11th at about seven o'clock off we went. Our orders were simple. We had to plant our mines in the middle channel at a dead reckoning position. After that we were to make a reconnaissance of Kiel Harbour to see how much shipping there was in that port, and also to check up at Middelfart and the amount of activity going on there at the railway sidings. Then we were to come home.

On no account were we to let our mines fall into the hands of the enemy. These were our secret weapons; we must not make Hitler a present of them, as he had to us. Special orders were issued to this effect. If we were unable to reach the right spot the mines were either to be brought back or jettisoned in deep water. If over land and something went wrong, we were to abandon ship so that it would crash in the right way and blow itself and its weapon to glory.

As we flew out I thought of these things. Pleased as Punch to be on ops, but hoping like hell that an engine wouldn't stop over land, as this meant abandoning ship, and that meant being a prisoner of war for the duration.

The trip itself was completely uneventful. We found the spot. We saw our mines gurgle into the black water. Then after we had made a quick reconnaissance at Kiel at a safe altitude (to find that low cloud blacked out all chance of a recco) we went up to Middelfart, where we noted fiendish activity at the railway station and wished for a couple of bombs. While we were there we noticed that the best landmark for miles around was the bridge – a magnificent steel structure, rather like the Firth of Forth Bridge, but not so large. We noticed plenty of ice clinging to the banks in these April months and thought it must have been pretty cold down there on the ground. Then after eight hours we came home.

Now in a Hampden the pilot can't move out of his seat, so after eight hours I was feeling pretty cramped. Eight hours on your bottom is a long time, but worse was to come, nine, ten, even eleven hours at a stretch – an awful long time.

This prompts the obvious question, and to the curious I would say the answer is usually 'No', but in an emergency, beer bottles or empty Very-light cases may be used. Sometimes a long rubber tube is utilized and this trails behind through a hole in the aircraft. However, ground crews who dislike their pilots have been known to tie a knot in this, with disastrous results, and most pilots usually avoid having anything to do with it. Anyway, I repeat to the curious that the answer is usually in the negative.

Two days later there was much excitement in the camp. Four ships full of troops were reported to have been sunk with all hands near where we had been gardening, ie, planting vegetables. This was very satisfactory. Everyone was pleased. Our weapon was working.

On the 14th we were ordered to lay mines at Middelfart. It was a big effort, consisting of about forty bombers all told. The weather was going to be bad, so the Met man said. He explained that a warm front was moving westwards towards England at fifteen miles an hour, bringing with it cloud and rain. When we took off it was about 100 miles out to sea, and this meant that we would have to land elsewhere on return. It was instrument-flying all the way there, then came a patch of clear and we saw Denmark ahead. It did not take Jackie Withers long to pinpoint on the southern point of Sylt. Then we set course for the Bottle. As we buzzed along about 2,000 feet above Denmark we ran into more low cloud. Although we were skimming the tops, its base must have been pretty well on the deck.

'You're sure we pinpointed at Sylt?' I yelled at Jackie.

'That was Sylt all right; I saw the seaplanes.'

'OK. I'll come down on ETA. Let me know when we start or about three minutes before if possible.'

A little later Jack told me to start easing down. Gradually at about 300 feet a minute the old Hampden slid into the murk. All the time came Jack's voice reading the altimeter.

'900 feet; 500 feet.'

There was a silence for awhile, still we were going down; outside the swirling cloud, inside the soft glow of the instrument. It was getting darker and darker. I saw my altimeter and it was reading nearly zero. 'Come on, Jack, what's the height?' I said, pressing the emergency intercom button. With a click his voice burst in, 'Sorry, my intercom plug came out. Christ, if my altimeter's reading right we're a ruddy submarine!'

Quickly we levelled out. Then I saw the bridge. It was Middelfart Bridge all right, straight in front of us. There was nothing for it, no question of recklessness. If we went up we would be back in the clouds and completely lost, we could only stay low down. And so Mac, in the mid-upper position, was very surprised when he saw a bridge whistle over him.

Then:

'Bomb doors open. We're here.'

'OK. Hold it.'

'Steady, steady, not too soon.'

'OK. Mines . . . GONE.'

There was a slap and a clonk as the mines shot out, then a flak-ship opened out on us. We were only about 100 feet, but soon we had pulled up into the cloud with A/C Tointon in the bottom rear position firing his guns like a man possessed at the invisible flak-ship. I didn't blame him; he had only come along as a passenger and he was getting his money's worth. These were the days when no air crews were NCOs. The Jeeps* were AC 1s and the gunners were AC 2s. Both got the grand sum of sixpence extra a day flying pay. Most of the gunners, such as Tointon, had never even been to a gunnery school, but had picked up what they could in the squadron in their spare time.

Soon we were on our way home. I shall never forget that journey. It rained all the way and was pitch black. Now and again the aeroplane became charged with static electricity and resembled a poor edition of Piccadilly Circus in peacetime. We had been diverted to Manston and a south-westerly gale was blowing into our nose, making our ground speed a little under 100 miles an hour. After two hours we passed over the lights of Holland. Then another two hours were in front of us before we could see Manston. Most pilots when flying on instruments sometimes get the funny feeling that their instruments are giving false readings and they are quite certain that they are about to turn upside down any moment. After a while I was no exception and I had repeatedly to shake my head, rather like a ballet-dancer does when coming out of a pirouette, in order to keep myself upright.

Then we were getting QDMs from Manston. Soon out of the low cloud and rain there suddenly came a green light, then another. It was Manston telling us to land, and we did not waste any time.

This trip took nine hours, mostly on instruments. No wonder I didn't wake up till four in the afternoon next day.

Sylvo did not come back. He had got his QDMs but had gone floating down the Channel into the Atlantic; they never found him.

In 49 Squadron two crews failed to return: both were married. I pitied the poor Adjutant, who had to break the news to their wives. Low, one of the Squadron-Leaders, had lost his way and crashed on the beaches near Newcastle, killing the rear-gunner. Taking things all round it had

---

* Wireless Operator.

been a terrible night, and of all the aircraft despatched, Jack and I were the only ones to lay mines in the right spot. Naturally, we were pretty pleased with ourselves and the next night we sat up late patting ourselves on the back – ignorant idiots that we were.

While we were fighting our way around at night, other squadrons were doing their stuff by day. Hampdens from No. 5 Group flew long sorties up to Norway to seek out German ships; usually cruisers lying in fjords.

On one occasion two squadrons had stood by all day to take off and carry out a medium attack on the cruiser *Leipzig*, which was lying off Hilversund. Three times they were ordered off, three times they had been cancelled. Whoever were giving the orders, and they thought it was the Admiralty, were behaving like schoolboys.

Next day they were ordered off at ten o'clock. Just as they were getting airborne a red Very light shot up from the watch office and those who were airborne had to land again overloaded with bombs as they were. This time it was, in fact, the Admiralty who had caused the delay. If some of the Admirals could have heard what the boys were saying, they would have scuttled themselves.

At last they all got away at about three in the afternoon. By the time they reached Norway it was dark in the fjords, the fog had come up, visibility was bad. After a fruitless search during which nothing was seen, they turned back.

Their Lordships were furious. Said AVM (Bert) Harris, the Group Commander: 'Order, counter-order, disorder . . .'

When, however, these Hampden squadrons were given their chance and did get to Norway in daylight it was pretty fierce slaughter. Their orders were to fly in a very tight box so as to bring as much defensive armament as possible to bear on oncoming fighters, but the Germans were no fools; they had found a weak spot in the Hampdens, for at that time there was a blind area on either side, and the Huns made the best of their knowledge.

One squadron, led by S/L Watts from Edinburgh, was 'bounced' near Stavanger. Far out to sea was some cloud cover, but it was a long way away. He immediately did his best go get the whole squadron into a tight fighting formation by diving towards the deck. If he had been foolish enough to try to climb for the cloud he knew the whole squadron would have straggled and would have been picked off one by one. But the Germans were flying in Messerschmitt 110 fighters, which have one gun which can fire sideways. Their mode of attack was to fly in formation with the Hampdens perhaps fifty yards out and slightly to the front, and pick off the outside men with their one gun aiming with a no-deflection shot at the pilot. The bomber boys could do nothing about it; they just had to sit there and wait to be shot down. If they broke away they were immediately pounced on by three Messerschmitt 109s waiting in the background. If they stayed, the pilot received a machine gun serenade in his face. One by one they were hacked down from the wing man inwards. Watts said it was a terrible sight to see them burst into flames at about twenty feet, then cartwheel one wing into the cold sea. First B beer went; that was poor old Peter.

Who was next? There was H Harry on the outside. The German gunner carefully took aim, then a few minutes later H Harry had disappeared beneath the flaming waves. That was poor old Charles.

One pilot made the hopeless gesture of pulling back his hood and firing his revolver at the enemy gunner, but it was no good, and his brave act was the last thing he did on this earth.

At last low cloud was reached and four out of the twelve managed to scrape home.

Poor old Watts. A few weeks later when returning from a raid on Hamburg he hit a balloon cable at Harwich and crashed into a grain elevator. His funeral pyre burnt for two days and two nights.

But despite their bad luck and despite the odds against them some squadrons met with success off Norway. For instance, Bud Malloy managed to hit a cruiser from about 10,000 feet with a 500-pound bomb. It burst into flames and reconnaissance later established that it had been sunk. I think this was the first time in its history the Royal Air Force had sunk a warship from 10,000 feet.

I could write much about the bravery of these pioneers, many of them fine, experienced pilots who met their end so prematurely off the grim coast of Norway. The lessons they learned, despite the price they paid, proved very useful to the lucky ones who survived.

Meanwhile, the battle of Norway was not doing so well. Our troops up in the north were having to contend with nearly non-stop dive bombing. This made the landing of supplies almost impossible. True, we had a few Gladiators out there on a frozen lake operating against the enemy, but they had to face the most awful series of setbacks which were nearly impossible to overcome.

They were just a group of keen pilots, fighting to the end, to the last aeroplane, and even when Hurricanes were flown off the *Glorious* to join battle with the Hun, it was no use; the Germans had complete and utter air superiority and there was no way out of it. Of these men also in the north I could write a lot, but it is not my job; my story must deal with the bombers of that time.

By the 19th it was obvious that Hitler had not missed anything. He may have missed the sea bus; he was certainly buying up return tickets on the airborne bus. All day long Junkers 52 transports were ferrying men and materials into southern Norway from aerodromes in northern

Denmark. Sometimes as many as 200 transports were seen at any time on any one field.

Aalborg was one of these aerodromes.

Oscar, Rossy and I were detailed to carry out the first bombing attack of the war on this vulnerable target. It was the first time, in fact, that British aircraft had been detailed to attack an aerodrome. There was some doubt about our load. Some said all incendiaries; others plumped for 500-pounders. In the end we carried 30 by 40-pound fragmentation bombs and one 250-pounder (for the hangar) and a few incendiaries (for luck). We were to attack from 1,000 feet at dawn on the 20th, aiming at the aircraft on the ground and destroying as many as possible. I asked myself at the time why so few aircraft were detailed. Why not the whole squadron? There were plenty available. Then we could have done the thing properly, but I suppose the idea was to conserve losses and this bogey was to dog the Air Force for a couple of years to come. We were always to nibble at targets and never destroy them. No one knew exactly why, no one asked. Certainly not the boys; it was merely our job to carry out orders.

There was a Mess party on the night of the 19th, and I remember sitting with Rossy drinking lemonades, watching the other boys getting tight. I was glad when Oscar walked over to us and lit his pipe. 'Let's go and get a meal,' he said. 'We will take off in two-minute intervals at one o'clock onwards.'

It was about ten minutes to one when I climbed into C Charlie. It was a lousy night, rain pouring down and cloud about 300 feet. When we turned on the intercom only a high-pitched buzz came to our ears. The rain had leaked into it and had made it completely unserviceable. While I was swearing at Mac, who was trying to get it working, Oscar went off with a roar, followed by Rossy. Mac did his best, but the water had done its worst, and we had to change to Jack Kynoch's aeroplane, which was the spare.

At about 2.15 we at last got airborne, all soaking wet; all browned off. We knew we were going to be late; we knew that the defences would be very hot when we got there, having been roused by the two other boys. And to crown it all, Jack's aircraft was so stiff on the ailerons that I could hardly move them.

When we reached the Danish coast we set course for Aalborg. After a while we passed over a convoy. This was wrong; we should have been over land. Where the hell are we? Jackie didn't know – I certainly didn't.

'When's the ETA up, Jackie?'

'About another five minutes.'

'OK, we will look around then.'

Then we found we were over water. I do not know how it had happened; we had somewhere mistaken our pinpoint, or perhaps there was another gale-head-wind which had slowed down our ground speed. We pushed on, hoping, not knowing quite what to do. Suddenly in the north, heralded by a bright fan-light glow of many colours, the sun came up in all its glory. We could now see we were over land, and, in fact, we could see everything – villages, farmhouses. We could see all we wanted – and more. Then Jackie's voice, slowly and carefully:

'I say, Guy, don't look now, but I think that's Copenhagen on the left.'

'You're damn right, it's Copenhagen,' I shouted.

Then we dived for the deck in a steep turn for home.

'We're miles off our course. How long will it be before we are over the sea?'

Jackie made a quick calculation.

'About an hour if you go flat out,' he said.

What a spot to be in! All thought of bombing Aalborg was now completely out of the question. Here we were with about 200 miles of enemy territory to fly over, going along in broad daylight, all alone. If those boys in Norway hadn't much chance in formation our prospects were pretty small. A few farmers were kind to us; they waved, but that didn't do any good. One policeman was not so kind. I saw him pull out his revolver, take steady aim, but I think he must have missed. Our orders at that time were not to fire on anything in occupied territory in case we killed civilians. So we could do nothing about it.

We were flying very low and all the time our shadow flew beside us, dancing over the fields.

God did not mean us to die that day. Up came a fog-bank and we were safe. A few minutes earlier I had never been so scared in all my life. Now I had never been so relieved. Away out to sea we saw a Heinkel, but it had the legs on us and we couldn't catch it up I think it must have been coming back from a shipping patrol. And four hours later we were circling Lossiemouth in Scotland.

Oscar had landed two hours before me. His attack had been successful. Rossy hadn't been too good. The flak gunners had been ready for him and gave him a tough reception at 800 feet and he had got holed fairly badly. I was the failure and was furious with myself and everybody else, but when told that the compass in my aircraft had some twenty degrees deviation I quietened down. So that was the reason for our failure to keep on track. Then it wasn't Jack's fault. I went up and told him that I was sorry for swearing at him, and everyone was happy.

On my return to Scampton I asked Chiefy about the stiff controls and he found that one of the self-sealing tanks had burst and was rubbing the control wires. Jack Kynoch had never noticed it, but without his strength I had found the going pretty difficult.

In the ante-room there was much joking at my expense, especially as we had been shooting a terrific line about our successful Middelfart

sortie. Air Vice-Marshal Harris, who met us in the Mess, had a good
laugh, too. I was tempted to tell him about the compass, but it is said
somewhere that a bad workman blames his tools. So we just sat there
and took it.

The next night we went to Oslo Fjord to lay mines in the harbour. I
had a pretty easy trip myself – but Joe Collier had to plant his vegetables
within a few yards of a battleship and said that he didn't enjoy the
experience very much. S/L Good, an Australian, was hit in the face and
arms by cannon-shells fired at pointblank range, and owed his neck to
his navigator's skill in pulling him out of his seat and taking over, an
amazing feat carried out at fifty feet at night while being blinded by
searchlights.

Poor old Crappie Kitson had some trouble, too. His pilot, Svenson, a
New Zealander, flew right over the battleship and got a packet for his
pains. Crappie got shot in the face and lost both his eyes, poor lad. He
was so full of life I felt quite miserable when I heard about it. Of all the
things to lose, your eyes.

Oslo was a pretty hot spot all right. Apart from these instances everyone
who went in got hit in some place or another. Three failed to return and
Johnnie Johnstone crashed in England on the way home, killing the
whole crew, including his second pilot, Taffy Vagg, the Welshman. Poor
old Johnnie was married. I knew him and his wife very well. Next day
it was a sad sight to see her, eyes rather red, collecting his kit from the
Mess. These poor wives who live near bomber aerodromes undergo a
continual strain. All day long they wait, knowing deep in their hearts
that one day they will get the bad news, and when it comes they behave
like thoroughbreds. I could write a lot about the wives, and perhaps I
will before I have finished.

By now, the end of April, it was obvious that it was all over in Norway.
We had begun to evacuate Trondheim. It had been found that it was just
not possible to land supplies in the continuous bombardment. Our troops
had had to retreat and now they were clearing out, poor lads. I pitied the
PBI. They fight all wars, and have to win them, unless they go under.
There can always be the air. There can always be the sea. But only the
infantry can conquer territory, and only the infantry can evacuate territory
at great loss of prestige and great loss of life.

In the beginning of May we made one more mine-laying sortie; the
last for some time. This time it was Copenhagen, which as Snaith said,
'Gibbo ought to know very well.' This time Jackie excelled himself and
we made the trip in six and a half hours. It was dawn when we came
in; neither of us felt tired and we opened a bottle of beer to celebrate our
success. After a while in walked Oscar.

'They are all back except Pitcairn. Nothing has been heard.'

Old Pitcairn was very popular in the squadron not only because he was a sportsman, but because he was as white as a man can be, and we all sat around waiting for news. An hour passed, then two hours. Then, hesitatingly, from the east came the dull drone of an aeroplane making heavy going. It was a Hampden all right, a speck in the distance getting nearer and nearer. Then we saw that it had its wheels down, then we could read the letters. Yes – B-O-L. – That was Pit all right.

'Good show, chaps,' said Oscar. 'Now we can go and have some bacon and eggs.'

Later Pit told his story. When he arrived at Copenhagen he found that he could not open his bomb doors and after trying many taps in his cockpit he had pulled the wrong one. He had pulled the emergency undercarriage bottle, which not only blows all the hydraulic oil out of the aircraft, but also forces down the wheels. Then he found that he had done it. He had pulled his ladder right up. It was getting light at Copenhagen. He could not raise his wheels and he could not open his bomb doors, and worst of all he still had his mines on board, and so was very heavily laden. He had turned his nose for home, making an air speed of only 120 miles an hour. He had flown across Denmark in broad daylight and many Huns had come up to have a look at him, but seeing that his wheels were down, they had sheered off, thinking, no doubt that he was one of their own. The journey across the sea had taken five hours. Poor old Pit, no wonder he didn't see the joke.

CHAPTER FIVE

BALLOON CABLES AND BOTTLES

Crosby was a funny type. For two years he had been my batman and had never put a foot wrong. He never even got browned off when I used to swear at him on certain occasions. He was a tall man with a slight deformity which screwed his head permanently on to one side. Bord and bred in Lincolnshire, he had little if any sense of humour. Ever since the beginning of the war he had taken it upon himself to give me the news with the morning cup of tea, and so at nine o'clock on May 10, when his voice roused me, I was not a bit surprised to hear that Germany had invaded Holland. Reaching across my bed I turned on the radio and heard the full story. How our troops were rushing forward to save Belgium; how the Maginot Line was invulnerable and how at last the tank had come into its own. But the military commentator pointed out that no matter how far a tank advances it must always run out of fuel some time or, on the other hand, it may advance so far that it will be cut off from its main sources and can then be dealt with easily. He warned the public not to worry too much should a bulge develop in our lines; this was a case of enemy fighting behind enemy and both sides were running great risks.

The news quickly brought everyone to their toes. Nobody knew quite what to believe, as there had been so much wishful thinking during the Norwegian *débâcle*. And so everyone was prepared for the worst. All leave was cancelled and we had to be ready to take off at half-an-hour's notice.

It was three days before anything happened and then we got our orders. Some of the boys were detailed to attack Hitler's oil reserves well behind the lines. I and three others were given special missions which involved the Kiel Canal.

As we sat in the crew room we were told of the importance of the plan, how we might block all traffic if we were successful in doing our job thoroughly. We were also told the uncomfortable news that there were balloon cables every 300 metres all along the Canal, and that all bridges were very heavily defended with light cannon and flak. It looked like being a sticky target, and long were the faces of Oscar, Joe, Pit and myself as we smoked our last cigarettes. Suddenly Oscar began to write something on the back of a cigarette packet. It did not take him long, then he handed it to Harris, the Adjutant, an elderly man with grey hair, who had fought in the last war. 'I want this will read in the Mess,' Oscar said quietly, 'if I don't come back. You will do it, won't you?' There was an uncomfortable silence. I stubbed out my cigarette. Then we went into the night.

That trip was lousy. None of us got there and we all brought our bombs back. The weather was the trouble. Low cloud had been on the hills all the way and made it quite impossible to find a tree, let alone a canal.

Next day Pit and I volunteered to go again and this time we were lucky. It wasn't a tough trip at all and we completed our job in a highly successful manner, but in those days there was no such thing as constant aerial reconnaissance, and whatever good we had done will never be known till after the war. Anyway, despite all this we were all pretty pleased with ourselves, and the whole of A Flight went into Nottingham to get plastered at the 'Black Boy'.

Meanwhile things were not going too well in the battle of France. In Holland German troops were quickly overrunning the country. Parachute troops, dressed as nuns and Hula girls, it was said, came floating down into the fields and captured anything they saw. In France the bulge had developed. German armoured forces sweeping round like a cow-catcher were pushing miles behind our rear lines. They had attacked across the

Forest of Ardennes and had driven the French back from the Meuse and
the great fort of Sedan, which had collapsed under heavy dive-bomber
attack. Their aircraft had complete air superiority in all directions. It
was said that the French General Staff were asking Great Britain for
more fighter aircraft, but we were loath to let our Metropolitan Air Force
go – a wise decision, as things turned out.

We home-based bomber-boys had watched with a certain amount of
trepidation the fate of our poor old Fairey Battles and Blenheims out in
France. We had seen them hacked down one by one regardless of
individual skill and bravery. There was the case of the Maastricht Bridge
which young Garland dive-bombed with his Fairey Battle, earning a vc.
This was a very gallant attack even though he perished in the attempt;
but his soul must have shuddered when he saw the crack German
engineers put up a pontoon bridge alongside his objective within a few
hours. No, the thought of sending us to France did not appeal one bit,
and apparently someone had some sense because they realized that we
just did not have the necessary air superiority. And so our job was to fly
out at night using the darkness to escape from fighters and using our
night-flying skill to bomb accurately. This policy at the time seemed all
wrong to armchair critics, but time has justified it. Those grim days and
nights were the playing-fields of Eton to the would-be night-flying pilot.
We learned the hard way, but we learned everything.

While the Dutch Commander-in-Chief was telling his Army to lay
down their arms and to surrender to the Germans: while the battle of the
Meuse was getting rather too far south for everyone's liking, the Air
Force was not idle. Fighter Command Squadrons, of which the most
famous were numbers 1 and 73, which included Cobber Kane and Co,
were meeting fearful odds, but were acquitting themselves very well,
shooting down four enemy for the loss of every one of their own. Coastal
Command Ansons and Hudsons were watching the U-boats in the North
Sea and elsewhere, and Bomber Command were getting down to the first
big raids of the war. The objectives were the oil-tanks in the docks at
Hamburg. None of us who sat around listening to the briefing ever
dreamt that almost exactly three years later this city was to be destroyed
by the same weapon, the bomb.

Snaith was speaking.

'Your target is the west side of the oil refinery at A 3, here on the map.
Your bomb load will be 4 × 500-pound bombs – fused instantaneous,
and you will carry full petrol. You can attack at any height from which
the target is visible, but remember the moon is in the south-west, so the
best direction for attack would be to come from the north-east side of
Hamburg so that you can see the reflection of the water in the dockyards.
Again I must warn you that on no account are you to bomb towns or
villages indiscriminately. Only this target may be attacked tonight. If you

cannot find it you must bring your bombs back. That is about all. You can fly to the target whichever route you wish and bomb at any time between 1200 hours and 0400 hours. Any questions?'

There was silence. Then he went on: 'The Navigation Officer has got the maps ready, so you can all get down to working out your routes.' He paused for a second. I think he wanted to go himself, but at that time Wing-Commanders' flying times were strictly limited. Then he smiled shyly and wished us good luck.

In came the Station-Commander and all crews jumped to their feet. Having told us to sit down he then described how we were going to help the situation in France by destroying Hitler's oil. There was no doubt that the offensive in Belgium was using up vast and prodigious quantities of this valuable fuel, and by bombing his supplies in the rear we would directly interfere with operations at the front. Such was the plan.

As Jackie and I wanted to get to a movie in Lincoln that night we decided to take off late. Our plan was to attack between three and four in the morning. We reckoned it would be getting light then and the glow in the north, coupled with the light of the moon, would make target identification very easy.

For a long time Jackie and I had been perfecting a dive-bombing attack in a Hampden. This consisted of a 60-degree dive from 6,000 feet, pulling out at 2,000 feet. We had found that we could get great accuracy and we also hoped that we would be quite immune from flak and searchlights. The only snag we had encountered so far, such was the speed we would get up in the final pull out, was that often the glass nose of the old Hampden would collapse, much to the embarrassment of the bomb-aimer.

The movie, *Babes in Arms*, was terrible, and neither Jackie nor I were in the right mood for it. When we got back we found most of the boys had gone; they all obviously had dates the next night.

Not long afterwards we were groping our way in the mist on the aerodrome, trying to find the flare-path. Then with a screech of brakes and the roar of the engines, old Admiral Foo-Bang, having first swung to the left in her usual style, lumbered into the air.

It was a clear night, and two hours later, above the hollow noise of the Pegasus engines, came Jack's voice.

'What height are we?'

'About 8,000 feet.'

'We are a bit low for oxygen, but I didn't bring my tube, anyway.'

'Nor did I.' This was Mac.

'Nor me,' said Watty, the rear-gunner, making his first trip. Flying-Officer Watson was a newly commissioned armament NCO who had just joined the squadron as a volunteer air crew. He was a cool fellow but keen as mustard to do his bit against the enemy, and a very likeable chap.

'That's all right, chaps. We are not an oxygen crew,' I called to them. We were proud of our crew and proud that A Flight were known as the low-level kings in the squadron. In most squadrons in those days there were always chaps who were willing to risk their necks and go in from a height from which they couldn't miss, and there was always the other crowd who used to stay high in the sky and drop their bombs at anything they thought they could see. Needless to say there was great rivalry between the two sides and many hot arguments ensued, but they all ended in the rash statement that the low-flying merchants would buy it, while the high-flying boys would live again to do another raid, a statement which has not been borne out by fact. To be successful, bomber pilots have to have a large amount of skill and dash; that is, if they wish to survive, and if they want to do any good work. This doesn't mean sitting up high, thinking one is safe, and of the bacon and eggs four hours later. Nor does it mean risking the crew's life unnecessarily. What it does mean is to try to get the bombs on to the target in the most expeditious way. Such was our creed at the time, and it hasn't altered very much.

Then we saw Hamburg for the first time. At first we thought it was another moon in the wrong place, just a small red sphere lying on the ground. When we got closer we could see the docks. Then we could see the town, a great sprawling mass spread for miles around, and at the northern end of our target we could see that one oil-tank was on fire. That was all, just one oil-tank; but the smoke reflecting the flames in many directions probably helped to magnify the damage. (This may have been the reason why most crews claimed the destruction of the target, while the German radio said no damage was done.) This was the great snag in night bombing, and it was only when daily photographic reconnaissance came along that we were able to know exactly what we had done.

Anyway, the target looked to us to be well ablaze and great whoops of joy came from the front position. There were a lot of searchlights about clumsily fingering the sky, and there was plenty of flak being shot up in a sort of elongated cone directly over the docks. We had de-synchronized our engines to that unmelodious 'Rhoom-rhoom' noise which we were told rendered searchlights ineffective, but all it did really was to cause unnecessary vibration on board.

There was more light flak here than I had ever seen in my life. Light flak is a pretty sight, curling gracefully up towards you, getting faster and faster as it comes until it goes by with a loud whistling hiss and a roar to explode a few hundred yards farther on. It makes a funny noise when it does that, a sort of 'Bok-bok' noise. Each shell has a different colour and they are usually in the same order, and so they come chasing towards you – green, white, red – rather like a waterfall upside down. Yes, pretty to watch, even harmless, but if they hit you there is a noise like a crash of thunder; a rending of metal and then the tinkling crash of broken glass. Everything becomes bright red as your tanks go up, and your stomach suddenly feels hollow, then you begin falling faster and faster. You try to get out, but the wind keeps you in. You yell to your crew to bale out and all the time the light flak is still pouring into you. Then it is all over and you hit the ground. Petrol flames come soaring up into the sky almost ready to meet you as though to rocket your soul to heaven. Then all is silent save a dull red fire on the ground. Soon one of your boys will come along and bomb your fire, thinking it another military objective. Such are the thoughts that pass through your mind as you see the tracers curling up, and I for one quickly banked the other way.

But poor old Robbo of B Flight (P. L. Roberts, New Zealand) was not banking at all, when I last saw him, and he went down like a blazing firecracker. You have to keep moving the whole time when there is light flak around.

At last we were in a position about one mile north-east of the tanks and at about 6,000 feet high. Down below I saw Peter Ward-Hunt of 49 Squadron going in about 2,000 feet and getting hell for it, but he got away all right. At the same time some other fellow was getting a few sundry shells lobbed up with him at some 15,000 feet or so.

At last just underneath the port engine I could see the oil-tanks clearly. Yes, only one was on fire; the rest looked like silver golf balls in the moonlight. Then down went the left wing and we were wheeling into our dive. Down went the nose and immediately the altimeter began to whizz round backwards as the air-speed indicator began moving forward to hit a new high.

In the front Jack sat there all set, waiting for the order to release the bombs in a stick (these were the days when we had no automatic stick droppers but the bomb-aimer did it by pulling a thing like a cheese-cutter). I was watching the golf balls getting larger and larger in my windscreen. Watty was wondering when his hatch would blow off, and in the top Mac was wondering what it was all about.

At last:

'Bombs gone,' I screamed at Jack.

'Bombs gone.'

Later:

'Did you see anything, Watty?'

'Not a thing; I don't think they fell off.'

'They must have.'

'No, they're still on.' This was Jackie. 'I can see them.'

When I had finished saying some very rude words about the hard-

working electricians we began to climb up again. With a load on this
was a long business, but we had to be quick because it was getting light.
At last with engines red hot we reached 5,000 feet. But when we got
there we could not find our oil-tanks, as smoke from the fire had begun
to blot them and everything else out. As we were circling round and
round to avoid searchlights and flak I noticed a lot of balloons floating
around above me – a not too pleasant sight. Suddenly on my right-hand
side I saw what we wanted and dived straight for them. Because the dive
was practically vertical we reached the phenomenal speed of 320 miles
an hour, and the pull-out was quite impossible, even though I put both
feet on the panel, but she came out all right by using the tail-trimming
tabs (which they say is very bad for an aeroplane), so quickly in fact that
we all blacked out.

This time our bombs hit the mark and something burst in flames
behind our tail. Then, because we had dived the wrong way, we were
in the thick of it. Two thousand feet over the centre of Hamburg is not
a healthy place. Flak was whistling all round us, making that aggressive
'Bok-bok' noise. Then some broad-beamed searchlights got us and we
were completely blinded. Jack was saying, 'Weave left, weave right,' in
front, but I knew he couldn't see a thing. I remember diving straight for
the searchlight on the ground, firing my fixed Browning gun all the way
down and yelling at the same time: 'I'll get you, you bastard!' Then it
went out and I hoped morbidly that I had killed the operator as well. I
remember glancing to the right and seeing the starboard wing on fire.
This was the end. We had better all bale out, and so I pressed the
emergency 'abandon aircraft' signal, but it wasn't working. Another look
and I cursed myself for a fool. This was no fire, only a large piece of
metal off the wing flapping in the light of an amber-coloured searchlight.
I said to Jack, 'I think we have been hit; she feels funny.'

'You bet she feels funny, there's a few hundred yards of balloon cable
on your wing,' he answered.

He was exaggerating, of course, but we had hit a balloon cable and
the 'funniness' was caused by the damage to the rudders by flak.

At last we were out of it, and save for the usual exchange of fire
between ourselves and flak ships we reached the coast safely. It was good
to see England down below in the early morning and someone said
something about bacon and eggs in half-an-hour's time.

Sunny Scampton under Hugh Walmsley was a fine station. Everyone
was very happy and everyone worked very hard, but the Station-Commander had one bee in his bonnet. He did not like aerodrome lights; he
hated them because he looked upon it as his own responsibility to prevent
his station being bombed, and so instead of a flare-path for returning
bombers, all we had to land on were two red lights, and this we had to
do without breaking too many aircraft. On this particular morning it

was foggy and we could not even see the tops of the hangars, so we were diverted to Abingdon, where we landed all in one piece, cursing the Station-Commander and his lights, and more than hungry for the bacon and eggs we had visualized two hours earlier.

Many boys had been well shot up on this raid, others had been wounded, but considering it was the first of its kind it had been successful. Most of them had gone in low to achieve their aim in the highest traditions of the Air Force. On the other hand, one Squadron-Leader had bombed from 16,000 feet, and by excellent bomb-aiming was responsible for the fires which led us to the target. He was awarded the DFC.

And so ended a typical early 1940 raid on Germany. I have described it in full to show how different were the raids to come. These early raids were haphazard. We could choose our own route; we could bomb from any old height; sometimes we could carry whatever load we wished; we could go off at any time. We were individuals, but to tell the honest truth we were not very efficient, and out of the total tonnage of bombs carried to A 3 that night I would say that the actual amount which fell on the target might have been at the most ten per cent.

A few nights later we went again to this place, but cloud was down to 500 feet – below the safety height for bombing. Oscar was the only one to go below and his rear-gunner reported an oil-tank rise in the air behind his tail and well above him. Poor Dennis Field, I think, tried to do the same but didn't come back. He was a grand type. I spoke to his wife, Joan, next day in the Mess. She had been collecting his things, packing them to take home. I remember she couldn't find his movie-camera, and at last found it in his flying locker in B Flight Office. Joan was very brave, but then they all are.

The next few days there was a lull in operations; this was strictly enforced by the weather and nothing to do with tactical necessity.

Things were going badly in Belgium and France, but over in England fog came up regularly, as if by the will of God to cover our fields and to prevent us operating. But the Huns, in their limited way, began to roam around England bent on mischief. One formation of twelve Dornier 17's crossed the coast of Yorkshire at Withernsea and swarmed inland to the big bomber base near Morpeth. This was a fine station built on the same lines as Scampton, but the Dorniers did their work well. They knocked down all the four hangars and destroyed every other large building, including the Officers' Mess, the workshops and the airmen's cookhouse. The only thing they missed was the Sergeants' Mess, and this because they had no bombs left. They must have been pleased with themselves, this squadron. So pleased, in fact, that they, no doubt thinking our fighters were busy in the south, came back next day to give their undivided attention to the Sergeants' Mess, but this time the fighter boys were ready. Although the Sergeants' Mess was damaged, not one of the

Dorniers reached Germany to report the fact. They were all shot down far out to sea. A few survivors were picked up by our armed trawlers, the crews of which were constantly asked the question, 'Where did those fighters come from? We thought they were all in France.'

As usual during these lulls we made the best of our time by going to Lincoln. In that city is a pub of some notoriety, with a bar which some call the small bar and others the 'Snake Pit'. In this den used to sit (they don't now, they've all been called up) young girls who spent their time with foolish young officers, tempting them, getting drinks off them; sometimes necking in the back of a car with them. We used to call them 'amorous amateurs', but few of our boys would have anything to do with them, mainly because we were in good health and wished to remain so. One officer, whose name I shall not mention, however, felt different, and leaving our party went over and asked a thin blonde girl to have a beer. After a while, during which we noticed he was in earnest conversation with her, it was evident that all was not running as smoothly as usual. Suddenly there was an explosive, 'Give me back my bloody beer' and he came strolling back towards us with his can and her half-drunk glass in his hands, while she rose and stormed out of the bar.

'What on earth's wrong?' someone asked.

'She won't play,' said the young Romeo, drinking up his two cans.

'God, you're a dirty old—,' growled Oscar. 'Come on, Gibbo, drive us up to the George – we can drink there until after hours and Jackie can hit the keys.'

The night was pitch black outside, the moon had not yet come up. Driving with masked headlamps was no joke, as I had found out before. But this time I was seeing two white lines which disappeared when I closed one eye, a tricky and embarrassing situation. In the end I took off my masks and we shot off at an alarming rate towards the George. The boys crowded into the back, singing bawdy songs. A policeman on lonely duty along the Wragby road must have been rather startled about that time when he saw a car shoot by, to the tune of 'Whip her knickers away', and to the light of two, as they must have looked to him, searchlights. He immediately phoned the next man on duty along the road.

While this was going on, I was carefully keeping to the left of the second white line, while Oscar was yelling, 'Faster, faster,' in my ear. Suddenly we came across a red light slowly waving from side to side in the middle of the road. The car wasn't taxed or insured; I knew that. I was also stinking; I knew that too. I was also broke; everyone knew that, and so there was nothing for it. I stepped on the gas; how we missed the law I do not know. I remember his lamp going one way and his legs the other. Then we were a long way past and I switched off all lights and glided slowly into a by-road. There was dead silence; the boys knew how to play when the time came and no one said a word. We hardly dared to breathe, feeling like a submarine which has penetrated into Hamburg Harbour before daybreak.

For a full fifteen minutes we waited: then one by one we crossed the fields to the George. The rest of the boys had arrived by then and there was a rip-roaring party going on when we came in. Later on in the evening I had the pleasure of buying a drink for a het-up country policeman who told me that he had nearly been knocked down by a drunken farmer coming back from Lincoln's market-day!

Although we had done nothing much at night for three or four days, during the day there had been some activity going on. Jackie, Dickie Bunker and Bill Tweddell had all taken on crews of their own to fill up the gaps caused by our own losses. This meant I was without a navigator, but Watty the rear-gunner said that he had done some in the year dot, and so I gave him his trial by stooging around in an Anson. He soon picked up the art of map-reading, and it did not take him long to learn the rudiments of flying, so that he could take over in case I caught a packet. In all we put in fifteen hours in two days, which was quite a feat, especially as Watty was a man of about thirty, long past the age of learning things quickly.

On the last day of the lull I phoned Eve to come up and meet the boys, as there wouldn't be any flying that night. As is usual on all these occasions, things went wrong, and I was 'dicing with death' the night she arrived, but my friend Ian stepped into the gap, and after they had watched me in old Admiral Foo-Bang take off with a lurch into the night sky, they went and had some dinner together.

The next few nights we alternated between Düsseldorf and the George, Mannerheim and Petwood, Kiel (where we started some good fires – the best, in fact, I had seen) and Lincoln. You can't burn a candle both ends, and I was no exception. By the end of the month I was worn out, and Willie Snaith gave me a week's leave. The night before I went Harris, the Adjutant, came up and told me I had got the DFC, together with Oscar, Rossy, Bill and Dickie. This was good news and worth waiting for. There were smiles all round. Quickly I phoned Eve to lay on a big party at the 'Snake-Pit'. All the boys were to be there; it would be terrific.

Of the party I shall say little except that it was a good one; of the next day I shall say less. Bruce woke me up at about nine o'clock.

'Good news about the boys,' he said cattishly.

'What boys?' I was sleepy; I didn't understand.

'Oscar and Co. They've got the DFC.'

I nearly asked him about mine, but instead reached for a paper. Yes, he was right. They had all got it except me.

I went to Brighton with Eve, disgusted that I had bought so many rounds the night before for nothing.

CHAPTER SIX

MAXIMUM EFFORT

Brighton was peaceful. In fact, just the same as it ever was – pretty girls with short skirts blowing in the sea breeze were still walking along the front, eyeing each man they passed with that well-known 'I-don't-first-time-but-I-like-boys' look. Little dark-haired maids with the same black stockings with holes in the heels, and stained pinafores, were still serving tea in cosy but small restaurants by the sea. The boarding-houses were open, the beaches were packed. It was hard to realize that a hundred miles away there was being enacted a grim drama, the one-act play of Dunkirk. Only the presence of soldiers and the barbed wire reminded one of the war.

My leave passed quickly, as leaves do. All day long I lay on the beach with Eve and another girl, Doreen, who was in the same show. *Come Out to Play* was having its pre-London trial, and Jessie Matthews, the star, was pretty busy flapping around getting everything on the top line. I hadn't met many stage folk before, but I must say that, taking things all round, I got on very well with them, especially in the evenings when the bars opened.

On my last night I picked up Eve and a few other girls at the stage door and we were walking along the promenade when suddenly an air-raid warning sounded. A bomb dropped in the distance, one or two guns fired into the night and a parachute flare lit up the headland. And so we all went into the Grand to have a drink until the flap had died down. As usual in these places the lounge was congested with people. They had all congregated to listen to the nine o'clock news. As we were standing there an Army officer came forward slowly, staring, his light blue eyes fixed on me like a madman. At first I thought he was drunk and prepared myself for just another row with one of those 'brown jobs'. But this poor chap wasn't drunk. He had had it. He had just come off Dunkirk that morning, after spending four days on the beaches, and was in as big a state of nerves as any man I have ever seen .

His lips began to move and at last he mouthed these words. It was the first time I had heard them, but not the last.

'Where was the RAF at Dunkirk?'

'I don't know; weren't they there?' I answered foolishly.

'*They* were – the Heinkels and the Messerschmitts, but not our fighters. I only saw one Spitfire in four days.'

'Perhaps they were fighting the enemy elsewhere,' I said.

'No, they weren't. We were bombed every hour. It was absolute hell. Bomb after bomb rained around us and we couldn't do a thing about it.'

I let him ramble on; sometimes his voice got louder, sometimes died away. Now and then he stopped. He was almost talking to himself.

Suddenly the wireless pips sounded and Bruce Belfrage began reading the news. But still this man mumbled on, completely unaware that he was causing a slight disturbance. At last an old man who looked of foreign extraction got up and took the officer by the arm. 'Do you mind if we listen to the news?' he said suavely, conscious of the fact that he had a sympathetic audience. The Army man blinked and seemed hurt. He couldn't quite understand what was going on. Now I had seen some sights in my time, but this one made my blood boil, and having gathered some Dutch courage from a couple of high-balls, this was enough for me.

I switched off the radio quickly and the room suddenly became very silent. Then I swung round on the old man. 'Listen, you stupid old bastard,' I said softly, though every man and woman in the bar could hear. 'Do you realize that while you are here sitting on your fat behind, eating the fat of the land, there are a few men fighting for your plump neck? Do you realize that at this very minute the bomber boys are risking their skins trying to delay Hitler's advance, and far out to sea convoys manned by the Merchant Navy and guarded by His Majesty's ships are bringing in your food, and only a hundred miles away over there an army, our British Army, is trying to get itself out of a mess caused by old men like you? Perhaps you don't realize that you're talking to a man who has just come away. He has probably seen things that you will never see in your lifetime, and you just want to sit there, thinking you are completely safe, and listen to the news.'

After making this long speech, or something like it, I was completely stymied for anything else to say. So I gave him a dirty look and ended up weakly: 'I think, sir, you are a complete bum.'

Then I went out into the dusk, and as I went I heard the Army type still muttering: 'Where was the RAF at Dunkirk?'

Next day I paid a loving goodbye to Eve. She thought it was the last time she would ever see me; there were tears and for a moment I felt awful. But then the train started up and we puffed our way out of the station.

I was glad to be going back, for this seemed to be the wrong time to be on leave. The enemy would soon be only a few miles from our shores. Perhaps within a month he would be invading us. Then it would be a case of every man doing his utmost. And as we passed Grantham I began to feel quite happy.

The boys were sitting in the rest room when I arrived; some looked terribly tired because they had just done three nights running.

Nevertheless, there was the usual chorus of rude greetings as I came in. The tension was there though, and Jack Kynoch and Sergeant Ollason both looked as if they could do with a week's rest. But who were we to grumble? Our job was easy compared with that of the Navy, who for nearly a week, backed up by volunteers, had fetched a large proportion of our battered Army back to England. And how about those fighter squadrons of the Air Component and the Metropolitan Air Force who had been flying sortie after sortie during the hours of daylight in order to maintain air superiority over the Channel? No sleep for them, just time to have a cup of coffee and perhaps a bit to eat while their aircraft were being refuelled and re-armed, and then up once again into the blue.

Suddenly I noticed two familiar faces missing. 'Where's Ian and Greenie?' I asked.

'Missing two days ago,' someone answered.

'What on?'

'Low level: Aachen.'

'Hell! how did poor old Dell take it?'

'Damn well – the Adj told her.'

'Poor old Ian.'

'Yeah; bad show.'

'Yeah.'

Suddenly Oscar came in breezily. 'Hello, Gibbo. Heard the news?' he asked. He was always pleased to see someone back from leave.

'No, but I've heard enough. What's new?'

'Churchill has been speaking in the House of Commons. He says we have rescued 335,000 men from the beaches. I reckon that's pretty good when they only expected to rescue about 20,000.'

There were murmurs of approval all round.

'What's he think of King Leopold?' asked Jackie.

'Thinks he's a bad type. He didn't say so, but said there is no reason why we should not form our own opinions on his surrender.'

'That might mean anything. That's political language.'

'Well, I think he's put up a black, anyway. He asked us to go in to save his country at the last moment. If he had had any sense he would have been in with us at the beginning.' This was Tony.

'The Army are saying the RAF had its finger in over Dunkirk. What did Churchill say about that?' asked Ollason, changing the subject.

'He says it's all rot, the fighter boys were fighting like hell miles away. What better targets could there have been for the German bombers than the ships at Dunkirk? And what a mess they would have made if they had been let loose among them'.

'I suppose a lot of bombers did get through,' I said. 'I met a chap at Brighton who said he saw nothing else.'

'Well, that's pretty natural,' Oscar pointed out. 'When the boys had to refuel, they had to fly a long way back to their bases. In any case, they were out-numbered three to one, and so it's quite natural that a few bombers slipped through.'

'Well, the Army are pretty browned off about it,' said Bill, who had just woken up and was lighting his pipe. 'I came up from Salisbury yesterday, and the chaps down there say it isn't safe to go into a pub unless in convoys of two or three. The brown jobs are beating up anything in blue they can see.'

'Oh, you can't blame them; they have had a hell of a time. They have been thrown out of Norway, kicked out of France. Where next?'

'God knows.'

'First thing to do is get a foothold somewhere.'

'Yes.'

'Oh, they've had a pretty tough break all right,' said Oscar. 'Being thrown out a second time is bad enough, but I honestly can't see what went wrong.'

Most flying fellows like to be armchair strategists, and Oscar was no exception. Getting out his cigarette case he began to expound his views.

Norway was just a case of too many aircraft on the other side. We didn't have enough bases close enough to Norway to even protect our troops, but this time I think we had enough but didn't use them all in close support of our army. Like ourselves.'

'But we would have been hacked down like flies,' I pointed out.

'Well, we could have been protected by our Metropolitan fighter strength.'

'Then the Luftwaffe would have bombed London flat.'

'Maybe you're right,' Oscar went on. He loved arguing. 'Let's say we could have done this with more close-support aircraft but didn't have them available. After all, the shortage of aircraft and the right type of aircraft dates back to Swinton days. But to go back to the land forces. In the first case, if those petty neutrals had come in with us right at the beginning, the situation might have been different.'

'That goes for Norway, too,' said Bill.

'It will go for all neutrals for ever,' said Oscar, lighting his cigarette. 'Then there was another snag. As soon as Germany invaded Belgium our armies rushed in to do their bit. However, they were too late to consolidate their lines of supply and the Germans were too quick for them. When the Jerries took Sedan and crossed the Meuse only a retreat right back to Amiens could have saved the situation. However, Weygand thought he could hold on and close the gap, but this type of blitz warfare was new to most of our commanders and strong point after strong point fell by the combined use of dive-bomber and tank. Moreover, the French soldiers, or some of them at least, surrendered on the slightest provocation.

Then came the kick in the stomach when King Leopold surrendered and left us a gap of thirty miles along the coast to defend.

'I suppose there was nothing for it, we just had to fall back; in fact, right back to Dunkirk, having lost a good deal of our allied strength. I believe seventeen French Divisions went for a Burton, and of course the whole of the Belgian Army, and I think about 30,000 of our own. Taking things all round I think it was a complete *débâcle*.'

'It was certainly that; but what's going to happen now?'

'Oh, I don't know. The French may hold out in the north until we can get a new army over.'

'Perhaps, but it's not going to be an easy job.'

'Churchill says we have lost all our equipment.'

There was a long silence. We often used to have discussions about the war; this was one of them now. Someone was thinking of something good to say.

Then the door opened and Willie walked in. There was a scuffle as we all scrambled to our feet.

'Sit down, chaps.' He was in a good mood. 'Any of you fellows any good at billiards or other games of skill?' he asked, as he stood there, eyebrows raised. No one said anything; we weren't quite sure what he meant.

'I want two volunteers,' Willie went on. Then he pointed to Pit and me. 'You and you.'

I groaned. What game could this be? I wanted to get cracking in the air, not playing billiards for some country fête.

Up in his office Willie took the lid off a small plasticine model. It was a miniature railway tunnel. He was serious now and began talking quietly.

'Your job tonight is to try out a new experiment that Air Vice-Marshall Harris has thought out. As you know, things have gone badly in France, and it is his idea to hold up the enemy attack by concentrating on severing his railway communications; the roads we are leaving to the day boys. As you know, the most vulnerable points of railways to attack are bridges and tunnels. The former are very hard to hit, but the latter resolve themselves into a simpler problem. Just now I asked whether you played billiards. Well, actually, I meant snooker, and what I want is just that. I want a couple of fellows who will drop their bombs so that they roll into the tunnels and explode a few seconds afterwards. This, of course, will block the railway for quite a few days and in turn might have quite an effect on the amount of supplies the Germans can get through. There will be many applications to this game,' he ended, 'but I leave them to you to find out. Take-off will be at ten tonight.'

No sooner had we left than a great smile lit up Pit's face. No snooker player himself, this was a game after his own heart.

We took off together and flew off across the sea, past smouldering Rotterdam on the left, across Belgium and badly blacked-out Brussels and on into Germany.

In fact, everywhere we noticed that the blackout was fairly bad and people were waving to us with torches. Away on the left an aircraft was being coned by searchlights at about 13,000 and being shot to hell by heavy flak. For some reason it had its bottom identification light on, and later we heard that this was some fellow in A flight who had forgotten to turn it out after taking off. No wonder he told the boys, 'You'd think I was the only aircraft in the sky . . . '

By map-reading carefully from canal to canal we at last came to our tunnel near Aachen. By now the moon had gone down, so I released a flare. Like striking a match in the dark to see the way so suddenly we saw our tunnel clear and sharp in the yellow light. There was no time to waste, as these flares only burn for about three minutes, and so we dived into the attack. Down the railway lines we went like a high-speed train, and I noticed almost subconsciously that the signals were up. Then, when the cliff face seemed to be towering high above us, we pulled right up and at the same time let go a couple of 500-pounders. A few seconds later, during which we saw trees miss our wingtip by inches, there came a welcome roar and turning round we saw the entrance to the tunnel had collapsed. This was fine and we still had two bombs on board. When we came to our next tunnel, about ten miles farther on, we encountered a snag. The other reconnaissance flare would not fall off. This was terrible. It was too dark to see without one. If the armourers had heard even a quarter of what we said in that aircraft in the next few minutes, even they would have been embarrassed.

In the end Watty and I hit upon a plan. We flew down on to the railway line as low as possible and then I turned on my landing light, which lit up the permanent way enough for me to see the sleepers rush by. At the same time Watty held the Aldis light straight forward, acting as a spotlight waiting for the tunnel to loom up in its light. All the while the cliff face drew nearer and nearer at 200 miles an hour. For a few minutes we flew like this, watching the shiny surface of the railway lines, while I prayed there would be no night-fighters about. While we were flying along like a Brock's Benefit, some lonely soul opened up with a machine gun nearby, but must have been squinting because it went about half a mile behind.

Then – 'Here comes the tunnel. Bombs . . . bombs gone.'

On the word 'gone' I slammed the throttles forward and remember seeing the tunnel spotlighted in our Aldis lamp before I yanked back the stick. The old Hampden, relieved of her bombs, went up like an elevator, and we just cleared a 400-foot cliff by a few feet. I remember this well because it was a white cliff with a chalk face, and we could see it quite clearly; eleven seconds later came that pleasant muffled crump, showing that we had reached our mark.

When we landed Pit had a better story to tell. He had been back an hour before and had had an even easier time, and in my opinion had done a much better job. When he found his tunnel he had noticed a train steaming into it. Full of cunning, he had quickly flown round the other end and by careful aiming had sealed it up: then he dashed back to the end the train had entered and had sealed down that entrance too. What a chap! especially for the son of a Scottish Presbyterian minister!

There is an entry in my log book which reads: 'June 13, 1940 – Hampden L.4070 – Pilot: self and crew – duty: bombing Ghent and England (nearly) – time: 7.15 hours.'

This was one of those occasions when you nearly put your foot in it, but not quite. We were returning from a mission which involved the bombing of a German military headquarters at Ghent at dawn. Usually in these cases we used to set course from a target in a south-westerly direction, so as to arrive over Unoccupied France in daylight when there wouldn't be any air opposition. Often on these trips you could see the confusion of the refugees packing the roads, trudging their lonely way towards the south coast. When we had arrived at a safe spot in this unoccupied area we would then set course direct to England.

On this occasion, however, we arrived a little early and Watty thought he could make it direct with the hours of darkness available. So we set course straight to base, i.e., north-west. Soon we ran into low cloud and after a while passed over a concentration of heavy guns and searchlights. We thought that this must have been Dunkirk, and we then turned due west. As daylight came we got closer and closer to the ground, every eye looking in all directions for enemy fighters. We thought we were still over France, and there was still no sign of the French coast coming up. When it was quite light we began to distrust our compass and turned north-west, steering as far as we could judge by the sun. By now we were flying right down among the trees, everyone on board completely scared stiff. Suddenly an aerodrome loomed up in front, and I opened my bomb doors in desperation. If I was to be forced down among the Hun the last thing I could do while still flying was to bomb a hangar, and we still had one bomb left. Just as my finger was playing with the button I thought I recognized the field. Yes, no doubt about it now. This was Harwell and this was England. I slammed the bomb doors shut and quickly turned on to a new course. After an hour we arrived at base to find that we were exactly three hours overdue. Most people thought that we had had it.

One Whitley pilot though wasn't so lucky and put up a real black. He did the same as I had nearly done, only this time he actually did let go a stick right across an English aerodrome. No sooner had he done this than both engines failed for lack of fuel. Quickly he slid his giant aircraft into a cabbage field and then proceeded to set fire to it, as one does on these occasions. When it was burning nicely he hid himself and his crew in a barn nearby, hoping to make a dash for the open country when night fell. Suddenly a Royal Air Force staff car drove up and out stepped a Group-Captain. Having watched the progress of the crew with binoculars from a control tower nearby, he had gone straight to the barn . . . I am told that the heat of the language from that wooden shack was only equalled by the heat of the blazing Whitley a few yards away.

The Germans, too, were quite good at this sort of thing. One crew, obviously not the very best types, got lost during one of their 'armed reconnaissance' patrols. At last they came to South Wales and in the moonlight saw the silver glow of the Bristol Channel to the south.

'Ach,' said the navigator. 'Good – English Channel.'

The pilot turned south and after a while they came to more land.

Said the navigator again: 'Good – France at last.'

But he was wrong – this was North Devon. By now it had got light and they were getting low in their fuel supply, so they landed at the first airfield they saw.

And so, a tired Army gunner nearly asleep in his sandbags must have been rather surprised to see, at about ten past six in the morning, a Ju 88 make a perfect landing on No. 2 runway, then taxi up to the Watch Office. No doubt he immediately began to make out a report.

But the pilot was a stooge. Still thinking he was in France, he got out and walked to the control tower. Here an airman standing at the door failed to salute him, not being quite sure of the uniform and not certain of the rank. The pilot gave him a raspberry in German.

The airman was a keen moviegoer and suddenly realized. Out came his revolver and that was that. One more prisoner had been added to a long list.

Many stories such as this can be told, but must wait until after the war.

These were the days when we were working at maximum effort with very little sleep. It was a question of bombing as often as possible; as often as humans could possibly take the strain. And so the villages of Lincolnshire and East Anglia were kept awake all night long as the bomber boys roared off and returned from missions.

It was with regret that we watched dear old Willie Snaith leave us, this time for good. A new chap. Sisson, came along to take over the squadron. Sisson was a small, quiet man with a pleasant personality who did not say much. Meanwhile, the other squadron had also got a new CO called Gillan. It was Gillan who, in 1938, flew a 335-mph Hurricane down from Scotland at the average speed of 408 mph. For this he earned the eternal name of Downwind Gillan. He was a forceful personality and for sheer contrast the two were as different as chalk from cheese.

Each day while we were doing our best to delay the Germans' advance, Crosby would wake me at the usual time whether I had been up all night or not. That cup of tea was always welcome, but his voice got more and more doleful every day, his face longer and longer. Each day it was the same, there was no variation. He was pessimism personified.

On the 10th. 'Italy's in, Sir. Shall I order breakfast, Sir?'

On the 12th. 'Rouen has fallen, Sir. Do you want your best uniform?'

On the 14th. 'Paris is out, Sir. You look a bit tired this morning, Sir.' And so on.

Doleful days. Bad and black days. England had never sunk so low, and yet in some ways she had never risen to such a fine height, for it seemed that soon this little country would be alone defending the world against Nazi tyranny.

On the night of the 17th we listened to Churchill's broadcast to the people. Pétain had just sued for peace.

'The news from France is very bad, and I grieve for the gallant French people who have fallen into this terrible misfortune. Nothing will alter our feeling towards them or our faith that the genius of France will rise again. What has happened in France makes no diffence to our actions and purpose. We have become the sole champions now in arms to defend the world cause. We shall do our best to be worthy of this high honour. We shall defend our island home and with the British Empire we shall fight on unconquerable until the curse of Hitler is lifted from the brows of mankind. We are sure that in the end all will come right.'

Great words by a great man, prophetic words. But who could tell then that all would come right? It seemed practically impossible. It seemed that anything might happen.

To refer to a very different sort of personality we come to a large fat man, Hermann Goering, who had made millions of Reichsmarks by getting his fat fingers into such huge organizations as Krupps and Linz. But Hermann was also, on the quiet, the proud owner of a small oil refinery near Hanover. In fact, it was his model refinery, not too large, not too small, but just right to bring in enough money to spend on his uniforms every year. It was said that the fat Marshal had built a canteen specially for his men with his name over the door in nine-feet letters.

Naturally, this juicy target was not overlooked by the planners of Bomber Command, and one day in June it was with great pleasure that 83 Squadron received the order to destroy it.

We took off, well overloaded so as to do as much damage as possible, and three hours later clearly saw the target in the light of the nearly full moon. Rather like moths around a flame, we circled at 2,000 feet, waiting for the right time. Walt Disney could not have created a better spectacle. Pit started it off. We saw him running in, quite level, taking his time, and then his bombs crumped on to the foundry and sent what looked like molten metal spraying out in all directions. That started it all. The boys came romping in and soon the foundry area was one mass of bomb-bursts. One by one the buildings caught fire and glowed dull red like a smouldering charcoal fire 500 yards below us. But we waited, Watty and I. We had a plan. At last, when we thought that all the boys had bombed and gone home, we cut off our engines and glided towards the oil storage tanks. As yet no one had touched them, as these are not the most important part of an oil refinery, but what we wanted to see was a good blaze. When we were about 300 feet high. Watty began to let go, trying, if possible, to put a separate bomb in each tank. Then, seconds later, there was a whoomph! and every tank blew up. The most wonderful sight that any man could ever hope to see, especially when you are responsible for it, and even more especially when they belong to Hermann Goering.

As I walked into the Intelligence Office later in the morning. Oscar had just finished writing his report. I noticed he had put 'Target destroyed', and this seemed queer, so I went up to him.

'What did you think of it, Oscar?' I asked.

'Damn fine blaze,' unemotionally.

'But there wasn't a blaze when the boys left,' I pointed out. 'I know because I waited. We went for the oil-tanks.'

'Well, what time did you bomb?' Oscar asked curiously.

'Twenty-five past one,' I answered.

'So did I. And I went for those tanks, too.'

Then I burst out laughing. So both of us had hit upon the same idea and we had both bombed at exactly the same time. It was lucky we hadn't both blown ourselves out of the sky. Three weeks later we heard from a reliable and secret source that Hermann Goering had moved his refinery far out to East Prussia.

Night after night it went on. Parties seemed things of the past, dreams of days gone by. All of us were averaging twenty sorties a month, and despite the fact that most of these were carried out at very low level the losses were not unduly high.

Nuisance raids on the Ruhr marshalling yards were the order of the day for a while, in order to delay German transport behind the lines, and as only about six aircraft were sent to each place the damage done by flak was considerable.

On one particular night Jack Kynoch, myself and Ross were sent to Soest; Oscar and three others to Gelsenkirchen, to try to destroy signal boxes, which, after all, are the most vulnerable part of any railway. By flying with the hood open at about 500 feet we at last got to the Ruhr

River, turned left, found the Möhne Lake and, of course, four miles north lies Soest. We bombed at 600 feet and nearly came to the end of a brief career there and then. There was much more flak than I thought possible in such a small place, and in a second I nearly had a baby as one shell took off the starboard wingtip, and then as we dived quickly for safety more shells pumped home, one severing both rudder cables. Getting out of the dive was quite a game without rudders, and why we did not hit a tall house standing at a crossroads I shall never know. Watty in the front said he thought I was cutting it a bit fine. This time I think perhaps he was right. The port engine had been hit and the oil pressure had dropped to 40 pounds per square inch. This meant if it failed, without rudders available, we would have to land at once. The trip home was a nightmare. Mac tapped out an SOS, the only one I have ever sent, so that should the engine seize we would be able to be 'fixed' and perhaps they might be able to rescue us.

But all went well and we landed safely, our rudders still flapping uselessly behind.

Rossy and Kynoch had not been so lucky and had bombed alternative targets, but Oscar and the rest of the boys had done some good work at the other place, although they had paid the price and all their aircraft received many holes in odd places. Someone in B flight had been so badly wounded that he had crashed while trying to land his aircraft and the whole lot had been killed.

Next night we went to another place on the Baltic coast called Wismar, where one of the big Dornier factories was situated, turning out seaplanes and bombers.

The Adjutant had just told me as I took off that I had been awarded the DFC, and I remember thinking at the time, this is a fine time to tell a chap a thing like that.

As it happened, the whole of our squadron reached and bombed the target, while not a soul in 49 Squadron found it. This was a great feather in our cap, but our rivalry was now disappearing with the coming of new faces.

The attack on Wismar was the same as all other targets, low level in the face of heavy light flak. My job, after I had bombed, was to beat up searchlights around the aerodrome. This was fine, and Mac shot out six, so he said, but when we got back both Pit's aircraft and mine had quite a few holes in them, and were both unserviceable for a week.

This was a memorable night, too, because there was a great argument in the briefing room when we got back as to who had started the only fire on the aerodrome. Sergeant Lister, one of the pilots, who had never started a fire before, kept on claiming it as his own, and on looking back I think he was right.

And so Aachen, Düren, Cassel, Amiens and all the rest, and a few military objectives such as aircraft factories, received half-a-dozen British bombers every night. Although the damage wasn't much, the strain on the crews was extraordinary, and some of the boys began to suffer from the first signs of over-strain and lack of sleep.

In the average Bomber Officers' Mess, what with batmen and waiters whistling, and banging doors, while penguins sing loudly in the mornings as they get up to shave, it was rather hard for the boys who had been up all night to get a good day's rest. To solve this problem and to try if possible to get the airmen among pleasant surroundings, a large country house had been requisitioned nearby: the idea being that the crews could sleep there and use it as a sort of club, while the officers were billeted in large country mansions all round the district.

It so happened, and not entirely by accident, that Oscar, Rossy, Jack, Tony and I were all billeted at a very nice old lady's whose name I shall not mention. She was tall and grey and psychic. She had a husband who was long since dead. Her house was one of the Lincolnshire paddock type with its own church and cemetery and acres of land; a fine rambling old place which had seen better days. I did not know what this lady's financial position was, but after a while I noticed she would be doing her own housework and that some of the chairs needed mending and that the carpets were frayed at the top of the stairs. Little things, I know, but whether I was wrong or not, I admired the spirit which enabled her to keep her home and her heritage going.

I am afraid we were not very good billettees; at least not very quiet ones. When we got back from a raid at night we were usually in very high spirits. Often we would make such a noise that we waked up the whole household. Often we played silly games in her garden, such as trying to plunge through the rhododendron bushes on bikes without hurting ourselves or rolling on the lawn in one great fighting mass cutting up all the grass, which must have broken her heart next day.

Soon I was to discover that this old lady was a firm believer in spirits and the occult. One night I sat up late with her talking about fear and faith and many other things until I had completely run out of conversation. I personally didn't have much to say on the subject, but she would ramble on for hours. In the end I stifled a yawn and went to bed, but not before she had confided in me that there were visible spirits in this very house, spirits which she knew by name and which visited her on occasion. Having seen death hurled about in four dimensions, and not wishing to see the fifth, I grabbed my candle and went upstairs.

It was an old house with no electricity, so when I had blown out my candle and got into bed I lay awake thinking a long time about what she had said. At last the country air took effect and I went to sleep.

Suddenly, in the middle of the night, something woke me up. I did not know what it was and I didn't care, but feeling thirsty I lit my candle again and groped my way to the bathroom to get a glass of water. Now this was in the summer and it was a very hot night. On such occasions I sometimes sleep without pyjamas, and tonight was one of these occasions. As I was tripping my way back from the bathroom, quite unashamed in my nakedness, my candle blew out. I grabbed the banisters and gingerly began feeling my way back to the door. Suddenly, unmistakably, from the depths of the house came the gentle swelling music of an organ played softly. I stood still. I was petrified. So these were the spirits. Then, as if someone had stuck a pin into my back, I made a dash for my room. I remember the first two steps – then, nothing, and I was falling head over heels into space.

When the noise subsided I realized I had fallen downstairs. Cursing, I began to crawl my way up. Suddenly at the top appeared a queer figure in a nightcap and old-fashioned nightgown. It was the old lady. A querulous voice broke the silence. 'Is that you, John, is that you?' she called out. She was peering into the darkness down below.

By now rather ashamed of my lack of clothes, I at last managed to blurt out that it wasn't John and that it was me, and would she kindly leave the candle at the top of the stairs so that I could find my way to my room.

When I at last got back into bed again Jack and Tony came in. They had just come back from a late raid and both had had a few glasses of beer.

'Nice organ in that church,' said Jack to Tony.

'Yeah, good organ that. I didn't know you played so well.'

I nearly leaped at them. So it was they who had been playing the organ in the middle of the night in the old chapel. And to think that for a moment I had been scared!

Next night John, with a very large lump on his head, was bombing Lorient, making great efforts to keep inside four dimensions and not slip into the fifth.

CHAPTER SEVEN

SUSTAINED EFFORT

By the beginning of July most of the bomber crews were just about all in. Lack of sleep night after night has a cumulative effect, and soon tempers began to get frayed and quarrels were picked on the slightest provocation. Many of the boys, especially old Jack Kynoch, would use one of the finest old British traditions to the full; that is, grumbling about everything: the weather, the aeroplanes, the bomb load, even the war.

However, had we been more wide awake we would have realized that the change of policy in our bombing technique was slowly making itself felt in Bomber Command. Up to now we had done our best to support land operations indirectly by concentrated attacks on military objectives in the rear, but France was now going under. Military objectives could no longer aid actions being fought at the front, and slowly but surely we began to bomb Germany on an organized pattern: part of a long-term policy. These co-ordinated blows were to fit into a big jigsaw puzzle of an offensive which was not to last one year, nor even two, but perhaps four. And so plans were changed. The Ministry of Economic Warfare had long consultations with the Chief of Bomber Command, and later orders were given out to Group-Commanders to hammer away at dockyards, at oil, at ships and at submarines. In these dark days this was our only offensive against Germany. Soon it was to become complementary to many others.

On July 5 the Pétain Government in Vichy broke off diplomatic relations with the British. No sooner had they done this than they laid the tortured, innocent people of France open to air attack as well. These men of Vichy, thinking no doubt that the days of Great Britain were numbered, were only too ready to flirt with their new German mistress. And so the factories of France began turning out goods in the shape of lorries, tanks and guns for the Reich.

One clear night in July, the skies of southern France reverberated with the din and heavy hum of many twin-engined bombers. I was in one of the leading aircraft and had been told to be extremely careful not to bomb French civilians. Our target was a lorry factory on the River Loire. As this was well away from any nearby town it seemed that we would be able to lay it flat without hurting anyone.

As we neared Nantes I saw the whole town light up like peacetime. There was no question of blackout; they just weren't expecting us. And even later on, moving down the river some distance towards Lorient, we at last came to our factory, and here we found the same thing. It was just one blaze of light. It was pleasant flying over a lit-up area again, so different from Germany and reminiscent of the good old days of peace.

After a time we circled until we were joined by the other aircraft. From about 2,000 feet – which is, after all, only 700 yards – we could quite easily see people moving around the factory roads in the light of the arc lamps and wondered when they would begin to take to their shelters, because we could not possibly bomb them before they had gone down below. Someone dropped a bomb in the river to let them know there was a raid on and to try to hurry them away from their lathes and furnaces. Then it started. Panic reigned down below and for about twenty minutes one by one the lights of the factory began to go out. Someone even opened up with a machine gun. It soon appeared that the place was quite empty. Then the boys proceeded to knock it flat.

On this occasion no one saw my own bomb-bursts, a sure sign that they fell in the river, and so old Watty, for the first time in his life, had under-shot.

On the way back we passed over St Malo. Only two years before I had spent a very nice holiday here, and I couldn't believe that we were now returning after such a mission. But it was lucky for the world that we were in a position to do these things.

The next night someone managed to get some flak down there, but whether it was manned by French Quislings or Nazis I do not know. Anyway, it was very inaccurate.

When this area had been heartily bombed, the boys moved farther south to Bordeaux. Here an attack on the oil-tanks at low level by about twenty-four aircraft burnt for two weeks. Rightly had the rear-gunner of the leading aircraft claimed that the target had been destroyed. However, most pilots had been taught not to believe the rear-gunner, because usually he is over-enthusiastic. After all, the pilot is always responsible for the final report and has to put his signature to it.

I know of a good instance where a certain pilot put up quite a black by making this mistake. He was in my squadron (no names, no pack-drill) and had been detailed to attack a factory near Strasbourg. It was a normal trip and everything went fine. There wasn't much flak and the bombing raid was made at extremely low level. As they turned away the rear-gunner reported flames and sparks up to 1,000 feet and, of course, saw the tall chimney fall down. Next day when the pilot made out his report he merely wrote 'Target obliterated' and strolled off to the Mess to have his morning can of beer. Later his CO sent for him while he was having his lunch. He was quite pleasant but a bit plaintive. 'Look,' he said. 'I know you have a good record, but why on earth did you claim to have destroyed that target last night?' The pilot was incredulous, he did not quite understand what the CO meant. Then the CO went on: 'You say that sparks and flames rose to a thousand feet, yet your Flight-Sergeant has just come in here and told me that you brought all your bombs back, except for a can of incendiaries.'

This story has two morals: 1. Never shoot a line until you have made certain your bombs have dropped; and 2. Never believe the rear-gunner.

Another time when attacking the *Scharnhorst*, which was lying in dry dock in Kiel harbour, Jack Kynoch bombed from 16,000 feet. When he came back his rear-gunner reported two direct hits near the funnel, one near miss on the dry dock and one in the water. This rear-gunner must have had mighty good eyes, because we were trying at the same time to dive-bomb the thing with a 2,000-pound armour-piercing bomb from

6,000 feet, and each time we couldn't see a thing. In all we made six dives and on the last one that great bomb fell off too late and dropped into the middle of Kiel town. This, of course, may have killed some civilians, but it was purely an accident, as we had been told carefully to avoid the town.

One thing puzzled us that night. We had not hit any balloon cables and surely such an important harbour would be absolutely bristling with them. Two weeks later we found out why. A high-flying Blenheim brought back some good pictures of Kiel after our attack, indicating that there had been a gap in the balloon barrage about a quarter of a mile wide and by sheer luck each time we dived we had gone through it. Why there should have been a gap no one ever knew. Perhaps least of all the Germans. The photographs also showed something else, that the *Scharnhorst* had been hit six times by small bombs. So perhaps that rear-gunner did have very good eyesight!

This sustained effort was very much easier than the other thing and everyone began to quieten down. We would fly one day and then have perhaps two days off. It was quite a pleasure to be able to go out to Lincoln again; perhaps get tight on the first night and rest on the second, ready for operations on the third. Mull, Rossy and I would often go to the celebrated Theatre Royal in Lincoln City, watch the first house of a road show, which was usually lousy, and then drink till ten o'clock in the Crown afterwards. A pleasant way of spending an evening and not too hectic.

Life became quite orderly and we felt rather like businessmen who spend their days in a year doing regular things. At the same time tempers calmed down and nerves became normal, and everyone was quite happy once more.

Every night between 100 and 150 bombers would leave England bent on bombing missions over Germany. Their course would take them over separate areas far and wide, from Denmark to Southern France. For these were the days when raids were spread over a period of the whole night, so that the sirens would blow everywhere all night long, causing as much disruption to war production as possible. For instance, in the vast steel mills in the Ruhr, scared workmen would be forced to leave the furnaces; in time the crucibles would cool down, the steel would harden. It would take some time to drill it all out.

Enemy night-fighters were practically non-existent, or at least we thought so, because they had no method of detection. But, on the other hand, German flak was extremely heavy and very accurate; it ought to have been because they had been making guns for eight years. One of their favourite tricks was to put a box barrage just above you which would creep down on top, forcing you to get lower and lower until you were in range of the light flak guns, where the searchlights would grab you, and you would be very lucky if you got out without being hit several times. Even in those days their method of detection was very sensitive and often above the clouds. It was nothing to see a shell burst 100 yards away dead level past one of the wingtips. But despite this night-bombing losses were very low, about 3½ per cent. On the other hand, accuracy was very low, too, not many bombs actually reaching the target. So both sides were satisfied.

For good or ill, therefore, every night when the weather was fine German sirens would wail in Hamburg, where lay the *Tirpitz*, in Wilhelmshaven, where the *Bismarck* was lurking, in Kiel, home of the *Scharnhorst* and *Gneisenau*, and in many cities from Aachen to Frankfurt.

On some occasions when conditions were ideal severe damage was done; other times, when cloud blocked all chance of getting a pinpoint, probably no bombs dropped within miles of their objective. The Germans, too, were beginning to lay out dummy cities, with dummy factories burning furiously inside them. Often a very heavy weight of bombs would fall around these places, while the Germans fired anything but dummy flak at the bombardier. But sometimes, strange to say, these dummies helped. There was one near 'X', a huge affair which looked almost too absurd for words; everything was set out in typical Hunnish fashion in straight lines and squares. The procedure here was simply to navigate to this place, which could be seen miles away, then, knowing that 'X' was only eighteen miles south-west, the rest was comparatively easy.

These trips to places inside Germany often meant spending a long time over enemy territory, especially in slow aircraft like Hampdens. Because we had no real navigation equipment, except sextants, which very few navigators knew how to use anyway, we would often stray off track and blunder over some enemy strong point and get heartily shot out of the sky for our pains. To overcome this snag many contrivances were devised, but the one which worked best of all was to carry the Luftwaffe emergency cartridge which signifies an aircraft in distress. Whenever their defences opened up we would fire one of these, and as soon as the red sparkling light left the aircraft in a gentle curve every gun and every searchlight would immediately pack up. The layman would think that such a trick could only be used once, but we went on using it for months. I think the explanation of this was simply that at that time the Luftwaffe in Germany was all-powerful and the simple rather brow-beaten Reichswehr AA gunners lived in constant fear of shooting down one of their own planes.

And so, with that new-fangled device 'George' flying the aeroplane all the way back from Mannerheim, it was quite pleasant to sit there and eat oranges while the rear-gunner periodically fired off one or two of these cartridges.

Towards the end of July word got around that a lot of Germany's armament reserves were being stored in scattered hangars in the Black Forest. A plan was accordingly set afoot to destroy these and other weapons and also Hitler's wood supply. Scientists put their heads together and soon the weapon was evolved. For some curious reason they named it razzle. It consisted of two square sheets of celluloid about six inches long, and in the middle, surrounded by damp cottonwool, was placed a piece of phosphorus. The idea was a simple one; the razzle fell into a wood or on to dry grass, the cottonwool would take about fifteen minutes to dry, the phosphorous would begin to smoulder and set light to the celluloid, which would burn with a very fierce flame for about ten seconds. Naturally the art of dropping this was called razzling.

These razzles were always carried supplementary to the bomb load, and no special mission was ever planned which would involve razzling alone. Mostly the pilots were told to arrange their routes to a target so that they passed over a large portion of the Black Forest or any other forests in Germany, when they could be dropped at will. Large conflagrations were caused which burned for weeks on end, for the summer was particularly dry at that time. To my mind this idea was quite a success, but one pilot, so the spies told us, made a navigational error while flying across the cloud and dropped his razzles in the middle of Bremen. The citizens of that gay city, having received a few leaflets the night before, thought this was more British propaganda coming down from the skies; knowing full well that the Gestapo's eyes were everywhere watching their movements, they stealthily crept along the streets, picked up the razzles, stuck them in their trousers pockets and took them home to read . . . The results must have been embarrassing.

Oscar, Rossy and I were having a good laugh about this story on day sitting on the lawn of our baronial hall when Jack Kynoch turned up.

'Hullo, chaps. I have been posted.'

'Where?' asked Rossy.

'Cottesmore.'

This was an operational training unit.

'Who else?' Oscar asked.

'Only Sergeant Ollason and myself. I don't know why. I suppose I am being rested or something. Well, I must rush off and pack now. Cheerio, chaps.'

And with these words Jack went off on his bike to the main camp.

'That's funny,' said Oscar. 'I hadn't thought of a rest. I thought we would go on for ever.'

'Me too.'

'And I reckon I could go on for ever, too,' Oscar went on. 'Anyway, I think I have got the answer to this night-bombing racket. As long as you keep alert the whole time and keep as far as possible out of defended areas, except over the target, there is no reason why you should not do a hundred trips. What do you think, Rossy?'

'I like high-level attacks,' Rossy replied in his Australian dialect, 'or else it must be the very low-level prang; but the main thing, without a doubt, is to keep right on the track.'

'I agree,' I said. 'But, of course, it takes a lot to beat a dive-bombing attack for sheer safety; the only snag is that you have to rely on the rear-gunner to find out where the bombs went.'

'That's OK,' said Oscar, rudely; 'they will always shoot a pretty good line for you.'

Rossy laughed, probably thinking of the chap in B Flight who had bombed Strasbourg.

'But seriously,' Oscar went on, 'if you are really in the know in this game, there's sweet FA danger to the whole thing.'

'Well, there's always the chance of a lucky hit.'

'Yes, but it will have to be pretty lucky to hit me,' said Oscar, lighting his pipe.

Just as he spoke a tremendous explosion came from the direction of Scampton, followed by a column of black smoke 3,000 feet high.

'Christ, what on earth's that?'

'That wasn't an aircraft.'

'Come on, let's see.'

When we got up to Scampton we found all ground personnel emerging from their shelters. At first we thought they had been bombed, but later a calm WAAF in the operations room told us what had happened. Eighteen magnetic mines in the bomb dump had just blown up and she said that the stones were still falling five minutes afterwards. It was certainly the biggest explosion I had ever heard.

At this time Hemswell had just carried out an attack with twenty-four aircraft on a very special military objective on the Ems Canal. They pressed home their attack from very low level. The raid was a success in so far as it destroyed one bridge, but it was necessary to destroy the second one which carried the Dortmund Canal over the River Ems. This bridge, of course, is very vulnerable to air attack, and when Hemswell carried out the raid it was practically undefended. However, there was every indication that the Huns had now put in a few searchlights and plenty of light flak all round to see that the attack was not repeated. Scampton, being at the time the best station in our bomber group, was, therefore, given the job of trying to destroy this important military objective.

Two teams, consisting of mixed crews from both squadrons, were selected; one team consisting of 'Babe' Learoyd, Pitcairn-Hill, Joe, Oscar and Mull, and the other made up of five equally good pilots as a sort of second eleven.

Training was carried out on canals in Lincolnshire the same width as the bridge which we were going to attack. Plasticine models were made and careful study was made of the lie of the land around this objective. During one of the practices Mull and I changed aircraft at the last minute. I was fairly proud of Watty as a bomb-aimer and was glad to see that during our attack he dropped his bombs exactly in the right spot. At lunch later on it was a bit of a shock when the Armament Officer came up to me and told me I had dropped the bombs on the bank, and had narrowly missed blowing his foot off. This was Mull flying in my aeroplane.

And so we trained on in moonlight until both teams were highly proficient. At the beginning of August everything was ready. Learoyd made a reconnaissance and found that the defences were fairly hot. In his estimation the job had better be done soon or not at all.

As it happened I went on leave down to Cornwall just when everything was being prepared. On my birthday, August 12, they set out. While I was drinking beers with the yokels in a pub down in Boscastle, Pitcairn, leading Learoyd, Mull, Rossy and Matthews, was droning his way towards his objective.

Much has been written about this attack, but there is no doubt that it was a very gallant effort. Pitcairn went in first, dropped his bombs in the right spot and got shot up very, very badly in the light flak defences. Next came Rossy. He went in low, and the next they saw of him was a flaming mass on the ground. Poor old Rossy was killed. Then came Mull. His port engine was set on fire, but he managed to climb up to 2,000 and was able to bale the whole of his crew out. Then came Matthews, and he too bombed accurately, but had to return on one engine. Lastly came Learoyd; in the face of blinding searchlights his bomb-aimer managed to put his bombs in the right spot.

Next day photographs were taken of the objective. The raid had been a complete success; the bridges had been breached and all the water had flowed out of the canal. This must have been a serious impediment to Hitler's barge transport.

Learoyd was given the VC, Pitcairn the DSO, and when they found that Mull was alive they gave him the DFC in his prison camp.

This raid was noteworthy because it was one of the first attacks of its kind during the war. A special attack trained for by crack crews; a completely successful attack planned by men who flew.

It was the first of many.

CHAPTER EIGHT

BATTLE OF THE BARGES

Down in Cornwall the air was good. Sitting back in my comfortable bed each morning I would look out of the window and try to realize that at that very moment the grimmest part of the Battle of Britain was being fought. Then we would go down and have breakfast and eat good food, and afterwards walk along the windswept cliffs, watching the pounding seas and trying to forget the thunder of enemy flak.

The papers rolled in about lunch time and each day I could read about the blitz on England which had just started. Eveyone remembers those early days. How on August 8 Marshall Goering sent his vaunted Luftwaffe towards London, rather like an armada Napoleon would have given a fortune to control. There were hundreds of bombers flying wingtip to wingtip in close formation, covered by a few fighters; later a few bombers would make hit-and-run raids covered by hundreds of fighters.

But they were being driven back. Everyone knows how our aircraft industry produced our fighters and equipped them with a new constant-speed propeller which made all the difference to the actual fighting. Everyone knows how our fighter boys went in. Standford Tuck, Douglas Bader, Shorty Lock and the rest of them, rallied their squadrons and went into the fight with their country at stake. They acquitted themselves well, these boys, and fought in the finest of all traditions with their backs to the wall. This battle, one of the most important ever fought, ended in a trouncing defeat for the Luftwaffe.

In the operations rooms great men watched the thin blue line slowly retreat, even as far as London, but it was never broken, and in the end it began advancing over the stratosphere towards Dover. We, like the infantrymen of old, had held the Hun and then threw them back over the other side of the Channel decimated and beaten, never to come back.

It was a great story, of which we should all be proud. Many speeches have been made about the boys concerned, many classic utterances published, such as Winston Churchill's – 'Never in the history of human conflict have so many owed so much to so few'. Songs were written and danced to in london nightclubs to celebrate the victory but let us pray, here and now, that those men will be remembered for ever; and especially in ten or twenty years' time.

While all this was going on I was slowly getting fit by sunbathing and even sometimes slipping into the cold Cornish sea, afterwards drinking quiet cans of beer with the locals in the Wellington Hotel at Boscastle. I did not feel the same as I had at Dunkirk. This time I knew that reserves were fast coming in; I knew that if they needed me they would quickly let me know. This was the time to rest, and I made the most of the chance. But at last it was over, and at Bristol we stood on the station, Eve and I, saying goodbye. Many were doing the same all round us, young people saying pre-invasion goodbyes, holding each other close and looking into each other's eyes before going into the unknown. For we were not to know that the Luftwaffe had been completely defeated; we were quite ready for the invasion. All of us had heard grim stories of the Nazi occupation of France, how they ruthlessly achieved their objectives; how callous and cruel they were as conquerors. We all know that if they set foot in England it would be the same, or worse.

At times like these one doesn't know quite what to say, and I am not very good, anyway, at saying these things, but I remember looking Eve straight in her shining eyes and holding her up to the railway carriage while the porter went running up and down the platform blowing his final whistle.

'Well, one thing, darling: if they invade Wales I will come straight down and take you away,' I whispered, not quite knowing how I'd do it; 'just send me a telegram and I will be there.'

Then there was a shrill whistle, a clanging of doors, and we began to move. Eve faded out of sight, tears streaming down her face.

Back at Scampton the sun was still shining; it was still hot, but there was a difference. A great change had taken place, at least it seemed so to me, from the Scampton I knew two weeks before. Rossy and Mull had gone, and so had some of the other boys. Sergeant Ollason had gone to his OTU. Learoyd was running around as PA to Brooke-Popham, and even some of the WAAF officers had been posted. It was a funny, depressing feeling, coming back after such a glorious leave, and a horrible feeling when I found that I was on Ops that night.

But Oscar was there as usual when I went into the Flight Office. 'Hello, Gibbo,' he said. 'We are all going to Lorient tonight, not much of a trip, just to lay mines off the U-boat basin; it ought to be pretty cissy because they have only got a couple of guns there.'

'Thanks, Oscar. Are all my crew back?'

'Yeah, they are all here, but I'm having Watty – my navigator was hit the other night. You can have the new bloke, Sergeant Houghton.'

'Well, thanks very much,' I said, feeling damned annoyed, as Watty was such a good navigator and I had got used to him. But as it happened Houghton was very good and it was poor old Watty who was to be unlucky.

It was a simple trip, and although we were laying mines very close to the shore the flak did not bother us much, and the whole squadron did a good job of work. Afterwards we looked around for some E-boats which we were told were operating in that area. We turned out to sea and stooged around with our navigation lights on so as to lull all and sundry into believing us to be friendly aircraft. Suddenly, in the long silver reflection of the moon in the calm water we saw one going at a rate of knots for a small harbour in the Île d'Eu; and Houghton pressed the button. However, at times like this, when bombing wasn't a highly organized affair, we weren't sure of our height and Houghton certainly wasn't sure of our level, and so the 2 × 250-pound bombs fell within a few yards but did not hit him; whether we damaged him or not we couldn't say, but there was some happy chatter on board as we turned for home.

But even better was to come. As we crossed over Cherbourg on the way home an aircraft passed us going in the opposite direction with his navigation lights on. This must have been a Hun which had been bombing England. Quickly we whipped around and by pushing the old Hampden to the limit so that she shuddered and quivered at the unknown horsepower she was developing, we at last caught him up just near to Lorient. For a while we flew in formation, about fifty yards away, trying to make out what type of aircraft it was, but the night was dark. At last, through the welcome beam of an enemy searchlight, we identified it as a Dornier 17. Moreover, both pilots on board seemed very happy; they had their full cockpit lights on and we could see them inside sitting motionless as they, no doubt, thought of the ersatz coffee and bacon and eggs they were going to get in a few minutes' time.

In the rear both my bottom and top guns slid slowly over to the starboard side and I told Mac to take careful aim. Then I counted slowly. 'One – two – three,' and then I yelled: 'Let him have it, Mac.'

There was a quick staccato roar as all four guns belched out tracers and the Dornier dived to the ground with one engine on fire. In doing so he flew low right over Lorient Docks, where his own flak, no doubt thinking he was one of ours, gave him a pretty good pasting, and the last we saw of him was a flaming mass going down behind some trees. Bomber Command credited us with a probable when we got home.

Next night, August 26, came the first raid on Berlin. Great excitement was caused when the target was announced. We had been waiting for this for a long time. Now we were going to get our chance. Many pilots who had been given an off-night immediately began to plead to have themselves put down on the list of the first crews to bomb the German capital. Even Downwind Gillan took an aeroplane over from one of his youngest pilots in order to be one of the first over the big city. But whoever chose August 26 chose a night when as good a head wind as any faced our medium range bombers.

The raid was in fact lousy. There was thick cloud over the target itself, and I don't suppose more than ten bombs actually landed in Berlin. On the way home the Germans, in their methodical way, had laid a line of flak which stretched in a straight line from Berlin to London and the going was very heavy. Many aircraft landed in the sea on the way home, and even in our own squadron we had three incidents. Tony Mills ran out of petrol off Flamborough Head and took to his dinghy with his crew, who were all violently seasick; Pitcairn-Hill, who was always doing things wrong but was always getting his bombs on the target, thought that he was going to be unable to make land and slid his Hampden into the sea opposite one of HM Trawlers thirty miles off Grimsby; a Canadian, called Pitt-Clayton, pulled off a dead-stick landing in the middle of an East Coast minefield and had to sit in his aeroplane for a long time, not daring to walk across the sand dunes himself in case he trod on one, while those on land watched him, not daring to walk out until a coastguard, who knew a channel, drove up and rescued them.

As soon as I landed I got my aircraft refuelled and took off to look for Tony. We were in the air six hours, but never saw a thing. When we finally landed back at Scampton I was annoyed to hear that he had been picked up a long time ago, having seen me pass over him twice, and was at the moment having a party with the boys in Grimsby.

Some nights later Joe Collier undershot when landing and crashed, giving himself very severe concussion. The next night Dickie Bunker crashed in a field near Norwich and split his skull open. Gradually our numbers were dwindling, and out of the great bunch of boys who had started to fight a war against Germany, only Pitcairn, Oscar and I were left.

Meanwhile in Hamburg harbour, where there is always a busy hum of activity from the shipbuilding yards, sat the *Tirpitz*, a great battleship of some 45,000 tons having the last fittings put on before she was to sail out on the high seas to challenge the British Fleet. Many heads in the Admiralty were put together to think out some method of disabling her before she made her first sortie.

Our capital ship situation was not good at the time and the war in the Mediterranan had seriously embarrassed our strategy. Someone had heard of our dive-bombing attacks, and on our off-nights it fell to some other boys and myself to take off early in the morning and make a dawn dive-bombing attack on the *Tirpitz* and return in time for breakfast.

Usually we would split up, some going to Wilhelmshaven, where the *Bismarck* was lying, and others to happy Hamburg. But these attacks were never much good, and owing to the fact that the bomb never fell off when we pushed the button it was lucky if we ever put one within half a mile of the dock she was lying in.

As we flew above the clouds in these early mornings over the cold North Sea, it seemed to me that the very anvil tops of the cumulas storm-clouds were all pointing the way to Germany, as if to say, 'That is the way; that is the way to Germany, and you won't come back.' Now and then a flash of lightning would make me jump vertically in my seat as at the same time I went into a vertical turn with Mac shouting: 'Flak, flak', in the background. I was getting nervy, there was no doubt about it; this bombing was beginning to get me down.

Sometimes over a German city we would make a half-hearted attack, knowing well in our hearts that we had not done our best. Even when back in bed I could not sleep, but used to lie awake at night tossing and turning, thinking of the noise of the engines and that bok-bok noise which was always in my ears. And when I did dream it was always slow-motion dreams of balloon cables, thick ones, like tree-trunks, which I would get past by landing my aircraft in the middle of Hamburg and cutting them down with an axe, then flying home as if nothing had happened.

In the middle of one night Gibby, a B Flight rear-gunner, came into my room when I was having one of these nightmares. Although I don't remember anything about it, he told me afterwards that I yelled at him to get out at the top of my voice for about five minutes, and he thought I was a raving lunatic. If ever there was such a thing as a war of nerves, then some of us in 83 Squadron were certainly beginning to get affected.

Meanwhile, although everything wasn't going dead according to plan for the Hun, he hadn't been exactly defeated in the air. No doubt Goering thought that in a few weeks' time we would come to our last reserves, and then Hitler could establish his headquarters in Buckingham Palace and the Marshal himself could take over the Savoy Hotel. In other words, the plans for the invasion of England were still on.

All the military strategists in Germany knew very well that the first thing on the programme was to obtain complete and absolute air superiority over the Channel ports. Then it would be possible to launch an invasion force, consisting of many thousands of 2,000-ton barges which would sail across one dark night, covered on either side by submarines, minesweepers and E-boats. Then, with the dawn of a September morning, unload under cover of air superiority. Once the bridgehead had been established, airfields would be improvised on the beaches and in the fields, consisting of wire-netting strips, and these no doubt would ensure the forward air support for the Invasion Force.

Marshall Rundstet, who commanded the Invasion Force, must have known that our Home Guard had not yet been equipped and that our Army was being reorganized and rebuilt. Like Napoleon, Hitler came all the way from Paris one sunny day to gaze at the white cliffs of Dover with powerful binoculars and survey his next victim.

By the beginning of September unusual activity was noticed on the canals in Germany. Barges of all kinds began to make their way to most of the invasion ports; many of these were ocean-going barges with 200-horse-power engines, capable of ploughing through the seas at 10 knots. They were laden with high explosives, tanks, field- and anti-aircraft artillery; troops stood by in the dockyards, waiting for the order to set sail. Everything was ready. Every port from Antwerp to Dieppe was packed like lumber floating in a river with thousands of these invasion barges. The Huns knew, of course, that our meagre bomber force would attack them. Light flak guns were brought from far and wide to put up a cordon of steel which would ensure that no bombs could be dropped within miles; flak towers were erected, balloon barrages were put up.

At the beginning of September the Battle of the Barges began. It went on day and night, Blenheims, Hampdens, Wellingtons all taking part in low-level attacks which not only destroyed many barges on the spot, but also killed many troops whose billets were in the warehouses nearby.

On one of these raids on Antwerp I flew for a while alongside an aeroplane which was on fire. It was a nasty sight because I could see it was one of our own. As flames and sparks came out like the wrong end of a rocket hanging in the air, I saw one chap bale out and land in the river, and I remember hoping that he could swim.

When we got back I asked young O'Connor, a Canadian boy, what sort of a trip he had had. He did not say much except that he had caught fire over the target and had got hell from the light flak. Later, I heard that Hannah, of our squadron, had been awarded the VC, for his attempt to stamp out the flames with his bare hands.

Two nights later we went again to Antwerp, and this city, with its heavy flak defences, shot down one of the few left. I saw him flying straight and level over one of the basins; taking his time about his run, making sure that all his bombs went into the right spot. Then he blew up – and Pitcairn-Hill had gone to join his forefathers.

These raids on the invasion ports were organized to destroy as many barges as possible. Each squadron was given a port which was to be considered its own particular port and the pet baby of all concerned; each crew was given a basin; in each basin there were so many barges, sometimes 200, sometimes even 400. Bomb-loads were organized so that the maximum amount of damage would be done per aircraft. Many small bombs were carried, even hand-grenades, which would, at least, do the job if they hit the right spot.

After each raid a reconnaissance was made, and the CO would call all crews together. 'I have got some pictures of C Basin at Antwerp. Yesterday there were 400 barges there; today's reconnaissance shows 350. Who is on C basin?'

Some pilot would shuffle to his feet.

'Well, you sank fifty, you and the rest, but that is not enough. You have got to put all your bombs in that basin, not a stick starting on the edge and then doing its job, but every single bomb. Otherwise those bastards over there are going to come and invade us, and then you will have to fight with your bare hands.'

Then we would go off again. Of course, sometimes this didn't work very well. In my particular basin – a thing shaped rather like a heart in the middle of Antwerp dockyards – I once gained 100 barges, and neither the CO or anyone else could tell that I was responsible for them. Taking things all round, we were sinking them fast despite all the anti-aircraft fire they could put up against us. But our losses were heavy and we all knew that we would have to win the Battle of the Barges before they started to move out. There were rumours that they actually had moved out and that we had sunk them. There were rumours that thousands of German soldiers were buried on the east coast of England; soldiers who had been hit by Bomber Command, who had been drowned and washed ashore. These rumours were untrue, and no one in this country will ever know anyone who saw a dead German soldier, although many a man will claim to know someone who knows someone else who buried one.

On September 15 the fighter boys pulled off their greatest victory. They shot down no fewer than 185 German aircraft for quite a small loss of their own, and no doubt after the war it will be known that the number destroyed was far greater.* It was the victory of superior fire-power, of superior aircraft, of superior men.

On that night we made our biggest raid on Antwerp. It was the night of the full moon; many barges were sunk, many blew up, destroying others around them. They were full of stuff and we could see, there and then, there was no doubt about it, the Germans were ready.

Flying low around these docks that night we could easily see the tanks on board, the guns on mountings at the stern of each invasion craft, the tarpaulins over sinister objects on the docks. 'Der Tag' was drawing near for the Hun, and September 15 was, perhaps, the day when they realized that it would be no use.

From now on we stepped up our trips to maximum effort and all our nerves seemed to vanish in the heat of the battle. It reminded us, perhaps, of those dark days in June. On September 17 we heard on the wireless Mr Churchill's report on the war situation in the House of Commons. The Italian Army had begun to advance in Libya, the two British platoons which had been holding Sollum had been withdrawn, but the enemy had still to reach our main line of resistance. He went on to warn us all that invasion might come at any moment.

Many will remember a few days after this a great invasion scare which swept the country. This may have been caused by one lonely Coastal

---

* Publisher's note: The true figure proved to be considerably less.

Command pilot on his moonlight patrol over the North Sea who made a slight error of observation. He was flying some 100 miles out from England, when glancing down he saw to his amazement many dark shadows moving on the sea. There were a few clouds above him, small clouds, but he did not notice these and immediately wirelessed back that the invasion was on.

Immediately everyone stood by. Fighter boys were aroused from their beds for a day's hard fighting, bomber pilots stood by till dawn, and it was only a subsequent reconnaissance by a more experienced pilot which revealed that the 'barges' in the sea were merely shadows of the small clouds reflecting on the water.

After the flap had died down there were a few sardonic laughs in the Mess, but we knew it would come one day, and although we thought we were ready, we were not quite sure about the rest of the country.

A few days later the AOC decided to give the squadron an extra night off duty. I was scared stiff that I would have to go on one of those lonely dawn missions to Hamburg to do a bit of dive-bombing, but luckily this did not happen. Jack Withers and I took ourselves to a quiet 'flick' in Lincoln because we knew that we would probably be on next afternoon. But Oscar, Tony Mills and a newcomer called Barker, whom we nicknamed 'Colonel' for obvious reasons, took themselves to Nottingham, where the story is that they got very drunk.

Next day we were on again for a large raid on Antwerp. As I was walking across the hangar, having fixed up the crews and ready to take Houghton up to the Mess for a cup of tea, the flight van drew up outside with the screeching of brakes. Out staggered the boys, somewhat the worse for wear from their night off. One was in a belligerent mood and ready to take a swing at anybody, but Jackie quickly ran forward and slapped him back in his van and drove him up to the Mess, where, with the help of a few more of the boys, he was tucked safely into bed.

Meanwhile, Tony Mills came into the Flight Office.

'Hello, Tony. You're late.'

'Yeah, I know. We had a hell of a party.'

'Well, that's OK; you're not on tonight.'

'Oh yes, I am. I'm all right.'

'Like hell you are! You're going to bed.'

The 'Colonel' joined in. They were both as high as anyone, in the sort of mood when they thought they were all right and very keen to fly. There was quite an argument. At last Jack and I with much diplomacy persuaded them that it was a cissy target and only the new boys were going, plus ourselves, to show them how. They were pleased then. Tony said:

'I would have been damned annoyed if you had kept us off because we went out last night.'

And they departed to the Mess, their honour satisfied.

And so off we went each to our own basins in Antwerp. Once again I had the pleasure of hearing that crump, crump, crump just behind my tail-plane as our bombs went off. Then, that illuminating flash which lit up the ground all round as some ammunition barge exploded. But this time something happened. There was a rending crack and a noise like the crash of thunder. At first I didn't know what had happened, and was rather frightened that Houghton in front had been killed. Then, as one does on these occasions, I suddenly realized that something was wrong with the aeroplane; she was flying in a queer way. There was no rudder bar. Then Houghton told me what was wrong. He had to crawl up to do so because the intercom had gone. A shell had entered by my feet, had got the toe-strap on my rudder bar and then had hit its pivotal point and knocked it spinning forward on to Houghton's head, where it had laid him out. Quite an unlucky shot.

When I got back to Scampton F/Sgt Langford examined the damage. I remember his words very well.

'Cor, sir,' he said, 'that's bloomin' providence, that's what I call it, bloomin' providence. It missed your foot by half an inch.'

I did not know quite what to say, but Houghton was up to the occasion and he replied, sardonically:

'No it wasn't, Flight; it was just a question of having short legs!'

Strangely enough the lad who had been put to bed was up when we got back and extremely rude. I think he was rather annoyed about his behaviour and didn't like someone taking care of him as we had. When Houghton told him about our trouble he just looked queer and said:

'What the hell do you need rudders for, anyway? You never use them, you know that, you old lineshooter.'

There was an awkward silence from the boys all round. Even the Intelligence Officers felt something was wrong. I thought for a minute I was going to say something really bad, then I realized that we were all tired out, and so I walked out of the room without saying another word.

The next night we went to Berlin. This was a big raid; the biggest so far of the war. About 200 aircraft were engaged and it looked as though it was going to be a good prang on the German capital. As we were standing around, ready to take off, I wanted to go up to Oscar and wish him 'good luck', but he hadn't said a word to me all day and I knew he was furious, so I went to my aircraft and took off.

It was one of those trips which were so common in those days. Cloud all the way, flak all the way; no one knowing where Berlin was, our loop bearings continually being jammed by the enemy and general chaos all round. Needless to say, we had to bomb at the end of our dead reckoning position where we estimated Berlin might be. Down below were several American journalists, and one of them, William Shirer, said afterwards that not many bombs actually dropped in Berlin itself. I can well believe it.

On the way home there was another head wind of gale strength, so we came back at 1,000 feet with our radio shot away. As I walked into the briefing room quite a few of the boys had already returned. Jackie Withers had had some trouble with flak over Hanover and had had to return early on one engine.

'Oscar's had it,' he said quietly and rather strangely, as I opened a bottle of beer.

'What do you mean?'

'About half an hour ago he sent out a signal, saying that one engine had been put on fire over Bremen and that he was baling out. Later another message came in that he was trying to get home. Since then there has been silence.'

'Did the messages come in strong?'

'Yes. Gorwood, his radio operator, was tapping them out as if nothing had happened.'

'Well, we had better get on to the Rescue Service and see if we can get anything.'

We waited all night; we waited until the grey darkness of the early hours became purple, then blue as the sun rose in the east over Lincoln Wolds and it became daylight. But Oscar never came back.*

And so I went to bed. I was the last one left, the last one out of a bunch of boys who belonged to 83 Squadron at the beginning of the war, to fight until the end of Hitlerism. They had all fought well, but they had paid the price. Some were prisoners of war, I knew, but many were dead. As I lay in bed thinking, I knew I was lucky to survive, but it would come to me any day now. We would go on and on until the whole squadron was wiped out, then there would be new boys to carry on our traditions, new squadrons, new gadgets and new ground crews to crack jokes with us as we took the air. I did not see any point in living. For the moment I didn't even care about Eve. All my friends had gone now – there were new people – different – with different views on life, different jokes and different ways of living. I was the last one left.

Houghton and I made one more dawn attack on Kiel. This time we carried a flare on our 2,000-pound bomb so that we could see it go into the sea. It missed by some 200 yards, so the rear-gunner said, and as we got hell beaten out of us for our attack, I swore then and there, at that moment, that I would never bomb the *Scharnhorst* again. It seemed so foolish to go there all alone. It seemed that we were the only ones fighting the war for England when you sit up there on top of a cone over a great harbour surrounded by coloured lights and smelling the flak. You feel

* Publisher's note: S/Ldr Bridgman survived, to be taken prisoner.

a long way from home, you feel you want to get back, you feel you never want to go again. And when you do come back it gets you and you want to have another crack. God knows why.

Once again we had to spend two hours over Hamburg city, dropping a bomb every thirty minutes in order to cause despondency and lack of sleep to the dwellers down below. Needless to say, we came back dithering wrecks. Never had so many guns fired at so few.

It was after this, when we were all sitting in the Mess, that Harris came in and read out Oscar's will. Someone switched off the wireless; there was silence save for the clinking of beer cans being put down on tables.

'Squadron-Leader Bridgman,' began Harris, 'asked me to read this out if he failed to come back from a raid. As you know, that has happened. So here goes.'

I looked across at Jackie Withers nervously; this was one of the moments when I would have preferred to be elsewhere. Then it began. He had left little things, such as his pipes, to Jackie, his note-book to me. He had asked one or two of us to write to his mother occasionally and then – "to —, of 49 Squadron, the biggest lineshooter of all, I leave one hearty kick in the crutch to be delivered by John Kynoch, who is the strongest man I know.'

But John Kynoch wasn't there, nor was the lineshooter.

There were one or two more raids. A few attacked the Channel ports. Others, some 300 strong, consisting of all types of bombers, made their way to such cities as Bremen, Kiel and Wilhelmshaven. Even now a change was apparent. In fact, some organization was being revealed. True, we could still choose our own routes; true, we could still bomb at any height we liked; but now the best crews began to carry flares to light up the target. Bomb-loads were scientifically worked out with a view to causing as much damage by incendiaries as possible. Bomber Command was getting organized; it was getting itself fit, it was beginning to shape itself for the years to come. But the German Bomber Command was already organized. Hitler, in a passionate speech to the German people, swore that he would raze every British city to the ground. From sundry bases in France they came, flying high and fast to begin a series of attacks on London. Such attacks made everyone's blood boil. What could we do about it? We were still told to bomb military objectives and to keep our bombs right on the target or not to bomb at all.

One night, however, the mother of one of our sergeant pilots was killed in an air raid on London when a bomb came through her window as she was lying asleep underneath the stairs. He came to me that afternoon; his eyes were wet, but he was not crying. He wanted to come with us that night, to avenge his mother.

Such a spirit spelt doom for German cities in 1943 and 1944.

The Battle of Britain and the Battle of the Barges drew to a close. The long arm of Bomber Command had begun already to reach far into Germany to smash war industries. We must never forget the boys who took part in those battles. We must never forget that they laid the foundation for all that was to come. It was a great victory and one of which England should forever be proud.

When the fighter boys showed the world that they possessed undisputed mastery of the air over the Channel and Great Britain, and when the twin-engined bombers gave the barges such a packet, William Shirer, in his *Berlin Diary*, wrote of the bombing of the Channel ports, 'But from what I saw of these bombings myself and from what I have been told by German airmen, I think it is highly improbable that the German Army would ever be able to assemble in the ports of Boulogne, Calais, Dunkirk, Ostend or on the beaches, enough barges or ships to launch an invasion in the force that would be necessary.'

Thus checked, after many days of continuous defeat, the Hun gave up his idea of invading England for a whole year and turned the might of the German army elsewhere. Future historians will say, and rightly so, in my opinion, that the Battle of Britain, coupled, in a lesser degree, with the Battle of the Barges, altered the future of the world.

CHAPTER NINE

INTERLUDE

When the Battle of Britain ended with the Luftwaffe beaten and baffled, thanks to the British aircraft industry and a few hundred pilots, new developments began to take place elsewhere. Italy, like a hungry jackal, looked round for some easy prey and found it, so she thought, in Greece. Immediately our forces in the Mediterranean, already hard-pressed, were dissipated even more by the formation of the third expeditionary force in just over one year.

While all this was going on, an interlude was taking place in Lincolnshire. This took the form of a bloodless battle royal between two age-old rivals – the Bomber Barons and the Fighter Glamour Boys. No lives were lost, no one was even injured (by a miracle) in this fight, but much cunning was used to bring about the defeat of the enemy. Like many battles, it ended with both sides saying they had won. To many it was known as the Battle of the 'Snake-Pit' and will, no doubt, go down in Air Force history as such.

Since the earliest days of the RAF there have always been two very different breeds, different both by temperament and by virtue of their job, the bombers and the fighters.

During the lull in between wars, the latter had it all their own way. At Hendon air displays everyone thrilled to the aerobatics of four Hawker Super-Furies as they looped and rolled in perfect box formation. No one noticed the heavy bomber pilot, except perhaps to say with sympathy, 'Look at the poor bloody bus-driver.'

With the advent of new and fast fighters such as the Hurricanes, there was much talk in the newspapers of 'young supermen who had to be corseted, so fast do they fly.'

All young would-be pilots at the flying training schools clamoured to be put on to single-seaters. Only a few, the very best, the cream of the Service, ever got there. One and all hero-worshipped the white-overalled Squadron-crested youth who had just stepped down from a Spitfire. If he had lowered himself out of a Handley-Page Harrow, they would have merely turned away and said to themselves: 'Poor sucker! he must be a Ham.'

Anyway, compare the thrills of flying in formation, beating up each other and ground-firing on fixed targets, to the drab training of the 'Hams' – straight runs over a camera obscura and level bombing from 10,000 feet.

Even in the cities, the fighters seemed to have all the fun, walking off with the women and drinking the beer, mainly because their stations were always close to a town, while a bomber base is miles from anywhere.

Naturally all this irked the boys of Bomber Command quite a lot. They began to take an active dislike to the flying-booted, scarf-flapping glamour boys; many a rude word was spoken between the two in practically every pub between Biggin Hill and Edinburgh.

Much of this rivalry may have arisen from the last war, when the feats of such great men as Bishop, Ball and McCudden captured everyone's imagination, while a bomber pilot hardly ever got his name in the papers.

Not surprisingly, the fighter boys became very cocky and full of their own importance, and the bus-drivers began to get quite an inferiority complex, knowing, as they did, that only the very best of them could be considered really good pilots.

Then came the war.

At first everything was forgotten in the common desire to beat the enemy. But as time wore on a few loose-fingered fighter boys would hoot down the odd bomber, and feeling began to run high again.

The trouble was that neither appreciated the other. The fighters never escorted the bombers, the bombers never saw the fighters in action. And so came the battle of the 'Snake-Pit'.

What precipitated the battle no one will ever know. Probably too much beer on both sides; anyway, the whole thing started in the small bar.

Next day three Hampdens took off from nearby Waddington, laden
to full capacity with lavatory paper and old leaflets. As they were circling
to gain altitude, a few miles away lay the aerodrome at Digby, an old
fighter station dating from the last war. Two squadrons were stationed
there at the time, a single-seater Squadron No. 141 and a twin-engined
Beaufighter Squadron, No. 29.

While the fighter boys were having their lunch, they were surprised
to hear an angry snarl of engines. The three Hampdens were beating up
the place in no mean style. As they ran out of the Mess, their mouths
gaped in astonishment. No Hampdens were to be seen, but the sky was
full of lavatory paper, floating quite slowly down on to their airfield.
Quickly the Flight-Commander swore that reprisals would follow. Being
fighters, they could not carry a sufficient quantity of paper, but they soon
hit upon a plan. Phase II would soon be in operation.

Next day there was rain and flying was cancelled. The bomber-boys
of Waddington sat around their crew-rooms, having a good laugh about
their successful venture the day before. They felt good; why, last night
even the 'Snake-Pit' had been clear of glamour boys. Everything was
fine.

At about eleven o'clock a Black Blenheim with no squadron markings
landed on their field and taxied up to the control tower.

'Hullo, Control,' it called. 'This is Group-Captain Biggleswade from
Bomber Command. I have an important message for OC 144 Squadron.
It is very urgent. Will you send him out to this aircraft immediately?'

In a few minutes the Wing-Commander's car appeared around the
perimeter track and soon he began to climb inside the Blenheim. No
sooner was he in than a bag was snapped over his head and willing
hands dragged him back into the spacious rear of the aeroplane. At the
same time the Blenheim became airborn with F/L Sandy Campbell of
A Flight 29 Squadron at the controls . . .

At Digby the Wing-Commander's instructions were simple. He was
given a long stick with a spike on it, and was politely asked to go around
and pick up all the paper his squadron had dropped the day before.
When this had been done, he was returned to his base as expeditiously
as he had come.

From then on the war raged fast and furious. Both sides had attacked,
and had drawn blood. Plans were made for the third phase.

A few days later, Digby entertained a few Mess visitors. There was
a padre from a Scottish station, an engineer officer and a few others.
They hadn't much to say and didn't stay very long. They had, they said,
to catch a train from Lincolnshire. Half-an-hour after they had gone
someone noticed that both squadron crests had disappeared from the hall.
Now, all squadrons are very proud of their crests and most of all, perhaps,

are fighter squadrons. Feeling ran high in the Mess, cars were sent to chase the padre and his gang, but no one was found.

At Waddington the crests were received with pleasure. They were set up against a tree in the Officers' Mess garden. Then all the boys gathered around with beer mugs, waiting patiently. The camera was adjusted, everything was ready. Then the camera clicked.

Next day, as mysteriously as they had vanished, the crests were returned. But stuck to the noticeboard was a picture; a picture which nearly sent the whole of Digby raving mad.

This was an outrage. Threats were hurled across the anteroom as the Digby War Cabinet met, when the bar opened, to discuss the situation.

Only two cans had been knocked back before the master plan was evolved. It seemed a cinch.

Back at Waddington, the bomber boys were puzzled. Nothing had happened for a few days and they had begun to wonder why. Next second they didn't have to worry any more, the fighter boys had come.

Screaming across the hangars they came in close formation, one jerking the motionless windsock into life, so close did he go, vapour swirling from his wingtips. For a quarter of an hour the beat-up went on, and even the bomber boys came out of their ante-room to have a look, admitting it was the best they had ever seen.

Suddenly they vanished as quickly as they had come with a final dive by the leader at the boys standing on the Mess lawn.

It was a good beat-up, but what was the point? Nothing had happened out of the ordinary. One by one the barons went back into the Mess.

When the time came to go to work they soon discovered what had happened. There were yells of chagrin throughout the bar. While they had been outside watching the beat-up, some smart type had slunk into their cloakroom and pinched all their hats.

Now a bomber boy is proud of his 'operational' peaked cap and wears it on every occasion, because he thinks he looks a stooge in a 'fore-and-after'. This manoeuvre by Digby successfully kept the bulk of the barons away from the Saracen's Head that night, and the fighter boys had the place almost entirely to themselves.

But worse was to come. Next day a Beaufighter shot up the Mess and cascaded the whole load of headwear into the mud. Immediately there was a rush to lay hands on and identify each other's hats, but the fighter boys had played their cards carefully. All nametabs had been removed.

From now on, the battle began to reach a climax; little moves were made by each side which caused inconvenience to the other. For instance, one fighter boy was going to rub out the white line in the middle of the road which leads from Lincoln to Waddington. The barons relied a lot on this white line, especially when returning from a sortie to Lincoln. They began to regard it as rather like 'being in the beam'. So much so that one fellow had a white line which went up the stairs and led to his bedroom. But this glamour boy had an even more diabolical plan. His intention was not only to rub out the correct line, but to paint in another which would gently swerve off the road and up a large oak tree. Such a move would have been detrimental to the war effort and was sadly abandoned by all concerned.

It was at this juncture that the respective COs took a hand. The barons, vastly superior in numbers, had begun to threaten the glamour boys that they would de-bag everyone of them who came into the Saracen's Head. Fearing, no doubt, that trouble would be caused by the civil authorities if this happened, and scared stiff that both sides might hurt each other, both Station-Commanders gave an order to cease fire. The battle ended on that day.

As a Scampton boy, I wasn't really mixed up in the whole show, but now and then I have been around in the 'Snake-Pit' when some fighter boy had come in wearing a roll-neck sweater. My part in the war had been brief, merely to be slightly rude to fighter types on certain occasions.

Despite this, my hand wasn't quite as steady as it might have been when one day in October I received a blunt telegram from the Air Ministry.

'Report to 29 (F) Squadron Digby for Flight-Commander (Flying) Duties. FORTHWITH.'

CHAPTER TEN

29 FIGHTER SQUADRON

It was a rainy, murky day in mid-November when Runt Reynolds,* a pal of mine from Upper Heyford, flew me in his old groaning Anson to bleak Digby Aerodrome. Here Lincolnshire is at its worst – a vast area of flatness, spreading out towards the East Fenlands of the Wash. Hardly a tree breaks the horizon, hardly a bird sings. Now and then large numbers of rooks croak their way above the barren earth. These are constantly being hacked down by ardent farmers.

On the aerodrome not a soul was in sight. The aircraft were all covered up and the windsock hung water-logged and motionless from one of the hangars. As I stood and watched Runt take off to climb towards the sunny south, I felt very lonely standing here, surrounded by a few suitcases, my worldly possessions. For a minute I wished I had never

* Now Wing-Commander Reynolds, DSO and Bar, DFC and Bar.

volunteered to be transferred to fighters, but that I was still residing in a warm OTU where life is pleasant and where I had a lot of pals from bomber squadrons.

I asked the first airman I saw the way to 29 Squadron offices. He was a friendly soul, as all airmen are, and soon we stood in front of a little wooden shack with a white notice on the door. I noticed it was peeling slightly and the door didn't fit very well either. All the notice said was 'CO and Adjutant: 29 Squadron,' and underneath was the cruder and more direct 'Knock and Enter.'

I went in. When my eyes had pierced the thick clouds of pipe smoke I saw a small man, a Pilot-Officer, walk towards me out of the haze. Sam France was the Adjutant. He was a man of about forty who had flown in the last war, but looked younger. It was nice and warm in his office and he was friendly. He held out his cigarette case.

'Good afternoon, sir. You're F/Lt Gibson, aren't you? Group told me you were coming.'

'Yes. How do you do? Miserable day.'

'Certainly is, sir. I am afraid the CO is away at the AOC. He will be back about teatime.'

'Good. What is he like?' Everyone asks this when posted to a new unit.

'A wizard type and a good pilot. He has put you in charge of A Flight, sir.'

'Fine.'

I was a bit puzzled, him calling me 'sir' the whole time, and asked him why. 'Well, this is a Fighter Squadron, sir, and you are a Flight-Commander and as such you are treated in the same way as a Squadron-Leader in a Bomber Squadron.'*

'I see. How many aircraft are there in each Flight?'

'Normally ten, but we are converting to Beaufighters at the moment and everything is upside down. We have three detachments at various places all round the country. There are two chaps at Turnhill to defend Liverpool; two at Kirton for Hull, and two at Wittering for Coventry.'

'What are the rest doing?'

'Oh, the rest are here converting on to Beaus.'

'This is a night-fighter squadron for all purposes, isn't it?' I asked.

'Yes, day and night. We operate in all weather; during the day when the Spitfire boys can't cope. Things are not going too well at the moment though. We haven't got anything much in the way of control and the airborne intercept devices are not working very well, but the technical blokes say they are coming along fine.'

I didn't know what he was talking about. Fighting procedure was

* A Bomber Flight is commanded by a Squadron-Leader, a Fighter Flight by a Flight-Lieutenant.

obviously very different from bomber. I thought I had better change the subject. I would find out about control and other stuff later.

We went on chatting for quite a while. He told me that we were operating from a little aerodrome near the village (of Wellingore) which, for some reason, was called WC1. That our Mess was in the village (at a place called The Grange). The corporal in charge was an ex-London chef and so the food was excellent. This suited me because in the last week or two I had become engaged and meant to bring Eve up here when we were married. Before he could tell me any more, Charles Widdows strolled in. He was the Squadron-Leader, and looked like it. In fact, I thought him a little pompous at first, but soon got to know and like him very much indeed. He was one of those officers who had been in the Service for years and regarded it as his career. He was very pleased to see me and began to ask many questions about the bomber war, and to find out my ideas on night-fighters. As I had never seen one I didn't have any.

When they had fixed up all the paper work, I was driven over to the Mess. This turned out to be a pleasant old country house set in its own grounds. Inside there was a pleasant warm atmosphere, no doubt due to low ceilings and log fires. It was an ideal house to enter on such a miserable day. But my reception was anything but warm. In fact, it was somewhat chilly. As we entered the anteroom, I noticed a few chaps sitting around; all dressed in the conventional attire of the fighter-boy – flying-boots with a couple of maps stuck in the top, roll-neck pullovers and/or sweaters, no ties or collars and, of course, dirty tunics, with top buttons undone. Personally, I like this type of dress; it is comfortable and when one has to be leaping into the air at odd times of the night it is sensible. I felt a little embarrassed standing there looking like Little Lord Fauntleroy. As Sam closed the door there was an uncomfortable silence. Then he spoke to the whole room.

'Er, er, this is Flight-Lieut Gibson, the new A Flight Commander.' Another silence. One or two put down their papers and said: 'Wotcha,' and 'Hi'yer'. Then buried their noses once more. Someone yawned.

It was obvious that these boys weren't pleased to see me, and I knew why. I was a bomber boy. Someone got up and walked out of the room; he was a fat man with a black moustache, whom I later got to know as Peter Kells. Later he came back and without saying a word picked up his beer and walked out again, slamming the door.

This was a highly embarrassing situation, and having just come from a squadron where everyone was very friendly, I nearly asked the CO if I could be posted on the spot. As Sam and I were standing by the fireplace saying very little, a long, lanky fellow who had a pleasant grin on his face turned up.

'My name's Graham-Little,' he said, without ceremony. 'I have just come too. Have a drink.'

This was a welcome break, and I spent the next hour talking to him. His father was an MP, but he seemed more proud of the fact that he was one of the best skin-disease specialists in the whole country. 'Very useful around here, you know.'

It seemed that the squadron consisted of a few new arrivals and some old hands, who had been flying around the night sky never shooting anything down and always grumbling about the hardness of their work. Graham introduced me to some of the newer ones. There was Ken Davison, a barrister; there was young Victor Lovell, who had just left school, and another tall, good-looking boy called Robin Miles, who I think had been a tea-planter in Burma. These fellows were all right, and we had supper together. Sam was right about the chef: the steaks were wonderful.

After supper Sam suggested that we should go and have one at the 'local', and here he told me the story.

'In the first place,' he began, 'you don't want to think that the squadron is bad just because of your first welcome. The trouble is, as you know, that these boys are very browned off; they have been flying since the beginning of the war in Blenheim aircraft, never shooting down anything, and watching all the other squadrons get the gongs. Then, of course, there was that "war" between Waddington and ourselves, which doesn't help matters, and above all, I am afraid they dislike bomber boys at the moment. The other great snag is that by coming here you are taking over A Flight from a very popular chap called Wynne, who has got to drop his acting rank. This has upset the boys quite a lot.' There was a funny feeling in my stomach as he went on:

'As I am a slightly older man than you, the best advice I can give you is to take things easy; they'll soon get to know you and everything will get smoothed over.'

He went on talking for a bit and then I went to bed. As I lay trying to get some sleep in my new surroundings, my thoughts were very mixed. No one minds a new job, but it is a bit tough to start off on the wrong foot. But at last I turned over, thinking of the days when I would be married to Eve and would be able to have a little home life, which I had missed so far.

The next day was my own, but that night the Huns began to come over in swarms to bomb some Midland town, and Widdows took me to the operations room. Operations rooms have been described so many times that I certainly won't try to do so here, but broadly they consist of a large sound-deadened room in the middle of which is a large table on which is drawn the sector map. WAAFs sit around with earphones on their carefully done hair, working small flags which indicate the position of enemy aircraft and, of course, our own fighters. Some of these girls are extremely pretty and have in Fighter Command been known since time immemorial as 'the beauty chorus'. As they worked the flags, I noticed there was a small board attached to each, indicating the height at which the aircraft was flying; a small arrow indicated its course.

Sitting on a raised dais watching the whole show was the controller, whose job it is to talk to the fighters and vector* them on to the incoming bombers. I couldn't help thinking, as I watched these little green flags move towards the city of Sheffield, that they were like so many green slugs, slugs of death. And as our red fighters moved in between them here was the last thing in modern warfare; the last word in efficiency.

However, it seemed that although the controller would tell a fighter that the bandit was only a few miles in front, no one ever saw anything; the night was too dark and the sky was too big. Much technical development would be required before we mastered the night bomber.

The controller this night was the Duke of Newcastle, a Squadron-Leader and a very likeable man. He was a good-looking man and I noticed that all the girls had quite an eye on him. He gave me a terse description of what was going on. 'Now and then,' he said, 'you will hear me say to an aircraft: "Hello, Bad Hat 14. Transmit for fix," and you will hear him count 1 to 10 quickly and then switch off. While he is doing that, these three radio-fixer stations get bearings on him which are plotted on that table over there. This plot is then handed to me and to those girls working on the main table; they then adjust his position into its right spot and I tell him where he is, so that should he get lost, he will know what course to steer for home. Of course, you can see the snag,' he went on. 'Although the fixing procedure is very quick, there is still a delay of a minute or so, and four miles in the air is a very great distance to see; that is why we are not having much success.'

'But can't you put up more fighters flying one behind the other, so that one is bound to see him?' I asked.

'No, I'm afraid that this method of control isn't accurate enough. Besides, there would always be the danger of someone shooting down his friend.'

'How about searchlights?'

'Well, they do their best, but they rely entirely on sound for their directions and usually illuminate the fighter flying behind.'

'Not so good.'

'No.'

And as I watched the green swarm slowly cluster around Sheffield, hang there for a few minutes, then disperse again to the coast, I realized that these raids were being carried out by the GAF almost without loss.

* Steer.

After a few days I began to settle down. When the boys had got over their first reactions to the revolting idea of having a bomber pilot as flight commander, they seemed to me to be quite normal types. In my flight there was Dave Humphries, who got on well with the ladies; there was young Anderson, who wasn't fond of women at all; there was a little man called Munn, who was always grumbling, and there was a very nice fellow called Buchanan, whom we nicknamed Jack; Graham-Little, the lad who had first spoken to me, was also one of the boys. He spent most of his time prowling around with a ·22 rifle, looking for hares.

The days passed fairly quickly, as I was working pretty hard, getting used to radio-telephony procedure. Air firing wasn't much of a snag, as we used to have a front gun on the Hampden, and though I wasn't good, I was not completely bad.

The Beaufighter was the new aeroplane of the day. It possessed a terrific punch in its armament of four cannons and six Browning guns, but these often used to freeze up, because as yet we had no cockpit heating. For its size the Beau was very heavy and its wing loading rather on the high side. For this reason the CO insisted on all pilots carrying out a lot of day flying before trying to fly it at night, especially as our landing run at WC1 was only 1,000 yards.

On November 22 there is an entry in my log book which indicates that a Blenheim, flown by myself, took off from WC1 to land on Cardiff aerodrome with P/O Lovell as a passenger, and in the duty column are three great words: 'To be married!' The only other comment I should like to make is that this was due to the courtesy of Cox and King's Bank, London, who granted me an overdraft of £5 for the occasion.

We returned from our honeymoon and tried to get a house in the neighbourhood. It was quite impossible, and at last we put up at the biggest pub in the village called the Lion and Royal. Its chief distinction was that it possessed a bath. Although it was pleasant to live with your wife on these occasions, I used to feel very sorry, as I would come back for lunch every day and find her sitting there all alone in our bedroom, the only room available for her, trying to keep warm in front of a gas fire, waiting for me. Lonely because there had been no one to talk to the whole morning. Some wives have to go through quite a lot to be near their husbands.

Christmas drew near, and I began to operate at night. As there were very few of us in the squadron who were in a position to fly the Beau at night, it was a question of being two nights on and one off. Although we rarely did more than four hours' flying each night, it was an awful bind having to sleep in the operations hut on the aerodrome with all one's heavy flying kit on, feeling dirty and unshaven. By the end of two nights on, one's bathwater was quite black.

One particular night, I remember, the Huns were bombing Coventry.

Everyone will remember the occasion because it was one of the first heavy raids made on a provincial town. I was above and saw it burn, and the only consolation was that I had seen Kiel burn better. There was very little flak, in fact none, but No. 5 Bomber Group had put in the air about fifty Hampdens whose job was to circle the city at 500 feet layers, above the city, and shoot down any twin-engined aircraft they saw. As there were about two hundred Huns as well floating around the night sky, someone thought that someone might see something, but this did not occur. I never saw a Hampden or a German bomber the whole evening, and this convinced me once and for all the night sky is very, very big.

Another time we went up to defend Sheffield, which was getting bombed, but instead were directed to Manchester. At this critical moment, the radio telephony failed. Cloud that night was down to 500 feet everywhere. We wandered around England all night, trying to find a flare-path, and I was just about to bale out when I saw an old Anson go in to land. By following him in and landing on the other side of the flare-path we just managed to scape down. It was a lovely feeling to stand on Mother Earth again; being lost is not a pleasant feeling.

Naturally, I arrived back at WC1 next morning, but no one had bothered to tell Eve of my misfortune and I found the poor girl almost in tears, not knowing what to do. I am afraid she thought I had had it.

Fighter stations are excellent for parties, and they know how to throw them in a really big way. There is always someone on a fighter station who knows some star in London who will bring up a really good show. One particular night a famous striptease artist was billed to appear in the Officers' Mess to give us an informal dance. Naturally everyone turned up. Unluckily, she caught cold or something, and couldn't be there; but someone else filled the bill fairly well. We had gone to this part in a convoy of three cars. The snow was just beginning to fall as we went on our way, but it didn't seem very heavy. When we left, however, at about three o'clock in the morning, the leading car led us down a country lane, which began to get deeper and deeper in snow. Then a blizzard started up. Suddenly our wheels began churning and we realized we could go no farther. Quickly we tried to reverse, but this was no use and we were stuck. From the other two cars we heard coarse words in the distance, which indicated that both were in the ditch. It was a pitch-black night and we were about three miles from any sign of habitation. With Eve and the other girl in their flimsy evening dresses which Dave Humphries and I had gallantly supplemented with our tunics, the prospect of wading thigh deep in snow for three miles wasn't very pleasant, but it had to be done. It was a question of 'march or perish'. That journey took two hours and I never want to see icicles hanging off my wife's nose again.

Another time we went into Lincoln in my new car which I had bought with some of my short-service commission gratuity and, of course, the darned thing conked out with about six miles to go on the way home. We had to spend all night in the car and I have never been so frozen stiff, except perhaps on certain occasions in Beaufighters. When it got light a meat-van came along and we rode back to our pub hanging on hooks beside large sirloins of beef, but the temperature inside that meat-van was tropical compared to what it had been a few hours before.

During all this time London had been getting its nightly blitz. There wasn't much flak and, taking things all round, I think the civil population were getting decidedly jumpy. I remember one occasion when I happened to be in London while it was getting a packet. The train I had come up in was three hours late, and it was about two o'clock in the morning when I tried to get a room at the Station Hotel. They had only one room at 24s 6d, which struck me as being too high, so I made my way to a tube shelter. As I walked along the rows upon rows of huddled figures, crouching on each side, I was aware of a certain animosity in the crowd. Suddenly one woman yelled out at the top of her voice, 'Why don't you get up there and fight those bastards?' I quickly turned and ran up the stairs again, not wishing to be torn limb from limb.

It was miserable wandering around London with the bombs crumping down, and I couldn't help thinking how much more pleasant it was to be up above in a warm cockpit thinking of home in a few hours' time. Yes, London was taking it all right, but I prayed in my heart that the Hun wouldn't go on bombing London forever because something was bound to happen.

Meanwhile, the Beau wasn't behaving itself. Although I never had any trouble with the Beaufighter myself, it had been a bit troublesome with other pilots. Don Parker, one of our fellows, himself an ex-bomber boy, had to bale out when an engine caught fire. Another time the CO was flying around above Northampton when suddenly one engine started banging at about 8,000 feet. He immediately throttled it back, then the other went. He started pulling taps and juggling petrol-cocks, but was unable to do very much about it, and so gave the order to bale out. The observer, sitting in the back, was a bit slow and caught his feet in the rear escape hatch. When Widdows looked round to see that he had gone safely, he was astonished to find him lying on the floor doing his best to free himself. During this time the aeroplane had lost some 5,000 feet in height. Old Charles then put up a very good show. He climbed back into his seat and although he didn't have time even to put his feet on the rudder bar, managed to pull off a good landing in a field with the aid of his landing lamp, missing some high-tension wires by a few feet. By his quick action not only did he save the life of his observer, but also brought the Beau down in more or less one piece, and thus enabled the experts to solve the mystery, which turned out to be some trouble with the blower.

But despite the small trouble we had had, other squadrons had begun to look upon it as a suicide ship. There is a story that one particular squadron in the north had got to the stage when they almost refused to fly it. They said that it stalled too quickly and that it was unmanageable in tight turns. They were sitting about one foggy day on their aerodrome when there was no flying possible, and were discussing the subject heatedly, when suddenly a Beau whistled over their heads at about 100 feet, pulled up in a stall turn, dropped its wheels and flaps and pulled off a perfect landing on the runway. Naturally, this attracted a lot of attention. They all thought that this pilot must have been one of the crack test pilots who had come up to show them how. As it taxied up to the watch office, they all crowded around to get the gen. However, a lot of faces dropped to the ground when from underneath the Beau crawled a figure in a white flying-suit, capped by blonde, floating hair; it was one the ATA girls. I am told that this squadron had no trouble from Beaus from that day on.

Time marched on. We had to wait for the scientists and the Boffins to complete the trials on our new weapons. They were coming along, there was no doubt about that, but as yet they weren't perfect. And they had to be just right if we were to beat the night Hun.

Many fantastic ideas were being put forward. Don came into my office one day and told me about one.

'Here's a chap with an idea to beat the night raider. He suggests we cover England with motor-car headlamps which will dazzle the enemy bomb-aimers.'

'What a cock-eyed idea. How about the cost?'

'Oh, he says it can be done pretty cheaply.'

'Well, what about the radio beams? The Hun doesn't aim much with the human eye; I think he relies more on wireless. That's why he can hit a city above the cloud.'

'Yes, I thought it was pretty silly myself,' Don agreed. 'The trouble with these old boys is they don't think in terms of modern science.'

'Then there's the other chap who believes in flares,' Jack Buchanan said. 'He wants us to go around the night sky in Fairey Battles, towing a flare behind – like a match-flame in a cathedral.'

'All right if there were enough of them.'

'Yeah, but there's not.'

Arguments and discussions would often take place at length, but it always boiled down to the same thing. The night raider must be beaten by the night-fighter. And we had a long way to go.

Meanwhile, the lowly Italian was finding that war was not all fun. In Greece they were being driven back everywhere. Those tough little fighters had already captured Argyrocastro. In Libya we had begun to advance again, under General Wavell, who seemed to be in a hurry. Sidi Barrani and Fort Capuzzo fell in a matter of days, yielded thousands of willing prisoners. No – it wasn't all fun for Mussolini; even his internal politics weren't too good. Badoglio had resigned.

But each night whenever the weather was reasonable the Huns droned over, intent on destroying Britain, city by city. We were always up, leaning forward in our cockpits, eyes pressed against the armour-plated windscreen, trying to see something. One night I actually did. We thought it was a Blenheim, and as Robin Miles was flying in one we thought it would be a good idea to shake him. We slunk up behind, then turned on our landing light. Quickly I grabbed the twister ring on my firing-button, but it was too late. Spotlighted in the beam was an iron cross and a very startled W op AG of a Ju. 88. Then it had gone, before either he or I could fire a shot. His pilot put her into a dive which I prayed he wouldn't pull out of. But apparently my prayer failed.

Towards the end of the year I had a chance to fire at my first enemy aircraft. It was one of the flare droppers over Hull, and I could see him quite clearly as flare after flare emerged from his bomb doors. I was so excited for the moment that I took bad aim and missed, but he jettisoned the rest of his load into the Humber, and I landed feeling very pleased with myself. It was obvious that I was a very bad shot, but at least it was a beginning.

CHAPTER ELEVEN

DUSK READINESS

The beginning of the year was marked by bad weather. Everyone in Lincolnshire will remember the continuous fog which lay on the ground for practically three weeks. It was, in fact, only possible to fly one night sortie throughout the whole of the month. The bombers, by landing on bases far from those from which they set off, had been able to get a few hearty punches in at the *Scharnhorst* and *Gneisenau*, which were lying at Brest. As I watched them drone overhead I couldn't quite honestly say that I would like to have been with them. But there was plenty of day patrolling for us, and as the Hun used to spend his spare time coming over England under cover of cloud and bombing whatever he could see, we would be up day after day trying to intercept them on the way home. Often these patrols would take us far out to sea, sometimes as far as the Dutch coast. But the great trouble was that as soon as his rear-gunner spotted you the bandit would disappear into a cloud. This misty weather was bad for morale, and everyone began to get very browned off.

In order to raise some spirit in the squadron, the CO decided to have a squadron party in the City Hall at Lincoln. Everything was organized so as to make it one of the biggest parties ever. Needless to say, it was a great success – even when someone passed out on his face in the middle of a cabaret and had to be carried out by two airmen. The only snag about the party was that it didn't make a very good impression on the Lincoln Watch Committee, who wrote a letter saying that never again must such parties be held in the City Hall.

With the coming of the good weather in February the squadron began to get really down to work. The Beaufighters were now running smoothly. A new sort of operational control had been introduced which could put the fighter on the track of the bomber, and yet another innovation had been devised by the scientists. This was a very secret weapon which cannot be described in full until after the war, but roughly, it consisted of two teams – a pilot and the observer. It was the pilot's job to fly carefully on instruments, while the observer sat in the back twiddling knobs and working dials 'picking' up the bandit ahead. When he had got within a certain distance he was able to give the pilot such directions as would bring the fighter within a few hundred yards of the bomber. It was then up to the pilot's eyes and his good shooting.

To carry out training we used to go up in pairs and fly hour after hour with about three operators on board who would each do an hour's work. At first the operators, as they were called, seemed to have no idea at all, but we all had to be very patient, and after a time some of them began to get very good. This went on day and night for the next two months.

Meanwhile the Huns were still coming in and training was complementary to operations. About six of us used to stand by every night in our dirty little operations hut waiting for the order to take off.

One wintry morning at about seven o'clock we went up after a Heinkel III which had dropped some incendiaries near Grantham. As he was flying very low, about 500 feet, there was nothing much we could do to intercept him except follow the advice of the controller from our radio fixing plots, but after half an hour, way out to sea, I suddenly saw him about 800 yards ahead, just moving from one cloud to another. Eight hundred yards is, of course, a long way even for cannon, but we gave him a squirt and as far as we could see nothing happened. When we landed, however, they showed me the radio plots which indicated our tracks converging on to one another and the exact moment we had opened fire the bomber had made a large circle and disappeared. Naturally we did not claim anything because no one could honestly say that it had been destroyed, or even damaged.

Another time Don Parker, in a daylight patrol, was actually vectored on to a bomber high above the clouds. It was a Junkers 88, but the pilot was good and had dived so speedily for the cloud that Don was unable to follow. This was the great limitation of the Beaufighters in daylight operations. At night it was good because it could slink up behind, unobserved, to deal the death-blow. By day it could always be seen, and provided that the enemy pilot took good evasive action, he would usually get away.

All this involved about sixty flying hours a month for each pilot in the squadron and was not without casualties. One pilot with a crowd of radio observers on board went into a wood upside down. Jack Buchanan mistook his air speed and stalled when coming in to land and crashed on the edge of the aerodrome, a burning mass. Another young pilot, Paul Tomlinson, who was never very fond of the Beau, crashed while taking off at Digby. The whole front of the aircraft caught fire, but the ground crew were up to the occasion. Led by F/Sgt Pease they dashed out and despite exploding ammunition hacked away at the fuselage until someone could get in and pull him out. Poor lad, he was coughing and spitting out black smoke for the next week.

I was never very squeamish about bodies, but one night Dave Humphries and I saw a sight which made us both turn and run. It was stormy and had been snowing, when suddenly a Wellington returning, no doubt, from a bombing mission tried to land on our flare-path. For some reason or other something went wrong and the great Wimpy crashed into a field and burnt up. Dave and I went out to look for it next morning. We were the first there and the wind was whistling fiercely, sending up snow-flurries round each foot as we tramped across the field towards the gaunt skeleton of the Wellington, its tail fin sticking up in the air like an accusing finger.

As we got closer and closer we could smell that unpleasant smell of burnt aircraft, but when we got really close we could see quite clearly the pilot sitting still at his controls, burnt to a frazzle, with his goggles gently swaying in the wind hanging from one hand. Without a word we began to retreat and were back in our operations hut within a few minutes.

As February turned into March and the snow melted away there came the full moon. We had fifteen crews ready to operate. It looked as if the Hun was going to begin bombing again after the short lull, and we were all looking forward to doing some really good work.

Widdows shot down the first one, a Junkers 88 which crashed in a field near Louth. A few hours later Bob Braham* had an exciting combat with a Dornier 17, which he chased down to sea level and watched blow up. I myself didn't have any luck that night. My special device was

---

* Now W/Cdr Braham, DSO and Bar, DFC and two Bars.

working badly, and when my operator gave me directions to go up I should, in fact, have gone down, with the result that we lost every Hun that we were vectored on to.

A quick night-flying test next day put that right and that night off Skegness I saw a fat Heinkel flying north. He didn't notice me and I dropped down into the darkness of the land which formed the background. I knew he hadn't seen me, but I could see him clearly – a black smudge against the stars. I adjusted my parachute harness and safety straps, then carefully turned on my ring sight and closed for the attack. When the centre spot was right in the middle of the Heinkel I pressed the button . . . Instead of a blinding flash there was nothing. The Heinkel flew on and I throttled back to avoid over-shooting; in doing so flames and sparks spat from my exhausts and I swore, anxiously hoping that he wouldn't dive away. The next time I got into position, I pressed the button again. This time only one cannon fired and again nothing happened. There was no return fire, so I reckoned my first burst must have killed the rear-gunner. The third time we got into position, no cannons fired. I began imploring Sergeant James to get one going so that I could finish him off. But it was some ten minutes before he was able to do so. The Hun, meanwhile, had turned out to sea and began diving for home.

It seemed quiet and ethereal up there, man against man. At the time I wouldn't have exchanged places with anyone else in the world. This, in a way, was better than a bombing mission; the only thing was it didn't happen often enough.

At last James got one cannon going and we aimed at the port engine. As shell after shell banged home there was a yellow flash. Sparks flew out and the engine stopped. Then we aimed at the starboard engine, and this stopped within a few seconds. And the great Heinkel was careering down towards the earth at 120 miles an hour. Someone baled out, but we were a long way out to sea. We followed it right down, and watched it land in the sea off Skegness pier, but I don't know to this day whether that Heinkel landed itself or if at the controls there was some wounded Hun trying to pull off a safe landing.

When I first saw him I had screamed over the RT full of excitement. When he was gliding down completely helpless I felt almost sorry for him. The whole combat had taken about twenty minutes, but Sam and I had no idea of time. We were so excited we could hardly speak, but both of us made a complete mess of the next interception.

That afternoon we collected the whole of the Heinkel tail assembly as a squadron trophy. Sam France and I drove over to Skegness. There we met the Chief Constable.

'Looking for your Heinkel?' he asked.

'Yes. Any bodies?' asked Sam.

'One. A Hauptmann with the Iron Cross. He's in the morgue. Head nearly shot off by a cannon shell. Care to see him?'

I was nearly sick. But I wanted the Iron Cross to send home to his people.

'I'm afraid that's been pinched: his watch, too. Talk about vultures. I've got some men out trying to find who did it.'

'Anything else?'

'A rubber dinghy in good condition. You can take that if you want.'

'Thanks.'

I've still got that dinghy, and sometimes, when basking off the sunny shores of Cornwall, I still wonder if some dying German airman made a vain attempt to save his life in it.

That was all we got for that moon party. Three destroyed, but it was certainly the beginning of things to come.

When the moon ended there was a squadron party to celebrate, and it was no mean party either. A large silver mug was bought on which were inscribed the names of the pilots concerned. It was the duty of those pilots to drink this mug full of beer without stopping – a job much harder than shooting down a Heinkel.

The party was a bit too good, really, because it had a sequel for me in court. All I had done was to take off my headlamp masks, as I had done once before in order to get home safely, but this time they got my number. Graham-Little and Ken Davidson gave me plenty of advice, but the police had me in their grip and there was no way out.

Eve and I went to court and appeared before a magistrate who looked like Colonel Blimp. He was a tall man with a large moustache and a bald head, and sat eyeing us from the bench with his spectacles as though we were objects of curiosity rather than offenders against the law. I had told Eve I would do all the talking. My defence was simple; I merely stated that the visibility was down to 400 yards, which is termed 'fog', and that in order to proceed safely on my way I had taken off my headlight masks. This was a fact, I could have brought a meteorological officer along with me to prove it, but instead had to listen to three policemen get up one after another and say that it was a clear night. Suddenly Eve spoke up from the back of the court. The magistrate was very pleasant. He let her say her piece, and no sooner had she done so than he tapped his hammer and said: 'You are fined four pounds five shillings. Will you pay now or by cheque?' I paid by cheque.

This little clash with the law quietened us down a lot. Eve and I spent our evenings off going to quiet flicks and sometimes listening to the wireless in our miserable bed-sitting-room. By now our pub was beginning to get us down, neither of us having ever lived in anything like it before. However, the news was good. The Italians were being given a tremendous pasting on all sides. Abyssinia was going; they had lost Benghazi, British

Somaliland was recaptured. In fact, Il Duce's Empire was about to drop off like a ripe plum. Moreover, there was a rumour that we were going to move south to defend London.

Working hours in a night-fighter squadron were easy, taking things all round. Each morning we could lie in bed and take it easy till eleven, when flying began. It was quite pleasant, reading the good, optimistic news in the morning papers and drinking tea brought up by Mine Hostess.

However, one day she put up a black. We had been given some smoked salmon, a rare delicacy, and Eve decided we would have it when we returned from Lincoln that night.

When we entered the pub at about nine o'clock we asked if we could have our salmon.

'I think so; it's nearly ready.' She went out to the kitchen.

'Nearly ready!' Eve's face began to drop.

With a 'Git out of my way, Artie' to her youngest offspring, in came mine hostess with a tray. *She had fried our salmon in batter.* Eve nearly fainted.

By now we could intercept often enough on practice nights, but this didn't mean we would get the enemy. When it came to the actual thing, something always seemed to go wrong. Either the airborne detector apparatus would fail, or the R.T. would get jammed, or the cannons wouldn't fire, and if all these were working, there would be no Huns about. It was a depressing job and everyone had to be very patient.

Cockpit heating had been introduced and this worked very well. It was pleasant to sit up there and listen to the directions of the controller.

'Hullo, Bad Hat 17. This is Digby Control. Bandit approaching you from the east. Vector 09 zero, Angels fifteen, about ten miles away.'

A little later:

'Hullo, Bad Hat 17. Bandit three miles from you. Prepare to turn sharp to port on 270 degrees. Angels ten.'

Then would come the order to turn, and with full throttle the Beau would swing around in a vertical turn and wait for further instructions. Then:

'Hullo, Bad Hat 17. You turned rather late. He is now about four miles ahead and slightly to port. Vector 425 for two minutes then back on to 280 degrees. Buster.'

This meant that I was going to get myself into position and at the same time would have to go much faster. All those of us who have sat down below and listened to a night raid will often hear a very high-pitched buzzing rather like the sound of an angry bee. This noise is usually a fighter trying to chase a bomber. After a while the Controller would come in again.

'Hullo, Bad Hat 17. He is now about one mile ahead. Prepare to use your apparatus. Let me know when you have got anything.'

You immediately throttle back and adjust your speed to one which you think will be overtaking him very slowly. Then your radio observer begins to work the dials at the back. After a while he will probably say: 'OK, Pilot, I have got an indication. He is straight ahead about a mile and a half.' And then a series of quick directions will gradually bring you into a position from which you should see him silhouetted against the night sky.

Yes, it is pleasant sitting there warm and comfortable, eating the odd spot of chocolate, waiting for a sight of the enemy. The big moment comes when you see him.

Once we were put on to an 88 and I had got exactly to this moment. I quickly swung to the left, as I was told he would be slightly on my left, but on looking the other way I found that we were flying practically alongside him, and he saw us first and disappeared. Another night we got so close that the operator said that we would collide any minute, but I couldn't see a thing. In desperation I fired all four cannons into space to try to make him fire back at me, and immediately back came the tracer from his rear-gunner from far below; something again was wrong with our airborne apparatus. This time the rear-gunner paid for his folly though, and I saw a lot of cannon shells pump into him before he managed to escape.

It was all a question of trial and error, and, I am afraid, a lot of trial and a lot of error. Many times our night-fighter aerodromes would get bombed. Often lonely Junkers 88 would sit above our flare-path at night, waiting for us to land, and would try to shoot us down. I myself had an affair of this kind with a Junkers 88; we had been returning from Manchester, where we had seen 'sweet nothing' except a lot of inaccurate flak, and were circling WC1, looking forward to bacon and eggs and coffee. I called up the control and asked them if there were enemy aircraft about.

No, there were no enemy aircraft, they said.

This was fine. So I turned on my navigation lights and began the approach. Down went the wheels and flaps according to plan. Meanwhile, down on the ground, watching events, but unable to do anything, as there were no RT facilities, stood Charles Widdows. He had been looking at a suspicious aeroplane which had been floating around for some time. Now he saw it get into position behind my tail. When about fifty feet off the ground the Junkers 88 let me have it. But he too was a bad shot and all we did was to crash through some trees on the far side of the drome, although one cannon shell went into the radio operator's leg and wounded him.

These things were happening every night and so there was nothing to shoot a line about. Sometimes, though, the intruders got more success with the bombers over their own aerodromes. In fact, Scampton a little later was to have quite an eventful evening. First of all an intruder tried to do the same thing, but got shot down for its pains, and rolled in a ball across the middle of the aerodrome. Then Tony Mills, returning from a mission, happened to collide with one of his own aircraft directly above the drome and both crashed in flames, everyone being killed. The final curtain came when a Hampden opened its bomb doors at the dispersal point and a 40-pound fragmentation bomb fell out, killing three people. There were fifteen bodies in the mortuary that night.

One night one lone Ju. 88 spent about two hours over Lincolnshire, prowling up and down between Hemswell and Cranwell, sometimes having a bang at a bomber, now and then getting among the 'Oxfords' at that very famous flying school. Each time his route took him over a certain fighter station. There, the Station-Commander stood up on top of one of his hangars and watched, swearing loudly each time he came over. He was a last war pilot and had won both the DSO and DFC flying Camels in France. The sight of this Ju. flying unmolested over his drome on this bright moonlight night irked him considerably.

At last he could stand it no longer. He ordered a Hurricane to be started up.

In its cockpit he sat, waiting patiently for the reappearance of the Hun. At last it came along, flying north at 2,000 feet. He took off.

Almost immediately he intercepted and got into a position astern for the kill. With memories of the sky above Amiens in 1917, he pressed the button. Nothing happened. Again. No cannon even clicked. He swore down the RT, but this wasn't working.

Suddenly the Hun turned out to sea and he followed it for some twenty minutes, all the time trying to get his guns to fire, but, needless to say, in vain. Regretfully he turned around for home, breathing dire threats to those on the ground.

Some say at this station that you could hear him shouting when he was coming in to land. Others say he put every armourer on the station under arrest. Whatever happened, he was very annoyed until the Squadron-Commander turned up. 'Did you turn the ring, sir?' he asked politely.

'What ring?'

'Why, the safety ring on the gun-button, sir. The guns won't fire unless you turn it anti-clockwise, like this – then press like this.'

Four cannons roared healthily into the night.

The Station-Commander went very red. He had tried to fire his guns in the 'safe' position.

The rest of the story must remain untold . . .

After a while the aerodromes of Lincolnshire were right in the front line. We had to change the flare-path, amidst exploding bombs, on many an occasion; often bombers returning from raids in bad weather would crash near our landing ground and our ground crews would put up magnificent shows trying to get the air crews out in a hell of blazing ammunition and bursting bombs.

These were the days, too, when the fighter-bomber feud closed down. Escorted by scores of Hurricanes and Spitfires, our new heavy bombers had made a worthy attack on Brest. It was a complete success. The fighters protected the bombers, and the bombers flew through heavy flak to do their job. Both sides came back swearing to high heaven about the prowess of the other. They were blood brothers at last.

Meanwhile, a word about security. Most people will have seen a poster depicting a young airman talking to a dumb blonde who tells the story to a not-so-dumb redhead – thence to the spy; underneath is the legend 'Careless Talk Costs Lives'.

Many, like ostriches like to bury their heads in the sand and say, 'This can't happen in England'. To these people I would like to tell this short story, of how such a thing did happen. At least, I think it did.

It was in the days of sweeps, when vast formations of Spitfires would patrol up and down the Pas-de-Calais area, looking for trouble. Sometimes they found it, sometimes they never saw a thing.

One day, in the early evening, I was having a quiet glass of beer in a certain pub. The bar was crowded mostly with RAF types, but with one or two civilians thrown in. Suddenly, my companion saw a fighter boy across the bar.

'Hullo, old boy. Have a beer?' he called.

'No, thanks. I'm on a big show early tomorrow.'

There was a hushed silence. Everyone had heard with a certain amount of uneasiness what had been said. Some were in the 'big show' as well. Then the bar became alive with conversation, and the incident was forgotten.

Next day they went off. Flying high in tight formation they crossed the coast somewhere between Dunkirk and Ostend. Behind, criss-crossing from side to side, flew the weavers, whose job was to keep a continual watch behind and to cover the rear rear of the formation.

Suddenly – 'Bandits diving astern' came the cry. Out of the sun came the Me.s, and fifteen of our boys failed to return. Later, I read the Intelligence report on the raid. 'It would seem,' it read, 'that enemy knew we were coming from sources other than radio. Some information must have leaked out.' Next night I looked for the boy who had talked, but he was one of the fifteen.

As on a cloudy day, when the sun has been shining for a few minutes then goes behind a storm-cloud and it begins to rain . . . we in England began to face bad news once again. First, the Germans retook Benghazi. Then began a long retreat for the tired, supply-starved British Army. Then Hitler invaded Greece and Jugoslavia. By the April 10 the British and Imperial Forces were in action over the entire Greek Front. Exactly seventeen days later Athens fell, and a day later, to the fanfare of trumpets, Hitler announced that Marshal Rommel had entered Sollum.

At home the Luftwaffe was doing its best to carry out Hitler's threat. Coventry, London, Birmingham and Plymouth all received the fury of the fire-bomb. Many were unprepared for such a blitz and severe damage was done. Sometimes whole blocks would be burnt-out shells with the coming of daylight.

Britain was getting it. And taking it.

The papers demanded reprisals. 'Bomb Berlin,' they shouted, 'Bomb Berlin.'

We did, on April 17, and thirty-seven of our bombers failed to return out of a couple of hundred. The trouble – icing.

No, we had a long way to go before we could reply in strength, but the might of our bombers was growing day by day. Some said we would have a thousand before the end of the year. Mr Churchill said, 'We will bomb the German enemy in ever-increasing measure.'

He spoke truly.

With the sure knowledge that one day we would be able to repay the compliment tenfold, we night-fighter boys did our best to protect our kith and kin down below, but we had to be patient. These were dark days, but perhaps they would get darker. Invasion time was looming up. We could only sit and wait. Sometimes a little tired – because, although this night-fighting business had nothing of the strain of night bombing, it was, when the blitz was on, quite a hectic job.

By the end of April Charles Widdows came in with good news, the first we had heard for some time.

'Good morning, chaps,' said he, puffing at his pipe. 'I have new gen for you. We are going to be moved out of 12 Group down to West Malling in 11 Group. As you know,' he went on, 'West Malling is in Kent and there ought to be bags of activity down there, especially as we are entrusted with the direct defence of London.'

In a week we had gone, and although we were not to know it, we were going to be very disappointed.

CHAPTER TWELVE

FIND THE HUN

West Malling is in Kent, near Maidstone. Of all the airfields in Great Britain, here, many say (including myself) we have the most pleasant. It is near London (one hour by Southern Railway) and it is also near the sea. Its location in the middle of the hop country makes it extremely attractive to Air Force fellows. For in this country are many pubs, and good ones at that, and the inmates are fine types who have toiled and cherished their land for many centuries. The local people are kind and generous, probably because they saw the Battle of Britain rage above their heads, and know more than most what the Air Force have done for this country.

The Huns in 1940 had done their best to destroy Malling, but it had been put up again quickly, this time among the trees, which made it hard to be seen from the air. Natural camouflage is always a good thing. Usually contractors insist on cutting down the trees around the aerodrome site, all except those which lie directly in the landing path. There is a well-known story which got around about that time which, I believe, originated from this aerodrome. Workmen had been imported from the North to do the renovation, and these were always grumbling about their pay and the long hours they had to work. One day a particularly badly shot-up Spitfire pilot landed there after a rather tough sweep. On his way to the watch office an old labourer stopped him. 'How did you get on?' he asked. The Spit boy told him: they had a cigarette together, and the conversation drifted to the subject of pay.

'Well, how much do you get?'

'About six pounds a week,' the boy answered. 'How about you?'

'I get eight pounds,' replied the workman, 'but, of course, I work through alerts.'

But Kent in the beginning of May is a sight to be seen. No one could have given this fair country a better name that the 'Garden of England'. As we flew over the orchards on our way to the drome we saw the apple-blossom was out. White and fragrant, it gave the impression of newly-formed snow. One by one the orchards came and went in continuous panorama, some large, some small, but all owned by the men of Kent. Now and then an oasthouse would flash by. This is where the hops are dried, and they say you can feel tight on the smell alone if you stay in long enough. And all over the country was the Mark of the Beast –

thousands of bomb craters that had left their holes in the white chalk, dropped in neat sticks miles from anywhere. This, we found out later, was known as the jettison area where many a windy Hun, pursued by fighters, would pull the plug, then leg it for home across the Channel.

Then there were the trees, green, impassive and tall, miles and miles of them. It takes more than a bomb to shift trees, and these had been here for hundreds of years and meant to stay. Green trees, green fields, green England. A lovely sight. We were glad, as we roared over the drome in a tight box, to be here.

It did not take long for us to settle down. Wing-Commander Wilkinson, the CO, a nice chap, had everything fixed. Our quarters were in the old Maidstone Flying Club clubhouse, comfortable and warm. He had taken over a fine Victorian country house, known as The Hermitage, which was to be used as an Officers' Mess; the ground crews were put up in an older castle nearby, and they were all very enthusiastic about it too, especially when they compared it with their drab quarters in Lincolnshire.

That night we stood by, but the weather was bad and Group released the squadron at about nine. Down to the Startled Saint we went, complete with ground crews, to sample the beer; it was good and everyone was happy.

The next night the Huns began to give Liverpool a week of blitz. In doing so, their route to the target usually took them over our sector, and we were ready. For a few nights we were unlucky, but then came the night. Above Brighton six of us circled, waiting . . . Then:

'Hullo, Bad Hat 25. Biggin Control calling. We have some customers for you. Vector 180 degrees to meet them across the Channel. Angels twelve. Buster.'

I heard Dave acknowledge the message and thought, lucky devil, he is going to get first chance.

'Hullo, Bad Hat 13. Biggin Control calling. Vector 170. Bandits.' That was Graham-Little.

'Hullo, Bad Hat 34. Vector 130 degrees. Angels twenty. Bandits' course zero-four-zero. Stand by to turn.'

One by one the boys were pulled out of their orbiting positions to chase the unseen enemy. I sat up there, cursing, waiting for my orders, impatient to be given the chance. Sergeant James, my radio observer, sat in the back, silently chewing gum.

We listened to the other voices, coming over the RT.

'Hullo, Bad Hat 25. You are right among them. Flash your weapon.'*

'Hullo, Bad Hat 34. Sharp turn on to zero – zero – zero. He is one mile in front.'

* This means 'Use A1.'

'Hullo, all Bad Hat aircraft. Bandits going for Liverpool – rough course three-four-zero. Stand by.'

Still no orders; round and round I went, getting almost dizzy. It was a lovely night, clear as a bell and just a small new moon. Ideal. But we must wait. Wait for orders.

I pictured the Controller sitting at his desk 100 miles away. On his table all the green slugs were moving north, among them a few red flags; that was us. He must have been harassed at all the activity, hoping that he was doing the right thing. He wasn't a pilot himself and hadn't flown much. He had a tough job.

Suddenly:

'Tally-ho, Tally-ho.' This was Bad Hat 34, a new fellow called Lance Martin.

'OK, 34. Good luck. Listen out.'

'Listen out.'

Silence in the air for ten minutes. Then:

'Hullo, Control. 34 calling. It was a Wimpy, blast it. I nearly cracked him down.'

'OK, 34. Stand by.'

Another problem for the Controller. What was a Wellington doing here? Was it friendly or was it one of ours flown by a German crew? They say they had captured some in Libya. What was he going to do? What must he say?

'Hullo, 34. Identify and challenge.'

'OK, Control. I have; it's friendly.'

'OK. Listen out.'

Plenty of OKs in this night RT, but the Controller wasn't worrying about this. He was cursing Bomber Command to all and sundry in the operations room. Why must they let their ruddy Wimpies fly around amidst Huns on a night like this? If they had to fly high, why couldn't they keep on their identification lights? He picked up the phone to have a word with the operations room.

The air was full of radio background 'mush' and now and again came an odd order from below. An unreal scene, a scene engineered by science. This was the twentieth-century war. The war of electricity.

Still more jabbering.

'He's four miles in front. Buster 34.'

'OK.'

'Flash your weapon.'

'Flashing weapon.'

'Hullo, 13. Any luck?'

'No, nothing yet.'

'Hullo, 25. Return to base.'

'Bad luck.'

'Hullo, Bad Hat 16. Change to button D and call Ragbag.'

Alan Grout, who was sixteen, acknowledged and then went off the air. He had changed his frequency to receive instructions from an advance control point known as Ragbag. Alan was new, a pleasant chap, who seemed to fly well. I wished him luck.

We were still circling Brighton. Away on the left I could see the searchlights flickering above Southampton, now and again supported by the odd amount of flak, nothing much, just a few shells. Away in the distance a red ball suddenly appeared in the sky. At first it looked like a flare, but soon we could see it was moving slowly – terribly slowly – then sparks began to come out from the back. So this was an aircraft on fire. Gradually the ball began to lose height, taking its time, but all the while going towards the ground. It had flown on like this for what seemed a lifetime, but actually perhaps for two minutes, and it suddenly got bigger and something fell off behind, a wing maybe. Then it was all over. It began to plummet down towards the earth like a rocket, leaving a long trail of white sparks and exploding Very lights. Was it a Hun? Perhaps it was one of the boys? Then it hit the ground with a tremendous yellow-orange explosion which lit up the countryside for about five seconds and then died out. All that was left was a dull red glow like a piece of red hot charcoal, burning solitarily in the darkness below.

If it had been a Hun there should have been a few incendiaries burning around the wreckage. But maybe he had already dropped his load. Maybe someone had shot down that Wimpy. Maybe everything. Anything can happen up here. Then:

'Hullo, Bad Hat 17. Are you receiving me?'

This was me.

'Yes, loud and clear.' I replied, waking up.

'Pres button B and call Kenley Control.'

On my left was a little box which has various buttons on it, just like an ordinary radio. I pushed, and immediately heard the voice of the Kenley Controller. A deep and hearty voice, as though he had just had a good dinner. He was talking to someone else.

'Well done, Binto 40. Return to base. Nice work.'

So it was the other squadron which had just had a kill. I called up quickly, anxious not to miss anything.

'OK, 17,' came the fruity voice. 'Vector 180 degrees.'

When we were in mid-Channel:

'They're still around you. They're coming in droves and convoys, crossing the coast at Hove.'

I nearly expected a voice to say 'Square four', but nothing happened.

'OK. Shall I orbit?'

'Yes, orbit and flash your weapon.'

We circled to the left, James in the back working his instrument, watching carefully, ready to shout instructions to me at the first opportunity.

'Any joy, Bad Hat 17?'

'Nothing yet, listening out.'

'OK.'

It was then I saw it. A black shadow with flames spitting out of the twin exhausts. He wasn't coming directly towards me, but rather more from left to right. For a minute I felt rather like one does when driving a car. You see another chap coming towards you, and you hoot your horn wildly to tell him to keep to his right side. A funny feeling of alarm, and I felt my thumb tighten against the gun-button as if to do the same, but there wasn't much time. A hard kick on the rudder-bar brought the Beau into the right position and I squinted through the ring-sight. One ring deflection. No, give it two. I didn't know much about this deflection business, anyway.

'Look out, Jimmy,' I found myself whispering, thinking for a second that the bandit might hear me, rather as one does, or might do, if you were slinking up on a sentry from behind.

Then my four cannons and six machine guns blazed into the night. The effect was startling. An enormous explosion rent the air and it became, quite suddenly, as light as day. For a moment I was rather stunned by what had happened as I watched my victim fall quickly towards the earth. We were away out to sea. No one had baled out. Even if they had, the sea was pretty cold.

I felt pleased and worried at the same time. Pleased to have shot down something; worried because I didn't know what it was. James was more excited than I and kept yelling at me from the back. Then a sort of anti-climax came over us both, and we wanted to land quickly and tell the boys all about it.

As we crossed the coast again:

'Hullo, 17. Bandit four miles ahead. Angels 10.'

We were at 18,000, so I put down my nose to gain speed. The Beau began to whistle (no wonder she is called 'whispering death'). Then a yell from James.

'OK, Pilot; he is straight ahead – a little below.'

We were now going quite fast: air speed about 330. I had to wind the trimming well to keep her in her dive. Then I saw him. He was going like a dingbat for Southampton at about 6,000 feet. But just before I could press the button, he suddenly rolled over on to his back and dived into a small village, a mass of burning incendiaries. We had followed him right down to the ground, and the explosion blinded us completely and at the same time rocked our wings, as though to shake them off.

It was some time before I could regain contact with Kenley. At last, when we had climbed enough, I told them the story – how the thing had pranged without my firing a shot.

'OK,' came that voice. 'I think she must be yours.'

'But I didn't fire a single shot!'

'I know. Ring me up when you land. Press button A and request a homing bearing. Good night.'

We flew home puzzled. Both combats – if you can call them such – were not organized as they should be, but complete flukes. We felt lucky and a little ashamed.

Next day, as usual, all pilots who had flown the night before reported to the Intelligence Officer. Unlike some RAF Intelligence Officers, F/Lt Hickman was intelligent. Unable to fly himself because of his eyes, he did everything humanly possible to help us pilots. Moreover, he was young and could drink beer.

'Well, chaps,' he said as we came in, 'last night was pretty good. In all eighteen Huns were brought down: a high percentage of all the numbers involved. It looks as though we are getting somewhere at last.'

This was true. I noticed one or two of the pilots fidgeting, anxious to get into the air to test their apparatus, ready for the night's work. I think Hickman noticed this, too, because instead of his usual *résumé* of current troop movements on the world map, he came right to the last point.

'Last night,' he went on, 'some of you were unlucky. Humphries's apparatus failed in the chase. Gordon Clegg got shot up by another Beau, and his observer's leg has just been amputated; he is doing all right, though. Martin's RT packed up, but the searchlights helped him to get home. The only real combat of the night was by Bad Hat 17.'

'Pretty lucky,' I murmured.

'Yeah, but your first one is confirmed by the Home Guards and Coastguards at Selsey Bill, who saw it fall into the sea at the exact time you yelled to the controller. So that's all right.'

'How about the second?' asked James.

'Well, this is the tricky part. First Fighter Command told us to credit you with both, so that the Gunners wouldn't claim it. Now we have heard that not a gun fired at it in the whole neighbourhood. So the AA boys are not claiming anything. But another fellow in the squadron at Tangmere says it was his.'

'Probably was. It certainly wasn't mine.'

'Then you don't want to have anything to do with it?'

'No.'

'Well, wait till you have heard what I have got to say. The crew of four baled out and were interrogated. They all say, independently, that they were first attacked by a twin-engine fighter which did them severe harm but did not send them completely out of control. They therefore abandoned the idea of bombing Liverpool and decided to drop their incendiaries on Southampton. It was while they were running in that something hit them and knocked off their wing. They have no idea what it was, but say they had to bale out in a hurry. Someone gave the pilot a cup of tea in the farmhouse where he landed. He was pretty shaken.'

'Well, I think it should go to the first pilot,' said Graham.

'I agree,' said James.

'Well, it is a mystery which may never be solved, but I think that's the best plan. That's all, chaps. Good luck tonight.'

James and I walked out feeling good. We were both pleased that our first one had been confirmed, even though it had been so lucky. It was a great job, this night-fighting business.

The last few nights Liverpool had got it badly. The fires that were started, despite the valiant efforts of the NFS, were still burning the next night, and all the Hun had to do was to aim at these. The resulting devastation was appalling. But by shooting down a large number during the time of the blitz, we had diverted the bombers to a route which took them far away from our sector up the Irish Sea; not all of them, but a few. This, being a longer journey, at least reduced their bomb-loads slightly, which, of course, gave Liverpool a slight break. But those that did fly up the Irish Sea managed to evade most night-fighters, although the few operating from the Isle of Anglesey did get one or two. This journey up the Irish Sea, it was said, resulted in Dublin being bombed.

When Liverpool had been left battered, the German Bomber Command laid off. They had done their work well, but had misjudged the calibre of the North-country Englishman. Although some ugly stories got around about the morale of the blitzed citizens, it left that city in the mood of war, a grim mood, longing for the day of reprisal. But except for the daily news of the bombing of Brest they had a long time to wait.

A few nights later the Luftwaffe sang its swan song of night bombing over the Houses of Parliament. The House of Commons was hit. About 250 long-range bombers swarmed over the capital at two-minute intervals, crossing the coast at all points between Dungeness and Beachy Head. They flew high across the coast, dived inland towards London to make their bombing attack and came out low. I think that was partly to avoid night-fighters and partly to avoid collisions. All had the same tactics; all did the same thing, and they received a severe rebuff. It was a full moon. Ideal for a fighter. Thirty-three failed to return, many others were damaged.

In my squadron Alan Grout got two, Bob Braham shot another one down over Croydon (his third) and others had combats. It was an eventful night and one which marked the turning-point of the air war over London.

I flew that night. I saw London burn, but it didn't seem too bad. Many bombers were dropping their loads far short among the suburbs, some even as far out as Dorking and Guildford. The bombing wasn't concentrated. If it had been London would have looked much worse. One load which fell in a wood in Alton burnt for a whole week, doing no real damage. No doubt some German observer claimed this as an aircraft factory burning.

The flak over London was really terrible, not enough of it and not even accurate. All we fighter boys used to take no notice of it at all, knowing that it would be extremely bad luck if it hit us. I remembered from my bombing days that even a French village would push up more. This wasn't the fault of AA Command so much as the fact that the Germans had started making guns eight years before us. But, nevertheless, if we were to be really successful in the night-fighting game, we would have to be backed up by real anti-aircraft ground defences which would prevent the Hun from straying around too much. Army gunners and searchlight crews at that time were always annoying the night-fighter pilot by their optimism. Often they would claim to have done their stuff on the flimsiest piece of wishful evidence. All we knew was that it would take a fighter to stop the night bomber, and so were very careful in what we said. Every piece of information was analysed, checked and re-checked. Each combat was carefully thought out. Could it have been better? Could our equipment have worked in another way? These were all filed into a master plan which eventually made Night Fighter Command what it became.

But I shall not say much of May 10/11. My log book tells the story. Here is an extract:

Date	a/c	No.	Pilot	Observer	Duty	Time Up
May 10	Beau	2250	Self	Sgt James	Night Defence London. We saw four Heinkels. Cannons jammed each time.	3.40

(There was also a very rude word written in the Remarks column, but this was blacked out by the CO with an appropriate note.)

The entries read on:

May 11. Tested cannons out at sea. No good.
May 12. Tested cannons. Only one fired.
May 13. Tested cannons. None fired.
May 13. Tested cannons. None fired.
May 15. To test cannons. All fired OK.

And the reason? Not the cannons at all, but a simple electrical solenoid in the firing-button becoming unserviceable. Sergeant James, who had, of course, been responsible for the interceptions, was furious! Four Huns! Four months we had stooged around, thinking ourselves lucky if we saw one. Then we had seen four fat ones with bomb-loads on, and they had all got away. We saw them – unlike most things that got away.

Despite our failure, the whole night's work was a great success for the defenders of the night sky. The percentage shot down was high and, despite what Goebbels said, they never again came over in strength on a bright moonlight night.

The rest of the month of May passed without incident. Few enemy aircraft crossed the coast, and although we never even dreamed that we had driven them away, everyone was puzzled as to their whereabouts. The weather was good, but the Luftwaffe seemed to have disappeared. Then came the news of the invasion of Crete.

We all thought that they had all gone down there for their summer holiday and to take that island in their stride. Many sea-minded men were saying, 'It is impossible, Hitler's really bitten off too much this time.' But air power conquered Crete in a few days by combined use of parachute troops, glider-borne troops, anti-flak fighters and bombers.

The Luftwaffe had not gone to Crete for a holiday. We got the answer a few weeks later. Every night we had stood by at dusk, in readiness, in our club quarters, waiting to take the air. The first one off usually patrolled up and down the French coast, ready for the early bird, but never saw a thing. These stooge patrols were browning us off, and sometimes we were even scared of being smacked down ourselves by a German night-fighter. Each morning I would cycle home to our little cottage, where Eve had breakfast ready for me. Her eyes would light up when I came in.

'Any luck?' she would ask.

'No, nothing about.'

'Well, here's your breakfast. You can have it in bed.'

Then in between clean sheets to snatch a few hours' rest before getting ready for the next night.

But on June 22 some of us had gone up before dawn to look for that odd Heinkel, making his early morning shipping recco. When it got light we landed back at base and the Spitfires took over. Graham was standing on the doorstep of the clubhouse, looking terrible. He had just got out of his sleeping-bag in the Readiness hut; his eyes were red (four hours' night flying), his hair looked like a mop and his face was covered with oil (unserviceable windscreen spray). We had all been on three nights running, and he hadn't shaved during that time. So you can imagine the rest, a grim sight to see so early in the morning.

'Hullo. Heard the news?' he asked, knowing that I hadn't.

'No. Been stooging around for the last two hours.'

'Germany has invaded Russia.'

There had been rumours of this for the last few days, so I wasn't too surprised.

'So that's where all the Huns are.'

'Must be. We may as well pack up for a few weeks,' said Lance, who had just landed.

'No, we can't. Our spies say the Huns are going to intensify their mine-laying in the estuary, so that we cannot get supplies up to Russia. We have got to get going at low-level interception. It is going to be a tough job.'

'Which?'

The mine-laying interceptions, of course.'

By then the morning papers arrived, and I pounced on one and took it home. Some said it would all be over in a matter of weeks. Russia's show against Finland hadn't been too impressive. Others said that Hitler was too late: the winter would begin long before he reached Moscow and he would perish like Napoleon. Only one paper made a really accurate statement. If, it said, Russia could survive the first hundred days, Germany would have had it. By then the Soviet would have been able to mobilize her full manpower reserves, which were prodigious, and even the might of the Wehrmacht would be halted.

During the next few days events moved quickly. The Russians became our allies. Brest-Litovsk and Riga fell as the Hun tide of terror moved slowly forward. Marshal Stalin broadcast his famous scorched-earth policy to his people. By the 7th the Russians had fallen back to the Dnieper, but left a trail of desolation behind them in their retreat. Another milestone in the war had been reached.

The Russians were now friends and allies of the British people, who were left blitz-free for many a moon. Most nightfighter squadrons now had plenty of time to perfect the new devices which might be able to beat the night-bomber, while we took up our role of anti-minelayers.

The enemy minelayers were hard to beat. They left their coast, flying low and fast until they came to a point about thirty miles from England, when they would climb up to about 4,000 feet, get a quick radio position, then dive down again to drop their mines. With our existing equipment it was necessary to make our interception at the exact place where they began to climb. Needless to say, this was very difficult. Moreover, it involved flying to almost unheard-of accuracy. When we were told to lose height at 250 feet per minute, we had to do so; if we did not, we would lose him. If we were told to fly 180 ASI, it meant that exactly. A special RT station was fixed up on the Kent cliffs which could talk to us as far as the Dutch coast. Beside it was a special station which could 'see' us almost as far. Day and night we began to practise, often within sight of the enemy coastline, often intercepting ourselves, but sometimes practising on enemy shipping raiders. Now and then the enemy would send up a fighter which would listen in to our frequencies and not only would follow the directions of our controller but would begin to chase us, with the result that it became a game of grim hide-and-seek among the low-lying clouds off the Dutch coast.

On our station, while vast changes to the British Cabinet were being announced, we, too, had our reshuffle. Charles Widdows took over the station. A new Wing-Commander, Ted Colbeck-Welch, became Squadron-Leader; he was a pleasant fellow with an outstanding personality and a nice wife. Bob and I were each given a Flight, at the same time being promoted to Squadron-Leaders.

A few days later the squadron had its first success at this new game. Bob got one near Southport, flying at 6,000 feet. All its mines blew up and it fell, a blazing wreck, into the sea. A few minutes later James put me on to a Heinkel at 4,000 feet, and after a two-second burst it caught fire and spun in off Sheerness. A third was shot down into the marshland near Harwich by another squadron. Considering this was about twenty per cent of the number sent over, it was a very good night, but the sky had been clear and the visibility good. Our next step was to do the same thing in bad weather.

Robin Miles and Lance Martin both did the trick within a week. Both had seen the glow from the enemy's exhaust underneath the cloud. Both had taken careful aim. Both Huns were blown up, and both Robin and Lance celebrated.

One of the survivors was interrogated by a special chap on the Station. I saw him in the Mess afterwards. He was fuming.

'I've never heard such a line of bull in all my life. The fellow must have been absolutely crazy. He said the Russians would be conquered in a month's time and Hitler would be in London by the end of the year.'

'What about America's supplies?'

'He said we're losing nearly all of them to the U-boats.'

This was partially true. The U-boat situation was critical, but, like us, Coastal Command was still persevering with the unseen enemy. An electric device was coming along, and they thought they would soon have the answer.

'Did he say anything else?'

'Nothing else,' the Intelligence Officer said grimly, 'except to tell me that I could put in a good word for him and get him to Canada, where he seems to think he could escape easily, he would see that I was well treated when the Germans marched in. I nearly smacked his teeth in,' he murmured, taking a long swig at his can.

So those were our enemies. Cocksure, brutal and full of graft. No wonder they stink.

As the summer began to pass away, something began to stir within me. God knows what it was. I was very happy in the squadron; they were an extremely friendly bunch with very high morale. There was no cattishness; no one talked about the other, and there was no jealousy. They loved flying and could do it well. They liked parties and, of course, they could do that very well. Night-flying was good fun and not too dangerous. There was absolutely no nerve-strain, and I felt I could go on for ever. Leave came regularly and frequently. Only last month Eve, Dave and I had driven down to St. Mawes in Cornwall, where our antics in a sailing-boat made the local sailors grin. They would spit and say, 'You may be able to fly a Spitfire, but you bain't able to sail a ruddy boat.' This was true enough, so we never argued; that was one of the reasons why we always had our Heinkel dinghy towing behind us, so that if anything went wrong we could always bale out. Needless to say it was a good holiday.

Our Station, under Charles Widdows, was happy. He and Nicky, his wife, knew how to entertain. The parties in the Mess were prodigious. No one even minded when Nigger, my new and lovely Labrador pup, would let himself go over the Mess carpet. A great flyer was Nigger; he used to go up on nearly every patrol. I think it made him thirsty, and he loved beer.

The local people had by now got to know us. Everyone wanted to have us, with our wives, in for a meal. Such names as Sheldon and Bincham were by-words in the district, and more than that, in our squadron the latter used to have the boys in every Monday night. I would usually work it that my Flight was 'off' that night, and we would go there in a convoy of cars up the winding hill to Ebbor House. There the beer flowed easily. Songs were sung. Lance played the piano well. A few men like Ken could do little acts, such as reciting some of Noël Coward's master-pieces in a certain manner, arousing great enthusiasm. These were really enjoyable days, and no matter what happens, I should like to record that in many ways they were the happiest I have ever had. But, somehow, in the back of my head was that little bug of restlessness.

The enemy bombers had almost ceased their activity both by day and night. Now and again they would come over to make quick attacks on our coastal towns. At one time they began to send Junkers 87s, making their first reappearance since the Battle of Britain. One night they came a little too early, when it wasn't yet dark, and I had the good fortune to damage two of them. A lonely watcher on the cliff said he saw one go into the sea, but it was never confirmed.

New devices were being fitted up in our aircraft which enabled us to land in fog. Bob Braham once went up when the visibility was no more than 300 yards. I did the same when it was about 600 yards, and found no difficulty whatsoever. Other devices were on the way which would enable us to shoot down enemy aircraft when they were flying very low. We would practise with these a lot and became, in the end, very successful.

Good fun, but it wasn't enough. That is why, towards the end of November, the duty pilot in Scampton Watch Office was surprised to see, at dusk, a Beau pull off a mediocre landing by the old A Flight dispersal point. He immediately picked up the phone and asked for the Mess.

Jack Kynoch, now a Squadron Leader, met me in the hall. He was back on Ops again in the same old squadron, but a lot of the old faces had gone. Gillan had transferred to Fighters and had been shot down on his first trip. 'Colonel' Barker had failed to return a few nights before. Jackie Withers had been killed by one of our own night-fighters. Charles Kidd had pranged himself in a Manchester. In fact, all of them: Tony Mills, young Dixon and the rest – that is, nearly all – just weren't there.

'Things are getting tougher there now,' said a fellow called Ord, in answer to my question. 'The flak's about the same, but those searchlights are absolute hell. They have put up a huge belt to cover the Ruhr, about twenty miles wide, from the Dutch coast down to Paris. We all have to go through it, both on the way in and on the way out. In fact, there is no avoiding it. A few say go in at low level, but none of us can fly high enough to get out of the beams; besides, the Hampden's getting pretty worn out.'

'How about targets? Do you still go for military objectives?'

'More or less. We have given up that old idea of bringing the bombs back if you can't see the Primary. These days we are given an aiming point in the middle of an industrial area; the idea being that even if the attack is scattered, some worthwhile object will be hit.'

'What sort of numbers are sent out now?'

'Oh, about 400 if it's to be a good prang. It would have been much more if it hadn't been for the Middle East offensive.'

'I suppose that's about 800 tons?'

'Yes, about 800 if a few Stirlings are with us. We can carry 3,000 pounds to the Ruhr now, because we knock off petrol.'

'Good idea! What about accuracy?'

'Well, some aircraft are fitted with cameras to show how we have got on. The effect of searchlight dazzle, coupled with decoys and deceptive lighting, and, of course, the flak, makes a good attack almost impossible, except on bright moonlight nights. The trouble is the weather is so bad, and we have to dive below the cloud if we want to do any good, but it is often so dark down there that we can never see the aiming point. More often than not bombs fall anywhere within ten miles.'

'Well, what do the cameras do?'

'As yet only a few carry them. We all take our turn. The idea is really to find out who are the best crews, so that they can go in and light up the aiming point, if possible with an incendiary load, but even if that happens the Hun will put up dummies which will look just like an incendiary light burning on the aiming point, which is, of course, miles away. I have carried one of these cameras, and the results have been startling,' he went on. 'Some chaps who come back shooting a hell of a line find they have taken a photograph of open country miles from anywhere; that's happened to me.'

'But does the photo show where your bombs fell accurately?' I asked.

'To within a few hundred yards. When you press the tit a flash-bomb goes off at the same time as the bombs; it explodes at about 3,000 feet and lights up the ground while the camera shutter is opened for just about the right time. It is quite simple, really.'

'I should think a camera fitted to all aircraft will not only increase bombing accuracy, but will make sure that all crews press home their attacks,' said my observer.

'That is just what it will do,' the bomber pilot went on. 'But there are several technical difficulties. However, the Boffins* are hard at work. What we do really need is a new aeroplane. These old Hampdens . . .'

We talked on for an hour or two, then went down to the flare-path to watch the boys take off. They were just the same. They still hit that large ridge in the middle of the field and jumped into the air prematurely, as if someone had kicked them in the pants; there was still the same little crowd of boys who weren't going, to wave them off from the first flare; the same spirit – the spirit of pioneers of an offensive.

Then I jumped into my sleek black Beau, which looked so handsome among those flying suitcases, pressed the self-starts and we were off.

My journey had been really necessary. I was convinced that it was Bomber Command for me any day.

A few days later Bob got another one. By now he was getting really good, and the way he handled his latest success showed that he was going to be a pastmaster at the art of shooting down Huns.

The Bandit had been flying far out to sea, just above cloud, now and then darting into it, probably as some gunners in the back saw a star and gave the alarm. Bob, on his way out to intercept, had noticed that the cloud broke some way from the coast. When his observer, Gregory, gave him a contact, instead of trying to close immediately, and therefore risking the chance of having a quick squirt before the Hun dived into the cloud, he told him to lay off. They followed about half a mile behind for some fifteen minutes, then the cloud broke. The rest was simple.

Bob was a dead-eye Dick as far as four cannons were concerned, and the Hun blew up smartly.

* Scientists.

But no such luck for me. I flew on night after night, never seeing any more. Once I did see a Heinkel going in the opposite direction just below me. I tried to turn, but it was no use, the thing had disappeared.

Each time I was on these stooge patrols I used to get more and more fed up. Poor old James in the back would take a whole harangue of 'this being a waste of time, etc, etc.' Each night I would long for the minute when my wheels would touch earth again, so that I could go back to see my little cottage.

Flying is great fun if there is some point in it; if something's going to happen. I don't think I should ever be able to take the long hours of Coastal Command, where boys have to be on the top line for sometimes eighteen hours, or even more.

And so came December. The third milestone of the war had arrived rather slowly, and very unexpectedly. On December 7 the radios of the world blared out the news that while negotiations were being carried on in Washington to make quite certain that Japan would not enter the war, she carried out a dawn attack on Pearl Harbor that Sunday morning. It was an attack aimed well below the belt, but, nevertheless, total war is all below the belt, and Big Powers have to realize this.

The general feeling among the boys was – good. Thank God the whole world's in now. There can't be any more surprises in this war now. Three milestones had passed; the last would be Victory. News began to pour in through the ticker tapes of London clubs, as quickly as it could be tapped out: to be read anxiously by members who had all returned, now that the blitz was over. They crowded around – knowing that history was being made.

On the 10th the *Prince of Wales* and *Repulse* were sunk by the Japanese. On the 11th Germany and Italy declared war on the United States. A few days later Hitler, no doubt not satisfied with the events in Russia, dismissed Field-Marshal Brauchitsch, while Mr Churchill crossed the Atlantic Ocean to confer for the second time with President Roosevelt.

On the 24th Benghazi was occupied. This was the only successful offensive waged by the British at that time; next day Hong Kong was forced to surrender. Many Canadians were taken prisoner.

And so the year came to a close. But there was worse news for me. I was playing billiards while standing by for 'dusk readiness' in the clubhouse. It was an important game because we had all got very good in our long hours of waiting, and this time I had half a crown on to win. Suddenly Ted Colbeck-Welch came in.

Hullo, Guy,' he said. 'I have got some gen for you.'

'Oh yes, what's that?' I asked, eyeing a pocket cannon I was about to pull off.

'You're being posted to an OTU,' he said. 'You're being rested.'

'Rested!' I nearly yelled. 'But I came on to night-fighters for a rest. Group must be barmy.'

'It's not Group,' said Ted. 'It's Fighter Command who feel you should be. You've got to go.'

I knew that Ted wasn't joking, so I picked up my cue to finish the game. But from then on I couldn't play another shot. Rested in an OTU! What a thought! I would ring up Bomber Command tomorrow. Then I could go back on to Ops. But you cannot play billiards when thinking of these things. I lost half a crown.

CHAPTER THIRTEEN

THE HEAVY BRIGADE

AOCs, Group Captains and the rest of them are very fine, powerful fellows; there is no doubt about that. By merely pushing a button they can launch into the air hundreds of aircraft to obey their immediate command. If the wine last night was good and their liver this morning bad, they can in one quick second give an order which will parade thousands of young airmen in best blue; all standing stiffly to attention, each one thinking the old thought, So this is an inspection. They can post men at will from John-o'-Groats to Baghdad. But when it comes to altering a posting, that is an entirely different matter.

'Ah! we must be careful here,' says one.

'Must not put our foot in this,' says another.

And the final result is nearly always the same – nothing happens. And so it was with me. A journey to Fighter Command brought no joy. A quick flight to Grantham, which used to be the Headquarters of No. 5 Group, was a waste of time. It looked as though I would have to go to the OTU.

My last week in the squadron alternated between Bob and me trying to 'pull as many strings' as possible, and a run of large and extensive farewell parties. I was sorry to leave fighters and very sorry to leave the boys. Someone said something about my taking over the squadron when I came back in six months' time. Ted hadn't been very well and might be rested himself about then. But I didn't intend to come back. Night-fighting was all very well, but it meant too much patience for me. I should think single-engine fighters are good, clean fun if you are lucky and a good shot. The best thing of all would be train-busting in Hurricanes, being both fairly safe and effective, but night-fighters were different. In a year's work, involving about seventy night sorties and thirty day patrols, I had in all seen about twenty Huns. Of these, I had opened fire on nine. Obviously I was not a very good shot. And bombing was still in my blood.

Many people have asked me which I prefer, bombers or fighters. The answer is obvious. They have also asked me many times what is the essential difference between the two. I may be wrong, but I think it lies in one's mentality and personal make-up.

But first let's separate the day-fighter from the night-fighter. The former is a single-engine flyer; the pilot has no responsibility save for his own skin and, of course, the responsibility which all team work involves in aerial combat. He does not have to undergo an awful lot of training. His is a happy-go-lucky existence, for the very reason that to him flying is fun, even though sometimes casualties are high.

In the case of a night-fighter crew we have a highly-skilled team, working together, pilot and observer. A Spitfire boy will always avoid flying in cloud, as it involves instrument-flying, but a Beaufighter pilot has to fly on instruments, often from the moment of take-off to the moment of landing. He has to spend most of his time practising both by day and by night. This involves a lot of hard work and practice, but he must be patient. For this reason, many night-fighters are ex-flying instructors with plenty of experience, perhaps married with a family, who wish to do their bit for their country, and a grand job they do too. And speaking of casualties (in Home Defence Squadrons, anyway) due to enemy action, I would say that his is the safest game of all. On the other hand, there is always the eternal enemy, the weather. Most people will agree that night-fighters have to fly, from take-off to landing, in worse weather than any other airmen. But provided the pilot can fly on instruments, it is not a dangerous job.

The degree of danger varies, of course, with the position of the squadron. Some squadrons hardly ever cross the sea, while we at West Malling spent most of our time stooging up and down the enemy coast at a time when we had no dinghys fitted to our aircraft, so that, should anything go wrong, we would have a long way to swim home. Even so, during the whole year I was with the 29th we had only one casualty due to enemy action. He was a radio observer who flew with Charles Widdows. They had over-shot when attacking a Junkers 88, whose rear-gunner had given Charles a good squirt. Then everything happened at once: an engine stopped, the radio inter-com went, Charles was wounded and the observer baled out. Unfortunately they were fifty miles out to sea. Charles put up a very good show in bringing his battered aircraft all the way back to base on a dark night with no instruments. And he didn't know, until he landed, that his fellow had baled out.

But the weather killed quite a few – Alan Grout, Robin Miles,

Sergeant Freer and some others – all through the unlucky roll of the dice. Most of them bought it in the high ground near West Malling.

Yes, the night-fighters' job was to beat the weather and to fly on instruments; they had to be good, if they wanted to survive.

Now let's take the bomber pilot. Here we have men with responsibility. They had a crew of about seven chaps, all of whom depend on the captain for their lives. They fly aircraft weighing about thirty tons and costing £35,000 sterling. They have to combine the skill of the night-fighter with the guts of the day-sweeper. They face all the hazards of bad weather, icing and low cloud. They have to endure the sagging effect on morale of high casualties due to enemy action, they have to wait weeks, perhaps, to know what has happened to their comrades; and all the time weighing on top of them is a deep sense of responsibility.

Perhaps that is why some bomber pilots are a little quieter than others. Perhaps that is why they stand in a corner of a bar, smoking their pipes, reserved and cautious. But not all are like that, especially the fellows whom I mix with. 'We must never let our job get us down,' they say. Nevertheless, they don't go around dressed like film stars, because the nature of their job is such that it can only be done by iron discipline and good morale. Good leadership will produce the latter, but discipline has to be made. Many members of bomber squadrons when they first arrive think that except for flying, life is all honey. That is not quite the case. They soon find that the other members of a squadron, feeling as they do that they captain the 'little ships' of the air, like to take a pride in their appearance; they like to keep their offices clean and tidy; their gardens growing; their aircraft polished. Such spirit breeds efficiency.

That, I think, is the difference between the two.

Some will have wondered why during my association with both types of pilot I have made so much mention of parties and of beer. The reason is simple and true. In a squadron the boys live, eat, sleep and face death together. Some are lucky and keep going and sometimes finish their tour of operations, others don't. If the lucky ones who get good at the game were to sneak out on their off nights with some girl, perhaps to a quiet movie, they would never get to know their squadron, and the squadron would never get to know them. The younger members would do the wrong things at night and squadron spirit would die. However, the one and only plan is to go out with the boys, drink with them, lead them into thinking they are the best; that they cannot die. Get them away from the atmosphere of 'Yes, sir', 'No, sir.' But make sure that atmosphere is very much present next day; be polite, listen to advice. The specialists in the squadron usually know much more than you. Then you will have high morale and a keen team spirit. Huns will be shot down; bombs will fall on the target.

Having risen during this war from a Flying Officer to a Flight

Commander, I knew such doctrine to be right. I had served under all types – quiet, noisy, mousy, forceful. But of all these men, Ted Colbeck-Welch was the boy who knew the game. Although I hadn't been extremely successful during my time in night-fighters, I had at least picked up some very useful tips from him on how to run a squadron in a happy way. And, moreover, the whole of Fighter Command is the same. It is a very happy Command.

And now I was leaving to go to an OTU. The idea was extremely distasteful, and I felt sorry for myself.

The weather was quite unflyable during the last week, and so the farewell parties to Dave, myself and Bob were on the hectic side. The final one came towards the end of the year, when the whole Station, including friends and wives, sat down to a Christmastide supper in the main Mess.

From then on it was free for all, and certainly the most outstanding party of all times in that district. Faces were blacked with cork, lipstick was used with abandon on all the unwary. The 'kneeling-behind' trick was performed again and again. Those from outside who had never seen anything like it before, looked on, amazed that human beings could act in such a barbaric way. But here was steam being let off, steam which had accumulated for a long time, owing to the Huns' inactivity, and I shall leave it at that, because I think enough has been said.

Next day the boys spent about an hour trying to wash my face. My wife had imprinted with lipstick two large question marks on either cheek during the latter part of the night, which looked very funny at the time, but next day it wouldn't come off. They even tried to use petrol, but it was no use. That afternoon I reported to Group Captain Fullergood at the OTU with a chapped face and two faint red lines still discernible. However, it was New Year, and I think he put it down to bad liquor, because he didn't say anything.

Days at the OTU passed slowly into weeks. I could never say I was happy, but Fullergood was an ideal CO for the job, and life was not unpleasant.

But the news was. We had started the year full of hope. The Russians had begun their counter-offensive against Kharkov and simultaneously General Auchinleck's advance into Libya went as far as the capture of Benghazi; then both petered out. And while ther Germans in Russia held their hand till the spring, the Afrika Korps began to counter-attack almost immediately, throwing us back as far as Gazala.

They had brought up a lot of reinforcements since the last battle. Now and again I met a few boys who belonged to the Desert Air Force. They said that the going was pretty tough. Dark days were ahead, there was no doubt about that.

We had little to set against the heavy disasters which befell us in the Far East. The crippling of the American Fleet in Pearl Harbor, coupled with the loss of the *Repulse* and *Prince of Wales* off the Malayan coast, had left the Japanese complete masters of the Pacific Ocean. With almost everything in their favour, they had landed troops in the Philippines, the Dutch East Indies and the Bataan Peninsula. The Allies fought well against tremendous odds, especially the Dutch, but it was no use; they were slowly forced under.

Then came the black week in February. Profiting by the treachery of Siam and the submission of French Indo-China, the Japs swept down on to the Malay Peninsula. There, the great fortress of Singapore, built solely for defence against the sea, surrendered unconditionally on February 15. Many white people vanished never to be heard of again. This was the greatest blow to Britain since Dunkirk – a blow against Britannia who used to rule the waves, against all free people fighting a long uphill battle.

The loss of prestige would have been almost unbearable had not another incident occurred during the same week. After a year of continuous bombing, the *Scarnhorst* and the *Gneisenau*, accompanied by the *Prinz Eugen*, had left their refuge in Brest and had steamed up the English Channel to their home ports in Germany. Immediately a storm of criticism swept the country. A vote of censure was demanded against the Government. First Bomber Command, then the Navy, then the Tories all got their share of bombastic language in editorial columns. Insolent cartoons appeared in our national papers. In America the people who had not yet got accustomed to their new Ally waxed furious. In Berlin they chuckled and waited for the summer.

Of the two disasters, I know little of the first, except that some men came back with horrid tales of inefficiency and apathy on the part of all concerned. One day we will know the truth, but let judgement be suspended until after the war. But of the escape of 'Salmon and Gluckstein', there is a small story to tell.

In the first place, these two ships were bombed both by day and by night as often as possible during the past year. 'Why,' asked the man in the street, 'hadn't they been hit, or even destroyed?' The answer is simple. The crews couldn't see them. Moreover, not only the glare of hundreds of searchlights, but the many decoys, coupled with thousands of flak-shells filling the sky above the very small target area, made it virtually impossible even to hit the docks, let alone the ships. Even when our bomber formations had bombed Brest by day, the Germans would fill the whole area with thick yellow smoke, which completely hid everything from view. When I say that in order to get the bombs anywhere near the docks it was necessary to do a five-minute timed run from an island nearby, it will perhaps be realized why no serious damage was done.

However, they were kept in port, probably by blast damage, for a whole year – thus saving many a 'murder' on the high seas.

On the day of their departure, which was carefully timed to coincide with some very bad weather up the Channel, it was sheer bad luck that prevented aircraft of Coastal Command, which had been watching the place as a cat watches a mouse, from detecting what was happening. The first person to see the ships proceeding up Channel was Group Captain Victor Beamish, looking for trouble in a Spitfire off the French coast. As soon as he wirelessed back what was happening, wheels of action began to revolve along the South Coast. Bomber Command loaded up for maximum effort. At the same time little ships, Swordfishes and destroyers made attempts to torpedo from close range. They all returned safely and undamaged except for the six Swordfish which, led by Lieutenant Commander Esmonde,* pressed home their attack in the most gallant way and were all shot down. The trouble was that the Germans chose a day when the cloud was down to 200 feet in places, while their fighters were swarming around the ships like bees around a honeycomb.

When our bombers made their attack, many of them found the ships, some made some gallant attacks, but the clouds were too low and often the bombs bounced off the armoured decks. Forty-two failed to return.

It looked as though the ships were going to get away. By now they were well past Den Helder and the Hook of Holland. But Air Marshal Pierse was up to the job. He gave an order. Armourers sweated blood; they immediately loaded up all aircraft again with magnetic mines, and that evening the greatest minefield ever was laid across the ships' paths which would lead them into the North German ports. Meanwhile, if they turned north to avoid the minefield, another force of the Royal Navy was waiting. They chose to go over the minefields, and this is what happened.

Both the *Scharnhorst* and the *Prinz Eugen* were damaged – to what degree has been hard to assess, but they at least each touched off a mine. To say that they had escaped scot-free is quite untrue, thanks to the work done by the minelayers. And to damage a ship the size of the *Gneisenau* was a major victory. The fact that she was later towed to Kiel, where she was again hit by a very heavy bomb, which blew a large hole immediately above her forward magazine, and the fact that she was later towed to Gdynia in Poland, where she was subsequently dismantled, are the answer to those critics who ignorantly attacked the Bomber Force.

However, the fact remained at the time that the two ships had sailed under our very noses – an unpalatable insult.

All could now watch the vast plan of the Axis, would-be world-conquerors, beginning to unfold itself. The ominous pattern of global

* Awarded posthumous VC.

warfare could be seen clearly on the map. Japan, unchecked, was driving west. Germany in the summer was to drive east both in Russia and in North Africa, to meet somewhere in the region of the Persian Gulf. First the Western World would go under, save perhaps Great Britain, which would be blockaded from all sides. Then South Africa, Australia and the rest of the islands. A short pause, consolidate, and then an attack on the New World from either side – the Japs on the Pacific, the Germans in from northern Canada. It wouldn't take long, although the free peoples would fight to the last. Then the whole world could come under the jackboot. England would collapse through starvation. The world would be conquered. What a prospect!

There is, when flying across the ocean, a point somewhere in the middle known as the 'point of no return', when the range of the aircraft is such that it would only enable you to go on to your destination; if you turn back you are lost. I think the Allies had reached that point by March 1942. It was now a fight to a finish.

With the news bad and with the whole country clamouring for a second front, with Malta the only British port in the Axis-held Mediterranean, the one and only offensive being carried on against Germany itself was still that of Bomber Command. Air Marshal Harris, who had now taken over command, was launching his plan of action with heavy attacks against the more lightly defended military objectives, partly to give the crews confidence and partly to dissipate the enemy's defences. The first of these was a heavy one made against the Renault works in Paris. I saw these pictures in the Mess, and having had a hectic morning testing doubtful pilots in an old Blenheim with a spluttering port engine, I decided I would have to get back somehow to bombers.

Two telegrams tell the story.

'To S/Ldr G. P. Gibson, RAF.
    Date: March 12, 1942.
Report PM today for interview C.-in-C. Bomber Command. Ends.'

Two days later:

    Copy: 'To S/Ldr G. P. Gibson, RAF.
    Date: March 14, 1942.
    Time: 12.15.
    Post S/Ldr Gibson (39438) DFC to 106 Squadron to command W/Cdr Post. Ends.'

I went.
It can be seen that the Air Marshal was certainly a fast mover.

My new squadron was in the North of England. Alick Worthington and Ginger Parkins flew me up there in a Dominie, after a farewell celebration with Group Captain Fullergood. I was sorry to leave, in a way, because at least it was a happy place where everyone saw the fun in life. But although it may seem foolish to say so, it was nice to be going back to Ops.

When we landed, Nigger immediately found that the parting Wing-Commander's dog was a playful type, too, and I didn't see him for a couple of days. The Station was commanded by Group Captain (Daddy) Rowe, DFC, a very pleasant, easy-going man. More the naval type than RAF was 'Daddy'. Stocky, pipe-smoking, he loved gardening, and especially his dahlias. His batman told me that his bathroom and sitting-room were so full of them you could hardly see him when he was changing.

In a few brief sentences he told me the facts. I was to take over 106 squadron from W/Cdr Bob Allen, DSO, DFC and Bar, who had held it for over a year. It was a good squadron, well known for its fine record in Hampdens, but was now equipped with Manchesters. Soon it would have Lancasters. The other squadron in the Station was already equipped, and was very proud of the fact, as it was the second in the Group to have them. The CO of this outfit was W/Cdr Joe Collier, who used to be in 83 Squadron with me. After his crash in September, 1940 he had come back to bombers again, and had done about sixty sorties to date. He went on talking for a while, and as I listened I realized that Daddy Rowe was commanding a happy station, even though there was a certain amount of rivalry between the two squadrons. But still, there always is.

As I walked up to the Mess, I think my chest was stuck out a little more than usual and I felt as though I was walking on air. This was my first command, my first squadron. I was the boss. I could put my own ideas into action at last, and I hoped I would be as good as dear old Ted of 29. I felt happy.

Nevertheless, it was rather lonely and strange walking into the Mess. I had been out of the Command for over a year and I couldn't say I expected to see anyone I knew. No one noticed me, no one said anything. Over in the corner was a fellow called Dunlop Mackenzie, who used to be in 83 Squadron. He had gone to his OTU in April 1940, where he had been the only chap who dared to fly the 48-cylinder masterpiece, the Hereford, at night. For reasons of ill-health, however, he hadn't done many trips. When I told him that I had come to take over the squadron—

'God! you're a clot,' he said, disrespectfully.

'Why?' I said, surprised.

'These Manchesters. They're awful. The actual kite's all right, but it's the engine. They're fine when they keep turning but they don't often do so. We have had an awful lot of prangs.'

'I had heard the Manchester had had some teething troubles, but thought they had all been cured.'

'No, they haven't,' he said. 'If you are hit in one engine you've had it.'

'But surely they will fly on one engine?'

'Some will, some won't. A fellow called "Kipper-Herring" from 61 Squadron brought one all the way from Berlin on one engine and got the DSO for it, but he's an exception.'

'Have you had a prang in one?' I asked, thinking perhaps that he had had some trouble which prejudiced his statements.

'Not me, but I've been darn lucky. I have seen enough of them. Bill Whamond—'

'Who's he?'

'A boy in A Flight. He piled up after a daylight mine-laying do. He got away OK, though.'

'I know – the CO told me. Just a belly landing.'

'Maybe, but you should have seen W/Cdr Balston prang on his return from a daylight raid on Brest.'

'What happened there?'

'Well, he was coming back pretty badly shot up and the weather was fairly heavy. All the rest of the boys had come in when he made his approach. It was then we saw that he had his elevators shot off, or most of them. Anyway, he came in, but was slightly high, about one hundred feet over the hedge. He opened his throttles to go round again, but the extra power forced the CG aft, and he began to climb with engines flat out. He went up to about five hundred feet until he was in a nearly vertical position. Apparently he couldn't do anything about it. Then the nose dropped slowly, oh! very slowly, and he went in vertically, dead in the middle of the aerodrome, a few hundred yards from the control tower, where everyone was watching. I believe his wife was there, too.'

'Flames?'

'God! yes, nothing left.'

'Must have been a horrible sight, especially as you could hear him on the RT.'

'It certainly was. Thing was, he could have baled out, only his rear-gunner was badly wounded.'

As we were talking there came the harsh roar of a Lancaster taking off.

'Now you watch this,' said Dunlop. 'This is a real aeroplane.'

Bob Allen was standing outside, and we watched, all three of us together.

The great tail came up, the engines screamed into full power, but she didn't leave the ground.

'He's going to prang,' said Bob quietly.

'I think you're right,' said I.

There was plenty of time to talk, no need to hurry. Quite slowly, at least it seemed so, the giant bomber rumbled across the aerodrome, at perhaps 120 miles an hour, but she wasn't getting airborne; something was wrong. Then, quite slowly, she struck one wing into the bomb dump and cartwheeled out of sight. A great cloud of dust arose, and seconds later there came a dull thud, as something finally hit something else.

'They've had it,' said Bob unemotionally. We waited for the black smoke, none came. Then we went back into the Mess again.

'Who was the pilot?' someone asked.

'Tommy Boylan.'

'Poor old Tommy!'

One of the navigators pressed the bell for the waiter, and there was a short silence.

Then in came Tommy. He was looking a little dirty and there was a lot of earth around his tunic; his hair was somewhat disordered, but otherwise he seemed none the worse for wear for his mishap. He was an Australian who had just left the squadron after doing sixty trips. He was a good type, and his hand was as steady as a rock as he grabbed the first can out of the waiter's tray.

'God! you're lucky,' said Bob.

'Too right I am,' said Tommy.

What had happened was simple, and certainly no structural failure. The leading edge of his port-wing hadn't been screwed down properly and had blown up on take-off, destroying most of the lift from that wing. It was just another of those thousand-and-one snags which are inevitable when re-equipping a bomber group; luckily Lancasters do not give so many. Nevertheless, I felt a bit doubtful about the future as I went down to the cookhouse to look for Nigger.

Later I met some of the boys. The circumstances were unusual for a new Wing Commander. But on looking back I know of lots worse. We met at the bar of the WAAFs' Mess, where they were throwing a dance. I was sober as a judge, being careful not to put a foot wrong. But they were high, and in this state I heard all their moans, which might have taken weeks to get out of them in the ordinary way. There were moans about this, moans about that, but all of them showing some signs of proportion and most of them well deserved.

There was John Hopgood – Hoppy they called him. He was a fair-haired chap about medium height, rather good-looking, except for one prominent tooth. The boys seemed to be always taking him off about this, but he took it very good-naturedly. He was a serious fellow at heart, though, even though he spent most of his time being with the boys. As soon as I saw him I thought, 'What an ideal squadron type. I like that chap.'

The rest were Rhodesians. All young, all keen, all pals. Bill Whamond, a Rhodes scholar, was learning to be a medico before he volunteered for flying. Bill Picken, always happy except when he was going to Hamburg; that was his moan tonight, there was too much flak at Hamburg. Harry Stoffer, just engaged to a WAAF officer, called Mary, on the Station. There were others there, all drinking and talking, whose names I just didn't pick up. But they were all the same – they were the boys – they were enjoying themselves.

Next day I saw the whole squadron on parade. They seemed a good lot and I told them my rough requirements. Then I had a word with the NCO air crews. When I walked in, none of them stood up. I suppose that they thought I looked a bit young, and they could afford to take a few advantages. I am afraid I was rather rude, but you have to be, so that they can know what you think and you can know what they think. Then I had a talk with the pilots, some of whom I had been drinking with last night. They were different now: standing stiffly to attention, careful not to say one word out of place. Tonight they were going to Lübeck, an important port on the Baltic coast. No drink for them; that was over until the next day; even in the Mess at lunchtime I noticed a complete reversal from last night. Now they were standing around in small circles, talking quietly, drinking soft drinks, some not drinking at all.

This, I might say, goes for all squadrons that I have ever known. Unlike some last war pilots, the boys will not touch a drop of alcohol before flying. They know the danger and respect it. Even the wild fighter boys were no exception. I have known them go all the way over to tell their host that they were 'on' that night and refuse, with an iron will, any attempt on his part to make them have one, even for the road. To them it would mean at the most death, at the least a raspberry from the CO. But, worst of all, they might injure somebody else.

And so they sat there, being very polite, while I got to know them. Later I had a talk with the two flight commanders. Both had obviously been doing too much. They were excellent types, but tired out from an operational point of view. One had already done about sixty trips and had begun to feel the strain. Tonight he had put himself 'on', and I could see at a glance what he was going through. He was jumpy, didn't listen to what was being said; his thoughts were miles away. Later, he got into his flight van and went off to see his wife, and I imagined the painful scene.

She had seen, for some time, the change that had come over him. All wives can. Now she knew he was going out. After the garden gate had slammed and after the noise of the van had died into the distance she would wait, first for the roar of them taking off, then the hours would pass slowly while she counted each one, until they came back later, faster and making an easier noise. Then she would know that they were landing at base, and that the weather was fit. Only one thing could stop him now, only one terrible thing. The minutes would seem like hours, and time would seem to stop until the noise of that van, the slam of the gate, and in he would walk. Then she would tick him off for not having his scarf on, in the cold of the morning. Something silly, anything to stop her going down on her knees and praying to God to stop him getting into the air any more.

I pictured all this because I, too, am married; but my wife was working in a war factory and didn't know whether I was flying or not.

As this fellow had done his bit, and done it well, I swore then and there that he would never have to do another trip after this one. I would also post the other fellow, and thus begin life in my squadron with a new nucleus at the top, which is all-important for efficiency.

The raid on Lübeck was a success. The Flight Commander got back all right with the rest of the boys. It had been a clear night with a full moon, each load had done its stuff, and the timing had been good. The whole raid was over in two hours; that meant 600 tons in two hours, nearly a record. The damage done was perhaps the most spectacular of the war, as the whole of the old town was burnt completely out.

Next night, while the GAF was bombing Exeter as a reprisal, we were giving young Harry Stoffer a bachelor party one the eve of his wedding to Mary. It was a good, almost sober party, and I thought at the time, as I watched this boy sitting there, laughing and joking, how young he was to be married. He had done a few trips and had got some experience, and I hoped that God would spare him his life – a life so young, so full and happy.

Next day he got married, with the blessings of all the boys. There were plenty of gags played on them as they went off on their honeymoon in his snorting old car. I think the jerry we tied on the back stayed there until they were well on their way.

Afterwards I went back to my office. These days there was plenty of paper work to do. Such a thing was quite new to me. In Fighter Command they don't have half so much, but we found it pretty easy, the Adjutant and I, owing to the amazing knowledge of the Orderly Room Corporal who, as Bob Allen said, 'practically runs the squadron'. But one Command order caught my eye. It was from the C.-in-C. himself, and forbade in clear-cut language any wife living within forty miles of her husband on a Bomber Base. Only those who were already living out were exempted, and a quick check-up with the Corporal revealed this as only four. This was the best news I had heard for a long time. You cannot fight a war and live at home, all at the same time. This order was to see that you didn't have to.

The Manchester was very heavy on the controls after the Beau. The take-off seemed to take hours and turns were so slow that it felt almost unreal. But she was smooth enought at 180 miles an hour, so long as her engines kept running. We found this out together, Robbo and I. He had just arrived, the same day as I. F/L Robertson was from New Zealand, a happy fellow, always smiling. Moreoever, he had done about thirty trips, so I immediately promoted him to Squadron Leader in charge of A Flight, with Bill Whamond as his deputy. He and I gave each other dual in the Manchester, and I think we shook each other equally much, I by handling it like a fighter and he by flying it like a bomber.

His promotion was a popular move, and Robbo began to shine as a leader, both in the air and on the ground.

After we had been in the squadron for a few days, we did our first trip together. It was a simple one, but I was being careful, as I hadn't seen real enemy flak for a year. All we had to do was to plant six mines in the water at the entrance to Kiel Harbour. There was no flak, there were no fighters, so we came away no more experienced than when we set out.

Two nights later we went back to Rostock. It was the third night of its blitz. The idea was that a force of bombers would attack the town and dock area, while we in No. 5 Group would bomb the factory which makes Heinkel 111s, about ten miles away. The plan being that when the factory people, who had probably been bombed out, went off to do some work next day, they would find that their factory had been bombed out too.

On the first night there had been no flak over the factory at all, but then only twelve bombers were detailed; little damage was done. On the second night we went there was quite a lot of light flak and about sixty bombers attacked the factory, causing fires and doing some damage. And on the last night of the blitz, I believe the whole force was put on to the factory to hit the central hangar.

After the briefing, Hoppy and Bill came up. 'Why the blazes,' they asked, 'didn't they put a large force on the factory the first night, when there was no flak? Then it would have been flattened first time!'

'I don't know,' I replied. 'It does seem rather stupid, though. I'll ring up Group.'

There was no answer from Group; they just didn't know. All they wanted, they said, was photographs. By now all our aircraft were equipped with cameras, but these would not take good pictures below 4,000. I couldn't understand at the time why they wanted photographs which would mean bombing from above 4,000, and so not being as accurate, when they could have given the order for all aircraft to bomb lower and hit the hangar, even though the photographic results would be negligible. Anyway, I told my boys to go in at 2,000 feet, hit the hangar and damn the photographs! A dawn reconnaissance showed that the factory was hit. But next night they went again to finish the job.

I sat up late in the Ops room waiting for them to return. A bomber Ops room is rather different from a fighter Ops room. The only things that hold your interest in it are, perhaps, the pretty girl behind the telephone and the large blackboard on the wall. On this board are written the various names of the captains who are undertaking operations that night. Much information is written against their name: bomb-load, time off, crew, etc. But the only important one was a space on top of which are the magnetic words, 'time landed'.

As I sat listening to the aircraft return, I watched the pretty girl mount the ladder and fill in those spaces. That pretty girl was Mary Stoffer.

Time passed.

One by one she would get up and fill in – X-X-ray landed 05.20; Y-Yorker landed 05.22 – until the whole board was complete except for that one small space. S-Sugar. Normally it is not very nice to sit there and watch that one space, waiting for it to be filled in. But tonight was even worse, for the name against that space was P/O Stoffer.

I sat there smoking cigarette after cigarette, until it became light and an orderly came in and drew the blackout curtains. It was hard to say anything. I wanted to go up to the crew room and talk to the boys, but I didn't like to leave her. She just sat there, staring at the space, a funny look – an incredible look. Someone came in with a cup of tea, but it had long since gone cold before she noticed it was there. Then there was a quick ray of hope, the phone rang. It was the Observer Corps to say that a Manchester had just crossed the coast coming in our direction. Could it be Harry? Her face lit up in a smile, hardly daring to say anything; then we heard it go over and pass on its way. Her face fell, her eyes began to glisten as she fought back her tears. An airman on the watch tower telephoned to say that it belonged to 50 Squadron. In the end I got up and took her by her arm and led her to my car. She wasn't crying, she was very brave. She insisted on stopping at the WAAF Officers' Mess to collect her shopping, which she had bought for their little home the morning before. Packed into the bag there was a cardboard packet of cornflakes, a two-pound jar of marmalade, some butter and some sugar, and a little bacon, their ration – simple things, little household things. She clutched them tightly as I dropped her at her house. There were nearly tears in my eyes as I drove home.

Despite the successful attacks on Warnemünde and Rostock, it was still obvious with the coming of spring that certain changes would have to take place in Bomber Command if we were to hit the target. One bad weather day in May a conference was called to discuss one thing, and one thing only: how to get more bombs into the target area. Air Vice-Marshal Coryton took the chair. He had sat in the Air Ministry for many years, and now was given his chance to command a Bomber Group. He was a keen, able, kind and inventive type, very popular with the whole Group. He was the sort, when driving round the aerodrome, who would look into an aircraft and discuss with an amazed electrician the full wiring diagram of an electrical revolution counter, much to the amazement of the man concerned. He knew everything. To me and the other Squadron Commanders in the Group he was the most popular Group Commander we had ever known and were ever likely to know. To all and sundry in the group, which he looked upon as his own pet baby, he behaved like a father. As often as possible his little Proctor aircraft would touch down at least once a week on each Station to make sure that everything was running smoothly.

Now he began to talk:

'As you know, we have in the past few weeks been having some success, but the point is that these targets which we have been attacking are not really heavily defended. I know that Warnemünde cost us a serious percentage, but I think this was due to collisions. It seems to me that in order to hit precision targets, we must raid them in daylight, such as the Augsburg raid (where Nettleton was awarded the VC), but on this type of thing we must have absolute surprise and security, and this is very hard to have when so many people are involved in Bomber Command. The other way is to have better bombing at night. Now, how are we going to do this and at the same time get our losses down to a minimum, so that we can operate day after day in ever-increasing strength?'

He went on to talk, and he talked a lot.

The first thing he talked about was cameras. All squadrons must get photographic-minded. In order to do so a certain number of points would be given to the squadrons who got most bull's-eyes. There would be a photographic ladder in the Group and in Bomber Command. From these ladders it would be easy to see which was the top squadron and which was the top crew. Moreover, it would introduce a high degree of competitive spirit between the squadrons: thus doing a good job in trying to make each beat the other. From the results of the photographic plots the best crew could be detailed to carry flares to illuminate the targets. Sometimes the best squadrons could go in first (which is normally safer). There must be more practice bombing, not from 6,000 feet but from 18,000 feet, which is more like the height from which we bomb in the actual thing. There had been little done before he arrived. He now wanted to introduce a squadron bombing competition. He went on for a bit, saying much more, then asked for some questions.

One by one the Squadron Commanders put their points forward. The

AOC listened attentively, then a long discussion would arise; all this being taken down by a shorthand typist, for further reference.

One of the moans was the old subject of routeing. W/Cdr 'Mary' Tudor of 83 Squadron was talking. 'As you know, sir,' he began in his rather high voice, 'all our routes to the target are now being planned by Bomber Command men, some who haven't seen the flak in Germany for six months or so. Well, as you know, this is anything but static: they are always moving it from one place to another. Even the searchlight belt has now disappeared within the last few weeks. They've put them all around the Ruhr towns, about two thousand of them.'

'The Battle of the Ruhr has yet to start,' said the AOC.

'I know, sir, we'll never be able to hit anything in the glare of all those light. I think they're worse than the flak. But what I want is this. Let the routes and the general Flight Plan be decided by the squadrons themselves. After all, they're the chaps who have to do the job. About an hour before each briefing, I suggest we have a conference over tie-line telephones, which will decide the final plan. Everyone will be able to put forward suggestions. A route to the target will be taken which will not lead the boys over two other defended areas as well. The height for bombing will be correct and in dead proportion to the amount of flak. I think in this way we will get the boys happier, and thus far more bombs on the target.' He sat down.

'Good idea,' said the AOC. 'We'll put this plan into action as soon as possible. But first, we must get the whole Group equipped with Lancasters. We can't do a thing until then. What shall we call your conference?'

'As it's about the Flight Plan, we may as well call it "The Flight Planning Conference",' suggested the SASO dryly.

'OK?' The AOC looked round: there was a murmur of assent, and he nodded to the typist.

Many problems peculiar to the difficulties of the time were discussed at length. First, training. We were equipping the Group with a large four-engined bomber; quite a change from the small Hampden. How was this to be done? First of all, each squadron had been given a third flight, commanded by an operationally rested pilot, such as Tommy Boylan. As often as possible with his three Lancasters available, he would convert pilots into the new aircraft. But then the man-power problem was terrific. New flights meant more men. There were none available. We had to rob our own operational flights. The Hampden used to carry a crew of four. The Lancaster carries seven. These extra, highly skilled air crews had to found from somewhere – where? The whole air-training programme stretching from the dusty offices of the Air Ministry to the far-off prairies of Canada had to be remodelled. And for one reason alone. Bomber Command was being reborn.

New navigational aids were coming along. These would enable us to find out where we were, above cloud, within a few seconds and to extraordinary accuracy. These, too, were very secret, and every aircraft had to be guarded day and night. This meant more men. Men from somewhere. But all the forces needed more men. It seemed a vicious circle.

Then they decided that a conversion flight was not good enough. This in itself was a waste of man-power. All flights would have to combine to form a conversion unit – which would supply every squadron with fully-trained crews. But would they? There was a shortage of trained flight engineers. Volunteers had been asked for, but it would take time. New airfields had to be taken over; larger runways to be built, for the longer landing run of the Lancaster.

Hundreds of problems confronted us, and I got up feeling quite dizzy after a four-hour session.

On my way back to the Mess a Lancaster roared overhead on its way to the sea. I noticed a couple of civilians who didn't even look up. They were used to the sight. But did they know even half the story? Of course not. Re-equipping a Bomber Group is a big job. But the whole of the Command was soon to be completely re-equipped and reorganized. To tell the story of hard work would need a full-sized book. Mention must be made of everybody who worked flat out for a long time to do the job. The factories who turned out the new aircraft under conditions peculiar only to this country. The contractors who make the fields. The equipment officers – the new petrol installation experts – the list would run on for ever. Let it be sufficient to say that there is much work done behind the headlines. Work which, though not so glamorous as combat action, is carried out by quiet men with stout hearts. Funnily enough, it is only the air crews who really appreciate them.

Within the next few days we got Lancasters. They came, flown over by the ATA five at a time, all ready for action except for a few modifications. My own squadron did not have a conversion flight, and the conversion unit had not yet got going. We had to do our training ourselves. Moreover we were told to hurry because there might be a maximum effort at the end of the month, in two weeks' time.

Hoppy, who had managed to pick up some training on an off day from the other squadron, had done more than other pilots, about ten hours. I asked him to show me how.

It was mostly a question of getting the cockpit drill dead right. The most important thing of all is this cockpit-drill business, when flying modern aircraft. All it means is getting to know the position of every tap so that you can fly the aircraft without having to look down for the controls. All movements have to be made automatically, as one does when driving a car. When flying a big bomber on a misty night, that split second when the pilot might turn his head away from the instruments might mean the difference between life and death.

As we climbed in I noticed the cockpit layout was much the same as that of a Manchester. Practically everything was in its usual place, only the four throttles and one or two refinements seemed to be the difference.

Hoppy climbed into the driving-seat while I stood behind him. Dave Shannon, a new chap who had just come, sat beside him in the second pilot's place to act as a Flight-Engineer. Hoppy explained the starting-up procedure in detail.

'Switches off,' he said into his mike.

'Switches off,' repeated Dave.

'Inner tanks on.'

'Inner tanks on.'

'Immersed pumps on.'

'OK, on.'

'OK, now read the list of checks,' said Hoppy, and I listened in silence as Dave read out aloud a list which seemed very long.

'Check seat secure,' said Dave.

'Checked seat secure,' doing so.

'Brakes on and pressure up.'

'OK. Brakes on and pressure up.'

'Undercarriage locked.'

One by one, Hoppy answered until the list was finished, then Dave turned his attention to the crew. From the bomb-aimer to the rear-gunner each one was carefully checked in his equipment. All this took some time. When all was done, Hoppy turned round to me.

'Of course, that's the complete drill, sir. If I were you I'd do it for the first few flights, then you'll find you'll want to slack off. It'll all come absolutely automatic. The next thing is the starting-up, take-off and air drill, which never varies. Most pilots do this, no matter how experienced they are.'

Then to the Flight-Engineer:

'Prepare to start up.'

'OK. Ready to start up.'

The ground crew had primed the engines and all was ready. Hoppy had his hand on the throttles. Dave was working the switches and booster coils.

'Contact – starboard outer,' Hoppy yelled through his window.

Dave pressed the button and one by one the four great engines roared into life with that harsh crackling, splitting noise peculiar to Merlin engines.

'Chocks away.'

'Chocks away.'

As I glanced down out of the side window, I saw, twenty feet below me, a small man dart in and out of the huge landing-wheels, pulling a long rope at the end of which was a chock. Funny things, chocks – everyone knows that they are there to prevent the aircraft running forward when its engines are running, but most people don't realize that, whereas aircraft have grown up in size since the last war, the good old chocks have still remained the same. This one had become wedged in the earth, and the little man was lying on his back underneath the huge propeller slicing through the air four feet above his head, trying to kick it free.

At last another man came running in front with his thumbs stuck up, and Hoppy released the brakes.

There was a hiss of air, and we began to sway and rumble our way along the taxi-track. At the entrance to the runway, Hoppy stopped and ran up his engines to full power, one by one, each time checking the two-stage blower, the airscrew pitch control and the magnetos.

Meanwhile, Dave called up the control tower.

'Hullo, Control. Y-Yoke calling. May we take-off, please? – over.'

'OK. Take off. Listen out.' This was a girl's voice, one of the many WAAFs who had taken over a man's job, thus releasing him for service elsewhere. A great crowd are the WAAFs.

Then came a string of orders from Hoppy.

'Flaps thirty.'

'Radiators closed.'

'Lock throttles.'

'Prepare to take-off.'

'OK behind, rear-gunner?'

'OK behind,' came a voice.

He ran up the engines all together, evenly, until one was showing Zero 600 st, then released the brakes. The acceleration was terrific, and I had to grab the back of his armour-plated seat to hold myself upright.

'Full power.'

'Full power,' answered Dave, opening the throttles wide.

Soon the ASI was showing a speed of 110 mph and the aircraft suddenly became steady. We were airborne.

'Climbing power.'

'Climbing power.'

'Wheels up.'

'Wheels up.'

'Flaps up.'

'Flaps up.'

'Cruising power.'

As Dave adjusted the engines to their correct revolutions for cruising, I noticed our air-speed was about 120. Pretty fast for a big bomber. She was flying perfectly, hands-off. On the controls she was as light as could be. This ship was certainly a honey. Hoppy showed me how to stop (feather) an engine simply by pressing a button, how it would fly quite well on only one, losing height very gradually the whole time, but good enough to get you well away from the enemy coast. He showed how to 'ditch' the aircraft, using slight flap and plenty of speed. The 'drink' we used for the occasion was a stretch of smooth cloud at about 4,000 feet.

After half an hour he had shown me everything, and he called up control and got permission to land.

'Now watch this carefully,' he pointed out. 'It's very important to get the landing drill wrapped up.'

As we were going downwind around the circuit, keeping about a mile from the runway and about 1,000 feet high, came some more orders:

'Flaps twenty.'

Dave put down twenty degrees of flap. The ASI dropped to 160.

'Revs up.'

The constant-speed propeller controls were pushed forward and a loud whine came from all engines.

'Wheels down.'

'Wheels down.'

We were now turning into the runway.

'Radiators closed.'

'OK. Closed.'

Suddenly two green lights came on in front of the pilot.

'Wheels locked down,' called Dave, seeing this.

By now we were pointing straight at the landing-strip, which looked about six feet wide from my position.

'Full flap.'

'Full flap.' Dave put down the lever and immediately the nose came up, while Hoppy struggled with the trimming wheels, to balance her in the glide.

'Airspeed, Flight-Engineer?'

'Speed 130 – 125 – 128 – 130,' chanted Dave, as we dropped towards the ground.

'You want to keep the nose well up when landing these things,' said Hoppy over his shoulder. Then:

'Height and speed, please,' he called.

Three hundred, one-twenty.'

'Two hundred, one-twenty.'

'One hundred, one-one-five.'

'Fifty. One-one-five.'

'OK,' jerked Hoppy; 'throttle back.'

Dave snapped back all four throttles while Hoppy, with both hands on the wheel, pulled off a good landing to the accompaniment of crackling and popping exhaust stubs.

When we had run about 1,000 yards we came to a stop. He pulled his oxygen mask off his sweating face and grinned.

'There, now you have a try.'

The next few days saw a lot of practice flying for my crew. There were only three regular members; the rest we used to beg, borrow or steal from other crews at the appropriate time. 'Junior' Ruskell was the navigator. He was very young, hence his name, but a very fine navigator, especially in the use of electrical navigation boxes. Junior's one weakness was beer. He could take about one pint, then he became comically light. When we used to go out together, perhaps to Boston, he usually drank lemonade. Sometimes he got tight on that! Johnny the rear-gunner was older, and as conscientious as any I knew. Hutch was the wireless-operator, and had just got his commission. I must make mention of one more fellow who used to fly with us. His real trade was wireless-operator, but he could do practically everything except land the aircraft. They called him Jordy, and a very lovable character he was. A real London Cockney, he would go off on Ops as often as possible. He once did seven trips running in different crews, flying as a gunner one night, a flight-engineer the next and a wireless-operator the next. Jordy was amusing to see before a trip. His dress was always alarming and would not bear description here, but over his head he always wore a dirty silk stocking à la French-sailor style. He used to vow he would never do a trip without it, and so far as I know he never has.

In the end we got more or less proficient, and so one day we flew down to an airfield in Cambridgeshire to collect Sir Archibald Sinclair, the Air Minister, and one or two brass hats. We were proud of this honour, but we were carrying, for our sins, a brand new flight-engineer. On the way home the Air Minister jabbed a finger in my back and told me to feather an engine. This was done, and he seemed very pleased. Then we feathered another one, and he seemed even more pleased.

After we had flown along like this for a few minutes, one of the brass hats came forward and told me to unfeather, as they were in a hurry. I gave the order, casually, to the flight-engineer. Suddenly, to the horror of both myself and the man with goggles on, looking over my shoulder, the two other engines began to feather themselves. Our new flight-engineer had pressed the wrong buttons. It was all right, though, because it didn't take a second to get all four going again. However, in that second I couldn't help thinking what stooges we'd look if we'd had to land in the middle of a field in England on a hot summer's day with nothing wrong with the aircraft at all, except finger trouble. All this with our Air Minister on board! However, he was testing the rear turret at the time, and I don't think he noticed anything amiss.

The two weeks which the AOC had hinted at came to an end. In that time, thanks to Hoppy, Bill and a few others, the whole squadron had been taught to fly Lancasters both by day and night. A flood of new flight-engineers had arrived, and we had no less than forty crews ready to operate.

On May 29 we were told what was happening. A major attack was to be made against Hamburg. All types of aircraft were to take part, including a few from Coastal and Training Commands. In all, about 1,300 aircraft would take off and drop something like 1,500 tons. It was to be the biggest air raid of all time.

However, the weather was kind to Hamburg and the show was put off until the next night, when the target was changed to Cologne.

Luck went all the way with the bombers and they did their job well. Towards the end of the attack the flak had been pulverized and the city resembled one mass of flames. Nearly 1,500 tons had been dropped in ninety minutes. An unheard-of concentration, so much so that Air Vice-Marshal Baldwin, who flew over the city, said he had never seen a sight like it before. We had sent thirty-eight aircraft from our squadron, and had dropped eighty-eight tons of bombs on the target for no loss. This was a record, and great entries were made in the squadron history to this effect.

The plan of the raid was partly to destroy the industrial area of Cologne and partly to pep up the weary British people. However, it was successful because it was carried out on a night when the moon was full and the visibility was good. The next night another force of nearly 1,000 bombers tried to do the same to Essen, but the complete opposite happened. There was cloud all the way, and bombs were scattered all over the Ruhr Valley. Nevertheless, those Germans who had country homes well away from the towns must have been considerably shaken.

There was only one more 1,000-bomber raid. This was on Bremen, towards the end of the month. It met with failure because of bad weather. They were abandoned mainly because of the great disruption to training they caused in Operational Training and Conversion Units. A smaller consideration must be given to the view that the proportion of bombs dropped on the target by the OTU crews could not justify the risk of the loss of an experienced instructor.

From now on we would get to war as often as possible with large forces varying between 400 and 600. I didn't do as much as the boys, but used to content myself with one trip every five nights. No Squadron-Commander can for that matter. Not only had he got to deal with the paper work, write long casualty letters and run the squadron generally, but has also to be up at nights. In fact, every night when the boys are out you will find him waiting in the Ops room for their return. But no lying in bed for him next day; after perhaps three hours' rest he must be up, ready to plan the next raid, arrange the bomb and petrol loads, organize the crews. But this applies to many others on a bomber station. Armament officers, navigation experts, intelligence officers, all of whom go about their work, looking very tired, but still keen to get more bombs on Germany.

Not many people realize in the outside world (and sometimes it does seem the outside world) that although the BBC will inform them that 'Last night a strong force of bombers were out for the first time in seven days', hard work has been done on the bases. On each of those days the crews have most likely been briefed, bombs have been loaded on aircraft, then taken off again; sometimes they even taxi out to take-off when a red light shoots up from the control tower, telling them that it has been cancelled.

Imagine their feelings. Most people will agree with me when I say the worst part of any bombing raid is the start. I, for my part, hate the feeling of standing around in the crew rooms, waiting to get into the vans that will take you out to your aircraft. It's a horrible business. Your stomach feels as though it wants to hit your backbone. You can't stand still. You laugh at small jokes, loudly, stupidly. You smoke far too many cigarettes, usually only halfway through, then throw them away. Sometimes you feel sick and want to go to the lavatory. The smallest incidents annoy you and you flare up on the slightest provocation. When someone forgets his parachute you call him names that you would never use in the ordinary way. All this because you're frightened, scared stiff. I know – because I've done all those things. I have always felt bad until the door of the aircraft clangs shut; until the wireless-op (Hutch) says 'Intercom OK,' and the engines burst into life. Then it's all right. Just another job.

But when that light goes up – then the spring is uncoiled. Some laugh. Others swear. A few get drunk.

'It's all very bad for them.'

Tommy Lloyd and I were talking about this one day. He was the Senior Intelligence Officer. He had been recalled into the Service during the early stages of this war; he had served in the front line in the last, winning the DSO. We were in a little club in Skegness, having a quiet glass of beer with the boys. We were all tired out, having been on duty for the past fourteen days, during which there had been fourteen briefings but only four raids. A civilian had just come up and said something about us having a rest. Something to do with Egypt. Perhaps?

I nearly exploded.

'It's all right,' said Tommy; 'they just don't understand.'

'I know they don't – if they had to exist on three hours' sleep for a fortnight there would be a terrific row. Their Unions would object. Still, I suppose it was worse in the last war for you infantry boys.'

'It was in a way – but we got our regular rests. But then, everybody knew about us – nobody seems to know what goes on on a bomber station today. Someone ought to tell them.'

'Someone should. Perhaps one day I will,' I replied.

Of parties: there weren't many these days, everyone was too busy. True we had a squadron party in the dancehall in Boston, but it was nothing like the old days. The only incident of note was Bill Whamond lending his tunic to a roadsweeper in a local pub. This individual then made his way into the dance and I, thinking he was one of my new officers, told him to go and get a shave. Much to his surprise and indignation!

At this time there was a rumour that the whole of our Group might move to the Middle East. Things had not gone too well in the last few months, and this rumour seemed quite a possibility. However, nothing came of it. Nevertheless, air-power was definitely needed in that part of the world. After the heavy battles of Knightsbridge, when many of our tanks had been knocked out, we had been forced to fall back to El Alamein, the only natural barrier before Cairo. There did not seem much of a chance of holding them even there, and it was said that Mussolini himself had crossed to a safe part of Africa, bringing with him a gorgeous braided uniform for his state entry into Cairo. But, bringing up reserves and displaying incredible guts, our army held Rommel, whose Afrika Korps was already beginning to feel the pinch of a 1,500-miles supply line.

In Russia the Germans had attacked and were sweeping up the Don at an alarming rate. It looked as though the end there was in sight.

Submarine warfare in the Atlantic was cutting great hunks out of our life-line with America. It seemed almost impossible to get the answer to an enemy that fights at night, under the sea. In my squadron we had even detached a flight of Lancasters to Ireland to help look for U-boats in the bay, thus diminishing the scale of attack against Germany. Such was the gravity of the U-boat menace.

Only in the Far East had the aggressor been slowed down, and this because of the skill and foresight of the admirals of the US Navy. Both the battles of Coral Sea and Midway were fought on new lines. Carrier-borne aircraft were used in great numbers, with decisive results. The Japs' thrust at Australia had been parried. Perhaps their next move was a drive into India?

Only time would tell, but the people of this country and in Parliament were getting restive. The strain of waiting for good news was beginning to tell. In the House a heavy attack was made on Mr Churchill and his conduct of the war. A vote of censure was taken, at the very time when he was planning with his Allies a vast enterprise which would be launched in the autumn.

But as the weeks passed and new crews came and went, the only permanent offensive was still that coming from a few score bomber squadrons.

The attacks on Hamburg and Düsseldorf on bright moonlight nights were partly successful, good concentrated bombing being achieved because the crews were in low to see the aiming points. But the full moon was beginning to be a danger. The German night-fighter force was growing every day. Soon it would become a serious menace, even worse than the flak. For protection some of us would fly in formation, but this had its difficulties when nearing the aiming point. One night Hoppy and I nearly collided over the docks at Hamburg when trying to fly in formation and look for the target at the same time.

But it had to be moonlight nights or nothing. The dark-night raids proved nearly useless and very dangerous. Crews, circling fo find a pinpoint over a town, would run a serious risk of colliding. Sometimes as many as 400 aircraft would be over the target at the same time. When you consider that in England we think it dangerous for twenty aircraft to circle a base, with lights off, what would be worse than Bremen on a dark night with scores of aircraft about? But on all nights crews had to face the danger of staying over a target too long. In daylight it is easy to see what you are going to hit from a long way off. You can go over the target in a straight line, and in the shortest possible time, thus in the safest time. But at night they had to stooge up and down looking for what they wanted, always being fired at and undergoing the risk of collision the whole time. Aircraft would inevitably split up, and thus fall easy prey to night-fighters on the way home.

Something had to be done. We had got everything else. We could carry the loads for a long distance; 4,000-pound and 8,000-pound bombs were the order of the day. Tons of incendiaries could be dropped in a 'stick' a mile long. We had the aircraft. We had the crews, who could bomb accurately with the new bomb-sights. Now we wanted the accuracy, so that we could 'apply' the vast concentration of bombs straight on to the aiming point. Then we could begin to do some real damage.

How?

First the best crews in the best squadrons began to carry flares.

These were carried in bundles of twelve, and when dropped would illuminate the ground well, but only for a few minutes. But sometimes these flares were more of a liability than an asset. Navigational errors on the part of the selected crews would cause the wrong city to be bombed, let alone the wrong target. Cloud would ruin everything and illuminate our bombers nicely for the night-fighters. But, nevertheless, they were a beginning. However, some targets, such as Krupps at Essen, which were surrounded by so many guns and searchlights that not even flares could pierce the glare, seemed quite immune from aerial attack.

One day we began to practise high-level formation in daylight. There were rumours immediately.

'We're going after the *Tirpitz* again.'

'No, airfields in France to stop the Baedeker raids.'

But I had an idea.

I spoke to Tommy Lloyd. Hoppy was there.

'What do you make of this high-level stuff?'

'I'm not quite sure – but I've got a good idea.'

'Krupps?'

'Yes.'

'I think so, too,' I agreed. 'The American boys have just started in their Fortresses. They're shooting the fighters down, too. I wouldn't be surprised if we were asked to go with them, protected by their guns.'

'Wouldn't be very nice,' said Hoppy. 'Why don't we have guns like their?'

'We don't need them at night. The range is too short. But it would be nice to have the hitting power.' This was Bill, who had just turned up.

'Well, how are we ever going to hit these heavily defended targets?' I asked.

'I can't ever see us getting Krupps. Day or night; it's just too heavily defended by flak.'

'Nor I,' said I.

But Tommy Lloyd had an idea.

'Well, I suggest,' he began, 'that a special squadron of Beaufighters or Mosquitos be formed out of crack crews. Their job would be to go in at dusk, just before the main force was due, and drop coloured incendiaries on the factory itself. These could be seen from high up, and the boys of the main force would be able to do steady bombing runs which would plaster the area with cookies.'

'Seems a good idea – but the suicide squadron losses would be high.'

'They probably would – but the target would be destroyed.'

'Yeah; that's the main thing,' said Hoppy.

It was lunchtime. I got up to go, when suddenly the telephone rang. Tommy picked it up.

'It's Group Ops,' he said, quietly.

We waited, wondering what it was. We had been released tonight. There had been a small party fixed up.

'OK,' said Tommy casually. 'I'll tell the Station-Commander.' Then he looked at us, his eyes dancing 'You were right,' he said. 'Your squadron's on Krupps today. Take-off as soon as possible.'

'What the hell!' I exploded.

'Oh, it's OK. It's only a cloud-cover raid.'

We went. Six of us, within an hour. Within three, we were all back again.

On July 8, a dark night, I took Dave Shannon as my second pilot to Wilhelmshaven. The winds were high and not as forecast. When we were sixty miles away flares began to go down. We immediately went over to have a look and saw nothing but open fields. More flares to the north; still open fields. In vain we looked around, hoping to find the target illuminated, but there was nothing doing. In the end we turned north, found the coastline and followed it along till we found the harbour. There wasn't even one fire burning there – twenty minutes after the attack was due to begin. Even Dave wasn't so sure whether we were over the right place ourselves.

The photographic plots for the night's work were disgusting. Bombs had been dropped all over north-western Germany. But worse than this, losses due to our lack of concentration had been high. The German News Agency said: 'Last night enemy aircraft dropped bombs at random over North-West Germany. No damage was done.'

From 106, P/O Broderick failed to return. I drove around to tell his wife after waiting until he was three hours overdue. As I approached the gate I saw a small white face looking out of the window. She opened the door before I even had time to press the bell. She knew what had happened. I could see that by her eyes. She just stood there as I told her, the world falling in a crumbled heap at her feet. Then she went upstairs without saying a word.

But as I went to my room I wasn't thinking of the painful scene which had just occurred. I was thinking of Bomber Command. This boy, like hundreds of others, had not come back, and I didn't suppose he had even seen the target. This would have to be altered. A new system like the scheme Tommy Lloyd mentioned. Perhaps even better.

FOURTEEN

TURNING OF THE TIDE

If mere squadrons were giving plenty of thought to the matter of getting more bombs on the target, let us say something of the activities of the Commander-in-Chief. It was learned from reliable sources that he spent a lot, even the whole, of his time sitting at his desk interviewing pilots, cursing scientists and leaping on Group-Commanders from great heights in order to try to get some information out of them about the subject of bombs on the target. Why had the raid on Bremen gone wrong last night? Because the crews couldn't see the ground. Why couldn't they navigate blind? Because they couldn't get any idea of where they were within twenty miles. Why? Because the Germans were jamming our RT and navigational aids. Why weren't the flares dropped over Bremen? They might have been, but the smokescreen was too good for them to see anything at all. Why did the few bombs that did fall anywhere near the area fall mostly south-west? Because the wind changed after take-off and there was no one to tell them about it.

And so it went on day after day. Everyone was interested; everyone was trying to see if there was any way in which it would be possible for a large bomber force to drop its bombs accurately on the target, without incurring any undue danger in doing so. And at last a plan was formed.

Meanwhile, in our squadron many of the faces which were there when I took over had gone, some for ever. But new ones had arrived. The conversion units had got into their stride and were turning out really good material: Bunny Grein, Wimpy Wellington, Johnny Coates, Taffy Williams and Ginger Crowfoot had all come within the last few weeks, and they will go down in history as the great men of 106 Squadron. Right from the start they began to get aiming point pictures of the target, and with the points gained by their photographs they brought our squadron up to the proud position of seventh in Bomber Command. Their keenness and skill were largely due to an excellent Flight-Commander who had just come to take the place of a vacancy in the other flight. Wooldridge was his surname, but he was rarely called that. He had been known as Dim ever since he learned to fly. He was a sort of 'Algy' of the air, with a large moustache and a drawling voice. He had amazing habits, and at the time he joined he was engaged in the doubtful art of composing a concerto for piano and orchestra. I think it was a ruse on his part to keep him away from the boys. He had stomach trouble. He couldn't drink a lot, and his excuse always was that he must sit down quietly in his sitting-room and write his concerto rather than go out and drink beer. Poetry was his line as well, but he was an excellent type, and, apart from all this, had done sixty-seven trips over the Third Reich. Dim was very good with the boys, but, I am afraid, rather unscrupulous with his Squadron-Commander, and even though I say so myself, he needed a lot of watching.

One day we were sent on a sudden daylight raid over North-West Germany. I strolled along to his office. 'Can I have my O-Orange?' I asked.

'Awfully sorry, sir,' he said, smugly; 'she's blown an engine. She'll be unserviceable for a few days.'

Cursing about maintenance, I went to Bill in A Flight (Robbo was missing from the previous week's Hamburg raid) and asked him for a reliable aircraft, but all the boys had had theirs and I was given a lousy job called B-Beer, dirty and oily inside and smelling strongly of disinfectant carried in the lavatory aft. Even Junior was upset having to navigate in such a queer ship, especially after our own perfectly maintained 'Queen of the Air'.

When we got as far as Antwerp we were recalled. The cloud-cover we had depended on for protection had begun to break. It had become perfectly clear, and we could see as far and wide as we wished. Not a very pleasant sight when all alone. As soon as we got the recall we screamed round in a turn and dived low over Flushing on our way out to sea, hoping to bomb a 4,000-ton steamer which was steaming along on its own about a mile off shore. Doing exactly the same thing a mile ahead was another Lancaster, and knowing well the Luftwaffe was up after us, I quickly caught it up in order to get mutual protection with our twelve guns. (In actual fact we got three Huns that day, all FW 190's.) For a while we flew in formation with him, and at last reached some cloud, but Johnny was the first to see the aircraft lettering on the other ship.

'Why, that's O-Orange!' he said.

Looking hard through the window I could see Dim sitting at the controls, his great moustache sticking out of his helmet as his Flight-Engineer handed him a cigarette. Seeing us, he smiled. Then I think he saw who was alongside and promptly dived into the clouds.

'So that was O-Orange,' I said to my boys. 'She looked pretty unserviceable, didn't she?'

Not only that, on many occasions my car would vanish on the slightest provocation; mysterious faces would appear in the squadron, postings which Don had engineered carefully without my knowledge – boys he wanted to have beside him. But, for all this, Dim was a good chap. He did a lot for our squadron. For too long we, including myself, probably more than anyone else, had thought too much in terms of tonnage and too little in terms of accuracy. But Dim had organized a lot of night bombing, and he got the boys up practically every night taking practice photographs.

All the time there was still the great problem of how to hit appointed objectives. The American Air Force had not yet begun to operate in force. We all knew they had a new bombsight, and we all knew that when they started bombing they would hit the target right on the nail, but at the moment it was up to Bomber Command. Meanwhile, the U-boat menace was still the big thing of the day. In Germany and their occupied ports they were building U-boats much faster than we could sink them.

Danzig was one of these ports.

Danzig lies in Poland, a long way from British shores, but order in to try to stem the tide of the Atlantic Battle, a daylight raid was planned on this place, where they were turning out at least twelve U-boats every month.

It was decided that Lancasters were to do the job. A long flight of some

1,500 miles over enemy territory in daylight was involved. If night-bombing had been accurate the job could have been done at night with the minimum amount of risk, but special orders had been given that we must avoid killing civilians at all costs. Thus extra risk had to be taken by flying unescorted over enemy territory in daylight. Such was the way of things.

Little need be said of that raid, the success of which as a precision bombing attack can best be gathered from a current newspaper report:

'Yesterday our Lancasters flew to Danzig in daylight to carry out a low-level attack on the submarine yards. Many searchlights were shot up by our gunners . . .'

There *were* flak and searchlights, because the timing had misfired. Most of us arrived over Danzig when it was pitch dark. In my aircraft, instead of bombing Danzig at night, where we couldn't even see the docks, let alone the street, we had bombed a small ship in the outer harbour and missed it by twenty yards from 1,000 feet. We had spared civilians, but we were still learning that raids must be planned carefully.

At that time there were rumours that a Pathfinder Squadron was to be formed, composed of the best bombing crews from all squadrons.

Dim said: 'It seems a good idea to me, but I can see many snags.'

'What are they going to do?' someone asked.

'Go in low and light up the targets for us with flares. We stay high and safe and bomb accurately,' said Johnny.

'That's good.'

'That's fine.'

'Yes, but here are the snags,' said Dim. 'First it is hard to form a new squadron quickly, and if you form it quickly it is hard to form it well, and speed is what they want. I think it would be better to take the best squadron in the Command and call it the "First Pathfinder Squadron".'

'That means us,' said Taff.

'No, we are about fifth now. I think 97 Squadron.'

A short argument followed in which it was generally agreed that 97 Squadron should be chosen.

'The second snag,' went on Dim, 'is losses. If they are going to go in low, their casualties are going to be high – very high. How are they going to get away with it? New crews will take a long time to train.'

'Squadrons will have to give up their best crews,' suggested Wimpy, 'on a strictly volunteer basis.'

'Then the best squadrons will either be deprived of all their crack crews, or no one will volunteer and the Pathfinders will be starved.'

'That's right. Keen squadrons will cough up their best crews and lose their place on the photographic ladder, while a lousy squadron will do nothing about it and go up to the top.'

'*C'est la guerre*,' said Dim. 'It will be fair enough in the long run. But the third great snag, as far as I can see, is promotion in the squadron. If there are heavy losses, then it won't matter, but if there aren't, then good chaps who would become Flight-Commanders in an ordinary squadron would be kept down because they had volunteered to become Pathfinders. They would lose their promotion, and the old hands would stay on and keep their rank. It seems rather unfair.'

'That goes for all special squadrons,' I pointed out.

'I suppose so. Anyway, I wish they would hurry up and get cracking. Our bombing certainly needs a spot of accuracy.'

Meanwhile, I am told, arguments, debates and discussions were taking place at length in Bomber Command. Some of the big noises were flat out for the day when Pathfinders would take the air. This included most of the Group-Commanders. Others, one or two of whom were in Bomber Command itself, were not so keen. It was a new idea. Why change three years' hard work? They argued and grumbled, grumbled and argued, hour after hour, day after day. Even the Prime Minister was consulted, and in the end it was he who did much to put the matter right.

Then came August 15, 1942, the day the Pathfinders came into being.

But let's go back just a few days. On the 9th and 10th we had all gone out to lay mines in the Baltic to try to stop the *Prinz Eugen* from slipping into the Atlantic. These were long trips in bad weather, both of seven or more hours' duration, and fifteen hours' flying in twenty-four was pretty tiring to the average pilot. The weather was so bad when we took off from England that we were cloud-borne before we even got our wheels up, and coming back we had to land on the beam in daylight.

On the 11th we rested, but on the next night, my birthday, we made the last Pathfinderless attack on Germany and queerly enough, it was a roaring success; 135 acres were destroyed. Every crew went below the clouds to find his objective; every crew bombed from 5,000 feet. I couldn't help thinking at the time that I couldn't, myself and the boys, have given a better birthday present to the Nazis.

But after four trips in five days we were all pretty tired out and the whole squadron was given a night off. We went to our usual pub, the Red Lion, and had a few beers.

Next day we heard which squadron had been selected to be the Pathfinder Squadron in No. 5 Group. There was a boy from this squadron with us at the time. He had landed at our place the night before with engine trouble, and he told us the gen.

'We are moving down south tomorrow,' he said, 'to a place in

Huntingdonshire. Quite a good spot, I believe: the beer's good and the girls aren't bad. Anyway, it will be jolly nice to get out of Lincolnshire.'

'Fine,' said Dim drily; 'but what are the conditions of the Pathfinder Service?'

'As far as I know, we can do up to sixty trips without a rest, but have to give up when we get tired, and no one will call it lack of moral fibre. When we are qualified Pathfinders – which means ten trips as an illuminator – we are allowed to wear a special pair of gold wings underneath our medal ribbons.' (He had the DFC).

At this there was a chorus of sarcastic cheers.

'What is an illuminator?'

'Perhaps I had better explain the whole procedure. The new crews merely carry incendiary bombs and no flares at all, but they attack in front of the main force, so that the first incendiaries fall accurately on to the target. The next lot of crews carry a full load of flares. The job of these boys is to find the target, and so they are known as "Finders". They fly out on a course extremely accurately, keeping to dead reckoning, and when the ETA is up they begin to drop a flare every thirty seconds, and so a long line of country is illuminated for perhaps ten miles. Meanwhile, the other Finders will spread out on either side, so that when zero hour arrives the whole German countryside for ten miles square is illuminated. Not very well, but enough for the next crowd of boys to see.'

'And the best crews?' I asked.

'They carry bundles of flares which they drop the moment they see the aiming point. In fact, they try to drop them on top of the aiming point. They fly right with the Finders, and they themselves are called the "Illuminators". When they see where the target is they drop a flew flares in a certain pattern, and the rest of the Pathfinders immediately come along and dump hundreds of flares right over the target, which will illuminate it, we hope, like daylight.'

'How about cloud?'

'We haven't got an answer to that yet, but the first thing we are going to do is to send a Mosquito out every night about an hour in front of us who will tell us exactly what the weather is like over the target. We may even send one out five hours before the raid is due to take off, so that we can be pretty sure that the weather will be OK when we get there.'

'And fog?'

'Well, if there is any thick fog we will probably drop pink pansies. These are 250-pound incendiary bombs which burn with a bright red glow on the ground and can be seen quite clearly through any fog.'

'How long do they burn?'

'Oh, quite a long time – about fifteen minutes.'

'That sounds good enough. At what height are you going to fly?'

'About the same as you. We may go in lower if the cloud is low, but we have had it impressed on us that the main thing is to be absolutely certain of our position.'

'But how can you be certain of knowing where you are? The Germans are jamming our Nav boxes so much that except for finding a position over the North Sea, we can't do a thing about it.'

'Our idea is to keep to dead reckoning as much as possible. In fact, dead reckoning is our motto. We will get a wind – a good wind – early on, and then fly absolutely accurately, and if you work it out you can't be more than ten miles out either way, after three hundred miles, provided the pilot is good and compasses are right. Then, of course, the Finders will take care of the rest.'

'It seems OK to me,' said Hoppy. 'But we still haven't got a point to aim at.'

'Yes, that's right; bombing will be scattered.'

'But it will be in the right place.'

'Yes, it will be in the right place all right, which is something.'

'I hope,' said Dim, doubtfully.

The Pathfinders led the main force into action two days later, on a very small-scale raid on Emden. This is not a large port and is not defended by many guns, so nothing much could be gained from the success of this raid, but it gave the whole of the Pathfinder force a lot of confidence in their job. They had lit up the place well and bombs had fallen, causing destruction, which the Emdenites had never seen before.

We didn't take part in this and the following raids, because for a time we had been shifted on to special duties.

The story had begun a long time ago, when in our old Hampdens we used to make lonely dive-bombing attacks on the *Scharnhorst* in Kiel Harbour. Now the *Scharnhorst* was in Gdynia having certain new gadgets put on. The *Gneisenau* was there, too, being dismantled, together with a new aircraft carrier, the *Graf Zeppelin*, which was being fitted out for its first voyage. The admirals of the Royal Navy were fearful that these ships, together with the battleship *Tirpitz* and a few scattered cruisers, might set sail as a formidable task force towards mid-Atlantic, where their presence might be undesirable. Especially so, bearing in mind new operations of considerable magnitude which were being considered at that time.

Meanwhile, after the episode of the *Scharnhorst* and *Gneisenau* slipping through the Channel, certain scientists had gone into action. A new bomb had been designed. It was known simply as the 'capital ship bomb'. How it worked and what it was supposed to do were, and still are today, well-kept secrets. But the rough idea was that one hit took care of one battleship. It was heavy, but like most new weapons it had its limitations. It was not a beautiful bomb; in fact, it was extremely ugly, and looked of all things rather like a turnip, and like most turnips its ballistics were not very good. When it was dropped at a high altitude, instead of following the path of a beautiful bomb it might easily swing out of its course. And so to hit a ship from 8,000 feet would require a lot of luck, even though the bomb-aiming was extremely good. The other alternative, and the only alternative, was to go in low. Unfortunately, this bomb had to be dropped, if we went in low, from exactly 1,000 feet if it was to do its stuff; and there is no future in flying straight and level over a battleship at 1,000 feet. I think most naval gunners will agree with me that few Lancasters would reach the release point, let alone the aiming point.

Air Marshall Harris had given this 'toy' to my squadron. We had been told to get on with a lot of practice in low- and high-level bombing. Two special bomb-sights had been acquired for the job. Now the Ministry of Aircraft Production, which works wonders in aircraft, can also always produce a good many other things when required, and they soon managed to get hold of two extremely accurate types. A high-level bomb-sight is very different from a low-level bomb-sight, but in any case we of the Royal Air Force have never made much of a song and dance of our bomb-sights, because night-bombing doesn't need a really accurate one. Anything within a quarter of a mile will do. However, the sight to which I am referring – the high-level sight – was really accurate, and soon we began to get, with practice, errors of only sixty yards from 10,000 feet. This was good enough for what we wanted.

This training had gone on without a pause for two months, and six crews in the squadron had become fairly proficient. When clouds were low we had also carried out low-level practice, so that we could drop our bombs to the tune of an accuracy of about fifteen yards. Should any German warship try to steal away under cover of low cloud we would still have been able to fix him, even though it wouldn't have been much fun. Every day for the last two months we always had three crews available, standing by in flying kit, who could take off immediately to do the job; sometimes I was one of them. But whoever we were and whatever we were like as pilots, I think they would all agree when I say that the boys owe their lives to the fact that no German admiral had the guts to put to sea.

'One thing,' said Dim; 'if we do go and attack those ships, one of us might get a posthumous VC.'

'Who wants that?' said Taffy.

'Not me,' said one of the boys; 'all I want is a Peace and Victory Medal.'

Most of us agreed.

Then came the moon period of August. Special intelligence reports had said that the *Graf Zeppelin* was almost ready; the crew was supposed to be on board; the aircraft had been taken over; they were ready to set sail. Now, a German aircraft-carrier was a thing that hadn't been known before, and it was our idea that it wouldn't be known very long. We knew how to drop our bomb; and we were ready.

On the full-moon night of August 27, while the rest of the boys were bombing Kassel, twelve of us set out for the 950-mile journey to Gdynia. We took off overloaded to the hitherto unprecedented weight of 67,000 pounds in all. In my crew we were carrying S/L Richardson as a bomb-aimer. He was a bombing instructor, and if anyone could drop a bomb accurately it was he, but he was making his first war flight since August 1918.

Our plan was to make accurate bombing runs from 6,000 feet in the moon. It should have been easy; the docks in the brilliant light should have been clear-cut squares in the bomb-sight. Everything seemed to point in our favour. Out of twelve bombs, one would surely fall in the right place. But old man weather turned against us. When we arrived over the target the south-westerly wind had blown all the haze away from Berlin straight over Danzig and Gdynia. It reduced visibility to about a mile. Moreover, there was a lot of light flak and searchlights about.

Hoppy was nearest, He missed by about fifty yards, causing one of the largest craters they had ever seen in those parts. We spent an hour over the target, and made twelve bombing runs. We never saw the *Graf Zeppelin* – but the *Gneisenau* was there, and Dicky Richardson aimed at that. Each time he made his run he was completely oblivious of the fact that the flak was all round. I think he thought he was over the practice range on the East Coast. The first time he said 'Dummy run' there was a silence; the tenth time he said it, a quick ejaculation came from Johnny Wickens in the rear turret. In the end, we saw our huge bomb fall into the water about 400 yards away from the *Gneisenau*. Dicky's remark was rather laconic, considering that by now we were alone over the target and the flak was giving us hell. He said:

'That's killed a few fish for the bastards,' and added as an afterthought, 'Blast it.'

Combie in the mid-upper turret said he thought we had better be going. Junior said it would be daylight when we recrossed the Danish coast. Hutch said he would send a message telling them we had just left the target, so that they wouldn't worry if we were a few hours late. Junior piped up again and said that he thought we should go a little north, so as to avoid Sylt on the way home – there were some fighters there. I said nothing, or very nearly nothing; just a few short words . . .

That's the worst of one big bomb: you go a long way to do your best; then you miss; then you have a five-hours bind on the way home. It is an infuriating business.

When we were circling base I looked at my clock. We had been in the air ten hours, and with no second pilot I felt pretty well all in. Ten hours' flying is a long time, but apart from our failure, the only worthwhile event was the Russians bombing Königsberg at the same time as we were bombing Gdynia. In the bright moonlight I saw over the target a funny-looking thing, rather like an elongated Heinkel. Next day some newspaper correspondent wrote of the 'aerial arms shaking hands over Danzig'. I am quite sure neither side knew the other was there.

A few days later we flew behind the Pathfinders to bomb Saarbrucken. We were carrying an 8,000-pound bomb for the first time, and great excitement prevailed on board as we waited in anticipation to see what it would look like. We had never flown behind the Pathfinders before, and we arrived a little early to see what they would do. Sure enough the Finders laid their long strings of flares, the illuminators hovered around and then dumped bunch after bunch of flares right over the town; the bombs, incendiaries first, began to fall thick and fast, about 1,000 tons of them. Soon the whole area was one mass of flames. Junior saw our cookie fall and said it caused 'an expanding mushroom of blue-red flame which seemed to cover an area of about half a mile square for a full five seconds'. Long words for Junior, but I wouldn't have cared to have been in it.

Everything was fine. We all got back safely, although we ourselves had some of the biggest holes knocked in our wings and fuselage I have yet to see in a Lancaster, and we went to bed pleased. Our photographs had shown one mass of flames.

But next day we heard very bad news from the photo-reconnaissance unit. The Pathfinder Force had boobed. They had lit up Saarlouis, a small town – in fact, a tiny town – ten miles from Saarbrucken, and the Recco boys said that, judging from the photographs, there wasn't even a sign-post left standing there. Those 1,000 tons had removed the place from the map. A few nights later the same thing happened at Frankfurt, when a small force had, through slight miscalculations on the part of the Pathfinders, bombed another small town nearby. But this time they destroyed by mistake a large and hitherto unknown factory making Opel trucks for the German Army.

But if some raids went wrong, others went right. The Pathfinders had already begun to pay good dividends under the command of Group-Captain Bennett, an ex-airline pilot. Devastation in industrial areas in many cities was on a scale hitherto unknown. The crews at last could see what they were aiming at, the area which they had set out for. The day had at last been reached when most of the bombs would fall in the right place, but unfortunately the right place was too big; bombing was still not concentrated. Marker bombs were still required to give the bomb-aimers a bull's-eye aiming point.

It soon became obvious that the pink pansies were no earthly use at all. The Germans hadn't been slow. They copied these pink pansies so quickly that soon they sprang up like poppies over all open fields in Germany.

So it went on. A step had been taken in the right direction. Improvements were being made every day. Towns in the Third Reich were being raided every night, and reading from my log book it can be seen that these were being raided with varying success:

On September 10th, Düsseldorf; target lit up well: many acres of industrial area were destroyed.

On the 13th, Bremen; a failure, we lost nineteen, including three from 106 – Taffy Williams, Dizzy Downer, S/L Howell – too much flak, target not illuminated, raids scattered.

On 19th, Ruhr area; cloud all the way; complete failure.

23rd, Flensburg; failure, due to haze, bombing not concentrated.

It was obvious that a snag had yet to be overcome. We had done everything else, but we hadn't beaten the weather. When it was good, a raid was successful; but when it was bad, the bombs were scattered far and wide.

On October 1 we moved to another airfield. As soon as we arrived we started training mass low-level formation under the able Command of Group-Captain Gus Walker of rugger fame, who had won the DSO and DFC. He used to lead us round the countryside, practising navigation at nought feet. There is no room in this book to say what a great man Gus is, but I know that all of 106 would like it to be said that he was one of the finest Station-masters they had ever served under.

We started off first in squadrons, then in wings, and finally in a sort of formation known as a group gaggle, meaning a flock of geese. We flew the length and breadth of England, never more than 300 feet up; mighty dangerous it was, too. In the beginning there were no set positions, and we flew through the air, wingtip to wingtip, rather like a crowd of workers elbowing their way into a bus. The only snag was that if anyone touched it would be 'curtains' to the two aircraft concerned. When we finally levelled out for the practice bombing run it was a question of closing our eyes and praying to God. Practice bombs whistled down all round, and one of my pilots, George Lace, flying on my left-hand side, once collected one in the mid-upper turret, but it merely fell through his gunner's legs without going off, much to his surprise.

On many occasions some of our Metropolitan Air Force fighters would carry out dummy attacks on us. Such was the nature of our formation that quite a few found it extremely difficult to get out of our slipstream once they had got in. More than one hit the deck making these dummy attacks.

All this culminated in one of the greatest low-level daylight raids of the war. It was carried out by ninety-four Lancasters flying in tight formation, and even though I say it myself, it was a fine raid, led, planned and executed by a fine group. My report next day, written while I was still in pyjamas in my bedroom, read:

For some days the squadron had been practising low-level formation flying – in threes, in sixes and with other squadrons in long cross-country flights. Quite obiously these exercises were leading up to something 'big,' something out of the ordinary – perhaps a mass formation raid in daylight. After several 'flaps', during which aircraft were de-bombed almost as soon as they were bombed-up, the day finally arrived when all conditions were favourable for such an attack. The day was Saturday, October 14, 1942, and the target was the Schneider Armament Factory at Le Creusot, almost on the border of occupied and Vichy France.

The raid was exclusively 5 Group's – a grand force of ninety-four Lancasters assembling and forming up soon after midday. The squadron supplied ten aircraft and all of them took off without a hitch. The route was over Land's End, far out to the Bay of Biscay and then turning into the French Coast, crossing it just south of Île d'Yeu and thence over some 200 miles of enemy-occupied territory, to the target. The formation flew the whole way between heights of 50 and 500 feet, climbing up to 4,000 feet as it neared the target.

The sun had set and it was getting dark when the objective was reached, soon after six o'clock, but the vast area of factories, workshops and warehouses was clearly seen. The attack lasted for nine minutes, during which time over 200 tons of high explosives and incendiaries were rained down with commendable precision. Huge fires broke out and terrific explosions were seen over a wide area and within a few minutes the whole town was blanketed with a thick pall of smoke.

In addition to the main target a formation of six aircraft were detailed to bomb the Montchanin Power Station – a vital target which if hit would cause widespread chaos and confusion. In this formation, No. 106 Squadron was represented by W/C G. P. Gibson, DFC, and F/L J. V. Hopgood, DFC. The attack was made from 500 feet, each aircraft carrying 10 × 500-pound bombs. Both crews claim that their bombs straddled the target – a claim which was justified by later reports which stated that the transformer house would take nearly two years to repair. Our two aircraft then circled the target and between them fired 1,000 rounds of ammunition into the transformers – a satisfactory and spectacular operation which brought forth vivid blue flashes each time a bullet hit a vital spot.

The attack completed, to the satisfaction of all concerned, the aircraft turned for home – independently since it was now dark, and by the shortest route. Weather, which had been favourable, was very bad over this country and the majority of aircraft were diverted to bases in the south.

Throughout the whole trip not a single enemy fighter offered combat (except to one aircraft limping home on three engines) and the opposition over the target itself was negligible.

All squadron aircraft returned safely and undamaged with the exception of W/C Gibson's (slightly holed) and F/L Hopgood's. This latter aircraft was damaged by the blast of its own bombs, F/L Hopgood (incidentally this was the last trip of his tour) being a little too enthusiastic and bombing from below safety height. All ten crews claim to have hit their target, so that from a squadron point of view the raid was 100 per cent successful.

Owing to the fading light, pictures of the actual bombing were not obtainable, but P/O Ruskell took several photographs of the outward journey from the Wing-Commander's aircraft, with an ordinary cine camera. Several of his pictures, the only ones taken on the raid, were subsequently published in the Press.

Captains of squadron aircraft taking part:

> W/C Gibson, DFC
> P/O Crowe
> Sergeant Lace, DFM
> P/O Shannon
> Sergeant Hamilton
> F/L Hopgood, DFC
> P/O Cassels
> P/O Healey, DFM
> Sergeant Phair
> P/O Wellington

Two days later we were briefed for Italy; this was to be the first raid here for some time. Because the Italians had no flak worth mentioning, and because the trip over France was similar to flying over England, Italy had always been popular with all bomber crews.

'Tonight it is Genoa,' said Gus Walker. 'I don't want to waste your time by making a speech, but it is the first time we have attacked Genoa for years. The targets, of course, are all in the dock area, where units of the Italian fleet are sheltering. You may wonder why we have been suddenly switched from Germany, and why you are going here tonight – I only wish I could come too. Well, all I can say is that you may, for all I know, be taking part in a large operation in the Mediterranean. For the first time in history you may be supporting land operations, hundreds of miles away. Anyway, off you go. Good luck.'

We went and we all came back. It was a good prang. The Pathfinders lit the targets just like daylight. We all watched our incendiaries burn merrily away on the concrete roofs of the Genoa houses, We watched our block-busters disintegrate the buildings on the dockyards. And when we came back we all decided that Genoa was pretty cushy.

Next day the offensive in the Western Desert started. Mr Churchill had given his orders. Gus had been right.

This was a great week from the start, because the next day we went off to Italy again. This time it was a daylight raid. Apart from the damage we were going to do, I think the whole idea was to show the Italians that the British Air Force was all supreme on the Western Front. We were going to attack Milan in daylight at teatime.

It is not being quite fair to the German fighters to say that we flew across France on the way to Italy completely unsupported. We crossed Selsey Bill at very low level and flew towards that flat part of land between Cherbourg and Le Havre. A warm front had been reported lying across France which would give us cloud-cover when we approached. We were to climb up for this cloud as soon as possible. In actual fact the cloud had receded from the French coast, and we all stormed up over the cliffs in bright daylight, climbing flat out with the clouds in the distance. Most of us had gone a long way into France before the motherly safeness of the blanketing white mist had been reached. They fired at us a bit over the French coast, but I think they were all surprised to see a hundred bombers supported by Spitfires flying so low. Then we heard the Germans chattering away on the RT. We heard the controller say: 'Hello, all German aircraft. The British bombers are too far south; you must land at the nearest bases.'

On we flew, this bright, sunny day; it was getting warmer and warmer as we flew south, and Junior helped me to take off my coat. We were carrying movie-cameras, and took many interesting pictures of little French villages, and some rather charming French people, who were all waving to us. One charming family group I remember stood in front of their white cottage – a young man, a little blonde daughter, about seven years old, and a sweet wife; at least she looked sweet from 100 feet, with her blonde hair flying in the breeze; they were all waving like mad. Another time we saw a flock of what I thought at first were geese, clustered together in the middle of the field. When we had gone over them Johnny told me they were nuns.

After three hours we climbed up high over the Alps and gathered in a fighting formation over Lake Annecy; then stormed down on to Milan, another sixty miles farther on, dropping our cookies from 3,000 feet. The sun was still well up; in fact, we could see our shadows before us moving along the ground. The confusion in Milan was something to be seen. A few flak-guns fired spasmodically; private cars ran on to the pavements;

people rushed to shelters; someone turned on a searchlight. But it was no use, the boys behaved like real gentlemen. They all went for military objectives, and they did a lot of military damage. As far as I know, not one civilian establishment was hit.

Then we turned around and came home again. The sun began to set over the Alps – a beautiful sight, a sight which perhaps we will never see again. An Italian fighter came in to have a look at us. His was a biplane with only two guns; we had six. Johnny Wickens kept on saying in the back, 'Come on, you beggar; come on, you beggar; come closer.' But he never came. And then the sun went down, and we were flying safely over France again on the way home.

Later that night Halifaxes bombed the place again, and the panic in this second raid was said to beat all records, even for the Italians.

It was a good raid, this daylight one on Milan, and must have shaken the Italians more than somewhat, especially as they relied on their great German partner to protect them from the Northern Approaches. But a few days later Genoa had it two nights running, and we all began to wonder what was happening. Were we trying to give the Pathfinders a break, or were we trying to give them confidence in illuminating weakly defended targets? Or was it to try to bomb Italy out of the war? The rumours had it that things were going pretty badly inside Italy. When the King visited Genoa, people were said to have gone down on their knees and prayed for peace. Some even said that most of the statesmen were entertaining the idea of making a separate peace. But why were we bombing Genoa the whole time? Why not Turin? We knew the Fleet was at Genoa, but Turin was the better target. There is not so much concrete there. Why bomb the Italian fleet the whole time – it never put to sea, anyway.

But on November 8 we got our answer. North Africa had been invaded.

We had been trying to prevent the Itie fleet from interfering.

From now on Italy began to get it whenever the weather was suitable for the occasion. Not only the fogs in England often stopped a raid, but the big cloud-banks over the Alps themselves made the trip almost impossible. We were briefed practically every night, but each time the Met man would walk in with his 'cloud board', which showed the heights of cloud all the way to the target. Icing cloud was marked in deep red and the non-icing variety in blue. When he walked in, as he usually did, with his board looking as if it had been dipped in red paint, nervous howls of laughter would go up from all the crews. Then the target would be changed to somewhere else, possibly in Germany. This meant last-minute flaps – a new briefing a new flight-planning conference, new maps and bad tempers all round. We were briefed many times, but the weather often held us back.

But despite the fact that Lancasters from our Group were the only ones capable of 'doing' Italy, we flew in the month of November no fewer than 1,336 sorties to that fair country for the loss of only two aircraft. If we should cast our minds back and say, for a matter of example, that an air line flew three flights a day to Italy for three years running and lost only two aircraft, they would consider themselves one of the safest air lines in the world.

Moreover, we had to contend with what little flak there was; but whatever damage our bombs did, it was certainly a good portent of the future of civil aviation and the complete reliability of British aircraft.

By now the Italians were getting jumpy; these raids were doing their stuff. We were, as they say, on a good wicket. It is a well-known fact that bombing accuracy and effect increase indirectly with the weakness of flak and morale. Italian flak, though bolstered up by certain Nazi flak regiments, was still bad. We would often bomb at very low level, picking out targets at will, and nothing could be worse for the people below than to see those great Lancasters flying around, making a tremendous noise, and dropping their cookies out one after another, on exactly the right spot.

On November 29 my crew and I dropped the first 8,000-pound bomb of the war on Italy. Turin received it with displeasure, and I took a movie picture to show it bursting, and also to show the boys what it was like when we got home.

After this 'Woe-Woe' Ansaldo reached a new high in moans about the war. He said that the whole thing was unfair, that there should be no such thing as aerial attack. Perhaps he had forgotten Abyssinia and gas.

'Darned good show, too,' said Johnny Searby, one of the new Flight-Commanders. He had taken the place of Dim, who had wangled a posting to a 'secret' place in London, probably the Savoy. Johnny was a little older than the average, rather taciturn – sometimes severe – but a very good-hearted fellow. He was married and had a baby. He had done a lot of work in Ferry Command. Now he wanted to fly on Ops badly, and was doing trips as often as possible.

'Yes, the Ities are getting absolute hell.' This was Charles Martin, the Adjutant. He was about forty-five years old and had won the Military Medal in the last war, and for his sins had done about twenty trips at the rear turret of a Wimpy in this one. Why they had never given him a gong, if only for the magnificent example he had shown, I cannot think.

We were sitting in the dining-room of the Black Boy Hotel at Nottingham. The food had been good, the wine even better. Now we were smoking cigars and drinking a modest brandy. Often we would treat ourselves like this, just to get away from the drab routine of station life. All the rest of the boys – Hoppy, Bill, Brian Oliver, my new gunnery officer, Gray Healey, Mike Lumley, his wireless-operator, Don Curtin, from Long Island, USA – were upstairs in the American bar, cracking jokes with the two barmaids and drinking a terrible potion known as the '106 Special', which I think consisted of every drink under the sun mixed into one glass. We had driven them in. They were having a noisy evening. We were having a quiet one.

'You know,' said Charles, 'it is amazing how this war has changed. Last year about this time things looked pretty grim. Last summer I think they looked even worse, and now everything seems fine; that is, at least, we don't look like losing it.'

'I wonder when it will be all over,' I said to myself, more than to the others.

'A long time yet,' said Charles.

'I agree,' said John, 'but when you mentioned just now that things had changed a lot since the summer, I think you can almost say that the turning point of the war was reached in the month between October 22, and when was it that the Russians started their Stalingrad offensive—?'

'November 22.'

'Yes, that's right, between October 22 and November 22 the course of this war changed completely. Last summer the Axis came to the limit of their advance; they had come as far as they could. Then they were held; their initiative died away at Stalingrad, at El Alamein and in the Solomons.'

'Go on.'

John took a sip at his brandy. Charles lit his cigar and I listened, watching his smoke curl into the air.

'Well, you know the rest,' he continued. 'On October 22 we attacked at El Alamein, and after a week broke through and turned the whole German line there into a complete rout. On the 8th they invaded North Africa, and although I am not quite sure of that man, Admiral Darlan, things seem to be going pretty well. On the 22nd Timoshenko counter-attacked at Stalingrad under Stalin's orders, and now what has happened? A vast German army is trapped, and the loss of men on the Eastern Front might make all the difference to the fighting. In North Africa both sides are going forward well. They look like meeting in a couple of months' time. Then another German army might be annihilated, or what is left of it. After all, we have complete sea-power in the Med now.'

'Yes, we have certainly got sea superiority,' said Charles. 'Then perhaps we will invade the fortress of Europe.'

'Perhaps next autumn.'

'Depends on how things go. The Russians are yelling for a Second Front, but we can't do a thing until we have beaten the submarine menace. Besides that, we've got to get air superiority on all fronts first. It is pretty easy for the Germans; they are tucked up inside their fortress,

and they can meet anyone on the outside rim by moving all their forces
to that point. Our job is to get complete and utter air superiority
everywhere.'

'Don't the Russians think the African campaign a Second Front?'

'No. It isn't killing enough Germans.'

'They like our bombing, though,' I said. 'It has quite an effect on
German morale at home.'

'But surely you don't think bombing could win the war alone?' asked
Charles.

'I don't know, Charles; that is what we are taught, as you know; but
we are dealing with the mass psychology of a nation – and a bad nation
at that. It is run, organized and controlled by Gestapo and SS police.
They might crack, if they can break out of the iron ring, or they might
not. No one can say.'

'And if our bombing gets heavier?'

'You are asking the impossible. The German people are extraordinary;
they have never faced devastation on their home front before. But the fact
still remains that if they were to give in, they would have everything to
lose and nothing to gain. I think myself they will fight till the end. A lot
of people go around talking so much bull about the crack appearing and
once the crack has appeared the foundation will weaken, etc, etc. In fact,
so much so that the British public is getting very much "win-the-war-
by-the-easiest-method" minded. The Yankee boys have already started
going farther and farther into France – Rouen had it the other day. No
one can tell where they will stop. Not, perhaps, until they reach Berlin.
At the same time we shall obviously be increasing our effort. The whole
Bomber Command is getting Lancasters and improved Halifaxes, but
even then, who knows?'

'It's funny they're not making any real attempt at reprisals for all
that,' put in John. 'That Canterbury raid was just a hate sortie. From
what I am told by eye-witnesses, they came in at teatime at low level in
the middle of the busiest shopping hour. Casualties were pretty heavy.'

Charles offered me a cigarette.

'That was a hate raid all right,' he said; 'but I think I agree with the
wingco in what he has just said. The Germans may get their cities
devastated, they may even get their cities wiped out, but they will never
understand war until an army marches in as it has never done before,
as far as we know, in our history. This army must not be made up of
cissies, but an army which will show these bastards exactly what we
mean by telling them that war doesn't pay. Hitler, Goering and the rest
of them must be dealt with in the appropriate manner – though God
knows what that is.'

'Let's hope the Russians get there first,' said John, feelingly; 'but if
they don't, then let's hope we do a really good job.'

There was a short silence. Then I changed the subject.

'I think Goering's a complete clot. He started off thinking the Luftwaffe was all-powerful and prepared it for a short war with a minimum of reserves. Now he is finding that his ambitious programme is not so good. All his boys have to fly old types with no guns on board which don't fly very well, anyway. He is backing a real loser.'

'Don't you let him hear you say that,' said Charles, laughing.

And so we sat there, talking over our cigars and brandy, mostly about the war, for there was little else to talk about. We went on to the Jap war: how the little yellow bellies themselves had been halted, and how the balance of sea-power had swung back in the Allies' favour; how once again the Japs were being beaten back; about the U-boat war; how aeroplanes were now being equipped with certain devices which would be able to attack the U-boat when they least expected it; the aerial war – we all had stories to tell, ideas to put forward. The liqueurs were doing their work well. Conversation flowed easily.

Up to now it had been a long road of defeat and failure; a long uphill road which had taken a lot of climbing. Now at last we were over the hump. It was pleasant to sit there and rest awhile and think that the worst was behind. Perhaps the Hun would now retire right into his European fortress. In fact, we knew that he had already begun to do so. The German leaders in their speeches were tacitly acknowledging this governing factor in their policy. They were now going to organize all Europe as an impregnable fortress, capable of resisting a definite siege until war weariness, or internal dissension, should cause the Allies to abandon any attempt to try to crack an impossible nut. Exploitation of conquered territories had become so ruthless as almost to shake the quislings. Italians, Hungarians, Rumanians and other vassal nationalities had been herded by their thousands to the death-pit of the Russian front. By cold-blooded murder and an unexampled campaign of cruelty a strong attempt had been made to obliterate the entire Jewish race. France had been made to enter into full collaboration with the Axis. Adolf Hitler had proclaimed himself above the law.

But we would attack that Festung Europa, and we were going to get inside for the first time. And this time we would be able to dictate to the German people in the language of the sword – their own language, and the only language they will be able to understand until we alter their entire educational ideas. After this would come the Japs. It would take a long time, but they, too, would earn the penalty meted out for aggression.

'It really does seem,' said John, yawning, 'that once we invade the end is in sight.'

'The executive word is "once"; in fact, a big word is "once",' said Charles.

We got up to go. The evening had been pleasant and we had practically 'won' the war. But we shouldn't have been so pleased if we had known of the long battles that were to be fought, the heavy casualties to be borne, and the fact that the war was to be so prolonged. The tide had turned, but had a long way to go back.

CHAPTER FIFTEEN

THE SHAPE OF THINGS

The raids on Italy ended as suddenly as they began – that is, for our Group. We began once more to bomb the Ruhr valley. On the other hand, a few Halifaxes and Stirlings would wend their lonely way down to the south over the Alps and drop a few tons on the industrial areas of Turin and Genoa, but these were more spasmodic than usual. In our Group we even made one heavy raid on Milan in which my 106 Squadron topped all previous records by obtaining six aiming-point pictures of the target, a feat which brought us up from third to the proud position of top of Bomber Command.

But taking things by and large, Italy was off, the battle of Germany was on.

While little had been done to Germany in the past few months, when most of the bomber force had been engaged elsewhere, the scientists had not been idle. 'Boffins', we call them, why I don't know. They are not long-haired, spectacled old men, as you might imagine. They are just ordinary types, some young, some middle-aged, who have not had the chance to fly but are doing the next best thing.

They were out to beat the weather. For months they had slaved with short-wave radio trying to work out a system. Now, at last, they had got it.

One day towards the end of December the Group Bombing Leader, F/Lt Bob Hay, explained exactly how it was to be done. He was speaking to us in our briefing-room in front of a large blackboard on which were drawn many complex diagrams. 'Now so far in this war,' he began, 'you have always bombed something on the ground.' I looked across at John Searby and smiled. Of course we had always bombed something on the ground; what else could we bomb? 'If you can see your target easily, you have always done your best to hit it; but when your target has been covered by cloud you know what happens – you just drop your bombs on ETA, or on a timed run from the nearest landmark, and this means that your bombs are scattered over the countryside.'

There was an expectant hush, everybody was listening.

'Now we've got something new. We're going to bomb through cloud, we're going to bomb completely "blind". You're going to aim at something in the air. This something will take the form of a coloured flare which will be dropped by the Pathfinders in a certain position right over the aiming point.'

Bomb a flare! Somebody laughed.

'It is nothing to laugh about,' Bob went on; 'wait till you hear the rest. These flares are going to be dropped by certain aircraft of the Pathfinder force who have been practising over England for some time, and I can't tell you how they do it. It's all a question of a super instrument. For the benefit of the bomb-aimers I might tell you that you use your sight in the normal way, except that you set up the following data.'

He went on for a while in his cut-and-dried manner expounding technical stuff about wind velocities, terminal velocities, trail angles and the rest of the thousand things that make up the information fed into the modern bomb-sight. Gone were the days when the Royal Air Force bombers had to use sights produced in 1932. Now the Mark XIV had come along. It did practically everything. You could fly at any angle, you could dive at any speed, but minute little gyros revolving at many thousands of revs per minute took care of everything except the wind, and the bombs were sure to fall near the target. Such was the character of our new bomb-sight that it became known as the all-singing, all-talking, all-dancing weapon.

One of the most enthusiastic persons about this new technique was Gus Walker. He, too, had had his fair share of bombing Germany when conditions were bad, hence his DSO and DFC, and he knew the game inside out. But, unfortunately, for a while Gus was not going to see this new system put into operation.

It all happened on one of the worst nights I can ever remember. We were sending a lot of aircraft off and it was dusk, just at the time when you cannot see very well. About thirty aircraft were taxiing around the perimeter track waiting for each other to take off. Gus and I were watching from the control tower. Suddenly, right on the far side of the aerodrome, we saw that a few incendiaries had dropped out of the gaping bomb-doors of one of the Lancasters. Gus, thinking that this aircraft had a 'cookie' on board, immediately rushed over to warn the crew to get out. I saw his car go speeding straight across the aerodrome, over the runways in front of aircraft taking off, to carry out his plan. But we knew it was a reserve aircraft, and I had to stay in the watch-tower, anyway, now that he had gone.

Watching him through field-glasses, I saw him get out of his car. I saw him run towards the aircraft, his arms waving against the lurid light cast up by the incendiaries. He was within twenty yards of the cookie when it went off.

There was one of those great slow explosions which shot straight into the air for about 2,000 feet and the great Lancaster just disappeared.

We turned away, trying not to think of the horrible sight; we thought that Gus had surely been blown sky high. But he was too tough for that. He had been bowled over backwards for about 200 yards; he had seen a great chunk of metal swipe off his right arm just below the elbow, but he had picked himself up and walked into the ambulance.

Ten other men, belonging to the fire-tender crew, were also injured, and now that I was acting Station-Commander, I arranged for the sick quarters to work at top speed in order to try to save their lives. The Station Medical Officer was away, but Doc. Arnold, our own doctor, worked wonders, and soon all the limbless men were tourniqueted up and, with lots of morphia in them, were fairly comfortable.

Gus's wife came over, having seen the explosion. I think she knew something had happened, and her face was a picture which cannot bear description, a picture of rapture, when she found out that Gus was not dead.

Before he was taken off to a base hospital he said two things. He asked me if I would look for his arm, which had a brand-new glove on it, and he gold me to ring up the AOC and ask him if he would take a one-armed Station-Commander in two months' time. And Gus came back in that time to the day.

Towards the end of the year came the night when we started our sky-marking technique raids on the Ruhr Valley. Essen was the target, Krupps the objective. Although the little city had had, up to date, hundreds of air-raid alerts, very few bombs had actually fallen in its built-up area: now we were going to try to do it 'blind'.

Twenty-five of us were going there, bombing from 23,000 feet. It was not a large number, in fact it was dangerously small, but this was because timing played such a big part in this new method of bombing.

The other Squadron-Commander did the briefing. 'You take off,' he said, 'and in the first hour and a half climb as high as possible. Then you set course at the exact second for Ijmuiden. From there you alter course and fly straight to point X, where two yellow blares will burn in the sky straight in front of you. These flares will be twenty-five miles from the target. You go straight on, taking no avoiding action until you come to point Y, when two red flares should be on either side of your wingtips. A few minutes later, straight in front of you, you will see a cluster of green flares. You are to aim your bombs at these on a correct heading of 170 degrees Magnetic. It doesn't matter a lot if you are two minutes late in bombing them, because the wind can only carry them a mile or two. But it is very important to bomb on that exact heading; if you are ten degrees off either way, your bombs will go about ten miles from the target.'

We set off, we saw our flares and we bombed them, and we came back, having beer. through the worst flak of all time.

There were too many troubles, many aircraft had turned back. We were not used to flying as high as this. And by these early returns the aircraft which did press on found that some 1,500 guns gave them their undivided attention for nearly half an hour. Not very pleasant.

There were oxygen failures, icing troubles, engines had overheated, guns had frozen up in a temperature of minus sixty degrees. Only ten out of twenty-five claimed to have bombed the target, but next day the German radio, for the first time in history, said that 'last night enemy bombers raided the town of Essen'.

It was a beginning, and from that day on the whole Group went on persevering, trying to solve our various difficulties. The plan itself was all right; the only failures were those due to the extreme conditions in which we were flying. The AOC quickly invented a special type of radiator flap which prevented the engines overheating. An instrument-maker fitted a gadget which prevented the oxygen failing. Guns were wiped quite free of oil so that there would be no friction at the highest altitudes; electrical flying kit was introduced so that the crews, especially in the turrets, would not suffer from cold.

But, for all this, the losses were extremely high. Although twenty-five aircraft would bomb the target within thirty seconds or so, there were so many guns in Essen that each aircraft was subjected to a veritable curtain of steel. One night we lost three from my squadron, and three very good fellows at that.

But the bombs were falling on Essen from above cloud, and the Germans were beginning to get worried. They even introduced a new kind of flak, which we called 'V' for Victory flak, because when bursting it looked like the Prime Minister's favourite sign, but they had a long time to wait if they thought that flak was going to stop what was now becoming a definite possibility.

A few weeks later the scientists introduced yet another innovation. This was the marker bomb. It took the form of a light-case 250-pound missile which burst at about 3,000 feet above the ground and cascaded on to the target hundreds of small red balls which burned for about five minutes. Moreover, the colours of these balls could be changed at will, and it was well-nigh impossible for the dummy target men in Germany to simulate anything like it on the ground. We called these bombs 'target indicating markers', or TI bombs for short. These were the bombs that put night bombing on the map.

From now on our plan began to shape itself. The jigsaw puzzle which had taken three and a half years to put together was almost complete. With the new year a new series of raids began which marked the end of German cities. Numbers were increased; bomb-loads were stepped up.

Extreme concentration and timing to seconds began to be their keynote of success.

On January 13 the target was Essen. The TI markers were seen clearly by all crews from a great height. An unknown concentration of bombs dropped on and around the doomed city. On the 16th and 17th Berlin was raided; here, once again, a limitation had crept into our weapons, in that they could not be used for a very long distance, and these markers fell this time about six miles south of the centre of the city, but, needless to say, great damage was done in the suburbs.

So it went on. We were just at the stage of transferring from the wrong to the right. It took about a month to get the new technique absolutely wrapped up by all crews. Now and then the effort was dispersed to Lorient, the centre of a vast system of U-boat pens. These raids were extremely devastating, and the whole dock area and town itself were wiped off the face of the earth. These Lorient raids, carried out under conditions of not too much flak, resulted in all crews getting to know the sky-marking and target-indicating method of attack so well that they would be able to do a good job when the time came to bomb Germany again.

With this technique at last buttoned up, the bomber boys once more turned their attention to the Ruhr.

Then came the real battle of Essen, and after three really heavy concentrated raids the famous Krupps works were almost wiped out. One after another, Nuremburg, Cologne, Düsseldorf and the rest of them began to get the real attack. At last the answer had been found, and whenever a German fire-watcher saw one of the deadly TIs come down on the right spot, he must have realized that the best place for him was below ground.

Meanwhile, with the increased bombing of those cities, to the German Herrenvolk came news on their radios, if they dared to listen, which must have made them apprehensive. The Russians were driving forward everywhere. On January 31, the German Sixth Army, under General von Paulus, surrendered before Stalingrad. Black flags were hung out in Berlin.

In Tunisia, the British and American armies had begun to squeeze the nutcracker. It looked as though the Axis would be driven into the sea, and they just did not have the sea superiority to take them off safely, as we had had at Dunkirk.

The Casablanca conference was in session. It was decided that only unconditional surrender was acceptable to the Allies. Also at Casablanca something else was being prepared for the Germans. General Eaker had flown there to plead the cause of the American daylight bomber, the Flying Fortress. He won, and the future of the Luftwaffe was sealed. All that the Germans knew was that a few days later a successful daylight raid was made by American bombers on Wilhelmshaven. The German people no doubt thought that Goering would soon drive them off. They did not know how wrong they were. No one had told them that my March their U-boat had been beaten at sea, that the Allies, thanks to the combined use of secret weapons, air and sea power, had at last settled accounts with their one and only successful weapon beneath the seas, and that our ships were now sailing to England and to North Africa practically without loss. All they did know, in fact, was that the systematic destruction of their country had begun. They could not help knowing that, no matter what their propaganda said. Soon even Goebbels had to change his tune and, instead of minimizing the damage, had begun to multiply it so that the whole world would look on the bomber as a murder weapon. This sort of article would appear from time to time in German newspapers:

'We know from experience gained in the towns afflicted by the air terror that civilian losses are heavy, and often very heavy! We cannot comply with the wishes of the population, however greatly interested they may be, by publishing any figures, since even now the enemy must not be able to estimate the results of his activities. The figures are high, but it must be stressed again that they are by no means as high as is stated by nervous and over-excited rumour-mongers in the Reich and even in Central Germany . . .

'Many towns which have now been partly destroyed by the enemy terror once believed that it would never be their turn because fog or their concealed position or other equally unfounded factors hampered the enemy's observation and prevented him from finding his way there. But the enemy found and hit some of these towns and some of these people.'

Yes, we found and hit those towns in fog and often from above the clouds. Old man weather, the last obstacle of all, had been overcome. Now it was the Germans' turn to moan. In fact, they were now squaling and wailing and appealing to the Pope to stop the bombings. But did they remember Warsaw, Rotterdam, Belgrade, Coventry, Bristol, Plymouth, Glasgow, Swansea and London? Did they remember Hitler's threat to raze every British city to the ground, to destroy Great Britain's population? If they did not, they had short memories – but that is typical of the Hun.

For year after year they had waged war on defenceless European countries, bleeding them, starving them, murdering them. They had done this for 150 years, and the German had never known what it was to have his own home destroyed. Wars had always been glorious, far from the fat Fräulein's doorstep. But now it was just starting. First the nearest German cities to our bomber bases began to get the new bombing; soon there would be new devices which would enable them to drop their TIs just as accurately as far as the long arm of the Lancasters could reach. Towns in the Ruhr Valley had already begun to disappear. The usual thick haze which hung over the river had dispersed, factories were beginning to close down, absenteeism by panic-stricken workers began to make itself felt on production.

But to destroy a big industrial area was a big job to tackle even for the bomber; nevertheless, it had been begun. Meanwhile, another raid which would help bring production in the Ruhr Valley to a standstill was being planned. Only a few men knew that the scientists had already begun their work. Orders had been given, special trials were to begin soon, but it was all very secret.

The Nazis spent most of their time attacking the British 'air pirates', calling them rude names and issuing dire threats of reprisal. But despite all their boloney, from travellers and other sources the news leaked out from Germany into the neutral Press that our bombing was doing serious damage now. Some of it was hard to believe; probably the correspondents let themselves go when writing their stories. They, too, probably had friends in Poland, Greece and Yugoslavia.

This was the sort of thing written about the fate of a certain town as seen by one neutral correspondent:

'The British bombardments have transformed the population with a high standard of living into troglodytes. Over two million people live in holes, cellars, in ruins or rough wooden hutments. Apart from a few tens of thousands who are anxiously awaiting the moment when they too will lose the roof over their heads, these two million people are about all that is left of the population of five million. The rest are scattered in all directions. Half a million are in Poland, hundreds of thousands are in Pomerania and Southern Germany, while still more hundreds of thousands are in Thuringia and Czechoslovakia. They are all living, squeezed close together, a prey to growing despair, increasingly attacked by the virus of nihilism because they are only pariahs, and for a long time now they have abandoned their belief in the wonderful promises of propaganda that would like to make them believe that with victory they would regain their possessions.

'There is also the question of looting. Clothes and furniture from bombed houses disappear magically from the pavements where they have been temporarily placed. Sometimes whole suites, grand pianos, sideboards complete with their silver, disappear without anyone knowing how. The authorities do not try to contest the facts, but for reasons of national pride they attribute them – to foreign workers. There probably are black sheep among the latter, but it may be asked, how do they manage to conceal sideboards, wardrobes and pianos in the barracks where most of them have to live?

'The population of this city lives in perpetual terror, terror of the police, terror of bombs, terror of looting and terror of foreign workers. All misdeeds that cannot be otherwise explained are imputed to the last named. For example, recently there were bands of saboteurs wandering through the blacked-out streets removing sewer gratings. The results of the 'jokes' can be imagined. The hurrying bombed-out people, rescue columns, even policemen on their beat fall through the openings into the sewers which swallow them up. The coin boxes in automatic telephone booths are mysteriously emptied of their contents. Water mains for fire fighting are blocked with cement.'

How was all this done? How was it organized? Who did all the work, and what were the aims of Bomber Command, anyway, if it was doing all this damage?

We never thought we could win the war by bombing alone. We were out to destroy German industry, to cut their transport system, to stop them building U-boats and ships and to make their channels unnavigable by mines. We were out to bomb them until they found themselves weak and punch-drunk from our blows, so that they would fall back before our invading armies. This in turn would save the lives of our own men – the young men of the Allies on whom the future of this world depends.

This was March 1943, the year when the grand Allied strategy went over to the offensive. This was the year that sealed the doom of the Nazi master race. The Americans, with their prodigious capacity for production, had begun to turn out a bomber force which soon would exceed our own. They had staked their own claim on daylight bombing. We would stick to the night, and so it would go on, day and night, city by city, until there was nothing much left, until the Luftwaffe was destroyed. This was the aim of Bomber Command. The formidable shape of 4,000 aircraft over Berlin – it would come to that – one day.

How was it being done?

Picture Bomber Command, a few brick buildings and a few trees. Inside sits Air Chief Marshal Harris, surrounded by his advisory staff, who have all done their fair share of duty over Germany. He has a conference with his staff, he gets the weather forecasts from meteorological experts, he decides that the target tonight will be Berlin, aiming point X. He picks up his telephone and asks to be put on to all Group-Commanders on a broadcast. He is a grim man, is Air Chief Marshal Harris, and looks even more grim as he sits at his desk, crouched over the telephone, his glasses perched on the end of his nose, his finger pointing to a place on the map of Berlin in front of him. He is speaking into the telephone: 'Hullo! Are you all there? Is that you, Alec? OK. Target tonight aiming point X.'

And he gives a code word over the telephone which means Berlin. 'All aircraft are to operate, maximum effort. Full instructions will follow in an hour's time. That is all. Goodbye.'

In the Group-Commander's office this curt message is given to Group Operations Officers, then down to stations, thence to squadrons. The Squadron-Commander is a young man with plenty of responsibility. He sits there quite calmly as he receives the message and presses the bell for his two Flight-Commanders. They come in, hats on the backs of their heads, smoking cigarettes, looking inquisitive. 'Berlin tonight, chaps,' says the Squadron-Commander. 'Maximum effort; get cracking.'

On the airfield a few minutes later there is a roar of engines as Lancaster after Lancaster takes off to be given its air test. These air tests take about half an hour each, and are very thoroughly done. Everything is tested – wireless, guns, navigational instruments, bomb doors. Sometimes even a few bombs are dropped for practice to make sure that the bomb-aimer will be on his target tonight.

Then comes lunch. A short, absent-minded meal taken in the minimum of time. Not much is said, most minds are preoccupied, often the Squadron-Commander does not have much time for lunch at all. The phone bell is ringing incessantly.

After this comes briefing. Here all the information is transmitted to the crews who are going to take part in tonight's big effort. The room is packed, many of the boys, in their roll-necked pullovers, are standing crowded up against the back of the room. In the corner there may be one or two war correspondents and perhaps a visiting army officer.

The Squadron-Commander comes in, followed by the navigation officer, and the crews get up and stop talking. The babble of conversation dies away and he begins his briefing. 'OK, chaps; sit down. Berlin tonight, aiming point X. This is the centre of a cluster of factories making Daimler-Benz engines. You can see it quite clearly here on the map.' He points to a position somewhere in Berlin. 'Tonight a total of 700 bombers are going. They are all four-engined types, so if you see anything twin-engined you can shoot at it. The bombload will be one 4,000-pounder and sixteen cans of incendiaries, so the total load will be about 2,000 tons. It ought to be a pretty good prang. The met man says the weather will be clear all the way, which is pretty phenomenal. Let's hope he's right. The Pathfinders are going to attack from zero hour minus one to zero plus 35; it is going to be a quick concentrated attack. Your bombing height will be 21,000 feet. Don't get out of this height band or you will run into other aircraft. As it is, we are very lucky not to be the bottom squadron; they will probably see a few bombs whistling past them on the way down. The route is the usual one marked on the board here. The Pathfinder procedure will be detailed by the navigation officer.' He cocks his head over to the corner of the room and calls, 'Nav.' The navigation officer, a big round man with the DFC and bar, gets up and begins talking. 'Zero hour is 1945 hours. At zero hour minus three and a third minutes the Pathfinders will sky-mark the lane to the target with red flares which will change to green after 120 seconds. At this time, too, they will mark a point on the ground exactly fifteen miles short of the aiming point. With the ground speed of 240 miles an hour this should give three and three-quarter minutes to go to the target. The timing has got to be done in seconds. If anybody is late, he will probably get a packet, so pilots must keep their air-speeds dead right. The target-indicating marker will go down at exactly zero minus one, and should be right on the factory roof. The sky above will also be marked by green flares in case the TIs are obscured by fog or smoke. I will see all navigators after the briefing to give them the tracks and distances.'

He turns round to the Squadron-Commander, who gets up again and gives his final orders. 'Now don't forget, chaps,' he begins; 'once you have reached the preliminary target indicator you turn on to a course of 135 degrees magnetic and hold it for four minutes. You are to take no evasive action, but to keep straight on past the target. Once you have dropped your bombs you may weave about slightly and gain speed by going down in a gentle dive. The Pathfinders will drop a cluster of green and red flares thirty miles beyond Berlin, and now are to concentrate on these, and return home in a gaggle. Now don't forget, no straggling. We've had pretty low losses so far and we don't want any tonight; and don't forget to twist your tails a bit so that you can see those fighters, which come up from below. I think that's about all. Don't forget your landing discipline when you come to base. I will see you down in the crew room before take-off. OK.'

The boys go out noisily. Some are on their first trip and look a bit worried. The veterans look as if they are just going to a tea-party, but inside they feel differently. After the briefing a war correspondent comes up and asks the Squadron-Commander a few questions.

'Why all this concentration?' he asks. 'What is the exact idea?' The Squadron-Commander is a busy man, but he gives him the whole answer. How there are so many guns in Germany, all depending on short-wave electricity for their prediction, so that if one aircraft were to go over every five minutes, each gun would have the aircraft all to itself. Similarly with the night-fighters. But if all the aircraft go over more or less simultaneously then the guns cannot pick out and fire at any one aircraft nor can the night-fighters be vectored on to any one aircraft. With the result that losses are kept down. Moreover, the bombing takes a more concentrated form when all aircraft bomb together.

'How about collisions?' the war correspondent asks.

'There won't be any,' says the Squadron-Leader, 'provided they all keep straight, and if the Pathfinders are on time. Sometimes this doesn't happen. One night at Stuttgart the Pathfinders were fifteen minutes late and there were some 400 bombers circling the target waiting for them; eighteen didn't come back. Some of those were collisions, I think.'

The time after the briefing is not very pleasant. No one knows what to do. Some sit in the Mess, listening to the radio, and wishing they were far away from all this. A few play billiards. But most of them just sit in chairs picking up papers and throwing them down, staring into space and waiting for the clock on the wall to show the time when they must go down to get on their flying-clothes.

The time passes slowly, minutes seem like hours, but it is a busy time for the Squadron-Commander and his Flight-Commanders. First Group telephones to confirm that there is the full number of aircraft on from the squadron. Then the maintenance officer to say that C Charlie has blown an engine, shall he put on the reserve? Yes, put on reserve.

A call from the armament officer – a cookie has dropped off Z Zebra. 'Is everyone all right?'

'Yes, everyone's all right.'

'Well, put it on again, then.'

The oxygen has leaked from G George – get on to the maintenance flight to have new oxygen bottles put in. And so it goes on, the phone ringing the whole time. He does not have time to think, and presently everyone is in the crew rooms dressing for the big raid, putting on their multiple underwear and electrically heated suits before going out to the aircraft.

All the boys are chattering happily, but this is only to cover up their true feelings. But they all know that they will be quite all right once they get into their aircraft.

'Prang it good, boys,' says an Australian who isn't coming tonight; one of his crew is sick.

Then comes the take-off. A thrilling sight to the layman. Exactly at the right time they taxi out, led by the Squadron-Commander in his own aircraft with a gaudy design painted on the nose. They come out one after another, like a long string of ducks, and line up on the runway waiting to take off. There is a cheery wave of goodbyes from the well-wishers on the first flare. Then the pilot slams his windows shut and pushes open the throttles. The ground underneath the well-wishers shivers and shakes, sending a funny feeling up their spine, and the Lancasters lumber off one after another down the mile-long flare-path. And off they go into the dusk.

Over to a farm labourer sitting on his tractor in a field . . . He has just done his ploughing and is about to go home. He is looking forward to his evening meal. Looking up, he can see hundreds of specks in the sky, black specks, all getting smaller and smaller as they climb higher and higher into the night air. He turns to his tractor and says, 'They be going out again tonight. I 'ope they give 'em bastards hell. May they all come back again, God bless 'em. Good boys they be.' Then he begins to trudge home.

Over to a girl typist about to get of a bus in the nearby city. She hears the roar of the aircraft and says to her companion, 'Oh, there they go again. I do hope they will come back early; otherwise they will wake me up . . .'

Over to one of our aircraft flying high . . . They have just reached their operational height. The engines are throttled back to cruising revolutions. 'Hullo, navigator. Skipper calling. What time must I set course for the rendezvous point?'

The navigator gets a quick fix. 'We are about sixty miles away. If you circle here for five minutes, then set course at 240 miles an hour, you will be there dead on time.'

'OK,' says the skipper. 'You all right, rear-gunner?'

'Yes,' comes the voice from the back.

In five minutes' time he sets course and the blunt nose of the Lancaster points towards the east. At that moment nearly all the bombers have done the same thing and, with navigation lights on at their various heights, they all converge on to the rendezvous spot at exactly zero minus two hours. They reach it more or less together, then all navigation lights go out simultaneously and they straighten up on their course for Berlin. The captain yells to his crew to check that all lights are out on board. The bomb-aimer fuses the bombs, the gunners cock their guns and they are on their way.

To describe this big bomber force flying out in this formation is not easy. But imagine a glass brick two miles across, twenty miles long and 8,000 feet thick, filled with hundreds of Lancasters, and move it slowly towards the Dutch coast, and there you have a concentrated wave on its way. The Dutch coast looms up incredibly soon, rather too soon . . .

It is now five o'clock. At this hour in Germany operational messages have come in from Gruppen and Staffeln of night-fighters scattered throughout German territory. Messerschmitt, Focke-Wulf and other types of fighters are fully loaded with fuel and ammunition, ready for take-off from the operational bases. Aircraft and personnel are ready, mechanics, engineers, armourers are on duty on many airfields ready to supply suddenly arriving aircraft with fresh fuel and more ammunition. Everything has been done to ensure the quickest possible employment of the night-fighter arm.

At this hour it is quiet at the German searchlight and flak batteries. Ammunition stocks have been made up again since the last raid. The enormous power-plants of the searchlights need only be switched on by the young Luftwaffe helpers to convert the electric current, enough to supply a medium-sized town, into shimmering light and send it up into the night sky. The sentries on the large 8.8-cm guns pace up and down and watch the approaching night. It will soon be pitch dark, as the sky is covered with heavy rain-clouds, and the crescent moon will not rise until later. Even then its light will scarcely pierce the dark clouds. The British prefer nights such as this.

1740 hours. A message comes into the centre near Berlin from the Channel coast. An alarm bell rings. Strong British bomber units are crossing the Dutch coast. A telephone call warns the air-defence forces of the Continent. The night-fighter units in Holland have already taken off and are on the look-out for the enemy on his eastern course, attach themselves to his units, and while the first night engagements between the German night-fighters and the British bombers are setting the stage for the great night battle, the ground crews of countless other Geschwader in the region of Central Germany are putting the final touches to the aircraft as they stand ready to take off.

Behind the great glass map stand female signals auxiliaries wearing head-phones and laryngophones, with a thick stick of charcoal in their right hands with which they draw in the positions of the enemy units. From the control room only their shadows moving behind the glass plate can be seen. Ceaselessly the strokes and arrows on the great map give place to new markings.

Every officer and man takes up his position. Each knows exactly what he has to do, and all work together without friction.

The glass map shows that the enemy is advancing along several different directions, but it is clear that the main force is continuing eastwards. The enemy bombers have crossed the frontier of Western Germany. Suddenly they swing round towards the south-east. A few weaker formations are flying southwards up the Rhine. Cascades are dropped over two West German towns; it may be that the main attack is to be directed against these towns, but it may also be that this is a feint movement designed to lure the German night-fighters into the wrong areas. The enemy hopes that a wrong German order will gain him valuable minutes to get his main attacking force into the prescribed target area, where he would then find weaker German night-fighter forces.

The control officer, who is fully acquainted with the many different problems and questions, the possibilities of attack and defence, makes his decision after conscientiously checking the situation and a brief talk with the OC. The British force is still on its way towards Central Germany. The main force of the bombers has made another turn and is again flying east. The last message reads: 'Front of enemy formation in Dora-Heinrich area, course east.'

1830 hours. At this moment fighter unit X, whose aircraft are ready at the end of the runway with their engines roaring, receives the order 'Unit X – village take off by visual beacon Y'.

A few minutes later the aircraft are racing over the ground, climbing rapidly, flying towards the flashing light of visual beacon Y. In Berlin the Underground is still running, and traffic goes on as usual. Then the population gets its first warning; the Deutschlandsender goes off the air. The bright lights at the marshalling yards are switched off. The great city sinks into darkness.

The enemy has meanwhile flown past to the north of the first large central German town. In a bare hour he may be over Berlin. At a height of 6,500 m the four-engine bombers are roaring on their way eastwards.

1845 hours. A message in the head-phones: the enemy has already lost seven aircraft before reaching Osnabrück.

Other night-fighter units are ready to take off to protect the capital. The meteorologist is describing the weather situation. Cloudless sky over South Germany, where night-fighters can land after the battle.

Meanwhile the night-fighter units, which have assembled in certain areas, are guided closer to the enemy. The German fighters have already made contact everywhere with the enemy bomber formations. Now the sirens are sounded in Berlin.

Important decisions are taken relating to the activity of the searchlight batteries, taking into consideration the weather situation. Orders are issued to the batteries of the Berlin flak division.

1916 hours. The enemy is 100 kilometres from Berlin. A large number of night-fighters are accompanying the British bombers.

The OC sits next to the IA (Intelligence) officer. In order to clear up a question quickly he asks to speak to the OC in another Luftgau; command priority call to X town. In a matter of seconds a female signals auxiliary has made the desired telephone connection.

On the great glass map the arrows draw closer and closer to Berlin. The positions of the night-fighter units are exactly known.

1941 hours. Is the enemy going straight for Berlin? At 1943 hours fire is opened by a heavy flak battery in the west. It is still impossible to say whether the mass of the enemy bombers will not again make a sharp turn short of Berlin and perhaps attack Leipzig.

Above the inner part of the town the enemy drops streams and cascades of flares. Strong forces are reported over various suburbs. A hail of HE shells from the heavy flak rushes up to the heights of the approaching bombers.

In spite of the difficulties of the weather the night-fighters hunt out the enemy. In the brilliant beams of the searchlights the British aircraft are clearly recognizable. The enemy drops his bombs on the city's industrial areas and then tries to get away as quickly as possible. At top

speed other German night-fighters chase after him to shoot up as many
of his forces as possible.

Over to the leading Pathfinder aircraft.

'How far are we from the target, Nav?'

'About twenty-five miles.'

'OK. Stand by to drop preliminary target marker.'

'Standing by.'

A voice from the mid-upper turret. 'Flak coming up port behind,
skipper.'

'OK.'

The guns are just beginning to open up down below. Ahead lies Berlin,
still and silent. Berlin seems to be lying down there like a gigantic mouse,
frightened to move, petrified. Suddenly it is galvanized into life; hundreds
of gun-flashes come up from its roofs, its parks and its railway flak.

'Don't weave, for Christ's sake, skipper; only another minute.' This
from the navigator.

Again the captain's voice, 'OK.'

He is not saying much. Both hands are on the wheel, his eyes are
darting everywhere, looking for trouble and hoping not to find it. His
aircraft seems huge, it appears to be the only one in the sky, every gun
down below seems to be aiming at him, the gun-flashes are vicious, short
and cruel.

Down below, to the Germans, he is the first many hundreds of small
spots on cathode-ray tubes. The civilians have long since gone to their
shelters, but those of the ARP, police and fire-watching services are
beginning to hear the loud, angry roar of the invading force.

'Coming up now, skipper. Steady – coming up – coming up – now!
OK. TI gone.'

A few seconds later it bursts and cascades on to the ground; a mass of
green bells, shining brightly, for all the world like a lit-up merry-go-
round, an unmistakable spot of light . . .

Over to one of the main-force aircraft.

'There she is, skip; straight ahead.' This from the bomb-aimer.

'Fine; the Pathfinders are dead on time.'

The navigator looks at his watch and makes a note to that effect. The
bomb-aimer starts his stop-watch. Three minutes and twenty seconds to
go. On all sides other bomb-aimers are doing the same, beginning their
straight fifteen-minute run through a curtain of steel. Flak is coming up
all round, leaving black balloons which float by at an alarming speed.
Searchlights are weaving, trying to pick up a straggler. The bomb-aimer
begins to count.

'Three minutes to go, skipper.'

Like a fleet of battleships the force sails in. Above are hundreds of
fighter flares, lighting up the long lane of bombers like daylight. Now

and then Junkers 88s and Me 110s come darting in and out like black moths trying to deliver their attack. The sky is full of tracer bullets, some going up, some going down. others hose-pipe out horizontally as one of our rear-gunners gets in a good squirt.

Two minutes to go.

More flares have gone down. It seems even lighter than day. Searchlights, usually so bright themselves, can hardly pierce the dazzling glow of flares up above. Now the tracers are coming up in all colours as combats take place left, right and centre. On all sides bombers are blowing up, as they get direct hits – great, slow flashes in the sky, leaving a vast trail of black smoke as they disintegrate earthwards. Someone bales out.

One minute to go – bomb-doors open.

The bomb-aimer is still counting.

'Fifty seconds.'

'Forty seconds.'

There is flak all round now. The leading wave of bombers has not been broken up, a few have been shot down, but the rest have held their course. But the short time they held that course seemed like a lifetime.

There comes the bomb-aimer's voice again. 'Red TIs straight ahead.'

'Good show; there's the sky marker too.'

'Thirty seconds.'

Still dead level. Someone in front has already started a fire. Great sticks of incendiaries are beginning to crisscross across the target-indicating marker. These sticks are a mile long, but from this height they look about the length of a match-stick.

'Twenty seconds.'

'Steady – hold it' – and then the bomb-aimer shouts: 'Bombs gone.' There is a note of relief in his voice.

The Lancaster leaps forward, relieved of its burden, diving, slithering. But it keeps straight on over the burning city. Throttles are slammed wide open, the engines are in fine pitch; they make a noise of an aircraft in pain.

A volcano is now raging down below, great sticks of incendiaries are still slapping across the point where the target-markers had first gone in. Now black smoke is beginning to rise, but as these target-markers burst and drop slowly into the flaming mass, the later bomb-aimers have a good chance of aiming at the middle. Cookies are exploding one after another with their slow, red flashes, photo-flashes are bursting at all heights as each aircraft takes it photographs. This is a galaxy of light, a living nightmare.

As the last wave of bombers roar over, the fires started by the first are beginning to take hold. Against their vivid light can be seen the bottom squadrons, flying steadily on, over the battered city.

The flak is beginning to die, the searchlights have gone out. Once again the ground defences have been beaten.

A few leaflets drift down through the bluish glare, only to be burnt in the flames of the burning houses.

Soon the area is one mass of flames and the last bomber has dropped its bombs. At last the rendezvous is reached and the surviving bombers turn for home.

That is how it is done, by young men with guts, by science and by skill. The Germans do everything in their power to stop it, but in vain. There are too many variations; feint attacks can be made, or the bombers can attack in waves. They can come in at hourly intervals; they might come over on a night when the German fighters cannot get up. And on every raid new devices are carried, made by scientists, to help defeat the German defences.

This was the beginning, the end of three years' hard experiment. The real answer had been found, and the bomber could at last hit hard. It could choose tactical or strategical targets. Both were allergic to bombs.

CHAPTER SIXTEEN

SQUADRON X

It was the middle of March.

The flak over France wasn't bad. It was coming up all around in spasmodic flashes as some straggler got off his course and struggled through a defended area. Otherwise the night was lovely. There was a three-quarter moon which shone brightly into my Lancaster, lighting the cockpit up almost as if it were day. Down below us the grey features of France were partially hidden by a thin layer of white cloud.

It was getting hot inside. I yelled to my wireless operator, 'Hey, Hutch. Turn off the heat.'

He said: 'Thank God for that.'

The heat in a Lancaster comes out somewhere round the wireless-operator's backside; hence the relief expressed by the long-suffering Hutch.

Around me, above, below and on every quarter, I could see the Lancasters moving forward towards their target, flying straight and flying fast, with their great chins thrust forward and looking to me more powerful than anything I had ever seen before.

I was feeling pleased because this was going to be my last raid before going on a few days' leave; for now I had done 173 sorties without having had much rest. It seemed almost too good to be true that after this raid on Stuttgart I should be able to go down to Cornwall with my wife and relax. Once again I should be able to walk down to St Ives with my pipe in my mouth and my dog, Nigger, running along by my side. Once again I should be able to stand and watch the sea when it became angry and fought with the north-west wind. In the evenings, instead of sitting up here with an oxygen mask over my face, I should be leaning back in my armchair looking at the ceiling and scratching the back of my dog. There would be no bomber raids to organize, no bomb-loads to think about.

As I was thinking these things, my Flight-Engineer yelled, 'Port outboard's going, sir!'

Sure enough, the port outboard-engine was packing up. I could feel it in the throttle control. There was no power coming from this engine. Rapidly, my heavy-laden Lancaster had to lose height.

This was bad. If I turned back now I should have to go out again tomorrow night. Maybe there would be no tomorrow night. Maybe the weather would be bad. Maybe I should have to wait four days; I should have to wait four days for my leave. Maybe it would be better to go on.

Scriv, my navigator, was standing at his station scratching his head and watching the air-speed needle drop rapidly.

I said, 'What shall we do, Scriv?'

'It's up to you, sir.'

'OK, Scriv; we are going on at low level. We will try to climb up to bomb when we get there.'

The Lancaster slid quietly out of formation, and like a wounded bird, dropped towards the earth. On all sides of me the flak was coming up from Mannheim, Frankfurt and Mainz. From where I was I had a grandstand view of the boys above getting shot at. But the Huns did not shoot at me. They did not even fire machine guns at me. Perhaps they thought that I was a night-fighter. Now and again I caught sight of a Lancaster far above, four miles above, as it got into the beam of a searchlight and as a light flashed on its wings; and I almost thought I could distinguish the separate aircraft as they flew over, merely from the light of the flames which danced through the streets of Stuttgart. The town was on fire.

An 8,000-pounder came whistling past my wingtip on its way down, and a few seconds later a great, slow, heavy flash came up from the ground where it had landed, and my aircraft was bounced and tossed about as though it were a leaf. I remember that once I distinctly saw a shower of incendiaries not 200 yards in front of me. It is indeed curious to be underneath a heavy bombing raid in an aeroplane.

We dropped our load, and my poor Lancaster on its three engines jumped into the air as the bombs fell out of its belly and I banked around and dived for the deck.

During these moments there had been little talk, but once we were clear of the target area all the boys on board started talking.

'Leave tomorrow.'

'Tomorrow we go on leave.'

'I'm going fishing.'

'I'm going to sleep.'

'Tomorrow we go on leave.'

My wife had been sweating it out in a factory near London for a long time without any rest, and now I should be able to take her home and let her breathe for a moment the fresh and pleasant air of Cornwall.

Soon, after dodging the night-fighters, we were back over England, and a few minutes later I was in my room, hurriedly packing my clothes before jumping into bed. As I dozed off, I thought of the morrow and of leave, and of the sound of the waves on the rocks down in Cornwall.

Next day I woke up late. My ears were still singing, my eyes felt red and sore as if I had rolled them through a gravel pit. I wanted to keep lying there in my warm bed, where it was quiet and peaceful. I wanted to think, and I wanted to be alone. After a year of this sort of thing I was getting a bit weary. It seems that no matter how hard you try, the human body can take just so much and no more.

Charles, the adjutant, came in. 'Is it important, Adj?' I said sleepily.

'It's your posting, sir.' He sounded rather sad, or else was a very good actor.

'My – my – posting? What on earth – where?'

'To 5 Group.'

I had heard that I was about due to be rested. The AOC had mentioned that I had done enough for a bit, but this was a bit of a surprise and a great shock. Posted to a headquarters, of all places.

I picked up the phone beside my bed and asked to speak to Group. Charles sat down in the corner, watching Nigger chewing one of my slippers on the mat in front of the fire.

A few words with the SASO and I found out the truth. John Searby was taking the squadron over and I had to be at Group the next afternoon. The reason, he said, was the AOC. He wanted me to help write a book for the benefit of the would-be bomber pilot.

'Write a book!' I had never done such a thing in my life; and what a time to begin, just when the real bomber offensive was starting.

At the most I had wanted a station, and at least thought that I would be given some job that would deal with operations exclusively. Worst of all, my leave was cancelled.

I asked Charles to send a wire to Eve and told him that the rest of the crew could go. When I had finished giving my orders, Charles quietly picked up the phone and booked a large private room at the Bridge Hotel, our local pub.

That night there was a party. Wine was drunk, many kind words were spoken. I staggered to my feet and made a rotten speech, looking nervously into my glass while the other boys sat around rather self-consciously.

I said I had been in the squadron over a year and I was sorry to go. I wished them good luck in whatever operations they would undertake after I had gone. They were still top squadron of Bomber Command and I thought they were the best. It is hard to say anything at a time like this, and when I sat down there were a few kind remarks of approval.

Then we got down to some solid drinking.

Next day I went to Grantham. Now Group Headquarters in particular, or any headquarters in general, are funny places. There is an air of quiet, cold efficiency about the whole place. WAAFs keep running in and out with cups of tea. Tired men walk through the corridors with red files under their arms. The yellow lights over the AOC and SASO's doors are almost always on, showing that they are engaged. Great decisions are being taken the whole time. There is not much time off, and I found it quite difficult to settle down.

I had been there one or two days and had tried to get down to the factual business of writing, when the AOC sent for me. Air Vice-Marshal Coryton had gone, to the deep regret of everyone in the Group, and the new Air Vice-Marshal was the Honourable Ralph Cochrane, a man with a lot of brain and organizing ability. In one breath he congratulated me on my bar to the DSO, in the next he suddenly said: 'How would you like the idea of doing one more trip?'

I gulped. More flak, more fighters; but said aloud:

'What kind of a trip, sir?'

'A pretty important one, perhaps one of the most devastating of all time. I can't tell you any more now. Do you want to do it?'

I said I thought I did, trying to remember where I had left my flying kit. He seemed to be in a such a hurry that I got the idea it was a case of take-off tonight.

But two days went by and nothing happened.

On the third he sent for me again. In his office was another man, one of the youngest Base commanders in the Group, Air-Commodore Charles Whitworth. The Air Vice-Marshal was very amiable. He told me to sit down, offered me a Chesterfield and began to talk.

'I asked you the other day if you would care to do another raid. You said you would, but I have to warn you that this is no ordinary sortie. In fact it can't be done for at least two months.'

(I thought, hell, it's the *Tirpitz*. What on earth did I say 'Yes' for?)

'Moreover,' he went on, 'the training for the raid is of such importance that the Commander-in-Chief has decided that a special squadron is to be formed for the job. I want you to form that squadron. As you know,

I believe in efficiency, so I want you to do it well. I think you had better use Whitworth's main base at Scampton. As far as air crews are concerned, I want the best – you choose them. W/C Smith, the SOA, will help you pick ground crews. Each squadron will be forced to cough up men to build your unit up to strength.

'Now there's a lot of urgency in this, because you haven't got long to train. Training will be the important thing, so get going right away. Remember you are working to a strict timetable, and I want to see your aircraft flying in four days' time. Now up you go upstairs to hand in the names of your crews to Cartwright; he will give you all the help you want.'

'But what sort of training, sir? And the target? I can't do a thing—'

'I am afraid I can't tell you any more just for the moment. All you have to do is to pick your crews, get them ready to fly, then I will come and see you and tell you more.'

'How about aircraft and equipment?'

'S/L May, the Group Equipment Officer, will do all that. All right, Gibson.'

He bent down to his work abruptly. This was a signal for me to go. There was a big raid to be organized that night. As I was closing the door, he looked up again. 'Let me know when you are ready; and remember, not a word to anyone. This is just an ordinary new squadron. Secrecy is vital.'

As we closed the door, 'See you at Scampton,' said Charles. 'If you come over in a couple of days I'll get everything fixed up for you. How many chaps are you going to bring?'

'About seven hundred.'

I was left standing alone feeling very bewildered. Charles went back to Scampton and I went upstairs to see various men who though unknown to the general public, are the very life-blood of the Royal Air Force. These men, most of them too old to fly themselves, deal in such things as equipment, bodies, erks, air crews.

The first man I saw was a fellow with a red moustache sitting behind a huge desk. This was Cartwright. His sales were air crews. It took me an hour to pick my pilots. I wrote all the names down on a piece of paper and handed them over to him. I had picked them all myself because from my own personal knowledge I believed them to be the best bomber pilots available. I knew that each one of them had already done his full tour of duty and should really now be having a well-earned rest; and I knew also that there was nothing any of them would want less than this rest when they heard that there was an exciting operation on hand. Cartwright helped me a lot with the crews because I didn't know these so well, but we chose carefully and we chose well. I think he was a bit puzzled either at the urgency in the matter or my desire to have the very best, perhaps both.

Then into another office to see the equipment officer. We would require ten aircraft to begin with, with all the gear. Later we would need more. This was a big job; there were trestles, trolleys, spare wheels and bumble motors. There were many other things, but I won't put them all down here. Enough to say that Cartwright knew his job inside out. He promised that they would be delivered at Scampton tomorrow.

Afterwards, back to another huge desk; here tools were arranged for, kit, motor transport, beds, blankets, kites, typewriters, tents, towels and beer. Also a few spare engines. All this took a long time, in fact the whole day.

Next morning to the personnel officer, to fix up the ground staff. We were taking a few ground crews from each squadron, but in the case of the NCOs it would be necessary to have the very best men available. I asked for them and got them. Then along to the WAAF officer to see that we got our fair share of MT drivers and cooks; very important.

By now things were beginning to get beyond me. I went to the stationery department and got a little book and wrote down everything to be done in a long column. Every time anything got fixed up I would tick it off, but by the end of the day there weren't many ticks to be seen. Then would come the visit to the SASO, and AOC's deputy. This was Air-Commodore Harry Satterly, a big, blunt man who had the habit of getting things done quickly and well. His help was invaluable – in fact, I don't know what could have happened without him.

And so by the end of two days the squadron was formed. It had no name and no number. We had worked too fast for that branch of the Air Ministry which gives squadrons new numbers and identification letters, and we decided to call it simply Squadron X.

All personnel were to be at Scampton by the next morning. Training would begin that afternoon. The AOC had said that we had not got much time. We had certainly started off pretty well, but it had been hard work.

But somewhere else in London the other men were working even harder. They were in a hurry, too. They didn't wear uniforms or medals. They were working on graphs, explosives and metal, and on reinforced concrete. Out in the open, away in the Welsh hills during those blowly March days, they stood with the wind whistling round them as if to howl down their experiments. But they went on, slaving, watching, waiting, praying, hoping . . .

Next night I arrived in the Mess at Scampton with Nigger sniffing his way along happily at my heels. I think he smelt a party. He was right. In the hall were the boys. I knew them all – that is, all the pilots, navigators and bomb-aimers – but there were a few strange gunners and wireless-operators knocking around.

Within a second a whisky was shoved into my hand and a beer put on the floor for Nigger, who seemed thirsty. Then there was a babbling of conversation and the hum of shop being happily exchanged: of old faces; old names; targets; bases; and of bombs. This was the conversation that only fliers can talk, and by that I don't mean movie fliers. These were real living chaps who had all done their stuff. By their eyes you could see that. But they were ready for more. These were the aces of Bomber Command.

All in all they probably knew more about the art of bombing than any other squadron in the world.

From all over the world they had come: from Australia, America, Canada, New Zealand and Great Britain. All of their own free will. All with one idea: to get to grips with the enemy. As I stood there talking to them and drinking beer with them I felt very proud; surely these were the best boys in the world. If there could come any better I should like to see them.

From 106 Squadron had come three crews. Hoppy, of course, and Dave Shannon from Australia. A Canadian Flight-Sergeant, Burpee, was the third. He had just married a young English girl and was busy trying to find her a house not too far away. He was telling me that he had found it a very difficult job. The rest, I am told, would have liked to have come, but it was the hard case of having the best and only the best.

From the Middle East came the senior Flight-Commander, 'Dinghy' Melvyn Young. Cambridge – California and sixty-five trips. 'Dinghy' because he had ditched twice in Mare Nostrum. A big man, Melvyn, and a very efficient organizer. I was to find out later that he could drink a pint of beer faster than any other man I know, with his elbow in the traditionally almost vertical position.

From New Zealand came Les Munro, ex-97 Squadron. Like all New Zealanders, he was a most charming fellow, with an excellent operational record. He was one of those types who can always be relied on to do the right thing at the right moment. There he was, standing quietly and drinking slowly and thinking a lot. Then there was David Maltby, large and thoughtful; a fine pilot.

Brooklyn gave us Joe McCarthy. He was one of the Americans who had volunteered to fly in the Royal Air Force before America was at war with the Axis. He had been given the chance to rejoin the United States forces, but had preferred to stay with the boys. He had just come from the same squadron as Les, and both were great pals. He had tried to get in my squadron once before, but despite all the strings we tried to pull between us it did not work. Now he was happy. We all were, standing there at midnight with our glasses in our hands initiating the historic walls of Scampton Mess with Squadron X spirit. The portraits of Babe Learoyd and Sergeant John Hannah stood looking down on us, as though wanting to join us. They were the two vcs that Scampton had already won during World War II, apart from many other decorations.

Eton gave us Henry Maudslay, the other Flight-Commander. A champion runner at school, he was one of the best pilots from 50 Squadron. He was standing there quiet and suave, and not drinking too much. Later on Henry became one of the mainstays of the squadron in supervising our training.

Then there were the others. Mickey Martin from Australia with his fellow diggers – Jack Leggo, crack navigator; Bob Hay, Group Bombing Leader. Toby Foxley, Les Knight, Len Chambers. All from Australia, all with the DFC, all feeling very pleased with themselves.

Playing with Nigger and trying to get him tight were some of my own crew. Terry, Spam, Trevor and Hutch had long since gone to bed with the rest. Nigger knocked back about four full cans, made a long, lazy zigzag trail of water down the corridor, then went to bed himself with his tail between his legs. The party went on till late, and Charles Whitworth joined in with Briggy, his second-in-command, to make us feel welcome, and in this they succeeded very well.

Soon it became obvious, even to the casual observer, that this was no ordinary squadron. The mess waiters had already begun eyeing us curiously. They had never seen a bunch of boys like this before, all in one squadron. Many of them had two DFCs, and most of them wore one, some had the DSO. No doubt while they were fetching the rounds they began to wonder what was happening. One of them told me that we had not been there three hours before the canteen buzzed with rumours:

'Heard about the new gen squadron?'

'They're going to Russia!'

'They've come from North Africa.'

'Something special?'

'Yeah, something special.'

The boys noticed it all. They felt curious and wondered. They also felt very proud to all be in the same crack unit, but they wanted to know why. They thought they had a right to know why. At last Coles, a Canadian navigator, wandered up and asked the inevitable question. It was late, but I remember my reply: 'I know less than you, old boy, but I'll see all air crews at 9.30 tomorrow and give you some gen.'

Next day I got them all together. There were twenty-one crews, comprising 147 men: pilots, navigators, wireless-operators, bomb-aimers, flight-engineers. Nearly all of them twenty-three years old or under, and nearly all of them veterans. I saw them in the same old crew room, which brought back many memories of 1939–40 days. Now it was packed full of young, carefree-looking boys, mostly blue-eyed, keen and eager to hear the gen. I felt quite old among them.

My speech to them was short. I said, 'You're here to do a special job, you're here as a crack squadron, you're here to carry out a raid on Germany which, I am told, will have startling results. Some say it may even cut short the duration of the war. What the target is I can't tell you. Nor can I tell you where it is. All I can tell you is that you will have to practise low flying all day and all night until you know how to do it with your eyes shut. If I tell you to fly to a tree in the middle of England, then I will want you to bomb that tree. If I tell you to fly through a hangar, then you will have to go through that hangar, even though your wingtips might hit either side. Discipline is absolutely essential.

'I needn't tell you that we are going to be talked about. It is very unusual to have such a crack crowd of boys in one squadron. There are going to be a lot of rumours – I have heard a few already. We've got to stop these rumours. We've got to say nothing. When you go into pubs at night you've got to keep your mouths shut. When the other boys ask you what you're doing, just tell them to mind their own business, because of all things in this game, security is the greatest factor.

'It will take a couple of days to get things organized, and I shall want you all to help. Most of you have been in squadrons some time, so you will know what is required. First thing I want done is to get our new aircraft tested, then you, Bill' (this was to Bill Astell, Englishman from Derbyshire, deputy Flight-Commander to Dinghy Young), 'I want you to take your crew and to fly over every lake you can see in England, Scotland and Wales and take photographs of them. Let me have the photographs in thirty-six hours.'

The AOC had told me to get this done by telephone earlier in the morning. What for I could not think, and I could see the boys were wondering why, too, so I went on:

'It's OK, chaps, don't go jumping to conclusions. The AOC wants this for his Conversion Units for cross-country practices; we're the only squadron with enough time to do it.'

This was the first of many white lies. Then I went on to say a lot more. I have forgotten what it was, but it was all on the same lines. About discipline – flying discipline – about working hours, about leave. There was to be no leave.

Then I handed over to Melvyn, the American, who with Henry began to divide the crews into flights, choosing those they knew best, allotting them flying lockers and crew rooms, sorting out the offices. And I went upstairs.

In my bare office were one chair, one telephone and one table; nothing more. It was cold and damp, as the hangar heating had not been turned on, but there was a lot of work to be done.

At Syerston there was a young man by the name of Humphreys who was doing an assistant adjutant's job. He had been in business in peace time and everything from orderly room clerk upwards in war. He was mad on flying, but his eyes had stopped him. Moreover, he was young and keen. Such men are the right type for this job, and a quick call by Charles to Group had him posted within forty-eight hours. But for the next few days we had to work without an adjutant, and the job of forming the entire squadron fell on the broad shoulders of three people of whom I must make special mention.

First there was F/Sgt Powell. He was the squadron disciplinarian, and he sat interviewing our new members, 700 of them, all day long, allotting them beds and bunks, getting their sections organized, supervising the unloading of the equipment. Chiefy Powell was small and dapper, not at all the bull-necked disciplinarian of the old days. He was something of a psychoanalyst and interviewed his men kindly, getting the best out of them. He did not know it, but he was laying down the foundation of the spirit which was to serve this squadron in such good stead later on. A great little man, and a king in his own way.

The second was Sergeant Hevron, boss of the orderly room. Group had been very efficient, and had given us everything in the way of equipment and air crews, but they had omitted to give us certain essential tools: typewriters and stationery and people to work them. So Hevron had to beg, borrow and sometimes steal from every imaginable source the much-required bumph so that he could start some form of filing system. Letters were already beginning to pour in. He was the only one who could type, and for a while he put in eighteen hours a day, filling in arrival reports, checking personnel documents and in the intervals pleading with me to get some help from somewhere.

The third was a WAAF. I don't know her name, but I think they called her Mary. She was plump and fair and the type that would make someone a very good wife some day. She had heard that we were in trouble, and so she had come over from one of the satellite airfields to give a hand with the typing. If she had been a civilian she could have put in a very reasonable claim for overtime.

And so they worked, these three, moulding the new squadron, while I sat in my bare office, slightly amazed at the way it was forming around me.

During those first two days Jack Leggo and Bob Hay were busy collecting the maps, setting up the bomb-sights, checking the bomb-stocks. They already knew that bombing was going to be one of our favourite occupations in the next two months. The Flight-Commanders were busy supervising their flights. There were many snags, too numerous to be detailed. There were no parachutes, there were no Mae Wests, there were no compass keys. But you cannot hope for everything when you form a squadron in two days.

The WAAF was still typing, Chiefy was still interviewing, ground crews were streaming like ants around our new aircraft. Air Ministry had at last woken up to the fact that a new squadron had been formed, and had given us a number – No. 617 Squadron. Our squadron marking letters were AJ. Now they were being painted on in big red letters.

Upstairs I sat meeting all the new operational crews. The captains would come in and introduce their boys to me. In the short conversation that followed I had a chance to get hold of some of their ideas. Then out they would go, and in would come another crew. So it went on. There were a few unlucky ones whom, for no discredit to them, I could not accept.

There were other troubles, too. Personal ones for me. Some of the squadrons which had been told by the SASO to supply us with tip-top men had taken the opportunity to get rid of some of their duds. From 106, the squadron which I commanded a week ago, came two men whom I myself had tried to get rid of. It was a rather plaintive voice that rung up Charles, the adjutant of 106, to tell him what I thought of him. The two men went – back to 106. Then another squadron supplied me, rather unkindly, with two pregnant WAAFs. They were both married, of course, but they weren't any use to me because they had to leave the service, anyway. There were other little games played on us which I won't mention.

By the third day everything was ready. We were all set to begin training, and I was not sorry. Nor, I am sure, were the rest of the boys.

In one of the big hangars Chiefy Powell got all the ground crews together, and I stood on top of my Humber brake and spoke to them. I said much the same as I said to the air crews, stressing that security was the most important thing of all. There was to be no talking.

Then Charles Whitworth got up and welcomed 617 Squadron officially to Scampton Base. He made a good speech, and I remember thinking that it would be a good idea if I could remember it, so as to copy him on some future occasion, but now I have forgotten what he said, except for one thing.

He said, 'Many of you will have seen Noël Coward's film, *In Which We Serve*. In one scene Coward, as commander of a destroyer, asks one of the seamen what is the secret of an efficient ship. The seaman answers, 'A happy ship, sir.' And that is what I want you to be here. You in the Air Force use a well-known verb in practically every sentence; that verb is to bind. I can promise you that if you don't bind me, I won't bind you!'

That afternoon Humphreys turned up and together we wrote out our first training report. It was very short, because little had been done. It read: 'Although the squadron was formed on 20.3.43 full facilities for training were not available until 25.3.43. Between these two days limited low-level cross-country flying was carried out. The squadron was organized into two flights on 22.3.43, but general deficiencies such as starter batteries and tool kits did not arrive until 26.3.43. No parachutes are available, but some have been borrowed from 57 Squadron. There are still no Mae Wests, but our crews don't seem to mind flying over the sea without them. Most of them feel that they are flying so low that they could not do anything about it, anyway. The aircraft are all serviceable, and training is expected to begin at maximum effort to-morrow.

'The following crews have finally been selected' [see over].

Next we started training in earnest. First there was a conference in my office, which by now wasn't so bare. Someone had put a carpet on the floor. Dinghy, Henry, Jack Leggo and Bob Hay sat around in chairs.

'The AOC has told me to get on with this low-level flying nonsense,' I began. 'We'd better limit the height at first to 150 feet because we don't want the chaps going round the countryside hitting trees. We had better lay down ten standard routes so that the Observer Corps won't have too much of a job. I'll let you know what sort of country we want to practise flying over later. Any routes will do at first, but none over three hours – it's going to be pretty hard work these bumpy days. We'll want to be able to fly day or night, so flying can go on into dusk, to give the boys practice in moonlight flying. After all, it's much the same. All navigators had better have a chart with the practices kept against their name so that we can see how they're getting along.'

I asked Jack if he had any problems, and Jack, the navigator, had some. The four of us discussed them. First there was the map problem. When flying at low level the ground goes by very quickly, and as you want large-scale maps, the navigator would have continually to keep changing them. The answer was roller maps. These were to be homemade. Jack said that he would get all navigators making their own. Then we got down to the refinements of low-level navigation. Jack said, 'As we're going to fly low, presumably far into Germany or somewhere, we won't get much navigational help from wireless. So I guess it will be all map-reading. I suggest that the bomb-aimer be the key map-reader, the navigator sticks to his chart, and both flight engineer and mid-upper gunners lend a hand in looking out when the time comes. In this way about eight pairs of eyes will be watching for landmarks, and everything should run pretty smoothly.'

I agreed to this and many other suggestions he put forward connected with his own job. Then I handed over to Dinghy to supervise further training while I took myself on a journey south.

We stopped, the driver and I, at Grantham, on the way, and I saw the SASO. He said, 'I'm sending you on a journey down south to meet a scientist who is working on your project. He's going to show you nearly

PILOT	F/ENG	NAVIGATOR	W/OPTR	B/AIMER	MID-UPPER	REAR-GUNNER
Leader: W/C Gibson, DSO, DFC	Sgt Pulford	P/O Taerum	F/L Hutchison, DFC	P/O Spafford	F/L Trevor-Roper, DFM	F/S Deering
'A' Flight S/L Young, DFC	Sgt Horsfall	Sgt Roberts	Sgt Nichols	F/O MacCausland	Sgt Yeo	Sgt Ibbotson
F/L Astell, DFC	Sgt Kinnear	P/O Wile	Sgt Garshowitz	F/O Hopkinson	Sgt Garbas	Sgt Bolitho
F/L Maltby, DFC	Sgt Hatton	Sgt Nicholson	Sgt Stone	P/O Fort	Sgt Hill	Sgt Simmonds
F/L Shannon, DFC	Sgt Henderson	P/O Walker, DFC	F/O Goodale, DFC	F/S Sumpter	Sgt Jagger	P/O Buckley
F/L Barlow	Sgt Whillis	P/O Burgess	F/O Williams	Sgt Gillespie	F/O Glinz	Sgt Liddell
P/O Rice	Sgt Smith	F/O MacFarlane	Sgt Gowrie	F/S Thrasher	Sgt Maynard	Sgt Burns
P/O Ottley	Sgt Marsden	F/O Barrett	Sgt Guterman	F/S Johnson	Sgt Tees	Sgt Strange
P/O Divall	Sgt Blake	F/O Warwick	Sgt Simpson	Sgt McArthur	Sgt Allatson	Sgt Murray
F/S Brown	Sgt Feneron	Sgt Heal	Sgt Hewstone	Sgt Oancia	Sgt Buntaine	F/S McDonald
Sgt Byers	Sgt Taylor	P/O Warner	Sgt Wilkinson	Sgt Whitaker	Sgt Jarvie	Sgt McDowell

Flight Bombing Leader: P/O Fort.   Flight Gunnery Leader: F/O Glinz.   Flight Navigation Officer: F/O MacFarlane

PILOT	F/ENG	NAVIGATOR	W/OPTR	B/AIMER	MID-UPPER	REAR-GUNNER
'B' Flight S/L Maudslay, DFC	Sgt Marriott	F/O Urquhart	Sgt Cottam	F/S Fuller	F/O Tytherleigh	Sgt Burrows
F/L Hopgood, DFC	Sgt Bronnan	F/O Earnshaw	Sgt Minchin	F/S. Fraser	P/O Gregory, DFM	P/O Burcher, DFM
F/L Martin, DFC	P/O Whittaker	F/L Leggo, DFC	F/O Chambers	F/L Hay, DFC	P/O Foxlee, DFM	F/S Simpson
F/L Munro	Sgt Appleby	F/O Rumbles	Sgt Pigeon	Sgt Clay	Sgt Howarth	F/S Weeks
F/L McCarthy	Sgt Ratcliffe	F/S MacLean	Sgt Eaton	Sgt Johnson	Sgt Batson	F/O Rodger
F/L Wilson	Sgt Johnson	F/O Rodger	Sgt Mieyette	P/O Coles	Sgt Payne	Sgt Hornby
P/O Burpee	Sgt Pegler	Sgt Jaye	P/O Weller	Sgt Arthur	Sgt Long	F/S Brady
P/O Knight	Sgt Grayston	F/O Hobday	Sgt Kellow	F/O Johnson	Sgt Sutherland	Sgt O'Brien
F/S Townsend	Sgt Powell	P/O Howard	F/S Chalmers	Sgt Franklin	Sgt Webb	Sgt Wilkinson
F/S Anderson	Sgt Paterson	Sgt Nugent	Sgt Bickle	Sgt Green	Sgt Ewan	Sgt Buck

Flight Bombing Leader: F/O Johnson.   Flight Gunnery Leader: F/O Tytherleigh.   Flight Navigation Officer: F/O Urquhart.

Signals Leader – F/L Hutchison, DFC   Nav. Officer – F/L Leggo, DFC
Bombing Leader – F/L Hay, DFC   F/Eng. – Sgt Johnson
Gunnery Leader – F/L Trevor-Roper, DFM   Spare: Sgt Williams (M. Upper)

everything, but remember only the AOC and myself and five others know anything about these matters, and you'll be the seventh. I can't stress too much the need for secrecy. It's absolutely vital.'

We went on, down the winding Great North Road, meeting very little traffic except vast army convoys going north: past London into the southern country and up to an old country railway station. There I caught my train. My destination was so secret that not even my driver was allowed to have any idea of where I was going. Half an hour later I was met by a tall man whom I shall call Mutt. He was the senior test pilot for a very well-known aircraft firm, and had himself been responsible for testing the prototypes of more than one of our most successful bombers. We drove in his little Fiat car quite a way, without saying a word. I don't think he expected to see such a young fellow, and I didn't expect to see a civilian, and I think we were both wondering what we were doing there, anyway. At last he pulled up at an old country house. Here our passes were checked and re-checked and I had to pull out my special buff-coloured pass (numbered seven) which the SASO had given me earlier in the day. Then a couple of tough policemen gave us both the once over and we entered this queer place. We went down a long, dimly lit corridor, down dark stairs, farther and farther into the earth. Mutt seemed to know the way, and at last we came to a large iron door. There were two more guards here, and once more we went through the same procedure. They were certainly being careful. Then one of them opened the iron door and we went in to a sort of laboratory. It was bright inside, much brighter than the dim corridors, and I blinked to try and get accustomed to the light.

Then I met a man whom I'm not going to try to describe in detail, for I know he wouldn't like it. But I'm going to call him Jeff, which of course is not his real name. He was a scientist, and very clever aircraft designer as well. Jeff was neither young nor old, but just a quiet, earnest man who worked very hard. He was one of the real backroom boys of whom little can be told until after the war, and even then I'm not sure their full story will be told. He looked around carefully before saying anything, then abruptly, but benignly, over his thick spectacles, 'I'm glad you've come; I don't suppose you know what for.'

'No idea, I'm afraid. SASO said you would tell me nearly everything, whatever that means.'

He raised his eyebrows. 'Do you mean to say you don't know the target?' he asked.

'Not the faintest idea.'

'That makes it awkward, very awkward.'

'But SASO said—'

'I know, but only very few people know, and no one can be told unless his name is on this list.' He waved a list in front of me. I could see there weren't many names on it.

'This is damned silly,' said Mutt.

'I know, but it can't be helped – but I'll tell you as much as I dare. I hope the AOC will tell you the rest when you get back.'

I said that I thought this would be all right and waited, very curiously, for him to go on. Then he said:

'There are certain objectives in enemy territory which are very vulnerable to air attack, and which are themselves important military objectives. However, these need a vast amount of explosive placed very accurately to shift them or blow them out – you know what I mean, viaducts, submarine pens, big ships and so on. I have had my eye on such things for a long time, but always the problem has been too great – much too great. First of all, there wasn't an aeroplane with a high enough performance to carry the required load at the required speed. Then along came the Lancaster bomber, and this problem was solved. The next one was the explosive itself. It would have to take the form of either a very large bomb or a very large mine. But if it was to be dropped accurately enough to do its job it would have to be placed within a few yards of the right spot. There are three snags to this. If bombing is to be as accurate as that, then the attack will have to be low level, which means below 300 feet. But with these great big bombs there's always the danger that they may explode on impact from this height, and you know what that means. And if they're dropped above that height, then accuracy diminishes and the job can't be done. It's a sort of vicious circle. The other two snags are, of course, the danger of flak at that level and balloons, and the difficulty of flying over water at low level.'

'Over water?' I said.

'Yes, over water at night or early morning, when the water will be as flat as a mill-pond backed up with a lot of haze or fog all round.'

I began thinking of possible targets. *Tirpitz*, U-boat pens? No future in this – but Jeff was still talking.

'For a month or two now we have had the go-ahead order from the War Cabinet to try and overcome these difficulties. So we've been working hard, Mutt and I, on a certain theory of mine. I discovered the idea quite simply, but you won't want to know about that. Come, I'll show you.'

The lights went out in the lab, and a small screen lit up with a flickering motion picture. The title was simple, 'Most Secret Trial Number One'. Then an aeroplane came into view, diving very fast towards the sea in a sort of estuary. When it got to about 200 feet it levelled out and a huge cylindrical object fell from it rather slowly towards the water. I was amazed; I expected to see the aircraft blown sky high. But when it hit the water there was a great splash, and then – it worked. That's all I can say to describe it – just that it worked, while the aeroplane flew over serenely on its way. Then came pictures of many more trials. Now and then Mutt or Jeff would explain a point, but it seemed to me that everything was behaving perfectly each time. And, what's more, it was hitting its target with amazing accuracy. Then the screen became white and the lights went up. 'You see,' said Jeff. 'That's my special mine to overcome our difficulties, and it does work. But I'm afraid it's only one quarter the size of the real thing which is required to do the job. When we get to the big fellows, I think we're going to run into a lot of difficulties.'

'Has any been made yet?' I interrupted.

'No, not yet; the first will be ready in about a week's time with a modified Lancaster to carry it. Avro's are doing a great rush job to get the special fittings put on; I believe they're working twenty-four hours a day. Now what I want to know from you is this. Can you fly to the limits I want? These are roughly a speed of 240 miles an hour at 150 feet above smooth water, having pulled out of a dive from 2,000 feet, and then be able to drop a bomb accurately within a few yards.'

I said I thought it was a bit difficult but worth trying. I would let him know as soon as possible. Then I was on my way. Out of this strange house and into the open air again. Mutt drove me to the station, a⌐ ⌐ four hours later I was back at Scampton.

There the boys were all flying, so I took Nigger for a long walk to think things over. It's always the best way to think things out, and as we walked the more the problem seemed to be insoluble. Nigger was the only happy one. He was catching rabbits.

Next day we had another conference. I told the boys what I knew about the accuracy required and the height at which we must attack, but nothing about the weapon I had seen. Then came the problem. Dinghy began speaking. 'The first big snag will be to get practice in moonlight. I suppose it will be moonlight or dusk, won't it?'

I said I thought it would be.

'Well, you know the difficulties in this country; there's not much moon, anyway, and if there is, the weather's sure to be bad, so we won't get much practice. We'll have to try and get some form of synthetic night-flying training.'

'Didn't the SASO tell us to fly around with dark glasses on?' This was Henry.

'Yes, I've tried that. It's no good. You can't see your instruments. But I've heard that the AAF have brought out a special form of synthetic night-flying. All the windows of the aircraft are painted blue, and the crews wear yellow goggles inside. These are complementary colours or something, and apparently you get the effect of soft moonlight with all the highlights outside on a bright, sunny day.'

'Well, that sounds fine to me. Go and find out from SASO where we can get hold of this stuff, will you?'

He came back with the information a few minutes later.

'I've been on to the SASO. The stuff's at Ford. He says we've got immediate priority, and we can have three aircraft fitted up right away if the maintenance unit can find the men. He's going to ring us back as soon as he has found out.'

Then Jack Leggo came back on his navigation problems again. There were routes to be considered. Would the routes take us over canals and lakes, so as to make it easier? Could slow bomb-aimers be put in crews as eighth men so as to get extra practice? They were already beginning to put in eight hours' flying a day, which is a lot.

Then Bob Hay got up. There were no bomb-carriers, and he understood we had to do a lot of bombing. There were no flame-floats, which are essential for oversea navigation. What sort of targets were required on the bombing range? And could we have priority on the use of the range from dawn to dusk? All these problems were solved by the ever-reliable SASO, who seemed to eat, sleep and live at his office desk. He fixed them all.

Trevor had his troubles, too. He wanted to get his gunners cracking. If we were to attack at low level, he wanted his gunners to be able to hit back. And for this he wanted maximum range tracer, so that although we were only firing ·303 bullets, they would look like cannon-shells to the flak gunners on the ground. The tracer he wanted was hard to get, but we got it – from the SASO.

Hutch was rather in a haze about the whole thing. He didn't quite know where his wireless-operators came in. I said to him: 'It's OK, Hutch. Just you concentrate on getting your wireless-operators on the top line, and your turn will come later. Now for a few general points, chaps. I've been speaking to the maintenance people, and they tell me that already a few aircraft have come back with leaves and tree-branches stuck in their radiators. This means the boys are flying too low. You've got to stop this, or else someone will kill himself, and I might also tell you that the Provost Marshals have already been up to see me about reported dangerous low flying. We all know we've got to fly low, and we've got to get some practice in, but for God's sake tell your boys to try and avoid going over towns and aerodromes and not to beat up policemen or lovers in a field, because they'll get a rocket if they do. Now, if you'll excuse me, I've got to do some trials on a certain reservoir, to find out if we can do the thing at all.'

Half an hour later we were on our way in my faithful G for George towards the reservoir called Derwent Water near Sheffield. This lake is in the Pennines, surrounded by high ground with just enough industrial haze blowing over it to make it ideal for the job; moreover, the water was always calm because there was no wind in that valley. Remembering what Jeff had said, we came screaming down at the right air-speed to pull out as near 150 feet as we could judge (Hoppy was sitting beside me), and released a missile. It fell short. Then we were twisting and turning our way through the valley, with high hills on either side. We climbed up again for several more tries, and in the end found it more or less fairly easy.

That night at dusk, with the fog already beginning to fill up in the valley, cutting visibility down to about a mile or so, we tried again. This time it wasn't so good. The water, which had been blue by day, was now black – we nearly hit that black water. Even Spam said, 'Christ! this is bloody dangerous,' which meant it was. Not only that. I said to Dinghy there and then, that unless we could find some way of judging our height above water, this type of attack would be completely impossible. 'But why must we fly at this dead height?' asked Hoppy.

'I'm afraid that's the snag. The scientist I met told me that in order to make this weapon work we would have to fly within a few miles an hour at the right air-speed and within a very few feet of the right height. That's our problem.'

The next day the AOC sent for me, and as I entered his office I noticed three large packing-cases on the floor; he handed me a screwdriver. 'There are models of your targets,' he said. 'Now I'm not going to tell you where they are, nor am I going to tell you what they are, although, of course, you will probably realize as soon as you see them. Jeff has rung me up and told me that you won't be able to train your squadron unless you know, and so I am leaving it to him to tell you all the details. However, don't forget that you have got to be the only man in the squadron who can possibly know the target until the day before the attack is made. Now let's have a crack at opening those cases.'

All of them were sealed up and marked 'Very Fragile'. Not being a carpenter by trade, I went to work gingerly, and at last had all the screws undone. Then, between us, we lifted off the heavy lids. The three models were perfect in every detail down to the smallest tree, and my first feeling was – thank God it's not the *Tirpitz*. This was something I did not expect. There were models of three dams, and very large dams at that. Then the AOC was talking.

'Now you've seen what you've got to attack, take an aeroplane and fly down and see our man right away, and report to me when you come back.'

Professor Jeff was in his office. He seemed pleased to see me.

'How did you get on with the trials?' he asked.

I told him that it was easy by day, but harder by night, and that flying level over water at 150 feet was very nearly impossible.

'But you could see the end all right?'

'Yes.'

'Good. Now to work. Mutt, will you get out my file on Downwood?'

'What's that?' I asked.

'It's the code name for the operation you're going to do. The AOC has told me that I can tell you the target.'

It was hard to analyse my feelings, because I wasn't sure where these dams were. The AOC had talked of haze and industrial smoke, which put them into a built-up area, and that wouldn't be too hot. Mutt gave me a cigarette, Jeff opened his his file and began: 'The dams which you saw in model form in the AOC's office are great barrage dams in the Ruhr Valley. The weapon you saw in my laboratory the other day is known as Downwood, and it's my idea that by really accurate use of this weapon we shall be able to knock down the concrete walls of these dams.'

'But surely a smaller bomb would do that easily?'

'No.' Jeff laughed. 'A lot of people think that; they think dams are just curved structures that hold back water by their shape, much the same as the.arch of a bridge. There are dams like that, but they are known as vault dams. These barrage dams are known as gravity dams, and hold back the water by their weight. As these are 140 feet thick of solid concrete and masonry and 150 feet high, you can see that there is a colossal amount of masonry to shift. But let me begin at the beginning.'

I was listening intently.

'As you know,' Jeff was saying, 'the Ruhr Valley is the most highly industrialized area in the whole of Germany, mainly because of the coal and heavy steel industries situated there. I know that a lot of Germany's factories are now dispersed, but as yet they have not moved many of their heavy industries, so the Ruhr Valley is still a very important target, even though you boys have done your best to knock it flat. However, there is one great snag to the Ruhr Valley itself, and this is the water supply. The Ruhr River itself is too small to supply much water, and the Rhine is a long way off for such big towns as Essen and Dortmund and the rest. So in 1911 the Germans, realizing this, built a mighty barrage dam blocking the Möhne Valley through which the River Ruhr flowed. The main idea of this dam was to create a storage of the surplus winter rainfall of the Ruhr catchment area – thus providing a reserve which could be released gradually during the summer months to maintain a fairly constant level in the river and protect the underground water-table which provided supplies for industrial and household purposes. This table had been gravely in peril prior to the dam's construction. The dam also provides improved navigability of the lower Ruhr, controls winter flooding and maintains a constant flow of water for electrical power. Needless to say,' he went on, 'the Germans are very proud of this dam. In fact, it is rather beautifully built, Gothic and all that. It is some 850 yards long and 140 feet thick, and as high as it is thick, and the lake it holds back is about twelve miles long, holding 140 million tons of water. At the same time they built another dam near by, called the Sorpe. This is very much smaller and is of earthen construction, which, if you know what I mean, consists of a sloping bank of earth 600 feet long on either side holding up a watertight concrete core. Between them they hold back about 77 per cent of the total water available in the Ruhr Valley. If they were to be breached, the consequent shortage of water for both drinking and industrial purposes might be disastrous. Of course, the damage done by floods if they were breached quickly would result in more damage to everything than has ever happened in this war.

'There is a third dam I must tell you about, and this is the Eder. This dam is some sixty miles away. It was built in 1914 primarily to prevent winter flooding of agricultural land and to assist in improving navigability of the lower Weser River. The dam also provides some water for the Mittelland Canal, which, as you know, is one of the main canals in Germany, running as it does on the main route from the Ruhr to Berlin. But, unlike the Möhne Dam, the Eder has no water-supply functions. However, it supplies a lot of hydro-electric power. This one's a little larger than the Möhne dam and lies in a valley 40 miles from Kassel. And it holds back 202 million tons of water. But to breach these things is an entirely different matter. You can imagine that many attempts have been made,' he went on, 'to devise some method of breaking down dam walls. But it's not so easy as it looks. When you consider that we in England here have ourselves been saved from an ordinary explosive bomb when we were behind 3 feet of concrete, you will begin to realize what I mean when I talk about shifting about 150 feet of the stuff.'

I said, 'Yes, I think I do.'

'Well, we have been making experiments and trying out the effects of explosives on such walls for some time. Now, let me show you something.'

He opened a book containing pictures of a small dam, some six feet across, which had been breached by a certain charge of explosive. 'You can see what we were after,' he said. 'Our next experiment was to try out our theories on a larger dam. We built out in the garden a dam some 200 feet across. This dam, I might tell you, was brick for brick in strength the same as the Möhne dam. The lake was filled with water, and by manipulation of certain charges, we intended to try out there the theories we had evolved from the smaller models.'

This, I thought, must have been fun. I could remember the times when I was a kid, when we used to go down to the beaches in Cornwall and shovel the sand across the little streams which ran down the granite cliffs. I could remember how we dammed up the water until it made a big pool behind the sand, and I could remember how, when it was time to go home for supper, I used to smash the whole thing with one sweep of my spade, letting the water rush out down the beach. I could also remember how angry my brother used to get when I did this.

'And what happened?' I asked.

'Well,' went on Jeff, 'after a lot of trouble we got a charge in the right place which we worked out a Lancaster on the same scale could carry, and the dam wall cracked. It cracked round about its base, and after a few more charges had been detonated the wall moved over backwards and water ran down into the garden. But this was not enough, we had to still make tests on a full-sized model. At that time we heard that a certain County Council in the Midlands had just built a new dam to supply their town with water. We heard about it and wrote to them and asked them if we could knock down their old dam, so that the water would run into their newly built one. After a lot of quibbling they agreed to let us do this, and once more after much trouble, we succeeded in knocking it down. Here are the pictures.'

I bent over his shoulder and studied them carefully. The dam had been breached right down to its foundations, a breach about three feet across. There was a dead frog lying on the mud bank.

'Well, after that experiment,' he went on, 'we knew more or less where we were. The next thing was to find the suitable weapon. Well, you've seen that. But we've not finished,' he added. 'Not nearly finished.' He paused and then went on quietly: 'My smaller-scale weapons have worked, but we haven't had a chance to try the big ones yet – they aren't ready. But I think they will be in a few days' time, and so the trials are set for the 16th. If the big ones work, Avro's will have to modify twenty-five Lancasters to carry them. This is quite a big job, because these mines weigh a lot and are about 11 feet in diameter. Then there's the time factor. The ordnance factory will have to construct the weapons, you'll have to plan a special method of attack, and all this will have to take place inside a month.'

'Why the urgency?' I asked.

'Because dams can only be attacked when they are full of water. Every day photo planes are going out to take pictures of these dams, and we are watching the water rising. At the moment it is 12 feet from the top, but we can only attack them when the water is 4 feet. This ensures that the maximum amount of water is in the dam and at the same time makes certain that there is four feet of free board on the lip against which you have to throw your mines. That is why you have to be so accurate. I have calculated that the water level will be suitable during the week 13th–19th May – that is, in about six weeks' time. This, as it happens, is a moon period – I think you will have to do it at night or dawn: you couldn't get into the Ruhr by day, could you?'

'God, no.'

'Then the moon will be useful, but if you want more light you'll have to do it at dawn – but that's up to you. But to get back to our side of things let me tell you more about these dams. Your projectiles will have to fall so that they sink into the water actually touching the dam wall itself about 40 feet down; if they are not touching, it'll be useless. Then, when the mine explodes by a hydrostatic fuse, I have calculated that a crack will appear just as it did in the models. By placing more mines in exactly the same spot you will be able to shift this wall backwards until it rolls over, helped, of course, by the water pressure. The Sorpe Dam requires rather a different technique, but we will go into that later.'

'So those are our three objectives?'

'Yes.'

'However did you arrive at this theory how to crack these things?'

'Mutt, you tell him; I'm hoarse.'

'Well,' said Mutt, reaching for the file. 'Jeff's always been playing about with things, large or small, since he was a small boy, and it came to him just like that one day when playing with his children in the garden.'

'And you think that this will have disastrous results?'

'I know it will. The Prime Minister is terribly keen on it.'

'You mentioned a special type of attack?'

'Yes; well, the first thing you've got to do is to get there. These mines are very heavy and you'll have to carry a lot of petrol because the operation may take some time. So you won't be able to fly very high. But again, that's up to you. The attack will have to be carried out at a dead height within a foot or so of 150 feet, and that's going to be hard. At the same time your air-speed's got to be bang on; remember that you've got to dive down into the valley and you may get up a hell of a speed, and your aiming has got to be perfect.'

'That's going to be mighty difficult.'

'Over black water at a constant height when you can't see the thing – in bad visibility.'

'Oh Christ!'

'And remember this, you'll have to drop your mines slightly before you reach the wall, so an ordinary bomb-sight won't do. If you under-shoot, nothing will happen; if you over-shoot, the mine will go over the top. But it's best to be accurate, because if you make a mistake the mine might hit the parapet and explode underneath you tail. That'll be pretty uncomfortable.'

'Where will it go off in the ordinary way?'

'About 100 yards behind. You'll be OK. There's not much blast from an underwater explosion. Besides, the parapet will protect you.'

'I see,' I said slowly.

I didn't see. I was completely and utterly bewildered. The limitations seemed almost impossible. But all we could do was to try. Jeff told me

to come down for the trials on the 16th, and in the meantime I would
be free to get on with training for the next two weeks. Half an hour later
a puzzled Wing-Commander and a thirsty dog were flying their way
back to Grantham in the communications aircraft. Perhaps baffled is a
better word than puzzled.

The next few days passed quickly. The synthetic night-flying aircraft
had arrived; we all had a crack, and found it perfect. It was funny,
though, flying along at night in day-time. It makes you quite sleepy. The
boys had begun to get good at their flying, and now I knew where and
what the targets were we could plan a route similar to the one which
would actually be used over Germany. This meant flying a lot over lakes,
but the excuse for these was always the same: they were good landmarks
and a good check on navigation. As we would have to fly to Germany at
tree-level height, keeping to track was most important, and it meant
navigation to the yard. There hadn't been any accidents – yet, but birds
were already beginning to get in our way, coming into windscreens and
getting stuck in the radiators; trees were being hit, and sometimes even
water. Many times out at sea the boys were getting fired on by His
Majesty's ships, who have notoriously light fingers, but they took it all
in good stead because, as Micky Martin put it, 'It's good practice. It
makes us flak happy.'

I pitied my own crew because I was busy all day and we could only
do our practice in the late part of the evening and at night. Many times
we would take off about six o'clock and fly up the west coast of England
to the northern tip of Scotland. It's a funny thing about England and
Scotland; many people think it's a small place and that we're overcrowded
in our little island, but it's amazing how unpopulated the country really
is. In the Western Isles, for instance, you can fly for miles without seeing
any sign of habitation. And so these long, lonely trips took place every
night, because if we were to lead the show we would have to be trained.
Funnily enough, the boys thought it was a good thing. I once heard
Trevor say, 'It's a good thing flying with the Wingco; it keeps us off the
booze.'

One fine day in April a Wing-Commander from MAP came up to see
me. I was sitting alone in my office when he came in. He began at once
to tell me of our sighting difficulties on the Eder and Möhne Dams. The
latest anti-submarine bomb-sight, he explained, would be no use when
carrying out our special form of attack, I was horrified.

'How the hell do you know all this?' I asked, rudely.

He went on to explain. He was the sighting expert and had been let
into the secret so that he could help us. No one else knew. I calmed
down. Between us we worked out a plan, although it was his original

idea. He took out a piece of paper and by drawing queer lines he explained what he meant – it took the form of a very simple bomb-sight using the age-old range-finding principles. From aerial photographs we had noticed that there were two towers on the dam, and when we measured these we found they were 600 feet apart. Our mines had to be dropped exactly a certain number of yards short of a certain position along the dam wall. He worked it all out. He was a mathematician. Then we handed it to a corporal with glasses, and within half an hour the instrument section had knocked up the prototype of the bomb-sight. It cost a little less than the price of a postage stamp.

That afternoon we went up, he and I, to try it over our dam in Sheffield. It worked. He was very pleased that he had been able to help, and took himself back to London. Just another backroom boy. His name? Dann.

Well pleased, I told Bob Hay to get cracking with all our bomb-aimers to teach them to make their own sights based on the prototype. From then on our bombing range at Wainfleet echoed to the thud of bursting practice bombs. Soon extraordinary accuracy was being achieved. F/Sgt Clifford sent down eight practice bombs from 150 feet – error four yards. He had free beer that night. Next day Les Knight managed to get this down to three yards. He was the pilot – the drinks were on him – but he didn't.

Soon we went on to night training, and again I found it very much harder, because although we could see the targets clearly enough, we couldn't see the water. It was practically impossible to fly at exactly 150 feet. A few went too low and rubbed their bellies along the water; others went too high and under-shot by miles. After the second night's bombing Dinghy landed, sweating. 'It's no use. I can't see how we're going to do it.'

I had to agree.

'Can't we get electric altimeters? Ours don't give the height to 50 feet. But personally I can't see the necessity, anyway, of flying to a few feet. It's easy enough to fly within ten feet of the height, why two feet?'

Melvyn, like all the boys, didn't know the target. I had hinted at U-boat pens or the *Tirpitz*. But an electric altimeter would only have worked over open sea or in a harbour. I knew it wouldn't work in a valley. There were too many hills around.

'I'll try,' I said, and left it at that. But this height question was to be one of our greatest difficulties for some days to come. In the end, however, it was to be solved as simply as the problem was complex, but more of this later.

By the end of the third week all crews had done about twenty cross-countries by night, and could now find the 'tree' which I had asked them to find. Their navigation was really expert. We had dropped about 1,500 practice bombs on our range, and the average error for all these was as low as 25 yards. With this basic training behind us we felt that the time had now come to plan our route to the target, so that we could imitate it as much as possible over this country. This would give the boys a chance to get there when it came to the real job – and getting there was the main thing.

We went down to see Charles Pickard of F for Freddie fame, who probably knew more about the light flak defences in the coastal areas of Holland and Belgium than any other man living. From his safe he pulled out a map on which all the defended areas along the coast were shown in red. There was a lot of red. But there were gaps. He showed me how to get through by means of a winding route in which nowhere did we get closer than one mile to the guns. Then Charles Whitworth and I, with the help of the SASO, sat down to imitate this winding journey, if possible, over England. This was easier than we expected. The flight out across the North Sea was simulated by a flight across the North Sea, but out in the middle our route turned round and came back towards England again. It crossed the coast inland over the Wash, which is similar to the Dutch islands. From then on it led from canal junction to river-rail crossings; from railway crossings over canals to road bridges, because all these show up well in moonlight and at dawn. But each turning point we selected because it looked exactly the same as the real thing. If we were to turn on a certain shaped bridge in Holland, then we turned on a similar bridge in Norfolk. For the River Rhine we had the River Trent, for the Ruhr Hills we had the Cotswolds, for the Möhne Lake we had Uppingham Reservoir, which was much the same shape though, of course, much smaller. Colchester Lake gave us a good idea of the calm waters of the Eder Reservoir. In fact, everything was much the same. On the way home our dummy route left England at the sand dunes near a point on the Norfolk coast, which corresponded exactly to our 'gap' near Egmond on the Hook of Holland. There was even a windmill nearby which was much the same as another windmill over there, and a wireless mast. Moreover, the total distance was nearly the same as the real thing, which was ideal. We knew all this because we took the trouble to fly around it and find out. And so the great imitation route was planned. I gave it to Jack Leggo and told him to get all crews so used to it that they could go around blindfold.

'But why the lakes? We're not going to pinpoint on lakes?'

'That's all right. I've told you – those are the checks.' Another white lie.

Meanwhile, it may well be imagined that the Germans would have liked to have known all about this. If they had known they would have improved their dam defences. But we knew that the defences were the same as at the beginning of the war. Even the double torpedo net was getting rusty from old age. The security measures were evidently efficient. All our telephone wires were tapped, all conversation was checked. One boy rang up his girl friend and told her that he could not come out that night because he was flying on special training. Next day, in front of the whole squadron, I told him that a lapse of this kind would end in a courtmartial. There was no more loose talk. Guards were stationed all round the vicinity; lectures were given on security to every man and woman on the station. All our letters were censored, and if anything which might give the game away was written, the letters found their way back to me. Special policemen in plain clothes were stationed in the vicinity. Their job was to eavesdrop. They did it well. Some say that even the local barmaid in the nearby pub was given three months' holiday. Everywhere – in the factories and on the testing grounds, in the Air Ministry – the same measures were in force. Taking things all round, I think every serviceman and every civilian co-operated very well. They knew that they had 125 lives on their hands. They did not talk.

And so, after three weeks, things were going pretty well. Operational training and security marched forward side by side. The weather had been kind – the aeroplanes were behaving themselves. The crews had begun to settle down to the dangerous art of low flying, and no one had killed himself yet. The pilots had begun to practise formation flying at night at low level to get used to their fighting formations. Bombing was generally very accurate and the speed of bombing was both high and constant. In fact, the only two great questions now remaining were, of course, the weapon itself, and the height problem. A high *esprit de corps* had already begun to creep into the squadron. The adjutant in his squadron diary wrote on April 14 'The whole of 617 has by now a feeling of solidity. The officers and NCO air-crew had shown remarkable enthusiasm for their job not only in flying alone, but in cleaning and painting the hangars and offices. We seem to have got tradition already.'

On the 15th, with one month to go, the SASO rang up. Bob Hay and I were to fly down to Parkstone, a place on the South Coast not very far from France, to witness the first trials of the new weapon. The first of the problems was about to be dealt with.

CHAPTER SEVENTEEN

BY TRIAL AND ERROR

Down at Parkstone, Bob and I sat in the sun and waited. We had been told that things weren't quite ready, so we drove round the town of Margate to see what it looked like in time of war. It was pretty hard to realize, as we lounged on the beach, that this was the same old sunshine resort of peacetime; the hotels were all closed, 'Dreamland' was an army barracks, barbed wire was everywhere and the place was full of soldiers. The only thing that had remained was the fish. We had just stuffed ourselves full of Dover soles and now felt pleasantly lazy in the early afternoon, listening to the screaming of the gulls as they glided over the harbour.

Suddenly there was a noise like the release of compressed air, then the chattering of cannon guns, followed by the full crump of bombs. Like a flash, glinting in the sun at 'nought' feet, four FW 190s rocketed over our heads going flat out towards France, followed closely by four Typhoons. The many Bofors parked along the front chattered after them, sending up red balls one after another in a gentle curve towards the whole ensemble, enemy and friend. This was the well-known tip-and-run raid. Bob said a rude four-letter word with emphasis. Then the sirens went. Later in the evening we heard that all four had been smacked down by the 'Tiffies'.

We also heard that the tide would be just right for the trials at seven o'clock next morning. We were told that after each mine had been dropped the scientists wanted to examine them to see how they had stood up to the shock of hitting the water at that very high speed. The idea was to drop one when the tide was on the ebb so that, when it went out, we could walk down the beach and examine it thoroughly at our leisure without the difficulty of recovering it from the sea.

Early next morning we stood together, Bob, Professor Jeff and I, on the range facing the sea, waiting. It was one of those white mornings with the cloud spread evenly over the sky; there was hardly a ripple on the water; it was cold and rather grim and our collars were turned up. Jeff looked at his watch and said, 'Shorty should be here any minute now.' Shorty was one of Mutt's test pilots – he was 5 feet 6 inches high and rejoiced in the name of Longbottom.

Behind us, round the barbed wire which surrounded the range, special policemen patrolled, their job to keep away strangers. No one else was meant to see these trials. Near us, a slow-motion movie camera sat angularly on its tripod with an operator panning its lens towards the east. Out at sea 100 yards away two white buoys bobbed up and down. These were the aiming markers. A small dinghy lay on the beach with a naval lieutenant asleep in it; he was the proud captain of this craft, whose job was to see to the repair of buoys if they got damaged.

Then out of the sun came the two Lancasters. They were both in fine pitch and making a very hearty noise for that time of the morning. They flew in formation; one the motion-picture aircraft, the other with one of our mines slung underneath. Inside the gaping bomb doors we could see it quite clearly painted black and white, looking large enough even against the massive black Lancaster itself. Down came the Lanc with Shorty Longbottom at the controls to about 150 feet, travelling at something like 270. We saw him level out for his run, then climb a bit to get his exact height over the calm water. We saw him tense at the controls, getting his horizon level on the cliffs farther on. Jeff stood beside Bob, crouching like a cat. The movie camera began turning. I picked up a pair of binoculars. Then the mine fell out quite slowly. It seemed to hang in the air for a long time before it hit the water with a terrific splash and a dull thud. In a minute we would know whether or not Jeff's calculations had been right or wrong, but for the moment there was nothing except that mighty wall of water which reached up to the aircraft's tail as if to grab it. Then it all subsided and we knew. The great mine could be seen taking its last dive smashed into six different fragments.

'Broken,' said Jeff, and looked at the ground. I said nothing. I knew the work he had put in, the hours of sitting at the desk with slide rule and calculator. Now it had failed. Would the mine have to be altered? Would the whole project fail? What next?

'They all said it wouldn't work,' Jeff was saying. 'They all said it was too big and too heavy, but I'll show them. We have got another in the hangars up there, and we'll strengthen it this afternoon and have some more trials this evening.'

In our secret hangar that afternoon there was feverish activity as the mine was strengthened by steel plates so that it wouldn't break when it hit the water. Small men with glasses toiled side by side with sweating airmen, none of whom knew the use for which the thing was intended. They had no meals, and worked through an alert without pause. At five o'clock that afternoon they straightened their backs. It was ready.

In the late afternoon we again stood waiting. Jeff was hopeful; the extra plating should do the trick. We had just had a look at the broken weapon, and it seemed it had hit so hard that the impact had broken the outer skin. By strengthening this outer skin with half-inch steel plate it seemed that we had got the answer.

Then over they came again; once more the suspense and once more the mighty splash. Then Mutt, who was flying it this time, banked steeply away to have a look. But we weren't looking at him, only at the bits of our smashed-up weapon which were hurtling round the sea like flying-fish. Then the foaming water settled down again and there was a long silence.

Jeff suddenly said, 'Oh, my God,' and I thought he was going to have a fit. But he soon calmed down, for he was not temperamental, and as we trudged along the shingle to the car park he began planning his next move. Here was a man who would not be beaten.

To make things worse, Bob and I took up a single-engine aircraft to fly back to Scampton. When we were about 300 feet over Margate the engine stopped. When an engine stops in a four-engine aircraft you do not have to worry much about it – you have always got three others, but when it happens in a single-engine aircraft, then the long finger of gravity points towards mother earth; and so we began coming down. In ordinary parts of the world this is quite easy, but at Hell's Corner they made quite certain that aircraft do not land safely in fields. There were abundant wires and other devices because German glider-borne troops were not very welcome. So we fell into the trap . . .

After the aircraft had rolled itself into a ball and we had stepped out of the dust, a man came running over to see if we were hurt. His words were memorable.

'I think they teach you young fellows to fly too early.' he said.

Then a policeman panted up and took a statement. 'I'm glad to see our anti-aircraft landing devices work,' he said without sympathy. We stumped back to the aerodrome.

Back at the squadron our great problem was the height. By now we had realized that we would have to get some method of flying accurately at 150 feet or the whole project would have to be called off. Many methods were tried; one of them consisted of a long wire which we trailed behind the aircraft with a heavy weight on it. The idea was that this weight would hang down exactly 150 feet at a certain speed and so, as the aircraft approached the water and the weight hit, there would be a jerk and the pilot would then know what height he was at. However, this method proved unsatisfactory because the weight has a nasty habit of trailing up straight behind the aircraft.

Then we tried to get practice by judging height. To do this we put a couple of men on the side of a hill overlooking a lake with a special instrument to measure aircraft height. One by one we dived over the water and were told afterwards whether we had been right or wrong. This was all right for daylight, but proved impossible at night. Then one day the problem was solved. Mr Lockspeiser of MAP paid the SASO a visit. He said, 'I think I can help you.' His idea was an old one; actually it was used in the last war. He suggested that two spotlights should be placed on either wing of the aircraft, pointing towards the water where they would converge at 150 feet. The pilot could see these spots, and when they merged into one he would then know the exact height. It all seemed too simple, and I came back to tell the boys. Spam's first words were: 'I could have told you that. Last night Terry and I went to see the show at the Theatre Royal, and when the girl there was doing her striptease act there were two spotlights shining on her. The idea crossed my mind then.'

I said, 'Never mind about striptease. You, Henry, take an aircraft down to Farnborough – I know it's a weekend; that doesn't count – and get two Aldis lights fitted up, one in the nose and one in the tail. Fly it back here as soon as it is ready and we will do some dummy runs across the aerodrome.'

Farnborough worked hard, and Henry was back within twenty-four hours. He took the aircraft up, and I stood out on the aerodrome to watch him. It was dusk when he came whistling across the aerodrome with his two thin beams of light shining down on the ground. He looked so low in his great aircraft that if he turned on to his side one wing would rip along the ground. It all looked very frightening, but when he landed he said it was quite easy and suggested that the navigator should get the height calculations and leave the pilot to concentrate on his instrument-flying.

Then a party of men descended on our workshops and all the aircraft were fitted within a matter of days. Night after night, dawn after dawn, the boys flew around the Wash and the nearby lakes and over the aerodrome itself at about 150 feet, while others with theodolites stood on the ground and measured their heights. Within a week everyone had got so good that they could fly to within two feet with amazing consistency. But as I stood there and watched them with their lights on, I knew that whatever losses there might have been before, we were certainly going to make it easier for the German gunners flying around with lights on.

Down in the South work was still going on. Every day dramatic experiments took place. One cold morning after another Shorty and Mutt flew over the range and dropped their missiles while this great little man, Jeff, stood in the shingle beside the water with his shoulders hunched and his hands in the pockets of his overcoat watching to see what would happen. One after another the experiments failed. The mines were not working. I can remember clearly the sight of that cold, quiet figure standing sometimes alone, sometimes with two or three others, on the brink of the water, looking up at the great Lancasters. There was a tenseness about the way in which he stood, with his legs apart and his

chin thrust out and a fearful expectancy about everything. There was
sometimes frost on the ground during these early mornings, which made
things sharp and bright and real.

For many days they worked and flew while he modified and experimented and the boys trained and trained and I watched and watched.
But every time it ended in the same thing – failure.

One day Shorty came up to collect me in a Mosquito. 'I have got to
take you to Brooklands,' he said. 'Jeff's there, and he wants to have an
urgent conference with you.'

I needn't say how much Shorty shook me going through the balloon
cables at Brooklands, nor need I say how tired Jeff seemed when I came
in. He said to me, 'The whole thing is going to be a failure unless we
jiggle around with our heights and speed.'

'What do you mean?'

'Simply this. From the slow-motion movie cameras which have taken
pictures of these things dropping, I have found out a few facts. I have
drawn this graph here to illustrate what I mean. It's all a combination
of speed and height. You see here that they will work and won't break
up if we drop them from 150 feet at a certain speed. On the other hand,
if we drop them from 40 feet at this speed they will also work. The best
height to suit your aircraft is here at the 60-feet level at 232 miles an
hour. But that is very low, and that's why I have asked you to come
down. Can you fly at 60 feet above the water? If you can't the whole
thing will have to be called off.'

I thought for a second and wondered if it could be done. If 150 feet
was low, 60 feet was very low. At that height you would only have to
hiccough and you would be in the drink. But I said aloud, 'We will have
a crack tonight.'

All this time we had reconnaissance aircraft flying out over Germany
watching the dams as a cat watches a mouse. They never flew straight
to them because then the Germans would know what they were looking
for, but always took a round-about route, crossing the dams as if by
accident. They were looking for two things; the first and more important
was the height of the water level. It was slowly rising. The second was
the state of the defences. If they were being intensified, the Germans
must know we were coming.

It was very thrilling in those cold spring evenings, watching the water
rise. By April 17 it was some 15 feet from the top of the dam wall. By
the beginning of May it was only ten feet, and so it went up and up. We
would have to be ready when it was four feet, and it looked as though
we were behind schedule.

When I got back to Scampton we immediately altered the spotlights
so that they converged at 60 feet and made our first trials over the Wash.
I think David Maltby was the first to take up the aircraft to experiment

at this height. He found it all right, but said that it seemed very low. We checked with our theodolites and found it was exactly right. Then I went up with Terry and flew along the calm waters of Uppingham Lake, and it seemed to me that we were a little higher than the height of the trees; it certainly was low, but there was no real danger because the spots were very accurate. When we were coming down Terry would say, 'Go down, go down,' very slowly, whereas if we were below 60 feet he would yell, 'Go up,' and a quick pull on the stick would shoot the Lanc up into the air.

We heard that these spotlights would work satisfactorily over water with a slight chop, but over glass calm the spots would shine through the water and converge underneath, so that there was very great danger of flying straight into the drink without knowing the danger.

Many a lonely bargee was frightened at the dead of night as we experimented like this along the still canals of Lincolnshire, and we found that the theorists were wrong. The spots did, in fact, keep on the surface. Within a few days all crews had tried it, and all crews were satisfied.

By May 1 I had rung up Jeff and told him that we could do it. He asked me to come down for the trials again.

Then one morning early in May, Mutt flew over and dropped one which worked. The man on the ground danced and waved his hands in the air and took out his handkerchief and waved it madly. I threw my hat in the air. I could see Mutt in his cockpit grinning as he banked around after his run, and I waved back at him and shouted into the noise of the engines. I believe, although I do not remember very well, that Jeff threw his hat into the air. This was a wonderful moment.

Then there were urgent telephone calls and many signals written in cipher, and messengers rushing to and fro, and factories receiving priority orders, so that men and women should work day and night making these things which we were to carry with us over to Germany to be dropped on the Möhne Dam. There was great excitement. One of the boys flew back to the squadron with the good news and there were smiles on all faces; we even persuaded Jeff to take a glass of beer afterwards. As he was sipping it one of the high officers of Bomber Command went up to him. I heard him say, 'It's OK. You seem to have got your weapons to work, but you will never knock down that rubble; it's completely impossible.' And Jeff smiled and I scowled and thought this officer was a bum, because he should have remembered that the barman was listening.

Meanwhile, Avro's began to churn out the new aircraft. Soon they were delivered by special pilots on to our aerodrome. The Engineer-Officer, F/Lt Capel – we always called him Capable Capel – began to delve into them; they were very different. There was mid-upper turret; this had been taken off because of the weight. A lot of armour had been taken out; there were new gadgets everywhere so that we could carry out our mission successfully. One by one they were allotted to crews who took great care of them, and I once heard a pilot swear lustily and go red in the face when his bomb-aimer got inside with muddy boots on! And at the same time in the early morning long eight-wheeled trucks arrived on our station covered with tarpaulins. These were our mines arriving. They were glistening new and still warm because they had just been filled with their very special explosive. Our armament officer, Doc Watson, had to deal with these, and it meant a lot of trouble because each one had to be treated like a diamond – they were very delicate and very hard to fuse and prepare. He and his armourers worked day and night getting them ready for our next trials.

Meanwhile, the whole squadron was beginning to get a bit tired. They had had nearly two months of continuous training, getting up at dawn and dusk so that they could fly in conditions which were nearly like moonlight. They had flown about a hundred hours of training, and because of the uncertainty of the whole thing the strain was beginning to get them down. For this reason I sent them off on three days' leave so that they could recover, but told them not to say a word to anyone outside. And I began to get ill too, and irritable and bad-tempered, and, of all things, there began to grow on my face a large carbuncle. I went to the doctor. He was very kind and he said: 'This just means you are over-worked. You will have to take two weeks off.' I just laughed in his face. Poor man! These medicos sometimes do not realize that there is a war on and when a job's got to be done personal health doesn't enter into the question. Nevertheless, I took part of his advice and began taking some tonic.

A few days later we went down to Parkstone again to watch the final handing-over trial. This was to see that our mines would actually explode in water. I flew in the camera aeroplane and Shorty flew the aeroplane which would drop it. It was a tense and dramatic moment watching the mine fall out, hit the water and not break up. And then, when Shorty had passed over it by about 100 yards, the whole surface of the sea shook as if by a mighty earthquake, and about five seconds afterwards a great column of snow-white water slowly rose into the air, beautiful to watch. It rose to a full 1,500 feet and stayed there for perhaps fifteen seconds, then slowly melted away in the spring sunshine. Our mines were ready.

On May 6th we held our last training conference. Both Capable Capel and Doc Watson were there because they were very much concerned. All the captains came too. I think they were now beginning to guess about targets, although none of them, of course, knew for certain. They sat in chairs round my office, smoking and talking – while Nigger sat in my place giving them the once over. I sat on the windowsill and began to talk.

'Well, chaps you know as well as I do it has been absolute hell getting
this right in the last few weeks, but now I think we are more or less set;
that is, we are set to begin co-ordinating our training in the one tactical
operation. When we began, navigation was the main problem. Now I am
satisfied you can fly to a target in the moonlight at low level. I am
satisfied you can reach it and identify it. As you may have realized, the
actual attack will be no ordinary one, and it will have to be closely
controlled by RT and WT so that everything runs smoothly.

'The purpose of this conference is to discuss this special attack so that
I can get out some form of operational plan when the time comes.'

'When will that be?' asked Dinghy.

'Within the next fortnight; but don't tell anyone, for God's sake,
because I can only repeat that if the Huns knew we were coming they
would take steps to see that we would never get away with it. Photo
aircraft have been over every day and have not yet reported any increase
in the defences. So far security must have been pretty good. But to go on.

'After our navigational problem we had three others:

    (1) how to fly over water at night;
    (2) how to bomb accurately in the special way that is required;
    (3) to find a suitable weapon for the job.

'Well, you boys between you solved the first two, and a crowd of test
pilots and scientists, whom I hope you will meet one day, solved the
other, and the time has now come when our very high standard of training
can be fitted in to carry out our special operation. SASO has given
permission for us to use the reservoirs at Uppingham and Colchester to
practise on. He has fixed up with a film studio or something to rig up
a special framework on the water barrage which will make them look
very much like our own objectives – that is U-boat pens, or whatever
they are.

'From now on we are going to carry out attacks against these places
using nine aircraft at a time. These attacks will begin tonight. The sort
of thing I visualize is three flights of three aircraft flying in formation
at night along our special route. We will reach the first lake; we will
then attack singly, according to my instructions on the RT, from exactly
60 feet and at exactly 232 miles an hour. I needn't tell you again how
necessary it will be to keep to these limits. If you don't, the whole thing
will be a failure. When we have destroyed the first objective, we will fly
down to the next and repeat the tactics. Then we will fly home out along
the special route as if we were actually leaving Germany.

'In the meantime, other crews are to keep their hands in with bombing
and spotlight flying over the Wash. Six other special crews will be sent
to another lake to carry out a special form of attack there.'

'Then you will need practically all serviceable aircraft?' asked Capable. 'Yes, we will want maximum serviceability. From now on your ground crews will have to work twenty-four hours a day, I'm afraid, to do it, but tell 'em it will be worth it in the end. And you, Doc – stop chewing gum – you will have to get your mines organized by the 12th because we will want to drop these on a final practice.'

'It will be a bit of a job, sir,' put in Doc. 'They haven't all arrived yet; that is, the modified ones, and they take twenty-four hours to prepare. You know how short of armourers we are, and my boys have been sweating blood as it is.'

'OK, I will ask the SASO to lend us a few more men; they can give us a hand during the last week. But don't forget that they can't leave the Station once they know that there is something special on.

'Now, another point. We want to practise flying at our proper all-up weight, so that I want the petrol load worked out. Don't forget some of the armour has been taken out. You can do that, Melvyn; get Pulford to work out the full load, and get another Flight-Engineer to check it. Don't exceed 63,000 pounds all up, because we won't get off otherwise.'

'OK,' said Dinghy. 'I believe you want the front gunner to remain in his turret the whole time so that he can deal with any flak guns we may meet. The snag about this is that his feet dangle in front of the bomb-aimer's face. It would be a good idea to fix up some stirrups for his legs, because he would be more comfortable himself and the wretched bomb-aimer wouldn't have to put with the smell of his feet.'

This was a good idea, and the long-suffering Capel was asked to fix up these things right away.

'Another point,' said someone. 'How about fixing a second altimeter in front of the pilot's face attached to the windscreen so that he can see it easily? It will save him looking down into the cockpit when he's near the drink.'

Another good idea, and the instrument boys again were asked to fit up all aircraft by the afternoon.

One by one the boys put forward their suggestions, and most of them were adopted because they were good ideas from chaps who knew their job. What they exactly were cannot be written here because they were and still are secret. Enough to say that many civilian workmen were moving around the hangars working on air-position indicators and other things which all helped navigation and bombing.

'How about radio telephony?' asked Dave Shannon. 'I am pretty hazy about this, not ever having been a fighter boy.'

'Well, as far as I can see, this is the procedure,' I replied. I took from my drawer something I had been working on the night before. 'The idea is that we use plain language, backed up by simple code words. If the radio should fail we will have to use WT as well. We won't use Air

Force code because wars have been lost in the past by the waste of time when decoding. We will invent our own simple code; it must be very simple and self-explanatory. Here's a slip of paper, giving the full gen.'

On this piece of paper were a few short code words which we were to use. For instance, the word 'Dinghy' would mean that the second objective had been destroyed. The word 'Nigger' would mean that the first objective had been destroyed. Words like 'Artichoke' and 'Beer' indicated that we would change frequency from Button A or B. There were many other words, and I told the boys to learn them off by heart.

'Now, the next thing is the procedure,' I went on. 'Hutch here has fitted up in the crew room twenty dummy aircraft headsets. In a minute we will go down there and run through the drill until we know it by heart. I will be the leader, Hoppy will be deputy-leader, and Mickey Martin will be the second deputy-leader. It is important to have two deputies because, you never know, one of us may get shot down. We will do this half an hour a day, and I think it will get us fully into the technique.'

For the next week we started by having our dress rehearsals, and at the same time practising our attack on the ground in the radio room. All this time the water was getting higher on the dams that we were going to attack. Now it was only five feet from the top. When we had all got fully trained in our special form of attack we held a full dress rehearsal which some few senior officers took an interest in. It was a complete failure. Aircraft went astray, some nearly collided, others went home browned off. The trouble was inter-communication. On attacks of this sort there must be no allowance for anything to go wrong, and things had gone wrong here. The radio-telephone sets which we were using were just not good enough. We would have to use fighter sets. When we got back I told the AOC that unless we were equipped with VHF* the whole mission would be a failure. I told him that I had been asking for it for some time. He said, 'I'll fix it.' He was as good as his word. Within a few hours a party of men landed on the aerodrome and went to work. Next day the whole squadron was equipped with the very best and most efficient radio-telephonic sets in the whole of the Royal Air Force. And not only this, but my aircraft and the deputy-leaders had two sets on board, so that if one should go wrong we would have the other.

Next night we carried out another dress rehearsal, and it was a complete success. Everything ran smoothly and there was no hitch: that is, no hitch except that six out of the twelve aircraft were very seriously damaged by the great columns of water set up when their mines splashed in. They had been flying slightly too low. Most of the damage was around the tails of the aircraft; elevators were smashed like plywood, turrets were

* Very High Frequency R/T.

knocked in, fins were bent. It was a miracle some of them got home. This was one of the many snags that the boys had to face while training. On the actual show it wouldn't matter so much because once the mines had dropped the job would be done and the next thing would be to get out of it, no matter how badly the aircraft were damaged by water or anything else. But the main thing was to get the mines into the right spot.

By now it was obvious that we would have to carry out the raid within the next few days – perhaps only two days, because the water level had been reported just right for the attack. The training was now complete. The crews were ready. In all we had done 2,000 hours of flying and had dropped 2,500 practice bombs, and all the boys were rather like a team of racehorses standing in the paddock, waiting for the big event. But the crews were working like slaves repairing the damage done to our aircraft.

Then there were visits to the Met Officer. Aircraft flew far out into the Atlantic, far out past Norway to see what was coming towards us in the way of 'fronts'. God was very kind to us; the weather was perfect. That was the last snag, and it seemed almost too good to be true that old man Met was behaving himself.

The AOC came over on May 15 and told me that we would take off the next night. As he left, a white aeroplane landed on our aerodrome and taxied up to our hangar. Out of it stepped Jeff and Mutt. They had come to see the end of all their work.

That night we stayed up late writing out the operation order. This was important because should the worst happen, and none of us got back, no one would know exactly what we had planned to do.

Hoppy was now told the target, so were Dinghy and Henry as well as Bob. And that night Hoppy saved our lives. The route that SASO and I had planned between us had taken us over Huls, a vast well-defended rubber factory on the edge of the Ruhr which wasn't marked on the flak map. He happened to know all this, and suggested that we should go a little farther north. If Hoppy hadn't known, we would have gone over that factory, and it would have been just too bad. We went to bed at midnight. As we were leaving Charles came rushing up with a white face.

'Look here, Guy, I'm awfully sorry, Nigger's had it; he has just been run over by a car outside the camp. He was killed instantaneously.'

And so I went back to my room on the eve of this adventure with my dog gone – the squadron mascot.

The Doc handed the boys some sleeping pills as they went to bed so that they should get a good night's sleep before they went off. Then I was alone in my room looking at the scratch-marks on the door Nigger used to make when he wanted to go out, and feeling very depressed.

Next day, on May 16, reconnaissance aircraft reported that the defences on the dam had remained unchanged and that the water level was just right for the attack. It was a great moment when the public-address system on the station said, 'All crews of No. 617 Squadron report to the briefing room immediately.' The boys came in hushed, having waited two and a half months to hear what it was they were going to attack. There were about 133 young men in that room, rather tousled and a little scruffy, and perhaps a little old-looking in spite of their youth. But now they were experts, beautifully trained, and each one of them knew his job as well as any man had ever known any job he was to do.

I let the scientist tell them all about it. In his gentle, benign way he repeated almost exactly the things that he had told me a long time before. He told them how and why the dam had been made and of what it was built. He told them how thick it was and how difficult it would be to crack, and he told them of the principles upon which we were going to work. He told them that it was not going to be easy, and everyone understood what he was trying to say. At the same time they were relieved to know at last what they were going to attack. This was not going to be too bad, they thought. The strain had begun to tell on them, because it is not a very pleasant feeling when you know you are training for a dangerous job and do not know what the target is.

The rest of the day was a terrific flap. There was testing of aircraft and checking of instruments; there were tractors driving round the aerodrome carrying the mines which were to be fitted to our aircraft. There was Doc Watson rushing round on his motor-bike looking worried. There was the engineer staff putting finishing touches to the aircraft which had been damaged; a new turret here, a repaired fin there. They finished the last one at five that afternoon. There were Jeff and Mutt walking round inspecting each aircraft and satisfying themselves that everything was perfect. There was a lot to be done and very little time to do it in. And while I was going out to my aircraft to give it a bounce round I gave instructions to Chiefy Powell about Nigger. I realized that this was a very bad omen, and told him to keep it dark. I asked him to bury Nigger at midnight that night, when we would be crossing the enemy coast. And while he was being buried I hoped that we would be going over to give his friendly little soul an uplift with the job we were about to do.

There was no lunch that day. Jeff came running up at the last minute and said in a strange voice:

'We have got the wrong oil.' He was nearly shouting. He said, 'Stores here haven't got any. We shall have to find some from somewhere else. If we cannot they may not work.'

I didn't understand what he was talking about, but an aeroplane was put at his disposal, and apparently the right stuff was found, because I heard nothing more about it.

It was a boiling hot day, but all air crews spent three hours of the afternoon studying the models of the dams. They studied and stared at them and drew them and photographed them on their minds until they knew exactly what they looked like. Then they asked each other questions from memory as to the position of the guns, the length of water and other vital points.

As the day cooled down we had our briefing. I will never forget that briefing. Two service policemen stood outside on guard. The doors were locked. No one was allowed in except the boys who were going to do the job and four other men. No one, not even Fighter Command or our own Group Headquarters, knew we were operating. They thought it was just a training operation.

I introduced Jeff to the boys, and he repeated more or less what he had said that morning, but this time he told them some of the difficulties he had had in developing the weapon. He was very worried, I knew, because he felt responsible for sending these boys off to this target and personally responsible for each and every one of their lives. He said to me, 'I hope they all come back.' I said, 'It won't be your fault if they don't.' He said, 'You know, I hardly look upon this as an operational mission. My job has just been to develop something which will break down a dam wall. I look upon this raid as my last great experiment to see if it can be done on the actual thing.'

While we were talking, the AOC was giving the boys a pep talk. He spoke well, but one remark I shall always remember.

'Now you are off on a raid which will do a tremendous amount of damage. It will become historic. Everyone will want to know how you did it, and it will be very difficult not to tell them. You must not do so because we have other uses for the weapon. I am giving you this warning now because, having watched your training from the beginning, I know that the attack will succeed.'

Then I got up and explained the type of attack which we were to use, although by now they knew it backwards because they had practised it so often. Nevertheless, I spoke for just over an hour and detailed the final plan. This was roughly as follows:

The Force was divided into three formations. The first consisted of:

> Myself,
> Hoppy,
> Mickey,
> Dinghy,
> Bill Astell,
> David Maltby,
> Henry,
> Les Knight,
> Dave Shannon,

and it was our job, being the best bomb crews in the squadron, to attack the Möhne Dam first and then carry on to the second dam, the Eder. When we had breached those, the attack would be over, but the big point was, we did not want a small breach; we wanted something really large; and so we were to carry on until we had used up all our mines. Our aim was to punch holes in them about 100 yards across.

The second formation consisted of:

> Joe McCarthy,
> F/Sgt Byers,
> F/Lt Barlow,
> P/O Rice,
> Les Munro.

This formation was really to act as a diversionary force and to attack the Sorpe. These boys were to fly out in formation and to cross the enemy coast far from where we were crossing it, so as to make a diversion and to split up enemy fighter forces. When they got to the Sorpe Dam they were to fire off Very lights and generally create a disturbance which would cause the fighters to go over there and draw them away from us. Their attack was a very special type which they had practised on their own for some time because the Sorpe was a different type of dam and required an entirely different technique.

The rest, consisting of:

> P/O Townsend,
> F/Sgt Anderson,
> P/O Brown,
> P/O Ottley,

were a rear formation which we would use to fill in gaps left in the first two. This would be easy because we would all be in radio touch. The other two crews which I have not mentioned had, unfortunately, fallen sick and couldn't fly. Nineteen of us were going to take the air.

So the briefing came to an end. Everyone knew exactly what to do; everyone knew the plan. We went up to the Mess and had some bacon and eggs.

Dinghy said to me, 'Can I have your egg if you don't come back?'

This was the well-known corny joke because each crew was allowed to have an egg after a successful operational mission, and eggs were considered delicacies because they were very scarce. I said 'Sugar off,' and told him to do something very difficult to himself. But there wasn't much time, and I went down to change.

Standing around for an hour and a half before the take-off, every one was tense and no one said very much. The long practice and the waiting and the business of being kept in the dark had keyed them up to a point where one could feel that they would have been better if they had stood on their toes and danced and shouted out loud, or even screamed to get rid of it, but they atood there with their hands in their pockets, smoking cigarettes and saying little.

I said to Hoppy, 'Hoppy, tonight's the night; tomorrow we will get drunk.'

We always said this, Hoppy and I, before going off on a mission. Then he jumped into a van which carried him out to his aircraft.

I could never hope to describe a time like this, and will leave it to what Humphreys, the Adjutant, wrote in his squadron diary:

'This was Der Tag for 617 Squadron. Hardly a soul with the exception of the crews knew the target. Very few people outside the squadron knew we were operating – not even the Waafs. From eight o'clock onwards the scenes outside the crew rooms were something to be remembered. It was not like an ordinary operational scene, all the crews on this occasion being aware of the terrific task confronting them. Most of them wore expressions varying from the "don't care a damn" to the grim and determined. On the whole I think it appeared rather reminiscent of a crusade.

'Dave was late, leaving the crew room quite a while after his own crew were in the plane and I anxiously wondered if our David, in his usual light-hearted manner, had forgotten all about it. The Wing-Commander turned up in his car prompt to time with crew. How they all got into that car beats me. He looked fit and well and quite unperturbed. [This was a complete lie. – G. G.] Our Favourite Yank, F/L McCarthy, caused quite a disturbance. He arrived at his aircraft and after finding she had hydraulic trouble came dashing back to our only reserve aircraft. When inside he noticed he had no compass card and came rushing back to the Flights frantically screaming for one. He had also pulled his parachute by mistake and the white silk was streaming all over the ground, trailing behind him. With perspiration dropping off his face, good old Mac ran back to his aircraft with everyone behind him trying to fix him up with what he wanted. He got off just in time.'

At exactly the right time Hutch fired a red Very light, and all the aircraft started up. There was to be RT silence until we crossed the enemy coast.

The AOC walked into my ship and wished me the best of luck, and I replied with a sickly grin. An RAF photographer came running up and asked to take a picture – these men certainly choose the queerest

times. Then we ambled out on to the runway in our formation and stood
there waiting to take off. Someone at the Control caravan waved a flag
and I opened the throttles and we were off for Germany. The Adjutant
wrote:

> 'The great machines with their loads trundled off in formation and
> left the grass surface while onlookers held their breath. All went well,
> however, but they all seemed to get airborne after extremely long runs.
> After they had gone and Lincoln was silent once more and the evening
> mist began to settle on the aerodrome, the squadron personnel sat
> around talking in groups for a short time and then dispersed to their
> respective quarters with the object of returning when the machines
> were due to land. It all seemed very quiet and we wished the boys over
> there Good Luck and a successful mission.'

CHAPTER EIGHTEEN

SOME WERE UNLUCKY

We had been flying for about an hour and ten minutes in complete
silence, each one busy with his thoughts, while the waves were slopping
by a few feet below with monotonous regularity. And the moon dancing
in those waves had become almost a hypnotising crystal. As Terry spoke
he jerked us into action. He said, 'Five minutes to go to the Dutch coast,
skip.'

I said, 'Good,' and looked ahead. Pulford turned on the spotlights and
told me to go down much lower; we were about 100 feet off the water.
Jim Deering, in the front turret, began to swing it from either way,
ready to deal with any flak ships which might be watching for minelayers off the coast. Hutch sat in his wireless cabin ready to send a flak
warning to the rest of the boys who might run into trouble behind us.
Trevor took off his Mae West and squeezed himself back into the rear
turret. On either side the boys tucked their blunt-nosed Lancs in even
closer than they were before, while the crews inside them were probably
doing the same sort of things as my own. Someone began whistling
nervously over the intercom. Someone else said, 'Shut up.'

Then Spam said, 'There's the coast.'

I said, 'No, it's not; that's just low cloud and shadows on the sea from
the moon.'

But he was right and I was wrong, and soon we could see the Dutch
islands approaching. They looked low and flat and evil in the full moon,

squirting flak in many directions because their radar would now know we were coming. But we knew all about their defences, and as we drew near this squat and unfriendly expanse we began to look for the necessary landmarks which would indicate how to get through that barrage. We began to behave like a ship threading its way through a minefield, in danger of destruction on either side, but safe if we were lucky and on the right track. Terry came up beside me to check up on Spam. He opened the side windows and looked out to scan the coast with his night glasses. 'Can't see much,' he said. 'We're too low, but I reckon we must be on track because there's so little wind.'

'Hope so.'

'Stand by, front gunner; we're going over.'

'OK. All lights off. No talking. Here we go.'

With a roar we hurtled over the Western Wall, skirting the defences and turning this way and that to keep to our thin line of safety; for a moment we held our breath. Then I gave a sigh of relief; no one had fired a shot. We had taken them by surprise.

'Good effort, Terry. Next course.'

'105 degrees magnetic.'

We had not been on the new course for more than two minutes before we came to more sea again; we had obviously just passed over a small island, and this was wrong. Our proper track should have taken us between the two islands, as both were fairly heavily defended, but by the grace of God the gunners on the one we had just passed over were apparently asleep. We pulled up high to about 300 feet to have a look and find out where we were, then scrammed down on the deck again as Terry said, 'OK – there's the windmill and those wireless masts. We must have drifted to starboard. Steer new course – 095 degrees magnetic, and be careful of a little town that is coming up straight ahead.'

'OK, Terry, I'll go around it.'

We were turning to the left now, and as we turned I noticed with satisfaction that Hoppy and Mickey were still flying there in perfect formation.

We were flying low. We were flying so low that more than once Spam yelled at me to pull up quickly to avoid high-tension wires and tall trees. Away on the right we could see the small town, its chimneys outlined against the night sky; we thought we saw someone flash us a 'V', but it may have been an innkeeper poking his head out of his bedroom window. The noise must have been terrific.

Our new course should have followed a very straight canal, which led to a T-shaped junction, and beyond that was the Dutch frontier and Germany. All eyes began looking out to see if we were right, because we could not afford to be wrong. Sure enough, the canal came up slowly from underneath the starboard wing and we began to follow it carefully, straight above it, for now we were mighty close to Eindhoven, which had the reputation of being very well defended. Then, after a few minutes, that too had passed behind and we saw a glint of silvery light straight ahead. This was the canal junction, the second turning point.

It did not take Spam long to see where we were; now we were right on track, and Terry again gave the new course for the River Rhine. A few minutes later we crossed the German frontier, and Terry said, in his matter-of-fact way: 'We'll be at the target in an hour and a half. The next thing to see is the Rhine.'

But we did not all get through. One aircraft, P/O Rice, had already hit the sea, bounced up, lost both its outboard engines and its weapon, and had flown back on the inboard two. Les Munro had been hit by flak a little later on, and his aircraft was so badly damaged that he was forced to return to base. I imagined the feelings of the crews of these aircraft who, after many weeks of intense practice and expectation, at the last moment could only hobble home and land with nothing accomplished. I felt very sorry for them. This left sixteen aircraft going on; 112 men.

The journey into the Ruhr Valley was not without excitement. They did not like our coming. And they knew we were coming. We were the only aircraft operating that night; it was too bright for the main forces. And so, deep down in their underground plotting-rooms, the Hun controllers stayed awake to watch us as we moved steadily on. We had a rough idea how they worked, these controllers, moving fighter squadrons to orbit points in front of us, sounding air-raid sirens here and there, tipping off the gun positions along our route and generally trying to make it pretty uncomfortable for the men who were bound for 'Happy Valley'. As yet they would not know where we were going, because our route was planned to make feint attacks and fox their control. Only the warning sirens would have sounded in all the cities from Bremen southwards. As yet, the fighters would be unable to get good plots on us because we were flying so low, but once we were there the job would have to take quite a time and they would have their chance.

We flew on. Germany seemed dead. Not a sign of movement, of light of a moving creature stirred the ground. There was no flak, there was nothing. Just us.

And so we came to the Rhine. This is virtually the entrance to the Ruhr Valley; the barrier our armies must cross before they march into the big towns of Essen and Dortmund. It looked white and calm and sinister in the moonlight. But it presented no difficulties to us. As it came up, Spam said, 'We are six miles south. Better turn right, skip. Duisburg is not far away.'

As soon as he mentioned Duisburg my hands acted before my brain, for they were more used to this sort of thing, and the Lanc banked steeply to follow the Rhine up to our crossing point. For Duisburg is not a healthy place to fly over at 100 feet. There are hundreds of guns there, both light and heavy, apart from all those searchlights, and the defences have had plenty of experience . . .

As we flew up – 'How did that happen?'

'Don't know, skip. Compass u/s?'

'Couldn't be.'

'Hold on, I will just check my figures.'

Later – 'I'm afraid I misread my writing, skip. The course I gave you should have been another ten degrees to port.'

'OK, Terry. That might have been an expensive mistake.'

During our steep turn the boys had lost contact, but now they were just beginning to form up again; it was my fault the turn had been too steep, but the name Duisburg or Essen, or any of the rest of them, always does that to me. As we flew along the Rhine there were barges on the river equipped with quick-firing guns and they shot at us as we flew over, but our gunners gave back as good as they got; then we found what we wanted, a sort of small inland harbour, and we turned slowly towards the east. Terry said monotonously, 'Thirty minutes to go and we are there.'

As we passed on into the Ruhr Valley we came to more and more trouble, for now we were in the outer light-flak defences, and these were very active, but by weaving and jinking we were able to escape most of them. Time and again searchlights would pick us up, but we were flying very low and, although it may sound foolish and untrue when I say so, we avoided a great number of them by dodging behind the trees. Once we went over a brand-new aerodrome which was very heavily defended and which had not been marked on our combat charts. Immediately all three of us in front were picked up by the searchlights and held. Suddenly Trevor, in the rear turret, began firing away trying to scare them enough to turn out their lights, then he shouted that they had gone behind some tall trees. At the same time Spam was yelling that he would soon be shaving himself by the tops of some corn in a field. Hutch immediately sent out a flak warning to all the boys behind so that they could avoid this unattractive area. On either side of me, Mickey and Hoppy, who were a little higher, were flying along brightly illuminated; I could see their letters quite clearly, 'TAJ' and 'MAJ', standing out like Broadway signs. Then a long string of tracer came out from Hoppy's rear turret and I lost him in the momentary darkness as the searchlights popped out. One of the pilots, a grand Englishman from Derbyshire, was not so lucky. He was flying well out to the left. He got blinded in the searchlights and, for a second, lost control. His aircraft reared up like a stricken horse, plunged on to the deck and burst into flames; five seconds later his mine blew up with a tremendous explosion. Bill Astell had gone.

The minutes passed slowly as we all sweated on this summer's night, sweated at working the controls and sweated with fear as we flew on. Every railway train, every hamlet and every bridge we passed was a potential danger, for our Lancasters were sitting targets at that height and speed. We fought our way past Dortmund, past Hamm – the well-known Hamm which has been bombed so many times; we could see it quite clearly now, its tall chimneys, factories and balloons capped by its umbrella of flak like a Christmas tree about five miles to our right; then we began turning to the right in between Hamm and the little town of Soest, where I nearly got shot down in 1940. Soest was sleepy now and did not open up, and out of the haze ahead appeared the Ruhr hills.

'We're there,' said Spam.

'Thank God,' said I, feelingly.

As we came over the hill, we saw the Möhne Lake. Then we saw the dam itself. In that light it looked squat and heavy and unconquerable; it looked grey and solid in the moonlight, as though it were part of the countryside itself and just as immovable. A structure like a battleship was showering out flak all along its length, but some came from the power-house below it and nearby. There were no searchlights. It was light flak, mostly green, yellow and red, and the colours of the tracer reflected upon the face of the water in the lake. The reflections on the dead calm of the black water made it seem there was twice as much as there really was.

'Did you say these gunners were out of practice?' asked Spam, sarcastically.

'They certainly seem awake now,' said Terry.

They were awake all right. No matter what people say, the Germans certainly have a good warning system. I scowled to myself as I remembered telling the boys an hour or so ago that they would probably only be the German equivalent of the Home Guard and in bed by the time we arrived.

It was hard to say exactly how many guns there were, but tracers seemed to be coming from about five positions, probably making twelve guns in all. It was hard at first to tell the calibre of the shells, but after one of the boys had been hit, we were informed over the RT that they were either 20-mm type or 37-mm, which, as everyone knows, are nasty little things.

We circled around stealthily, picking up the various landmarks upon which we had planned our method of attack, making use of some and avoiding others; every time we came within range of those bloody-minded flak-gunners they let us have it.

'Bit aggressive, aren't they?' said Trevor.

'Too right they are.'

I said to Terry, 'God, this light flak gives me the creeps.'

'Me, too,' someone answered.

For a time there was a general bind on the subject of light flak, and the only man who didn't say anything was Hutch, because he could not see it and because he never said anything about flak, anyway. But this was not the time for talking. I called up each member of our formation and found, to my relief, that they had all arrived, except, of course, Bill Astell. Away to the south, Joe McCarthy had just begun his diversionary attack on the Sorpe. But not all of them had been able to get there; both Byers and Barlow had been shot down by light flak after crossing the coast; these had been replaced by other aircraft of the rear formation. Bad luck, this being shot down after crossing the coast, because it could have happened to anybody; they must have been a mile or so off track and had got the hammer. This is the way things are in flying; you are either lucky or you aren't. We, too, had crossed the coast at the wrong place and had got away with it. We were lucky.

Down below, the Möhne Lake was silent and black and deep, and I spoke to my crew.

'Well, boys, I suppose we had better start the ball rolling.' This with no enthusiasm whatsoever. 'Hello, all Cooler aircraft. I am going to attack. Stand by to come in to attack in your order when I tell you.'

Then to Hoppy: 'Hello, "M Mother". Stand by to take over if anything happens.'

Hoppy's clear and casual voice came back. 'OK, Leader. Good luck.'

Then the boys dispersed to the pre-arranged hiding-spots in the hills, so that they should not be seen either from the ground or from the air, and we began to get into position for our approach. We circled wide and came around down moon, over the high hills at the eastern end of the lake. On straightening up we began to dive towards the flat, ominous water two miles away. Over the front turret was the dam silhouetted against the haze of the Ruhr Valley. We could see the towers. We could see the sluices. We could see everything. Spam, the bomb-aimer, said 'Good show. This is wizard.' He had been a bit worried, as all bomb-aimers are, in case they cannot see their aiming points, but as we came in over the tall fir trees his voice came up again rather quickly. 'You're going to hit them. You're going to hit those trees.'

'That's all right, Spam. I'm just getting my height.'

To Terry: 'Check height, Terry.'

To Pulford: 'Speed control, Flight-Engineer.'

To Trevor: 'All guns ready, gunners.'

To Spam: 'Coming up, Spam.'

Terry turned on the spotlights and began giving directions – 'Down – down – down. Steady – steady.' We were then exactly sixty feet.

Pulford began working the speed; first he put on a little flap to slow us down, then he opened the throttles to get the air-speed indicator exactly against the red mark. Spam began lining up his sights against the towers. He had turned the fusing switch to the 'ON' position. I began flying.

The gunners had seen us coming. They could see us coming with our spotlights on for over two miles away. Now they opened up and the tracers began swirling towards us; some were even bouncing off the smooth surface of the lake. This was a horrible moment: we were being dragged along at four miles a minute, almost against our will, towards the things we were going to destroy. I think at that moment the boys did not want to go. I know I did not want to go. I thought to myself, 'In another minute we shall all be dead – so what?' I thought again, 'This is terrible – this feeling of fear – if it is fear.' By now we were a few hundred yards away, and I said quickly to Pulford, under my breath, 'Better leave the throttles open now and stand by to pull me out of the seat if I get hit.' As I glanced at him I thought he looked a little glum on hearing this.

The Lancaster was really moving and I began looking through the special sight on my windscreen. Spam had his eyes glued to the bomb-sight in front, his hand on his button; a special mechanism on board had already begun to work so that the mine would drop (we hoped) in the right spot. Terry was still checking the height. Joe and Trev began to raise their guns. The flak could see us quite clearly now. It was not exactly inferno. I have been through far worse flak fire than that; but we were very low. There was something sinister and slightly unnerving about the whole operation. My aircraft was so small and the dam was so large; it was thick and solid, and now it was angry. My aircraft was very small. We skimmed along the surface of the lake, and as we went my gunner was firing into the defences, and the defences were firing back with vigour, their shells whistling past us. For some reason, we were not being hit.

Spam said, 'Left – little more left – steady – steady – steady – coming up.' Of the next few seconds I remember only a series of kaleidoscopic incidents.

The chatter from Joe's front guns pushing out tracers which bounced off the left-hand flak tower.

Pulford crouching beside me.

The smell of burnt cordite.

The cold sweat underneath my oxygen mask.

The tracers flashing past the windows – they all seemed the same colour now – and the inaccuracy of the gun positions near the power-station; they were firing in the wrong direction.

The closeness of the dam wall.

Spam's exultant, 'Mine gone.'

Hutch's red Very lights to blind the flak-gunners.

The speed of the whole thing.

Someone saying over the RT, 'Good show, leader. Nice work.'

Then it was all over, and at last we were out of range, and there came over us all, I think, an immense feeling of relief and confidence.

Trevor said, 'I will get those bastards,' and he began to spray the dam with bullets until at last he, too, was out of range. As we circled round we could see a great 1,000-feet column of whiteness still hanging in the air where our mine had exploded. We could see with satisfaction that Spam had been good, and it had gone off in the right position. Then, as we came closer, we could see that the explosion of the mine had caused a great disturbance upon the surface of the lake and the water had become broken and furious, as though it were being lashed by a gale. At first we thought that the dam itself had broken, because great sheets of water were slopping over the top of the wall like a gigantic basin. This caused some delay, because our mines could only be dropped in calm water, and we would have to wait until all became still again.

We waited.

We waited about ten minutes, but it seemed hours to us. It must have seemed even longer to Hoppy, who was the next to attack. Meanwhile, all the fighters had now collected over our target. They knew our game by now, but we were flying too low for them; they could not see us and there were no attacks.

'At last – 'Hello, "M Mother". You may attack now. Good luck.'

'OK. Attacking.'

Hoppy, the Englishman, casual, but very efficient, keen now on only one thing, which was war. He began his attack.

He began going down over the trees where I had come from a few moments before. We could see his spotlights quite clearly, slowly closing together as he ran across the water. We saw him approach. The flak, by now, had got an idea from which direction the attack was coming, and they let him have it. When he was about 100 yards away someone said, hoarsely, over the RT: 'Hell! he has been hit.'

'M Mother' was on fire; an unlucky shot had got him in one of the inboard petrol tanks and a long jet of flame was beginning to stream out. I saw him drop his mine, but his bomb-aimer must have been wounded, because it fell straight on to the power-house on the other side of the dam. But Hoppy staggered on, trying to gain altitude so that his crew could bale out. When he had got up to 500 feet there was a vivid flash in the sky and one wing fell off; his aircraft disintegrated and fell to the ground in cascading, flaming fragments. There it began to burn quite gently and rather sinisterly in a field some three miles beyond the dam.

Someone said, 'Poor old Hoppy!'

Another said, 'We'll get those bastards for this.'

A furious rage surged up inside my own crew, and Trevor said, 'Let's go in and murder those gunners.' As he spoke, Hoppy's mine went up.

It went up behind the power-house with a tremendous yellow explosion and left in the air a great ball of black smoke; again there was a long wait while we watched for this to clear. There was so little wind that it took a long time.

Many minutes later I told Mickey to attack; he seemed quite confident, and we ran in beside him and a little in front; as we turned, Trevor did his best to get those gunners as he had promised.

Bob Hay, Mickey's bomb-aimer, did a good job, and his mine dropped in exactly the right place. There was again a gigantic explosion as the whole surface of the lake shook, then spewed forth its cascade of white water. Mickey was all right; he got through. But he had been hit several times and one wing-tank lost all its petrol. I could see the vicious tracer from his rear-gunner giving one gun position a hail of bullets as he swept over. Then he called up, 'OK. Attack completed.' It was then that I thought that the dam wall had moved. Of course we could not see anything, but if Jeff's theory had been correct, it should have cracked by now. If only we could go on pushing it by dropping more successful mines, it would surely move back on its axis and collapse.

Once again we watched for the water to calm down. Then in came Melvyn Young in 'D Dog'. I yelled to him, 'Be careful of the flak. It's pretty hot.'

He said, 'OK.'

I yelled again, 'Trevor's going to beat them up on the other side. He'll take most of it off you.'

Melvyn's voice again. 'OK. Thanks.' And so as 'D Dog' ran in we stayed at a fairly safe distance on the other side, firing with all guns at the defences, and the defences, like the stooges they were, firing back at us. We were both out of range of each other, but the ruse seemed to work, and we flicked on our identification lights to let them see us even more clearly. Melvyn's mine went in, again in exactly the right spot, and this time a colossal wall of water swept right over the dam and kept on going. Melvyn said, 'I think I've done it. I've broken it.' But we were in a better position to see than he, and it had not rolled down yet. We were all getting pretty excited by now, and I screamed like a schoolboy over the RT: 'Wizard show, Melvyn. I think it'll go on the next one.'

Now we had been over the Möhne for quite a long time, and all the while I had been in contact with Scampton Base. We were in close contact with the Air Officer Commanding and the Commander-in-Chief of Bomber Command, and with the scientist, observing his own greatest scientific experiment in Damology. He was sitting in the operations room, his head in his hands, listening to the reports as one after another the aircraft attacked. On the other side of the room the Commander-in-Chief paced up and down. In a way their job of waiting was worse than mine.

The only difference was that they did not know that the structure was shifting as I knew, even though I could not see anything clearly.

When at last the water had all subsided I called up No. 5 – David Maltby – and told him to attack. He came in fast, and I saw his mine fall within feet of the right spot; once again the flak, the explosion and wall of water. But this time we were on the wrong side of the wall and could see what had happened. We watched for about five minutes, and it was rather hard to see anything, for by now the air was full of spray from these explosions, which had settled like mist on our windscreens. Time was getting short, so I called up Dave Shannon and told him to come in.

As he turned I got close to the dam wall and then saw what had happened. It had rolled over, but I could not believe my eyes. I heard someone shout, 'I think she has gone! I think she has gone!' Other voices took up the cry and quickly I said, 'Stand by until I make a recco.' I remembered that Dave was going in to attack and told him to turn away and not to approach the target. We had a closer look. Now there was no doubt about it; there was a great breach 100 yards across, and the water, looking like stirred porridge in the moonlight, was gushing out and rolling into the Ruhr Valley towards the industrial centres of Germany's Third Reich.

Nearly all the flak had now stopped, and the other boys came down from the hills to have a closer look to see what had been done. There was no doubt about it at all – the Möhne Dam had been breached and the gunners on top of the dam, except for one man, had all run for their lives towards the safety of solid ground; this remaining gunner was a brave man, but one of the boys quickly extinguished his flak with a burst of well-aimed tracer. Now it was all quiet, except for the roar of the water which steamed and hissed its way from its 150-foot head. Then we began to shout and scream and act like madmen over the RT, for this was a tremendous sight, a sight which probably no man will ever see again.

Quickly I told Hutch to tap out the message, 'Nigger', to my station, and when this was handed to the Air Officer Commanding there was (I heard afterwards) great excitement in the operations room. The scientist jumped up and danced round the room.

Then I looked again at the dam and at the water, while all around me the boys were doing the same. It was the most amazing sight. The whole valley was beginning to fill with fog from the steam of the gushing water, and down in the foggy valley we saw cars speeding along the roads in front of this great wave of water, which was chasing them and going faster than they could ever hope to go. I saw their headlights burning and I saw water overtake them, wave by wave, and then the colour of the headlights underneath the water changing from light blue to green, from green to dark purple, until there was no longer anything except the water bouncing down in great waves. The floods raced on, carrying with them as they went – viaducts, railways, bridges and everything that stood in their path. Three miles beyond the damn the remains of Hoppy's aircraft were still burning gently, a dull red glow on the ground. Hoppy had been avenged.

Then I felt a little remote and unreal sitting up there in the warm cockpit of my Lancaster, watching this mighty power which we had unleashed; then glad, because I knew that this was the heart of Germany, and the heart of her industries, the place which itself had unleashed so much misery upon the whole world.

We knew, as we watched, that this flood-water would not win the war; it would not do anything like that, but it was a catastrophe for Germany.

I circled round for about three minutes, then called up all aircraft and told Mickey and David Maltby to go home and the rest to follow me to Eder, where we would try to repeat the performance.

We set our course from the southern tip of the Möhne Lake, which was already fast emptying itself – we could see that even now – and flew on in the clear light of the early morning towards the south-east. We flew on over little towns tucked away in the valleys underneath the Ruhr Mountains. Little places, these, the Exeters and Baths of Germany; they seemed quiet and undisturbed and picturesque as they lay sleeping there on the morning of May 17. The thought crossed my mind of the amazing mentality of German airmen, who went out of their way to bomb such defenceless districts. At the same time a bomb or two on board would not have been out of place to wake them up as a reprisal.

At the Sorpe Dam, Joe McCarthy and Joe Brown had already finished their work. They had both made twelve dummy runs and had dropped their mines along the lip of the concrete wall in the right spot. But they had not been able to see anything spectacular, for these earthen dams are difficult nuts to crack and would require a lot of explosive to shift them. It looked as if we would not have enough aircraft to finish that job successfully because of our losses on the way in. However, the Sorpe was not a priority target, and only contributed a small amount of water to the Ruhr Valley Catchment Area.

After flying low across the treetops, up and down the valleys, we at last reached the Eder Lake and, by flying down it for some five minutes, we arrived over the Eder Dam. It took some finding because fog was already beginning to form in the valleys, and it was pretty hard to tell one part of the reservoir filled with water, from another valley filled with fog. We circled up for a few minutes waiting for Henry, Dave and Les to catch up; we had lost them on the way. Then I called up on the RT.

'Hello, Cooler aircraft – can you see the target?'

Dave answered faintly, 'I think I'm in the vicinity. I can't see anything. I cannot find the dam.'

'Stand by – I will fire a red Very light – right over the dam.' No sooner had Hutch fired his Very pistol than Dave called up again. 'OK – I was a bit south. I'm coming up.'

The other boys had seen the signal too, and after a few minutes we rendezvous'd in a left-hand orbit over the target. But time was getting short now; the glow in the north had begun to get brighter, heralding the coming dawn. Soon it would be daylight, and we did not want this in our ill-armed and unarmoured Lancasters.

I said, 'OK, Dave. You begin your attack.'

It was very hilly all round. The dam was situated, beautifully, I thought, in a deep valley with high hills all around densely covered with fir trees. At the far end, overlooking it, was rather a fine Gothic castle with magnificent grounds. In order to make a successful approach our aircraft would have to dive steeply over this castle, dropping down on to the water from 1,000 feet to 60 feet – level out – let go the mine – then do a steep climbing turn to starboard to avoid a rocky mountain about a mile on the other side of the dam. It was much more inaccessible than the Möhne Valley and called for a much higher degree of skill in flying. There did not seem to be any defences, though, probably because it was an out-of-the-way spot and the gunners would not have got the warning. Maybe they had just been warned and were now getting out of their beds in the nearby village before cycling up the steep hill to get to their gun emplacements. Dave circled wide and then turned to go in. He dived down rather too steeply and sparks came from his engine, as he had to pull out at full boost to avoid hitting the mountain on the north side. As he was doing so . . .

'Sorry, leader. I made a mess of that. I'll try again.'

He tried again. He tried five times, but each time he was not satisfied and would not allow his bomb-aimer to drop his mine. He spoke again on the RT 'I think I had better circle round a bit and try and get used to this place.'

'OK, Dave. You hang around for a bit, and I'll get another aircraft to have a crack – Hello, "Z Zebra" ' (this was Henry). 'You can go in now.'

Henry made two attempts. He said he found it very difficult, and gave the other boys some advice on the best way to go about it. Then he called up and told us that he was going in to make his final run. We could see him running in. Suddenly he pulled away; something seemed to be wrong, but he turned quickly, climbed up over the mountain and put his nose right down, literally flinging his machine into the valley. This time he was running straight and true for the middle of the wall. We saw his spotlights together, so he must have been at 60 feet. We saw the red ball of his Very light shooting out behind his tail, and we knew he had dropped his weapon. A split second later we saw something else; Henry Maudsley had dropped his mine too late. It had hit the top of the parapet and had exploded immediately on impact with a slow, yellow, vivid flame which lit up the whole valley like daylight for just a few seconds. We could see him quite clearly banking steeply a few feet above it. Perhaps the blast was doing that. It all seemed so sudden and vicious and the flame seemed so very cruel. Someone said, 'He has blown himself up.'

Trevor said, 'Bomb-aimer must have been wounded.'

It looked as though Henry had been unlucky enough to do the thing we all might have done.

I spoke to him quickly, 'Henry – Henry. "Z Zebra" – "Z Zebra". Are you OK?' No answer. I called again. Then we all thought we heard a very faint, tired voice say, 'I think so – stand by'. It seemed as though he was dazed, and his voice did not sound natural. But Henry had disappeared. There was no burning wreckage on the ground; there was no aircraft on fire in the air. There was nothing. Henry had disappeared. He never came back.

Once more the smoke from his explosion filled the valley, and we all had to wait for a few minutes. The glow in the north was much brighter, and we would have to hurry up if we wanted to get back.

We waited patiently for it to clear away.

At last to Dave – 'OK. Attack now, David. Good luck.'

Dave went in and, after a good dummy run, managed to put his mine up against the wall, more or less in the middle. He turned on his landing light as he pulled away and we saw the spot of light climbing steeply over the mountain as he jerked his great Lancaster almost vertically over the top. Behind me there was that explosion which, by now, we had got used to, but the wall of the Eder Dam did not move.

Meanwhile, Les Knight had been circling very patiently, not saying a word. I told him to get ready, and when the water had calmed down he began his attack. Les, the Australian, had some difficulty too, and after a while Dave began to give him some advice on how to do it. We all joined in on the RT, and there was a continuous back-chat going on.

'Come on, Les. Come in down the moon; dive towards the point and then turn left.'

'OK, Digger. It's pretty difficult.'

'Not that way, Dig. This way.'

'Too right it's difficult. I'm climbing up to have another crack.'

After a while I called up rather impatiently and told them that a joke was a joke and that we would have to be getting back. Then Les dived in to make his final attack. His was the last weapon left in the squadron. If he did not succeed in breaching the Eder now, then it would never be breached; at least, not tonight.

I saw him run in. I crossed my fingers. But Les was a good pilot and he made as perfect a run as any seen that night. We were flying above him, and about 400 yards to the right, and saw his mine hit the water. We saw where it sank. We saw the tremendous earthquake which shook the base of the dam, and then, as if a gigantic hand had punched a hole through cardboard, the whole thing collapsed. A great mass of water began running down the valley into Kassel. Les was very excited. He kept his radio transmitter on by mistake for quite some time. His crew's remarks were something to be heard, but they couldn't be put into print here. Dave was very excited and said, 'Good show, Dig!' I called them up and told them to go home immediately. I would meet them in the Mess afterwards for the biggest party of all time.

The valley below the Eder was steeper than the Ruhr, and we followed the water down for some way. We watched it swirling and slopping in a 30-foot wall as it tore round the steep bends of the countryside. We saw it crash down in six great waves, swiping off power-stations and roads as it went. We saw it extinguish all the lights in the neighbourhood as though a great black shadow had been drawn across the earth. I. all reminded us of a vast moving train. But we knew that a few miles farther on lay some of the Luftwaffe's largest training bases. We knew that it was a modern field with every convenience, including underground hangars and underground sleeping quarters . . . We turned for home.

Dave and Les, still jabbering at each other on RT, had by now turned for home as well. Their voices died away in the distance as we set our course for the Möhne Lake to see how far it was empty. Hutch sent out a signal to Base using the code word, 'Dinghy', telling them the good news – and they asked us if we had any more aircraft available to prang the third target. 'No, none,' I said. 'None,' tapped Hutch.

Now we were out of RT range of our base and were relying on WT for communication. Gradually, by code words, we were told of the movements of the other aircraft. Peter Townsend and Anderson of the rear formation had been sent out to make one attack against the Sorpe. We heard Peter say that he had been successful, but heard nothing from Anderson.

'Let's tell Base we're coming home, and tell them to lay on a party,' suggested Spam.

We told them we were coming home.

We had reached the Möhne by now and circled twice. We looked at the level of the lake. Already bridges were beginning to stick up out of the lowering water. Already mudbanks with pleasure-boats sitting on their sides could be seen. Below the dam the torpedo nets had been washed to one side of the valley. The power-station had disappeared.

The map had completely changed as a new silver lake had formed, a lake of no strict dimensions; a lake slowly moving down towards the west.

Base would probably be panicking a bit, so Hutch sent out another message telling them that there was no doubt about it. Then we took one final look at what we had done and afterwards turned north to the Zuider Zee.

Trevor asked a question – Trevor, who had fired nearly 12,000 rounds of amunition in the past two hours. 'I am almost out of ammo,' he called, 'but I have got one or two incendiaries back here. Would you mind if Spam tells me when a village is coming up, so that I can drop one out? It might pay for Hoppy, Henry and Bill.'

I answered, 'Go ahead.'

We flew north in the silence of the morning, hugging the ground and wanting to get home. It was quite light now, and we could see things that we could not see on the way in – cattle in the fields, chickens getting airborne as we rushed over them. On the left someone flew over Hamm at 500 feet. He got the chop. No one knew who it was. Spam said he thought it was a German night-fighter which had been chasing us.

I suppose they were all after us. Now that we were being plotted on our retreat to the coast, the enemy fighter controllers would be working overtime. I could imagine the Führer himself giving orders to 'stop those air pirates at all costs'. After all, we had done something which no one else had ever done. Water when released can be one of the most powerful things in the world – similar to an earthquake – and the Ruhr Valley had never had an earthquake.

Someone on board pointed out that Duisburg had been pranged the night before and that our water might put the fires out there. Someone else said – rather callously, I thought – 'If you can't burn 'em, drown 'em.' But we had not tried to do this; we had merely destroyed a legitimate industrial objective so as to hinder the Ruhr Valley output of war munitions. The fact that people were in the way was incidental. The fact that they might drown had not occurred to us. But we hoped that the dam wardens would warn those living below in time, even if they were Germans. No one likes mass slaughter, and we did not like being the authors of it. Besides, it brought us in line with Himmler and his boys.

Terry looked up from his chart-board. 'About an hour to the coast,' he said.

I turned to Pulford. 'Put her into maximum cruising. Don't worry about petrol consumption.' Then to Terry – 'I think we had better go the shortest way home, crossing the coast at Egmond – you know the gap there. We're the last one, and they'll probably try to get us if we lag behind.'

Terry smiled and watched the air-speed needle creep round. We were now doing a smooth 240 indicated, and the exhaust stubs glowed red hot with the power she was throwing out. Trevor's warning light came on the panel, then his voice – 'Unidentified enemy aircraft behind.'

'OK. I'll sink to the west – it's dark there.'

As we turned – 'OK. You've lost it.'

'Right. On course. Terry, we'd better fly really low.'

These fighters meant business, but they were hampered by the conditions of light during the early morning. We could see them before they saw us.

Down went the Lanc until we were a few feet off the ground, for this was the only way to survive. And we wanted to survive. Two hours before we had wanted to burst dams. Now we wanted to get home – quickly. Then we could have a party.

Some minutes later Terry spoke. 'Thirty minutes to the coast.'

'OK. More revs.'

The needle crept round. It got very noisy inside.

We were flying home – we knew that. We did not know whether we were safe. We did not know how the other boys had got on. Bill, Hoppy, Henry, Barlow, Byers and Ottley had all gone. They had all got the hammer. The light flak had given it to most of them, as it always will to low-flying aircraft – that is, the unlucky ones. They had all gone quickly, except perhaps for Henry. Henry, the born leader. A great loss, but he gave his life for a cause for which men should be proud. Boys like Henry are the cream of our youth. They die bravely and they die young.

And Burpee, the Canadian? His English wife about to have a baby. His father who kept a large store in Ottawa. He was not coming back because they had got him, too. They had got him somewhere between Hamm and the target. Burpee, slow of speech and slow of movement, but a good pilot. He was Terry's countryman and so were his crew. I like their ways and manners, their free-and-easy outlook, their openness. I was going to miss them a lot – even when they chewed gum.

I called up Melvyn on the RT. He had been with me all the way round as deputy-leader when Mickey had gone home with his leaking petrol tank. He was quite all right at the Eder. Now there was no reply. We wondered what had happened.

Terry said, 'Fifteen minutes to go.'

Fifteen minutes. Quite a way yet. A long way, and we might not make it. We were in the black territory. They had closed the gates of their fortress and we were locked inside; but we knew the gap – the gap by those wireless masts at Egmond. If we could find that, we should get through safely.

Back at the base they would be waiting for us. We did not know that when they received the code word 'Dinghy' there was a scene in the operations room such as the WAAF Ops Clerks had never seen before. The Air Officer Commanding had jumped up and had shaken Jeff by the hand, almost embracing him. The Commander-in-Chief had picked up the phone and asked for Washington. At Washington another US-Great Britain conference was in progress. Sir Charles Portal, the CAS, was giving a dinner-party. He was called away to the telephone. Back at Scampton the C.-in-C. yelled, 'Downwood successful – yes'. At Washington, CAS was having difficulty in hearing. At last members of the dinner-party heard him say quietly, 'Good show'. From then on the dinner-party was a roaring success.

We did not know anything about the fuss, the Press, the publicity which would go round the world after this effort. Or of the honours to be given to the squadron or of trips to America and Canada, or of visits by important people. We did not care about anything like that. We only wanted to get home.

We did not know that we had started something new in the history of aviation, that our squadron was to become a byword throughout the RAF as a precision-bombing unit – a unit which could pick off anything from viaducts to gun emplacements, from low level or high level, by day or by night. A squadron consisting of crack crews using all the latest new equipment and the largest bombs, even earthquake bombs. A squadron flying new aeroplanes, and flying them as well as any in the world.

Terry was saying, 'Rotterdam's 20 miles on the port bow. We will be getting to the gap in five minutes.' Now they could see where we were going, the fighters would be streaking across Holland to close that gap. Then they could hack us down.

I called up Melvyn, but he never answered. I was not to know that Melvyn had crashed into the sea a few miles in front of me. He had come all the way from California to fight this war and had survived sixty trips at home and in the Middle East, including a double ditching. Now he had ditched for the last time. Melvyn had been responsible for a good deal of the training that made this raid possible. He had endeared himself to the boys, and now he had gone.

Of the sixteen aircraft which had crossed the coast to carry out this mission, eight had been shot down, including both Flight Commanders. Only two men escaped to become prisoners of war. Only two out of fifty-six, for there is not much chance at 50 feet.

They had gone. Had it been worth it? Or were their lives just thrown away on a spectacular mission? Militarily, it was cheap at the price. The damage done to the German war effort was substantial. But there is another side to the question. We would soon begin our fifth year of war – a war in which the casualties had been lighter than the last; nevertheless, in Bomber Command there have been some heavy losses. These fifty-five boys who had lost their lives were some of many. The scythe of war, and a very bloody one at that, had reaped a good harvest in Bomber Command. As we flew on over the low fields of Holland, past dykes and ditches, we could not help thinking, 'Why must we make war every twenty-five years? Why must men fight? How can we stop it? Can we make countries live normal lives in a peaceful way?' But no one knows the answer to that one.

The answer may lie in being strong. A powerful, strategic bomber force based so that it would control the vital waterways of the world, could prevent and strangle the aggressor from the word 'Go'. But it rests with the people themselves; for it is the people who forget. After many years they will probably slip and ask for disarmament so that they can do away with taxes and raise their standard of living. If the people forget, they bring wars on themselves, and they can blame no one but themselves.

Yes, the decent people of this world would have to remember war. Movies and radio records should remind this and the future generations of what happened between 1936 and 1942. It should be possible to keep this danger in everyone's mind so that we can never be caught on the wrong foot again. So that our children will have a chance to live. After all, that is why we are born. We aren't born to die.

But we ourselves must learn. We must learn to know and respect our great Allies who have made the chance of victory possible. We must learn to understand them, their ways and their customs. We British are apt to consider ourselves the yardstick upon which everything else should be based. We must not delude ourselves. We have plenty to learn.

We must learn about politics. We must vote for the right things, and not necessarily the traditional things. We want to see our country remain as great as it is today – for ever. It all depends on the people, their common-sense and their memory.

Can we hope for this? Can all this be done? Can we be certain that we can find the answer to a peaceful world for generations to come?

'North Sea ahead, boys,' said Spam.

There it was. Beyond the gap, in the distance, lay the calm and silvery sea, and freedom. It looked beautiful to us then – perhaps the most wonderful thing in the world.

We climbed up a little to about 300 feet.

Then – 'Full revs and boost, Pulford.'

As he opened her right up, I shoved the nose down to get up extra speed and we sat down on the deck at about 260 indicated.

'Keep to the left of this little lake,' said Terry, map in hand.

This was flying.

'Now over this railway bridge.'

More speed.

'Along this canal . . .' We flew along that canal as low as we had flown that day. Our belly nearly scraped the water, our wings would have knocked horses off the towpath.

'See those radio masts?'

'Yeah.'

'About 200 yards to the right.'

'OK.'

The sea came closer. It came closer quickly as we tore towards it. There was a sudden tenseness on board.

'Keep going; you're OK now.'

'Right. Stand by, front gunner.'

'Guns ready.'

Then we came to the Western Wall. We whistled over the anti-tank ditches and beach obstacles. We saw the yellow sand-dunes slide below us silently, yellow in the pale morning.

Then we were over the sea with the rollers breaking on the beaches and the moon casting its long reflection straight in front of us – and there was England.

We were free. We had got through the gap. It was a wonderful feeling of relief and safety. Now for the party.

'Nice work,' said Trevor from the back.

'Course home?' I asked.

Behind us lay the Dutch coast, squat, desolate and bleak, still squirting flak in many directions.

We would be coming back.

The
Last Enemy

Richard
Hillary

'The last enemy that shall be destroyed is death'

Corinthians xv, 26

PROEM

September 3 dawned dark and overcast, with a slight breeze ruffling the waters of the Estuary. Hornchurch aerodrome, twelve miles east of London, wore its usual morning pallor of yellow fog, lending an added air of grimness to the dimly silhouetted Spitfires around the boundary. From time to time a balloon would poke its head grotesquely through the mist as though looking for possible victims before falling back like some tired monster.

We came out on to the tarmac at about eight o'clock. During the night our machines had been moved from the dispersal point over to the hangars. All the machine tools, oil, and general equipment had been left on the far side of the aerodrome. I was worried. We had been bombed a short time before, and my plane had been fitted out with a new cockpit hood. This hood, unfortunately, would not slide open along its groove; and with a depleted ground staff and no tools, I began to fear it never would. Unless it did open, I shouldn't be able to bale out in a hurry if I had to. Miraculously, 'Uncle George' Denholm, our squadron leader, produced three men with a heavy file and lubricating oil, and the corporal fitter and I set upon the hood in a fury of haste. We took it turn by turn, filing and oiling, oiling and filing, until at last the hood began to move. But agonizingly slowly: by ten o'clock, when the mist had cleared and the sun was blazing out of a clear sky, the hood was still sticking firmly half-way along the groove; at ten-fifteen, what I had feared for the last hour happened. Down the loud-speaker came the emotionless voice of the controller: '603 Squadron take off and patrol base; you will receive further orders in the air: 603 Squadron take off as quickly as you can, please.' As I pressed the starter and the engine roared into life, the corporal stepped back and crossed his fingers significantly. I felt the usual sick feeling in the pit of the stomach, as though I were about to row a race, and then I was too busy getting into position to feel anything.

Uncle George and the leading section took off in a cloud of dust; Brian Carbury looked across and put up his thumbs. I nodded and opened up, to take off for the last time from Hornchurch. I was flying No. 3 in Brian's section, with 'Stapme' Stapleton on the right: the third section consisted of only two machines, so that our squadron strength was eight. We headed south-east, climbing all out on a steady course. At about 12,000 feet we came up through the clouds: I looked down and saw them spread out below me like layers of whipped cream. The sun was brilliant and made it difficult to see even the next plane when turning. I was peering anxiously ahead, for the controller had given us warning of at least fifty enemy fighters approaching very high. When we did first sight them, nobody shouted, as I think we all saw them at the same moment. They must have been 500 to 1,000 feet above us and coming straight on like a swarm of locusts. I remember cursing and going automatically into line astern: the next moment we were in among them and it was each man for himself. As soon as they saw us they spread out and dived, and the next ten minutes was a blur of twisting machines and tracer bullets. One Messerschmitt went down in a sheet of flame on my right, and a Spitfire hurtled past in a half-roll; I was weaving and turning in a desperate attempt to gain height, with the machine practically hanging on the airscrew. Then, just below me and to my left, I saw what I had been praying for – a Messerschmitt climbing and away from the sun. I closed in to 200 yards and from slightly to one side gave him a two-second burst; fabric ripped off the wing and black smoke poured from the engine, but he did not go down. Like a fool, I did not break away, but put in another three-second burst. Red flames shot upwards and he spiralled out of sight. At that moment I felt a terrific explosion which knocked the control stick from my hand, and the whole machine quivered like a stricken animal. In a second, the cockpit was a mass of flames: instinctively, I reached up to open the hood. It would not move. I tore off my straps and managed to force it back; but this took time, and when I dropped back into the seat and reached for the stick in an effort to turn the plane on its back, the heat was so intense that I could feel myself going. I remember a second of sharp agony, remember thinking 'So this is it!' and putting both hands to my eyes. Then I passed out.

When I regained consciousness I was free of the machine and falling rapidly. I pulled the rip-cord of my parachute and checked my descent with a jerk. Looking down, I saw that my left trouser leg was burnt off, that I was going to fall into the sea, and that the English coast was deplorably far away. About twenty feet above the water, I attempted to undo my parachute, failed, and flopped into the sea with it billowing round me. I was told later that the machine went into a spin at about 25,000 feet and that at 10,000 feet I fell out – unconscious. This may well have been so, for I discovered later a large cut on the top of my head, presumably collected while bumping round inside.

The water was not unwarm and I was pleasantly surprised to find that my life-jacket kept me afloat. I looked at my watch: it was not there. Then, for the first time, I noticed how burnt my hands were: down to the wrist, the skin was dead white and hung in shreds: I felt faintly sick from the smell of burnt flesh. By closing one eye I could see my lips, jutting out like motor tyres. The side of my parachute harness was cutting into me particularly painfully, so that I guessed my right hip was burnt. I made a further attempt to undo the harness, but owing to the pain of my hands, soon desisted. Instead, I lay back and reviewed my position: I was a long way from land; my hands were burnt, and so, judging from the pain of the sun, was my face; it was unlikely that anyone on shore had seen me come down and even more unlikely that a ship would come by; I could float for possibly four hours in my Mae West. I began to feel that I had perhaps been premature in considering myself lucky to have escaped from the machine. After about half an hour my teeth started chattering, and to quiet them I kept up a regular tuneless chant, varying it from time to time with calls for help. There can be few more futile pastimes than yelling for help alone in the North Sea, with a solitary seagull for company, yet it gave me a certain melancholy satisfaction, for I had once written a short story in which the hero (falling from a liner) had done just this. It was rejected.

The water now seemed much colder and I noticed with surprise that the sun had gone in though my face was still burning. I looked down at my hands, and not seeing them, realized that I had gone blind. So I was going to die. It came to me like that – I was going to die, and I was not afraid. This realization came as a surprise. The manner of my approaching death appalled and horrified me, but the actual vision of death left me unafraid: I felt only a profound curiosity and a sense of satisfaction that within a few minutes or a few hours I was to learn the great answer. I decided that it should be in a few minutes. I had no qualms about hastening my end and, reaching up, I managed to unscrew the valve of my Mae West. The air escaped in a rush and my head went under water. It is said by people who have all but died in the sea that drowning is a pleasant death. I did not find it so. I swallowed a large quantity of water before my head came up again, but derived little satisfaction from it. I tried again, to find that I could not get my face under. I was so enmeshed in my parachute that I could not move. For the next ten minutes, I tore my hands to ribbons on the spring-release catch. It was stuck fast. I lay back exhausted, and then I started to laugh. By this time I was probably not entirely normal and I doubt if my laughter was wholly sane, but there was something irresistibly comical in my grand gesture of suicide being so simply thwarted.

Goethe once wrote that no one, unless he had led the full life and realized himself completely, had the right to take his own life. Providence seemed determined that I should not incur the great man's displeasure.

It is often said that a dying man re-lives his whole life in one rapid kaleidoscope. I merely thought gloomily of the squadron returning, of my mother at home, and of the few people who would miss me. Outside my family, I could count them on the fingers of one hand. What did gratify me enormously was to find that I indulged in no frantic abasements or prayers to the Almighty. It is an old jibe of God-fearing people that the irreligious always change their tune when about to die: I was pleased to think that I was proving them wrong. Because I seemed to be in for an indeterminate period of waiting, I began to feel a terrible loneliness and sought for some means to take my mind off my plight. I took it for granted that I must soon become delirious, and I attempted to hasten the process: I encouraged my mind to wander vaguely and aimlessly, with the result that I did experience a certain peace. But when I forced myself to think of something concrete, I found that I was still only too lucid. I went on shuttling between the two with varying success until I was picked up. I remember as in a dream hearing somebody shout: it seemed so far away and quite unconnected with me. . . .

Then willing arms were dragging me over the side; my parachute was taken off (and with such ease!); a brandy flask was pushed between my swollen lips; a voice said, 'OK, Joe, it's one of ours and still kicking'; and I was safe. I was neither relieved nor angry: I was past caring.

It was to the Margate lifeboat that I owed my rescue. Watchers on the coast had seen me come down, and for three hours they had been searching for me. Owing to wrong directions, they were just giving up and turning back for land when ironically enough one of them saw my parachute. They were then fifteen miles east of Margate.

While in the water I had been numb and had felt very little pain. Now that I began to thaw out, the agony was such that I could have cried out. The good fellows made me as comfortable as possible, put up some sort of awning to keep the sun from my face, and phoned through for a doctor. It seemed to me to take an eternity to reach shore. I was put into an ambulance and driven rapidly to hospital. Through all this I was quite conscious, though unable to see. At the hospital they cut off my uniform, I gave the requisite information to a nurse about my next of kin, and then, to my infinite relief, felt a hypodermic syringe pushed into my arm.

I can't help feeling that a good epitaph for me at that moment would have been four lines of Verlaine:

> Quoique sans patrie et sans roi,
> Et très brave ne l'étant guère,
> J'ai voulu mourir à la guerre.
> La mort n'a pas voulu de moi.

The foundations of an experience of which this crash was, if not the climax, at least the turning point were laid in Oxford before the war.

BOOK ONE

CHAPTER ONE

UNDER THE MUNICH UMBRELLA

Oxford has been called many names, from 'the city of beautiful nonsense' to 'an organized waste of time,' and it is characteristic of the place that the harsher names have usually been the inventions of the University's own undergraduates. I had been there two years and was not yet twenty-one when the war broke out. No one could say that we were, in my years, strictly 'politically minded.' At the same time it would be false to suggest that the University was blissfully unaware of impending disaster. True, one could enter anybody's rooms and within two minutes be engaged in a heated discussion over orthodox versus Fairbairn rowing, or whether Ezra Pound or T. S. Eliot was the daddy of contemporary poetry, while an impassioned harangue on liberty would be received in embarrassed silence. Nevertheless, politics filled a large space. That humorous tradition of Oxford verbosity, the Union, held a political debate every week; Conservative, Labour, and even Liberal clubs flourished; and the British Union of Fascists had managed to raise a back-room and twenty-four members.

But it was not to the political societies and meetings that one could look for a representative view of the pre-war undergraduate. Perhaps as good a cross-section of opinion and sentiment as any at Oxford was to be found in Trinity, the college where I spent those two years rowing a great deal, flying a little – I was a member of the University Air Squadron – and reading somewhat.

We were a small college of less than two hundred, but a successful one. We had the president of the Rugby Club, the secretary of the Boat Club, numerous golf, hockey, and running Blues and the best cricketer in the University. We also numbered among us the president of the Dramatic Society, the editor of the *Isis* (the University magazine), and a small but select band of scholars. The sentiment of the college was undoubtedly governed by the more athletic undergraduates, and we radiated an atmosphere of alert Philistinism. Apart from the scholars, we had come up from the so-called better public schools, from Eton, Shrewsbury, Wellington, and Winchester, and while not the richest representatives of the University, we were most of us comfortably enough off. Trinity was, in fact, a typical incubator of the English ruling classes before the war. Most of those with Blues were intelligent enough to get second-class honours in whatever subject they were 'reading,' and could thus ensure themselves entry into some branch of the Civil or Colonial Service, unless they happened to be reading Law, in which case they were sure to have sufficient private means to go through the lean years of a beginner's career at the Bar or in politics. We were held together by a common taste in friends, sport, literature, and idle amusement, by a deep-rooted distrust of all organized emotion and standardized patriotism, and by a somewhat self-conscious satisfaction in our ability to succeed without apparent effort. I went up for my first term, determined, without over-exertion, to row myself into the Government of the Sudan, that country of blacks ruled by Blues in which my father had spent so many years. To our scholars (except the Etonians) we scarcely spoke; not, I think, from plain snobbishness, but because we found we did not speak the same language. Through force of circumstances they had to work hard; they had neither the time nor the money to cultivate the dilettante browsing which we affected. As a result they tended to be martial in their enthusiasms, whether pacifistic or patriotic. They were earnest, technically knowing, and conversationally uninteresting.

Not that conversationally Trinity had any great claim to distinction. To speak brilliantly was not to be accepted at once as indispensable; indeed, it might prove a handicap, giving rise to suspicions of artiness. It would be tolerated as an idiosyncrasy because of one's prowess at golf, cricket, or some other college sport that proved one's all-rightness. For while one might be clever, on no account must one be unconventional or disturbing – above all disturbing. The scholars' conversation might well have been disturbing. Their very presence gave one the uneasy suspicion that in even so small a community as this while one half thought the world was their oyster, the other half knew it was not and never could be. Our attitude will doubtless strike the reader as reprehensible and snobbish, but I believe it to have been basically a suspicion of anything radical – any change, and not a matter of class distinction. For a man from any walk of life, were he athletic rather than aesthetic, was accepted by the college at once, if he was a decent sort of fellow. Snobbish or not, our attitude was essentially English.

Let us say, therefore, that it was an unconscious appreciation of the simple things of life, an instinctive distrust of any form of adopted aestheticism as insincere.

We had in Trinity several clubs and societies of which, typically, the Dining Club was the most exclusive and the Debating Society the most puerile. Outside the college, the clubs to which we belonged were mostly of a sporting nature, for though some of us in our first year had joined political societies, our enthusiasm soon waned. As for the Union, though we were at first impressed by its great past, and prepared to be amused and possibly instructed by its discussions, we were soon convinced of its fatuity, which exceeded that of the average school debating society.

It was often said that the President of Trinity would accept no one as a Commoner in his college who was not a landowner. This was an exaggeration, but one which the dons were not unwilling to foster. Noel Agazarian, an Armenian friend of mine in another college, once told me that he had been proposed for Trinity, but that the President had written back to his head master regretting that the College could not accept Mr. Agazarian, and pointing out that in 1911, when the last coloured gentleman had been at Trinity, it had really proved most unfortunate.

We were cliquy, extremely limited in our horizon, quite conscious of the fact, and in no way dissatisfied about it. We knew that war was imminent. There was nothing we could do about it. We were depressed by a sense of its inevitability, but we were not patriotic. While lacking any political training, we were convinced that we had been needlessly led into the present world crisis, not by unscrupulous rogues, but worse, by the bungling of a crowd of incompetent old fools. We hoped merely that when war came it might be fought with a maximum of individuality and a minimum of discipline.

Though still outwardly complacent and successful, there was a very definite undercurrent of dissatisfaction and frustration amongst nearly everyone I knew during my last year.

Frank Waldron had rowed No. 6 in the Oxford Crew. He stood six-foot-three and had an impressive mass of snow-white hair. Frank was not unintelligent and he was popular. In my first year he had been president of the Junior Common Room. The girls pursued him, but he affected to prefer drink. In point of fact he was unsure of himself and was searching for someone to put on a pedestal. He had great personality and an undeveloped character. Apart from myself, he was the laziest though most stylish oarsman in the University, but he was just that much better to get away with it. He did a minimum of work, knowing that it was essential to get a second if he wished to enter the Civil Service, but always finding some plausible argument to convince himself that the various distractions of life were necessities.

I mention Frank here, because, though a caricature, he was in a way representative of a large number of similarly situated young men. He had many unconscious imitators who, because they had not the same prowess or personality, showed up as the drifting shadows that they were.

The seed of self-destruction among the more intellectual members of the University was even more evident. Despising the middle-class society to which they owed their education and position, they attacked it, not with vigour but with an adolescent petulance. They were encouraged in this by their literary idols, by their unquestioning allegiance to Auden, Isherwood, Spender, and Day Lewis. With them they affected a dilettante political leaning to the left. Thus, while refusing to be confined by the limited outlook of their own class, they were regarded with suspicion by the practical exponents of labour as bourgeois, idealistic, pink in their politics and pale-grey in their effectiveness. They balanced precariously and with irritability between a despised world they had come out of and a despising world they couldn't get into. The result, in both their behaviour and their writing, was an inevitable concentration on self, a turning-in on themselves, a breaking-down and not a building-up. To build demanded enthusiasm, and that one could not tolerate. Of this leaning was a friend of mine in another college by the name of David Rutter. He was different not so much in that he was sincere as in that he was a pacifist.

'Modern patriotism,' he would say, 'is a false emotion. In the Middle Ages they had the right idea. All that a man cared about was his family and his own home on the village green. It was immaterial to him who was ruling the country and what political opinions held sway. Wars were no concern of his.' His favourite quotation was the remark of Joan's father in Schiller's drama on the Maid of Orleans, '*Lasst uns still gehorchend harren wem uns Gott zum König gibt*,' which he would translate for me as, 'Let us trust obediently in the king God sends us.'

'Then,' he would go on, 'came the industrial revolution. People had to move to the cities. They ceased to live on the land. Meanwhile our country, by being slightly more unscrupulous than anyone else, was obtaining colonies all over the world. Later came the popular Press, and we have been exhorted ever since to love not only our own country, but vast tracts of land and people in the Empire whom we have never seen and never wish to see.'

I would then ask him to explain the emotion one always feels when, after a long time abroad, the South Coast express steams into Victoria Station. 'False, quite false,' he would say; 'you're a sentimentalist.' I was inclined to agree with him. 'Furthermore,' he would say, 'when this war comes, which, thanks to the benighted muddling of our Government, come it must, whose war is it going to be? You can't tell me that it will be the same war for the unemployed labourer as for the Duke of Westminster. What are the people to gain from it? Nothing!'

But though his arguments against patriotism were intellectual, his pacifism was emotional. He had a completely sincere hatred of violence and killing, and the spectacle of army chaplains wearing field-boots under the surplice revolted him.

At this time I was stroking one of the trial crews for the Oxford boat just previous to being thrown out for 'lack of enthusiasm and co-operation.' I was also on the editorial staff of the University magazine. David Rutter once asked me how I could reconcile heartiness with aestheticism in my nature. 'You're like a man who hires two taxis and runs between,' he said. 'What are you going to do when the war comes?'

I told him that as I was already in the University Air Squadron I should of course join the Air Force. 'In the first place,' I said, 'I shall get paid and have good food. Secondly, I have none of your sentiments about killing, much as I admire them. In a fighter plane, I believe, we have found a way to return to war as it ought to be, war which is individual combat between two people, in which one either kills or is killed. It's exciting, it's individual, and it's disinterested. I shan't be sitting behind a long-range gun working out how to kill people sixty miles away. I shan't get maimed: either I shall get killed or I shall get a few pleasant putty medals and enjoy being stared at in a night club. Your unfortunate convictions, worthy as they are, will get you at best a few white feathers, and at worst locked up.'

'Thank God,' said David, 'that I at least have the courage of my convictions.'

I said nothing, but secretly I admired him. I was by now in a difficult position. I no longer wished to go to the Sudan; I wished to write; but to stop rowing and take to hard work when so near a Blue seemed absurd. Now in France or Germany one may announce at an early age that one intends to write, and one's family reconciles itself to the idea, if not with enthusiasm at least with encouragement. Not so in England. To impress writing as a career on one's parents one must be specific. I was. I announced my intention of becoming a journalist. My family was sceptical, my mother maintaining that I could never bring myself to live on thirty shillings a week, which seemed to her my probable salary for many years to come, while my father seemed to feel that I was in need of a healthier occupation. But my mind was made up. I could not see myself as an empire-builder and I managed to become sports editor of the University magazine. I dared not let myself consider the years out of my life, first at school, and now at the University, which had been sweated away upon the river, earnestly peering one way and going the other. Unfortunately, rowing was the only accomplishment in which I could get credit for being slightly better than average. I was in a dilemma, but I need not have worried. My state of mind was not conducive to good oarsmanship and I was removed from the crew. This at once irritated me and I made efforts to get back, succeeding only in wasting an equal amount of time and energy in the second crew for a lesser amount of glory.

Mentally, too, I felt restricted. It was not intellectual snobbery, but I felt the need sometimes to eat, drink, and think something else than rowing. I had a number of intelligent and witty friends; but a permanent oarsman's residence at either Putney or Henley gave me small opportunity to enjoy their company. Further, the more my training helped my mechanical perfection as an oarsman, the more it deadened my mind to an appreciation of anything but red meat and a comfortable bed. I made a determined effort to spend more time on the paper, and as a result did no reading for my degree. Had the war not broken, I fear I should have made a poor showing in my finals. This did not particularly worry me, as a degree seemed to me the least important of the University's offerings. Had I not been chained to my oar, I should have undoubtedly read more though not, I think, for my degree. As it was, I read fairly widely, and, more important, learned a certain *savoir-faire*; learned how much I could drink, how not to be *gauche* with women, how to talk to people without being aggressive or embarrassed, and gained a measure of confidence which would have been impossible for me under any other form of education.

I had the further advantage of having travelled. When very young I had lived abroad, and every vacation from school and the University I had utilized to visit the Continent. It is maintained by some that travel has no educational value, that a person with sensibility can gain as rich an experience of life by staying right where he is as by wandering around the world, and that a person with no sensibility may as well remain at home anyway. To me this is nonsense, for if one is a bore, I maintain that it is better to be a bore about Peshawar than Upper Tooting. I was more fortunate than some of my friends, for I knew enough French and German to be able to move about alone; whereas my friends, though they were not insular, tended to travel in organized groups, either to Switzerland for ski-ing in winter or to Austria for camping in summer.

It was on one of these organized trips that Frank Waldron and I went to Germany and Hungary shortly before the war. Frank was no keener on organized groups than I, but we both felt the urge to travel abroad again before it was too late, and we had worked out the cheapest way of doing so. We wrote to the German and Hungarian Governments expressing the hope that we might be allowed to row in their respective countries. They replied that they would be delighted, sent us the times of their regattas (which we very well knew), and expressed the wish that they might be allowed to pay our expenses. We wrote back with appropriate surprise and gratification, and having collected eight others, on July 3, 1938, we set forth.

Half of us went by car and half by train, but we contrived somehow to arrive in Bad Ems together, two days before the race. We were to row for General Goering's Prize Fours. They had originally been the Kaiser Fours, and the gallant General had taken them over.

We left our things at the hotel where we were to stay and took a look at the town which, with its mass of green trees rising in a sheer sweep on either side of the river, made an enchanting picture. Down at the boathouse we had our first encounter with Popeye. He was the local coach and had been a sergeant-major in the last war. With his squat muscled body, his toothless mouth sucking a pipe, the inevitable cap over one eye, his identity was beyond dispute. Popeye was to prove our one invaluable ally. He was very proud of his English, though we never discovered where he learned it. After expressing a horrified surprise that we had not brought our own boat, he was full of ideas for helping us.

'Mr Waldron,' he said, 'I fix you right up tomorrow this afternoon. You see, I get you boat.'

The next day saw the arrival of several very serious-looking crews and a host of supporters, but no boat. Again we went to Popeye.

'Ah, gentlemen,' he said. 'My wife, she drunk since two years but tomorrow she come.'

We hoped he meant the boat. Fortunately he did, and while leaky and low in the water, it was still a boat and we were mighty relieved to see it. By this time we were regarded with contemptuous amusement by the elegantly turned-out German crews. They came with car-loads of supporters and set, determined faces. Shortly before the race we walked down to the changing-rooms to get ready. All five German crews were lying flat on their backs on mattresses, great brown stupid-looking giants, taking deep breaths. It was all very impressive. I was getting out of my shirt when one of them came up and spoke to me, or rather harangued me, for I had no chance to say anything. He had been watching us, he said, and could only come to the conclusion that we were thoroughly representative of a decadent race. No German crew would dream of appearing so lackadaisical if rowing in England: they would train and they would win. Losing this race might not appear very important to us, but I could rest assured that the German people would not fail to notice and learn from our defeat.

I suggested that it might be advisable to wait until after the race before shooting his mouth off, but he was not listening. It was Popeye who finally silenced him by announcing that we would win. This caused a roar of laughter and everyone was happy again. As Popeye was our one and only supporter, we taught him to shout 'You got to go, boys, you got to go.' He assured us that we would hear him.

Looking back, this race was really a surprisingly accurate pointer to the course of the war. We were quite untrained, lacked any form of organization, and were really quite hopelessly casual. We even arrived late at the start, where all five German crews were lined up, eager to go. It was explained to us that we would be started in the usual manner; the starter would call out 'Are you ready?' and if nobody shouted or raised his hand he would fire a gun and we would be off. We made it clear that we understood and came forward expectantly. 'Are you ready?' called the starter. Beside us there was a flurry of oars and all five German crews were several lengths up the river. We got off to a very shaky start and I can't ever remember hearing that gun fired. The car-loads of German supporters were driving slowly along either bank yelling out encouragement to their respective crews in a regulated chant while we rowed in silence, till about quarter-way up the course and above all the roaring and shouting on the banks I heard Popeye: 'You got to go, boys, you got to go. All my dough she is on you.' I looked up to see Popeye hanging from a branch on the side of the river, his anxious face almost touching the water. When Frank took one hand off his oar and waved to him, I really thought the little man was going to fall in. As we came up to the bridge that was the half-way mark we must have been five lengths behind; but it was at that moment that somebody spat on us. It was a tactical error. Sammy Stockton, who was stroking the boat, took us up the next half of the course as though pursued by all the fiends in hell and we won the race by two-fifths of a second. General Goering had to surrender his cup and we took it back with us to England. It was a gold shell-case mounted with the German eagle and disgraced our rooms in Oxford for nearly a year until we could stand it no longer and sent it back through the German Embassy. I always regret that we didn't put it to the use which its shape suggested. It was certainly an unpopular win. Had we shown any sort of enthusiasm or given any impression that we had trained they would have tolerated it, but as it was they showed merely a sullen resentment.

Two days later we went on to Budapest. Popeye, faithful to the end, collected a dog-cart and took all our luggage to the station. We shook the old man's hand and thanked him for all he had done.

'Promise me one thing, Popeye,' said Frank, 'when the war comes you won't shoot any of us.'

'Ah, Mr Waldron,' he replied, 'you must not joke of these things. I never shoot you, we are brothers. It is those Frenchies we must shoot. The Tommies, they are good fellows, I remember. We must never fight again.'

As the train drew out of the station he stood, a tiny stocky figure, waving his cap until we finally steamed round the bend. We wrote to him later, but he never replied.

We were greeted at Budapest by a delegation. As I stepped on to the platform, a grey-haired man came forward and shook my hand.

'My dear sir,' he said, 'we are very happy to welcome you to our country. Good-bye.'

'Good-bye,' I said, introducing him rapidly to the others, half of whom were already climbing back into the train.

We were put up at the Palatinus Hotel on St Margaret's Island where Frank's antiquated Alvis created a sensation. Members of our party had been dropping off all the way across Europe and it was only by a constant stream of cables and a large measure of luck that we finally mustered eight people in Budapest, where we found to our horror that we had been billed all over town as the Oxford University Crew. Our frame of mind was not improved by the discovery that we had two eights races in the same day, the length of the Henley course, and that we were to be opposed by four Olympic crews. It was so hot it was only possible to row very early in the morning or in the cool of the evening. The Hungarians made sure we had so many official dinners that evening rowing was impossible, and the food was so good and the wines so potent that early-morning exercise was out of the question. Further, the Danube, far from being blue, turned out to be a turbulent brown torrent that made the Tideway seem like a mill-pond in comparison. Out in midstream half-naked giants, leaning over the side of anchored barges, hung on to the rudder to prevent us being carried off downstream before the start. We had to keep our blades above the water until they let go for fear that the stream would tear them out of our hands. Then at the last moment Sammy Stockton, the one member of our rather temperamental crew who could be relied upon never to show any temperament, turned pale green. A combination of heat, goulash, and Tokay had proved too much for him and he came up to the start a very sick man. Once again we were pinning all our faith on our Four, as the eight in the bows had an air of unco-ordinated individualism. We were three-quarters of the way down the course and still in front, when John Garton, who was steering, ran into the boat on our left. There was an immediate uproar of which we understood not one word, but it was, alas, impossible to misconstrue the meaning of the umpire's arm pointing firmly back towards the start. Once again we battled upstream and turned around with a sense of foreboding. Again we were off, half-way down the course and still ahead: a faint hope began to flutter in my agonized stomach, but it was not to be. The spirit was willing, but the flesh was weak. Behind me I heard Sammy let out a whistling sigh like a pricked balloon and the race was over. The jubilation of the Hungarians was tempered by the fact that our defeat nearly caused a crisis, for at the Mayor's banquet that night we were to be presented with medals struck in honour of our victory, and it was doubtful whether any others could be manufactured in time. But they were. The evening passed off admirably. Frank rose to his feet and delivered a speech in fluent if ungrammatical German. He congratulated the Hungarians on their victory, apologized for, but did not excuse, our defeat and thanked them for their excellent hospitality. There were, fortunately, no repercussions apart from a cartoon in the *Pesti Hirlap*, showing eight people in a boat looking over their left shoulders at a naked girl in a skiff with the caption underneath: WHY OXFORD LOST?

The others returned to England shortly afterwards, but I stayed on an extra month with some people I knew who had an estate at Vecses about twelve miles out of Budapest. They were Jews, and even then very careful about holding large parties or being in any way publicized for fear of giving a handle to the Nazi sympathizers in the Government. With them I travelled all around Hungary and found everywhere an atmosphere of medieval feudalism: most of the small towns and villages were peopled entirely by peasants, apart from a bored army garrison. In Budapest there was a sincere liking for the English tempered by an ever-present memory of the Treaty of Trianan, and a very genuine dislike of the Germans; but there was a general resignation to the inevitability of a Nazi alliance for geographical reasons. Any suggestion that there was still time for a United Balkans to put up a solid front as a counter to German influence was waved aside. The Hungarians were a proud race; what had they in common with the upstart barbarians who surrounded them and who had so cynically carved up their country?

I left with a genuine regret and advice from the British Embassy not to leave the train anywhere on the way through Germany.

Before the outbreak of the war I made two more trips abroad, each to France. As soon as I got back from Hungary I collected the car and motored through Brittany. My main object was, I must admit, food. I saw before me possibly years of cold mutton, boiled potatoes, and Brussels sprouts, and the lure of one final diet of cognac at fourpence a glass, oysters, coq-au-vin, and soufflés drew me like a magnet. I motored out through Abbeville, Rouen, Rennes, and Quimper and ended up at Beg Meil, a small fishing village on the east coast, where between rich meals of impossible cheapness and nights of indigestion and remorse I talked with the people. Everywhere there was the same resignation, the same it's-on-the-way-but-what-the-hell attitude. I was in Rouen on the night of Hitler's final speech before Munich. The hysterical 'Sieg Heils!' of his audience were picked up by the loud-speakers through the streets, and sounded strangely unreal in the quiet evening of the cathedral city. The French said nothing, merely listening in silence and then dispersing with a shrug of their shoulders. The walls were plastered with calling-up notices and the stations crowded with uniforms. There was no excitement. It was as though a very tired old man was bestirring himself for a long-expected and unwelcome appointment.

I got back to England on the day of the Munich Conference; the boat was crowded and several cars were broken as they were hauled on board. The French seemed to resent our going.

During 'peace in our time' I made my final trip. The Oxford and Cambridge crews were invited to Cannes to row on the bay and I had the enviable position of spare man. Café society was there in force; there were fireworks, banquets at Juan-les-Pins, battles of flowers at Nice, and a general air of all being for the best in the best of all possible worlds. We stayed at the Carlton, bathed at Eden Rock and spent most of the night in the Casino. We gave a dinner for the Mayor which ended with Frank and the guest of honour rolled together in the tablecloth singing quite unintelligible ditties, much to the surprise of the more sober diners. We emerged from some night club at seven o'clock on the morning of our departure with a bare half-hour left to catch our plane. Over the doorway a Union Jack and a Tricolour embraced each other in a rather tired *entente cordiale*. Frank seized the Tricolour and waved it gaily above his head. At that moment the smallest Frenchman I've ever seen rushed after us and clutched hold of Frank's retreating coat-tails.

'*Mais, non, non, non!*' he screeched.

'*Mais, oui, oui, oui,* my little man,' said Frank, and, disengaging himself, he belaboured the fellow over the head with the emblem of his Fatherland and cantered off down the road, to appear twenty minutes later on the airport, a sponge bag in one hand and the Tricolour still firmly clasped in the other.

This, then, was the Oxford generation which on September 3, 1939, went to war. I have of necessity described that part of the University with which I came in contact and which was particularly self-sufficient, but I venture to think that we differed little in essentials from the majority of young men with a similar education. We were disillusioned and spoiled. The Press referred to us as the Lost Generation and we were not displeased. Superficially we were selfish and egocentric without any Holy Grail in which we could lose ourselves. The war provided it, and in a delightfully palatable form. It demanded no heroics, but gave us the opportunity to demonstrate in action our dislike of organized emotion and patriotism, the opportunity to prove to ourselves and to the world that our effete veneer was not as deep as our dislike of interference, the opportunity to prove that, undisciplined though we might be, we were a match for Hitler's dogma-fed youth.

For myself, I was glad for purely selfish reasons. The war solved all problems of a career, and promised a chance of self-realization that would normally take years to achieve. As a fighter pilot I hoped for a concentration of amusement, fear, and exaltation which it would be impossible to experience in any other form of existence.

I was not disappointed.

September 3, 1939, fell during the long vacation, and all of us in the University Air Squadron reported that day to the Volunteer Reserve Centre at Oxford. I drove up from Beaconsfield in the late afternoon and discovered with the rest that we had made a mistake: the radio calling-up notice had referred only to ground crews and not to pilots. Instead of going home, I went along with Frank to his old rooms and we settled down to while away the evening.

Frank was then twenty-five and had just finished his last year. We had both rowed more than we had flown, and would have a lot to learn about flying. The walls of Frank's rooms were covered with oars, old prints, and the photographs of one or two actresses whom we had known: outside there was black-out and the noise of marching feet. We said little. Through that window there came to us, with an impact that was a shock, a breath of the new life we were to be hurled into. There was a heavy silence in the air that was ominous. I was moved, full of new and rather awed emotions. I wanted to say something but could not. I felt a curious constraint. At that moment there was a loud banging on the door, and we started up. Outside stood a policeman. We knew him well.

'I might have known,' he said, 'that it would be you two.'

'Good evening, Rogers,' said Frank. 'Surely no complaints. Term hasn't begun yet.'

'No, Mr Waldron, but the war has. Just take a look at your window.'

We looked up. A brilliant shaft of light was illuminating the street for fifty yards on either side of the house. Not a very auspicious start to our war careers.

CHAPTER TWO

BEFORE DUNKIRK

For some time we reported regularly every fortnight to the Air Centre at Oxford, where we were paid a handsome sum of money and told to stand by. Then we were drafted to an initial training wing. We were marched from the station to various colleges and I found myself supplied with a straw bed and command of a platoon. My fellow sergeants were certainly tough: they were farmers, bank clerks, estate agents, representatives of every class and calling, and just about the nicest bunch of men it has ever been my lot to meet. There could have been few people less fitted to drill them than I, but by a system of the majority vote we overcame most of our difficulties. If ignorant of on what foot to give a command, I would have a stand-easy and take a show of hands. The idea worked admirably and whenever an officer appeared our platoon was a model of efficiency. We never saw an aeroplane and seldom attended a lecture. This was the pre-Dunkirk 'phoney war' period, but life was not dull. Soon afterwards I was commissioned on the score of my proficiency certificate in the University Air Squadron, and was moved to another wing. Here I found myself amongst many old friends.

Frank Waldron was there, Noel Agazarian, and Michael Judd, also of the University Squadron. Michael thought and felt as egocentrically as I did about everything, but his reaction to the war was different. It did not fit into his plans, for he had just won a travelling fellowship at All Souls: to him the war was in fact a confounded nuisance. Although we were officers, route marches were nevertheless obligatory for us; but by some odd chance Frank and Noel and I always seemed to be in the last section of threes on the march. Prominent and eager at the start, we were somehow never to be seen by the end. London, I fear, accounted for more than enough of our time and money. That our behaviour was odd and unco-operative did not occur to us, or if it did, caused us few pangs. We had joined the Air Force to fly, and not to parade around like Boy Scouts. We didn't bother to consider that elementary training might be as essential as anything that we should learn later, or that a certain confusion of organization was inevitable at the beginning of the war. We rented a large room in a hotel and formed a club, pleasantly idling away six weeks in drinking and playing cards.

Then one day it was announced that we were to move. The news was greeted with enthusiasm, for while the prospect of flying seemed no nearer, this station was notoriously gay and seemed a step in the right direction. There had been pictures in the Press of young men diving into the swimming-pool, of Mr Wally Hammond leading a parade, and of Len Harvey and Eddie Phillips boxing. David Douglas-Hamilton, who boxed for England, and Noel, who boxed for Oxford, were particularly pleased.

I drove down with Frank in his battered old Alvis and reported. We were billeted in boarding-houses along the front. I had never quite believed in the legend of seaside boarding-houses, but within two days I was convinced. There it all was, the heavy smell of Brussels sprouts, the aspidistras, the slut of a maid with a hole in her black stockings and a filthy thumb-nail in the soup, the communal table in the dining-room which just didn't face the sea, the two meals a day served punctually at one o'clock and seven-thirty.

We found that Nigel Bicknell, Bill Aitken, and Dick Holdsworth had been billeted in the same boarding-house. The way in which they took the war deserves to be mentioned.

Nigel was a year or two older than I. He had been editor of the *Granta*, the University magazine at Cambridge. From Nigel's behaviour, referred to a little later, it will be seen that the attitude of Cambridge to the war was the same as ours. He had had a tentative job on the *Daily Express*, and by the outbreak of the war he had laid the foundations of a career. For him as for Michael Judd, the war was a confounded nuisance.

Bill Aitken was older. He had the Beaverbrook forehead and directness of approach. He was director of several companies, married, and with considerably more to lose by joining the RAF as a pilot officer than any of us. The immediate pettiness of our regulations and our momentary inactivity brought from him none of the petulant outbursts in which most of us indulged, nor did he display the same absorption with himself and what he was to get out of it.

Dick Holdsworth had much the same attitude. He was to me that nothing short of miraculous combination, a First in Law and a rowing

Blue. He, too, was several years older than most of us and considerably better orientated: his good-natured compliance with the most child-like rules and determined eagerness to gain everything possible from the course ensured him the respect of our instructors. But the others were mostly of my age and it was with no very good grace that we submitted to a fortnight's pep course.

We went for no more route marches, but drilled vigorously on the pier; we had no lectures on flying, but several on deportment; we were told to get our hair cut and told of the importance of forming threes for the proper handling of an aircraft; but of the sporting celebrities we were told nothing and saw little, until after much pleading a boxing tournament was arranged. Noel and David both acquitted themselves well, David hitting Len Harvey harder and more often than the champion expected. We applauded with suitable enthusiasm, and marched back to the pier for more drill.

At the end of a fortnight our postings to flying training schools came through and our period of inactivity was over. Dick Holdsworth, Noel, Peter Howes, and I were to report at a small village on the north-east coast of Scotland. None of us had ever heard of it, but none of us cared: as long as we flew it was immaterial to us where. As we were likely to be together for some months to come, I was relieved to be going with people whom I both knew and liked. Noel, with his pleasantly ugly face, had been sent down from Oxford over a slight matter of breaking up his college and intended reading for the Bar. With an Armenian father and a French mother he was by nature cosmopolitan, intelligent, and a brilliant linguist, but an English education had discovered that he was an athlete, and his University triumphs had been of brawn rather than brain. Of this he was very well aware and somewhat bewildered by it. These warring elements in his make-up made him a most amusing companion and a very good friend. Peter Howes, lanky and of cadaverous good looks, had been reading for a science degree. With a permanently harassed expression on his face he could be a good talker, and was never so happy as when, lying back smoking his pipe, he could expound his theories on sex (of which he knew very little), on literature (of which he knew more), and on mathematics (of which he knew a great deal). He was to prove an invaluable asset in our Wings Exam.

Peter, Noel, and I drove up together. We arrived in the late afternoon of a raw, cold November day. When we had reported to the Station Adjutant, Peter drove us down to the little greystone house in the neighbouring village that was to be our home for many months. Our landlady, a somewhat bewildered old body, showed us with pride the room in which we were to sleep. It was cold and without heating. The iron bedsteads stood austerely in the middle of the room, and an enamelled wash-basin stood in the corner. An old print hung by the window, and a bewhiskered ancestor looked stonily at us from over the wash-stand. The room was scrupulously clean. We assured her that we should be most comfortable, and returned, a little chastened, to the camp.

At the beginning of the war there was a definite prejudice in the Air Force against Volunteer Reserve Officers, and we had the added disadvantage of an Oxford attitude to life. We were expected to be superior; we were known as week-end pilots; we were known as the long-haired boys; we were to have the nonsense knocked out of us. When I say 'we' I don't include Dick Holdsworth. He settled down at once and was perfectly content: he was obviously willing to co-operate to the full. Noel, Peter, and I, less mature and more assertive, looked for trouble and found it. It came in the form of the Chief Ground Instructor, who took to his task of settling our hash with enthusiasm; but our innate laziness, added to a certain low cunning, proved equal to the situation, and we managed to skip quite a number of morning parades and lectures. There admittedly can be no excuse for our behaviour, but there is, I think, an explanation, to be found in the fact that Dunkirk had not come: the war was still one of tin soldiers and not yet of reality. Nevertheless, thanks to the fact that we got on well with our co-pilots, and to Noel's infectious good humour and lack of affectation, we gradually settled down to a harmonious relationship with our instructors, who were willing enough to help as soon as we showed signs of co-operation. Our lives quickly became a regular routine of flying and lectures. Dick Holdsworth started in on bombing training, but through making a nuisance of ourselves we three managed to fly Harvards, American fighter trainers.

In our flying instructors Noel and I were very lucky. Noel was handed over to Sergeant Robinson, I to Sergeant White. They were great friends, and a rivalry immediately began to see who could first make a pilot out of the unpromising material that we represented. White was a dour, taciturn little Scot with a dry sense of humour. I liked him at once.

Noel's flying was typical of the man: rough, slapdash, and with touches of brilliance. Owing to the complete blank in my mind on the subject of anything mechanical, I was at first bewildered by the complicated array of knobs and buttons confronting me in the cockpit. I was convinced that I might at any moment haul up the undercarriage while still on the ground, or switch off the engine in the air, out of pure confusion of mind. However, thanks to the patience and consideration of Sergeant White, I developed gradually from a mediocre performer to a quite moderate pilot. For weeks he sat behind me in the rear cockpit muttering, just loud enough for me to hear, about the bad luck of getting such a bum for a pupil. Then one day he called down the inter-comm., 'Man, you can fly at last. Now I want you to dust the pants of Agazarian and show our friend, Sergeant Robinson, that he's not the only one with a pupil that's not a half-wit.'

My recollection of our Scottish training is a confusion of, in the main, pleasant memories: Of my first solo cross-country flight, when I nearly made a forced landing down-wind in a field with a large white house at the far end. A little red light inside the cockpit started winking at me, and then the engine cut. The red light continued to shine like a brothel invitation while I racked my brain to think what was wrong. I was down to 500 feet, and more frightened of making a fool of myself than of crashing, when I remembered. It was the warning signal for no petrol. I quickly changed tanks, grateful that there were no spectators of my stupidity, and flew back, determined to learn my cockpit drill thoroughly before taking to the air again.

Of my second solo cross-country flight when the engine cut again, this time due to no fault of mine. Both the magnetos were burned out. I was on my way back from Wick and flying at about 2,000 feet when the engine spluttered twice and stopped. By the grace of God I was near a small aerodrome backed by a purple range of mountains and opening on to the sea. There was no time to make a circuit, so I banked and, feeling decidedly queasy, put down right across two incoming machines to pull up six yards from the sea.

Of cloud and formation flying. I shall never forget the first time that I flew really high, and, looking down, saw wave after wave of white undulating cloud that stretched for miles in every direction like some fairy city. I dived along a great canyon; the sun threw the reddish shadow of the plane on to the cotton-wool walls of white cliff that towered up on either side. It was intoxicating. I flew on. Soon I could see nothing and had to rely on my instruments. I did a slow roll. This was extremely stupid apart from being strictly forbidden. My speed fell off alarmingly. I pushed the stick forward: the speed fell still further and I nearly went into a spin. I could not tell whether I was on my back or right way up, and felt very unhappy. I lost about 2,000 feet and came out of the cloud in a screaming spiral, but still fortunately a long way above the earth. I straightened up and flew home with another lesson hard learned.

Formation flying was the most popular and exciting part of our training. At first I was very erratic, perilously close to the leader one minute and a quarter of a mile away the next. But gradually I began to improve, and after a few hours I was really enjoying myself. We had a flight commander who, once we were steady, insisted on us flying in very tight formation, the wing-tip of the outside machine in line with the roundel on the leader's fuselage. He was a brave man, and it certainly gave us confidence. Landing was a simple ritual of sign language; undercarriage down, engine into fine pitch, and flaps down, always without taking one's eyes off the leader. There was a tendency to drift away slightly before touching down, but we invariably landed as close as we dared, even among ourselves, until one day the CO of advanced training stood and watched us. I think he nearly had a stroke, and from then on we confined our tight formations to less public parts of the sky.

Of the scenery, which was superb. Many times of an evening I would stand on the shore and look out to sea, where a curious phosphorescent green was changing to a transparent blue. Behind the camp the setting sun, like a flaming ball, painted the mountains purple and gold. The air was like champagne, and as we were in the Gulf Stream the weather was beautifully mild. While violent snowstorms were raging in England, we were enjoying the most perfect flying weather and a day which lasted for nearly twenty-four hours.

On leave for four days, Noel and I drove across Scotland to the west coast and took the ferry over to Skye. The small stone quay was spotted with shops; a bus was drawn up by the waterside, a hotel advertisement on its side. I looked at Noel and he nodded. We had come prepared to be disappointed. But we had not driven far before the road gave way to a winding track and the only signs of habitation were a few crofters' cottages. It was evening when we drew up outside the Sligachan Inn at the foot of the Coolin mountains. The innkeeper welcomed us and showed us our rooms. From every window was the same view, grey mountains rising in austere beauty, their peaks hidden in a white mist, and everywhere a great feeling of stillness. The shadows that lengthened across the valley, the streams that coursed down the rocks, the thin mist turning now into night, all a part of that stillness. I shivered. Skye was a world that one would either love or hate; there could be no temporizing.

'It is very beautiful,' said the landlord.

'Yes,' I said, 'it's beautiful.'

'But only mountaineers or fools will climb those peaks.'

'We're both fools,' Noel said shortly.

'So be it. Dinner is at eight-thirty.'

We stood a while at the window. The night was clear and our heads felt clear and cold as the air. We smelled the odour of the ground in the spring after rain and behind us the wood smoke of the pine fire in our room, and we were content. For these are the odours of nostalgia, spring mist and wood smoke, and never the scent of a woman or of food.

We were alone in the inn save for one old man who had returned there to die. His hair was white, but his face and bearing were still those of a mountaineer, though he must have been a great age. He never spoke, but appeared regularly at meals to take his place at a table tight-pressed against the window, alone with his wine and his memories. We thought him rather fine.

In the morning we set off early, warmed by a rare spring sun which soon dried the dew from the heather. We had decided on Bruach-na-Free, one of the easier peaks, but it was lunch-time before we reached the base of the first stiff climb and the muscles in our thighs were already taut. We rested and ate our sandwiches and drank from a mountain stream. The water was achingly cold. Then we started to climb. In the morning we had taken our time and talked, now we moved fast and said nothing. With feet and hands we forced our way up the lower grey crumbling rock to the wet black smooth surface, mist-clouded above. There was no friendship in that climb: neither of us had spoken, but each knew that the other meant to reach the top first. Once I slipped and dropped back several feet, cutting open my hand. Noel did not stop; he did not even turn his head. I would not have forgiven him if he had. Gradually I brought him back. Nothing disturbed that great stillness but the occasional crash of a loose stone and the sobbing of our breath. We were no longer going up and around the face of the mountain but climbing straight. We could see nothing in the mist, but my thigh muscles were twitching with the strain and my arms were on fire. Then I felt a cold breeze blowing down on my upturned face and knew we were near the top. I practically threw myself up the last few yards, but Noel hung on to his advantage and hauled himself up the last ledge with a gasp of relief, a second or two before me. We lay on our backs, and felt the black wet rock cold against us, felt the deep mist damp against our faces, felt the sweat as it trickled into our eyes, felt the air in deep gulps within our lungs. The war was far away and life was very good.

We could see nothing below us, but started off down, jumping and slithering on the avalanche of rocks that cascaded beside us, making a great thunder of noise in that deep stillness. We soon felt again the sun, warm on our faces, and saw below us the bed of a mountain stream leading away into the distance, and scarcely visible, a mere speck at the far end, the inn. We did not hesitate to follow the stream, as it was running low, and we made quite good time until we came to a drop of some twelve feet where the water fell in a small torrent. This we managed to negotiate without getting too wet, only to be met a few yards farther on with a sheer drop of some twenty feet. The stream had become a river and dropped down into a shallow pool some two feet deep. It was impossible to go back and there was only one way of going on. 'You first,' I said to Noel. 'Give me your clothes and I'll throw them down to you with mine.'

Now early March is no time for bathing anywhere, but there can be fewer colder places that we could have chosen than the mountain streams of Skye. Noel stripped, handed me his clothes, and let himself down as far as possible. Then he let go. He landed on all fours and scrambled out unhurt, a grotesque white figure amidst those sombre rocks.

'For Christ's sake hurry up: I'm freezing.'

'I'm right with you,' I shouted, and then with Noel's clothes firmly clutched under my arm, and still wearing my own, I slipped. I had a short glimpse of Noel's agonized face watching the delicate curve of one

of his shoes through the air and then I was under the water with two
grazed knees. It was freezingly cold, but I managed to grab everything
and wallowed painfully out.

'You bastard,' said Noel.

'I'm sorry, but look at me: I'm just as wet.'

'Yes, but you're wearing your clothes: I've got to put these bloody
things on again.'

With much muttering he finally got dressed, and we squelched our
way onwards. By the time we reached the inn two hours later we were
dry, but mighty hungry.

Over dinner we told the landlord of our novel descent. His sole
comment was 'Humph,' but the old man at the window turned and
smiled at us. I think he approved.

Of crashes. It was after an armament lecture in one of the huts when
we heard, very high, the thin wailing scream of a plane coming down
fast. The corporal sat down and rolled himself a cigarette. He took out
the paper and made of it a neat trough with his forefinger, opened the
tin of tobacco and sprinkled a little on to the paper, ran his tongue along
the paper edge and then rolled it. As he put it in his mouth we heard the
crash, maybe a mile away. The corporal lit a match and spoke: 'I
remember the last time we had one of those. I was on the salvage party.
It wasn't a pretty sight.'

We learned later that the man had been on a warload height test and
had presumably fainted. They did not find much of him, but we filled
up the coffin with sand and gave him a grand funeral.

And again night flying. It was a dark night, but cloudless. Noel and
I walked down together from the Mess. A slight carpet of snow covered
the ground and gave an almost fairy-like appearance to the wooden
living-huts. Through a chink in the black-out a thin ray of light shone
out from one of the windows. A dry wind rustled over the bleakness of
the field as we crunched our way across the tarmac and pushed open the
door of the hangar.

I pulled on my sidcot and gloves and slipped my feet into the comforting
warmth of my fur-lined boots. I was to be off first. Sergeant White strode
in smoking a cigarette:

'Well, you couldn't want a better night. Even you shouldn't make a
mistake with this carpet on the ground.'

'Bet you need more than three dual circuits,' said Noel. (He meant
three times in with the instructor before I could do it solo.)

I took the bet and we walked out on to the field. I could see the
machine, a squat dark patch against the grey of the horizon. I hauled
myself up on to the wing, buckled on my parachute harness, and climbed
into the front cockpit, while the fitter stood by to strap me in. I settled

myself comfortably into the box seat, glanced over the dimly shining
instrument panel, and plugged in my ear-phones.

'All set.'

'Right, Hillary. Run her up.'

I lifted my hand to the rigger and he disappeared. I pulled the stick
back into my stomach and gradually opened the throttle, automatically
checking engine revs, oil pressure, and temperature. The engine burst
forth from a stutter to a great even roar of sound, hurling a scream of
defiance into the night. I throttled back, waved away the chocks from
under the wheels, and let the machine roll gently forward to the taxi-ing
post.

Across about a hundred yards from us lay the flare path, a straight
line of dimly glowing light. The officer in charge of night flying and a
sergeant with the Aldis lamp sat huddled in their greatcoats at the near
end. There was no landing beacon. I tapped out my letter on the Morse
key, had it returned in green by the lamp, and swung the machine into
wind. I pushed the throttle wide open and eased the stick forward. As
we gathered speed and the flickering lights of the flare path tore past in
a confused blur, I knew that I was too tense. I could feel my hand
hard-clenched on the control stick. I was swinging into the flare path and
I felt White give a slight push on the rudder. The tail came up and then
with one slight bump we were off the ground.

Reassuringly came White's voice: 'Climb up to a thousand feet and do
a normal circuit. Watch your speed.'

Automatically as we climbed I hauled up the undercarriage, and
pushed the pitch lever into coarse. I straightened out at a thousand feet,
and, with my eyes fixed on the turn-and-bank indicator, pushed rudder
and stick together to do a gentle turn to the left. Then I looked around
me. Below lay the flare path, a thin snake of light, while ahead the sea
was shot with silver beneath a sky of studded jewels. I could just make
out the horizon and it gave me a feeling of confidence. I relaxed back into
my seat, lifted my head from the cockpit, and took a lighter hold of the
stick. Behind me I could hear White humming softly. I tapped out my
letter and a flash of green answered from the ground. I banked again,
and flying down-wind, released the undercarriage: another turn and I
changed into fine pitch, throttling back slowly. In the silence that followed
turning into the flare path, I saw the lights rushing up to meet us and
could feel myself tensing up again.

'Watch your speed now.'

'OK.'

We were up to the first flare and I started to ease the stick back.

'Not yet, you're too high.'

I felt the pressure on the stick as White continued to hold it forward.
We were up to the second flare and still not down. I had a moment of

panic. I was going to stall, we were going too fast, couldn't possibly get down, I was making a fool of myself. Then a slight bump, the wheels rumbling along the runway, and White's voice, 'Hold her straight, man.' We were down.

Twice more we went round before White climbed out and poked his head into the front cockpit: 'Think you can take her round yourself now?'

'Sure.'

'Well, off you go, then, and for God's sake don't make a mess of it. I want some sleep tonight.'

For the first few minutes I flew automatically, but with a subdued feeling of excitement. Then again I lifted my eyes from the instrument panel and looked for the horizon. I could not see it. Heavy clouds obscured the stars, and outside the dimly-lighted cockpit lay pitch darkness. I looked for the flare path and for a moment could not pick it up. I glanced back at the instruments. I was gaining speed rapidly. That meant I was diving. Jerkily I hauled back on the stick. My speed fell off alarmingly. I knew exactly what to do, for I had had plenty of experience in instrument flying; but for a moment I was paralysed. Enclosed in the small space and faced with a thousand bewildering instruments, I had a moment of complete claustrophobia. I must get out. I was going to crash. I did not know in which direction I was going. Was I even right way up? I half stood up in my seat. Then I saw the flare path. I was not lost: I was in a perfectly normal position. I dropped back into my seat feeling thoroughly ashamed of myself. The awful feeling of being shut in was gone, and I began to enjoy myself. I was released, filled with a feeling of power, of exaltation. To be up there alone, confident that the machine would answer the least touch on the controls, to be isolated, entirely responsible for one's own return to earth – this was every man's ambition and for a moment I had nearly lost it.

I had to make a couple more circuits before I could get the signal to land. Two machines came in before me. Then I was down, the wheels skimming the ground. I turned off at the end of the flare path and taxied slowly back, swinging the machine gently from side to side. I made my second solo circuit, brought off an adequate landing, and climbed out. White met me as I walked into the hangar.

'OK ,' he said, 'you'll do.'

We sat down and he handed me a cigarette. Outside someone was coming in to land. He was given a green on the Aldis lamp and throttled back, only to open up and go round again. We watched the glimmer of his navigation lights as he made a quick circuit and once again throttled back. He was past the first flare, past the second, past the third and still not touching down when the engine roared into life and he was off again.

'Christ,' said White, 'he's in coarse pitch.'

Again we watched the navigation lights, but we soon lost them and could just hear the hum of the engine headed towards the sea. Ten minutes went by; twenty minutes. Nobody spoke. Then the officer in charge of night flying walked into the hangar.

'I've sent up for some more airmen. Meanwhile you all spread out and look. Move out to the sea.'

'Who was it?' someone asked.

'Ross. Get moving. We don't want to be here all night.'

We found him on the shore, the machine half in and half out of the sea. The officer in charge of night flying climbed on to the wing and peered into the cockpit.

'In coarse pitch,' he said, 'as I thought.' Then after a slight pause, 'Poor devil.'

I remembered again that moment of blind panic and knew what he must have felt. In his breast pocket was ten pounds, drawn out to go on leave the next day. He was twenty years old.

Of people. The other pilots on our course were a diverse and representative lot. They ranged from schoolboys of eighteen to men of twenty-six. They had taken on their short service commissions, because they were bored with their jobs, sensed the imminence of war, or, amongst the youngest, simply for the joy of flying. To my surprise, I discovered that they nearly all had a familiarity with mechanics and a degree of mathematical perception well ahead of my own. I consoled myself with the thought that I had always despised the mathematical mind and that few great men had possessed one. This was cold comfort; but what did seem more to the point was that if anything were to go wrong with my engine in mid-air I could hardly climb blithely out on to the wing and mend it. I was cheered to discover that Charlie Frizell, the most competent pilot on the course, was almost as mathematically imbecile as I. He had, however, an instinct for flying and a certain dash which marked him out as a future fighter pilot. He was nineteen and had joined the Air Force because he wanted a job.

While Charlie Frizell was nineteen and flying Harvards, Bob Marriott was twenty-six and training for bombers; yet they had much in common. They were both lazy (we took to them at once) and about as successful at dodging parades and lectures as we. Bob's instructor was the same age as Charlie Frizell, but this age juxtaposition between pupils and instructors was nothing rare and seemed to work out well enough. Then there was Giddings, an ex-school teacher, tall, ungainly, and oppressively serious-minded, who would never appear in the Mess with the others, but always retired to his room to pore over his books on navigation and theory of flight. There was Benbow, a merchant seaman all his life who had given up freighters for bombers, with an inexhaustible supply of dubious sea stories; Perkins, once a lawyer in South Africa, small, quiet, monosyllabic, and the soul of courtesy when sober, an unrecognizable glass-chewing trouble-maker when drunk; Russell, a mustachioed, swash-buckling, would-be leader of men, convinced that he was the best pilot on the course, but a sound enough fellow underneath. He amused us and mortified himself by landing his Harvard with the undercarriage up, quietly oblivious of the warning hooter inside the machine. Finally, Harry M'Grath and Dixie Dean.

I mention them together, but they could not have been more unlike. Harry, vast, genial, and thirty-two, with a cigarette permanently glued to his lower lip, was married and had a child. He had an Irish temper that flared up and then as quickly changed to shrill trumpetings of elephantine laughter. He had been on the Reserve for some time, having once flown Vickers Virginias'. In Ireland before the war he had been in some job connected with civil aviation. Dixie, diminutive, desperately keen, and nineteen, with, off duty, the most startling taste in clothes, and shoulders to his suits that you could ski off, was just out of school and adolescing self-consciously all over the place. He was as yet no great performer in the air, but pathetically keen to prove himself. When the others laughed at him, his narrow little face would tighten up with the determination to be the best pilot of them all.

This was a cross-section of the raw material out of which must be welded officers competent to take their place in Fighters, Bombers, and Coastal Command. After the day's work was over we would gather in the mess or adjourn to some neighbouring pub to pass the evening talking and drinking beer. And there as the months went by one could watch the gradual assimilation of these men, so diverse in their lives and habits, into something bigger than themselves, their integration into the composite figure that is the Air Force Pilot. Unknown to themselves, the realization of all this was gradually instilled in the embryo pilots who lived together, laughing, quarrelling, rapidly maturing in the incubator of that station.

Much that is untrue and misleading has been written on the pilot in this war. Within one short year he has become the nation's hero, and the attempt to live up to this false conception bores him. For, as he would be the first to admit, on the ground the pilot is a very ordinary fellow. Songs such as 'Silver Wings'—

> They say he's just a crazy sort of guy,
> But to me he means a million other things,

make him writhe with very genuine embarrassment.

The pilot is of a race of men who since time immemorial have been inarticulate; who, through their daily contact with death, have realized, often enough unconsciously, certain fundamental things. It is only in the air that the pilot can grasp that feeling, that flash of knowledge, of insight, that matures him beyond his years; only in the air that he knows suddenly he is a man in a world of men. 'Coming back to earth' has for him a double significance. He finds it difficult to orientate himself in a world that is so worldly, amongst a people whose conversation seems to him brilliant, minds agile, and knowledge complete – yet a people somehow blind. It is very strange.

In his village before the war the comfortably-off stockbrokers, the retired officers and business men, thought of the pilot, if they thought of him at all, as rather raffish, not a gentleman. Now they are eager to speak to him, to show him hospitality, to be seen about with him, to tell him that they, too, are doing their bit. He's a fine fellow, the saviour of the country; he must have qualities which they had overlooked. But they can't find them. He is polite, but not effusive. They are puzzled and he is embarrassed.

He wants only to get back to the mess, to be among his own kind, with men who act and don't talk, or if they do, talk only shop; of old So-and-So and his temper, of flights and crashes, of personal experiences; bragging with that understatement so dear to the Englishman. He wants to get back to that closed language that is Air Force slang.

These men, who in the air must have their minds clear, their nerves controlled, and their concentration intense, ask on the ground only to be allowed to relax. They ask only to get out of uniform; in the Mess, to read not literature, but thrillers, not *The Times*, but the *Daily Mirror*. Indeed, Popeye has been adopted by the Air Force. As these men fight the war they have no particular desire to read about it. They like to drink a little beer, play the radio and a little bridge. On leave they want only to get home to their wives and families and be left to themselves.

On some stations, officers, if they are married, live out. On others it is forbidden. This depends on the Commanding Officer, some believing the sudden change from night-bombing attacks over Berlin to all the comforts of home to be a psychological error, other believing it to be beneficial. In most squadrons the pilots live on the station, going home only on leave. It is always possible to apply for compassionate leave in the event of serious domestic trouble, and this is nearly always granted, though the 'passionate leave' applied for by some squadrons doesn't receive quite the same sympathy.

It might be imagined that there would be some lack of sympathy between the pilots and the ground staff of an aerodrome, that the pilots would adopt a rather patronizing manner towards the stores officers, engineers, signal operators, and adjutants of a station, rather similar to that condescension shown by the more highfalutin regiments towards the Royal Army Service Corps. But this is hardly ever true. On every station that I know there is an easy comradeship between pilots and technicians. Each realizes the essential value of the other – though I must admit on one occasion hearing a pilot define the height of impertinence as a stores officer wearing flying boots.

While on duty most pilots drink nothing and smoke little; when on leave they welcome the opportunity for an occasional carouse in London. They get a somewhat malicious pleasure in appearing slightly scruffy when dining at the smartest restaurants, thus tending to embarrass the beautifully turned out, pink-and-white-cheeked young men of the crack infantry regiments, and making them feel uncomfortably closely related to chorus boys.

But though these men may seem to fit into the picture of everyday life, though they seem content enough in the company of other men and in the restfulness of their homes, yet they are really only happy when they are back with their squadrons, with their associations and memories. They long to be back in their planes, so that isolated with the wind and the stars they may play their part in man's struggle against the elements.

The change in Peter Howes was perhaps the most interesting, for he was not unaware of what was happening. From an almost morbid introspection, an unhappy preoccupation with the psychological labyrinths of his own mind, his personality blossomed, like some plant long untouched by the sun, into an at first unwilling but soon open acceptance of the ideas and habits of the others. Peter had a biting tongue when he chose to use it. I remember one night we were discussing Air Force slang and its origins. I started off on some theory but he cut me short. 'Nonsense,' he said. 'You must understand that in our service we have a number of uneducated louts from all over the world none of whom can speak his own language properly. It thus becomes necessary to invent a small vocabulary of phrases, equipped with which they can carry on together an intelligible conversation.' At this time he was a very bad pilot, though his English was meticulous. In three months he was an excellent pilot and his vocabulary was pure RAF. I don't know if there is a connection, but I wonder. With enthusiasm he would join in the general debunking when an offender was caught 'shooting a line.'

Of the war. From time to time without warning a squadron of long-range bombers would come dropping out of the sky. For a week or so they would make our station their headquarters for raids on Norway, the heavy drone of their engines announcing their return as night began to fall. One day nine set out and four returned. I watched closely the pilots in the mess that night, but their faces were expressionless: they played bridge as usual and discussed the next day's raid.

Then one day a Spitfire squadron dropped in. It was our first glimpse of the machine which Peter, Noel, and I hoped eventually to fly. The trim deceptive frailty of their lines fascinated us and we spent much of our spare time climbing on to their wings and inspecting the controls. For while we continued to refuse to consider the war in the light of a crusade for humanity, or a life-and-death struggle for civilization, and concerned ourselves merely with what there was in it for us, yet for that very reason we were most anxious to fly single-seater fighters.

The course drew to a close. We had done a good many hours' flying on service types. We had taken our wings examination and somehow managed to pass. Giddings, our ex-schoolmaster, was way out in front, and I, thanks to Peter's knowledge of navigation and Noel's of armament, just scraped through.

We had learned something of flying and the theory of combat, but more important, we had learned a little of how to handle ourselves when we got to our squadrons. We awaited our final postings with impatience, but their arrival was a bitter disappointment. Only Charlie Frizell and two others were to go into fighters: at this early stage there had been few casualties in Fighter Command and there was little demand for replacements. Noel, Peter, and I were all slated for Army Co-operation. This entailed further training at Old Sarum before we should finally be operational, operational on Lysanders, machines which Peter gloomily termed 'flying coffins'. Giddings and a few other good sober pilots were to be instructors; the remainder were split up between bombers and Coastal Command.

And so we said good-bye to Scotland and headed south.

CHAPTER THREE

SPITFIRES

Noel and I spent one night in London. Peter Howes collected us at about ten o'clock and we drove down to Old Sarum. During the drive we talked ourselves into a belated enthusiasm for Army Co-operation, and as we came on to the road skirting the aerodrome and saw the field slanting downhill from the hangars with machines picketed around the edge, we gazed at them with interest. There were an equal number of Hectors and Lysanders, heroic enough names though the machines might belie them in appearance. The Hectors were slim biplanes, advanced editions of the old Hart, but it was the Lysanders, the machines in which it seemed probable that we should be flying for the duration, that really caught our attention. They were squat, heavy, high-winged monoplanes and looked as though they could take a beating. We were less impressed by the two solitary guns, one fixed and firing forward and the other rotatable by the rear gunner.

The road running up to the mess took us close by Salisbury, and the towering steeple of its cathedral was a good landmark from the aerodrome. The countryside lay quiet in the warm glow of the summer evening. A few minutes' flying to the south was the sea, and across from it France, equally peaceful in the quiet of the evening; within a few weeks Britain's army was to be struggling desperately to get back across that narrow stretch of water, and the France that we knew was to be no more.

The course was run with great efficiency by a dapper little squadron leader by the name of Barker. We were divided into squads and spent from nine o'clock in the morning to seven in the evening alternating between lectures and flying our two types of aircraft.

To our delight, on the second day of the course Bill Aitken appeared from Cranwell to join us. We had not seen him since together with most of our friends he had been posted to his FTS several months before. He was the same as ever, rather serious, with deep lines across his broad forehead and little bursts of dry laughter. He did his best to answer all our questions, but when we got around to Frank Waldron and Nigel Bicknell he was inclined to become a little pompous. It appeared that the regulations at Cranwell had been somewhat more strictly enforced than in Scotland. Frank and Nigel had set off with much the same ideas as Noel and I up in Scotland, but with more determination as the rules were stricter, and consequently they had come up against more trouble. They had consistently attempted to avoid lectures, and Frank had crowned his efforts by oversleeping for the wings exam. He was also violently sick whenever he went up (which was not his fault), so the Air Ministry raised little objection when he applied for a transfer to the Scots Guards.

Nigel, it appeared, had found the restrictions an irresistible attraction, and no notice could appear without him hearing of it; he would solemnly produce pieces of red tape from his pocket and pin them around the board. This did not tend to encourage cordial relations with the higher authorities, and when he finally wrote an extremely witty but hardly tactful letter to the Commanding Officer pointing out that Volunteer Reservists had joined the RAF to fight the Germans and not to be treated like children, his stock was at its lowest ebb. He was not actually kicked out, but his record sheet was the blackest of the course and his action resulted in a tightening-up of all restrictions.

'When I left Cranwell,' said Bill, 'he was trying to hook himself a job as Air Force psychologist.'

It was obvious that Bill did not approve, and one could not blame him. He thought their actions represented something deeper than mere fooling-about, a disinclination to face up to the war and a desire to avoid fighting it for as long as possible. He thought further that there were a dangerous number of young men with pseudo-intellectual leanings in the same direction – this last with a significant glance at me.

I disagreed with him. I thought he had made a superficial assessment and said so. I went further: I prophesied that within six months he would have to take those words back, that those very people who were being so unstable at the moment would prove themselves as capable as anyone of facing an emergency when the time came. 'I doubt it,' he said. 'Anyway you know that war has been described as "a period of great boredom, interspersed with moments of great excitement." The man who believes enough in what he's fighting for to put up with the periods of boredom is twice as important in the winning of a war as the man who rises to a crisis.'

Besides Bill we discovered two other familiar figures, Peter Pease and Colin Pinckney. They had both been in the Cambridge Air Squadron before the war. Peter was, I think, the best-looking man I have ever seen. He stood six-foot-three and was of a deceptive slightness, for he weighed close on thirteen stones. He had an outward reserve which protected him from any surface friendships, but for those who troubled to get to know him it was apparent that this reserve masked a deep shyness and a profound integrity of character. Soft-spoken, and with an innate habit of understatement, I never knew him to lose his temper. He never spoke of himself, and it was only through Colin that I learned how well he had done at Eton before his two reflective years at Cambridge, where he had watched events in Europe and made up his mind what part he must play when the exponents of everything he most abhorred began to sweep all before them.

Colin was of the same height but of broader build. He had a bony, pleasantly ugly face and openly admitted that he derived most of his pleasure in life from a good grouse-shoot and a well-proportioned salmon. He was somewhat more forthcoming than Peter but of fundamentally the same instincts. They had been together since the beginning of the war and were now inseparable. I was to become the third corner of a triangle of friendship the record of which will form an important part of the rest of this book. It is therefore perhaps well to stress that Peter Pease, and not Peter Howes, is the peak of this triangle.

The work at Old Sarum was interesting. We studied detailed map-reading, aerial photography, air-to-ground Morse, artillery shoots, and long-distance reconnaissance. The Lysander proved to be a ponderous old gentleman's plane, heavy on the controls but easy to handle. It seemed almost impossible to stall it.

Of flying incidents there were few, though once I did my best to kill my observer. We were on our way back from a photography sortie when I decided to do some aerobatics. As our inter-comm. was not working, I turned round, pointed at the observer, and then tapped my straps, to ask him if he was adequately tied in. He nodded. I started off by doing a couple of stall turns. Behind me I could hear him shouting away in what I took to be an involuntary access of enthusiastic approval. After the second stall turn I put the machine into a loop. On the dive down he leaned forward and shouted in my ear. I waved my hand. On the climb up, I saw him out of the corner of my eye letting himself low down into the rear seat. Then we were up and over. I straightened up and looked back. There was no sign of my observer. I shouted. Still he did not appear. I had a sudden feeling of apprehension. That shouting – could it mean . . .? I peered anxiously over the side. At that moment a white face emerged slowly from the back cockpit, a hand grabbed my shoulder and a voice shouted in my ear: 'For Christ's sake don't do a slow roll, I'm not strapped in!'

He had taken my signals for a query whether I was strapped in. His cries had been not of joy but of fear, and when we had started down on our loop he had dived rapidly to the bottom of the cockpit, clutched feverishly at the camera on the floor for support and convinced that his last hour had come.

I headed back for the aerodrome and, after making a quick circuit, deposited him gingerly on the field, landing as though I had dynamite in the back.

Noel nearly cut short a promising flying career in a Hector. He opened up to take off with the pasteboard instructions for his second Morse exercise on his knee. As the machine gathered speed across the aerodrome the card had dropped from his knee on to the floor. He bent to pick it up, inadvertently pushing the stick farther forward as he did so. The long prop touched the ground and the machine tore its nose in and somersaulted on to its back. It did not catch fire. As the ambulance shot out from the hangars, I remember muttering to myself: 'Pray God, don't be a bloody fool and undo the straps.' Fortunately he did not and escaped with a badly cut tongue and a warning from the CFI that a repetition of the episode would not be treated lightly.

A surprising number of people have managed to kill themselves by putting on their brakes too hard when coming in to land, toppling on to their backs, and then undoing the straps – to fall out on their heads and break their necks.

Every night at nine o'clock the mess was crowded with Army and Air Force officers, men who commonly never bothered to listen to the news, parked round the radio with silent expressionless faces, listening to the extermination of France and the desperate retreat of the British Expeditionary Force.

Privately we learned that Lysanders were hopping across the Channel two or three times daily in an effort to drop supplies to the besieged garrison in Calais, sometimes with a solitary one-gunned Hector for fighter support. As the Lysander was supposed to operate always under a covering layer of fighters, we could imagine how desperate the situation must be.

Then came Dunkirk: tired, ragged men who had once been an army, returning now with German souvenirs but without their own equipment; and the tendency of the public to regard it almost as a victory.

After days on the beaches without sight of British planes these men were bitter, and not unnaturally. They could not be expected to know that, had we not for once managed to gain air superiority behind them, over Flanders, they would never have left Dunkirk alive. For us the evacuation was still a newspaper story, until Noel, Howes, and I got the day off, motored to Brighton, and saw for ourselves.

The beaches, streets, and pubs were a crawling mass of soldiers, British, French, and Belgian. They had no money but were being loyally welcomed by the locals. They were ragged and weary. When Howes suddenly met a blonde and vanished with her and the car for the rest of the day, Noel and I soon found ourselves in various billets acting as interpreters for the French. They were very tired and very patient. It had been so long. What could a few more hours matter? The most frequent request was for somewhere to bathe their feet. When it became obvious that there had been a mix-up, that some billets looked like being hopelessly overcrowded and others empty, we gave up. Collecting two French soldiers and a Belgian dispatch rider, we took them off for a drink. The bar we chose was a seething mass of sweating, turbulent khaki. Before we could even get a drink we were involved in half a dozen arguments over the whereabouts of our aircraft over Dunkirk. Knowing personally several pilots who had been killed, and with some knowledge of the true facts, we found it hard to keep our tempers.

In fairness to the BEF, it must be said that by no means all returned as rabble. A story of the Grenadier Guards was already going the rounds. In columns of three they had marched on to the pier at Dunkirk with complete equipment, as though going for a route march. A Territorial officer, seeing them standing at ease, advanced and started to distribute spoons and forks for them to deal with the food that was being handed out. His efforts were summarily halted by the acid comment of a young Grenadier subaltern:

'Thank you,' he said, 'but the Grenadiers always carry their own cutlery.'

The French were less bitter, possibly out of politeness, but more probably because while they had seen few British aircraft, they had seen no French. But it was our Belgian dispatch rider who surprised and delighted us by endorsing everything we said.

'How could we expect to see many British fighter planes?' he asked. 'There was a heavy fog over the beaches and they were up above.'

One fight, however, he had seen – a lone Spitfire among four Junkers. For him, he said, it had been symbolic, and he admitted having prayed. If that Spitfire came out on top, then they would all be rescued. His prayer was answered. It shot down two Germans, crippled a third, and the fourth made off.

We sat on till well into the night, talking, arguing, singing, getting tight; they, tired and relaxed, content to sit back, their troubles for the moment over, we taut and expectant, braced by our first real contact with the war, eager to get started.

Finally, through an alcoholic haze, we made our farewells and staggered out into the street. Somehow we located both Howes and the car and set off back for Old Sarum. We were late and Howes drove fast. There was no moon. Coming out of a bend, he took the bank with his near-side front wheel, skidded, touched the brake, and hit the bank again. We were still travelling fast. For a moment we hung on two wheels, and then we turned over, once, twice. There was a crash of splintering glass, a tearing noise as two of the doors were torn off, and then, but for the sound of escaping petrol, silence. That week I had bought myself a new service cap and I could see it wedged under Noel's left knee.

'Get off my cap, blast you!' I shouted, thus destroying the silence and bringing down on my head a storm of invective, from which I gathered that none of us was seriously hurt. It turned out that we hadn't even a scratch. 'It looks,' said Howes, 'as though Fate doesn't want us to go out this way. Maybe we have a more exciting death in store for us.' Looking back, unpleasantly prophetic words.

A day or so later all leave was cancelled, no one was allowed farther than half an hour's call from the aerodrome, and the invasion scare was on. An order came that all officers were to carry side arms, and at the station armoury I was issued with an antiquated short-nosed forty-five and six soft-lead bullets. I appealed to the armament sergeant.

'Sorry, sir,' he said, 'but that's the regulation. Just content yourself with six Jerries, sir.'

That in itself would not have been so bad if only the ammunition fitted, which I soon found it did not. With only six bullets there was little temptation to waste any of them practising, but one day by low cunning I managed to get myself another twelve and loosed off. The first round fired but the second jammed. I had .455 bullets for a .45 revolver.

The Government's appeal to the people to stay put and not to evacuate, printed on the front page of every newspaper, roused England to the imminence of disaster. It could actually happen. England's green and pleasant land might at any moment wake to the noise of thundering tanks, to the sight of an army dropping from the skies, and to the realization that it was too late.

In Government departments, city offices and warehouses, in farms, schools, and universities, the civilian population of England woke up. It was their war. From seventeen to seventy they came forward for the Home Guard. If they had no arms – and usually they hadn't – they drilled with brooms. The spirit was there, but the arms and the organization were not.

At Old Sarum we had completed our six weeks and were ready for drafting to our squadrons. Then the inevitable happened, though at that time it seemed more like a miracle. It started as a rumour, but when the whole course was called together and the chief instructor rose to his feet, rumour became reality.

Owing to the sudden collapse of France and our own consequent vulnerability it had been decided that a number of us were to go to fighter squadrons. The Air Ministry had ordered fifteen to be transferred. We each looked at our neighbour as though he were suddenly an enemy. There were twenty of us, and the five who were to continue in Army Co-operation were to be drawn from a hat. It was my worst moment of the war, and I speak for all the others.

Bill Aitken and Peter Pease were both drawn, together with three others. The rest of us almost groaned with relief. But it seemed hard on Peter, though he made no complaint. It would mean his separation from Colin and the loss of a potentially great fighter pilot.

For Bill it did not matter: he was older, that type of flying appealed to him, and he was admirably suited for it. I think he was not too disappointed. The fighter pilots were to go to an Operational Training Unit in Gloucestershire close to the Welsh border, for a fortnight. Then our training would be complete and we would be drafted to fighter squadrons.

Of us all, I think Noel was the most elated. His face wore a permanent fixed grin which nothing could wipe off.

'Spitfires at last,' he kept repeating.

'Spitfires or Hurricanes,' I said meanly.

He continued to grin.

'Don't give a damn. They're both good enough for me.'

We were to leave at once. At the last moment one other man was required and Peter Pease was selected; so it was in a contented frame of mind that we set off.

To our delight our instructors were No. 1 Squadron, back from France, and being given a rest. There is little need for me to say much about them, for through Noel Monk's account in *Squadrons Up* of the part they played at Maastricht Bridge and elsewhere at the front, they must be about the best-known squadron in the RAF.

'Bull' Halahan was still their commanding officer, and Johnnie Walker was in charge of flying. They were the first decorated pilots of this war that we had seen and we regarded them with considerable awe. They were not unaware of this and affected a pointed nonchalance. The Bull was so much what one had expected as to be almost a caricature. A muscled stocky figure with a prominent jaw and an Irish twinkle in his eye, he would roll into the lecture room and start right in with whatever he had to say.

These men treated us as junior members of a squadron. They were friendly and casual, but they expected co-operation and they got it. It was a pleasant change from Training Command. Time was short and we had much to learn.

We learned many things then new, though perhaps no longer true, so swiftly do fighter tactics change. We learned for the first time the German habit of using their fighter escorts in stepped-up layers all around their bombers, their admitted excellence in carrying out some prearranged manoeuvre, and their confusion and ineffectiveness once this was in any way disturbed.

We learned of the advantage of height and of attacking from out of the sun; of the Germans' willingness to fight with height and odds in their favour and their disinclination to mix it on less favourable terms; of the vulnerability of the Messerschmitt 109 when attacked from the rear and its almost standardized method of evasion when so attacked – a half roll, followed by a vertical dive right down to the ground. As the Messerschmitt pilots had to sit on their petrol tanks, it is perhaps hard to blame them.

We learned of the necessity to work as a squadron and to understand thoroughly every command of the Squadron Leader whether given by mouth or gesture.

We learned that we should never follow a plane down after hitting it, for it weakened the effectiveness of the squadron; and further was likely to result in an attack from the rear. This point was driven home by the example of five planes over Dunkirk all of which followed each other down. Only the top machine survived.

If we were so outnumbered that we were forced to break formation, we should attempt to keep in pairs, and never for more than two seconds fly on a straight course. In that moment we might forget all we had ever learned about Rate-1 turns and keeping a watchful eye on the turn-and-bank indicator. We should straighten up only when about to attack, closing in to 200 yards, holding the machine steady in the turbulent slipstream of the other plane, and letting go with all eight guns in short snap bursts of from two to four seconds.

We learned of the German mass psychology applied even to their planes, of how they were so constructed that the crews were always bunched together, thus gaining confidence and a false sense of security.

We learned the importance of getting to know our ground crews and to appreciate their part in a successful day's fighting, to make a careful check-up before taking off, but not to be hypercritical, for the crews would detect and resent any lack of confidence at once.

And we learned, finally, to fly the Spitfire.

I faced the prospect with some trepidation. Here for the first time was a machine in which there was no chance of making a dual circuit as a preliminary. I must solo right off, and in the fastest machine in the world.

One of the squadron took me up for a couple of trips in a Miles Master, the British trainer most similar to a Spitfire in characteristics.

I was put through half an hour's instrument flying under the hood in a Harvard, and then I was ready. At least I hoped I was ready. Kilmartin, a slight dark-haired Irishman in charge of our Flight, said: 'Get your parachute and climb in. I'll just show you the cockpit before you go off.'

He sauntered over to the machine, and I found myself memorizing every detail of his appearance with the clearness of a condemned man on his way to the scaffold – the chin sunk into the folds of a polo sweater, the leather pads on the elbows, and the string-darned hole in the seat of the pants. He caught my look of anxiety and grinned.

'Don't worry; you'll be surprised how easy she is to handle.'

I hoped so.

The Spitfires stood in two lines outside 'A' Flight pilots' room. The dull grey-brown of the camouflage could not conceal the clear-cut beauty, the wicked simplicity of their lines. I hooked up my parachute and climbed awkwardly into the low cockpit. I noticed how small was my field of vision. Kilmartin swung himself on to a wing and started to run through the instruments. I was conscious of his voice, but heard nothing of what he said. I was to fly a Spitfire. It was what I had most wanted through all the long dreary months of training. If I could fly a Spitfire, it would be worth it. Well, I was about to achieve my ambition and felt nothing. I was numb, neither exhilarated nor scared. I noticed the white enamel undercarriage handle. 'Like a lavatory plug,' I thought.

'What did you say?'

Kilmartin was looking at me and I realized I had spoken aloud. I pulled myself together.

'Have you got all that?' he asked.

'Yes, sir.'

'Well, off you go then. About four circuits and bumps. Good luck!'

He climbed down.

I taxied slowly across the field, remembering suddenly what I had been told: that the Spitfire's prop was long and that it was therefore inadvisable to push the stick too far forward when taking off; that the Spitfire was not a Lysander and that any hard application of the brake when landing would result in a somersault and immediate transfer to a 'Battle' squadron. Because of the Battle's lack of power and small armament this was regarded by everyone as the ultimate disgrace.

I ran quickly through my cockpit drill, swung the nose into wind, and took off. I had been flying automatically for several minutes before it dawned on me that I was actually in the air, undercarriage retracted and half-way round the circuit without incident. I turned into wind and hauled up on my seat, at the same time pushing back the hood. I came in low, cut the engine just over the boundary hedge, and floated down on all three points. I took off again. Three more times I came round for a perfect landing. It was too easy. I waited across wind for a minute and watched with satisfaction several machines bounce badly as they came in. Then I taxied rapidly back to the hangars and climbed out nonchalantly. Noel, who had not yet soloed, met me.

'How was it?' he said.

I made a circle of approval with my thumb and forefinger.

'Money for old rope,' I said.

I didn't make another good landing for a week.

The flight immediately following our first solo was an hour's aerobatics. I climbed up to 12,000 feet before attempting even a slow roll. Kilmartin had said 'See if you can make her talk.' That meant the whole bag of tricks, and I wanted ample room for mistakes and possible blacking-out. With one or two very sharp movements on the stick I blacked myself out for a few seconds, but the machine was sweeter to handle than any other that I had flown. I put it through every manoeuvre that I knew of and it responded beautifully. I ended with two flick rolls and turned back for home. I was filled with a sudden exhilarating confidence. I could fly a Spitfire; in any position I was its master. It remained to be seen whether I could fight in one.

We also had to put in an oxygen climb to 28,000 feet, an air-firing exercise, formation attacks, and numerous dog-fights.

The oxygen climb was uneventful but lengthy. It was interesting to see what a distance one ended up from the aerodrome even though climbing all the way in wide circles. Helmet, goggles, and oxygen mask gave me a feeling of restriction, and from then on I always flew with my goggles up, except when landing. The results of this were to be far-reaching.

The air-firing exercise was uneventful, but as short as the oxygen climb had been long. We were given a few rounds in each gun and sent off to fire them into the Severn. All eight guns roared out from a quick pressure on the fire button on the control stick. The noise through the enclosed cabin was muffled, but the recoil caused a momentary drop in speed of forty miles per hour.

For our formation attack practices we usually needed six machines. We flew in two sections of three with an instructor heading each. One section would fly along in V formation representing the enemy and the other would make an attack. The attacking section would also fly in V formation until the enemy were sighted. Then the section leader would call out over the radio-telephone 'Line astern!' and the pilots to right and left of him would drop behind.

A section in line astern is in its most manoeuvrable formation. The leader would then come up on the enemy formation, taking care to keep

well out to one side (usually to starboard) and a few hundred feet above
them. When still some distance off, he would call out 'Echelon starboard!'
and the two following machines would draw out to his right, still keeping
fairly tight formation. When about 300 yards astern and to starboard of
the enemy, he would call out 'Going down!' and all three machines, still
in echelon formation, would dive down and come up behind the target
aircraft. At about 250 yards' range they would open fire (theoretically),
and close in more slowly to about 100 yards when the leader would call
out 'Breaking away!' and with an abrupt movement of stick and rudder
go tearing downwards and sideways beneath the enemy machines, thus
giving the rear gunners, if they were still alive, a double factor to allow
for when taking their aim. The other two machines would follow and
form up again in line astern, this time to port of the enemy and in a
position to repeat the attack. We came up in echelon to avoid cross-fire
– assuming the target aircraft to be bombers – and we broke away
downwards to avoid presenting the bellies of our machines to the rear
gunners. If the target aircraft were fighters, we broke away upwards, as
they had no rear gunners, and by doing so we at the same time gained
height.

When we were sent up for a dog-fight, two of us would go off together
for forty minutes and endeavour in every way possible to 'shoot' each
other down. One learned most from this exercise, of course, when an
instructor was in the other plane; but there were many pilots and few
instructors, so this was a rarity. On one occasion I went up with
Kilmartin. We climbed to 10,000 feet, and he intimated that he would
attempt to get on my tail. He succeeded. In frenzied eagerness I hurled
my machine about the sky. Never, I felt, had such things been done to
a plane. They must inevitably dislodge him. But a quick glance in my
mirror showed that he was quietly behind me like a patient nursemaid
following a too boisterous charge. Only once did I nearly succeed. I did
a particularly tight turn and inadvertently went into a spin which took
me into a cloud. For a moment I had lost him, but I had lost myself, too,
and thus restored the *status quo*.

When we re-established contact, he signalled to me to get on his tail
and stay there. I carried out the first part of my orders admirably and
started to pursue him round in ever-tightening cicles. I attempted to get
him in my sights, but could not quite succeed in doing so. But that did
not prevent me from wondering why he calmly allowed me to follow him
without taking any evasive action: these circles were becoming monotonous
and making me dizzy. I glanced in my mirror and understood. I was
dead long ago, and I could almost imagine that I saw him smile. I was
very glad it was a practice.

I landed considerably mortified and prepared for some withering comments. Kilmartin climbed out of his machine with a sly grin at the corner of his mouth.

'Do you feel as dead as you should?' he asked.

I nodded.

'That's all right,' he said. 'I meant you to. Now I'll give you a few tips for the text time.'

He told me then of the uselessness of all aerobatics in actual combat. Their only value was to give a pilot a feeling of mastery over his machine in any position, upright or inverted. To do a loop was to present a slow-moving sitting target to your opponent, who need only raise the nose of his machine slightly to keep you permanently in his sights. A slow roll was little better. For complete evasion the two most effective methods were a half roll and a controlled spin – especially if you had been hit, for it gave an impression of being out of control. For the rest it was a question of turning inside your opponent (sometimes pulling up and above him, the more effectively to dive down again), of thinking quickly and clearly, of seizing every opportunity and firing at once, and of a quick break-away. All this and more he impressed upon me, and I did my best to carry it out on my subsequent flights. These were less one-sided, but then I never flew with him again.

On these dog-fights we would also practise beam attacks, probably the most effective and certainly the most difficult means of bringing down an enemy machine. The attacking Spitfire would overhaul his target, well out to the side and about 500 feet or so above. When some little way ahead he would bank and turn in, to let the other machine come through his sights almost at right-angles, and with a double deflection (twice the diameter of his sights) he would let go in a long burst. He thus opened fire in front of the enemy's nose and raked him all the way down the side where he had the least protection and the smallest field of fire, while himself presenting a very small and awkwardly moving target for the gunners. He could then drop in behind and deliver another attack from the rear.

But my clearest memory of the course was the bridge. It was across the Severn and linked England to Wales. It was a narrow bridge with close-set arches, and it was the occasion of a long-brewing quarrel for Noel and me.

Noel, Peter Howes, and I had been together now for some time and were beginning to get on one another's nerves. There was soon to be a parting of the ways. It happened at the very end of our training, when we were about to join our squadrons, and was to have consequences which none of us core foresee, which all three of us vaguely sensed, but yet could do nothing to stop. With Howes it took the form of withdrawing into himself, of saying little and of avoiding our company. For Noel and me, fundamentally closer together and considerably quicker-tempered, it could not end like that. There had to be a showdown: the bridge provided it.

Noel, low-flying down the Severn, came to the bridge and flew under it. He came back and told me. From then on the bridge fascinated and frightened me. I had to fly under it. I said as much to Peter Pease. He gave me a long, quizzical stare.

'Richard,' he said, 'from now on a lot of people are going to fly under that bridge. From a flying point of view it proves nothing: it's extremely stupid. From a personal point of view it can only be of value if you don't tell anybody about it.'

He was right, of course.

To fly under the bridge now simply to come back and say that I had done so would be sheer exhibitionism. It would prove nothing. Yet I knew I would fly under it. I had to for my own satisfaction, just as many years before I had had to stand on a twenty-five-foot board above a swimming-pool until I dived off.

There was a strongish wind blowing, and as I came down to a few feet above the river I saw that I had on quite an amount of drift. The span of the arch looked depressingly narrow; I considered pulling up, but forced myself to hold the stick steady. For a moment I thought I was going to hit with the port wing, and then I was through.

It was later in the mess and we were playing billiards when Noel asked me if I had done it. By now we could not even play billiards without the game developing into a silently bitter struggle for supremacy. As Noel nearly always won, he could not have chosen a worse moment to speak.

'Well did you?' he asked.

I played a deliberate shot and didn't answer.

He laughed.

'Surely our little winged wonder isn't getting soft? I was expecting to hear how narrowly you missed death.'

I put down my cue.

'Listen, Noel,' I said. 'For months you've been smugly satisfied that you're a better pilot than I am, and just because I soloed before you here you have to go off and make a bloody fool of yourself under some bridge just to prove that your're still a hell of a pilot. You make me sick.'

He looked at me bitterly.

'Well, little Lord Fauntleroy, this *is* a new angle. And from you, the biggest line-shooter I've ever known. All right. Stick around the hangars cadging extra flights and crawling to the instructors. Maybe they'll give you a good assessment yet.' And with that he slammed red into a corner pocket to win the game and I stalked out of the room and slammed the door.

Next day squadron vacancies were announced. I walked down to the

Adjutant's office with Peter Pease and Colin Pinckney. 603 (City of Edinburgh) Squadron had three vacancies. It was out of the battle area (the first battle over Dover had already been fought), but it was a Spitfire squadron and we could all three go together. We put our names down.

Noel decided to go to Northolt to 609 Squadron to fly Hurricanes, and Peter Howes to Hornchurch to 54 Squadron.

The following day we left. I was to drive up with Peter Pease and we were to make an early start. I piled my luggage into his car and prepared to climb in after it. Then I hesitated and turned back. I found Noel packing. He got up as I came in. We were both embarrassed. I held out my hand.

'Good-bye and good luck,' I said.

'Good-bye, Dick,' he said. 'We've drifted rather a long way apart lately. I'm sorry. Don't let's either of us drift up to Heaven. That's all.'

While he was speaking Peter Howes had come in to say good-bye, too. 'You two needn't worry,' he said. 'You both have the luck of the devil. If the long-haired boys are to be broken up, I have a hunch that I'll be the first to go.' We both told him not to be a fool and agreed to meet, all three of us, in three months' time in London.

They came out to the car.

'Take care of yourself,' said Peter Howes.

'Your courage amazes me,' said Noel. 'Going back to that bloody awful country, and voluntarily!'

I waved and then Peter Pease and I were round the corner on our way. I sat silent most of the way to London, confused by a number of disturbing emotions.

CHAPTER FOUR

THE WORLD OF PETER PEASE

We had two days in which to get to Edinburgh and we spent one night in London, a London still unscarred and carefree, before driving up to Yorkshire, where we intended to break our journey at the Peases'.

Peter drove fast and well, without any of the sudden bursts of acceleration which characterize most fast drivers. For some reason I was surprised. Upright in his seat, his existence was concentrated in his hands on the wheel and in the sole of his foot on the accelerator. There was little traffic on the roads and as we moved out into the open country all nature seemed to sing with the rhythm of the tyres on the hot asphalt. Gradually the countryside turned from a soft green warmth to a gaunt bleakness. I was a little depressed, for we had heard a rumour that Scottish squadrons would not cross the Border. To kick our heels in Scotland with the war at last about to break in the south was not my idea of a design for living. Peter was unruffled and satisfied that we should be in the thick of it before many weeks were past, but with every mile my depression deepened.

'God, how I hate the north,' I said, 'the country, the climate, the people; all craggy, dour, and shut-in. I can go south to France, Italy, or where you will and feel perfectly at home; but north of Oxford I'm in a foreign country.'

Peter laughed. 'That's because at heart you're a man of the capital. You live in London, and you understand it and like it and like the people; but you get up to Manchester or Birmingham, and you see their ugliness with unprejudiced eyes. It appals you. I don't blame you, it appals me, too; but then so does ugliness in London. I'm not prejudiced in London's favour, as you are.'

'Oh, no, it's not only the towns, it's the country, too. What could you have more beautiful than Buckinghamshire – or if it's not beautiful, it's warm and attractive, which is much more important. But as for this—' I waved my hand vaguely out of the window, where the Black Country stretched out wet and dreary on either side.

Peter nodded. 'Yes, it looks pretty ghastly, doesn't it? Yet it all fits in. The people who live here love the grime and the stench and the living conditions. They've never known anything else and it's a part of them. That's why they'll fight this war to the end rather than surrender one inch of it.'

I thought for a moment I was going to get him into an argument about the war, but as soon as he saw what I was after he steered the conversation politely away, and it was not for another six weeks that I was to break down his silence.

We arrived in time for dinner, and the crunch of the tyres on the drive as we swung through the gates prepared me for the comfortably substantial house in front of which we drew up. Colin Pinckney arrived half an hour later, having driven up in a more leisurely manner, and we went in to dinner. The Peases were a devoted family and Peter's parents quite obviously adored him. In that quiet dining-room with just the five of us gathered round the table it occurred to me that if Peter were killed it would be important – not only to his family, but indeed for me, as the deaths of the majority of my friends many of whom I knew better could not be. I was confused and disturbed by this.

After dinner Lady Pease was discussing an offer she had had to send one of her boys, now at Eton, to America, an offer which she had turned down. She felt that it was a bad precedent for well-to-do children to be sent abroad and a very bad preparation for life in a post-war England.

THE LAST ENEMY 319

I agreed with her. I thought of the surprising number of men in responsible positions who seemed determined to get their wives and children out of the country. I didn't quite understand it. The natural reason would be that they didn't want them hurt, but I wasn't sure that that was the whole of it. I didn't believe that a man with something important to do in this war wanted the responsibility of a wife, more especially if he loved her. She was a distracting liability and he would be far happier with her out of the way. Then he could concentrate his whole mind on his job without having to wonder the whole time whether she was safe. All he needed was the purely physical satisfaction of some woman, and that he could get anywhere.

Now, at the Peases', on the way to bed, I asked Colin if he thought that were true. 'To a certain extent,' he replied, 'but like all your generalizations, it doesn't by any means apply universally. For example, how do you fit in all these hurried war marriages with your theory?'

'I admit they don't seem to fit into the picture at first, but I think we can explain them. I don't know if you've noticed it, and again this is one of my generalizations, but it's been almost entirely the little men who have got married.'

'What do you mean,' he asked, 'the little men?'

'Well, as far as I can see, in the Army, and certainly in all squadrons, it's been the nonentity, the fellow who was unsure of himself, standing drinks, always laughing and singing songs in the mess, trying to be one of the chaps and never quite succeeding. He doesn't feel himself accepted by the others and somehow he's got to prove himself, so he does it by marrying some poor, clinging little girl, giving her a child to justify his manhood and then getting killed. She's left with ninety pounds a year, and, I hope, a pleasant memory.'

But Colin, muttering about cynics and how late it was, was already on his way to bed.

Early next morning we were on our way. It was cold in Edinburgh and the damp mist lay heavy on the streets. We drove straight out to the aerodrome at Turnhouse and reported to our CO, Squadron Leader Denholm (known by the squadron as Uncle George). From him we learned that the squadron was operating farther north, 'A' Flight from Dyce and 'B' Flight from Montrose. There was one Spitfire replacement to be flown up to Dyce; Colin got the job and so it came about that Peter and I drove up together to join 'B' Flight at Montrose.

The aerodrome lay just geyond the town and stretched parallel to the sea, one edge of the landing field merging into the dunes. For a few miles around the country was flat, but mountain peaks reared abruptly into the sky, forming a purple backdrop for the aerodrome.

The first person to greet us in the mess was Michael Judd, whom neither of us had seen since our initial training. He was an instructor.

He took us down to the dispersal point to introduce us to the Squadron. Montrose was primarily an FTS where future pilots crowded the air in Miles Masters. As the only possible enemy raids must come from Norway, half a squadron was considered sufficient for its protection.

At our dispersal point at the north-west corner of the aerodrome there were three wooden huts. One of these was the Flight Commander's office; another was reserved for the RT Equipment and technicians; the third, divided into two, was for the pilots and ground crew respectively. It was into this third hut that Michael led us.

From the ceiling hung several models of German aircraft, on the back wall by the stove were pasted seductive creatures by Petty, and on a table in the middle of the room a gramophone was playing, propped at a drunken angle on a pile of old books and magazines. In a corner there was another table on which there were a couple of telephones operated by a corporal. Two beds standing against the longer walls, and several old chairs, completed the furniture.

As we came in, half a dozen heads were turned towards the door and Rushmer, the Flight Commander, came forward to greet us. Like the others, he wore a Mae West and no tunic. Known by everyone as Rusty on account of his dull-red hair, he had a shy manner and a friendly smile. Peter, I could see, sensed a kindred spirit at once. Rusty never ordered things to be done; he merely suggested that it might be a good idea if they were done, and they always were. He had a bland manner and an ability tacitly to ignore anything which he did not wish to hear, which protected him alike from outside interference from his superiors and from too frequent suggestions from his junior officers on how to run the Flight. Rusty had been with the Squadron since before the war: he was a Flight Lieutenant, and in action always led the Red Section. As 603 was an Auxiliary Squadron, all the older members were people with civilian occupations who before the war had flown for pleasure.

Blue Section Leader Larry Cunningham had also been with the Squadron for some time. He was a Scotsman, tall and thin, without Rusty's charm, but with plenty of experience.

Then there was Brian Carbury, a New Zealander who had started in 41 Squadron. He was six-foot-four, with crinkly hair and a roving eye. He greeted us warmly and suggested an immediate adjournment to the mess for drinks. Before the war he had been a shoe salesman in New Zealand. Sick of the job, he had come to England and taken a short service commission. He was now a Flying Officer. There was little distinctive about him on the ground, but he was to prove the Squadron's greatest asset in the air.

Another from overseas was Hugh Stapleton, a South African. He hoped to return after the war and run an orange farm. He, too, was over six feet tall, thick-set, with a mass of blond hair which he never brushed.

He was twenty and married, with a rough *savoir-faire* beyond his years, acquired from an early unprotected acquaintance with life. He was always losing buttons off his uniform and had a pair of patched trousers which the rest of the Squadron swore he slept in. He was completely slap-happy and known as 'Stapme' because of his predilection for Popeye in the *Daily Mirror*, his favourite literature.

Pilot Officer Berry, commonly known as Raspberry, came from Hull. He was short and stocky, with a ruddy complexion and a mouth that was always grinning or coming out with some broad Yorkshire witticism impossible to answer. Above that mouth, surprisingly, sprouted a heavy black moustache, which induced me to call him the organ-grinder. His reply to this was always unprintable but very much to the point. Even on the blackest days he radiated an infectious good-humour. His aggressive spirit chafed at the Squadron's present inactivity and he was always the first to hear any rumour of our moving south.

'Bubble' Waterson was twenty-four, but he looked eighteen, with his short-cropped hair and open face. He, too, had been with the Squadron for some time before the war. He had been studying in Scotland for an engineering degree. He had great curiosity about anything mechanical, and was always tinkering with the engine of his car. His unquestioning acceptance of everyone and his unconscious charm made him the most popular member of the Squadron.

Then there was Boulter, with jutting ears framing the face of an intelligent ferret, always sleepy and in bed snoring when off duty; 'Broody' Benson, nineteen years old, a fine pilot and possessed of only one idea, to shoot down Huns, more Huns, and then still more Huns; Don MacDonald, who had been in the Cambridge Squadron and had an elder brother in 'A' Flight at Dyce; and finally Pip Cardell, the most recent addition to the Squadron before our arrival, still bewildered, excited, and a little lost.

For the first week or so Peter and I were not to be operational. We would have a chance to utilize the Squadron's comparative inactivity to acquaint ourselves thoroughly with the flying idiosyncrasies of the others.

All that we had on duty at a time was one Readiness Section of three machines: the rest of the Squadron were either available (ready to take off within half an hour of a call) or released (allowed off the aerodrome). With a full complement of pilots, it was nearly always possible for two of us to get up into the hills for a couple of days a week, where we shot grouse. The same system applied to 'A' Flight at Dyce.

At this time the Germans were sending over single raiders from Norway, and with six Spitfires between Dyce and Montrose there was little difficulty in shooting them down. Operations would ring through, the corporal at the telephone in the pilots' room would call out, 'Red Section scramble base,' one of us would fire a red Very light to clear the air of all training aircraft, and within a couple of minutes three machines would be in the air climbing rapidly. The leader, in constant radio touch with the ground, would be given a course on which to fly to intercept the enemy. So good was the ground control that it was not infrequent to make an interception forty miles out to sea. The Section would then carry out a copy-book attack; the bomber would come down in the sea, and her crew, if still alive, would push off in a rubber boat, waving frantically. The Section would radio back the derelicts' position, turn for home, and that would be that.

On one occasion, when I was still not operational, I was flying up the coast when I heard Operations order our Blue Section into the air and start radioing the bomber's position. I should have returned to the base; but instead I grabbed my map and pin-pointed its position – about four miles south of me and heading out to sea. Without reporting my intention, I set off after it, delighted at the prospect of returning and nonchalantly announcing its destruction single-handed.

It was a cloudy day and a fair guess that the enemy machine would be flying just in the bottom of the cloud base. Up to this minute I had behaved fairly rationally, but I now began a series of slow climbs and dives in and out of the clouds in search of my quarry. Finding nothing, I turned back and landed, to discover that two minutes earlier the enemy machine had flown right across the aerodrome at 1,000 feet. It was not until Brian Carbury landed with his Section and inquired sweetly whether I'd had fun that I learned how nearly I had been killed. Having received no notice of any other friendly aircraft, and seeing a machine popping in and out of the clouds, he had put his Section in 'line astern' and had been about to open fire when he recognized me as a Spitfire.

Next day Rusty made both Peter and me operational. 'I think it will be safer for the others,' he explained apologetically.

My first assignment, though not exciting, was for me particularly interesting. It meant flying down to Oxford. I had not been back since the war began and I was curious to see how different it would all seem now.

Noel had been there recently to see his family and had written to me: 'Richard, whatever you do, don't go back. It would take a book to explain how it's changed; but to sum it up in one sentence – in the Randolph Bar there is a notice saying: "No unaccompanied ladies will be served with drinks." '

I flew down with one halt on the way and arrived in the early evening. I came down low and circled the city, looking for familiar landmarks. I picked out the Isis, a tiny mud-puddle, and the barges dotted along its bank; the Broad, and Trinity, with its well-kept gardens obvious from even that height; Longwall and Magdalen Tower. I made a couple of circuits and came in. This, the first part of my visit, was entirely satisfactory, for my bank manager was a member of the Home Guard and on duty at the time. He was suitably impressed with me as a pilot, and when next morning I called upon him, without much hope, for an extension of my overdraft, he was more than obliging.

On landing I called up Rusty and reported, then I hailed a taxi and drove straight down to Trinity.

Superficially it was unchanged. Huckins, the porter, was still at the gate. 'Good evening, Mr Hillary,' he said, in the same lugubrious tone in which he would announce that one was to be reported to the Dean. The windows of my rooms over the chapel still looked out on the quad and caught the evening rays of the sun, and a few old college servants raised friendly hands to their forelocks. But, apart from them, not a familiar face. It was, of course, out of term, but Trinity, unlike most colleges, had not been amalgamated or handed over to the Government, and I had hoped to see a few dons I knew. The old place was tired; it had the left-over air of a seaside resort in winter. I walked into the garden quad and looked around at the uncurtained windows.

There was Algy Young's old room in which I had spent many an agreeable evening. Algy had looked like playing rugger for the University. Of a serious disposition, he could not make up his mind whether to go into politics or business. I remember how often we had laughed at him for his enjoyment of food and getting fat. Well, it was doubtful if he was enjoying either now in Oflag VII C, having been captured along with the rest of the Highland Division at Dunkirk.

And there was Staircase 15. Alwyn Stevens had had a room there. We had rowed together in the Head of the River Boat for two years. Moody and of uncertain temper as he was, the rest of us had not gone out of our way to understand him, and he had wrapped himself up in his work, surprising everyone when it was understood that he had a good chance of a First in Law. He had been killed flying.

Peter Krabbé had also been on that staircase. Boisterous, amusing, and sarcastic, he had not come back from France.

I climbed to my old room, intending to find someone to make me up a bed for the night. All the furniture lay heaped in a corner, a mounted oar still hung over the fireplace, exaggerating if anything the bareness of the room. Geo. Coles had had the rooms before me. With his enormous shoulders he had had been heavy-weight boxer for the University and a Rugger Blue. Of no enormous mental stature, he had not let it worry him and had led the life which amused him. At the beginning of the war he had managed to get a permanent commission in the Air Force: it was only a week since he had been seen going down in flames over France.

I kicked a chair-leg dispiritedly and went back down the stairs, intending to take a room for the night at the Randolph. I had no luggage. I hoped they'd try to stop me. At the bottom of the stairs I ran into the President's wife. She offered to put me up for the night. I accepted gratefully, explaining I might be late as I must go to the depot to make some arrangements. I then set off to survey the town. My first stop was the Randolph, where the truth of Noel's warning was forcibly brought home to me. The bar was full, but of strange faces, and Mary was no longer there to serve drinks. Some harassed creature pushed me a pink gin and forgot my change. I was about to give up and leave when I saw Eric Dehn. Eric and I had been to school together and we had done two years together at Oxford. He was in battle dress, and as amusing as ever. He had been in France but had got out at Dunkirk. He was as depressed as I, but we went along to the George for an excellent dinner and then on to the Playhouse to look up some of Eric's girl friends, with whom we passed a pleasant enough evening. It was very late when I got back to Trinity and took off my shoes, the more quietly to climb the President's stairs (one's education dies hard).

I was slightly drunk as I got undressed and crawled into bed. 'This,' I thought to myself hazily, 'symbolizes everything. Tonight you sleep in the President's linen in your underpants; tomorrow God knows!' And with that I fell asleep. I was glad to go back to Montrose.

At this time we were still using Spitfires as night fighters. Now the Spitfire is not a good machine for night fighting. Its landing run is too long and the flames from its own exhaust make the pilot's visibility uncomfortably small. Shortly afterwards the whole problem of night interception was radically revised (with great success), but for the moment night fighting in Spitfires produced little more than hours to go in one's log-book. Three of us would spend the night in the dispersal hut waiting for a 'flap'. When it came, one machine would take off, and I as the junior squadron member would canter down the flare path, putting out all the lamps until the second machine took off some ten minutes later, when I would put them all on again. Meanwhile, there would be the uneven hum of a German bomber circling above, an experience which always gave me prickles down the spine.

For the most part, life at Montrose was very agreeable. We knew that at no very distant date the war would be upon us; but momentarily it was remote and we were enjoying ourselves. In the time when it was possible to get away from the station for a couple of days, most of us motored up to Invermark where Lord Dalhousie had kindly turned over his shooting lodge to us. Here in the deep stillness of the mountains it was possible to relax, and the war, if it penetrated at all, was wafted up as the breath of the vulgarity of another world. We shot grouse and fished on the loch, and on one occasion after an arduous day's stalking I shot a stag; but I am no sportsman and the dying look in the beast's eyes resolved me to confine my killing to Germans.

I was therefore relieved and grateful when Stapme and Bubble let me in on their preciously guarded secret. We three flew together and therefore had the same time off. Stapme and Bubble would both come up to Invermark, but neither of them shot. How they employed their few hours of freedom will, I think, come as a surprise to a number of people, for they must have seemed from the outside as typical a pair of easy-going pilots as one could expect to meet anywhere. Stapme with his talk of beer, blokes, and carburettors, and Bubble with his absorption in things mechanical, might have been expected to spend their leaves, respectively, in a too fast car with a too loud blonde, and in getting together with the chaps in the local pub. In point of fact they played hide-and-seek with children.

Tarfside was a tiny hamlet a few miles down the road from Invermark. and to it this summer had come a dozen or so Scots children, evacuated from the more vulnerable towns in the district. They went to school at Brechin, a few miles from Montrose, but for the holidays they came to the mountains, under the care of Mrs Davie, the admirable and unexacting mother of two of them. Their ages ranged from six to sixteen.

How Stapme and Bubble had first come upon them I never discovered, but from the moment that I saw those children I, too, was under their spell. That they really came from Brechin, that thin-blooded Wigan of the north, I was not prepared to admit; kilted and tanned by the sun, they were so essentially *right* against that background of heather, burns, and pine. They were in no way precocious, but rather completely natural and unselfconscious. In the general confusion of introductions, one little fellow, the smallest, was left out. He approached me slowly with a grave face.

'I'm Rat Face,' he said.

'How are you, Rat Face?' I asked.

'Quite well, thank you. You can pick me up if you like.'

I gave him a pick-a-back, and all day we played rounders, hide-and-seek, or picknicked, and as evening drew on we climbed up into the old hayloft and told stories, Stapme, Bubble, and I striving to outdo one another.

I lost my heart completely to Betty Davie, aged ten. She confided to me that I was her favourite, and I was ridiculously gratified. She was determined to be a school teacher, but with those eyes and the promise of those lips I did not doubt that her resolution would weaken.

It was with regret that we drove back to the aerodrome, and with a latent fear that we should not get back to Tarfside. We drove always straight to the dispersal point, each time expecting the greeting: 'Tomorrow we move south.' Out before the huts crouched our Spitfires, seemingly eager to be gone, the boldly painted names on their noses standing out in the gathering dusk. Nearly every plane was called by name, names as divergent as Boomerang, Valkyrie, and Angel Face. Mine I called Sredni Vashtar, after the immortal short story of Saki.

Sredni Vashtar was a ferret, worshipped and kept in the tool-shed by a little boy called Conradin: it finally made a meal of Conradin's most disagreeable guardian, Mrs De Ropp. Conradin in his worship would chant this hymn:

> Sredni Vashtar went forth,
> His thoughts were red thoughts and his teeth were white,
> His enemies called for peace, but he brought them death,
> Sredni Vashtar the Beautiful.

I thought it appropriate.

The legend of the children at Tarfside soon spread through the Squadron, and no three machines would return from a practice flight without first sweeping in tight formation low along the bed of the valley where the children, grouped on a patch of grass by the road, would wave and shout and dance in ecstasy.

Although our leaves did not coincide, I saw a fair amount of Peter Pease, but I found him exasperatingly elusive. I had an urge to get behind that polite reserve, and by drawing him into argument to discover how his mind worked. The more reserved he was the more sarcastically aggressive I became. It was to no avail. I would throw him the ball and he would quietly put it in his pocket. Whenever I thought I had him cornered he would smilingly excuse himself and retire to his rooms to write letters. What I did not know, but might have guessed, was that he was in love.

One occasion, however, we drove up to Aberdeen to see Colin and had dinner together in the town. Once Colin and I conspired to get him into some dance hop. We both expressed an eagerness to go in, and rather than be awkward he agreed to go with us. The smell of humanity was oppressive, and we sat on the balcony watching the closely-packed couples slowly circling the floor. A young woman, powerfully scented and with startlingly blonde hair, was sitting next to me.

'You do look mournful,'' she said. 'Come and have a dance.'

I pointed apologetically to my foot and sighed:

'Twisted my ankle, I'm afraid, but my friend here is a good dancer.'

I turned to Peter Pease and said, 'I want you to meet Miss— I'm sorry, I didn't get your name?'

'McBride. Dolly, my friends call me.'

'Miss McBride, Mr Pease.'

Peter got to his feet.

'I'm afraid I don't dance a tango very well, but I'd like to try.'

They went off down the stairs, to appear a moment later on the floor. Colin and I craned our necks. Dolly was looking eagerly up at Peter and they were talking and laughing. At the end of the dance Peter led her from the floor, thanked her, and started back up the stairs.

'It's no good,' said Colin mournfully. 'I might have known: the laugh's on us.'

I resented Peter's self-confidence, for while he was shy, he was perfectly assured. I rather prided myself on my self-sufficiency, on my ability to be perfectly at ease with people of any standing or any age, but with Peter I felt, as it were, that at any moment he might discover me wearing a made-up tie. He would, of course, not be so tactless as to mention it, would in fact put himself out to be even more charming than before. But there it would be: no getting round it, the fellow knew. Well, damn it, why shouldn't I wear a made-up tie if I wanted to?

I resented this assurance, basically because here was a man better orientated than I, and as the result of an upbringing and a system of education which I deeply distrusted and had in the past despised as being quite incapable of producing anything but, at the best, congenital idiots, and at the worst, fox-hunting bounders. For he was a product of the old-school-tie system in its most extreme form. He was more than comfortably off; his father owned property which in due course, as the eldest son, he would inherit; he had been brought up in the orthodox Tory tradition and in the belief that this was as it should be.

I often attacked him and accused him of living in an ivory tower, but he refused to be drawn; indeed, there was little reason why he should be, for it was only too obvious that he was liked and respected by everyone in the squadron. It was in fact almost impossible to draw him into an argument on any subject, though I tried everything, from apparently harmless conversation to attempts to make him lose his temper.

I wanted particularly to make him talk about the war, and in this I was determined to succeed. I knew that I need not expect any glib arguments. He was religious, and, I felt pretty certain, would not attempt to put forward any but the orthodox Christian views. Yet I wanted to hear his arguments from his own lips. I had an idea that the issue for him was an apprehension of something related to faith and not to any intellectual concept.

My chance came when we were sent down from Montrose to Edinburgh by train to fly up a couple of new Spitfires. We had the compartment to ourselves. I didn't temporize but asked him straight out his reasons for fighting the war. He gave me that slow smile of his.

'Well, Richard,' he said, 'you've got me at last, haven't you?'

He sat back in his corner and thought for a moment. Words didn't come easily to him, and I am bound to confess that in reconstructing his argument I do a certain violence to his expression. He was not as fluent as I shall make him. But what follows is at any rate the substance of his position.

'I don't know if I can answer you to your satisfaction,' he said, 'but I'll try. I would say that I was fighting the war to rid the world of fear

– of the fear of fear is perhaps what I mean. If the Germans win this war, nobody except little Hitlers will dare do anything. England will be run as if it were a concentration camp, or at best a factory. All courage will die out of the world – the courage to love, to create, to take risks, whether physical or intellectual or moral. Men will hesitate to carry out the promptings of the heart or the brain because, having acted, they will live in fear that their action may be discovered and themselves cruelly punished. Thus all love, all spontaneity, will die out of the world. Emotion will have atrophied. Thought will have petrified. The oxygen breathed by the soul, so to speak, will vanish, and mankind will wither. Does that satisfy you?'

'It's a good speech,' I said, 'but it's all big words. It's all negative. Isn't there something positive you want?'

Peter flushed slightly. He who was the last person to clothe his feelings in big words had done so out of regard for me; and I had reproached him. But he was persistent. What he had started he would finish.

'Something positive I want? But of course. Only, saying what it is means big words again, confound you, Richard! What I want is to see a better world come out of this war.'

'What do you mean by *better*? ' I challenged him. 'Christian, I suppose.'

'Now who is using the big words?' he wanted to know. 'You've used the biggest word of all. Yes, Christian, of course. Nothing else. It isn't only that I am a Christian by faith. It's that I don't know any other way of life worth fighting for. Christianity means to me, on the social plane, freedom, man's humanity to man. Everything else I see as man's inhumanity to man. I believe that we should all make our contribution, even though it's a mere drop in the ocean, to the betterment of humanity. I know that, put into words, it sounds sentimental, and, of course, you don't agree. I can see that.'

I nodded. 'You're quite right,' I said. 'I don't. I think that your Christianity clouds the issue, makes it harder to see what we're talking about. As I see it there are three possible philosophies. First, there is hedonism, living purely for pleasure. The rich, by and large, did nothing but that here in England until practically the other day – that is, the non-industrial rich. And that life is over. Only the rich could live that way, and now the poor aren't going to allow it any longer. Secondly, one can live for the good of the community – or for the betterment of mankind, as you would put it. Though how one is to be certain that one's contribution *is* bettering humanity, God only knows.'

'Yes,' Peter said, 'He unquestionably does.'

I threw up my hands. 'There you go,' I said. 'All you religious people are alike. In the end you always fall back upon infallible faith. 'I feel it here,' you say, with a hand on your stomachs. Well, I may feel just the same thing; but with me it's indigestion, or the exaltation I get from an hour of great music, or from Lear and Cordelia.'

Peter stared out of the window. I was a little ashamed of that crack about the hand on the stomach. It smelled of Hyde Park oratory. And I could have gone on more easily if I felt that I had hurt him, or angered him. I knew that what was disturbing him was simply the distance between us, the gulf.

'Look at your missionary,' I went on. 'He goes off to Bunga Bunga land to convert the blacks to bowler hats and spats. He's quite certain that he has the call to dedicate himself to humanity. In point of fact he's probably putting into practice the third philosophy, the only one in which I can believe. That is, to live for the realization of one's self. Some do it by preaching, some by making love, others by building locomotives or smashing stock markets.'

'If I gather what you mean,' Peter said, 'you mean something I should call rather base. In fact I couldn't imagine a lower form of life. Can you be more explicit?'

'Well,' I said, 'to be perfectly brutal about it – though actually it isn't in the least a brutal thing – I mean using the world as opposed to being used by the world. Every single artist who ever lived, every great scientist, did exactly that. You couldn't find a better example than Goethe, for instance, or Newton, or Leonardo. Would the world be poorer or richer if Goethe had been killed fighting for his native Frankfurt, or Leonardo had been stuck in the ribs by some petty Italian tyrant's lance? Or if Einstein had been beaten to death by the Gestapo because his "soul" commanded that he fight for the Jewish peoples?'

Peter, who was not ordinarily witty or mischievous, smiled almost maliciously.

'And is our Richard planning to be a Goethe or a Newton?' he asked. Before I could break in he had gone on: 'There was Joan of Arc, you know.'

'You couldn't cite a better instance of what I mean,' I said quickly. 'Obsessed with self-realization, she was. The Voices were *her* voices, the king of France was *her* king, the French were *her* people. God! What an egomaniac!

'But let me go on. You don't have to be a Goethe. I'm not concerned with genius. I'm concerned with my own potentialities. I say that I am fighting this war because I believe that, in war, one can swiftly develop all one's faculties to a degree it would normally take half a lifetime to achieve. And to do this you must be as free from outside interference as possible. That's why I'm in the Air Force. For in a Spitfire we're back to war as it ought to be – if you can talk about war as it ought to be. Back to individual combat, to self-reliance, total responsibility for one's own fate. One either kills or is killed; and it's damned exciting. And after the war, when I shall be writing, I'll again be developing faster than the rest of you. Because a writer is constantly digging into himself, penetrating the life and nature of man, and thus realizing himself.'

'Richard, I don't understand you,' Peter said. 'All your talk is hard-boiled; you as much as proclaim yourself a realist. And yet you are so fuzzy-minded as to assume that you'll be allowed to dig into yourself and the rest in a German-dominated world. You're not a medieval mystic, you know. You'll be able to think, perhaps, in a concentration camp, but not to write and impart what you think.'

'Of course I won't. Don't take me for a bloody fool. Besides, we're agreed about the necessity for smashing the Germans. It's the purpose that we're arguing about. I want to smash them in order to be free to grow; you in order to be free to worship your God and lead your villagers in prayer.'

'Suppose we go in to lunch,' said Peter. 'I could do with something to eat.'

We made our way along to the dining-car, clambering over feet, kit-bags, and suitcases, tossed from compartment door to window and back again by the motion of the train. We were passing through rough river-scored mountains, deceptively clothed with a soft brown moss. 'No place for a forced landing,' I thought automatically.

The dining-car was full, one or two business men but mostly uniforms. We managed to get ourselves a couple of seats and I took a look at them. I wondered if these people asked themselves such questions as I was asking Peter – probably not, if what foreigners say about the English is true, that we hate thinking, analysis. Peter certainly did, and I left him alone through lunch.

When we had got back to our compartment Peter gave a sigh of content and settled back in the corner, happy in the belief that his ordeal was over. But I hadn't said the half of what was on my mind. I knew that I should surely never get such a chance at him again. So I started.

'Look here, Peter,' I said. 'Let's begin by agreeing that I am a selfish swine, and am in the war only to get what I can out of it. But what about you? You're a landowner – a sort of dodo, a species nearly extinct. . . . No, don't stop me! Even though you may not own half England, you're representative of the type. I'm quite ready to agree that you're not fighting to maintain the present system of land tenure. You're fighting for all the ideals you mentioned earlier. I know that. Do you expect me to make the world a better place for your dependants to live in, solely through Christianity; and if so, how?'

Peter rather pointedly opened a window and stood staring out at the passing countryside. He was struggling to arrange his thoughts, to find words; and what he said came out so slowly, in such fragments of discourse, that I shall not attempt to give it shape. It was nothing new, and it came to this. He would be as decent to those in a less fortunate position as he possibly could, more especially to those dependent on him. He hoped that his rôle would consist in helping them, protecting them, keeping alive that ancient sturdy self-reliance of the true-born Englishman that had made England what she was.

About this I must say one thing. While Peter's words were all clichés on the surface, all copybook talk, underneath they were terrific. He was saying what was to him almost the most important thing he could say, something as intense as a prayer to his God. What he said was, if you like, stupidly English. But what he would *do*, the lengths to which he would go, the probity and charity with which he would live that extinct form of existence, would also be English; and magnificently English. Extinct is the word: Peter was the very parfit knyght.

I realized all this as he spoke, but I had no intention of pulling my punches because of it. 'Well,' said I, 'if I had your altruism I'd try economics and not religion as my nostrum. I'd say to myself, we must do away with this unemployment, muck, under-nourishment, and the rest of the horror that is the chief characteristic of every Christian State since Constantine became a Christian. And it differs from the non-Christian State only in that the others haven't been such raging persecutors of men of other faiths. Of course, there will still be what you'd call original sin. You still won't be able to prevent one man wanting to pop into bed with another man's wife. But on balance I should say you would be getting nearer to saving the world by economics than by religion, the greatest instrument of persecution ever devised.'

'Oh, now wait a minute!' Peter protested. 'I don't know much about either religion or economics, but I know this. Religious persecution has been periodic, but economic persecution has been constant, uninterrupted, never-ending. There's no evidence in history of men being better disposed towards one another because of economics, but there is some evidence of their being so through religion.' Now he was on a subject he could warm to. Where he got his fresh eloquence from I don't know; but he went on more or less in this vein: 'We're talking about two different things, you and I. You are talking about material misery and crime, and so on; whereas I am talking about something you're not interested in – sin, and the harm man does to himself. What I'm trying to say is this, that men who possess the religious sense know that you can't injure others without doing harm to yourself. You agree that there has always been economic misery. You're almost ready to admit it can't be altogether done away with. Well, make men Christians, I say, and they won't hurt others because they won't want to hurt themselves, their immortal souls.'

It was queer how I, who had taken the offensive from the beginning, was now being put on the defensive by the conviction behind Peter's words. I was convinced, too; but I was not half as collected in that

compartment as I am now, writing the debate out from memory. I recall
that we rambled round the subject a good deal, and that Peter admitted
he'd perhaps try to stand for Parliament. I pointed out to him that he
would have either to vote with his Party on every issue – if there still was
a dear old-fashioned Parliament – or retire a disappointed reformer.
Suppose, I said, he turned out like Neville Chamberlain, acted as his
conscience prompted and then found out he'd been a – well, never mind
the epithet. I told him that as a writer I should be content to go my own
way and be governed by any set of politicians he or his political enemies
could dish up for the misguidance of the perhaps excessively patient
British people.

But Peter had an answer to this. 'Do you realize,' he asked, 'that your
lofty political irresponsibilities are exactly what the Nazis are drilling
into the German people? You reject their system because you're an
individualist and don't like taking orders. But if you are politically
irresponsible, you have to take orders. I reject Nazism not only because
I have a sense of history, but also because, unlike you, I believe its
purpose is to stamp out the divine spark in Man.'

We should be pulling into Edinburgh soon. I wasn't satisfied. Politics
was an easier subject than the immortal soul, and I went back at him on
that tack.

'How,' I asked, 'are you going to reconcile your moral and religious
convictions with being a loyal Party member? Especially if you were
successful, and were taken into the Cabinet, some of the acts you
committed in the name of the State would get you put away for life if you
committed them as an individual.'

'Now, Richard,' Peter started to protest; but I stopped him.

'No, no. Let me go on. In time of need – and politics are continuously
in times of need – the rulers, the ruling classes, are always able to evoke
exceptional circumstances and glibly plead the need of exceptional measures. They are for ever in a state of self-defence. You may define reform
by saying that it indicates a weak state of ruling-class defence. Revolution
you may define by saying that it represents the breakdown of ruling-class
defence. You, as a Cabinet member, would spend your life defending a
class interest – by a concession to the common people when the defences
were weak, by a disguised persecution when your defences were strong.
Yes, you would! You wouldn't be able to help yourself. You'd be a cog
in the Party machine – or, as I've hinted before a mere overseer of your
baronial acres who hadn't been able to stand the gaff in Whitehall.'

My tirade had freshened me. I was feeling 'fine,' as Hemingway would
say; as fine as one of his heroes when a well-born girl offers him a bottle
of precious brandy if only he will go to bed with her. Peter stared at me
with a glint of curiosity in his eye. The day was darkening, and in the

half-light his bony face had taken on a decidedly ascetic look, so that I felt more than ever in contact with an alien spiritual world.

'You're not a Communist, Richard,' he said –

'God knows I'm not!'

'– but you are an anarchist.'

'Nonsense!' said I. 'It's simpler than that. You are going to concern yourself with politics and mankind when the war is over: I am going to concern myself with the individual and Richard Hillary. I may or may not be exactly a man of my time: I don't know. But I know that you are an anachronism. In an age when to love one's country is vulgar, to love God archaic, and to love mankind sentimental, you do all three. If you can work out a harmonious synthesis, I'll take my hat off to you. The really funny thing is that I, as an individual, shall certainly do less harm to the world writing than you as a Party member, a governor of the nation, are bound to do in office.'

'That,' said Peter, 'is most certainly not true. I don't read much myself; but lots of people round me do. And the harm done them by their reading these past few years has been absolutely appalling. It is taking this war to correct the flubdub of the nineteen-twenties' pacifism. All due to writers! Was there a single poet in Oxford who didn't write surrealist economics, who didn't proclaim that he refused to fight for king and country, instead of sticking to his cuckoos and bluebells? Not one! Besides, wasn't it your friend Goethe who said that while an artist never writes with a moral end in view, the effect of a work of art is always moral?'

'Yes, my good Peter,' I said. 'But that's where I have you, because I don't care. The mass of mankind leaves me cold. My only concern outside myself is my immediate circle of friends, to whom I behave well, basically, I suppose, because I hope they'll behave well towards me. That's merely oiling the wheels of an agreeable existence. Thus if I were asked to contribute to a friend of mine about to go down from Oxford through lack of money I would do so willingly, but if I were asked to subscribe to some African chief's wife because she was being beaten up by her husband I should refuse as I wouldn't know the good lady. But that in effect is what you're asking us all to do.'

'Oh, but you're such a fraud, Richard,' he said cheerfully. 'What about those children at Tarfside?'

'For God's sake,' I said, 'they gave me more pleasure than I gave them. I was taking, not giving.'

Peter groaned.

'I know, I know,' I said. 'You are about to tell me that in time, looking at the world and its featherless bipeds, studying the machinery that animates them, and describing it, I shall grow very fond of them. I shall end up with whiskers and a rage for primitive Christianity, like Tolstoi;

or bald and sitting in homespuns among my worshippers, like Gandhi. But I shan't, and if you live long enough I'll prove it to you.'

Peter said: 'I can see that neither of us going to convince the other. And I don't mind at all admitting that I am sure you will change your tune. It won't be long either. Something bigger than you and me is coming out of this, and as it grown you'll grow with it. Your preconceived notions won't last long. You are not entirely unfeeling, Richard. I'm sure it needs only some psychological shock, some affront to your sensibility, to arouse your pity or your anger sufficiently to make you forget yourself.'

'I doubt it,' I said; and at that we left it.

We spent the night at Turnhouse, collected the two Spitfires and flew back to Montrose. Before I had switched off, Bubble was climbing up on to the wing.

'Get your things packed and hand them over to Sergeant Ross. We're on our way. You'd left before we could stop you.'

It had come at last. The whole Squadron was moving down to Turnhouse. That was only Edinburgh, but with the German offensive in full swing in the south, it could mean only one thing. In a very few days we should be farther south and in it. Broody Benson was hopping up and down like a madman.

'Now we'll show the bastards! Jesus, will we show 'em!'

Stapme was capering about shaking everyone by the hand, and Raspberry's moustache looked as though it would fall off with excitement. 'Eh, now they'll cop it and no mistake,' he chortled. 'I've had just about enough of bulling about up here!' Even Boulter was out of bed, his ears twitching uncontrollably. Our relief squadron was already coming in, plane after plane engining down over the boundary. Rusty quickly allocated us to sections, and 'B' Flight roared twelve strong across the aerodrome, dipped once over the mess, and headed south.

For a moment I thought Rusty had forgotten, but then I heard his voice down the RT, 'Once more, boys,' and in four sections of three we were banking to starboard and headed for the mountains.

They had heard the news, and as we went into line astern and dived one by one in salute over the valley, none of the children moved or shouted. With white boulders they had spelt out on the road the two words: 'Good Luck.'

We rejoined formation and once again headed south. I looked back. The children stood close together on the grass, their hands raised in silent farewell.

CHAPTER FIVE

THE INVADERS

After kicking our heels for two days at Turnhouse, a reaction set in. We were like children with the promise of a trip to the seaside, broken because of rain. On the third day I allowed myself to be persuaded against my better judgment to take up a gun again.

The Duke of Hamilton, the Station CO, had offered the Squadron a couple of days grouse-shooting on his estate. Colin, of course, was eager to go as were two other 'A' Flight pilots, Sheep Gilroy and Black Morton. Sheep was a Scotsman and a farmer, with a port-wine complexion and features which gave rise to his name. I finally agreed to go in place of Peter Pease, who was on duty, and the four of us set off. It was pouring with rain when we arrived, to be greeted by the usual intimidating band of beaters, loaders, gillies, and what-not. We set off at once for the butts, an uphill climb across the moors of a mere couple of miles, the others apparently in no way put out by the weather. We climbed in single file, I bringing up the protesting rear, miserable, wet, and muddy from repeated falls into the heather. After about an hour we reached the top and disposed ourselves in four butts, while the beaters, loaders, gillies, and what-not squelched away into the mist. After the first half-hour, during which my hands turned blue and my feet lost all feeling, I sat down and resigned myself to the sensation of the wet earth steadily seeping through my breeches. From time to time I got up and looked over at the others, alert, guns gripped firmly, staring eagerly into the mist, and I was ashamed of my craven spirit: I chid myself. Were there not gentlemen – and the right type of gentlemen too – who paid £30 a day for the privilege of just such suffering? My musings were interrupted by a series of animal cries, and from out of the mist emerged the beaters, beating. As a result of this lengthy co-ordination of effort one hare and two rather tired-looking birds put in an apologetic short-lived appearance, to be summarily dispatched by our withering fire. The prospect of lunch cheered me, and my hunger was such that I was undismayed at the thought of the long walk back, but my illusions were rudely shattered when we set off purposefully for a second lot of butts where a larger flock, flight, covey, or what-have-you was expected. Once again the beaters vanished into the mist, once again we were left damply to our meditations, and once again a discreet flutter of wings rewarded our vigil. This time my cries of hunger were accorded a grudging attention and we set off for the brake, parked some miles away and containing whisky and sandwiches. Sheep and Black Morton had to return to Turnhouse that evening for duty, but Colin and I were to stay overnight and shoot again in the morning (on condition it wasn't raining). Back at the lodge I got out of my wet clothes and sank gratefully into a hot bath, allowing the steam to waft away the more acute memories of the day's discomforts. Colin at dinner stretched out his legs contentedly, and his face wore the rapt expression of the madman who, when asked why he banged his head against the wall, replied that it was such fun when he stopped.

We retired early to bed and slept until, at two o'clock in the morning, a gillie banged on the door. Colin got up, took from the gillie's hand a telegram, opened it, and read it aloud. It said: SQUADRON MOVING SOUTH STOP CAR WILL FETCH YOU AT EIGHT OCLOCK DENHOLM. For us, the war began that night.

At ten o'clock we were back at Turnhouse. The rest of the Squadron were all set to leave; we were to move down to Hornchurch, an aerodrome twelve miles east of London on the Thames Estuary. Four machines would not be serviceable until the evening, and Broody Benson, Pip Cardell, Colin, and I were to fly them down. We took off at four o'clock, some five hours after the others, Broody leading, Pip and I to each side, and Colin in the box, map-reading. Twenty-four of us flew south that tenth day of August 1940: of those twenty-four, eight were to fly back.

We landed at Hornchurch at about seven o'clock to receive our first shock. Instead of one section there were four squadrons at readiness; 603 Squadron were already in action. They started coming in about half an hour after we landed, smoke stains along the leading edges of the wings showing that all the guns had been fired. They had acquitted themselves well although caught at a disadvantage of height.

'You don't have to look for them,' said Brian. 'You have to look for a way out.'

From this flight Don MacDonald did not return.

At this time the Germans were sending over comparatively few bombers. They were making a determined attempt to wipe out our entire fighter force, and from dawn till dusk the sky was filled with Messerschmitts 109s and 110s.

Half a dozen of us always slept over at the dispersal hut to be ready for a surprise enemy attack at dawn. This entailed being up by four-thirty and by five o'clock having our machines warmed up and the oxygen, sights and ammunition tested. The first Hun attack usually came over about breakfast-time and from then until eight o'clock at night we were almost continuously in the air. We ate when we could, baked beans and bacon and eggs being sent over from the mess.

On the morning after our arrival I walked over with Peter Howes and Broody. Howes was at Hornchurch with another squadron and worried because he had as yet shot nothing down. Every evening when we came into the mess he would ask us how many we had got and then go over miserably to his room. His squadron had had a number of losses and was due for relief. If ever a man needed it, it was Howes. Broody, on the other hand, was in a high state of excitement, his sharp eager face grinning from ear to ear. We left Howes at his dispersal hut and walked over to where our machines were being warmed up. The voice of the controller came unhurried over the loud-speaker, telling us to take off, and in a few seconds we were running for our machines. I climbed into the cockpit of my plane and felt an empty sensation of suspense in the pit of my stomach. For one second time seemed to stand still and I stared blankly in front of me. I knew that that morning I was to kill for the first time. That I might be killed or in any way injured did not occur to me. Later, when we were losing pilots regularly, I did consider it in an abstract way when on the ground; but once in the air, never. I knew it could not happen to me. I suppose every pilot knows that, knows it cannot happen to him; even when he is taking off for the last time, when he will not return, he knowns that he cannot be killed. I wondered idly what he was like this man I would kill. Was he young, was he fat, would he die with the Fuehrer's name on his lips, or would he die alone, in that last moment conscious of himself as a man? I would never know. Then I was being strapped in, my mind automatically checking the controls, and we were off.

We ran into them at 18,000 feet, twenty yellow-nosed Messerschmitt 109s, about 500 feet above us. Our squadron strength was eight, and as they came down on us we went into line astern and turned head on to them. Brian Carbury, who was leading the Section, dropped the nose of his machine, and I could almost feel the leading Nazi pilot push forward on his stick to bring his guns to bear. At the same moment Brian hauled hard back on his own control stick and led us over them in a steep climbing turn to the left. In two vital seconds they lost their advantage. I saw Brian let go a burst of fire at the leading plane, saw the pilot put his machine into a half roll, and knew that he was mine. Automatically, I kicked the rudder to the left to get him at right angles, turned the gun-button to 'Fire,' and let go in a four-second burst with full deflection. He came right through my sights and I saw the tracer from all eight guns thud home. For a second he seemed to hang motionless; then a jet of red flame shot upwards and he spun out of sight.

For the next few minutes I was too busy looking after myself to think of anything, but when, after a short while, they turned and made off over the Channel, and we were ordered to our base, my mind began to work again.

It had happened.

My first emotion was one of satisfaction, satisfaction at a job adequately done, at the final logical conclusion of months of specialized training. And then I had a feeling of the essential rightness of it all. He was dead and I was alive; it could so easily have been the other way round; and that would somehow have been right too. I realized in that moment just how lucky a fighter pilot is. He has none of the personalized emotions of the soldier, handed a rifle and bayonet and told to charge. He does not even have to share the dangerous emotions of the bomber pilot who night after night must experience that childhood longing for smashing things. The fighter pilot's emotions are those of the duellist – cool, precise, impersonal. He is privileged to kill well. For if one must either kill or be killed, as now one must, it should, I feel, be done with dignity. Death should be given the setting it deserves; it should never be a pettiness; and for the fighter pilot it never can be.

From this flight Broody Benson did not return.

During that August-September period we were always so outnumbered that it was practically impossible, unless we were lucky enough to have the advantage of height, to deliver more than one squadron attack. After a few seconds we always broke up, and the sky was a smoke trail of individual dog-fights. The result was that the Squadron would come home individually, machines landing one after the other at intervals of about two minutes. After an hour, Uncle George would make a check-up on who was missing. Often there would be a telephone-call from some pilot to say that he had made a forced landing at some other aerodrome, or in a field. But the telephone wasn't always so welcome. It would be a rescue squad announcing the number of a crashed machine; then Uncle George would check it, and cross another name off the list. At that time, the losing of pilots was somehow extremely impersonal; nobody, I think, felt any great emotion – there simply wasn't time for it.

After the hard lesson of the first two days, we became more canny and determined not to let ourselves be caught from above. We would fly on the reciprocal of the course given us by the controller until we got to 15,000 feet, and then fly back again, climbing all the time. By this means we usually saw the Huns coming in below us, and were in a perfect position to deliver a squadron attack. If caught at a disadvantage, they would never stay to fight, but always turned straight back for the Channel. We arranged a system whereby two pilots always flew together – thus if one should follow a 'plane down the other stayed 500 feet or so above, to protect him from attack in the rear.

Often machines would come back to their base just long enough for the ground staff, who worked with beautiful speed, to refuel them and put in a new oxygen bottle and more ammunition before taking off again. Uncle George was shot down several times but always turned up unhurt; once we thought Rusty was gone for good, but he was back leading his flight the next day; one sergeant pilot in 'A' Flight was shot down four times, but he seemed to bear a charmed life.

The sun and the great height at which we flew often made it extremely difficult to pick out the enemy machines, but it was here that Sheep's experience on the moors of Scotland proved invaluable. He always led the guard section and always saw the Huns long before anyone else. For me the sun presented a major problem. We had dark lenses on our glasses, but I, as I have mentioned before, never wore mine. They gave me a feeling of claustrophobia. With spots on the wind-screen, spots before the eyes, and a couple of spots which might be Messerschmitts, blind spots on my goggles seemed too much of a good thing; I always slipped them up on to my forehead before going into action. For this and for not wearing gloves I paid a stiff price.

I remember once going practically to France before shooting down a 109. There were two of them, flying at sea-level and headed for the French coast. Raspberry was flying beside me and caught one half-way across. I got right up close behind the second one and gave it a series of short bursts. It darted about in front, like a startled rabbit, and finally plunged into the sea about three miles off the French coast.

On another occasion I was stupid enough actually to fly over France: the sky appeared to be perfectly clear but for one returning Messerschmitt, flying very high. I had been trying to catch him for about ten minutes and was determined that he should not get away. Eventually I caught him inland from Calais and was just about to open fire when I saw a squadron of twelve Messerschmitts coming in on my right. I was extremely frightened, but turned in towards them and opened fire at the leader. I could see his tracer going past underneath me, and then I saw his hood fly off, and the next moment they were past. I didn't wait to see any more, but made off for home, pursued for half the distance by eleven very determined Germans. I landed a good hour after everyone else to find Uncle George just finishing his check-up.

From this flight Larry Cunningham did not return.

After about a week of Hornchurch, I woke late one morning to the noise of machines running up on the aerodrome. It irritated me: I had a headache.

Having been on every flight the previous day, the morning was mine to do with as I pleased. I got up slowly, gazed dispassionately at my tongue in the mirror, and wandered over to the mess for breakfast. It must have been getting on for twelve o'clock when I came out on to the aerodrome to find the usual August heat haze forming a dull pall over everything. I started to walk across the aerodrome to the dispersal point on the far side. There were only two machines on the ground so I concluded that the Squadron was already up. Then I heard a shout, and our ground crew drew up in a lorry beside me. Sergeant Ross leaned out:

'Want a lift, sir? We're going round.'

'No, thanks, Sergeant. I'm going to cut across.'

This was forbidden for obvious reasons, but I felt like that.

'OK, sir. See you round there.'

The lorry trundled off down the road in a cloud of dust. I walked on across the landing ground. At that moment I heard the emotionless voice of the controller.

'Large enemy bombing formation approaching Hornchurch. All personnel not engaged in active duty take cover immediately.'

I looked up. They were still not visible. At the dispersal point I saw Bubble and Pip Cardell make a dash for the shelter. Three Spitfires just landed, turned about and came past me with a roar to take off downwind. Our lorry was still trundling along the road, maybe half-way round, and seemed suddenly an awfully long way from the dispersal point.

I looked up again, and this time I saw them – about a dozen slugs, shining in the bright sun and coming straight on. At the rising scream of the first bomb I instinctively shrugged up my shoulders and ducked my head. Out of the corner of my eye I saw the three Spitfires. One moment they were about twenty feet up in close formation; the next catapulted apart as though on elastic. The leader went over on his back and ploughed along the runway with a rending crash of tearing fabric; No. 2 put a wing in and spun around on his airscrew, while the plane on the left was blasted wingless into the next field. I remember thinking stupidly, 'That's the shortest flight he's ever taken,' and then my feet were nearly knocked from under me, my mouth was full of dirt, and Bubble, gesticulating like a madman from the shelter entrance, was yelling, 'Run, you bloody fool, run!' I ran. Suddenly awakened to the lunacy of my behaviour, I covered the distance to the shelter as if impelled by a rocket and shot through the entrance while once again the ground rose up and hit me, and my head smashed hard against one of the pillars. I subsided on a heap of rubble and massaged it.

'Who's here?' I asked, peering through the gloom.

'Cardell and I and three of our ground crew,' said Bubble, 'and, by the Grace of God, you!'

I could see by his mouth that he was still talking, but a sudden concentration of the scream and crump of falling bombs made it impossible to hear him.

The air was thick with dust and the shelter shook and heaved at each explosion, yet somehow held firm. For about three minutes the bedlam continued, and then suddenly ceased. In the utter silence which followed nobody moved. None of us wished to be the first to look on the devastation which we felt must be outside. Then Bubble spoke. 'Praise God!' he said, 'I'm not a civilian. Of all the bloody frightening things I've ever done, sitting in that shelter was the worst. Me for the air from now on!'

It broke the tension and we scrambled out of the entrance. The runways were certainly in something of a mess. Gaping holes and great gobbets of earth were everywhere. Right in front of us a bomb had landed by my Spitfire, covering it with a shower of grit and rubble.

I turned to the aircraftman standing beside me. 'Will you get hold of Sergeant Ross and tell him to have a crew give her an inspection.'

He jerked his head towards one corner of the aerodrome: 'I think I'd better collect the crew myself, sir. Sergeant Ross won't be doing any more inspections.'

I followed his glance and saw the lorry, the roof about twenty yards away, lying grotesquely on its side. I climbed into the cockpit, and, feeling faintly sick, tested out the switches. Bubble poked his head over the side.

'Let's go over to the mess and see what's up: all our machines will be landing down at the reserve landing field, anyway.'

I climbed out and walked over to find that the three Spitfire pilots were quite unharmed but for a few superficial scratches, in spite of being machine-gunned by the bombers. 'Operations' was undamaged: no hangar had been touched and the Officers' Mess had two windows broken.

The Station Commander ordered every available man and woman on to the job of repairing the aerodrome surface and by four o'clock there was not a hole to be seen. Several unexploded bombs were marked off, and two lines of yellow flags were laid down to mark the runways. At five o'clock our Squadron, taking off for a 'flap' from the reserve field, landed without incident on its home base. Thus, apart from four men killed in the lorry and a network of holes on the landing surface, there was nothing to show for ten minutes' really accurate bombing from 12,000 feet, in which several dozen sticks of bombs had been dropped. It was a striking proof of the inefficacy of their attempts to wipe out our advance fighter aerodromes.

Brian had a bullet through his foot, and as my machine was still out of commission, I took his place in readiness for the next show. I had had enough of the ground for one day.

Six o'clock came and went, and no call. We started to play poker and I was winning. It was agreed that we should stop at seven: should there be a 'flap' before then, the game was off. I gazed anxiously at the clock. I am always unlucky at cards, but when the hands pointed to 6.55 I really began to feel my luck was on the change. But sure enough at that moment came the voice of the controller: '603 Squadron take off and patrol base: further instructions in the air.'

We made a dash for our machines and within two minutes were off the ground. Twice we circled the aerodrome to allow all twelve planes to get in formation. We were flying in four sections of three: Red Section leading, Blue and Green to right and left, and the three remaining planes forming a guard section above and behind us.

I was flying No. 2 in the Blue Section.

Over the radio came the voice of the controller: 'Hullo, Red Leader,' followed by instructions on course and height.

As always, for the first few minutes we flew on the reciprocal of the course given until we reach 15,000 feet. We then turned about and flew on 110° in an all-out climb, thus coming out of the sun and gaining height all the way.

During the climb Uncle George was in constant touch with the ground. We were to intercept about twenty enemy fighters at 25,000 feet. I glanced across at Stapme and saw his mouth moving. That meant he was singing again. He would sometimes do this with his radio set on 'send,' with the result that, mingled with our instructions from the ground, we would hear a raucous rendering of 'Night and Day.' And then quite clearly over the radio I heard the Germans excitedly calling to each other. This was a not infrequent occurrence and it made one feel that they were right behind, although often they were some distance away. I switched my set to 'send' and called out *'Halt's Maul!'* and as many other choice pieces of German invective as I could remember. To my delight I heard one of them answer: 'You feelthy Englishman, we will teach you how to speak to a German.' I am aware that this sounds a tall story, but several others in the Squadron were listening out and heard the whole thing.

I looked down. It was a completely cloudless sky and way below lay the English countryside, stretching lazily into the distance, a quite extraordinary picture of green and purple in the setting sun.

I took a glance at my altimeter. We were at 28,000 feet. At that moment Sheep yelled 'Tallyho' and dropped down in front of Uncle George in a slow dive in the direction of the approaching planes. Uncle George saw them at once.

'OK. Line astern.'

I drew in behind Stapme and took a look at them. They were about 2,000 feet below us, which was a pleasant change, but they must have spotted us at the same moment, for they were forming a protective circle, one behind the other, which is a defence formation hard to break.

'Echelon starboard,' came Uncle George's voice.

We spread out fanwise to the right.

'Going down!'

One after the other we peeled off in a power dive. I picked out one machine and switched my gun-button to 'Fire.' At 300 yards I had him in my sights. At 200 I opened up in a long four-second burst and saw the tracer going into his nose. Then I was pulling out, so hard that I could feel my eyes dropping through my neck. Coming round in a slow climbing turn, I saw that we had broken them up. The sky was now a mass of individual dog-fights. Several of them had already been knocked down. One I hoped was mine, but on pulling up I had not been able to see the result. To my left I saw Peter Pease make a head-on attack on a Messerschmitt. They were headed straight for each other and it looked as though the fire of both was striking home. Then at the last moment the Messerschmitt pulled up, taking Peter's fire full in the belly. It rolled on to its back, yellow flames pouring from the cockpit, and vanished.

The next few minutes were typical. First the sky a bedlam of machines; then suddenly silence and not a plane to be seen. I noticed then that I was very tired and very hot. The sweat was running down my face in rivulets. But this was no time for vague reflections. Flying around the sky on one's own at that time was not a healthy course of action.

I still had some ammunition left. Having no desire to return to the aerodrome until it had all been used to some good purpose, I took a look around the sky for some friendly fighters. About a mile away over Dungeness I saw a formation of about forty Hurricanes on patrol at 20,000 feet. Feeling that there was safety in numbers, I set off in their direction. When about 200 yards from the rear machine, I looked down and saw 5,000 feet below another formation of fifty machines flying in the same direction. Flying stepped up like this was an old trick of the Huns, and I was glad to see we were adopting the same tactics. But as though hit by a douche of cold water, I suddenly woke up. There were far more machines flying together than we could ever muster over one spot. I took another look at the rear machine in my formation, and sure enough, there was the Swastika on its tail. Yet they all seemed quite oblivious of my presence. I had the sun behind me and a glorious opportunity. Closing in to 150 yards I let go a three-second burst into the rear machine. It flicked on to its back and spun out of sight. Feeling like an irresponsible schoolboy who has perpetrated some crime which must inevitably be found out, I glanced round me. Still nobody seemed disturbed. I suppose I could have repeated the performance on the next machine, but I felt that it was inadvisable to tempt Providence too far. I did a quick half roll and made off home, where I found to my irritation that Raspberry, as usual, had three planes down to my one.

There was to be a concert on the station that night, but as I had to be up at five the next morning for Dawn Readiness, I had a quick dinner and two beers, and went to bed, feeling not unsatisfied with the day.

Perhaps the most amusing though painful experience which I had was when I was shot down acting as 'Arse-end Charlie' to a squadron of Hurricanes. Arse-end Charlie is the man who weaves backwards and forwards above and behind the squadron to protect them from attack from the rear. There had been the usual dog-fights over the South Coast, and the squadron had broken up. Having only fired one snap burst, I climbed up in search of friendly Spitfires, but found instead a squadron of Hurricanes flying round the sky at 18,000 feet in sections of stepped-up threes, but with no rear-guard. So I joined on. I learned

within a few seconds the truth of the old warning, 'Beware of the Hun
in the Sun.' I was making pleasant little sweeps from side to side, and
peering earnestly into my mirror when, from out of the sun and dead
astern, bullets started appearing along my port wing. There is an
appalling tendency to sit and watch this happen without taking any
action, as though mesmerized by a snake; but I managed to pull myself
together and go into a spin, at the same time attempting to call up the
Hurricanes and warn them, but I found that my radio had been shot
away. At first there appeared to be little damage done and I started to
climb up again, but black smoke began pouring out of the engine and
there was an unpleasant smell of escaping glycol. I thought I had better
get home while I could; but as the wind-screen was soon covered with
oil I realized that I couldn't make it and decided instead to put down at
Lympne, where there was an aerodrome. Then I realized that I wasn't
going to make Lympne either – I was going at full boost and only
clocking ninety miles per hour, so I decided that I had better put down
in the nearest field before I stalled and spun in. I chose a cornfield and
put the machine down on its belly. Fortunately nothing caught fire, and
I had just climbed out and switched off the petrol, when to my amazement
I saw an ambulance coming through the gate. This I thought was real
service, until the corporal and two orderlies who climbed out started
cantering away in the opposite direction, their necks craned up to the
heavens. I looked up and saw about fifty yards away a parachute, and
suspended on the end, his legs dangling vaguely, Colin. He was a little
burned about his face and hands but quite cheerful.

We were at once surrounded by a bevy of officers and discovered that
we had landed practically in the back garden of a Brigade cocktail party.
A salvage crew from Lympne took charge of my machine, a doctor took
charge of Colin, and the rest took charge of me, handing me double
whiskies for the nerves at a laudable rate. I was put up that night by the
Brigadier, who thought I was suffering from a rather severe shock, largely
because by dinner-time I was so pie-eyed that I didn't dare open my
mouth but answered all his questions with a glassy stare. The next day
I went up to London by train, a somewhat incongruous figure, carrying
a helmet and parachute. The prospect of a long and tedious journey by
tube to Hornchurch did not appeal to me, so I called up the Air Ministry
and demanded a car and a WAAF. I was put on to the good lady in
charge of transport, a sergeant, who protested apologetically that she
must have the authorization of a Wing Commander. I told her forcibly
that at this moment I was considerably more important than any Wing
Commander, painted a vivid picture of the complete disorganization of
Fighter Command in the event of my not being back at Hornchurch
within an hour, and clinched the argument by telling her that my

parachute was a military secret which must on no account be seen in a train. By the afternoon I was flying again.

That evening there was a terrific attack on Hornchurch and, for the first time since coming south, I saw some bombers. There were twelve Dornier 215s flying in close formation at about 12,000 feet, and headed back for France. I was on my way back to the aerodrome when I first sighted them about 5,000 feet below me. I dived straight down in a quarter head-on attack. It seemed quite impossible to miss, and I pressed the button. Nothing happened; I had already fired all my ammunition. I could not turn back, so I put both my arms over my head and went straight through the formation, never thinking I'd get out of it unscratched. I landed on the aerodrome with the machine, quite serviceable, but a little draughty.

From this flight Bubble Waterson did not return.

And so August drew to a close with no slackening of pressure in the enemy offensive. Yet the Squadron showed no signs of strain, and I personally was content. This was what I had waited for, waited for nearly a year, and I was not disappointed. If I felt anything, it was a sensation of relief. We had little time to think and each day brought new action. No one thought of the future: sufficient unto the day was the emotion thereof. At night one switched off one's mind like an electric light.

It was one week after Bubble went that I crashed into the North Sea.

BOOK TWO

CHAPTER SIX

SHALL I LIVE FOR A GHOST?

I was falling. Falling slowly through a dark pit. I was dead. My body, headless, circled in front of me. I saw it with my mind, my mind that was the redness in front of the eye, the dull scream in the ear, the grinning of the mouth, the skin crawling on the skull. It was death and resurrection. Terror, moving with me, touched my cheek with hers and I felt the flesh wince. Faster, faster. . . . I was hot now, hot, again one with my body, on fire and screaming soundlessly. Dear God, no! No! Not that, not again. The sickly smell of death was in my nostrils and a confused roar of sound. Then was all quiet. I was back.

Someone was holding my arms.

'Quiet now. There's a good boy. You're going to be all right. You've been very ill and you mustn't talk.'

I tried to reach up my hand but could not.

'Is that you, nurse? What have they done to me?'

'Well, they've put something on your face and hands to stop them hurting and you won't be able to see for a little while. But you mustn't talk: you're not strong enough yet.'

Gradually I realized what had happened. My face and hands had been scrubbed and then sprayed with tannic acid. The acid had formed into a hard black cement. My eyes alone had received different treatment; they were coated with a thick layer of gentian violet. My arms were propped up in front of me, the fingers extended like witches' claws, and my body was hung loosely on straps just clear of the bed.

I can recollect no moments of acute agony in the four days which I spent in that hospital; only a great sea of pain in which I floated almost with comfort. Every three hours I was injected with morphia, so while imagining myself quite coherent, I was for the most part in a semi-stupor. The memory of it has remained a confused blur.

Two days without eating, and then periodic doses of liquid food taken through a tube. An appalling thirst, and hundreds of bottles of ginger beer. Being blind, and not really feeling strong enough to care. Imagining myself back in my plane, unable to get out, and waking to find myself shouting and bathed in sweat. My parents coming down to see me and their wonderful self-control.

They arrived in the late afternoon of my second day in bed, having with admirable restraint done nothing the first day. On the morning of the crash my mother had been on her way to the Red Cross, when she felt a premonition that she must go home. She told the taxi-driver to turn about and arrived at the flat to hear the telephone ringing. It was our Squadron Adjutant, trying to reach my father. Embarrassed by finding himself talking to my mother, he started in on a glamorized history of my exploits in the air and was bewildered by my mother cutting him short to ask where I was. He managed somehow after about five minutes of incoherent stuttering to get over his news.

They arrived in the afternoon and were met by Matron. Outside my ward a twittery nurse explained that they must not expect to find me looking quite normal, and they were ushered in. The room was in darkness; I just a dim shape in one corner. Then the blinds were shot up, all the lights switched on, and there I was. As my mother remarked later, the performance lacked only the rolling of drums and a spotlight. For the sake of decorum my face had been covered with white gauze, with a slit in the middle through which protruded my lips.

We spoke little, my only coherent remark being that I had no wish to go on living if I were to look like Alice. Alice was a large country girl who had once been our maid. As a child she had been burned and disfigured by a Primus stove. I was not aware that she had made any impression on me, but now I was unable to get her out of my mind. It was not so much her looks as her smell I had continually in my nostrils and which I couldn't dissociate from the disfigurement.

They sat quietly and listened to me rambling for an hour. Then it was time for my dressings and they took their leave.

The smell of ether. Matron once doing my dressing with three orderlies holding my arms; a nurse weeping quietly at the head of the bed, and no remembered sign of a doctor. A visit from the lifeboat crew that had picked me up, and a terrible longing to make sense when talking to them. Their inarticulate sympathy and assurance of quick recovery. Their discovery that an ancestor of mine had founded the lifeboats, and my pompous and unsolicited promise of a subscription. The expectation of an American ambulance to drive me up to the Masonic Hospital (for Margate was used only as a clearing station). Believing that I was already in it and on my way, and waking to the disappointment that I had not been moved. A dream that I was fighting to open my eyes and could not: waking in a sweat to realize it was a dream and then finding it to be true. A sensation of time slowing down, of words and actions, all in slow motion. Sweat, pain, smells, cheering messages from the Squadron, and an overriding apathy.

Finally I was moved. The ambulance appeared with a cargo of two somewhat nervous ATS women who were to drive me to London, and, with my nurse in attendance, and wrapped in an old grandmother's shawl, I was carried aboard and we were off. For the first few miles I felt quite well, dictated letters to my nurse, drank bottle after bottle of ginger beer, and gossiped with the drivers. They described the countryside for me, told me they were new to the job, expressed satisfaction at having me for a consignment, asked me if I felt fine. Yes, I said, I felt fine; asked my nurse if the drivers were pretty, heard her answer yes, heard them simpering, and we were all very matey. But after about half an hour my arms began to throb from the rhythmical jolting of the road. I stopped dictating, drank no more ginger beer, and didn't care whether they were pretty or not. Then they lost their way. Wasn't it awful and shouldn't they stop and ask? No, they certainly shouldn't: they could call out the names of the streets and I would tell them where to go. By the time we arrived at Ravenscourt Park I was pretty much all-in. I was carried into the hospital and once again felt the warm September sun burning my face. I was put in a private ward and had the impression of a hundred excited ants buzzing around me. My nurse said good-bye and started to sob. For no earthly reason I found myself in tears. It had been a lousy hospital, I had never seen the nurse anyway, and I was now in very good hands; but I suppose I was in a fairly exhausted state. So there we all were, snivelling about the place and getting nowhere. Then the charge nurse came up and took my arm and asked me what my name was.

'Dick,' I said.

'Ah,' she said brightly. 'We must call you Richard the Lion Heart.'

I made an attempt at a polite laugh but all that came out was a dismal groan and I fainted away. The house surgeon took the opportunity to give me an anaesthetic and removed all the tannic acid from my left hand.

At this time tannic acid was the recognized treatment for burns. The theory was that in forming a hard cement it protected the skin from the air, and encouraged it to heal up underneath. As the tannic started to crack, it was to be chipped off gradually with a scalpel, but after a few months of experience, it was discovered that nearly all pilots with third-degree burns so treated developed secondary infection and septicaemia. This caused its use to be discontinued and gave us the dubious satisfaction of knowing that we were suffering in the cause of science. Both my hands were suppurating, and the fingers were already contracting under the tannic and curling down into the palms. The risk of shock was considered too great for them to do both hands. I must have been under the anaesthetic for about fifteen minutes and in that time I saw Peter Pease killed.

He was after another machine, a tall figure leaning slightly forward with a smile at the corner of his mouth. Suddenly from nowhere a Messerschmitt was on his tail about 150 yards away. For two seconds nothing happened. I had a terrible feeling of futility. Then at the top of my voice I shouted, 'Peter, for God's sake look out behind!'

I saw the Messerschmitt open up and a burst of fire hit Peter's machine. His expression did not change, and for a moment his machine hung motionless. Then it turned slowly on its back and dived to the ground. I came-to, screaming his name, with two nurses and the doctor holding me down on the bed.

'All right now. Take it easy, you're not dead yet. That must have been a very bad dream.'

I said nothing. There wasn't anything to say. Two days later I had a letter from Colin. My nurse read it to me. It was very short, hoping that I was getting better and telling me that Peter was dead.

Slowly I came back to life. My morphia injections were less frequent and my mind began to clear. Though I began to feel and think again coherently I still could not see. Two VADs fainted while helping with my dressings, the first during the day and the other at night. The second time I could not sleep and was calling out for someone to stop the beetles running down my face, when I heard my nurse say fiercely, 'Get outside quick: don't make a fool of yourself here!' and the sound of footsteps moving towards the door. I remember cursing the unfortunate girl and telling her to put her head between her knees. I was told later that for my first three weeks I did little but curse and blaspheme, but I remember nothing of it. The nurses were wonderfully patient and never complained. Then one day I found that I could see. My nurse was bending over me doing my dressings, and she seemed to me very beautiful. She was. I watched her for a long time, grateful that my first glimpse of the world should be of anything so perfect. Finally I said:

'Sue, you never told me that your eyes were so blue.'

For a moment she stared at me. Then, 'Oh, Dick, how wonderful,' she said. 'I told you it wouldn't be long'; and she dashed out to bring in all the nurses on the block.

I felt absurdly elated and studied their faces eagerly, gradually connecting them with the voices that I knew.

'This is Anne,' said Sue. 'She is your special VAD and helps me with all your dressings. She was the only one of us you'd allow near you for about a week. You said you liked her voice.' Before me stood an attractive fair-haired girl of about twenty-three. She smiled and her teeth were as enchanting as her voice. I began to feel that hospital had its compensations. The nurses called me Dick and I knew them all by their Christian names. Quite how irregular this was I did not discover until I moved to another hospital where I was considerably less ill and not so outrageously spoiled. At first my dressings had to be changed every two hours in the daytime. As this took over an hour to do, it meant that Sue and Anne had practically no time off. But they seemed not to care. It was largely due to them that both my hands were not amputated.

Sue, who had been nursing since seventeen, had been allocated as my special nurse because of her previous experience of burns, and because, as Matron said, 'She's our best girl and very human.' Anne had been married to a naval officer killed in the *Courageous*, and had taken up nursing after his death.

At this time there was a very definite prejudice among the regular nurses against VADs. They were regarded as painted society girls, attracted to nursing by the prospect of sitting on the officers' beds and holding their hands. The VADs were rapidly disabused of this idea, and, if they were lucky, were finally graduated from washing bed-pans to polishing bed-tables. I never heard that any of them grumbled, and they gradually won a reluctant recognition. This prejudice was considerably less noticeable in the Masonic than in most hospitals: Sue, certainly, looked on Anne as a companionable and very useful lieutenant to whom she could safely entrust my dressings and general upkeep in her absence. I think I was a little in love with both of them.

The Masonic is perhaps the best hospital in England, though at the time I was unaware how lucky I was. When war broke out the Masons handed over a part of it to the services; but owing to its vulnerable position very few action casualties were kept there long. Pilots were pretty quickly moved out to the main Air Force Hospital, which I was not in the least eager to visit. Thanks to the kind-hearted duplicity of my house surgeon, I never had to; for every time they rang up and asked for me he would say that I was too ill to be moved. The Masonic's great charm lay in that it in no way resembled a hospital; if anything it was like the inside of a ship. The nursing staff were very carefully chosen, and during the regular blitzing of the district, which took place every night, they were magnificent.

The Germans were presumably attempting to hit Hammersmith Bridge, but their efforts were somewhat erratic and we were treated night after night to an orchestra of the scream and crump of falling bombs. They always seemed to choose a moment when my eyes were being irrigated, when my poor nurse was poised above me with a glass undine in her hand. At night we were moved into the corridor, away from the outside wall, but such was the snoring of my fellow sufferers that I persuaded Bertha to allow me back in my own room after Matron had made her rounds.

Bertha was my night nurse. I never discovered her real name, but to me she was Bertha from the instant that I saw her. She was large and gaunt with an Eton crop and a heart of gold. She was engaged to a merchant seaman who was on his way to Australia. She made it quite clear that she had no intention of letting me get round her as I did the day staff, and ended by spoiling me even more. At night when I couldn't sleep we would hold long and heated arguments on the subject of sex. She expressed horror at my ideas of love and on her preference for a cup of tea. I gave her a present of four pounds of it when I was discharged. One night the Germans were particularly persistent, and I had the unpleasant sensation of hearing a stick of bombs gradually approaching the hospital, the first some way off, the next closer, and the third shaking the building. Bertha threw herself across my bed; but the fourth bomb never fell. She got up quickly, looking embarrassed, and arranged her cap.

'Nice fool I'd look if you got hit in your own room when you're supposed to be out in the corridor,' she said, and stumped out of the room.

An RASC officer who had been admitted to the hospital with the painful but unromantic complaint of piles protested at the amount of favouritism shown to me merely because I was in the RAF. A patriotic captain who was in the same ward turned on him and said: 'At least he was shot down defending his country and didn't come in here with a pimple on his bottom. The Government will buy him a new Spitfire, but I'm damned if it will buy you a new arse.'

One day my doctor came in and said that I could get up. Soon after I was able to totter about the passages and could be given a proper bath. I was still unable to use my hands and everything had to be done for me. One evening during a blitz, my nurse, having led me along to the lavatory, placed a prodigiously long cigarette-holder in my mouth and lighted the cigarette in the end of it. Then she went off to get some coffee. I was puffing away contentedly when the lighted cigarette fell into my pyjama trousers and started smouldering. There was little danger that I would go up in flames, but I thought it advisable to draw attention to the fact that all was not well. I therefore shouted 'Oi!' Nobody heard me. 'Help!' I shouted somewhat louder. Still nothing happened, so I delivered myself of my imitation of Tarzan's elephant call of which I was quite proud. It happened that in the ward opposite there was an old gentleman who had been operated on for a hernia. The combination of the scream of falling bombs and my animal cries could mean only one thing. Someone had been seriously injured, and he made haste to dive over the side of the bed. In doing so he caused himself considerable discomfort: convinced of the ruin of his operation and the imminence of his death, he added his cries to mine. His fears finally calmed, he could see nothing humorous in the matter and insisted on being moved to another ward. From then on I was literally never left alone for a minute.

For the first few weeks, only my parents were allowed to visit me and they came every day. My mother would sit and read to me by the hour. Quite how much she suffered I could only guess, for she gave no sign. One remark of hers I shall never forget. She said: 'You should be glad this has to happen to you. Too many people told you how attractive you were and you believed them. You were well on the way to becoming something of a cad. Now you'll find out who your real friends are.' I did.

When I was allowed to see people, one of my first visitors was Michael Cary (who had been at Trinity with me and had a First in Greats). He was then private secretary to the Chief of Air Staff. He was allowed to stay only a short time before being shoo'd away by my nurses, but I think it may have been time enough to shake him. A short while afterwards he joined the Navy as an AB. I hope it was not as a result of seeing me, for he had too good a brain to waste polishing brass. Colin came down whenever he had leave from Hornchurch and brought me news of the Squadron.

Ken MacDonald, Don's brother who had been with 'A' Flight at Dyce, had been killed. He had been seen about to bale out of his blazing machine at 1,000 feet; but as he was over a thickly populated area he had climbed in again and crashed the machine in the Thames.

Pip Cardell had been killed. Returning from a chase over the Channel with Dexter, one of the new members of the Squadron, he appeared to be in trouble just before reaching the English coast. He jumped; but his parachute failed to open and he came down in the sea. Dexter flew low and saw him move. He was still alive, so Dexter flew right along the shore and out to sea, waggling his wings to draw attention and calling up the base on the RT. No boat put out from the shore, and Dexter made a crash landing on the beach, drawing up ten yards from a nest of buried mines. But when they got up to Pip he was dead.

Howes had been killed, even as he had said. His Squadron had been moved from Hornchurch to a quieter area, a few days after I was shot down. But he had been transferred to our Squadron, still deeply worried because as yet he had failed to bring anything down. The inevitable happened; and from his second flight with us he failed to return.

Rusty was missing, but a clairvoyant had written to Uncle George swearing that he was neither dead nor captured. Rusty, he said (whom he had never seen), had crashed in France, badly burned, and was being looked after by a French peasant.

As a counter to this depressing news Colin told me that Brian, Raspberry, and Sheep all had the DFC, and Brian was shortly to get a bar to his. The Squadron's confirmed score was nearing the hundred mark. We had also had the pleasure of dealing with the Italians. They had come over before breakfast, and together with 41 Squadron we were looking for them. Suddenly Uncle George called out:

'Wops ahead.'

'Where are they?' asked 41 Squadron.

'Shan't tell you,' came back the answer. 'We're only outnumbered three to one.'

Colin told me that it was the most unsporting thing he had ever had to do, rather like shooting sitting birds, as he so typically put it. We got down eight of them without loss to ourselves and much to the annoyance of 41 Squadron.

Then one day I had an unexpected visitor. Matron opened the door and said 'Someone to see you,' and Denise walked in. I knew at once who she was. It was unnecessary for her to speak. Her slight figure was in mourning and she wore no make-up. She was the most beautiful person I have ever seen.

Much has been written on Beauty. Poets have excelled themselves in similes for a woman's eyes, mouth, hair; novelists have devoted pages to a geometrically accurate description of their heroines' features. I can write no such description of Denise. I did not see her like that. For me she had an inner beauty, a serenity which no listing of features can convey. She had a perfection of carriage and a grace of movement that were strikingly reminiscent of Peter Pease, and when she spoke it might have been Peter speaking.

'I hope you'll excuse me coming to see you like this,' she said; 'but I was going to be married to Peter. He often spoke of you and wanted so much to see you. So I hope you won't mind me coming instead.'

There was so much I wanted to say, so many things for us to talk over, but the room seemed of a sudden unbearably full of hurrying jolly nurses who would not go away. The bustle and excitement did little to put her at her ease, and her shyness was painful to me. Time came for her to leave, and I had said nothing I wanted to say. As soon as she was gone I dictated a note, begging her to come again and to give me a little warning. She did. From then until I was able to get out, her visits did more to help my recovery than all the expert nursing and medical attention. For she was the very spirit of courage. It was useless for me to say to her any of the usual words of comfort for the loss of a fiancé, and I did not try. She and Peter were two halves of the same person. They even wrote alike. I could only pray that time would cure that awful numbness and bring her back to the fullness of life. Not that she was broken. She seemed somehow to have gathered his strength, to feel him always near her, and was determined to go on to the end in the cause for which he had given his life, hoping that she too might be allowed to die, but feeling guilty at the selfishness of the thought.

She believed passionately in freedom, in freedom from fear and oppression and tyranny, not only for herself but for the whole world. 'For the whole world.' Did I believe that? I still wasn't sure. There was a time – only the other day – when it hadn't mattered to me if it was true or not that a man could want freedom for others than himself. She made me feel that this might be no mere catch-phrase of politicians, since it was something to which the two finest people I had ever known had willingly dedicated themselves. I was impressed. I saw there a spirit far purer than mine. But was it for me? I didn't know. I just didn't know.

I lay in that hospital and watched summer turn to winter. Through my window I watched the leaves of my solitary tree gradually turn brown, and then, shaken by an ever-freshening wind, fall one by one. I watched the sun change from a great ball of fire to a watery glimmer, watched the rain beating on the glass and the small broken clouds drifting a few hundred feet above, and in that time I had ample opportunity for thinking.

I thought of the men I had known, of the men who were living and the men who were dead; and I came to this conclusion. It was to the Carburys and the Berrys of this war that Britain must look, to the tough practical men who had come up the hard way, who were not fighting this war for any philosophical principles or economic ideals; who, unlike the average Oxford undergraduate, were not flying for aesthetic reasons, but because of an instinctive knowledge that this was the job for which they were most suited. These were the men who had blasted and would continue to blast the Luftwaffe out of the sky while their more intellectual comrades would alas, in the main be killed. They might answer, if asked why they fought, 'To smash Hitler!' But instinctively, inarticulately, they too were fighting for the things that Peter had died to preserve.

Was there perhaps a new race of Englishmen arising out of this war, a race of men bred by the war, a harmonious synthesis of the governing class and the great rest of England; that synthesis of disparate backgrounds and upbringings to be seen at its most obvious best in RAF squadrons? While they were now possessed of no other thought than to win the war, yet having won it, would they this time refuse to step aside and remain indifferent to the peace-time fate of the country, once again leave government to the old governing class? I thought it possible. Indeed, the process might be said to have already begun. They now had as their representative Churchill, a man of initiative, determination, and no Party. But they would not always have him; and what than? Would they see to it that there arose from their fusion representatives, not of the old gang, deciding at Lady Cufuffle's that Henry should have the Foreign Office and George the Ministry of Food, nor figureheads for an angry but ineffectual Labour Party, but true representatives of the new England that should emerge from this struggle? And if they did, what then? Could they unite on a policy of humanity and sense to arrive at the settlement of problems which six thousand years of civilization had failed to solve? And even though they should fail, was there an obligation for the more thinking of them to try to contribute, at whatever personal cost 'their little drop,' however small, to the betterment of mankind? Was there that obligation, was that the goal towards which all those should strive who were left, strengthened and confirmed by those who had died? Or was it still possible for men to lead the egocentric life, to work out their own salvation without concern for the rest; could they simply look to themselves – or, more important, could I? I still thought so.

The day came when I was allowed out of the hospital for a few hours. Sue got me dressed, and with a pair of dark glasses, cotton-wool under my eyes, and my right arm in a sling, I looked fairly presentable. I walked out through the swing-doors and took a deep breath.

London in the morning was still the best place in the world. The smell of wet streets, of sawdust in the butchers' shops, of tar melted on the blocks, was exhilarating. Peter had been right: I loved the capital. The wind on the heath might call for a time, but the facile glitter of the city was the stronger. Self-esteem, I suppose, is one cause; for in the city, work of man, one is somebody, feet on the pavement, suit on the body, anybody's equal and nobody's fool; but in the country, work of God, one is nothing, less than the earth, the birds, and the trees; one is discordant – a blot.

I walked slowly through Ravenscourt Park and looked into many faces. Life was good, but if I hoped to find some reflection of my feeling, I was disappointed. One or two looked at me with pity, and for a moment I was angry; but when I gazed again at their faces, closed in as on some dread secret, their owners hurrying along, unseeing, unfeeling, eager to get to their jobs, unaware of the life within them, I was sorry for them.

I felt a desire to stop and shake them and say: 'You fools, it's you who should be pitied and not I; for this day I am alive while you are dead.'

And yet there were some who pleased me, some in whom all youth had not died. I passed one girl, and gazing into her face became aware of her as a woman: her lips were soft, her breasts firm, her legs long and graceful. It was many a month since any woman had stirred me, and I was pleased. I smiled at her and she smiled at me. I did not speak to her for fear of breaking the spell, but walked back to lunch on air. After this I was allowed out every day, and usually managed to stay out until nine o'clock, when I drove back through the blitz and the black-out.

'London can take it' was already becoming a truism; but I had been put out of action before the real fury of the night attacks had been let loose, and I had seen nothing of the damage. In the hospital, from the newspapers, and from people who came to see me, I gained a somewhat hazy idea of what was going on. On the one hand I saw London as a city hysterically gay, a city doomed, with nerves so strained that a life of synthetic gaiety alone prevented them from snapping. My other picture was of a London bloody but unbowed, of a people grimly determined to see this thing through, with manpower mobilized; a city unable, through a combined lack of inclination, facility, and time, to fritter away the war in the night-haunts of the capital. I set out to see for myself.

London night-life did exist. Though the sirens might scream and the bombs fall, restaurants and cocktail bars remained open and full every night of the week. I say restaurants and cocktail bars, for the bottle parties and strip-tease cabarets which had a mushroom growth at the beginning of the war had long been closed. Nor was prostitution abroad. Ladies of leisure whose business hours were from eleven till three were perhaps the only citizens to find themselves completely baffled by the black-out. London was not promiscuous: the diners-out in a West End restaurant were no longer the clientele of café society, for café society no longer existed in London. The majority of the so-called smart set felt at last with the outbreak of war a real vocation, felt finally a chance to realize themselves and to orientate themselves to a life of reality. They might be seen in a smart restaurant; but they were there in another guise – as soldiers, sailors, and airmen on forty-eight hours' leave; as members of one of the women's services seeking a few hours' relaxation before again applying themselves wholeheartedly to their jobs; or as civil servants and Government workers who, after a hard's day work, preferred to relax and enjoy the bombing in congenial company rather than return to a solitary dinner in their own flats.

While the bombs were dropping on London (and they were dropping every night in my time in the hospital), and while half London was enjoying itself, the other half was not asleep. It was striving to make London as normal a city by night as it had become by day. Anti-aircraft crews, studded around fields, parks, and streets, were momentarily silhouetted against the sky by the sudden flash of their guns. The Auxiliary Fire Service, spread out in a network of squads through the capital, was standing by, ready at a moment's notice to deal with the inevitable fires; air-raid wardens, tireless in their care of shelters and work of rescue, patrolled their areas watchfully. One heavy night I poked my nose out of the Dorchester, which was rocking gently, to find a cab calmly coasting down Park Lane. I hailed it and was driven back to the hospital. The driver turned to me: 'Thank God, sir,' he said, 'Jerry's wasting 'is time trying to break our morale, when 'e might be doing real damage on some small town.'

With the break of day London shook herself and went back to work. Women with husbands in Government jobs were no longer to be seen at noon draped along the bars of the West End as their first appointment of the day. They were up and at work with determined efficiency in administrative posts of the Red Cross, the women's voluntary services, and the prisoners of war organizations. The Home Guards and air-raid wardens of the previous night would return home, take a bath, and go off to their respective offices. The soldier was back with his regiment, the airman with his squadron; the charming frivolous creatures with whom they had dined were themselves in uniform, effective in their jobs of driving, typing, or nursing.

That, I discovered, was a little of what London was doing. But what was London feeling? Perhaps a not irrelevant example was an experience of Sheep Gilroy's when flying with the Squadron. He was sitting in his bath when a 'flap' was announced. Pulling on a few clothes and not bothering to put on his tunic, he dashed out to his plane and took off. A few minutes later he was hit by an incendiary bullet and the machine caught fire. He baled out, quite badly burned, and landed by a parachute in one of the poorer districts of London. With no identifying tunic, he was at once set upon by two hundred silent and coldly angry women, armed with knives and rolling-pins. For him no doubt it was a harrowing experience, until he finally established his nationality by producing all the most lurid words in his vocabulary; but as an omen for the day when the cream of Hitler's Aryan youth should attempt to land in Britain it was most interesting.

All this went on at a time when night after night the East End was taking a terrible beating, and it was rumoured that the people were ominously quiet. Could their morale be cracking? The answer was provided in a story that was going the rounds. A young man went down to see a chaplain whom he knew in the East End. He noticed not only that the damage was considerable but that the people were saying practically nothing at all. 'How are they taking it?' He asked nervously. The chaplain shook his head. 'I'm afraid,' he said, 'that my people have fallen from grace: they are beginning to feel a little bitter towards the Germans.'

The understatement in that remark was impressive because it was typical. The war was practically never discussed except as a joke. The casual observer might easily have drawn one of two conclusions: either that London was spent of all feeling, or that it was a city waiting like a blind man, unseeing, uncaring, for the end. Either conclusion would have been wide of the mark. Londoners are slow to anger. They had shown for long enough that they could take it; now they were waiting on the time when it would be their turn to dish it out, when their cold rage would need more than a Panzer division to stamp it out.

Now and then I lunched at home with my mother, who was working all day in the Prisoners of War Organization, or my father would leave his desk long enough to give me lunch at his club. On one of these occasions we ran into Bill Aitken, and I had coffee with him afterwards. He was still in Army Co-operation and reminded me of our conversation at Old Sarum. 'Do you remember,' he asked, 'telling me that I should have to eat my words about Nigel Bicknell and Frank Waldron? Well, you were certainly right about Nigel.'

'I haven't heard anything,' I said, 'but you sound as though he had renounced his career as Air Force psychologist.'

Bill laughed. 'He's done more than that. He was flying his Blenheim to make some attack on France when one engine cut. He carried on, bombed his objective, and was on his way back when the other engine cut out, too, and his machine came down in the sea. For six hours, until dawn when a boat saw them, he held his observer up. He's got the DFC.'

'I must write to him,' I said. 'But I was right about Frank too. Do you remember your quotation that war was 'a period of great boredom, interspersed with moments of great excitement'; and how you said that the real test came in the periods of boredom, since anyone can rise to a crisis?'

'Yes, I remember.'

'Well, I think I'm right in saying that Frank has come through on that score. He's in the Scots Guards with very little to do; but he's considerably more subdued than you'll remember him. When he first got out of the Air Force he thought he could waltz straight into the Guards, but they wouldn't take him until he had been through an OCTU. That was his first surprise. The second was when there was no vacancy in the OCTU for three months. Our Frank, undismayed, hied himself off to France and kicked up his heels in Megève with the *Chasseurs Alpins*, and then in Cannes with the local lovelies. But he came back and went through his course. He was a year behind all his friends – or rather all those that were left, and it sobered him up. I think you'd be surprised if you saw him now.'

Bill got up to leave. 'I should like to see him again,' he said with a smile, 'but of the ex-bad boys, I think you are the best example of a change for the better.'

'Perhaps it's as well that you can't stay,' I said. 'I'm afraid it wouldn't take you long to see that you're mistaken. If anything, I believe even more strongly in the ideas which I held before. Sometime we'll discuss it.'

I spent most evenings with Denise at the house in Eaton Place. It was the usual London house, tall, narrow, and comfortable. Denise was living there alone with a housekeeper, for her father was about to marry again and had moved to the country. At tea-time I would come and find her curled up on the sofa behind the tray, gazing into the fire; and from then until eight o'clock, when I had to drive back to the Masonic, we would sit and talk – mostly of Peter, for it eased her to speak of him, but also of the war, of life, and death, and many lesser things.

Two years before the war she had joined the ATS. Sensibility and shyness might well have made her unsuited for this service, but when her family said as much, they merely fortified her in her determination. After she was commissioned, she fainted on her first parade, but she was not deterred, and she succeeded. She had left the ATS to marry Peter. I was not surprised to learn that she had published a novel, nor that she refused to tell me under what pseudonym, in spite of all my accusations of inverted snobbery. She wished to see nobody but Colin and me, Peter's friends; and though often she would have preferred to be alone, she welcomed me every day, nevertheless. So warm and sincere was her nature, that I might almost have thought myself her only interest. Try as I would, I could not make her think of herself; it was as if she considered that as a person she was dead. Minutes would go by while she sat lost in reverie, her chin cupped in her hand. There seemed nothing I could do to rouse her to consciousness of herself, thaw out that terrible numbness, breathe life into that beautiful ghost. Concern with self was gone out of her. I tried pity, I tried understanding, and finally I tried brutality.

It was one evening before dinner, and Denise was leaning against the mantelpiece, one black heel resting on the fender.

'When are you coming out of mourning?' I asked.

She had been standing with her chin lowered; and now, without lifting it, she raised her eyes and looked at me a moment.

'I don't know,' she said slowly. 'Maybe I never shall.'

I think she sensed that the seemingly innocent question had been put deliberately, though she couldn't yet see why. It had surprised her; it had hurt her, as I had meant it to. Up to now I had been at pains to tread delicately. Now the time had come, I felt, for a direct attack upon her sensibility under the guise of outward stupidity.

'Oh, come, Denise,' I said. 'That's not like you. You know life better than that. You know there's no creeping away to hide in a dream world. When something really tragic happens – the cutting-off of a man at a moment when he has most reason to live, when he has planned great things for himself – the result for those who love him isn't a whimpering pathos; it's growth, not decline. It makes you a richer person, not a poorer one; better fitted to tackle life, not less fitted for it. I loved Peter, too. But I'm not going to pretend I feel sorry for you; and you ought to be grateful to the gods for having enriched you. Instead, you mope.'

I knew well enough that she wouldn't go under, that this present numb resignation was transitory. But I had been worried too long by her numbness, her rejection of life, and I wanted to end it. She said nothing, and I dared not look at her. I could see her fingers move as I went doggedly on.

'You can't run away from life,' I said. 'You're a living vital person. Your heart tells you that Peter will be with you always, but your senses know that absence blots people out. Your senses are the boundaries of your feeling world, and their power stops with death. To go back and back to places where you were happy with Peter, to touch his clothes, dress in black for him, say his name, is pure self-deception. You drug your senses in a world of dreams, but reality cannot be shut out for long.'

Still she said nothing, and I had a quick look at her. This was far worse than badgering Peter in the train. Her face was tense, slightly flushed, and her eyes were wide open and staring with what I hoped was anger, not pain. I wished to rouse her, and prayed only that I would not reduce her to tears.

'Death is love's crucifixion,' I said brutally. 'Now you go out with Colin and me because we were his friends, we are a link. But we are not only his friends, we are men. When I leave you and say good night, it's not Peter's hand that takes yours, it's mine. It's Colin's touch you feel when he helps you on with your coat. Colin will go away. I shall go back to hospital. What are you going to do then? Live alone? You'll try, but you won't be able. You will go out again – and with people who didn't know Peter, people your senses will force you to accept as flesh and blood, and not fellow players in a tragedy.'

She went over to a sofa opposite me and sat looking out of the window. I could see her breast rise and fall with her breathing. Her face was still tense. The set of her head on her shoulders was so graceful, the lines of her figure were so delicate as she sat outlined against the light, that I became aware with a shock of never before having thought of her as a woman, a creature of flesh and blood. I who had made the senses the crux of my argument had never thought of her except as disembodied spirit. Minutes passed; she said no word; and her silence began almost to frighten me. If she should go on saying nothing, and I had to do all the talking, I didn't know quite what I should end by saying. I was about to attack her again when she spoke, but in a voice so gentle that at first I had trouble hearing her.

'You're wrong, Richard,' she said. 'You are so afraid of anything mystical, anything you can't analyse, that you always begin rationalizing instinctively, in self-defence, fearing your own blind spots. You like to think of yourself as a man who sees things too clearly, too realistically, to be able to have any respect for the emotions. Perhaps you don't feel sorry for me; but I do feel sorry for you.

'I *know* that everything is not over for Peter and me. I know it with all the faith that you are so contemptuous of. We *shall* be together again. We are together now. I feel him constantly close to me; and that is my answer to your cheap talk about the senses. Peter lives within me. He neither comes nor goes, he is ever-present. Even while he was alive there was never quite the tenderness and closeness between us that now is there.'

She looked straight at me and there was a kind of triumph in her face. Her voice was now so strong that I felt there was no defeating her any more, no drawing her out of that morass of mysticism from which I so instinctively recoiled.

'I suppose you're trying to hurt me to give me strength, Richard,' she said; 'but you're only hurting yourself. I have the strength. And let me explain where it comes from, so that we need never revert to the subject again. I believe that in this life we live as in a room with the blinds down and the lights on. Once or twice, perhaps, it is granted us to switch off the lights and raise the blinds. Then for a moment the darkness outside becomes brightness, and we have a glimpse of what lies beyond this life. I believe not only in life after death, but in life before death. This life is to me an intermission lived in spiritual darkness. In this life we are in a state not of being, but of becoming.

'Peter and I are eternally bound up together; our destinies are the same. And you, with your unawakened heart, are in some curious way bound up with us. Oh, yes, you are! In spite of all your intellectual subterfuges and attempts to hide behind the cry of self-realization! You lay in hospital and saw Peter die as clearly as if you had been with him. You told me so yourself. Ever since Peter's death you have been different. It has worked on you; and it's only because it has that I tell you these things. Colin says he would never have believed that anyone could change as you have.'

'That,' said I, 'was pure hallucination. I don't pretend to account for it exactly, but it was that hundredth example of instinct, or intuition, that people are always boasting of while they never mention the ninety-nine other premonitions that were pure fantasy.'

'Please, Richard,' she said, 'let's not talk about Peter and me any more. Your self-realization theory is too glib to stand a real test. To pass coldly through the death and destruction of war, to stand aloof and watch your sensibility absorb experience like a photographic plate, so that you may store it away to use for your own self-development – that's what you had hoped to do. I believe?'

'Of course it is,' I admitted. She was really roused now, and I was pleased.

'Well, you can't! You know you can't, despite that Machiavellian pose of yours. You tell me women are not as I am. I tell you, men are not as you are. Or rather, were. You remember those photographs taken of you before the crash that I saw the other day? Well, I believe that then, before the crash, you could and possibly did feel as you say you still do. I could never have liked you when you looked like that, looked like the man of the theory you still vaunt. Have you read Donne's *Devotions*?'

'Looked through them,' I said.

'In one of them he says this: "Any man's death diminishes me, because I am involved in Mankind." You, too, are involved, Richard; and so deeply that you won't always be able to cover up and protect yourself from the feelings prompted in you by that involvement. You talk about my self-deception: do you really believe you can go through life to the end, always taking and never giving? And do you really imagine that you haven't given to me, haven't helped me? Well, you have. And what have you got out of it? Nothing! You have given to me in a way that would have been impossible for you before Peter's death. You are still giving. You are conferring value on life by feeling Peter's death as deeply as you do. And you are bound to feel the death, be recreated by the death, of the others in the Squadron – if not in the same degree, certainly in the same way. Certainly you are going to "realize" yourself; but it won't be by leading the egocentric life. The effect that you will have on everybody you meet will come not only from your own personality, but from what has been added to you by all the others who are now dead – what you have so ungratefully absorbed from them.'

She spoke with great feeling and much of what she said struck home. It was true that Peter was much in my thoughts, that I felt him somewhere near me, that he was in fact the touchstone of my sensibility at the moment. It was true that the mystical experience of his death was something which was outside my understanding, which had still to be assimilated, and yet, and yet . . . I could not help but feel that with the passage of time this sense of closeness, of affinity, must fade, that its very intensity was in part false, occasioned by being ill, and by meeting Denise so shortly afterwards; a Denise who was no mere shadow of Peter, but

Peter's reincarnation; thus serving to keep the memory and the experience always before my eyes. While here were two people of an intense lyrical sensibility, two people so close in thought, feeling, and ideals, that although one was dead and the other living they were to me as one, yet I could not feel that their experience was mine, that it could do more than touch me in passing, for that I had been of any help to Denise was in a large part due to the fact that we were so dissimilar. While her thoughts came trailing clouds of glory, mine were of the earth earthy, and at such a time could help to strike a balance between the mystical flights of her mind and the material fact of high-explosive bombs landing in the next street. But though we might travel the same road for a time, lone voyagers eager for company, yet the time must come when our ways should part. Right or wrong, her way was not mine and I should be mistaken in attempting to make it so. We must live how we can.

CHAPTER SEVEN

THE BEAUTY SHOP

I had now been in hospital something over two months and it was thought that I was sufficiently recovered for operation.

Shortly after my arrival at the Masonic the Air Force plastic surgeon, A. H. McIndoe, had come up to see me, but as I had been blind at the time I could recollect his visit but vaguely, remembering only that he had ordered the gentian violet to be removed from my eyes and saline compresses to be applied instead, with the result that shortly afterwards I had been able to see.

He was expected this time at about eleven o'clock, but I was ready a good hour before, bathed and shaved and dressings elaborately correct. The charge nurse ushered him in fussily. Of medium height, he was thickset and the line of his jaw was square. Behind his horn-rimmed spectacles a pair of tired friendly eyes regarded me speculatively.

'Well,' he said, 'you certainly made a thorough job of it, didn't you?'

He started to undo the dressings on my hands and I noticed his fingers – blunt, capable, incisive. By now all the tannic had been removed from my face and hands. He took a scalpel and tapped lightly on something white showing through the red granulating knuckle of my right forefinger.

'Bone,' he remarked laconically.

He looked at the badly contracted eyelids and the rapidly forming keloids, and pursed his lips.

'Four new eyelids, I'm afraid, but you're not ready for them yet. I want all this skin to soften up a lot first. How would you like to go to the south coast for a bit?'

He mentioned the official RAF convalescent hospital on the south coast, generally supplied with golf courses, tennis and squash courts. But as I could not use my hands, and abhorred seaside resorts in winter, I wasn't very enthusiastic. I asked instead whether I could go down to a convalescent home a couple of miles from his hospital. He raised no objection and said that he would fix it with the Commandant.

'And I'll be able to keep an eye on you there,' He added. He had got up to go when I asked him how long it would be before I should fly again. I had asked the same question on his previous visit, and when he had said 'Six months' I had been desperately depressed for days. Now when he said, 'Next war for you: those hands are going to be something of a problem,' I wasn't even surprised. I suppose I had known it for some time. I felt no emotion at all.

He took his leave and I went off to have lunch with my mother.

Two days later, after the disentangling of a few cross wires in official circles, Air Ministry permission came through and I was driven down to Sussex.

The house was rambling and attractive, and ideal for a convalescent home. I was greeted at the door by Matron and led in to tea. There were about twenty other inmates drinking tea, mostly Army men, not particularly exciting and with not particularly exciting complaints. About them hung the listless air and furtive manner of undertakers, born no doubt of their prolonged inactivity combined with the dreary nature of their intestinal afflictions. By dinner-time I was preparing to resign myself to a comfortable if not stimulating period of relaxation, when a couple of genial souls came rolling in very late and I met Colin Hodgkinson and Tony Tollemache.

Hodgkinson was twenty and in the Fleet Air Arm: it was not until he got up after dinner that I noticed his two artificial legs. While training in an Albacore he had come into collision with a Hurricane. His two companions and the Hurricane pilot were killed instantly and Colin was found in a field six hours later.

Tony Tollemache had crashed in March, night flying. Coming in to land, his Blenheim had turned over and caught fire, throwing him free. His passenger was also thrown free and killed; but under the impression that he was still inside, Tony had climbed in again and wandered up and down the flaming machine, looking for him. He had been badly burned on his face, hands, and, above all, legs. For this action he got the Empire Gallantry Medal and nearly a year in hospital. He had already had several operations, and he was due at the hospital in another two days for a graft on his left hand.

We sat long by the glow of the open fire talking of many things and it was late when we finally climbed the stairs to bed. As I turned on my side and closed my eyes I was content. Tomorrow I should have my breakfast in bed, be given a bath, and come down only for lunch: I was the autocrat of the bolster, the aristocrat of fine linen: there were many worse ways of spending the war.

The following afternoon an eye specialist took a look at me: the pupil of my left eye, dilated by regular treatment with belladonna, interested him particularly.

'Can't close your eyes at all, can you?' he asked.

'No, sir,' I said.

'Well, we'll have to get some covering over that left eye or you'll never use it again.'

He went into the Commandant's office where there was a telephone, and returned a few minutes later.

'McIndoe is going to give you a new pair of top lids,' he said. 'I know your eyes are still infected, but we'll have to take that chance. You're to go in with Tollemache tomorrow.'

At the Masonic I had been the only action casualty. I had been very ill and in a private ward; subsequently I had been outrageously spoiled. Having little previous experience of hospitals, I had taken it all as a matter of course. At the convalescent home the food was exceptional and the living conditions bordering on the luxurious: as a result the new hospital was something of a shock. It was one of several hundred Emergency Medical Service hospitals. Taken over by the Ministry of Health at the beginning of the war, these were nearly all small country-town hospitals in safe areas. Erected by subscription for the welfare of the district and run by committees of local publicity-loving figures in the community, they had been perfectly adequate for that purpose. They were not, however, geared for a war-time emergency; they were too small. To overcome this difficulty the Ministry of Health had supplied them with 'blisters' to accommodate the anticipated flow of troops. I had heard of these 'blisters' and was vaguely aware that they were huts, but this hospital provided my first introduction to them.

It was of fairly recent construction and of only one story. There were two main wards: one reserved for women and filled with residents of the district; the other for men, one-half for local civilians and the other (eight beds) for action casualties. Then there were the 'blisters'; a dental hut, and two others set at an angle to the main building.

Ward Three, housing some of the worst cases, stood about fifty yards away from the hospital. It was a long, low hut, with a door at one end and twenty beds down each side. The beds were separated from each other only by lockers, and it was possible without much exertion to reach out and touch the man in the next bed. Towards the far end the lockers degenerated into soap-boxes. They constituted the patients' furniture.

Windows were let into the walls at regular intervals on each side: they were never open. Down the middle there was a table with a wireless on it, a stove, and a piano. On either side of the entrance passage were four lavatories and two bathrooms. Immediately on the left of the entrance passage was the saline bath, a complicated arrangement of pipes that maintained a constant flow of saline around the bathed patient at a regulated temperature. McIndoe had been using it with great success for the rapid healing of extensive burns. Next to this, in a curtained-off bed, was a little girl of fifteen, by name Joan, terribly burnt by boiling sugar her first day in a factory. Joan was in this ward because there was no other saline bath in the hospital (there were only three in England), and she could not be moved any distance. She screamed fairly regularly, and always before being lifted into the bath; her voice was thin and like that of a child of seven. As the time for her bath approached there was a certain tension throughout the hut; and then everyone would start talking rather loudly, and the wireless was turned up.

For the rest, there was a blind man at the far end learning Braille with the assistance of his wife, a Squadron Leader, several Pilot Officers, a Czech, and sundry troops unlikely to forget Dunkirk as quickly as most.

But my first taste of Ward Three was not yet. It was to the main building that I went for my new eyelids, and with little graciousness. Tony and I came in late, a fair measure of whisky inside us, and started noisily to get undressed. Our beds were next to each other: opposite us were two Hurricane pilots, one with his legs badly burned and the other with a six-weeks' growth of beard and a thick surgical bandage over his eyes. He was being fed by a nurse.

'Is he blind?' I whispered to Tony.

'Blind?' he roared. 'Not half as blind as we are, I'll bet. No, me boy. That's what you're going to look like tomorrow when McIndoe's through with you.'

'Are you daft, Mr Tollemache, coming in here late and making all that noise? If it's trouble you want you'll get it when Sister Hall sees you. And tell your fine friend to take his shoes off the bed.'

This was my first introduction to the Ward Charge Nurse. She rose from feeding the man with the bandaged eyes and stood feet apart and hands on hips, her cap awry, one tooth nibbling her lower lip as though it was lettuce.

Tony turned to me.

'Begad,' he said, 'I forgot to warn you, it's back in Hell's Kitchen we are. The ward is lousy with Irish and 'tis better to lie and rot than let them lay a finger on your dressings. They'll give you a dig for De Valera as soon as look at you.'

'Ach! you needn't show off now, Mr Tollemache. That's not funny and I'm not laughing.'

She drew herself up to her full five feet and stalked majestically from the ward, somewhat spoiling the effect by a shrill cackle of laughter when she caught sight of the pair of red pyjamas that I was unpacking.

'It's the wrong address you're at with those passion pants,' she said. 'This is a hospital, not an English country house week-end.'

'Be off with you, woman,' I said, and putting on the offending garments I climbed into bed and settled down to read.

Shortly afterwards Sister Hall came into the ward, her dark-blue uniform proclaiming her rank.

'More Ireland,' whispered Tony as she approached.

She stopped at the foot of my bed and I noticed that she was short, that her hair was grey, and that a permanent struggle between a tight-lipped mouth and smiling eyes was at the moment being very definitely won by the mouth.

'Good evening, Mr Tollemache,' she said.

'Good evening, Sister Hall,' said Tony in his blandest manner.

She turned to me.

'Mr Hillary, both you and Mr. Tollemache are to be operated on tomorrow morning. As you know, you should have been in earlier for preparation; now it will have to be done in the morning. I hope you will settle in here quickly; but I want it understood that in my ward I will tolerate no bad language and no rudeness to the nurses.'

'My dear Sister,' I replied, 'I've no doubt that you will find me the mildest and most soft-spoken of men,' and sitting up in bed I bowed gravely from the waist. She gave me a hard look and walked through the ward.

Tony waited until she was out of earshot. Then: 'A tough nut, but the best nurse in the hospital,' he said. 'I don't advise you to get on the wrong side of her.'

Shortly after the lights were put out McIndoe made a round of the ward followed by half a dozen assistants, mostly service doctors who were training under him. 'You're first on the list, Tony,' he said, 'and you're second. By the looks of you both we'll need to use a stomach pump before we can give you any anaesthetic.'

He took a look at my eyes. 'They're still pretty mucky,' he said, 'but I think you'll find it a relief to have some eyelids on them.' He passed on through the ward and we settled down to sleep.

In the morning we were wakened early and 'prepped' by Taffy, the Welsh orderly. 'Prepping' consists of sterilizing the area of skin to be used for the graft and shaving completely any surrounding hair. My eyelids were to be a 'Thiersch' graft (a layer of skin thin as cigarette paper) taken from the inside of my left arm, so Taffy shaved the arm and armpit, then sterilized the arm and bound it up in a loose bandage. He did the same thing to Tony's leg, from where the skin was to be taken for his hand, and we were both ready to go. The Charge Nurse then trundled in a stretcher on wheels, parked it beside Tony's bed, pushed his feet into an enormous pair of bed-socks, and whipped out a hypodermic needle. This contained an injection to make one drowsy half an hour before being wheeled into the operating theatre.

'Bet you she's blunted the needle,' said Tony; 'and look at her hand; it's shaking like an aspen leaf.'

'Be quiet, Mr Tollemache, let's have less of your sauce now.'

After much protesting she finally caught his arm and stuck him with the needle. He then climbed on to the trolley, which was screened off, and after about half an hour he was wheeled away.

I hoped that the operation would not be a lengthy affair, for I was hungry and could have no food until after I had been sliced up. Finally Tony was wheeled back, very white on the unburned patches of his face and breathing ether all over the room. It was my turn for the trolley. The injection did not make me particularly drowsy, and feeling bored I asked for a cigarette from one of the others and puffed away contentedly behind the screen. But I had not counted on the sharp eyes of Sister Hall. For a second she stared unbelievingly at the thin spiral of smoke; then she was inside the screen, the confiscated cigarette glowing accusingly in her hand and herself looking down on me with silent disapproval. I gazed back innocently; but pulling the screen to with a jerk, she walked on, her measured tread the silent voice of outraged authority.

It was time for me to go. Two nurses appeared at either end of the trolley and I was off, Tony's stertorous breathing and the coarse cries of the others following me down the ward. I was welcomed by the anaesthetist, vast and genial, with his apparatus that resembled a petrol station on wheels. As he was tying up my arm with a piece of rubber tubing, McIndoe came in sharpening his knife and wearing a skull-cap and multi-coloured gown, for all the world like some Bedouin chieftain. The anaesthetist took my arm and pushed the needle in gently. 'Well, good-bye,' he said. A green film rose swiftly up my throat and I lost consciousness.

When I came round I was not uncomfortable, and, unlike Tony, I was not sick. I could not see; but apart from a slight pricking of the eyes I had no pain, and but for the boring prospect of five days without reading I was content. Those of us with eyelid grafts had, of course, to be fed and given bed baths, but we could (thank God) get up and walk to the lavatory, escorted by a nurse. Were there no nurses about, the others would sing out instructions to the needy one until he arrived safely at his destination.

Being unable to see, had, I discovered, some distinct disadvantages. As

I could not read, I talked; and as everyone knows, there are few more
pleasant pastimes when one is indisposed than grousing and swearing.
After a few unfortunate incidents I always asked Tony if any nurses
were about before opening my mouth, but Tony was unreliable, getting
a hideous pleasure out of watching the consequences. Then – I think it
was on the third day of my incarceration – some nurse farther down the
ward dropped a bed-pan with a crash that made me start up in bed.

'Jesus Christ,' I said, 'what a hospital! It stinks like a sewer, it's about
as quiet as a zoo, and instead of nurses we've got a bunch of moronic
Irish amazons.'

'Mister Hillary!' The voice was so close that I almost fell out of bed.

'That's done it,' I thought; and I was right.

'Not another dressing do you get until you apologize.' Sister Hall was
standing at my elbow. Tony, of course, was delighted and I could hear
him chuckling into the bed-clothes. I opened my mouth to apologize, but
no words came. Instead, I realized with horror that I was laughing,
laughing in a manner that could in no way be passed off as a mere
nervous titter, that could be taken, indeed, for nothing but what it was
– a rich, fruity belly-laugh.

Nothing was said, but I had a sense of impending doom. A few minutes
later my suspicions were confirmed: I felt my bed begin to move.

'What goes on?' I asked.

'Two orderlies are shipping you off next door,' said Tony. 'They're
going to separate us.'

Now I had no wish to be separated from Tony. He was amusing to
talk to, and especially at a time when I could not see, I felt the need of
his presence. Further, there is nothing more depressing than being moved
in hospital just after getting the feel of a ward. So I got out of bed. The
orderlies were for a moment nonplussed; but, as Tony explained to them,
their orders were to move the bed, not me. I could almost see their faces
clear and I heard the bed being pushed through the door.

'Trouble ahead,' said Tony. 'Haven't enjoyed myself so much for ages.'

Sure enough, a few minutes later Sister Hall returned accompanied
by one of the younger surgeons, unhappy and embarrassed by the whole
thing.

'Now, what's all this?' he asked nervously.

'Well, among other things,' I said, 'I have told Sister Hall that I object
to being treated as though I were still in kindergarten.'

'He said more than that, Doctor,' said Sister Hall with some truth.
'He and Mr Tollemache together make it impossible to run the ward.'

By this time the pettiness of it was boring me, and when the harassed
doctor said that he could not interfere with Sister Hall's running of the
ward I made no demur and allowed myself to be led off to the all-glass
covered-in balcony extension of the ward to which my bed had been

moved. I made some remark to Tony as I passed his bed, but Sister had the last word.

'And we'll have no bad language while I'm in charge here,' she said, and shut the door firmly behind me.

I found myself next to an Army doctor with smashed insides, sustained running into a stationary lorry in the black-out. He had difficulty in getting his breath and roared and whistled all night. I began to regret the haste of my outburst.

The hospital visiting hours were from two till four in the afternoon, a change from the Masonic and an arbitrary rule which in my present state of mind I considered nothing short of monstrous. Denise, who was now back in the ATS with an important job, could get off only at odd moments, but wanted to come and see me. I asked the Matron if she might be allowed to come in the morning if she could get down from London, and the Matron very reasonably agreed. Denise duly arrived and called up from the station to ask when she might appear. Due to a misunderstanding, she was told that visiting hours were from two till four, and she had therefore to kick her heels for several hours in the town. By this time I was so enjoying my sense of persecution that, even if I had realized that it was a misunderstanding, I should doubtless have chosen to ignore the fact. When, therefore, on the stroke of four Sister Hall entered and said coldly, 'All visitors must leave now,' I would willingly have committed murder, but Denise laid a warning hand on mine and I held my peace.

The next day McIndoe took down the dressing from my eyes and I saw again.

'A couple of real horse blinkers you've got there,' he said; and indeed for a day or so that is what they felt like. In order to see in front of me I had to turn my face up to the ceiling. They moulded in very rapidly, and soon I could raise and lower them at will. It was a remarkable piece of surgery, and an operation in which McIndoe had yet to score a failure.

Shortly afterwards I was allowed to have a bath and soak the bandage off my arm from where the graft had been taken. This laborious and painful process had already taken me half an hour when Sister Hall came in. I was down to the last layer, which I was pulling at gingerly, hurting myself considerably in the process.

'Well, really, Mister Hillary!' she said; and taking hold of it she gave a quick pull and ripped the whole thing off cleanly and painlessly.

'Christ!' I started involuntarily, but stopped myself and glanced apprehensively at Sister's face. She was smiling. Yes, there was no doubt about it, she was smiling. We said nothing, but from that moment we understood each other.

Tony's graft had been a success, and within a few days we were allowed out for a fortnight's convalescence before coming in again for further operations.

As I was getting ready to go, Sister took me on one side and slipped a small package into my hand.

'You'll be wanting to look your best for the girls, Mr Hillary, and I've put in some brown make-up powder that should help you.'

I started to protest but she cut me short.

'You'll be in again in a couple of weeks,' she said. 'Time enough for us to start quarrelling then.'

We returned after a short but very pleasant convalescence – Tony for his last operation, one top lid, and I for two lower ones.

This time when the dressings were taken down I looked exactly like an orang-outang. McIndoe had pinched out two semi-circular ledges of skin under my eyes to allow for contraction of the new lids. What was not absorbed was to be sliced off when I came in for my next operation, a new upper lip. The relief, however, was enormous, for now I could close my eyes almost completely and did not sleep with them rolled up and the whites showing like a frightened negro.

Once again we retired to our convalescent home, where our hostess did everything possible to relieve the monotony of our existence. She gave a large party on Christmas night, and every few weeks brought down stage or screen people to cheer up the patients.

There had been some changes among the other inmates since our last visit, and two of de Gaulle's Frenchmen had arrived from an Aldershot hospital. One of them, an Army officer, had been in plaster since Dunkirk, where he got an explosive bullet in the arm. The other had been in the French Air Force but had decidedly un-Gallic features. When I first saw him he was wearing a beard and looked like a Renaissance Christ. Later he shaved it off and was indistinguishable from any chorus-boy in the second row.

When France fell he was completing his flying training in Morocco. He had taken off in an antiquated trainer and landed at Gibraltar. Eventually he managed to reach England and to continue his training on Magisters with French instructors whom he described as old, blind, and incompetent. Apparently he was sent up to practise spins without having been told how to come out of them. His command of English was picturesque and somewhat erratic, yet he managed to convey to me a vivid picture of his crash.

'I am diving at about 4,000 feet,' he said, 'when I start the spin. I am told only two turns, so after these I think I centralize the stick and rudder and come out. Nothing happens, so I cross the controls, open the gas and push the stick further forward. I do not wish to jump out, you understand, as I have done this before and do not like. So I try an inverted loop but nothing happens. By this time I have done many turns and am feeling dizzy, so I say to myself, "I must now bale out," and I undo my straps and stand up. When I look over the side a haystack is spinning round the plane and I am stepping over the side, when crash! And we are no more.'

A most remarkable recital! His back and one foot were broken. His body and leg were swathed in plaster of Paris, and his fellow-countryman, who was an artist, had painted the picture of the crash across his chest.

On Tuesdays and Thursdays the inmates always drove into town in the station wagon to go to the pictures. This involved sitting in the local tea-shop for an hour afterwards, eating sickening cakes and waiting for the car to drive them back. As tea-shops have the most appalling effect on me, depression descending like a fog, I seldom went along. Eliot has said the final word about them:

> Over buttered scones and crumpets
> Weeping, weeping multitudes
> Droop in a hundred A B C's.

But on our first Thursday out of the hospital our two Frenchmen asked Tony and me to accompany them, and we duly set off.

We were having tea when a pretty waitress came up and said to my bearded friend, '*Vous êtes Français?*'

'*Oui, et vous?*'

'*Canadienne-Française.*'

'*Dommage que je n'aille mieux. J'aimerais vous prouver que je vous trouve gentille.*'

'*Faudrait aussi que je le veuille!*'

'*N'importe. J'aimerais toujoirs tenter la chance.*'

The rest of us sat there like cold suet.

Tony and I went often to London, where we settled ourselves down in some restaurant, ordered a most excellent dinner, and surveyed the youth and beauty around us with a fatherly eye. For while we were now medically fit and perfectly content, yet we were still naturally enough drained of any exuberance of youthful vitality.

One night over a particularly good dinner I summed it up to Tony. 'Well,' I said, waving a vague hand at the crowded dance floor, 'we're a lucky pair. Here we are enjoying all the pleasures of old men of sixty. To us it has been granted to pass through all the ages of man in a moment of time, and now we know the joys of the twilight of man's existence. We have come upon that great truth, that the warmth in the belly brought on by brandy and cigars leaves a glow that is the supreme carnal pleasure. Not for us the exacerbation of youthful flesh-twitchings, not for us palpitations and agony of spirit at a pretty smile, a slender waist. We see these things with pleasure, but we see them after our own fashion – as beauty, yes, and as a joy for ever, but as beauty should be seen, from afar and with reverence and with no desire to touch. We are free of the lusts of youth. We can see a patch of virgin snow and we do not have to rush out and leave our footprint. We are as David in the Bible when "they brought unto him a virgin but he gat no heat." '

Tony nodded owlishly and lit a cigar. Then, jabbing it through the air to emphasize his words, he spoke. Slowly and deliberately and with great sorrow he spoke.

'Alas,' he said, 'it is but a dream, a beautiful, beautiful dream, but still a dream. Youth will catch us up again. Youth with all her temptations, trials, and worries. There is no escape.' He lowered his voice and glanced nervously over his shoulder. 'Why, even now I feel her wings fluttering behind me. I am nearly the man I was. For you there is still a little time, not much but a little. Let us then enjoy ourselves while yet we may. Waiter, more brandy!'

One night when we were in town we walked around to see Rosa Lewis at the Cavendish Hotel. Suddenly caught by a stroke, she had been rushed to the London Clinic, where she refused to allow any of the nurses to touch her. After a week she saw the bill and immediately got up and left.

When we arrived, there she was, seventy-six years old, shrieking with laughter and waving a glass of champagne, apparently none the worse. She grabbed me by the arm and peered into my face. 'God, aren't you dead yet either, young Hillary? Come here and I'll tell you something. Don't you ever die. In the last two weeks I've been right up to the gates of 'eaven and 'ell and they're both bloody!'

A few weeks later a heavy bomb landed right on the Cavendish, but Rosa emerged triumphant, pulling bits of glass out of her hair and trumpeting with rage. Whatever else may go in this war, we shall still have Rosa Lewis and the Albert Memorial at the end.

Thus did I while away the time between operations, living from day to day, sometimes a little bored, a little depressed, aware of being restless, but analysing this restlessness no further than as the inevitable result of months in bed.

CHAPTER EIGHT

THE LAST OF THE LONG-HAIRED BOYS

It was already January of 1941 when I returned to the hospital for the removal of the ledges under my eyes and the grafting of my new upper lip.

I had lunch at home, saying good-bye to London with two dozen oysters and a bottle of Pol Roger, and just caught my train. On the way down I began to regret the richness of my lunch and I was in no way cheered by the discovery that the only available bed was in Ward Three. McIndoe came round on his tour of the ward, and asked if I might be first on the list, feeling that the great man would be at his best in the early morning. It was true that he never seemed to tire. Indeed he had been known to operate all day, and finally at ten o'clock at night, stretch himself comfortably and say to an exhausted theatre staff, 'Now let's *do* something!'

I was wakened early to have my arm 'prepped' by one of the orderlies. I had decided on the arm, and not the leg, in order to be spared the bother of shaving my new upper lip. We chose a piece of skin bounded on one side by a vaccination mark and on the other by the faint scar of what are now my upper lids.

Sister gave me an injection at about nine o'clock, and an hour later, wearing my red pyjamas for luck, I climbed on to the trolley and was wheeled across the fifty yards of open space to the hospital. There was something a little lowering about this journey on a cold morning, but I reached the theatre feeling quite emotionless, rather like a business man arriving at his office. The anaesthetist gave me an injection and I lost consciousness.

On coming round, I realized that I was bandaged from forehead to lip and unable to breathe through my nose. At about three o'clock Tony Tollemache and his mother came to see me. I had by then developed a delicate froth on both lips and must have resembled a perhaps refined stallion. They were very kind, and talked to me quite normally. I'm afraid I replied little, as I needed my mouth to breathe with. They went at about four. After that the day was a blur: a thin wailing scream, the radio playing 'Each day is one day nearer,' injections, a little singing, much laughter, and a voice saying, 'Naow, Charlie, you can't do it; naow, Charlie, you *can't* do it; naow, Charlie, you can't *do* it.' After this, oblivion, thank God.

The next morning I awoke in a cold sweat after a nightmare in which
my eyelids were sewn together and I was leading the Squadron in an
Avro Tutor. In the evening one of the doctors took the bandages off my
eyes. I was left with a thick dressing across my upper lip which pressed
against my nose, and two sets of semicircular stitches under my eyes.
Peering into a mirror, I noticed that my right eyebrow had been lifted
up higher to pair it off with the left. This was also stitched. Later
McIndoe made a round and peered anxiously at the scar under my right
eye, which was blue and swollen. He moved on. There was comparatively
little noise, but the ward smelt and I was depressed.

The next few days remain in my memory as a rather unpleasant
dream. Rumour started that eight of us were to be isolated, owing to
suspicion of a bug. It proved true. We climbed on to trolleys and were
pushed across the yard to one of the main wards, from which a bunch
of protesting old women had been evacuated. On the way over I passed
a new victim of tannic acid being wheeled in to take my bed; all I could
see was an ebony-coloured face enveloped in a white cowl. As we were
pushed up the steps to our new quarters we were greeted by four nurses
wearing masks, white aprons, and rubber gloves. Our luggage followed,
and was tipped into the store-room outside.

Opposite me was Squadron Leader Gleave with a flap graft on his
nose and an exposed nerve on his forehead: in Ward Three he had been
unable to sleep, nor could the night nurse drug him enough to stop the
pain. Next to him was Eric Lock, a tough little Shropshireman who had
been with me at Hornchurch and collected twenty-three planes, a DSO,
a DFC and a bar: he had cannon-shell wounds in the arms and legs. On
my left was Mark Mounsdon who trained with me in Scotland and was
awaiting an operation on his eyelids. Beyond the partition was Joseph,
the Czech sergeant pilot, also with a nose graft; Yorkey Law, a bombardier, blown up twice and burned at Dunkirk, with a complete new
face taken in bacon strips from his legs, and no hands; and Neft, a clever
young Jew (disliked for it by the others), with a broken leg from a
motor-cycle accident.

We were of course allowed no visitors and could write no letters.

On the second day Neft's face began to suppurate and a small colony
of streptococci settled comfortably on the Squadron Leader's nose. The
rest of us waited grimly. Neft showed a tendency to complain, which
caused Eric Lock to point out that some of us had been fighting the war
with real bullets and would be infinitely grateful for his silence.

On the third day in our new quarters the smell of the bandage under
my nose became so powerful that I took to dosing it liberally with eau-
de-cologne. I have since been unable to repress a feeling of nausea
whenever at a party or in company I have caught a whiff of this scent.

Our heads were shorn and our scalps rubbed with special soap and anointed with M. & B. powder. We submitted to this with a varying amount of protestation: the Squadron Leader was too ill to complain, but Eric Lock was vociferous and the rest of us sullen. A somewhat grim sense of humour helped us to pass this day, punctuated by half-hours during which Neft was an object of rather cruel mockery. He had been a pork butcher before the war and of quite moderate means, but he made the mistake of mentioning this fact and adding that foul-mouthed talk amused him not at all. From that moment Yorkey Law, our bombardier, gave him no peace and plied him with anecdotes which even curled what was left of my hair. By the evening Neft had retired completely under the bed-clothes, taking his suppurating face with him.

After the huts our new ward was luxurious: the beds were more comfortable, and above a pair of earphones hung on the wall. A large plain window ran the whole length of one side and ensured an adequate ventilation: the ward was kept dusted and tidy.

The nurses were efficient and not unfriendly, though the enforced wearing of masks and rubber gloves made them a little impersonal. Our language was always rough and sometimes offensive; Eric, with an amiable grin on his face, would curse them roundly from dawn till dusk, but they seldom complained. They did their best to make up to us for our lack of visitors. Tony Tollemache came down once from the convalescent home and said good-bye through the window: he was returning to Hornchurch. Otherwise we saw nobody.

It was announced that our swabs had returned. We all clamoured to know who was, and who was not, infected. Apparently two were not, but which two the doctors would not say.

On February 14 I developed earache. Short of breath and completely blocked in the nose, I gave a snort and felt something crack in my right ear. Never having had earache before, I found the experience disagreeable to a degree: it was as though someone with a sharp needle was driving it at regular intervals into the side of my head.

An ear, nose, and throat man, on a course of plastic surgery under McIndoe, came along to see me. He regarded me dispassionately for a minute, and then withdrew with Sister to the other end of the ward. That night I was put on to Prontosil and knew beyond any doubt that I had the streptococcus.

I slept fitfully, aided in my wakefulness by the pain in my ear, Eric's snores, and the groans of the Squadron Leader.

In the morning the pain in my ear was considerable and I felt sick from the Prontosil. But it was now eight days since my operation, and the dressing on my lip was due to be taken down. For this mercy I was grateful, as the smell under my nose was proving too strong for even the most frequent doses of eau-de-cologne. At lunch-time one of the doctors took off the bandages and removed the stitches, at the same time cutting the stitches from under my eyes to the accompaniment of appreciative purrs from his satellites. I asked for a mirror and gazed at the result. It was a blow to my vanity: the new lip was dead white, and thinner than its predecessor.

In point of fact it was a surgical masterpiece, but I was not in the mood to appreciate it. I fear I was not very gracious. The lip was duly painted with mercurochrome, and the doctors departed. The relief at having the bandages removed was enormous, but I still dared not blow my nose for fear that I should blow the graft away. I took a bath and soaked the bandage off the arm from which my lip had been taken. This was a painful process lasting three-quarters of an hour, at the end of which time was revealed a deep narrow scar, neatly stitched. Sister then removed the stitches. During this little operation an unfortunate incident occurred. As soon as the stitches were out, instead of behaving in an approved and conventional manner and remaining pressed together, the two lips of the wound opened out like a fan, exposing a raw surface the size of a half orange. Everyone clustered round to inspect this interesting phenomenon but were hastily ordered back to bed by a somewhat harassed Sister.

That night I slept not at all: the pain in my ear was a continuous throbbing and I felt violently sick from the Prontosil. At about two o'clock I got up and started pacing the ward. A night nurse ordered me back to bed. I invited her to go to hell with considerable vigour, but I felt no better. She called me a wicked ungrateful boy and I fear that I called her a cow. Finally I returned to bed and attempted to read until morning.

In the conversation of the next twenty-four hours I took little part but lay, propped up in bed, watching the Squadron Leader rubbing his eye with pieces of cotton-wool. The hair from his scalp was making it acutely uncomfortable. This is not so odd as it sounds, for during a flap graft on the nose the scalp is brought down to the top of one's eyebrow where it is neatly rolled and feeds the new nose. It is of course shaved but the hair tends to grow again.

February 17 was a Friday, the day on which an ear, nose, and throat specialist was in the habit of visiting the hospital. It was arranged for me to see him, and putting on my dressing-gown, I walked along to the Out-patients' Department. His manner was reassuring. He felt behind my ear and inquired if it pained me. I replied that it did.

That being so he regretted the necessity, but he must operate within half an hour for what appeared to be a most unpleasant mastoid. I asked if I might be moved to Sister Hall's ward, and after one look at my face the doctors very decently agreed.

I went back, changed into my red pyjamas and climbed once more on to the trolley. I was wheeled along to the Horsebox, the title affectionately bestowed on the emergency theatre which was the converted end of the children's ward. McIndoe was already at work in the main theatre.

With the usual feeling of relief I felt the hypodermic needle pushed into my arm, and within five seconds I was unconscious.

For the next week I was very ill, though quite how seriously I could only judge by the alacrity with which all my requests were granted. I was again in the glass extension of Sister Hall's ward and she nursed me all day and most of the night. I had regular morphia injections and for long periods at a time I was delirious. The bug had got into my lip and was biting deep into the skin at three places. I remember being in worse pain than at any time since my crash. After the plastic operations I had felt no discomfort, but now with the continuous throbbing agony in my head I thought that I must soon go mad. I would listen with dread for the footsteps of the doctors, knowing that the time was come for my dressings, for the piercing of the hole behind my ear with a thin steel probe to keep it open for draining, a sensation that made me contract within myself at the mere touch of the probe on the skin.

It was during my second night in the glass extension that a 2,500-lb bomb landed a hundred yards away but did not explode. I heard it coming down with a curious whirring rustle, and as I heard it I prayed, prayed that it would be near and bring with it peace, that it would explode and take with it me, the extension, the ward, the huts, everything. For a moment I thought it had, so great was the force of impact, but as I realized slowly that it had not exploded I found that the tears were pouring down my face: I was sobbing with mingled pain, rage, and frustration. Sister immediately gave me another morphia injection.

It was decided that while the excavation squad was digging it out, everybody possible must be evacuated to the convalescent home. Those who were too ill to be moved would go to Ward Three on the far side of the hospital. I imagined that I would go along with the others, but after taking a look at me McIndoe decided that it would be too dangerous to move me. Sister Hall offered to send a special nurse with me, but they thought even so the risk was too great.

Sister looked at me: 'I'm afraid that means the huts,' she said. At that something exploded inside me. McIndoe's chief assistant came into the ward to arrange for me to be moved and I let fly. I had not spoken since my operation and I saw the surprise in his face as I hauled myself up in bed and opened my mouth. Wild horses, I said, would not drag me back to that garbage-can of human refuse. If anyone laid a finger on my bed I would get up and start to walk to London. I preferred to die in the open rather than return to that stinking kitchen of fried flesh. I had come into the hospital with two scars on my upper lip: now I had a lip that was pox-ridden and an ear with enough infection in it to kill a regiment. There was only one thing to be said for the British medical profession:

it started where the *Luftwaffe* left off. An outburst to which I now confess with shame, but which at the time relieved my feelings considerably.

'You're not making this very easy,' he answered mildly.

'You're damn right, I'm not,' I said, and then felt very sick and lay down.

It was then that Sister Hall was magnificent.

'I think perhaps he should stay here in his present state, sir,' she said. 'I'll see if I can fix up something.'

The doctor, only too willing to have the problem off his hands, looked grateful, and left. I saw that she was smiling.

'Well, Mr Hillary,' she said, 'quite like old times,' and went off to see what she could arrange. Somehow she obtained permission to convert one of the consulting rooms further down the hospital into a ward, and my bed was pushed along.

That night McIndoe came in to see me. He was still wearing his operating robes and sat down on the end of the bed. He talked to me for some time – of the difficulties of running a unit such as this, of the inevitable trials and set-backs which must somehow be met. He knew, he said, that I had had a tough break, but I must try not to let it get me down. I noticed that he looked tired, dead tired, and remembered that he had been operating all day. I felt a little ashamed. The next day my mother and Denise motored down to see me. I was grey in the face from all the Prontosil that I was taking and they both thought that I was on the way out, though of this they gave no sign. Poor Mother. The crash, the sea, the hospital, the operations – she had weathered them all magnificently. But this last shock was almost too much. She did not look very well.

During the last five months I had gradually built up to my usual weight of twelve stone, but in the next week I sweated my temperature down to normal and my weight down to nine stone. I also began to feel more human, and as the bomb had been removed and the evacuated ones brought back, I returned to the main ward and the regular hospital routine.

If there is one thing I really loathe it is to be awakened an hour earlier than necessary with a cup of cold brown tea. Unfortunately I could not approach Tony's imperious sarcasm, which was proof against all nurses until nine o'clock, but I finally hit on an idea for stopping this persecution. Nurse Courtney promised that if I made no more remarks about Ireland, she would no longer wake me with tea. I agreed with alacrity, saying that I could easily dispense with both. She at once bristled but was calmed down by Sister.

My God, I thought, who would be a nurse! They must suffer all the inconveniences of convent celibacy without the consolation of that inner glow which I take to be an integral part of the spiritual life.

It was shortly after this that Edmonds was re-admitted to the hospital and placed in the bed next to mine. He was the worst-burned pilot in the Air Force to live. Taking off for his first solo in a Hampden at night, he had swung a little at the end of his run and put a wing in. The machine had immediately turned over and burst into flames. He had been strapped inside and fried for several minutes before they dragged him out. When he had first been brought to McIndoe he had been unrecognizable and had lain for months in a bath of his own suppuration. McIndoe performed two emergency operations and then left it to time and careful dressings to heal him enough for more.

Never once had Edmonds complained. After nine months McIndoe had sent him away to build up his strength. Now he was back. It would take years to build him a new face. He was completely cheerful, and such was his charm that after two minutes one never noticed his disfigurement.

He was first on the list for operation the day after his re-admission. Both his top lids and his lower lip were done together and he was brought back to the ward, even-tempered as ever. The man on his other side diverted him for most of the day with endless funny stories of crashes. Sometimes I think it would be very pleasant to be invested with the powers of life and death.

Three days went by and I noticed an ominous dribble down Edmonds' right cheek from under the dressing across his eyes. That night McIndoe took the dressing down: the right eyelid graft had not taken. He took it off and threw it away: it was the streptococcus at work again, and bitterly ironical that McIndoe's first eyelid failure should be on Edmonds. He was immediately put on to Prontosil and by the next morning was a greeny blue, with his lower lip jutting out like an African tribeswoman's.

After lunch some idiotic woman came in and exclaimed at how marvellously well he looked. I held my breath but I need not have worried. Instead of turning his face to the wall or damning her soul, he managed to smile and said:

'Yes, and I'm feeling much better too.'

I could not but marvel at his self-control and unruffled good manners. I remembered a few of my own recent outbursts and felt rather small.

Here was a twenty-six-year-old South African with no ties in this country, no mere boy with his whole life to make, terribly injured without even the satisfaction of having been in action. Sometimes he behaved as though he had been almost guilty not to have been shot down, as though he were in the hospital under false pretences; but if ever a pilot deserved a medal it was he. He read little, was not musical, yet somehow he carried on. How? What was it that gave not only him but all these men the courage to go on and fight their way back to life? Was it in some way bound up with the consciousness of death? This was a subject which

fascinated me and I had discussed it with McIndoe. Did people know
when they were about to die? He maintained that they did not, having
seen over two hundred go, none of them conscious that their last moment
had come.

'How about Charles the Second's apology for being such an uncon-
scionable time a-dying?'

He admitted that in some cases people might have a premonition of
death, but in cases of terrible physical injury he would say never. Their
physical and mental conditions were not on a different plane: the first
weakened the second (if I report him accurately), and there was neither
consciousness of great pain nor realization of the finality of physical
disintegration.

That, then, would account for my calmness when in the sea. I knew
well enough, meanwhile, that sheer anger had pulled me through my
mastoid complication. But what of the men who, after the first instinctive
fight to live, after surviving the original physical shock, went on fighting
to live, cheerfully aware that for them there was only a half-life? The
blind and the utterly maimed – what of them? Their mental state could
not remain in the same dazed condition after their bodies began to heal.
Where did they get the courage to go on?

It worried me all day. Finally I decided that the will to live must be
entirely instinctive and in no way related to courage. This nicely resolved
any suspicion that I might recently have behaved rather worse than any
of the others, might have caused unnecessary trouble and confusion.
Delighted with my analysis of the problem, I settled myself to sleep.

The following day my ear surgeon told me that I might go back to the
convalescent home in a week, McIndoe told me that he would not operate
on me again for three months, and my mother came down from town and
told me that Noel Agazarian had been killed.

At first I did not believe it. Not Noel. It couldn't happen to him. Then
I realized it must be true. That left only me – the last of the long-haired
boys. I was horrified to find that I felt no emotion at all.

CHAPTER NINE

'I SEE THEY GOT YOU TOO'

I was back at the convalescent home when the letter came. I was very
comfortable, but I had a flat, let-down feeling. I suppose it was natural
enough after the mastoid; but I knew it went deeper than that. The last
few months in the hospital had most certainly been an experience. I had

asked no more than that of the war. I was by no means regretting it, but
it was still too near in time for me to focus it clearly. I had, I thought,
observed the people around me disinterestedly. Their suffering and pain
had in no way affected my attitude to the war. I had come through it
without falling a victim to the cloying emotions of false pity. I could
congratulate myself that I was self-centred enough to have survived any
attack on my position as an egocentric. I had a fleeting suspicion that
that might be because the others had been so much an integral part of
my own experience that I could consider them only in relation to myself;
but I dismissed the idea. And yet something was wrong.

My thoughts were no longer tuned to Peter: there was no contact, not
even through Denise. All this was now as nothing. I was back where I
had started. It had been a mere passing emotional disturbance, occasioned
by my weakened condition. With the passage of time, as I had foreseen,
the whole relationship took on its normal proportions, Indeed I was a
little irritated with Denise. What had seemed sensibility now seemed
sentimentality: life was not all giving and selflessness, and no projection
of the imagination could make it so. The realization that I had felt so
deeply the need for the ghostly awareness of Peter now angered me. Still,
I had not expected it to last. Why, then, this absurd feeling of futility?

I was suddenly tired. The first intimation of spring was in the air and
I went for walks in the garden. Crocuses were bursting out of the ground,
the trembling livingness of the earth seemed urgent through the soles of
one's shoes; it was the time of poetry and the first glance of love; yet I
turned from it. It seemed to me that my mind was dry bone. I had an
idea for a play to be called *Dispersal Point*, a study in Air Force mentality
more or less on the lines of *Journey's End*, but the idea was stillborn. I
was cold and emptied of feeling. It was as though I were again at school,
at school and for Sunday lunch: the bars of the windows, the cracked
plaster above the empty grate, the housemaster surreptitiously picking
his teeth with a penknife, and the boys, their long-tailed coats drooping
over the hardwood benches, crouched dispiritedly above sickening plates
of cold trifle. And then one morning, the letter.

It was from David Rutter: he had read the notice about Noel in the
paper and asked if I could come to see him. David Rutter, a man with,
in a different way, as great an integrity as Peter's; David and the awful
sincerity of his pacificism, rationalized at Oxford by talk of the Middle
Ages, field-boots under the surplice, a different war for the unemployed
labourer and the Duke of Westminster; but with an instinctive, deep-
rooted hatred of killing which no argument could touch.

I had not seen him since that day more than a year before when Noel
and I had got our commissions. We were in the bar of a London club,
celebrating. David Rutter had come in. His first appeal as a conscientious

objector had been turned down by the board that morning. We told him our news.

'You always were the lucky bastard, Richard,' he said, and laughed. He had a drink with us and left. And now he was working on the land. I was eager to see if and how he had changed. I remembered our conversation at Oxford: I wasn't going to get hurt; I should get killed or win some putty medals while he went to jail. Well, I had to admit it hadn't worked out quite like that.

The letter came as a relief. I was eager to go, was sure that something would come of the visit. I thought I might go to London for the night afterwards: it would be a change. I applied for two days' leave and caught a train to Norfolk.

David met me at the station. A lock of hair hung over his forehead and he wore an old tweed jacket and corduroy trousers: he looked very fit. He seemed glad to see me, and as we climbed into his small car he told me shyly that he was married. I said little while we drove. I was uncertain what approach to take and felt it safer to let him make the first move. He was uneasy and I felt guilty: I had such an unfair advantage. We drew up outside a square brick bungalow and got out.

'Well, here we are,' said David with an attempt at a smile. 'Come and meet Mary.'

His wife greeted me politely but defensively. She was a large, good-looking girl, blonde hair hanging loosely forward over her shoulders. She began at once to talk about birds and their use as an alarm clock. She resented my face. I was amused and relieved, for the usual feminine opening of 'Poor boy, how you must have suffered' embarrassed me; embarrassed me not because it was tactless, but because I could not immediately disabuse my sympathizers of their misplaced pity without appearing mock-modest or slightly insane. And so I remained an impostor. They would say, 'I hope someone got the swine who got you: how you must hate those devils!' and I would say weakly, 'Oh, I don't know,' and leave it at that. I could not explain that I had not been injured in their war, that no thoughts of 'our island fortress' or of 'making the world safe for democracy' had bolstered me up when going into combat. I could not explain that what I had suffered I in no way regretted; that I had welcomed it; and that now that it was over I was in a sense grateful for it and certain that in time it would help me along the road of my own private development.

Well, here at least I need not worry.

Mary was still talking, this time about books, in an aggressive monologue which I was pretty certain masked a rawly sensitive nature.

But David cut in.

'It's all right, Mary,' he said in a tired voice, 'Richard's not belligerent.' He turned to me apologetically: 'I'm afraid I don't see many of my old friends any more and when I do there's usually a scene, so Mary's a bit on the defensive.'

We talked for a while on safe subjects – his work on the land, the district, and his evening visits to the local pub to gossip with the villagers. David was restless, pacing continuously up and down the room and rubbing a nervous hand over his hair. His wife followed his every movement; her eyes never left him. I realized that she was a very unhappy woman. It was not that she had no faith in David, for she was desperately loyal; it was that he no longer had any faith in himself.

I wanted to start him off, so I asked him what the CO boards had been like.

'Oh, moronic but well-meaning,' he said. 'Yes, they were certainly moronic; but they were right. That's the hell of it.'

He sat down and stared moodily into the fire.

Then: 'I'm sorry about Noel,' he said.

'Yes,' I said.

For a moment he sat in silence. Then he lay back in his chair and began to talk. From time to time he would glance up at my face, and as he talked I realized that while I might carry my scars for a few years, the scars of his action would be with him always. For he was a broken man. In the last year he had stood by and watched his ideals shattered, one by one. As country after country had fallen to Hitler his carefully reasoned arguments had been split wide open; it was as much the war of the unemployed labourer as of the Duke of Westminster. Never in the course of history had there been a struggle in which the issues were so clearly defined. Although our peculiar form of education would never allow him to admit it, he knew well enough that it had become a crusade. All this he could have borne. It was the painful death of his passionate fundamental belief that he should raise his hand against no man which finally brought his world crumbling about his ears.

It started as a suspicion, at first faint, then insistent, and finally a dominant conviction, that in this too, this in which he believed above all things, he had been wrong.

'After much heart-searching,' he said, 'I finally decided that with the outbreak of war I had failed in my own particular struggle. I had not now the right to refuse to fight: it was no longer a question for personal conscience but for the conscience of civilization. Civilization had decided, and it would be intolerable arrogance for me to question that decision.'

He gave me a wry smile.

'It is to be regretted,' he said, 'that it has taken me more than a year to see this. Now I suppose I shall join up. Do you think I should?'

I started: the question had caught me unawares. I looked at David's set face and the taut, expectant figure of his wife, and sitting there smugly with the 'honourable' scars of a battle that was not mine I felt of a sudden very small.

'I don't know, David,' I said. 'That's a question which only you can decide.'

When I rose to leave it was already dark. I said goodbye to his wife, and David drove me to my train up to London. As we got out of the car the searchlights were making a criss-cross pattern of light in the sky: all around us was the steady roar of anti-aircraft fire.

David held out his hand.

'Good-bye, Richard,' he said. 'You always were the lucky bastard.'

And this time he meant it.

There was a heavy raid on and the train crawled interminably, only the dull-blue light in the ceiling and the occasional glow of a cigarette revealing the presence of the passengers. David by now would be home again pacing the floor, up and down, up and down, while Mary sat by helpless. David, so lost and without purpose; I had never expected to find him like that. I thought of Noel, of the two Peters, of the others in the Squadron, all dead; and now the David that I had known was dead too. They had all, in their different ways, given so much: it was ironical that I who had given least should alone have survived.

Liverpool Street Station was a dull-grey blur of noise and movement. I managed somehow to get hold of a taxi and make a start across London, but my driver seemed doubtful whether we should be able to go very far. Some machine dropped a flare, and in the sudden brightness before it was put out I saw that the street was empty. What cars there were, were parked along the kerb and deserted.

'I'm afraid we'll be stopped soon, sir,' said the taxi-driver. At that moment there was a heavy crump unpleasantly close and glass flew across the street.

'See if you can find a pub and we'll stop there,' I shouted.

A few yards farther on he drew in to the kerb and we got out and ran to a door under a dimly lit sign of The George and Dragon. Inside there was a welcoming glow of bright lights and beery breaths and we soon had our faces deep in a couple of mugs of mild and bitter.

In one corner on a circular bench that ran round a stained wooden table sat a private in battle-dress and a girl, the girl drinking Scotch. She had light-brown hair and quite good features. I suppose if one had taken her outside and washed her face under a pump she would have had a rather mousy look, but she would still have been pretty. She was pretty now in spite of the efforts she had made to improve on nature, had made and continued to make, for every few minutes she would take out a vanity case, pull a face into the mirror, lick her lower lip and dash her lipstick in a petulant streak of scarlet across her mouth. She was also talking very loud and laughing immoderately. I caught the barmaid's eye. She gave me a conspiratorial wink and shook her head knowingly; ah yes, we understood, we two. But she was wrong: the girl was not drunk, she was very, very frightened, and, I thought, with good reason. For though at the Masonic I had dozed off regularly to the lullaby of the German night offensive, I had never before heard anything like this. The volume of noise shut out all thought, there was no lull, no second in which to breathe and follow carefully the note of an oncoming bomber. It was an orchestra of madmen playing in a cupboard. I thought, 'God! what a stupid waste if I were to die now.' I wished with all my heart that I was down a shelter.

'We'd be better off underground to-night, sir, and no mistake.' It was my taxi-driver speaking.

'Nonsense,' I said. 'We couldn't be drinking this down there,' and I took a long pull at my beer.

I was pushing the glass across the counter for a refill when we heard it coming. The girl in the corner was still laughing and for the first time I heard her soldier speak. 'Shut up!' he said, and the laugh was cut off like the sound track in a movie. Than everyone was diving for the floor. The barmaid (she was of considerable bulk) sank from view with a desperate slowness behind the counter and I flung myself tight up against the other side, my taxi-driver beside me. He still had his glass in his hand and the beer shot across the floor, making a dark stain and setting the sawdust afloat. The soldier too had made for the bar counter and wedged the girl on his inside. One of her shoes had nearly come off. It was an inch from my nose: she had a ladder in her stocking.

My hands were tight-pressed over my ears but the detonation deafened me. The floor rose up and smashed against my face, the swing-door tore off its hinges and crashed over a table, glass splinters flew across the room, and behind the bar every bottle in the place seemed to be breaking. The lights went out, but there was no darkness. An orange glow from across the street shone through the wall and threw everything into a strong relief.

I scrambled unsteadily to my feet and was leaning over the bar to see what had happened to the unfortunate barmaid when a voice said, 'Anyone hurt?' and there was an AFS man shining a torch. At that everyone began to move, but slowly and reluctantly as though coming out of a dream. The girl stood white and shaken in a corner, her arm about her companion, but she was unhurt and had stopped talking. Only the barmaid failed to get up.

'I think there is someone hurt behind the bar,' I said. The fireman nodded and went out, to return almost immediately with two stretcher-bearers who made a cursory inspection and discovered that she had escaped with no more than a severe cut on the head. They got her on to the stretcher and disappeared.

Together with the man in the AFS, the taxi-driver and I found our way out into the street. He turned to us almost apologetically. 'If you have nothing very urgent on hand,' he said, 'I wonder if you'd help here for a bit. You see it was the house next to you that was hit and there's someone buried in there.'

I turned and looked on a heap of bricks and mortar, wooden beams and doors, and one framed picture, unbroken. It was the first time that I had seen a building newly blasted. Often had I left the flat in the morning and walked up Piccadilly, aware vaguely of the ominously tidy gap between two houses, but further my mind had not gone.

We dug, or rather we pushed, pulled, heaved, and strained, I somewhat ineffectually because of my hands; I don't know for how long, but I suppose for a short enough while. And yet it seemed endless. From time to time I was aware of figures round me: an ARP warden, his face expressionless under a steel helmet; once a soldier swearing savagely in a quiet monotone; and the taxi-driver, his face pouring sweat.

And so we came to the woman. It was her feet that we saw first, and whereas before we had worked doggedly, now we worked with a sort of frenzy, like prospectors at the first glint of gold. She was not quite buried, and through the gap between two beams we could see that she was still alive. We got the child out first. It was passed back carefully and with an odd sort of reverence by the warden, but it was dead. She must have been holding it to her in the bed when the bomb came.

Finally we made a gap wide enough for the bed to be drawn out. The woman who lay there looked middle-aged. She lay on her back and her eyes were closed. Her face, through the dirt and streaked blood, was the face of a thousand working women; her body under the cotton nightdress was heavy. The nightdress was drawn up to her knees and one leg was twisted under her. There was no dignity about that figure.

Around me I heard voices. 'Where's the ambulance?' 'For Christ's sake don't move her!' 'Let her have some air!'

I was at the head of the bed, and looking down into that tired, blood-streaked, work-worn face I had a sense of complete unreality. I took the brandy flask from my hip pocket and held it to her lips. Most of it ran down her chin but a little flowed between those clenched teeth. She opened her eyes and reached out her arms instinctively for the child. Then she started to weep. Quite soundlessly, and with no sobbing, the tears were running down her cheeks when she lifted her eyes to mine.

'Thank you, sir,' she said, and took my hand in hers. And then, looking at me again, she said after a pause, 'I see they got you too.'

Very carefully I screwed the top on to the brandy flask, unscrewed it once and screwed it on again, for I had caught it on the wrong thread. I put the flask into my hip pocket and did up the button. I pulled across the buckle on my great-coat and noticed that I was dripping with sweat. I pulled the cap down over my eyes and walked out into the street.

Someone caught me by the arm, I think it was the soldier with the girl, and said: 'You'd better take some of that brandy yourself. You don't look too good'; but I shook him off. With difficulty I kept my pace to a walk, forcing myself not to run. For I wanted to run, to run anywhere away from that scene, from myself, from the terror that was inside me, the terror of something that was about to happen and which I had not the power to stop.

It started small, small but insistent deep inside of me, sharp as a needle, then welling up uncontrollable, spurting, flowing over, choking me. I was drowning, helpless in a rage that caught and twisted and hurled me on, mouthing in a blind unthinking frenzy. I heard myself cursing, the words pouring out, shrill, meaningless, and as my mind cleared a little I knew that it was the woman I cursed. Yes, the woman that I reviled, hating her that she should die like that for me to see, loathing that silly bloody twisted face that had said those words: 'I see they got you too.' That she should have spoken to me, why, oh Christ, to me? Could she not have died the next night, ten minutes later, or in the next street? Could she not have died without speaking, without raising those cow eyes to mine?

'I see they got you too.' All humanity had been in those few words, and I had cursed her. Slowly the frenzy died in me, the rage oozed out of me, leaving me cold, shivering, and bitterly ashamed. I had cursed her, cursed her, I realized as I grew calmer, for she had been the one thing that my rage surging uncontrollably had had to fasten on, the one thing to which my mind, overwhelmed by the sense of something so huge and beyond the range of thought, could cling. Her death was unjust, a crime, an outrage, a sin against mankind – weak inadequate words which even as they passed through my mind mocked me with their futility.

That that woman should so die was an enormity so great that it was terrifying in its implications, in its lifting of the veil on possibilities of thought so far beyond the grasp of the human mind. It was not just the German bombs, or the German Air Force, or even the German mentality, but a feeling of the very essence of anti-life that no words could convey. This was what I had been cursing – in part, for I had recognized in that moment what it was that Peter and the others had instantly recognized as evil and to be destroyed utterly. I saw now that it was not crime; it was Evil itself – something of which until then I had not even sensed the existence. And it was in the end, at bottom, myself against which I had raged, myself I had cursed. With awful clarity I saw myself suddenly as I was. Great God, that I could have been so arrogant!

How long I had been walking I don't know, but the drone of aircraft had ceased, so the All Clear must have sounded. I had a horror of thinking of allowing my mind to look back armed with this new consciousness, but memories of faces, scenes, conversations flooded in, each a shock greater than the last. I was again in the train with Peter, on the way to Edinburgh, sitting forward on the seat, ridiculing his beliefs with glib patronizing assurance. Once again I was drawing from him his hopes and fears, his aspirations for a better life, extracting them painfully one by one, and then triumphant, holding them up to the light, turning them this way and that, playing with them for a moment only to puncture them with ridicule and, delighted with my own wit, to throw them carelessly aside. Once again Peter was sitting opposite me, unruffled and tolerant, saying that I was not quite unfeeling, predicting that some shock of anger or of pity would serve to shake me from the complacency of my ivory tower, Peter quoting Tolstoi to me:

Man, man, you cannot live entirely without pity!

words which I had taken it upon myself to dismiss as the sentimental gub of an old man in his dotage.

Oh, God, that memory might be blotted out; but it was remorseless. Peter's death lived by me in all its vivid intensity, offering me yet again the full life by all its implications, but rejected by me later to Denise. Rejected brutally, 'Let the dead bury their dead,' close the door on the past, be grateful for the experience, use it, but understand that there is no communication, no message, no spiritual guidance, no bridge between life and death. Go on, do not look back, there is nothing there, nothing; it is all over. Denise, who had not been angry, who was now working day and night with Peter beside her, who had shown me the way, who with patience and understanding had let me look into her heart that I might learn. And I who, having looked, closed my eyes and turned away not wishing to believe, turned away irritated. Something there to be absorbed perhaps, an experience which might be useful; very interesting emotionally, of course, but nothing more. No, decidedly not. Dangerous morbid introspection; must get away.

Noel, Peter Howes, Bubble, and the others – their deaths. Not felt quite as fully as one had expected perhaps, but then there was a war on, people dying every minute, one must harden one's heart. They were gone; good friends all of them, but there it was, nothing there for me, no responsibility, no answering to them for my actions before or after.

And the hospital. I saw myself again that first day in Sussex, standing in the doorway and looking down Ward Three. Once again I saw Joan in the bed by the saline bath, saw her hairless head, her thin emaciated face, and heard that voice like a child of seven's whimpering, saw myself register it vaguely and pass on to look with interest at the others. The blind man learning Braille, utterly dependent on his wife; bad that, should be helping himself. Joseph the Czech and his nose growing from his forehead; his hands messy stumps and his eyes stupidly trusting. The one with practically no face at all, just a pair of eyes; unable to talk, of course, but interesting, oh, yes, particularly interesting: Yorkey Law the bombardier, later to be invalided out, but quite fascinating with all those bacon strips off his legs gradually forming a face. And the others; one after another I remembered them until finally Edmonds – Edmonds and his year of pain and disfigurement and my nice comfortable little theory on his will to live.

I remembered them all, remembered how at first they had interested me in their different ways, and then how they had irritated me with their dumb acceptance of the hospital conditions, their gratitude for what was being done for them, and above all their silent, uncomplaining endurance. It had baffled me. I had felt their suffering a little, had seen it, but through a glass darkly. They were too close to me, too much a part of my own suffering for me to focus it like this thing tonight.

Tonight. Had it really been such a short time ago, had it been today that I had talked to David Rutter?

Again memory dragged me back. It had been I this very day who had sat back smoking cigarettes while David had poured out his heart, while his wife had watched me, taut, hoping. But I had failed. I had been disturbed a little, yes, but when he was finished I had said nothing, given no sign, offered no assurance that he was now right. I saw it so clearly. 'Do you think I should join up?' On my answer had depended many things, his self-respect, his confidence for the future, his final good-bye to the past. And I had said nothing, shying away from the question, even then not seeing. In the train I had crossed my legs and sat back, amused, God help me, by the irony of it all. They had given so much and were dead. I had given so little and was alive. Ah, well!

I was very grateful for the night and my solitude. I who had always repeated the maxim 'Know theyself' was seeing now what it meant to live by that maxim: '*Le sentiment d'être tout et l'évidence de n'être rien.*' That was me. The feeling that I was everything and the evidence that I was nothing.

So Peter had been right. It was impossible to look only to oneself, to take from life and not to give except by accident, deliberately to look at humanity and then pass by on the other side. No longer could one say 'The world's my oyster and the hell with the rest.' What was it Denise had said? 'Yes, you can realize yourself, but not by leading the egocentric life. By feeling deeply the deaths of the others you are conferring value on life.'

For a moment I had had it, had that feeling, but I had let it go, had encouraged it to go, distrusting it, and now, and now . . . was it, then, too late?

I stopped and looked up into the night. They were there somewhere, all of them around me; dead perhaps, but not gone. Through Peter they had spoken to me, not once, but often. I had heard and shrugged my shoulders; I had gone my way unheeding, not bitter, either on their account or mine, but in some curious way suspended, blind, lifeless, as they could never be.

Not so the others. Not so the Berrys, the Stapletons, the Carburys. Again instinct had served. They hadn't even the need of a Peter. They had felt their universe, not rationalized it. Each time they climbed into their machines and took off into combat, they were paying instinctive tribute to their comrades who were dead. Not so those men in hospital. They, too, knew, knew that no price was too dear to achieve this victory, knew that their discomforts, their suffering, were as nothing if they could but get back, and should they never get back they knew that silence was their rôle.

But I! What had I done? What could I do now?

I wanted to seize a gun and fire it, hit somebody, break a window, anything. I saw the months ahead of me, hospital, hospital, hospital, operation after operation, and I was in despair. Somehow I got myself home, undressed, and into bed and fell into a troubled sleep. But I did not rest; when I awoke the problem was still within me. Surely there must be something.

Then after a while it came to me.

I could write. Later there would be other things, but now I could write. I had talked about it long enough, I was to be a writer, just like that. I was to be a writer, but in a vacuum. Well, here was my chance. To write I needed two things, a subject and a public. Now I knew well enough my subject. I would write of these men, of Peter and of the others. I would write for them and would write with them. They would be at my side. And to whom would I address this book, to whom would I be speaking when I spoke of these men? And that, too, I knew. To Humanity, for Humanity must be the public of any book. Yes, that despised Humanity which I had so scorned and ridiculed to Peter.

If I could do this thing, could tell a little of the lives of these men, I would have justified, at least in some measure, my right to fellowship with my dead, and to the friendship of those with courage and steadfastness who were still living and who would go on fighting until the ideals for which their comrades had died were stamped for ever on the future of civilization.

Reach
for the Sky
The Story of Douglas Bader
CBE DSO DFC

Paul
Brickhill

TO
THELMA

CHAPTER ONE

In 1909 the doctor warned Jessie Bader during her second pregnancy that the baby might not be born alive and that it would be risky for her to go ahead with it, but, rather imperiously, she resisted any interference. A tall and strikingly attractive girl of twenty with a cloud of black hair piled in thick Edwardian waves, Mrs Bader was sometimes emotional and generally wilful.

Frederick Bader[1] brought his young wife and the other baby, Frederick, or 'Derick, home to England from India on furlough for the birth and they took a house at St John's Wood. The doctor and midwife arrived on 21 February, 1910, and Frederick Bader walked restlessly round the house. Jessie's sister, Hazel, and the German nursemaid waited hours outside the bedroom door until a thin but persistent cry broke the quiet; a little later the door opened and the doctor came out with the pleased look of a family GP who has seen his friends through a crisis.

'The little trouble-maker has arrived,' he said benignly. 'It's a boy.' The squalling kept sounding through the door and the doctor observed that the 'little trouble-maker' seemed to have a talent for expressing himself forcibly. (The doctor is not alive now to marvel at the unwitting accuracy of his foresight.)

They christened the baby Douglas Robert Steuart; and the 'Steuart,' from his maternal great-grandfather, was not all that the baby inherited from the intractable John Steuart Amos, who drove to the Liverpool docks in the family carriage one day in the 1840s, got out pulling a kitbag after him, and told the coachman, 'You may tell the family I will not be returning.' He walked on board a windjammer, talked himself into a job as ship's carpenter (though he knew nothing about either ships or carpentry) and worked his passage to India.

Ambition fortified his unruly spirit and in a few years John Amos was an officer in the Indian Naval Service. A photograph shows his character: within a fringe of crisp, black beard, large eyes with a bold dominating stare, and thin, straight lips clamped together. Not the face of a compromiser. He married, and later appalled his family of daughters by telling them how he watched the ringleaders of the Mutiny lashed across the cannon's mouth and blown out of this world. A detached hand flying

---

[1] Pronounced Bahder.

through the air slapped him across the face and (he told the shuddering girls) dropped into his pocket.

His eldest daughter, Jessie, was least appalled by the story. She had her father's bold eyes and tight mouth and was impervious to fear. In the eighties she married a gentle engineer in India called McKenzie, and they had two daughters, Jessie and Hazel. Mr McKenzie died then, and his wife brought up the two girls with a resourceful hand. They lived in Kotri, in the troublesome north-west (now Pakistan), but having no man in the house did not daunt the formidable Mrs McKenzie. One night she and the two little girls were woken by a sound downstairs. She handed each terrified child a golf club, shepherded each into a strategic point behind a door and said, 'Stand there and if anyone comes past . . . hit him.' Then she strode through the house brandishing a niblick and shouting in a menacing voice, 'Where are you? Come out at once.'

No one came out. The thief, if it was a thief, vanished into the night.

Another time a face appeared at a window in the middle of the night. Mrs McKenzie swung out of bed and ran, not away, but at the window. The owner of the face ran the other way.

Hazel was not fond of the dark but her mother brushed such fears aside, saying boldly, 'I'd walk through a grave-yard at midnight.' Hazel shuddered. 'Have no fear, God is near,' said her mother. Hazel wanted to say that that would be all very well if she could see God, but prudently left it unsaid. She was a pretty girl who had inherited her father's gentleness, but it was becoming clear that her sister, Jessie, had inherited the mettle of John Steuart Amos and her mother. She had the large bold eyes, but this time long-lashed, darker and wide-set under arching brows. Her lips were full but had the same compressed look, and the jaw was substantial.

She was seventeen when she met Frederick Roberts Bader at the club which was the usual social centre for the district, and she was eighteen when she married him. He was twenty years older, a gruff, heavily moustached, almost confirmed bachelor captivated by the vital girl. Where Jessie was tall and slim, Frederick Bader was heavy-set, a civil engineer of note with thinning hair and a capacity for expressing himself forcefully (he and his temperamental bride had that in common). They lived comfortably in the hot, dry plains around Sukkur and Kotri, and a year later the first baby was born. They christened him Frederick and called him 'Derick to distinguish him from his father. Both of them doted on 'Derick and within a year all three were on their way back to England for Jessie to have the second baby.

Three days after Douglas was born in St John's Wood, both mother and baby caught measles, and as soon as both were better Jessie had to have a major operation. From the start baby and mother were virtually separated. Jessie recovered, though she had no more children, and then the family was due back in India. Douglas was only a few months old; a little young, they thought, for India's climate, so they left him with relatives on the Isle of Man.

He was almost two by the time he was taken out to join the family in Sukkur and that may have been the beginning of the loneliness that has been deep within him ever since. He was a stranger in India, like an affectionate puppy before he has been smacked for wetting the floor. 'Derick had been receiving the attention lavished on an only child and the new boy did not fit in. Their Aunt Hazel, visiting the Sukkur bungalow from Kotri one day, saw Douglas's face covered in little sores. Jessie said 'Derick had been pinching bits of skin off his face. 'Derick at four had vitality from both parents. Douglas, two and a half, was sweet-tempered but subdued.

Six months later, servants were constantly on duty to keep them apart — Douglas had begun fighting back like a tiger. It seemed that he, too, had inherited a bold vigour. From then on he always fought his own battles and never cried if he lost. The only times he cried were when his father and mother and 'Derick went visiting in the car and left him behind, which they often did.

In 1913 his father resigned his job in India to study law, and the family left for England and took a house in Kew, breaking three generations of residence in India. In that twilight year before war came to write an ending and a new beginning to England's ways, the Bader household was adjusting to a life where servants were not so plentiful. Jessie and Frederick still had their matrimonial differences which they aired with vigour, and the two boys, together in the care of one nanny instead of separated by servants, were a handful. Douglas could usually hold his own in scuffles, but when crises had to be resolved by parental judgment, 'Derick had an advantage: in Jessie's indulgent eyes he could do little wrong.

Then the war came and Frederick Bader was commissioned in the Royal Engineers and went to France. Douglas, now a spirited five-year-old, was ever ready to show his mother and 'Derick that he was no minor underling, and 'Derick, finding he would leap at any challenge, used to dare him to carry out hazardous or punishable exploits. Never refusing a dare, Douglas came to be considered as much the naughtier of the two. Soon he regarded punishment as an inevitable part of life and so was able to endure it stoically.

One hurtful incident was when a ball bounced over tall, spiked railings into a locked churchyard near Kew Bridge. Dared by 'Derick to climb over the railings, Douglas ran at them and pulled himself to the top, where his foot slipped and his behind was impaled on one of the sharp spikes. White-faced, he hung on with his hands, unable to move. At last the nanny arrived and prised him clear and he walked silently half a mile to the house, gripping her hand with pain. The doctor put eight stitches in his rump without the patient letting out a murmur.

Soon Douglas joined 'Derick at Colet Court, a nearby prep. school. Their Aunt Hazel was back from India and usually escorted them to and from school in the bus, a series of nightmare journeys which she still remembers vividly as they seldom stopped fighting in their struggle for supremacy. Though 'Derick was spirited, Douglas was even more so, and as he had never enjoyed the same attention, felt he had to assert himself. Yet he only became combative when affairs threatened his *amour propre*. Otherwise he bubbled with life, warm-hearted, impulsive, and insulated against rebuffs.

At Colet Court he had his first fights and they were always with bigger boys. Always the same story: bigger boys expect smaller boys to know their place and Douglas would not be forcibly put there. After a while there were not so many fights because he never lost one, though he fought several bloodstained draws: then the generosity showed because he had a tendency to stop fighting when he had hurt someone.

'Derick went on to prep. school at Temple Grove, near Eastbourne, and there was a little more peace in the house, except during the holidays when 'Derick was home and Douglas was relegated again to second place.

The boys seldom saw their father, who was in the thick of it in France. In 1917 shrapnel wounded Major Bader badly in the head. They could not get all the shrapnel out, but he recovered without home leave and went back into the fighting.

Douglas followed 'Derick to Temple Grove and fairly soon scored his first knock-out. A bigger boy twisted his arm and Douglas clouted him across the face with his free hand. Honour demanded a proper fight, in which the bigger boy rushed at him. Douglas stood his ground, ducked his head, thrust both fists out together, and the boy rammed his chin against them and went down, out cold for several seconds. Thinking he had killed him, Douglas knelt contritely by the body and was most relieved to see the eyelids flicker and open.

Temple Grove was a pleasant old school with plenty of playing fields. The regime quickly drew the new boy into organised games and overnight he seemed to flare up like a Roman candle with eagerness. It was the perfect outlet for his mercurial nature and he literally threw himself into rugger, a gritty and indestructible small boy bouncing up as fast as he was knocked down, which was often. Fast on his feet and fast-thinking, he shone as fly-half, and after the first few games was promoted to more senior teams, finding himself now, as in all fights, matched against bigger boys. It only made him more determined to hold his own.

In the gym he limbered up on the parallel bars or the horizontal bar, the vaulting horse or in the boxing ring; he would try anything, not just once but till he had mastered it, hating to let anything beat him. Or anyone. People lost count of the times he fell off the parallel bars, but he learned to fall without hurting himself; in fact he lost all fear of falling, and that, as he later discovered, was one of the most important things that ever happened to him.

At home in the holidays without the outlet of sport, the favoured 'Derick talked his mother into buying them bows and arrows. They started shooting at each other first, and then as they became too accurate for comfort took to ambushing passers-by. A hedge ran along one side of the house just high enough for hats to bob invitingly over the top as men passed, and irate men with arrow-dented bowlets kept banging on the door-knocker.

Now the war was over but still they rarely saw their father, who was still in the Army, still on the Continent and busy helping repair war damage. Even after that he was retained in France on the War Graves Commission.

Meanwhile Hazel had married an RAF flight lieutenant, Cyril Burge, who had flown most of the war in the Royal Flying Corps. He fascinated Douglas by the wings and ribbons on his tunic and his stories of the war. Burge was likewise attracted by the boy who seemed at times so vital as to be 'almost on fire,' a good-looking youngster with large clear blue eyes and frank gaze, a mouth that grinned easily, crisp curly hair and a square jaw, an oddly commanding face for a small boy. 'Derick looked very like him, but without quite the same intensity in the face.

Back at school, Douglas shone at cricket too, being a reasonable bowler, miraculously quick as a fieldsman and a batsman who believed that the ball was there to be hit, not blocked.

By tradition at Temple Grove all boys carved their names on desks. Douglas tried but made a botch of it, and 'Derick was a shade scornful. They were walking near the garden where the headmaster grew huge vegetable marrows. 'I bet I could do a corker carving on that,' Douglas said, not very seriously, eyeing the largest marrow.

'Bet you're not game,' said 'Derick provocatively. 'I dare you.' Douglas carved 'D. Bader' in large and immature print on the headmaster's prize marrow. He deserved no sympathy. Nor did he get any.

Though he always tried to the limit at games he never tried hard in the classroom. He did not really have to because his mind was quick and receptive; he picked up Latin and Greek with ease and was often top of his form, but never worked harder than just enough. Academically, he was lazy because he was not interested. Maths and other modern subjects he detested and did the barest minimum of work on them so that his reports usually said, 'Very good, but could do better if he tried.' He was turning out to be impregnably obstinate about things he did not want to do, having, like his mother, a will of his own.

The PT instructor, Crease, a retired chief petty officer with a beard, who looked like the man on a Player's cigarette packet, taught him to shoot. Crease drilled it into him to get his bead and shoot quickly before the sight became blurred with concentration, and he became accurate and fast in shooting (which years later cost men their lives).

Once they put him in a hockey team against some girls from a neighbouring school, and he played robustly, scorning chivalry. One of his shots missed either the goal or girl at which it was aimed and bounced off a slow-moving master's skull with a satisfying thud which brought Bader Minor some hero-worship. He was barred from playing against girls any more and that delighted him.

In 1922 a War Office telegram came to the house in Kew regretting that Major Bader had died of his wounds in St Omer—the shrapnel which had wounded him in the head in 1917. Though the boys had seen little of their father, it did not make Douglas feel any more secure. Later, a more practical effect had to be faced. 'Derick had already gone on to King's School at Canterbury. Now there was doubt whether funds were enough to send Douglas to public school too. The one solution was a scholarship, and a very loath boy began studying, in the galling position of having to prove his reports: 'could do better if he tried.'

Not for a moment did he slacken his sporting activity. Not Bader Minor. In that last year he was captain of cricket, captain of rugger, captain of soccer, and in the school sports in the final term won every senior race he could enter for, the 100 yards, 220, quarter mile, half mile and hurdles, then set a new school record for throwing the cricket ball. At term's end the headmaster, with real pleasure, told him he had also won a scholarship to St Edward's School, Oxford.

About this time Jessie Bader, dark and vividly good-looking at thirty-two, remarried. The boys' step-father was the vicar of Sprotborough (Yorkshire), the Reverend Ernest William Hobbs, who had been a gentle bachelor of thirty-seven before his life was so radically stirred up. Jessie was devoted to him but still had her outspoken wilfulness, while the two boys resented going up to Yorkshire to live in the rambling rectory with its eight bedrooms, two kitchens, servants' quarters (mostly empty), pump (no running water), lamps (no electricity) and all-pervading cold in winter. Acres of garden and elm-studded grass spread between the house and the handsome church that dated back to the eleventh century and, like the rectory, was too big for the small village of scattered cottages near Doncaster.

The vicar was too mild for his intransigent new family. He suggested that 'Derick and Douglas might like to mow some of the grass but they flatly refused, and that was that. Jessie was firmer, insisting that the two boys take it in turns to pump the water in the kitchen, and they did so. The vicar tried to institute family prayers after breakfast, but Douglas and 'Derick scuffled and fidgeted and giggled so much that he gave it up. Jessie was inclined to blame Douglas, and he began to feel more at home out of doors.

That summer he was packed off for a week with Cyril and Hazel Burge at Cranwell, where Cyril was adjutant of the Royal Air Force College (in fact, he was Cranwell's first adjutant, having helped open the RAF's equivalent of Sandhurst in 1919). It was not then the grand place it is now: no fine white façades planted four-square in tailored acres but a few weedy buildings and barrack huts straggling along the side of a large field which was the aerodrome.

From Hazel and Cyril the welcome was warm. Only just thirteen, Douglas had never been near aeroplanes before, and when the quiet, good-humoured Cyril sat him in the cockpit of an Avro 504 trainer the thick hair almost vanished as the boy bent over the controls and dials like a terrier. Later he stood for hours in Cyril's garden watching the bellowing Avros taking off over his head as the cadets practised 'circuits and bumps.' Every morning at 6.30 he joined the cadets in training runs, doggedly trying to keep up. He admired them enormously; they seemed so fit, and after a couple of days, he spent less time watching the flying and more time with the cadets at cricket and athletics.

When Hazel and Cyril were putting him in the train for Sprotborough he said with what sounded like a catch in his voice (though it was probably only the voice breaking), 'Crumbs I want to come back to Cranwell as a cadet.' Cyril thought he had a convert then but he was a little premature. The flying bug was not in Douglas as yet. Interest—yes, as a boy likes dogs and catapults: but it was the games that drew him. Soon he forgot even that because he went to St Edward's, and there was all the sport he wanted.

CHAPTER TWO

A mile or two along the Woodstock Road outside Oxford, St Edward's School lay behind a high stone wall, a little world of its own. They boys seldom saw much of Oxford. If they went outside the gates in the stone wall it was usually to cross the road to the playing fields, acres and acres of rugger fields and cricket pitches, five courts and a swimming pool. Behind the wall the school buildings stood around the quad with its clipped lawns and gravel paths, the Warden's house, School House, Big Hall, Big School, and the other houses. And a little apart, away from the road, Cowell's House, into which the new boy, Bader, in new blue suit and new bowler hat, walked on a late summer morning in 1923. The new boys always arrived a day before the school reassembled. A dozen or so were allotted to Cowell's and for a while they and Douglas stood meekly in the lower hall, lonely and strange, waiting for their next directions. Upstairs, the housemaster had some guests for sherry before lunch. The matron was bustling around, too busy to be motherly. Douglas dropped his new bowler hat, which was part of the school uniform. He did not like it very much. He gave it a kick to express what he felt. Very satisfying. He kicked it again. And again. That was better. He kicked it round the hall, his shoes scraping and clumping on the stone.

A voice above said crisply: 'Boy!'

He looked up. A lean face peered over the landing balustrade, cold eyes behind spectacles.

'Stop kicking your hat about. Pick it up and be quiet.'

'Yes, sir,' said the boy, abashed.

The face vanished. For seconds the hall was quiet. Then Douglas dropped his hat and kicked it once more to establish independent self-respect.

Above, the voice rasped louder: 'Boy!'

In the hall the new boys froze. The face of the housemaster, wise in the ways of boys, peered again over the balustrade where he had lingered a few seconds with unerring suspicion. 'Come here, boy!' he said.

The sherry guests were impressed to see the housemaster return, excuse himself briefly, draw a cane from behind the grandfather clock and make his resolute exit. They did not witness the six strokes on the tightened trousers seat. Nor for that matter did they hear anything. Douglas never yelped. It was not in his character, though his first day at public scool certainly was.

He lost any shyness at school within a couple of days. People liked his zest and transparent honesty, and he, feeling he was liked, responded warmly as always. With a willingness that might have surprised his mother he submitted to the rules, even to that mark of inferior status inflicted on all new boys of always having the three jacket buttons done up for the first team.

Games instantly claimed his interest and absorbed excess energy. He played house cricket down on the canal fields, clouted a punching ball in the gym and swam in the pool, screened by shrubs and hedges, where everyone splashed about naked. School became his real life, not only the playing fields but the little things in the background — the red blankets on the iron beds in the dormitories, the overgrown patch in the middle of the quad known as 'The Jungle,' the 'San,' the 'Crystal Palace' (main lavatories), 'Hell' (the mysterious basement room where the text-books were stored), and Hall, where they clattered in to the long refectory tables and ate and chattered like sparrows till the gavel rapped on the wooden block, and everyone stood while the Warden intoned a Latin prayer.

He had to 'fag' for a prefect, which was a bore, but there was not much more to it than running messages or polishing a pair of shoes occasionally, and that left plenty of times for games. Or even for study? As a winner of a scholarship he was expected to shine in the classroom but, as at Temple Grove, he did no more work than the minimum required to avoid trouble. His darting mind picked up lessons easily, and at prep., half-hidden from prefectorial eyes in the battered 'horse-boxes' of the day-room, his mind wandered to more sporting matters.

In his second term things were better in two ways — he could leave one button of his jacket undone and the rugger season was in. As fly-half in the House second team, he showed such dash that they promoted him to the House first team, though it meant playing against boys much bigger and older.

Back home for the holidays, 'Derick and Douglas bought air-guns, and a reign of terror began in Sprotborough until the day Douglas saw through a bathroom window the pale form of a noted local lady about to step into the bath. Someone dared him, and a moment later the pellet smashed through the splintering glass, followed by a squeal. The sharp-shooter vanished and later had a heated argument with 'Derick about the suffering inflicted by an air-gun pellet. 'Derick demonstrated by shooting Douglas in the shoulder at point-blank range, and that started a scuffle which ended with Jessie confiscating the guns.

Douglas simply could not resist a challenge, even daring himself to do anything that seemed to daunt him. With the air-guns locked away, poaching attracted him, but night in the woods was alarming for a small boy, so he dared himself to enter them at night and forced himself to walk slowly through without turning or jumping at noises or shadows.

The year 1924 was trouble-free at St. Edward's because he was busy on the playing fields. At Christmas time the boys put on a Shakespearian play in Big School and a youngster called Lawrence Olivier outshone the others so much that he came in for a little deprecating comment for ostentatious acting.

In 1925 Douglas was more games-mad than ever, and, as a corollary, more fidgety in class. It was not easy to pin charges on him because with no effort he still shone at Latin and Greek, showed interest in history and absorbed pages of poetry with obvious pleasure. (Shakespeare, however, he was inclined to resist because he felt it was forced down his throat; he preferred the astringent Swinburne.) Maths was his weakness; he still hated them and refused to bother, so that several times he was 'carpeted' by his new housemaster, A. F. Yorke.

'Bader, you aren't doing any work in class.'

'I'm awfully sorry, sir. I'll try and do better next week.'

'That's exactly what you told me last week.'

The boy used to become disarming then, confessing his sins with engaging simplicity and suggesting that Mr. Yorke cane him to teach him a lesson. Yorke could rarely beat him after that. ('I hardly ever caned him. It wouldn't have had any effect if I had. He had a *very* thick hide.') Yorke finally accepted that Bader had an incisive and sensitive brain and would never bother to exercise it hard academically.

Simple misdemeanours such as indoor rugger and debagging, combined with his academic reluctance, brought him occasionally to the attention of the Warden (headmaster), the Rev. H. E. Kendall, a ruddy-faced, brisk and cheerful cleric who tolerantly believed that boys have a right to be reasonably naughty. Punishments were minor matters of a hundred lines here and there because Kendall considered that Douglas, whatever his peccadilloes, was generally 'on the side of the angels,' an increasingly strong-willed boy who could only be reasoned into the mould, never pressed into it.

In the summer holidays 'Derick persuaded Jessie to let them have the air-guns again, and the boys used them for poaching, keeping a sharp eye open for Scott, the gamekeeper. An accurate snapshooter, Douglas once got a partridge on the wing, a rare feat with an air-gun. They were never actually caught red-handed, though Franklin, the village constable, and Scott were often on the rectory doorstep with suspicion. Jessie confiscated the guns again and scolded bitterly that their behaviour was undermining her authority as vicar's wife. That amused Douglas, which infuriated his mother all the more. The two boys were good friends now, making common cause against authority, though they were beginning to have affection for 'Bill' Hobbs, the gentle vicar, who tolerated their peccadilloes with resignation and was not above taking off his clerical collar and going off to the races for the day.

Back at school, Douglas was 'capped' for cricket, aged only fifteen and the youngest boy in the team. He finished the season top of both batting and bowling averages for the First Eleven (batting 34, bowling 41 wickets for 8.63 runs) and set up a new school record for throwing the cricket ball. For the first time he really had status in the hierarchy of his world behind the stone wall on the Woodstock Road.

But it was winter he was waiting for. He like the aggressive rough and tumble of rugger above everything. On the Thursday before the first game the captain pinned the names of the First Fifteen on the board under the cloisters of Big School, and Douglas, looking over the heads of the huddle round it, saw his own name scrawled there as fly-half. He did not shout or make any outward show, but a glow flushed right through him and he walked away soaked with quiet, fulfilled happiness.

It was the warmest moment of life. Now there was no mad hurry for the game. The list was up and he was on it. Barring some appalling accident he was going to play on Saturday, and for the next couple of days he kept passing by the board, taking a little peek at his name. On the Saturday he played, almost broke his nose in a tackle, had blood drawn from a gashed lip, scored a try and thoroughly distinguished himself by his fiery vigour. He was still only fifteen, again the youngest in the school team, and thereafter was never dropped except through illness.

A report in the *School Chronicle* of a match not long after said, 'Bader did as he chose and scored seven tries.' (No question now of him being second to 'Derick, or second to anyone else.) The Warden clearly remembers his jaunty figure striding around the quad, hands in pockets, 'absolutely full of beans.'

Pride cometh before a fall. In the charabanc returning from an away match he fell and hit his head on the edge of a seat. It was rumoured he gave cheek to an older boy, who then pushed him, but Bader insisted that it was his own fault; that he had merely tripped. He was six weeks in the San recovering from concussion before he took the field again. The boys he played against, the seniors of other schools, were older and invariably bigger so that he took more hard bumps, but that only seemed to increase his ardour.

At Easter his mother told him she did not think they would be able to keep him on at St Edward's after the next term. On a parson's stipend they could not afford the fees. 'Derick was leaving King's School and though Douglas's scholarship had helped so much, it still cost an extra £100 a year to keep him at St Edward's. Though school was the only thing he cared about, Bader was not greatly upset. He was showing a peculiar capacity for shutting his mind to disagreeable things until he had to face them (maths was another example). He was clearly too fond of enjoying the present and ignoring the future.

Half-way through the next term, Walter Dingwall, a reserved young history master who also acted as bursar for the school, sent for him and said, 'I'm very sorry, Bader, but we've just had a letter from your mother to say that she does not think you will be able to return here next term.'

For a few minutes the words brought the reality unpleasantly close.

'Don't worry,' Dingwall said. 'I feel it would be a pity if you had to leave. We'll see what we can do about it.'

A week later Bader had put it right out of his mind. He was playing for the First Eleven again, boxing and running for his House, and Yorke had just made him a House prefect. At the end of term he went home for the holidays, but no one said anything about leaving school and after the holidays he went back to St Edward's again. By this time he had filled out and was giving as many bumps at rugger as he received.

The Warden made him a school prefect with the privilege of wielding a cane and of possessing a study in the 'Beehive,' a quaint little octagonal building where the rooms were tiny triangles just big enough for a boy, a desk and chair and trunk covered with cushions. One or two thought Bader was getting bumptious, but the Warden felt it was mostly that he was too full of vitality to sit in the background. Underneath Kendall detected a sense of responsibility that should be fostered. Other boys all respected him greatly, an acid test, and Kendall liked his spontaneous friendliness and the way he could talk to a master without being 'on guard.'

The authority in Bader's character developed fast. He seldom had to use his cane as a prefect; his mere presence in a day-room doorway compelled instant quiet in a scuffling crowd of boys. Sometimes his eagerness at rugger led him into individualism that amounted to selfishness: he would try to run through the whole of the opposition. Arthur Tilley, the sportsmaster, partly cured him of that by saying tartly, 'You might get through five people, Bader, but the sixth will usually get you if you don't pass the ball out.' Now he was also playing fives for the school. Without a glove, of course. That would not have been in character.

Early in summer he went to the San one day and said he thought he was getting 'flu. They found he had a temperature and put him to bed, and as he lay there be began to feel light-headed and then his heart began to pound. It got worse, every beat seemed to hammer through him, the blows coming faster and faster, vibrating in his ears till his body seemed to be thumping like a compression engine. He was drifting away from the room and reality, withdrawing into himself; vague illusions chased nightmarishly through his mind. The nurse found him delirious with rheumatic fever.

For several days he wandered in delirium, close to death. They sent for his mother and she came down from Sprotborough and stayed nearby. In the chapel the whole school prayed for him. Then the fever broke one night and the crisis passed. His memory of new consciousness starts when the Warden stood by his bed and told him that the school had prayed for him. A glow spread through him; there was something deeply warming in knowing that so many people had cared enough about him to do that. He had never had that before, unless one counted the occasional resented voice asking (as though it were hopeless) that God forgive him for his many sins.

The doctor told him as gently as he could that rheumatic fever affected the heart and that he must lie quietly for a long time and try to repair some of the damage, but the boy declined to accept that, insisting that he was perfectly well already and was going to play rugger in the coming season. It was a trying time in the San; Bader, feeling fit and confined to bed, was not tractable. The crisis came one hot night when the nurse found his bed empty. People rushed everywhere looking for him and finally saw him sleeping peacefully on the lawn, where he had dragged his mattress. It was cooler there, he said.

Out of the San he quietly began training again, swimming at first, then gym and running. Soon after the rugger season started the doctor examined him and, a little surprised, found he was fit enough to play. So fit, as it happened, that Arthur Tilley made him captain of the First Fifteen.

This was Bader's first real taste of leadership, and he seemed to blossom instantly. He lived for the team, full of a breezy, non-stop enthusiasm both on the field and off that infected everyone else. Some captains had been known to hold themselves a little aloof, especially from the lesser members of the team. Not Bader. Every player was a brother (slightly junior) to be exhorted and coached and fired with enthusiasm from dawn till lights out. Douglas lived for them — with one proviso: they must also live for the team, dedicated, tireless and fearless. If a boy did not, he was no longer on the team. It was as simple as that. Tilley noticed that Bader's paternal concern for his team was overshadowing his own ego; he was not so selfish with the ball now—only rarely when his exuberance carried him away. Being captain obviously nourished his sense of responsibility.

He sat near the Warden at lunch in Hall, and Kendall watched with interest how his will and generosity combined with his vigour to make a commanding personality. Here was no doubting Hamlet, but a young chieftain who evoked co-operation as well as obedience. At lunch one day the Warden asked him what he was going to do when he left school, and Bader said simply that he did not know. Lately he had begun asking himself the same question. Go on to Oxford? He could probably win a scholarship, but that would mean hard study, which was repulsive. Besides, what would he read at Oxford? Classics? History? Neither appealed. Certainly not maths. Anyway, too many undergraduates had long hair. 'Derick was talking of going out to South Africa in engineering but that did not appeal either. As he did so often with tedious things like text-books, he put the problem out of his mind and lived on in the agreeable present.

Shortly before Christmas an old boy, Roy Bartlett, now at Cranwell, visisted the school, and Bader remembered his own visit there five years earlier, especially the games. Flying might be fun. That night he wrote to Uncle Cyril asking what his chances were of getting into Cranwell as a cadet.

Cyril Burge had left Cranwell and was now personal assistant to Air Chief Marshal Sir Hugh Trenchard, Chief of the Air Staff. With the satisfaction of a match-maker, Cyril wrote back saying that Douglas was just the type they wanted and he would do everything he could to help (which, from the p.a. to the CAS, sounded considerable). There was one catch — Cyril pointed out that it would cost Jessie and the vicar about £150 a year[1] to send him to Cranwell, and the course lasted two years. Could they afford it?

Douglas took the question home and Jessie quickly settled it. (a) She did not like flying, (b) she did not think Douglas should go into the Air Force, and (c) they could not possibly afford £150 a year.

She added, 'You wouldn't even be at St Edward's now but for the kindness of Mr Dingwall.'

'What d'you mean?' He was puzzled.

'I didn't want you to know yet,' his mother said, 'but Mr Dingwall has been paying the rest of your fees since 1926.'

The news staggered him, more so as he knew his mother had never met Dingwall, who was such a reserved person that he himself hardly knew Dingwall. He had never been in one of Dingwall's classes and had seldom encountered him.

Back at school he went to thank Dingwall, and the master, looking very embarrassed, shrugged it off with a deprecating laugh and got off the subject by asking him what he was going to do when he left. Embarrassed himself, Bader mentioned that he had hoped to get into the RAF.

'Something might be arranged,' Dingwall said thoughtfully.

Shortly another letter came from Burge saying that six prize cadetships were given every year to Cranwell, which meant virtual free entry. Several hundred boys fancied them, there was a stiff eliminating examination and the academic standard was high. Did Douglas really think it worth trying? (It was tantamount to a dare — as Burge knew.)

Bader tapped on the housemaster's door. Did Mr Yorke think he was good enough to win a prize cadetship?

'I think you *could* get one, Bader,' Yorke said, a little meaningly.

'But I'm no good at maths, sir.'

'You're darned lazy at maths, I know that.'

'If I worked hard, sir, and you coached, d'you think I could catch up?'

'If you worked hard,' said Yorke, 'I *know* you could do it. But I'm not going to waste time coaching you unless you *will* work. Are you prepared to?'

Bader took a breath and said, 'Yes, sir, I'll have a shot.'

He joined the small circle of boys, sometimes known as 'the Army Sixth,' whom Yorke coached in maths. They were all trying for the Services. After his day's work, duties and games, Bader spent a couple of hours every night 'cramming' maths, hating it but sticking to it. By day he still exhorted and captained the rugger team, dispensed prefectorial

---

[1] In those days Cranwell was like a public school in that it charged fees. Now the system is different and no fees are charged; in fact, modern cadets are even paid properly.

justice, boxed, exercised as an under-officer with the OTC, shot with the school rifle team, played fives and even found time to be a leading member of the school debating society. He did not regard debating as a mental fag; it stimulated him because the element of contest was in it. In debate his mind had a habit of cutting through irrelevancies to the heart of the matter, sometimes imperiously, sometimes with a sudden charm that glowed out of him with compelling vitality, and always plausibly. In his face one could see signs of evolving character, a hint of pleased yet defiant pride, and in the bearing an amiable swagger. If beneath there was insecurity, it was well hidden, or well compensated; only if he were challenged did it flash out and make him combative. Whether, after schooldays, the mould would sufficiently curb the sparkling nature no one knew, though it was felt that the mould would have to stretch a little now and then.

That spring (1928) he became captain of cricket, then early in June a letter called him to London for RAF examination, interview and medical. Another letter came from Cyril telling him what sort of answers the selection board usually liked to hear.

He sat for the exam in a comfortless room in Burlington Place, glad to find the papers were not difficult but knowing that scores of other boys were likewise rejoicing. The maths paper, happily, was almost a replica of those that Mr Yorke had been setting for him, and he finished on time, reasonably content. After lunch he stood to attention in front of a long table while five elderly men in civilian clothes gazed steadily at him. Some of the questions seemed foolishly irrelevant: 'How often do you brush your teeth?' — 'What is the capital of Sweden?' — but all the time the eyes were on him. Some questions he was ready for (thanks to Cyril):

'Why do you want to join the Air Force?'

'I think it would suit my temperament, sir ... and so does my housemaster.'

(Satisfied nods.)

'What do you do in your holidays?'

'Oh, games, sir. *Team* games usually. Cricket or rugger. I like rugger best.'

(True up to a point, but he had a sudden quaking fear that they might have inquired about him at Sprotborough and heard lurid tales about the poaching and the air-guns. Apparently they hadn't. They beamed.)

He came out knowing he had done well. (Out of a maximum of 250 points for the interview he had, in fact, scored 235, a figure which is seldom approached.)

Then to the doctors. They looked down his throat, into his eyes and ears, tapped his knees for reflexes, tapped him all over, made him blow a column of mercury up a fuse and hold it, holding his breath, listened to his heart and took his blood pressure. When it was over, the man in the white coat looked thoughtfully at the papers on his desk. 'I see you've had rheumatic fever,' he said. 'I'm afraid it's left your blood pressure a little high.'

Bader asked in dismay. 'Does that mean I'm turned down?'

The doctor said, 'Not necessarily, but high blood pressure is not very good for high flying. Come back in a few weeks and we'll see how it is then. I suggest you keep fairly quiet in the meantime.'

He went back to school and for a while was almost sedate. Then back to London, where the doctor wrapped the cloth round his arm and pumped it up three times. He felt his heart beating with anxiety. The doctor scratched his chin. The seconds dragged. 'I'm a bit keyed up,' Bader said. 'That might have affected it.'

'Yes.' The doctor closed the lid of his blood pressure gadget with a detached professional air. 'It's still up a bit, you know, but we'll pass you.'

It was a good moment, till he remembered he still had to win selection.

About a week later another letter came from Air Ministry and he made himself open it slowly. The unemotional, numbered paragraphs told him he had come fifth in the examinations, had won a prize cadetship and would be required to present himself at Cranwell in September with a change of underclothes, bowler hat and toilet articles. Stilted prose has seldom had such an electrifying effect. Mr Yorke, very pleased, said:

'I'm delighted for you, Bader, but remember you have another two years of academic work to do now.'

He was proud when he told Dingwall.

'From what I know of Cranwell, all the chaps there have motor-bikes,' Dingwall observed. 'I think you'd better have one, too, as a reward for your work.'

He pressed the point over the boy's reluctance with discreet insistence, and soon Bader had a second-hand, flat-twin Douglas motor-cycle for which Dingwall had paid £30 and fended off any thanks with his usual deprecating laugh.

A day or two later the school broke up for the summer holidays and Bader said good-bye to St Edward's. The Warden had him to tea before he left and observed: 'Don't become over-confident. Keep a hold on those high spirits of yours.'

At Sprotborough his mother, though proud of him, was still dubious about the Air Force as a career. As 'Derick had gone off to South Africa, Douglas got more attention than usual and responded warmly to it.

In the second week in September, Douglas, boisterously cheerful, strapped two small suitcases to the pillion of the motor-cycle, rammed a new bowler hat rakishly over the headlight, kissed his mother, shook the vicar's hand, and pelted with exhaust blaring down the highway towards Cranwell. Two hours later, roaring down the Ancaster straight four miles from Cranwell, he saw a cow wander across the road ahead and swerved; his front wheel hit the grass verge and the motor-cycle kicked over the steep bank and cartwheeled on the other side. Thrown clear on the grass, he got groggily to his feet, shaken and bruised but otherwise, surprisingly, unhurt. Watched vacantly by the idiot cow, he hauled the motor-cycle upright, wheeled it back to the road and kicked the self-starter. The engine blurted healthily and everything seemed all right till he noticed the headlamp sticking through the top of the bowler hat where the crown had burst and a flap at the top gaped open like a tin lid. Instead of dismay he felt a wicked satisfaction, flung a leg over the saddle and roared off again. Eight minutes later he rode through the gates of Cranwell and into the Royal Air Force.

A confused couple of hours then, waiting, coming to attention and saying 'Sir,' filling in forms, saying a few brief and guarded words to other new boys, trying to size them up, and then a corporal led four of them like sheep to a hut, into an end room where four iron cots covered with khaki blankets stood thin-legged against the wooden wall. Rough bedside tables, four lockers — an impression of bareness.

'Like school, isn't it,' said one.

They talked till well after Lights Out, and in the morning went on parade for the first time. Wearing bowler hats. Bader was not so happy about his hat now. He tried to tuck the loose flap inside the crown, but when they were snapped to attention on the gravelled square he had a feeling (later confirmed) that the torn flap was sticking up like a lid again. A warrant officer with a red and bony face walked down the line, inspecting each face. In front of Douglas he stopped and stared and the arid voice said, 'And what is *your* name, sir?'

'Bader, sir.'

The voice crunched again, 'And what do you think you are, Mr. Bader? ... A comedian?'

'I had an accident on the way yesterday,' he started. ... After five seconds or so the warrant officer cut him short. 'I don't think I wish to hear any more.' He gazed once more at the hat, once more into the young man's eyes, turned and walked frigidly down the ranks.

Bader stayed rigid and poker-faced, remembering his other bowler hat on his first day at St Edward's and the six weals that it produced. But now they were not boys. They were gentlemen on probation spending hours every day on parade having discipline drilled into them by straight-backed NCOs who called them 'Sir' and 'Gentleman' and blistered their ears with invective. Cranwell had grown a little but still looked much as he remembered it; still with the cavernous hangars squatting beside the two landing grounds that straddled the camp of long wooden huts.

On parade the NCOs took it in turn to comment raucously on Bader's bowler hat. He considered gumming the lid down with sticky paper and then stubbornly decided to leave it as it was, until, after a week when the joke had worn thin, they got their uniforms, rough serge tunics (as still worn), breeches worn with puttees and a cap with shiny peak and the white cadet band round it. They paraded again to draw flying kit and a new excitement stirred as he stood in the QM store and a sergeant slapped a Sidcot flying suit on the counter in front of him, stood a pair of flying boots beside them, added a scarf and gauntlets, slapped a pair of goggles on the pile and handed over a helmet to try on. It fitted snugly and suddenly he wanted urgently to try this flying which was to be his career. He had never been in the air yet.

A couple of days later — a sunny afternoon late in September with the trees still in summer leaf — he reported to the flight hangar with flying kit. A chunky little man came into the cadet pilots' room and introduced himself in a quiet voice as Flying Officer Pearson. Bader was to be his pupil. They went out on the tarmac and Pearson led him, self-conscious in his new flying kit, to a flimsy-looking biplane, fabric-covered wings harnessed together with struts and wires. It was an Avro 504, the same type he had sat in at Cranwell five years earlier.

'We're going up for half an hour,' Pearson said. 'You won't touch the controls this time. It's just to get you used to the idea of flying.' He explained briefly why and how the machine flew, pointed out the controls, strapped him in the rear cockpit (all open in those days) and slipped into the front cockpit himself. The propeller spun into noisy life, and in a little while they were bouncing across the field. Gently the grass sank below, wing-tips tilted, and Douglas, leaning over the leather-padded rim of the cockpit, wind whipping at his face, looked down on green country, exhilaration bubbling in him. Soon they dipped towards the landing ground, and the Avro, swaying a little in the afternoon thermals, slid down the glide-slope to check, check, touch the grass and rumble.

'How did you like it?' Pearson asked, and found his answer in gleaming eyes.

Next afternoon Flight Cadet D. R. S. Bader took the control column in the air for the first time, gingerly at first, then too tightly, till Pearson's voice nudged at him to relax. Stick gently forward and the nose dipped; gently back and it rose; stick to each side and it tilted. Then feet on the rudder bar and the first co-ordinated turns. Taut concentration for a few minutes: it was strange; one had to think before one could tentatively act. Then the athlete's eye, mind and muscle began to combine in harmony and he had the feel of it. Pearson himself was a classically smooth pilot who never showed off to his pupil like some other instructors. He kept quietly drilling into Bader: 'Never be brutal with your aeroplane. Guide it. Don't shove it.' And another time: 'I never want to hear you call it a plane or a kite. The word is aeroplane or aircraft.' (Never since that day has it ever been anything else from Bader's lips. Pearson taught him to look on an aeroplane as a man might regard his favourite horse.)

After a landing in October, when the pupil had had only six and a half hours' dual instruction, Pearson got out and said: 'D'you think you could take it around on your own?' Douglas grinned and nodded, and Pearson casually waved him off, saying: 'All right. Don't bend it.' It is always done like that, before a pupil has time to start worrying. Bader did not worry; he opened the throttle and eased the Avro into the air, revelling to be up alone and guiding the vibrating thing round the perimeter. Gently he turned upwind, slanted her down towards the field and now memory and tension faded from the rapt and lonely moments as he jockeyed her down, flattening, holding off, off, as the tail sank until the little aeroplane settled in a velvety and somewhat flukey three-pointer, giving him the same stab of joy a man has at the click of his first perfectly hit golf ball.

'Pretty smooth,' said Pearson tolerantly when he had taxied in. 'I bet you don't do another one as good for a couple of months.'

Pearson nearly took his words back because his pupil was consistently smooth in his flying, landings as well, and the instructor fairly soon realised that he had the eye and timing of a natural pilot. Perhaps too much exuberance? But under that lay a disciplined zeal to shine at the things that stirred him — in this case to fly with delicate accuracy. Some day rashness might for a few moments overrule the discipline. It happens among pilots trained for war who are not recruited for their caution; usually it happens only once to each — he lives and learns or, if they can reassemble enough of him, is buried.

Now he had gone solo, Flight Cadet Bader wanted to be a fighter pilot, and flying vied with rugger for his devotion. He liked Cranwell exceedingly. It was like school but even better because, in spite of the discipline, they were treated more as adults and did not have to behave responsibly like prefects. Sometimes they could stay out until midnight, they could ride motor-bikes (though cars were strongly forbidden), smoke and be men of the world. After a couple of puffs at a cigarette he had tossed it away with distaste. Besides, it was not good for one's fitness. He tried a pipe, liked it, decided it would not clog his lungs if he did not inhale, and soon was an addict, seldom seen (at permissible times) without a stub pipe between his teeth.

The only catch was the schoolroom part. Theory of flight, engines, signals, armaments and such things were reasonably interesting, but the maths! He ignored them. Besides, the rugger season had arrived. He was picked for the First Fifteen, and for the first time Cranwell beat both Sandhurst and the Woolwich Military Academy.

The flight cadets were paid £4 a month pocket money, but every twelve weeks the post brought Bader cheques for a further £12 from Walter Dingwall, with a brief note when the first cheque arrived saying that there was no reason why Bader should have less than the others. He wrote several letters of thanks, deeply touched and amazed at Dingwall's generosity, and got pleasant little notes back, but Dingwall always stayed remotely in the background. One never seemed to know what he was thinking, but he seemed to find pleasure in quiet altruism. Bader never saw him after leaving St Edward's, but he did discover that Dingwall had intended to pay his fees at Cranwell had he failed to win his prize cadetship.

He found a new pleasure in the schoolroom side of the course — reading the stories of the Great War 'aces' — McCudden, Bishop, Ball and others. Their accounts of air fighting fired him more than ever with the ambition to be a fighterpilot, and his spirit thoroughly approved of their tenets—get up close as you can and let him have the lot.

In the air Pearson was initiating him into aerobatics, teaching him not to throw the Avro about but to coax her immaculately through every antic in the book. As well as the thrill, Bader began to find the joy of an artist, in a slow roll, for instance, of revolving her evenly about her axis without losing height. Yet not all his flying was copybook. An enterprising fellow-cadet named Hank More (who later won a DFC and was killed in the Far East) evolved a hair-raising trick of climbing out of his rear cockpit in mid-air and crawling forward to tie a handkerchief about the joystick in the empty front cockpit, then getting back into the rear cockpit. One had to take one's parachute off to do it. A crony of Bader's, an old Etonian called John Chance, did it then. On his next solo flight, of course, Cadet Bader did it too, finding it diverting to be straddled across the fuselage like a bare-back rider, holding on with the heels while the hands were busy tying the handkerchief. Naturally then nearly every other cadet did it. One could not do it while an instructor was in the front cockpit because the instructor would (a) get in the way, and (b) have the cadet thrown out of the college. The riskiest part was considered to lie in the chances of being found out.

As well as flying and rugger, he was playing hockey now and also boxing. His first fight he won by a knock-out in the first round. A sergeant instructor had told him that if you hit a man on the chin very hard at the beginning of a fight, when he is cold, he would go 'out' far more easily than later when he had warmed up and was sweating, when his body could absorb a punch better. Next fight Bader lunged out of his corner at the gong, bashed through the other's man guard with a storm of punches and knocked him out within a minute. His fights were on the same pattern after that, and word of his toughness spread. He had just the body and temperament for a middleweight fighter. By his twentieth birthday he had filled out to a muscular 5 feet 10 inches, with strong-fingered, square hands, ruggedly handsome with an arresting vitality in the eyes that seemed to glow vividly blue in large clear whites under the dark brow. Some of the other cadets were beginning to look upon him as a super-youth and some of the Cranwell staff as an *enfant terrible*.

The fact is the discipline alone was never enough to curb him. He needed responsibility or some positive purpose to harness him, but he lacked both and enjoyed the sport of flouting minor regulations. They 'gated' him for roaring round the district at high speed on his motor-bike, and when he was freed from barracks he did it again, more culpably, by having John Chance or his particular friend, the dark, slight Geoffrey Stephenson, on the pillion (pillion riding was strictly forbidden). Chance bought an old Morris car for £50, and the three of them kept this banned luxury hidden in an old barn about a mile from the camp. Often they got back from Grantham after their midnight passes had expired, and climbed back to bed over the seven-foot spiked fence. More than once they were caught, but that only made the sport more attractive. It was all a game.

After a year they sat for exams. He struggled with his maths, hoped for the best, and afterwards, with Chance, Stephenson and Denys Field,[1] rattled off to a dance at Grantham in the old Morris. They arrived back at the barn with three minutes to sign in at the guardroom a mile away. Bader alone had his motor-cycle there, but that was a detail; all four festooned themselves on it, and two minutes later, after a crazy ride, he was pulling up a hundred yards from the guardhouse to let the others off to walk the rest when suddenly a torch shone on them, held by an advancing policeman. It was a fair cop. Service police came down from the guardhouse and there was a solemn period of name and note-taking.

In the morning the four of them had a menacing interview with the squadron commander. In the afternoon Bader was fined £2 for being in improper control of his motor-cycle, and next morning the four of them went out in the car again. As they returned to the barn a hawk-eyed instructor, coming in to land just overhead, spotted them. At this trying moment the results of the exams came out and Cadet Bader, scholarship winner, was nineteenth out of twenty-one.

This time he stood alone on the carpet in front of the desk, and after a crisp homily the squadron commander concluded by saying: 'I'm fed up with you. If you don't change considerably I shall take steps to have you and your friends removed from the college.'

There was no doubt he meant it. Bader emerged a disturbed young

---

[1] A big, excitable young man who could break evens for the 100 yards and became a scratch golfer before being killed over Hamburg in 1941.

man and received a message to report to the commandant immediately. Unhappily he went.

Air Vice Marshal Halahan was a square-faced, grey-haired former heavyweight boxing champion who spoke in a quiet voice. Bader, rigidly at attention, listened to a dispassionate review of his misdemeanours and winced at the end when Halahan said, almost laconically: 'You're young. I can understand your trouble, but the Air Force won't go on understanding. They don't want schoolboys here. They want men.'

He almost crept out feeling he had shrunk to about half size. To have his manhood challenged! And even worse, to know that Halahan was right! He was honest enough to face that. After a couple of days' heavy thinking Flight Cadet Bader was a different young man, with radically changed views of Cranwell and a potent desire to justify his place there. He even began studying maths.

Some of the staff regarded the transformation suspiciously at first, but eventually even they recognised that a permanent change had occurred. Like any convert, he steered a rigidly straight path, his maths kept improving and his flying, as always, was deft and accurate.

Now the course was flying single-seater Siskins, biplane fighters odd to modern eyes, but they made Bader keener than ever to be a fighter pilot. (Not much doubt that he would be. Fighter pilots are picked from individualists, and Cranwell knew an individualist when they saw one.)

He stuck to his studies, but without missing a moment from games, and in both his years at Cranwell got his 'blues' for cricket, rugger, hockey and boxing. (Rupert Leigh, a cadet on the junior course, gave this appraisal of him: 'To us he was a sort of god who played every conceivable game and was the best player on every team.')

Young tyros in the RAF have not always been noted for temperance, but Bader was. Once he tried beer, and once each sherry and whisky, but never finished any of them. He did not like them; therefore he ignored them. In any case, at a party he had his own spirits to exhilarate him, and any temptations liquor might have held were easily repelled by the thought that abstinence would keep him fitter.

Everyone knew how fit he was. When the Sandburst boxing team came to joust with them again the visiting middleweight climbed into the ring looking pale and ill-at-ease. Bader ducked through the ropes a few seconds later looking sure of himself and obviously relishing the coming fight. The gong sounded and in seven seconds the Sandhurst man was unconscious on the canvas. He spent the next two weeks in hospital with concussion. Rupert Leigh remembers Bader having about twenty fights at Cranwell, of which he won all on knock-outs but the last one. This last bout was against a man called Jock McLean, Inter-Services light-heavyweight champion and somewhat heavier than Bader. At the gong Bader rushed out in his usual way and within a minute McLean was down. But not out. He got up again and a fierce mutual slogging went on. At the gong for round two Bader tore out again, ran smack into a rigid fist on the chin and went down, out cold. When he came to he wanted to fight McLean again but it was too late. Playing rugger a few days later he tore a cartilage in his knee and that put a stop to more boxing. He has mourned ever since that he did not have a second try against the only man who ever beat him.

The damaged cartilage was a curb that helped him focus on less robust affairs, even maths, and early in 1930 his persistent new virtue was rewarded when he and another outstanding cadet, Paddy Coote, were appointed under-officers of 'A' and 'B' Training Squadrons. Once again he was a leader with responsibilities and once again he rose to it, tending his cadets with a firm and friendly hand and setting an example even in studies.

In June they sat for their final exams and this time he had no qualms about his work. A couple of days later, while waiting for the results, he led 'A' Squadron in the last cricket match against 'B' Squadron (whose team had nine of the Cranwell First Eleven). 'B' Squadron scored 238. Bader took five of their wickets and opened the batting for his own team. On a sodden pitch, wickets fell fast: soon 4 for 23. Bader began lambasting the bowling and in less than an hour it was six for 126 — Bader's share being 97 not out. Three 'ducks' followed, and the last man, Reed came in with the score at 135. The first ball shaved Reed's off-stump. The next shaved his leg-stump. He never received another ball. Bader kept jumping down the pitch slamming at everything, hitting fours and sixes during the overs, and singles or threes off the last balls. The 200 came up with Reed not out 0, and Bader not out, 171. Excitement was mounting continuously. Soon Bader clouted a ball to the square leg boundary, bringing the total to 227. Two more sixes would do it. Next ball, he jumped out of this crease and drove it like a bullet knee-high to short mid-off, where Paddy Coote held a brilliant catch.

The score-sheet read:

Emson	8
Morrison	5
Cleland	0
Bader	194
Doran	0
Moore	8
More	8
Andrews	0
Widdows	0

Edwards	....	0
Reed	....	0
Extras	....	4

Next day the exam results came out, and Paddy Coote just beat him for the Sword of Honour. No one could mind being second to a man like Coote.

In reticent official terms the report on Bader summed him up neatly: 'Plucky, capable, headstrong.' His flying rating was 'above average,' which is RAF understatement for a natural pilot (the only higher rating is 'exceptional,' which is such a rarity as to be almost a myth). Then the postings:

'P/O Bader, D. R. S., to 23 Squadron, Kenley.'

He rode his motor-cycle to London and traded it in for his first car, a second-hand Austin Seven that looked like a lacquered biscuit box on pram wheels. In this, on an August morning in 1930, he drove to Kenley, brimming with content. No. 23 Squadron flew Gloster Gamecock fighters.

CHAPTER THREE

Before the age of runways Kenley was a large, grass field and behind the hangars on the rim lay the graces of a station built in peace for an Air Force that was small and select, like a club whose members in the red-brick officers' messes scattered across the land (and outposts) more often than not knew one another. Less encrusted by years than the Navy or Army, the RAF accent was on youth: even the core, the 1914–18 veterans who had made its first traditions, were still young enough to play rugger. A mess waiter, with the deference reserved for qualified officers, showed Bader to his own room, an austere enough affair with an iron bed, leather chair and simple furniture which he viewed with pleasure. It was home; the life he wanted lay before him and down the corridor lived his friend Geoffrey Stephenson, posted to the same squadron.

In the morning B Flight commander sat him in a Gamecock and showed him 'the taps;' not much to show, no brakes, no retractable undercart lever, no flaps, no variable pitch propeller, no gyro instruments, no trimming tabs. She was a tubby little thing and from the cockpit he felt he could almost touch the tips of the two braced and strutted wings. Top speed was 156 mph, but the stumpy fuselage made her the most agile little aeroplane in the RAF. He took her up that morning, rolled and tumbled her about the sky for half an hour and joyfully agreed with that. For the past two years two of 23 Squadron's Gamecocks had been picked to do the combined aerobatics at Hendon pageant. Bader decided he wanted to be one of those two pilots next time.

He slid effortlessly into squadron life, perhaps a shade too confident for a new boy, but too friendly and vital to irk anyone. On 'dining-in' nights when, immaculate in mess kit, they passed the port decanter, Douglas, strictly sober, joined as wildly and hilariously as anyone in the subsequent games of rugger in the ante-room with a waste-paper basket for a ball; or highcockalorum; or 'desert warfare,' when they grabbed the assegais off the wall and stalked their fellow-men through oases of aspidistras on the floor while others beat tom-tom rhythms on the table-top. Life was idyllic, with flying, games and fellowship, buttressed by the tangible prestige and comfort of a permanent commission from Cranwell. Most of all he liked aerobatics in the Gamecock. That same August he arrived at Kenley he was picked for the RAF cricket team.

A month later, when cricket was finished, the Harlequins, famous amateur rugger club, asked him to play in a trial game. The knee cartilage stood up to it well, and so the Harlequins acquired a new centre-threequarter. Thereafter in *The Times* one not infrequently read little headlines such as 'Bader Brilliant,' 'Bader Excels,' often with the remark that he was the best player on the field. A few weeks later he was picked for the RAF. Fifteen, and again as fly-half he was in both senses head and shoulders above the ruck. By his twenty-first birthday in February, 1931, his name was becoming widely identified with a sinewy, beautifully-tuned human machine that weighed eleven stone six pounds stripped, and had the temperament of a dynamo. His present to himself was to trade in his little Austin biscuit-box for an MG sports car, which he cherished.

All other fighter squadrons now had the Bristol Bulldog or the Siskin; only 23 Squadron was left with Gamecocks, and that was partly why they were chosen again to do the combined aerobatics at Hendon that year. Woollett picked C Flight Commander, Harry Day, to lead the team, and all the other pilots started training hard for selection. One man killed himself flying upside down, and slowly the selection narrowed. In April Woollett told Douglas that he was to be second man in the team, with the inseparable Geoffrey Stephenson as number three, in reserve. Harry Day was a lean, glint-eyed man who had fought as a youngster in the Great War, and now, a hawk-faced thirty, commanded instant obedience. Prone to occasional turbulence, he thought it was time to change Hendon's traditional aerobatics, so he invented five new routines of 'synchronised aerobatics.' The first was typical of the other four — two aircraft would dive together, then pull out in two consecutive loops, wing-tip to wing-tip (three feet between, Day said), then up again, stall-turn away on each side into a vertical dive, aileron turn inwards so that they faced and crossed each other, wing-tip to wing-tip again, then up, up and roll off the top of a loop together (going different ways) to dive to each side of the airfield, turn back and race at each other head-on to start a new routine which included some upside down formation. It was safe enough provided no one made a mistake and provided the wind stayed kind. Day would not have tried it with pilots less cool and accurate than Bader and Stephenson.

Strict orders said they were not to go below 500 feet, though Bader made a nuisance of himself wanting to go lower. Typically, one of his favoured occupations was to do slow rolls 'on the deck' at about fifty feet. One tends to lose height in a slow roll and the engine tended to cut upside down. The trick was not to fly into the ground, and part of the charm was that to try this trick was a court-martial offence.

During practice one day Stephenson fell out of a slow roll but luckily was just beyond the end of the Kenley escarpment and had enough space to recover. Another day his engine failed and he made a neat forced landing in the grounds of a large country house. Bader drove over to pick him up and met there the daughter of the house, a dark and vividly pretty girl whom we shall call Patricia. The attraction was prompt and mutual and they began to meet after that.

Day tolerated Bader's 'press-on' spirit good humouredly. Other pilots might do bone-headed things on the spur of the moment, but he felt that Bader, even in his wilder moments, was always practical, would always know in advance exactly what he was going to do and would then do it with judgment.

There were still other activities — cricket, for instance. Early in June, Bader was picked to play for the Air Force again and soon there was a picture of him in the paper hitting a six almost out of the ground at the Oval. In that innings he hit 65 in thirty minutes — a six, a five and twelve fours made up 59 of that. Later that month Day confirmed that he was to be his number two at Hendon.

The Times said that 175,000 were inside Hendon Aerodrome on the day of the display and that 'hundreds of thousands of others crowded hillsides and fields outside.' In bright sunshine they saw what *The Times* also declared was 'the event of the day' as Day and Bader in the Gamecocks 'provided the most thrilling spectacle ever seen in exhibition flying ... ten minutes full of the cleanest trick flying, synchronised to a fraction of a second ... the most successful of the Hendon displays yet held.'

Pilot Officer Bader was an object for youthful hero-worship — dashing airman, brilliant rugger player and cricketer, and vitally handsome, especially at a Service dance in the tight blue trousers and the short mess jacket with blue silk lapels and gilt buttons. Many young women sighed over him and made what decorous advances convention allowed. From time to time he played escort to several: Patricia, of course, and there was a quiet, blue-eyed girl with classic features called Hilda, a pert little blonde called June and a giggly blonde as well. His main interests were still flying and games, but he *did* enjoy the adulation and the Press notices — all very stimulating to the self-confidence of a young man who was once the somewhat rejected Bader Minor.

The aerobatics team flew north to Cramlington for a display, and on the way back, strictly against orders, Bader dropped out of the formation to spend an hour skimming over the hedges and along the floors of the valleys. When they landed, Day read him an angry lecture on flying discipline, though Bader turned on his usual disarming charm and averted the worst of the wrath.

A couple of weeks later he heard through the orderly room that he was on the 'A List,' a roster of young officers due for posting overseas. That had nothing to do with the low flying; it was routine that after a year on a squadron a young permanent officer would go overseas. He seemed slated for Iraq in the autumn, and late in summer, sitting in the pavilion at Aldershot with the pads on waiting to bat, he mentioned a little sadly to Squadron Leader Brian Baker,[1] of 32 Squadron, that it would probably be his last game in England for a long time. Baker commented: 'I don't think so. You probably won't be going till next year.' Bader wanted to know why and Baker said he fancied they were going to keep him at Kenley all winter to give him a chance to get his 'cap' for England at rugger.

Bader felt the electric thrill a man would get on drawing a horse in the Irish Sweep. Rugger for England was the summit of ambition, something breathtaking in the 'too good to be true' class. Some overseas postings came out but he was not on them.

At last 23 Squadron was getting Bristol Bulldog fighters to replace Gamecocks. The Bulldog was the last word in fighters. She could do 176 mph. There were minor drawbacks; she was not as manoeuvrable as a Gamecock, for instance, being heavier, which gave her a tendency to sink faster on her back in the middle of a slow roll. Low aerobatics were strictly banned, though some people good-humouredly ignored that. Then one of the pilots spun into the ground and killed himself.

Squadron Leader Woollett left the squadron and Harry Day took over command for the time. Another pilot crashed and killed himself. Day called all the others together and read them a lecture on low aerobatics in the Bulldog. 'Fighting Area Regulations say that you must not aerobat below 2,000 feet,' he said. 'Well, you know my views about some

---

[1] Now Air Chief Marshal Sir Brian Baker.

regulations – they're written for the obedience of fools and the guidance of wise men. Now if you're going to aerobat under 2,000 feet, first of all – don't. If you decide to ignore that advice, don't do it where any senior officers can see you. And remember these three things: first of all, make up your mind exactly what you're going to do, then get properly settled down, and *then get your speed right* so you don't spin off or lose height. The only thing you have to worry about then is if your engine stops. If it stops – you're dead, but if you're going to start worrying about that stop flying anyway.'

It was sound advice, if a little ambiguous, but Day was not out to make decorous airmen; he wanted to turn out pilots with the 'guts' and judgment for war. Otherwise the RAF was meaningless. Besides, people were not in the habit of ignoring a warning from Harry Day.

Pilot Officer Bader did. In November a flight commander spotted him doing low aerobatics and 'beating up' the airfield. Day had him on the mat and told him crisply and at length to watch his step and not to show off. After a chastened Douglas went out Day wondered whether perhaps he should not have slapped him down harder. Bader was getting into the dangerous phase of over-confidence which comes to so many pilots after a year or two. What with his Hendon success and other things on top of the volatile nature he was too outspoken. One or two resented the 'white-haired Cranwell boy' and thought he was conceited. Day recognised it more as a coltish, super-vitality and also recognised what others did not always see, that under the buoyant front lay sensitivity. Perhaps he could be slapped down too much? You could not force him – he would only become stubborn. Very likely, with a little firmness, he would correct things himself. But the red light was there. It was a problem. Day was still thinking about it (and other squadron problems) when he went on leave.

As it happened, Day's remark about 'showing off' had given Bader the sort of jolt he had had from Halahan at Cranwell; he began to watch what he was saying and shy away from ostentatious aerobatics. Also the Springboks had arrived from South Africa for a series of rugger tests against England, and with that goal in front of him he was training harder than ever before. He wanted his 'cap' so much he wouldn't even admit he had a chance for it.

On Saturdays he played for the Harlequins, knowing that the international selectors were watching, and was dismayed to feel that he was over-trained and not playing well. The other pilots kept reassuring him, telling him he would be out of his misery as soon as the selectors named the Combined Services team to play the early match against the Springboks. Last season's England fly-half was also fly-half for the Navy. If they chose Bader instead of him for the Combined Services – he was probably in for England.

At the end of November the Combined Services team was named and there it was —' 'Fly-half: D. R. S. Bader.' It was like the moment he had seen his name on the board for the First Fifteen at school; the same kind of brimming joy, but even deeper. For days he savoured the prospect, and on the Saturday played with a dashing, high-geared vigour. Just after half-time he flung himself at a huge Springbok who was trampling for the line, brough him down, but broke his nose at the same time. They'd be picking the England team in about three weeks. Too much at stake to worry about a broken nose: he played on.

The following Saturday he played again for the Harlequins, not even bothering to plaster his nose first, and though he tried his hardest, kept fumbling passes and spent the rest of the week-end worrying about his uneven form.

The Monday morning, December 14, 1931, was bright and clear with a nip in the air and a little scattered cumulus about 4,000 feet. About ten o'clock Bader was curing his gloom with some aerobatics not far from the airfield when he saw two Bulldogs taking off and remembered that two of the pilots, Phillips and Richardson, were flying over to Woodley Aerodrome near Reading to see Phillips' brother, who helped to run the aero club there. Bader tacked on to make a threesome, and half an hour later they settled on the grass in a neat vic at Woodley. In the clubhouse some young pilots, drinking coffee and talking shop as usual, asked Douglas, the Hendon star, questions about aerobatics, and then someone suggested he give a demonstration beat-up of the airfield. Bader said no, he didn't want to. The Hendon show had been in a Gamecock and the Bulldog was not quite the same (and uncomfortably he remembered Harry Day's 'show-off' remark). The matter was dropped until they were leaving, and a young man suggested it again. Bader again said no, and someone grinned and made some barbed joke about being 'windy.' He made it sound like a dare.

Richardson took off first, and then a tight-lipped, angry Bader. As Phillips left the ground Bader was banking steeply, turning back, and slanting down for a low run across the field. A knot of young men watched from the clubhouse. Just above the grass, rocking a little in the thermals, the Bulldog, engine bellowing, swept across the boundary fence, rushing at a spot beside the clubhouse. The nose lifted a fraction and she began rolling to the right.

He had the stick well over . . . a little top rudder to hold the nose up . . . stick forward to keep it up and as she rolled upside down throttle back to keep the engine alive. He felt her starting to drop.

Stick *hard* over now; the wings were vertical, glinting in the sun, and she was dropping fast. Grimly he was reefing her round and she was rolling out of it fast when the left wing-tip hit the grass and jerked the nose down. As propeller and cowling exploded into the ground the engine tore out, bouncing in a cloud of flying dirt, and the Bulldog seemed to crumple and cartwheel into a tangle very fast. Pinned by his straps, Bader did not feel anything but heard only a terrible noise.

All the airfield was suddenly still, except for the fierce boil of dust round the awkward heap in the middle that looked like crushed brown paper. As the dust began to drift the men by the clubhouse were running.

CHAPTER FOUR

After the noise everything was suddenly quiet and still. The cockpit was tilted. That was odd: it leaned him sideways. He must have crashed; but it was only a hazy idea and not very interesting because pain was stabbing at his back. Slowly it ebbed, leaving a passive torpor, and sitting in the straps, hands in his lap, he was placidly aware of the cockpit: beyond that, nothing.

Gently as the mind came into focus he was aware that his knees were buzzing as though he had hit his funnybone. The eyes wandered down and absorbed with curiosity that his legs were in peculiar positions. At least his right leg was. He could not see the left leg and forgot about it. (It had buckled under the collapsed seat so that he was sitting on it.) His right foot was tucked over in the far, right-hand corner and the clean white overalls were torn at the knee and staining in blood that was pumping in slow little squirts and spreading in filmy waves. There was his knee through the blood, and something sticking through it. Looked a bit like the rudder bar. Very odd. He regarded it in an abstracted way, and for a while it made no impact until an ugly thought crystallised: 'Damn! I won't be able to play rugger on Saturday.'

After a while that did not seem to matter so much and he was content again.

For the first time he became aware of things beyond the cockpit: voices, and people moving, but they seemed shadowy and remote.

A man in a white coat was standing beside the cockpit. Right at his elbow. There was a face and a white coat and a hand holding out a glass. A voice said: 'Here you are, sir. Have a bit of this brandy.' (It was a steward from the clubhouse.)

Automatically, with no effort, he answered casually: 'No, thanks very much. I don't drink.'

The man leaned over to urge him and saw the blood spurting in the cockpit. He turned very pale and then he stood back and drank the brandy himself.

A big ruddy-faced young man stood there instead of the man in the white coat, and leaned in and started undoing his harness, saying things in a gentle voice. He let him go ahead, and then became unconscious for a while.

Jack Cruttenden, the big man, an Australian student pilot at the club, found he could not lift Bader out of the crushed cockpit. He started tearing at bits of the wreckage and other men did the same. Someone brought a hacksaw and cut away a twisted centre-section strut. Bader partly came to and sensed more than knew that Cruttenden was gently lifting him out.

Consciousness was lapping and receding in waves. He was lying on the grass. Someone was taking his shoes off. Cruttenden's hands were doing something to his right knee: they felt very strong and were covered in blood. He felt no pain. A little to one side two white doors with red crosses opened and the crosses went out of sight. He supposed it was an ambulance.

Then he was lying in it on a stretcher and men were bent over his legs. He tried to sit up but could not get very far and watched the men with detached interest. The legs of his overalls and trousers had gone somewhere, and Cruttenden's fingers seemed to be on his right knee (holding the femoral artery). After a few moments he got bored with watching. He could feel the ambulance was moving and wanted to see what was happening outside. He said to Cruttenden: 'Look, I think I'll get up now. I want to get out of here.'

He started struggling up on his elbows and Cruttenden said: 'Take it easy. Won't be long now.'

Bader said petulantly: 'Oh, to hell with this. I want to get out now. This is damn' silly.'

He tried to struggle up again, and Cruttenden took one hand from the knee and pressed it gently against his chest to hold him down.

Being held down by a stranger was irritating. He twisted a shoulder off the stretcher, hooked his right fist up and hit Cruttenden on the chin. He felt he could not hit very hard lying down.

Cruttenden, looking at him with a pacifying grin, said: 'Ease it up, mate.'

Having hit him, Bader felt suddenly feeble and foolish. But honour was satisfied – he'd made the gesture – and anyway he'd completely lost interest in getting up now. He lay back and did not remember any more.

The ambulance weaved swiftly through the Reading traffic, swung into Redlands Road and stopped in front of the Casualty door of the Royal Berkshire Hospital. Within a minute he was on a table with the duty doctor tying the artery and swabbing the pulpy mess in both legs where the bones had torn through. The right leg looked nearly off at the knee and the left shin was broken and badly splintered, the torn flesh full of oil and dirt. The patient's pulse was getting weaker, very thready, so that the doctor could hardly feel it and broke off to give a heart stimulant. He straightened both legs and put them in box splints, then got Sister Thornhill in Benyon Ward on the house phone.

'There's a young man coming up with multiple injuries, shock and loss of blood from an aeroplane crash. Get him warm in bed to ease the shock. I don't think there's much we can do.' (Sister Thornhill recognised the tone. After messages like that the patient was sometimes dead by the time he arrived.) Soon they wheeled Douglas in, now deeply unconscious, and she packed hot-water bottles and blankets round the body, which was very cold.

The resident surgical officer examined him briefly. No chance of operating yet, he said when he straightened up. Perhaps later, if he lasted, but there was no real hope.

Thornhill remembered that Leonard Joyce, who was probably the best surgeon in England, was operating at the hospital that day and rang the theatre, but they said he had just left. Hurrying as fast as she dared, she found him in the entrance hall putting on his coat to go. She said: 'Excuse me, Mr Joyce, but we've just admitted a young Air Force officer after a bad crash. Could you have a look at him?'

The rest was understood: she had assisted Joyce at many operations and he was a man of few words. He took his coat off and followed her back to the ward, and shortly was saying that he would wait and see if the patient came out of shock enough to try and operate. He was young and strong. They must at least try.

When Harry Day rang the hospital from Kenley they were very guarded and he understood perfectly clearly that Bader was dying. He sent a telegram to Jessie, at Sprotborough, and, on the hospital's advice, to Cyril Burge, who was at Aldershot and could reach the hospital in an hour.

About two o'clock Sister Thornhill noticed that the patient was breathing more noticeably and his pulse was also stronger. Gradually his condition kept improving, and Joyce, surprised, put it down to his physical fitness. At 3.30 he decided to try and operate, and on the way to the theatre they first wheeled the patient into the X-ray room.

On the operating table Bader came to and lay looking up at a large light and a white ceiling, not knowing where he was or caring, becoming aware of a hospital smell and a man in a long white surgeon's coat and cap standing by his head who looked scholarly and said in a quiet voice: 'Hallo, old chap. I see you've had a bit of an accident. Don't worry. Just lie back and we'll soon have you fixed up.'

Bader looked at him vaguely, and as this sank in he said: 'Don't give me an anaesthetic, will you. I can't stand the stuff.'

'Don't worry,' the man said, 'we'll see things are all right.' He seemed to exude warmth and compassion.

Afterwards Bader could not remember getting the anaesthetic. As he was going 'under,' the plates came in from the X-ray room and Joyce held them up, still wet, to the light. First the right leg. He passed it almost instantly to the nurse, saying briefly: 'That must come off.' He hesitated over the left leg and finally passed it across without comment. The plates of the abdomen and head showed only two ribs broken, though the face was gashed and a tooth had come through the upper lip.

Joyce worked fast. The patient was too shaky for thorough surgery; there was time only to try and patch things temporarily in a race with the imminence of more shock and fatal collapse. He severed the right leg above the smashed knee, but that did not take long because it was almost off already. When he turned to the left leg the patient was sinking and there was just time to clean the torn mess and seal it, hoping no infection would set in, and inject a saline solution. Bader was close to death when they got him to a private room and started working on him for post-operative shock.

Cyril Burge reached the hospital and waited. By nine o'clock Bader was still alive, but shock was draining him of the last resistance and he was nearly pulseless, cold to the touch and still deeply unconscious. Joyce told Burge he was not expected to live till the morning and a matron gave Burge a room to sleep in, promising to call him when the time came. He lay on the bed in his clothes to wait.

A nurse woke him out of a doze about 2 am and said softly: 'Will you please come down now.' He got up and followed her without a word. Outside the patient's door two girls stood, both crying. One was Patricia and the other Hilda, though in the emotion of the moment there were no introductions. He put his head in the door and saw two doctors in white coats and two nurses bending over a bed doing something to the shape in it. One of the doctors saw him and came over and murmured: 'Would you wait outside, please? He seems to be holding on.'

Half an hour later the doctor came out again and said they might as well go and rest for a while. He would call them if anything happened. The girls went away. Burge went back to his room and was called again an hour later, but when he got there the doctor said the patient had suddenly rallied again, and after a while Burge once more went back to bed.

In the morning Bader was still alive but it seemed only a matter of time. His mother, Mrs Hobbs, arrived but was so overwrought that the matron gave her a room and a sedative. At nightfall Bader was still holding on, but at midnight they called Burge again, then sent him back to rest. By morning the patient still lingered with a finger-tip hold on life. He had not recovered consciousness since the operation. Joyce told Burge that if he lasted another day he might have a chance, provided the left leg did not become septic. There might even be a chance of saving the remaining leg.

Twenty-four hours later Bader's eyes quietly opened and gave him an extraordinary experience that started with knowing again and seeing things for the first time like a puppy at the moment its birth blindness lifted. It was like being born again, being alive without knowing what alive meant, unaware of the world or even his name. Sunshine flooded the room. He was conscious of objects that meant nothing for a while but then slowly focused into meaning: a cream ceiling, white sheets and then a tall girl in white and a red cape standing by a window with her back to him. It was like a fade-in of a film scene that suddenly stops and is frozen. Imperceptibly comprehension came without any effort, and the film came to life and meaning, but with no pain and no concern, no backward memory to give depth or disquiet. After a while he murmured: 'What the hell am I doing here?'

Sister Thornhill turned and came over smiling. She had been given Bader as a 'special' and had been with him nearly all the time. He saw she was about twenty-five, nicely rounded with a strong, capable face, healthily attractive.

'Oh, you're awake, are you?' Her voice was pleasant and steady. He looked up at her impassively.

'You've had an accident,' she said.

'An accident?'

'Yes. You crashed in an aeroplane.'

'Oh, did I?' He pondered vacantly. 'What a bloody silly thing to do.'

She laughed and said she must go because Mr Joyce wanted to see him as soon as he was awake.

He did not know who Mr Joyce was nor cared if he came. Nothing seemed to matter. He became aware that there was an enormous mound in the bed-clothes, and remembered a similar mound when 'Derick had broken his leg at prep. school and they had put a cradle over it.

'Must have broken my leg,' he thought. But he was not really interested.

The door opened and Joyce came in, but he did not recognise the pointed, sensitive face.

'Hallo,' Joyce said. 'Glad to see you're awake.'

Bader looked at him composedly but did not speak. Joyce made a few more cheerful sounds and then said: 'I'm very sorry, old chap, but I'm afraid we've had to take off your right leg.'

Bader gazed placidly at him. He had heard and understood the words but not the meaning. Politely he said: 'That's all right. I hope I haven't been a nuisance.'

Thornhill leaned over his body to block his view while Joyce lifted the bed-clothes and started unwrapping the dressings. It gave Bader his first reaction: an urgent curiosity to see this most interesting sight of a severed leg. But he did not want to look while the others were in the room: for some crafty quirk he wanted them outside so he could lift the bed-clothes in privacy.

Joyce looked at the right stump first. It seemed all right. He unwrapped the dressing on the left leg and saw the red puffiness of incipient septicaemia and the dead, grey signs of gangrene. After a while he wrapped it up again, smiled at Bader: 'I'll see you again soon,' and went out to find Mrs Hobbs and Cyril Burge.

As soon as the door had closed, Bader lifted the blankets and looked. Yes, there it was. A short stump of thigh with a rather bloody bandage round it. He thought it would look like that. They hadn't given him any pyjama pants.[1] Oh, well . . . he put the blankets down, not even noticing the left leg.

Mrs Hobbs collapsed into a chair when Joyce told her the second leg had to come off. In near hysteria, she wanted everyone to go away and leave Douglas alone so she could look after him herself.

Joyce found Cyril Burge and told him the situation plainly and lucidly. The boy would certainly die if the left leg stayed. He would probably die from operative shock if they tried to take it off, but it was the only chance. It would have to be done immediately. Burge nodded.

The door opened and Joyce walked into the sick-room again and said: 'We've got to re-set your left leg, old chap. I'm awfully sorry about that. It might hurt a bit, so we'll put you to sleep for a while.' He looked like a sympathetic housemaster.

'That's all right, Doc,' Bader murmured obligingly, supremely placid. It did not seem to be particularly his business. Other people had charge and he was drifting with the stream.

A burly man in a violent check suit and yellow pullover came in. He had a big nose, a cheery face and a tremendously breezy and matey manner that made Bader feel like getting up to shake hands. Commander Parry Price, RNR (Ret'd), the anaesthetist, said: 'By Jove, old boy, you look fine. Now let's see, what do you weigh?'

'I used to box at eleven stone six.'

'That's fine. Just about what I thought you were.'

Price went out, and soon Thornhill came in with a phial of pink liquid that she injected into him. Soon he felt consciousness withdrawing to a little speck in the back of his mind, and then he was asleep.

In the operating theatre Joyce worked fast again, taking the left leg off about six inches below the knee. As he lifted it away a young nurse

[1] He never wore pyjama pants again because trouser legs get tangled round a short stump.

started crying, and then as Joyce was sewing the flap of skin over the bone, Parry Price, who had been watching like a hawk, said quietly: 'The heart's stopped.'

Joyce looked up, motionless. The room was suddenly still. In a dead silence Price jabbed with a needle and took the wrist. The silence lingered on, and then Price felt the little thready flutter start again.

Joyce finished quickly and they wheeled him back to the room. Every ten minutes they kept taking his pulse and it kept palpitating with thin, fast persistence.

Some time in the night, about eighteen hours later, Bader's eyes opened. Vaguely on the rim of a dim circle of light that played round him a nurse was sitting. It was soothing to feel that he was not alone, and the eyes closed and he sank into oblivion again.

Six hours later he came to again, conscious only of pain. His left leg was hurting with a bitter, steady ache that sharpened the torpid mind and began to distress him. After a while Sister Thornhill came in and said: 'Oh, you're awake.'

'My left leg's hurting,' he complained, and she said soothingly that it would probably ease after a while. The leg kept on hurting keenly and remorselessly. Thornhill gave him a little morphia to ease it, but it seemed to make no difference: the terrible hurting went on, stabbing stronger and stronger till it was shredding his nerves all over and beginning to obsess him with agony to the point of feeling he could stand no more. But he had to stand it because it went on and on, and there were no defences and no relief. The mind was sharper now, but still not caring about the loss of the right leg, only about the cruel pain in the left. Sweat began to glisten on his face, and then he was sweating all over and groaning now and then. Thornhill gave him more morphia and the pain went relentlessly on.

By nightfall his eyes were sunken and restless in dark hollows, and the face was grey and waxy, glistening with a film of sweat. For a while he slept under more morphia, but soon awoke to more pain. The following morning he drifted into unconsciousness but now and then revived for brief spells, when his eyes rolled with the constant ache and his mind wandered in a vague half-world. Once he was briefly aware of his mother sitting by the bed, and then she had changed into Cyril Burge. Joyce looked in and told Burge that they were giving all the morphia they dared and doing all they could, but he did not sound hopeful. It would depend on the patient's youth and constitution; in short, his lasting power and resilience.

That night they sent for Burge again at the hotel where he was now staying, but Bader did not die and towards dawn Burge was able to go back to his own room.

Later the young man woke and the pain had gone. He could not feel his body at all, but for some reason his mind was perfectly clear. He lay still, eyes open and head raised on a pillow, looking straight out through the top of a window at a patch of clear blue sky, and into his mind crept a peaceful thought: 'This is pleasant. I've only got to shut my eyes now and lean back and everything's all right.' Warm peace was stealing over him, his eyes closing and his head seeming to sink into the pillow. It did not occur to him that he was dying; only that he was letting go, drifting down and wanting to. In a dreamy haze the mind was shrinking into a soft, deep pinpoint.

Through the slightly open door of the room a woman's disembodied voice slid into the receding clarity: 'Sssh! Don't make so much noise. There's a boy dying in there.'

The words quivered in him like a little electric shock that froze the drifting dream and sparked a sharp thought: 'So that's it. Hell, am I!' Feeling began flickering out through his body like ripples from a pebble tossed in a pool. He stopped letting go and the mind was clearing; the body did not move but the brain began gripping thought and reality. It was the challenge that stirred him. His eyes opened and, instead of looking unseeing through the window, began moving, taking note of things in the room. Sister Thornhill came in. He noted her stiff white cap and dress under the red cape. She stood by the bed looking down at him and then smiled and moved away.

As he lay thinking, quite clear-headed, the pain came back to his leg. Somehow he did not mind this time; it was almost satisfying because he felt he was normal again and had slipped away from the ethereal spirit that had been floating him to Limbo. Another thought came: 'I mustn't let that happen again. Apparently it wasn't as good as it felt.'

Some instinct told him that he had been dying in that moment. (Ever since then he has been convinced of it, and from that moment has never been frightened of dying. Later this was to have a vital effect on his life.)

The pain began to increase agonisingly again till it gripped him so that he wanted to die because it was unbearable, but now he could not die because the tortured mind could not sink back in peace. Thornhill gave him more morphia.

That night delayed shock took effect and he sank into unconsciousness that lasted two days. His mother and Cyril Burge were asked to keep in close touch with the hospital. Joyce was non-committal about the prospects. Thornhill kept rolling him over in bed from time to time to avoid lung congestion that would lead to pneumonia. It had become a personal fight with her and other nurses to save the young man's life. Usually they were impartial and impersonal about patients, but this one somehow was different. He seemed too young and handsome to die, and everyone kept asking about him. On the second morning she was turning the limp body with the help of another nurse when he suddenly sat up and kissed her, then sank back into unconsciousness again. She was petrified with amazement. 'Not so unconscious after all,' observed the other nurse slyly. Thornhill lifted his eyelid back with a gentle thumb but he *was* unconscious.

Later, Joyce (who had heard from the other nurse about the incident) came round on his inspection and asked whether the patient had shown any signs of reviving. Thornhill, still a little confused, said no, there hadn't been, and Joyce looked at her and said dryly to no one in particular: 'Sister isn't giving much away this morning, is she?'

Bader came to that afternoon and they kept injecting so much morphia into him that he lay in a drugged stupor for two more days. Several times in the nights he had moments of near clarity, aware of a pretty young probationer giving him a drink out of something with a spout that she held in his lips. Every time he opened his eyes she seemed to be leaning over him and he thought she was wonderful.

Slowly the shock subsided and he came out of the coma. Morphia helped deaden the pain of the leg and the face lost some of its greyness, though it was still waxy, with eyes sunk in dark sockets and a dark stubble of beard. Thornhill changed the dressings that day, and he rose with a sharp and quivering groan of agony as she whipped away the last lint that stuck bloodily to the raw wound. She leaned her body carefully over so that he could not see that he had lost both legs. The whole hospital seemed to be aware with a sort of fascinated dread that he would have to find out soon. Thornhill was frightened that he would find out accidentally himself and be thrown back into danger by the shock.

The next day he winced as usual when she was changing the dressings and asked: 'How are they?'

Now! she thought. Do it casually.

In an off-hand way she said: 'Well, they took one off the same day and the other one came off below the knee a couple of days later when septicaemia set in. Don't worry about it. A man with your guts can overcome that. They've got pretty good artificial legs nowadays.'

She waited nervously for the answer and was amazed when he said quite casually:

'I suppose so.' He was quite calm about it, and after the moment of relief and anti-climax she wondered how he had known.

In fact, Bader had not known, and still did not know. He had heard her words and answered automatically, but they had not registered a meaning in his drugged mind because he could still feel his toes and did not know anything about the phantom sensations that lead a man to feel his foot so realistically after losing his leg that he can waggle his toes in his mind. With the phantom feeling he was in a never-never land of unreality, as in a dream when anything can happen, when a man can lose both legs and still walk on them.

Later that day when Cyril Burge sat with him and the left leg was hurting again, he said despairingly: 'Why does it hurt so much: Why don't they cut it off like the other leg?' Burge, a little sick at heart, did not try to tell him.

It was the following day that the boy found out, and he only discovered it then because in spite of the morphia he was in torment that sharpened the brain into a little clarity. Squadron Leader Woollett had come in to ask how he was, and Bader said: 'All right, sir, but my left leg's hurting like hell.'

'I expect it's bound to hurt for a bit,' Woollett said sympathetically.

'Well, I wish to God they'd cut it off like the right leg,' he groaned, 'that doesn't hurt at all. I'm sick to death of this left one.'

'Would you really like them to cut it off?' Woollett asked.

'I don't give a damn what they do as long as they stop it hurting.'

'You mightn't want it off if it didn't hurt.'

'I don't know what I'd want if it didn't hurt. All I know is that I'm sick of the damn' thing now and I wish to God it were off.'

Sitting on the chair by the bed, Woollett leaned forward, elbows on his knees, and he said quietly, nervously aware of the drama: 'As a matter of fact, Douglas, they *have* cut it off.'

CHAPTER FIVE

That time it sank into his brain, but distorted with the morphia and the pain it made no impact. Only the pain mattered: nothing else. He only said petulantly: 'Well, why does the damn' thing hurt so much?'

It shook Woollett and he switched to the safety of squadron gossip, though he did not mention that most of them felt it would have been better for Bader to have been killed outright.

The impact of losing his legs never hit Bader in one moment, or even in a day or a week. The realisation formed slowly in a doped mind, which was merciful. Against the agonising urgency of the pain it was only a detail, and when the pain ebbed and allowed other things to matter his feelings were cushioned by dope that left him floating easily and somewhat detached in a tranquil unreal present, unmindful of any future. Joyce came in later that day and said: 'Sorry, old man, but I had to take the other leg off below the knee. I couldn't save it. You're really lucky to be in the world still.'

'That's all right, sir,' Bader said. 'I'll get some longer legs. I always wanted to be taller.'

Next day, Christmas Eve, as the patient seemed disinclined to die yet, Joyce had him moved a hundred yards across a courtyard from the main hospital to Greenlands, the private nursing home in the hospital grounds. They put him in a friendly little room on the ground floor looking out on the lawns and a green deodar tree. There were gay curtains, deep chairs and a bookcase to give it warmth of atmosphere. Nurses kept injecting dope to quell the outraged nerves in the left leg, and Christmas Day was a blank to him. So were the next two days. Joyce was still afraid he would die from either thrombosis or sepsis.

On the fourth morning he was conscious of a new nurse by his bed saying that she would have to change his dressings, and he started sweating again, remembering the last times, but she brought hot water and spent twenty minutes soaking them off so that he did not feel a thing. It endeared him to the new girl from that moment. Dorothy Brace was petite, with a friendly laugh and used her hands tenderly.

The pain was under control now, and about this time he remembered talking to his mother for the first time, though she had been sitting by the bed for days dabbing sweat off the grey face. They never mentioned the legs and most of the talk was a stilted fumbling for safe subjects. Patricia and Hilda came to see him too, both overflowing with a girl's warmth and sympathy for a wounded warrior, though Patricia, the more attractive of the two, was normally a rather brittle type. The more sensible Hilda said: 'Look, Douglas, don't worry about losing your legs. If you'll take me as a typical young woman, the fact that you've lost your legs doesn't make any difference at all. You're still my favourite boy.'

'I don't give a damn about losing my legs,' he said amiably. 'Honestly, it doesn't worry me a bit.' In his drugged state he obviously meant it. Another time he said to Hazel Burge. 'I can't always believe I've lost them, you know. I can still feel my toes.'

Just before New Year Joyce took the stitches out. Bader braced himself for it, but there were only a couple of snipping sounds and a faint but painless sensation when the threads were pulled out. Suddenly and quite rapidly he began to get better. The face filled out and got some colour, and the dark rings went from round the eyes. So did the pain in the left leg and they tapered off the morphia. He felt well and alert, yet still unconcerned about the loss of his legs. There were several reasons for this. Over the days through the soothing morphia and the monopolising pain the loss had slowly infiltrated his mind so that he had digested it gradually, absorbing it into his mentality through a cushioned pressure that did not jar. By the time it had clarified into reality he was already temporarily adjusted to it.

Another reason was that he did not – yet – miss his legs. He was

comfortably in bed where legs were only remote extensions, and surrounded by attractive girls who brought him anything he wanted like
devoted and adoring angels. There was no need to move a finger; he had
chicken and egg-flips, fruit and cream, books, friends paying court, and
a gramophone which gave him bliss by grinding out 'Trees' or 'Abdul
the Bul-Bul Emir,' nearly all day. Old friends from the squadron popped
now and then through the window, assuring him by their presence that
he still belonged and making jokes about his beard, which, as no one had
shaved him yet, was beginning to look impressive rather than scruffy.
Harry Day said: 'You look like one of the apostles,' which shocked
Bader's firmly religious mother. Hilda stroked his brow. Dorothy Brace
was a cheerful and gentle lieutenant who gurgled at his jokes and was
deliciously horrified at bolder things he frequently said. He lived most
agreeably in the present.

The past was past, the present was good and the future had not yet
intruded. Let it wait. His nature, nearly always so practical, still had the
capacity for dealing with first things first and shutting out others. The
first thing was to get well again and that he was obviously achieving.

Possibly the most powerful reason lay in the kindness that enveloped
him (largely due to Sister Penley-Cooper, who ran Greenlands, hand-
picked his nurses and relaxed hospital rules for his benefit). The warm
and reassuring affection on all sides satisfied a deep need that he was not
consciously aware of. To all the nurses, as well as to Hilda and Patricia,
he was inevitably attractive, not only because he was young, virile and
handsome, but because he was a heroic figure cheerfully enduring tragedy
with a courage that stirred deep feminine feelings in their normally
impersonal and professional bosoms.

With the two girls (plus occasional others) and his mother always
popping in there was seldom a dull moment. Mrs Hobbs did not
wholeheartedly approve of the girls, nor they of each other. As none
would submit to the indignity of calling by roster it fell to Dorothy Brace
to juggle the callers in the interests of peace, so that when one was in
session with the patient she kept guard and diverted any others of the
female sex. There was one hectic day when the two girls arrived within
a minute of each other while Mrs Hobbs was with her son. The nurse
had no sooner steered Hilda into a waiting-room than Patricia arrived,
and she bundled Patricia quickly into a refrigerator room, thinking,
'That'll cool her off.'

Dorothy Brace much preferred Hilda, who was devoted and completely
unselfish, though Douglas, as a young man will, was becoming a little
smitten by the more glittering, if less enduring, Patricia.

On January 15, he got up for the first time – a month and a day after
the crash. He put on a dressing-gown in bed, Dorothy Brace pushed a
wheel-chair to the bed and he heaved himself into it with his hands and

sat there beaming with satisfaction. He wheeled himself to the window and sat looking out, but found he quickly became tired and was put back to bed in a couple of hours. Yet within a week he had the bandages off his stumps and was able to wheel himself down the ramps into the garden and spin around talking cheerfully to the gardeners.

At the end of January, Joyce said he could have a peg-leg on the left stump and try getting about with crutches. Bader wanted to start off with a 'real' artificial leg, but Joyce said that would be a waste because the stump would probably shrink later. The real reason was that he had to operate on the stump again to cut more bone away, but he did not mention that.

A thin-faced little man in a white coat came into the room next day to take a plaster cast of the stump for the socket into which it would fit on the peg-leg (he called it a 'pylon' – that was the trade name). Bader bared his stump and the man slapped the plaster on. In five minutes it had set, and as the man pulled it off all the hairs in the stump were dragged out by the roots with it, in a thousand little pin-pricks of torture. Taken by surprise, Bader's shocked bellows of agony reached to the farthest cranny of the hospital and the language made people blanch. The little man apologised, nearly in tears; he had forgotten, he confessed, to put a thin sock over the stump first.

The little man was back in a couple of days with the 'pylon,' a short smoothly turned piece of wood, painted black, and with a rubber pad on the bottom. At the top was a leather socket made from the plaster cast and above this two metal arms stuck up on each side, hinged where the knee went and ending in a leather corset to be laced round the thigh. Bader strapped it on, with the little man explaining that the weight was taken on the sides of the leather socket, not on the bottom of the stump.

It felt very odd when he put it on. The stump fitted neatly into the moulded leather, but it felt strange to the unaccustomed skin, and the thigh corset gripped firmly. Sitting on the edge of the bed with the little man, Dorothy Brace and a big Irish nurse watching, he bent his knee to waggle the pylon and get a little used to it. Brace passed him a pair of crutches and said:

'Now don't forget, you won't have any strength in that leg at all for a while.'

One on each side, they helped him up from the bed to ease his weight on the crutches. Tentatively he let his weight sink on to the pylon and the knee buckled like a piece of paper. It had no strength at all. They held him up while he shuffled each crutch forward in turn, and like that they lurched all over the room, giggling. It seemed a great joke. After half an hour he was tired out. Later he tried again and again, but it was three days before he was able to hobble a couple of steps without help, with the left knee feeling it would collapse at any moment. Apart from that the strangeness was going and it did not seem very difficult. He took to new crutches with rings round the elbows instead of pads under the armpits and they were more manageable.

A day or two later came a milestone in his career when he was able to stump down the corridor and take a bath – the first since his accident. He had worked out in advance how he would get into it – sit on the edge, unlace the pylon and then lower himself into it with hands on each side. Sinking into the hot water was ecstasy and he lay there a long time and got Brace to scrub his back. Getting out was not very difficult either. When he heaved himself up with a hand on each side, he was surprised to find how easy it was and remembered that Joyce had told him he would be about thirty pounds lighter without his legs.

Soon he was independent of outside help and spent hours stumping about the garden. It felt really good to be moving round again, and in the limited world of the garden the loss of his legs still did not seem at all serious, though the skin over each stump was contracting and stretching tightly over the bone-ends that he could clearly feel protruding. Joyce said one day: 'We'll have to trim these off a bit soon, you know. Otherwise they might split the skin. We didn't have time to do them properly before and you can't get your proper legs until the stumps are all right.'

'Another operation?' Bader asked.

'Yes. But it'll be all right this time. You're as strong as a young bull.' Joyce's manner seemed to be trying to soothe him, but it was unnecessary, partly because Bader had complete faith in him and partly because his mind was still comfortable and secure from the weeks of protective kindness.

He said flippantly: 'That's all right, Doc. I'm all for you having your fun.'

Joyce, professional dignity ruffled, remarked a little severely: 'It isn't exactly fun, old chap.'

'Well, I don't mind, Doc. You can cut my head off if you like.'

'Would the day after to-morrow suit you?' Unused to this attitude, the surgeon was a little formal.

'Fine. Any time you like.' He genuinely felt no nervousness at all.

On the chosen morning Parry Price breezed in again in the same check suit. 'You look disgustingly fit,' he boomed. 'What d'you weigh now?'

'Ten stone two.'

'Getting disgustingly fat,' boomed Price and breezed out again.

Brace came in with the pink liquid and injected it. Bader said: 'That sugar water won't send me to sleep.'

'Won't it?' she said. 'You wait and see,' but there was no answer from the sleeping patient.

Joyce sawed about two inches off the bone of the right stump, pulled the muscles down over the bevelled edges to make a pad at the base and sewed them underneath. On the left leg he took about an inch off the fibula, the little bone behind the shin. There was no hurry this time; the patient stood it easily.

Bader woke drowsily back in his bed, noted that the blankets were humped with the cradle again, and drifted off to sleep again. Hours later, nagging pain brought him more sharply awake; this time it was the right stump. The pain grew till it was like sharp teeth gnawing and tearing ceaselessly at the raw nerves and he was rolling his head from side to side in instinctive and futile struggles to get away from it. Dorothy Brace gave him morphia, but soon the pain cut through the drug and he began to sweat and make little involuntary sounds.

At intervals that he longed for, the morphia gave brief relief and then the attack started again, focused round the blunt end of the stump, where some major nerve seemed to be stretched on a rack. His mother and other visitors came, but, obsessed with the pain, he could not talk properly to them and did not want to be bothered. Even the top of the thigh seemed to have a sore patch, though they discovered the reason for that the first time Dorothy Brace changed his dressings; he flinched when she pulled out the top safety pin and she saw that the bandage had been pinned accidentally through his flesh.

The pain kept on and after a day or two visitors were discouraged. The patient was going downhill again, losing weight rapidly, the face growing grey and waxy under the sweat and the eyes sinking into the dark sockets. After a while his mind wandered into delirium and they began to get worried and increased the morphia to a maximum until he was unconscious for long stretches until resurgent pain or nightmares brought him out of it.

Night and day had no meaning and the nightmares came even in the stupor. Brace always knew when one was starting because he began twitching, then he would start waving his arms in front of his face as though he were trying to ward off something and call out: 'Get me out of here! I can't get out! I can't get out!' It was nearly always the same, but there was no escape from the pain. Joyce guessed that internal sutures must be pressing on the sciatic nerve, and it was a question of time until the sutures absorbed and relieved the pressure.

It was nearly a week before the pain began to ease, and then one day when Joyce looked at the stump he said: 'You've got a bit of haematoma here, old chap.'

Bader was too weak and exhausted to bother about what a haematoma was.

'Hang on to something,' Joyce went on. 'This might hurt a bit.' Almost before Bader was aware of it, he was sliding something sharp into the wound, and in the shock punch of agony, Bader grabbed the back of the bed in such a frenzied spasm that he bent the iron frame. The pool of blood that had been trapped tightly inside began seeping out, easing further pressure, and from that moment the last of the pain began to ebb. The fluid seeped for ten days, gradually turning almost white before it stopped. By that time the stitches were out and the physical battle was over. Then the mental battle started.

Perhaps it would not have been so bad if everyone had not tried so hard to reassure him. He himself had accepted that he was legless and in some ways the future was a challenge that was almost exciting. That perennially stimulating aspect made him eager to be out of bed and into the world to get at it; also a lot of encouraging pamphlets had arrived in the post from artificial limb-makers and they had braced him. Perhaps, through a little wishful thinking, he had read into them a little more than the authors intended or perhaps they were too rosy anyway. At any rate he had the feeling that when he got his new legs he would be able to carry on a reasonably normal life, not, perhaps, playing rugger, but playing cricket (with a chap to run when he was batting), maybe some squash, certainly walking and dancing (with a bit of a limp perhaps), driving a car, of course, and flying too. No reason why not. Flying was mostly eyes and hands and co-ordination, not feet. He'd be able to stay in the Air Force. After all, he knew of a Service pilot who had lost a leg in the war and still flew. Thornhill used to come over and tell him about a friend of hers who had lost a leg and still played tennis. One leg. Two legs. No legs! What the hell! He had strength and balance and with the latest tin legs he would be quite mobile.

Lying in bed he had begun working out a way to drive his car again. The short right stump would probably not be sensitive or quick enough to guide a leg working both accelerator and brake. But his left leg would. All right – he'd have the outside pedals transposed; work the clutch on the right with his right leg and use the left for both foot-brake and accelerator. The seat would slide back on runners so that he could climb in easily and then lock it in the driving position.

But gradually the drip-drip of grave but well-meant encouragement began to have a sinister effect.

'Of *course* you'll be all right,' they said. 'Of *course* . . .' trying just too hard to be convincing. . . . 'Of *course* they'll let you stay in the Air Force . . .' (They'll *let* me stay . . . Charity!) 'Even if you can't fly, they'll let you do a ground job.'

'For God's sake they *can't* throw me out of the RAF,' he used to say. 'I *know* I'll be able to fly still.'

'Of course you will,' they said soothingly.

The thought of a ground job while his comrades flew revolted him. They kept telling him about one-legged people who had made successes but he began to notice that no one seemed to know of anyone who had lost *both* legs and made a go of it. His mother said he was not to worry because she had signed a paper to look after him for the rest of his life and his insides seemed to twist at the thought of always being dependent on her. He began having dreams, and always in them he had his own legs, dancing or flying, playing rugger or running around doing all sorts of carefree things as he used to. It was such a cruel shock when he woke and remembered where he was. That kept happening night after night because his subconscious knew nothing about life without legs and so it ignored the loss.

Dorothy Brace noticed he was getting less open and cheerful, and sometimes for hours would lie back with his eyes open, silent and moody. It worried her because she guessed what was happening. The first spoken sign came on a day when he heard that Johnson, a friend on the squadron, had crashed and was killed.

She said to Douglas: 'You're darned lucky you didn't do that,' and he turned his head and said bitterly:

'*He's* the lucky one. He's dead. I'd rather be killed outright than left like this.'

Sometimes he was his cheerful self and at others, when he thought too much, the moodiness and silence would settle. He swung like an uncertain pendulum between the two. Out of the blue he said to Brace one day:

'They won't have me back in the Air Force, you know. And they won't give me a pension because they'll say it was my own fault.'

'You don't *know* anything of the sort,' she answered with practical sense. 'Anyway, you could still make yourself a new career in an office.'

'An office,' he said scornfully. 'Shut up in an office all day, tied to a desk and getting constipated on a stool! There'll be no life for me if I have to leave the Air Force.'

In one way separation from the Air Force would hurt him more than separation from his legs. The Air Force became a kind of symbol: return would mean that he was a normal man: rejection would mean that he was a helpless cripple.

Yet Brace was the only one who ever saw his depression and bitterness, and with unflagging warmth and an instinctive sympathy that never hurt she unobtrusively soothed, cheered and encouraged him in the way that is a woman's special gift. The two were so closely identified that they were virtually fighting the battle together (to such an extent that Bader ever since has claimed that Dorothy Brace saved his life). To others, the other nurses, his mother, Hilda, Patricia, Cyril Burge or his squadron friends he always cracked hardy, putting on a brash front, saying that he would rather lose both legs than one hand, that he was not disfigured, not helpless, and that he had seen chaps with one leg gone who were worse than he would be. There was never any self-pity and he never looked back thinking, If only I hadn't done it. He *had* done it, and knew it, and it could not be undone. It was that attitude which made his future possible.

Only once he said wryly to Dorothy Brace: 'Never do anything in a temper.'

He took to reading his old favourite, Swinburne, who appealed to some secret and cynical streak bred of juvenile hurt.

'Listen to this,' he said once and read to her:

> 'Thou hast conquered, O pale Galilean; the world has
> grown grey from thy breath;
> We have drunken of things Lethean, and fed on the
> fullness of death.
> Laurel is green for a season, and love is sweet for a
> day;
> But love grows bitter with treason, and laurel outlives
> not May . . .
> For the glass of the years is brittle wherein we gaze
> for a span;
> A little soul for a little bears up this corpse which is
> man.'

'He doesn't know love,' Brace said, giving a woman's viewpoint. 'I don't know whether you know it, but Hilda has been in love with you for a long time. The legs might worry you but they'll never worry her. She's ready to marry you, you know. You've only got to ask her.'

'Yes,' Bader said, 'I know. She's so utterly decent and kind. If I asked her to marry me she would . . . out of pity. They're all stirred by pity and hers would last, but I couldn't face it. If I ever marry it's got to be someone I meet for the first time just as I am now. Or no one.' Then he covered up with a brazen laugh: 'And if no one'll have me – hell, I'll marry *you*,' which reduced her to demonstrative indignation.

Yet he was increasingly attracted to Patricia and she, in her own impulsive way, to him. About this time her mother took her away to South America for three months. Neither she nor Douglas had any illusions about the reason for the trip. Her mother liked Douglas in an abstract way but did not approve of her growing feeling for a legless man; a trip away might be the best solution. It was a practical thing for a mother to do but it hurt Bader for a while, increasing his moodiness.

Slowly he began to emerge from his brooding. A stream of affectionate letters from the ship helped and so did the prospect of artificial limbs, but the greatest and most constant factor in his endurance and resilience all through the months since December lay in his eternal and aggressive response to any challenge, the quality in him that is least elegantly and most effectively expressed as guts.

Senior Air Force officers visited him at the hospital to hold a court of inquiry into the accident. It did not promise to be a cheerful affair and,

impressed by the braid and alarmed for her patient, Brace whispered to
him: 'If you're getting in an awkward spot ring the bell and I'll come in
and say you're not well and they must go.'

The door closed on the court and she spent a troubled hour until the
bell suddenly rang and she hurried grimly in to protect him. The officers
were sitting round the bed, everyone laughing and joking in great humour.
Bader called: 'Ah, tea for four, please, Nurse,' and, fear somersaulting
into feminine umbrage, she said severely: 'What d'you think this is – a
Lyon's cafe?' and swept primly out.

The Court of Inquiry's finding slid adroitly round the question of
blame, considering that whatever had happened, Bader had suffered more
than enough.

Soon he was up in the wheel-chair again, and a week after that was
stumping about the hospital garden on the pylon (luckily the left stump
still fitted into the leather socket). Now it was late March and stimulated
by the sunshine, the early spring air and the first green buds, he was
feeling eager to face the world again. One day he went outside the main
gate into Redlands Road, into the world again for the first time, and as
he stood on the pavement a peculiar sensation of naked insecurity suddenly
welled up as though a strong light were beating on him. He made himself
stump a hundred yards down to the other gate and thankfully went inside
again to the safe, home pasture. Trying it again that afternoon, he got
the same feeling of exposed vulnerability as soon as he got outside the
gate, and this time it was a shade worse because two people passed him,
staring at the peg-leg and the right trouser leg pinned high above the
knee. But after doing the same thing for three days the unpleasant feeling
eased a little.

The day came when he had to cross the road to meet Hilda, and as
he stood on the kerb a car whizzed past and a wave of dread chilled his
insides. It felt like stepping helplessly into a snakepit, but he made himself
do it, waiting till no cars were in sight and then hobbling across as fast
as he could, dimly realising that there would be a lot of strange and
terrifying plunges to take from now on and that, for a while at least, there
would be as many mental barriers to overcome as physical ones.

One important day Dorothy Brace and another nurse called a taxi and
took him to a cinema in Reading, and he was like a small child bubbling
with glee until the taxi pulled up outside the cinema. As he struggled out
in a tangle of peg-leg, crutches and helping nurses, people stopped and
stared: he did not see them until he straightened up, and then the cod-
like eyes seemed to hit him. Clustered faces of pity and vacuous curiosity
gave him the feeling of nakedness again, and he hobbled into the foyer
shrinking from it. Inside the darkened auditorium he sank into a seat
and felt all right again, normal and belonging with all the others, but

later, as he ran the gauntlet across the pavement to a waiting taxi, he heard a woman say: 'Oh, look, Jean, he's lost both of them.'

Dorothy Brace squeezed his hand in the taxi and said: 'Don't worry. You'll get used to it.'

After a few more days swinging along Redlands Road he found that he did, at least to some extent, being able to shut his mind to the curious stares almost completely.

About this time Audrey and Adrian Stoop several times drove him for tea to their home at Hartley Wintney about sixteen miles from Reading, and these sallies into the world were noteworthy for their pleasantness. Adrian Stoop, secretary of the Harlequins, was one of the best fly-halves ever to play for England, and his home was a lovely rambling red mansion set in acres of lawns and parkland where Bader was surrounded by friendliness with no prying eyes to stare.

In the middle of April came the time to leave Greenlands for good. He was still the Air Force's responsibility and they sent a car to take him to their hospital at Uxbridge. The nurses seemed more affected than the patient; most of them gathered on the steps, some in sentimental tears, and he kissed them all with his cheerful enthusiasm and was driven off to face whatever the future held.

CHAPTER SIX

Uxbridge was pleasant enough, but different. They were mostly male nurses, enlisted men, respectful but remote. In the ward, however, he was among old chums again; Flying Officer Victor Streatfeild with his arm in a cradle, Odbert, who had played rugger with him and was in with a slipped cartilage, and others of his own ilk, all barely mobile 'crocks' in some way so that he felt naturally at home among them. In fact, the RAF *was* his home; no other place gave him the same feeling and it linked him again with the past to which once more he belonged.

For a few days the usual Service restrictions irked a little, especially the hot day he stumped three-quarters of a mile to the Group Captain's house for 'elevenses' and struggled sweatily all the way back to arrive five minutes late for lunch. At the door a senior doctor, a wing commander, greeted him testily, 'Oh, Bader, I do wish you'd try to be on time for meals. It's an awful nuisance for the staff when you people come in late.'

He said, 'Yes, sir,' thought, 'You—!' and stumped into lunch fuming. It would never have happened at Greenlands; but then again, he thought philosophically, he would not have had quite the same companionship there. In any case, if he wanted to be a normal chap again he should expect that sort of thing.

His mother drove down from Yorkshire in the family car for a fortnight and took him for a drive most afternoons. The first time they went out she was driving along a quiet stretch of road in Great Windsor Park when he said: 'Stop a minute, Mother, will you?'

She stopped, and he said: 'Now let's change places. I'd like to have a crack at driving.'

She looked at him in horror but he bullied her until before she quite knew what was happening he was in the driver's seat and she was sitting in the passenger's, saying, 'But you can't. And what will happen if the police catch you?'

'We'll have a damn' good argument,' he said. 'Now, just put your foot on the clutch, will you?'

After more vain protests she did so. He selected the gear (the car had a pre-selector gear on the steering wheel) and said: 'Right. Now let it up.' She lifted her foot slowly, he pressed his peg-leg on the accelerator and off they went. It worked like a charm and as they went along he worked out a drill for changing gear. He'd say, 'Mother!' Her foot would go on the clutch, he would select the new gear, say, 'Right,' her foot would come up and that was all there was to it, apart from practice, concentration and co-ordination. After a couple of hours the team-work was quite good and his mother became enthusiastic. 'What a pity you can only drive with a partner beside you,' she said.

Pondering this limiting factor he thought out loud: 'If only I had something to prod the clutch with.'

'Well, dear, would my umbrella do?'

'Yes! That's a wonderful idea.'

She passed across her short, black umbrella, a very practical implement. He took it in his left hand, selected the next gear, held the wheel with the right while he felt for the clutch with the ferrule, pressed it down, let it up again and the car had changed gear smoothly. For several days he drove his mother like that and it seemed to open new windows in his limited world. This was being normal!

But there was still a catch. He could only use the umbrella on a car with a pre-selector gear. There was no way on a normal car of working both umbrella and gear lever with his left hand at the same time.

Patients at Uxbridge were not supposed to have cars but Peel, a young flying officer with a broken left leg in plaster, had an old Humber parked in a garage a few hundred yards away and he suggested to Bader and Streatfield that they should go for a surreptitious spin. In the safe period after lunch when the doctors had vanished for coffee the three cripples clumped down the road to the car. Peel's claim that he could still use his plastered leg on the clutch pedal turned out to be correct and cheerfully they cruised about the district. As the car had a normal gear lever Bader had no ambitions about driving it until going through Windsor Great Park again he noticed that it had a hand throttle on the steering wheel. It occurred to him that a hand throttle would spare the peg-leg to work the clutch.

'I could drive this car,' he said. 'Pull up and let's have a go.'

Peel very agreeably did so and left the engine running while Douglas slid behind the wheel. Streatfeild in the back started muttering: 'God, if I'm going to have my arm broken again I'd rather have a surgeon do it.' Bader pressed the clutch down with his peg, put the gear lever into first, and let the clutch up again, working the hand throttle, and they moved off smoothly. After a while he found that changing gear with two movements of the clutch called for tricky co-ordination but with the occasional crashes from the gear box, winces from Peel, and insults from Streatfeild, he managed reasonably well, though in due course they ran into Slough where the traffic was heavy and he began sweating with the concentration of slowing, stopping, restarting and slowing as they moved jerkily and noisily in the stream. It was easier to try and keep the car moving at all costs, even if only slowly in first gear, so he ploughed remorselessly on, butting, weaving and honking, carving a kind of bow-wave of squealing brakes on other cars and pedestrians jumping like startled springboks out of the way. Shouts of abuse rose in their trail but they blundered on with Streatfeild leaning out the back yelling: 'So are you! So are you! So are you!'

In due course in great good humour, Streatfeild said: 'It's four o'clock. How about stopping somewhere for a cuppa?'

'Good idea,' Peel said. 'Stop at the next place, Douglas.'

Bader promised to do so if he could.

As they came over a little bridge on the outskirts of Bagshot, Streatfeild said: 'There's the Cricketers pub. Let's stop there.'

But the pub was on the other side of the road and just as they neared it a stream of cars came the other way making it too awkward for the unpractised driver to ease up and swing behind them, so he took the easy way and said: 'Oh, hell. Let's go on a bit. Bound to be another place soon.'

Chance hangs on such slender threads. It was purely fortuitous that the other cars should be passing at that moment to force him on, but it was the luckiest thing that ever happened to him. A hundred yards on he saw a sign hanging out on the same side as the car: 'The Pantiles.' 'Morning Coffee. Lunches. Cream Teas.' He eased the car and swung off the road on to the gravelled apron in front of an attractive converted barn with leaded windows, surrounded by garden, shurbs and ornamental trees. Outside, people, mostly elderly women, were sitting sedately at little tables in the sun sipping their cups and delicately pronging bits of cake into their mouths. Streatfeild got out of the back with his arm in a cradle and they all looked up at him with mild curiosity. Peel stiffly clambered out of the front passenger's seat with his conspicuously plastered leg, hobbling with a pair of sticks, and the converging eyes softened in sympathy. Streatfeild leaned in, took the crutches out of the back and handed them to Bader as he got out, and when the women saw the third cripple emerge from the driver's seat and prop himself up on the crutches and a single peg-leg, the eyes stuck out like organ stops and an awed silence seemed to echo round the place.

No one said a word while the three hobbled to a table as though everything were quite normal, sat down and distributed sticks and crutches around them. They looked up as a waitress arrived at the table and the interest of all three quickened. She was a slim girl with a delicately modelled face and a sensitive, expressive mouth – very good looking. Bader was first off the mark, flashing his glowing smile and saying: 'Can we have three teas, please?'

'Cream or plain?' asked the girl.

The three men giggled faintly. 'Cream,' Bader said. (He never forgot the first words that he and the girl spoke to each other. It always seemed such a ludicrously banal start.)

As the girl went away Bader said to the others: 'And very nice too!'

'Wonder if there are any more like her,' Streatfeild said, looking round, but deciding soon that there were not.

The girl came back with the tea and laid it out in a faintly strained silence, conscious of being watched. Later when she came back with the bill Bader made a couple of facetious comments and once, briefly, she permitted herself a faint and dignified smile.

As the strange procession stumped back to the car everyone gaped again, especially when the one with the peg-leg got back into the driver's seat. With a grinding of gears the car jerked into motion and vanished into the traffic. The girl watched it go from the serving-hatch, feeling that the bold-eyed one with the peg-leg had an arresting personality.

On the way back to Uxbridge Bader was both concentrating on driving and thinking about the girl.

Next day when his mother took him out he artfully contrived that they should arrive at the Pantiles for tea and sit at the same table. The girl came over looking more attractive than ever and after some cogitation and discussion Mrs Hobbs decided on cream tea. As the girl went away Douglas said as casually as he could: 'That looks a jolly nice girl,' but his mother only said absently: 'Yes, dear. Rather a sulky mouth, though.' He concluded that she had not really noticed the girl at all.

A day or two later came the moment he had been waiting for. One of the Uxbridge doctors said: 'It's about time you got your new legs, Bader.

Your stumps should be all right by this so we're sending you over to Roehampton for measuring.'

Roehampton was a hospital in London where the Ministry of Pensions carried out its obligations. In the grounds were several wooden huts occupied by artificial limb makers, some specialising in legs and some in arms. The RAF car took Bader to the hut of the Dessoutter Brothers who used to make aeroplanes until Marcel Dessoutter lost his leg in an early crash and became interested in artificial limbs. Bader was introduced to the other brother, Robert, a short, thickset, vivacious man with a big face and a shock of dark, grey-streaked hair.

'You *are* an ass getting both of 'em messed up,' Dessoutter said. 'Let's have a look.'

Bader took his trousers down and showed the stumps. Dessoutter inspected them professionally and said: 'By jove those are good. Who did them for you?'

Bader told him about Leonard Joyce and added: ' . . . so now if you can trot me out a pair of pins I'll bung 'em on and get cracking.'

'Ha, we don't take 'em off the peg,' Dessoutter said. 'We tailor 'em to the stumps pretty carefully. It'll take a couple of weeks. How tall used you to be?'

'Five feet ten and a half in socks.'

'I see.' Dessoutter did some measuring and then slid thin socks over each stump and slapped plaster over them. Ten minutes later when he slid the casts and socks easily off, not a single hair came away. Bader watched the procedure with interest, beginning to be fascinated by the business.

'Right,' said Dessoutter when he had finished, 'I'll let you know in a couple of weeks when we're ready for a fitting. Send me an old pair of your shoes so I can give you the right-sized feet.'

'Get 'em fixed as soon as you can, would you?' Bader asked. 'There's rather a nice girl I want to take dancing.'

'We'll do the best we can for you,' Dessoutter said, thinking, incorrectly, that he was joking.

During those next two weeks Bader, unlicensed and uninsured, drove the Humber a lot in defiance of Air Force and Civil regulations, becoming quite competent and usually steering it to the Pantiles for tea till it became a kind of ritual which Peel and Streatfeild bore tolerantly. The girl always served him and every day the little chit-chat between them increased, though legs were never mentioned.

She was becoming rather important to him and he was beginning to realise that the situation was raising a new mental hurdle. Driving a car with companions in the normal world had lifted him out of the bitter moods of Greenlands but a girl, in the serious sense, was a different thing altogether. Though not depressed he was well aware that his future relationship with life was uncertain and somehow he did not feel justified yet in making any sort of advances. With confidence and bravura he could pat any other girl's bottom and kiss her till she giggled and said: 'Stop,' unconvincingly, but this girl was different and disturbing. He wanted to make advances and yet shrank from it, feeling that first he must sort things out, and also not wanting to spoil things by an ill-timed approach. All very complicating. Besides, there were Hilda and other girls, and affectionate letters coming from Patricia in South America. Outwardly as brash as ever, he was confused inside.

Some of the other girls took him driving and usually he steered them blandly to the Pantiles where the slim waitress, already very conscious of him, brought tea and went away thinking dubiously he was somewhat of a Casanova, legs or no legs.

The new legs might be his solution – when he got them! He yearned for the day they would be ready and he could put them on and walk out of Dessoutter's hut, free and exultantly independent again, almost like he used to be, except, he supposed, for a bit of a limp. He could stand with other people, with equality and with the blessing that they did not have of appreciating what it meant to be like them, however ordinary. He would drive his own MG straight to the Pantiles, walk in with full-length trousers and no crutches and sit at the old table. Then it would be different. He wrote to the garage at Kenley where the little MG was stored and told them to change the brake and clutch pedals and have it ready.

Dessoutter rang one day. He was ready for a fitting.

The first thing Bader saw when he stumped into the hut on the pylon were the new metal legs standing up incongruously without a body by the wall. Unpainted they looked shiny and new and covered in little rivets, nuts and screws, and he was amused to see that they wore socks and his own shoes.

'Ah,' said Dessoutter; 'handsome, aren't they? Look at those muscular calves.'

Bader grinned.

'You'll be about an inch shorter than you used to be,' Dessoutter went on.

The grin faded. 'Why?' Bader demanded indignantly.

'Gives you better balance. We always do that. If you want them longer we can always lengthen them.'

'As long as I can be as tall as any girl-friend.'

'You can marry an Amazon if you like,' Dessoutter said. 'We can make you seven feet tall.'

They went into the fitting-room, a long rectangular place with large mirrors at the end and what looked like parallel bars, but so low that a man could walk between them, holding on to the bars for balance. A middle-aged very fat man was standing there in shirt tails with a strap over one shoulder and a belt round his bulging abdomen to which a tin leg hung by straps. He looked so odd that Bader said with youthful and tactless impudence: 'I must say you look damn' funny.'

Justifiably annoyed, the fat man said: 'You won't think it so damn' funny when you try these things.' He stumped clumsily along to the far end and began pulling on his trousers.

'Sit down here.' Dessoutter indicated a stool and Bader, with a hand grabbing a crutch and another on the stool, eased his rump on to it and began the aggravating task of wriggling his trousers down over the buttocks he was sitting on. Dessoutter introduced two of his white-coated assistants, a jovial little man called Charlie Walker, and Tulitt, a big man with glasses. They made him strip to vest and underpants and then Walker, the 'below-the-knee' specialist, pulled a short woolly 'sock' over the left stump and slid it into a leather socket sunk in the calf of his new left leg. Above the calf, metal bars came up on each side like the ones on the peg-leg, hinged at the knee and ending in a lace-up leather corset. Walker laced the corset round the thigh.

'You'll find it a bit different to the pylon,' Dessoutter said. 'You've got ten inches of fairly rigid foot sticking out at the bottom and you'll have to lift your leg a big higher to get the toe clear.'

'All right,' Walker said. 'Hups-a-daisy.' He put the crutches under Bader's armpits and he and Tulitt helped him up. Bader stood firmly on the leg and it felt fine. Just fine. Much more solid, somehow, than the pylon. Leaning experimentally on it he felt a slight 'give' in the foot and Dessoutter explained that it was hinged at the instep with little rubber pads inset to allow a faint, resilient movement. The toe was jointed with a rubber pad too. Confidently Bader took a pace forward on the crutches and the wooden left toe caught on the mat and he nearly tripped.

'See what I mean about the stiffish foot,' Dessoutter said.

He tried again, lifting his leg like a high-stepping horse, and walked up and down the room like a one-legged man with crutches. 'Right,' he said with satisfaction. 'Let's have a go at the right leg.'

Tulitt brought it over. The thigh was a shaped metal cylinder that came right up to the groin and strung to it were straps leading up to a thick belt. With more straps looped on the top like a double military Sam Browne. Tulitt pulled a 'sock' on the right stump, eased the stump into the deep socket of the thigh and then buckled the belt to which it was attached round Bader's lower abdomen over his underpants. Over each shoulder he buckled the leather braces and then strapped the thigh corset of the left leg to the body-belt.

Bader sat in growing dismay, feeling he was being trussed into a strait-jacket. There seemed to be strap after strap and he felt irksomely constricted and uncomfortable.

'I'm afraid you'll have to have all this harness,' Dessoutter said; 'but you'll get used to it. Everybody does.'

Tulitt stepped back. 'All right,' he said. 'You'll do. No, never mind the crutches. Hups-a-daisy.'

This was the moment!

Walker and Tulitt took each arm round their shoulders and hauled him to his feet for the first time. As his weight came on both, especially the right stump, it was the worst shock he ever had. He felt absolutely hellish, wildly unbalanced and strange. His right stump was utterly helpless and uncomfortable to the point of hurting and the harness itself seemed to cripple him.

In stung despair he burst out: 'Good lord, this is absolutely impossible.'

'That's what they all say the first time,' Dessoutter said. 'You get used to it. Don't forget your right stump has done no work for nearly six months.'

Bader said grimly: 'I thought I'd be able to walk out of here and start playing games and things.'

'Look,' Dessoutter said gently, 'I think you ought to face it that you'll never walk again without a stick.'

Bader looked at him with tense dismay, and then as the challenge stirred him he said pugnaciously: 'Damn that! I'll never, *never* walk *with* a stick!'

In his stubborn anger he meant it.

'Try a step or two,' Dessoutter suggested.

Feeling he would be more secure staying on the left leg he tried to swing his right leg forward, but it did not move.

'How the hell do I get it to move?' he demanded.

'Try kicking the stump forward,' Dessoutter said. 'The right knee will bend automatically. Then when it's forward, kick the stump downwards and it'll straighten out on the heel. It's like cracking a whip.'

He kicked the stump forward and the metal knee bent as the leg went forward. He jerked the stump down and the knee straightened as the heel hit the mat.

'That's better,' Dessoutter said. 'Now come forward.'

Bader suddenly felt paralysed, unable to move. It was like having a chair back stuck under a door handle.

'How the devil *do* I?' he asked irritably. 'I *can't* move.'

'That's the big lesson you've just learned,' Dessoutter said. 'You haven't got any toe or ankle muscles now to spring you forward as you used to. That's the secret of it. Or the catch. That right leg is a firm barrier that you have to push yourself over, on top of, by leaning forward and by your momentum when you're moving.'

Bader said to Tulitt and Walker: 'Pull me forward over this damn' leg.'

They heaved him forward till he was precariously balanced on the weak right stump. Having his own knee, he was able quite easily to swing the left leg forward and then he stuck again, unable to push forward with toe and ankle.

'Pull me, for God's sake,' he said.

They pulled and he flicked his right stump forward again, and they pulled him on to it and he got his left leg forward once more; so it went on in clumsy, stiff, jerky movements as they pulled him the length of the room. There was no natural automatic movement at all; he had to think each step out in advance and then signal his mind to make the move. Whenever they eased the forward tug he felt that the stiff leg out in front would push him over backwards. At the end he lowered himself on to another stool and uttered with grim feeling: 'This is – awful.'

'It always is the first time,' Dessoutter said. 'Don't be too depressed. The first steps always feel like that. It's learning to walk all over again with an entirely new system and you can only learn it by practice, like playing the piano. Don't worry. You'll do it, but it might take you six months.'

Bader looked at him with a humourless grin. 'Don't be silly. There's a girl I want to see in a couple of days and I want to be walking with these things then.'

Dessoutter broke a slightly appalled silence: 'You'll find a stick useful in pushing yourself over the leg in front.'

Bader stuck his jaw out aggressively. 'Not me! Come on, you two. Let's have another go.'

They hauled him to his feet again and this time they took his elbows instead of having his arms round their shoulders. 'Try taking very short steps,'[1] Walker said. 'It'll be easier to lean forward over a short step.'

He tried that and the improvement was immediate. They still had to pull him forward, but he did not get quite the feeling of coming to a dead stop whenever he put a leg forward, especially the right leg. They went up and down the room several more times and slowly, subconsciously, he began to get the hang of it, leaning the top of his body well forward so that his unbalanced weight tended to carry him on to the leg placed just in front.

Dessoutter said after a while, 'Let's try taking half an inch off that right leg. Might make it a bit easier.'

Bader sat down and unstrapped it. Walker and Tulitt took it away for half an hour and lowered the thigh about half an inch into the knee socket. Bader put it on again and without so much height to overcome found that he could transfer his weight with a little less trouble. It was not so much that it was easier but just a little less impossible, still wildly

---

[1] This is one of the real secrets at the beginning.

clumsy and unnerving. They helped him up and down the room several more times and then he said: 'All right, now let me go.' They were too cautious to do so, so he shrugged his elbows to push them away and took his first steps alone, three or four jerky stumbles that ended with him just grabbing the parallel bars before he fell over. He hung on to them, grinning all over his face where the sweat was shining again. Turning to Dessoutter, he said: 'There you are. You can keep your damn' sticks now.'

Dessoutter was laughing in genuine delight. 'I've never even seen a chap with *one* leg do that before first time,' he said. Walker and Tulitt were openly surprised, obviously not pretending.

'I think you've done enough for to-day,' Dessoutter said; 'you must be feeling pretty tired.'

That was true enough. He was hot, and sweaty, beginning to feel exhausted, and the right stump was stiff and sore. As he strapped on the peg-leg again Dessoutter suggested he come back for more practice in a couple of days; meanwhile he would 'pretty up' the legs with paint and other finishing touches. Bader got up with his crutches to leave and this time the peg-leg felt strange in an unpleasant way, unsteady and uncomfortable. Back at Uxbridge when he hobbled in Streatfeild bellowed: 'Hallo, here's Long John Silver again. I thought you were coming back on your own two pins this time?'

'I was going to,' Bader said; 'but I forgot to take a clean pair of socks.'

Thinking in bed that night, he did not feel so flippant. It was not like he thought it was going to be at all. Little needles of doubt were pricking him. He supposed, a little doubtfully, that it would be all right with practice.

Back at Roehampton in a few days he found the legs painted a smart yellow. 'Looks more natural than any other colour through a thick sock,' Dessoutter explained. 'Don't ask me why.'

Walker and Tulitt walked him up and down the room again and it was still hellish, but not quite as bad as the first time he had tried. After a while he made them loosen their grip and with their hands hovering by his elbows he was able to walk the length of the room. Standing facing the wall he found a new problem – he could not turn. In exasperation, hands steadying him against the boards, he said to the wall, 'What the hell does a man do now?' The others turned him round and back at the parallel bars the same thing happened. It seemed impossible to turn his feet round. He lurched back to the other wall and this time as he neared it he teetered round in a tight semi-circle, fending himself off against the wall. For two hours he practised that morning until he was almost too tired to stand.

'I honestly think you're incredible,' Dessoutter said as he unstrapped the legs. 'None of us have ever seen anyone like you before.'

Walker and Tulitt inspected the stumps for raw patches of chafing, but they seemed all right. Bader wanted to take his legs away there and then, but Dessoutter said there were still a couple of adjustments he wanted to make.

It was a glorious spring morning when Bader drove back to Roehampton to take delivery and his spirits were soaring at the prospect. He thought it must be the way a woman felt on her way to pick up a new fur coat. Dessoutter had a set of three shallow wooden steps with bannisters in a corner of the room and when he had put the legs on and tried a couple of circuits round the room, he made his first attempt at the steps. With the bannister to support him, it turned out to be relatively simple – hand on the rail to steady him, left foot on the first step, bring up the right foot to the same step, and then lift the left foot again. Thank God he still had one knee left to raise himself with or it would have been impossible. Coming down was the same thing. He called it the 'dot-and-carry' system and he never used any other for stairs. That morning he learned how to get up out of a chair without help too – lean forward, a good shove on the seat of the chair with both hands and the left knee took the strain and lifted him.

'Well, there you are,' Dessoutter said. 'They're all yours. It's a bit soon to let you have them really, but I suppose you'll only start complaining if you don't take them.' He grinned. 'Shall I wrap them for you?'

'Not on your life,' Bader grinned back. 'I'm walking out on 'em. Here, catch this . . .' He threw him the peg-leg and nearly fell over in the process. 'You can do what you like with that.'

'Now what about a stick,' Dessoutter suggested persuasively.

'Never!' he answered crisply. 'I'm going to start the way I mean to go on.'

For the first time he began putting the rest of his clothes on over the legs and harness, the shirt over the belt and shoulder straps, the trousers over the legs. Ah, here was another catch! He had to lift the right leg with a hand round the thigh to do it, and then found that with the foot sticking rigidly out he could not point his toes to slide into the trouser leg. The heel and toe caught and he had to ease the foot through the cloth by tugging on each crease alternately.

'Oh, another point,' Dessoutter said. 'Never try and walk barefoot. It's difficult and you'll probably fall flat on your back. You'll notice that the feet slope down at a slight angle. That's because shoes have thick heels and you'll always need a heel underneath to put you on an even keel.'

He put on his tie and jacket, stood up and teetering round, looked at himself in the mirror. He looked *quite* normal. It was a terrific moment. Heart-swelling! He was *standing up* – dressed like an ordinary chap –

looking like one. And, after seven months, suddenly feeling like one again. Perhaps he looked a bit shorter than before, about five feet nine and a half now so that the trousers crinkled slightly at the ankles. A detail. With great satisfaction he said: 'It looks damn' good to be standing up like this again.'

As Walker and Tulitt helped him totter out to the waiting car he became irksomely conscious of the harness. Under his clothes it seemed worse than before cripplingly uncomfortable, as bad as walking with a stone in one's shoe . . . in the circumstances a ridiculous comparison, he thought wryly. But he'd have to wear it for the rest of his life! A grim thought. Maybe he'd get used to it . . .

As they handled him into the car Dessoutter said: 'Don't worry if you have a bad time for a while. You've done amazingly well so far, but don't expect it to go on as fast as that. Everyone feels desperate for a while.' They shouted 'Good luck!' through the glass and the car moved off. He relaxed, satisfied, on the soft seat and discovered a new catch. He could not cross his legs.

CHAPTER SEVEN

When the car pulled up just before lunch in front of the Uxbridge hospital doors an orderly helped him out and the wing commander who had once ticked him off for being late for lunch was standing by the door talking to another doctor. Bader pushed away the orderly who was fussing at his elbow and lurched with tense concentration about six paces to the door feeling snugly proud, like a girl in a new party dress which is bound to be noticed.

The wing commander briefly turned his head, said curtly: 'You ought to have a stick, Bader,' and turned back to the other doctor. Bader tottered angrily through the door, praying that he would not fall.

In the dining-room the greeting was hearteningly different. There were roars of welcome and ribald remarks. Streatfeild bawled: 'Long John's got his ruddy undercarriage back.' He walked across to them, concentrating too much to make any answer and feeling that he was going to spoil his entrance at any moment by making a three-point landing and denting his tail-skid. One of them pulled out a chair and he just made it. Lunch was eaten in great jollity.

'No doubt any moment now you'll be wanting to dash off to the Pantiles,' Streatfeild suggested banteringly.

'Not on your life,' he said. 'I'm going to learn to walk on these pins first and the next time I go there I'll be driving my own car.'

His ward was on the first floor and after lunch he tottered out to the stairs. They looked appallingly high and steep, but he dragged himself up and was sweating at the top. In the ward he tried to give a demonstration of walking, lurching a precarious way from bed to bed, grabbing each bed-rail as he reached it, and encouraged by cheerful barracking from patients in the beds. But after a few minutes he was so tired he could hardly stand and the right stump was trembling and aching with weakness. He tried again an hour later but after one circuit sweat was soaking him all over and the right stump was threatening to collapse under him, the muscles shrunken, weak and flabby after so long without use. He was beginning to realise that it was not going to be so easy and for the rest of the day he relaxed to give the stumps a chance to recover.

At dinner-time he was able to struggle downstairs, but when he went to climb back he just could not do it; the strength was drained out of him and he was aching all over. A burly orderly carried him up with Bader's arms round his neck, body dangling over his back, and lowered him on to his bed. Lying there, Douglas undressed and with enormous relief unstrapped his harness and carefully leaned the legs against the wall where they would be nicely within reach. He thought it was smart of him to remember that, but the thought was interrupted by a minor clatter as the legs fell over on to the floor, looking obscene and disembodied with shoes and socks on. Too tired to pick them up, he swore and crawled between the sheets.

Shortly another thought stirred. Damn! He hadn't cleaned his teeth. Oh, let it go till morning for once. A little later he came out of a doze wanting to go to the toilet. Damn! He'd forgotten that too. Well, it would *have* to wait till morning. Sinking down again he wanted to blow his nose and found he did not have a handkerchief. That was the last straw and he started muttering unprintably. In that mood there was not going to be any sleep and at last he testily reached out for his legs but could not reach them on the floor. He rang for an orderly who picked them up and offered to carry him, but no – he laboriously strapped on all the harness, got a handkerchief, tottered into the bathroom and did all he wanted to, then tottered back to bed, making sure this time that the legs stood up within reach. Very tired he was drifting off to sleep when he began to feel thirsty. Firmly he put it out of his mind and rolled over, but the desire for a drink of water crept insidiously back and the more he tried to forget it the more he wanted a drink and the angrier he became. Damn and blast! No drink – no sleep, that was obvious. But he was damned if he was going to strap that flickering harness on again. Tossing the blankets back, he lowered his rump on to the floor by taking his weight with hands on the bed and the bedside table, then swinging himself along on his hands and bottom he got to the bathroom.

Then he couldn't reach the tap.

Muttering, he pulled a stool across, hoisted his rump on to it with a hand on the edge of the bath, took a drink from a tooth-glass and 'walked' on hands and rump back to his bed where with a last strenuous effort, hands on bedside table and bed, he hoisted himself back on to the sheet. Temper cooling off as he drifted tiredly into sleep he realised that going to bed would have to be an organised ritual before removing the legs.

In the morning as he woke he remembered with satisfaction that he was mobile and, after the previous night's lesson, lay a while planning procedure. Was it worth putting on his legs to walk to the bath, taking them off and putting them on again afterwards? No. He went to the bathroom on his rump and put his legs on afterwards. Clutching the banister rail he dot-and-carried alone down the stairs to breakfast and after that teetered out into the garden, where he got another shock as he stepped on to a patch of grass and instantly felt as dismayingly insecure as the first time he had stood on the legs. It was fairly level grass, but it was no firm level floor and he felt that he would topple if he moved. He took a step, the right toe immediately hit a clump of grass and he pitched forward – his first fall. He took the shock on his hands. That part was all right, but now he had to get up again. He lay for a while thinking about it. A man came running up and said sympathetically: 'Hang on to me, old boy. Soon have you up.'

'Go away,' he snapped. 'I'll do this.'

He took his weight on his hands and lowered the rear weight on to his left knee, then pushed hard. In a moment he had fallen back on his hands again. He tried again, pushing up on the left toe, straightening his left knee, and pushing his hands back towards the toe, and came uneasily but without too much difficulty to his feet again. Then he took another step and fell again.

That morning he fell at least twenty times but managed to stumble up and down the grass again and again, arms flailing to keep his balance like a novice on ice skates, but persisting until his legs were aching and trembling with exhaustion again. Worse, the right stump was sore in spots – obviously chafing. The difficulty of walking on anything but the smoothest floor was worrying him. That was the worst part of all. There would be more rough paths than smooth paths in life, and the airy confidence he had had was rattled.

After lunch he got the orderly to carry him upstairs to the ward where he practised from bed-rail to bed-rail again. Soon he was in agony from the chafed right stump and had to struggle to his bed. Unstrapping all the harness and taking off the stump sock he found that the skin round

the groin was rubbed raw in a couple of places. If the future was going
to be like that . . .

With a sudden idea he called an orderly to bring him some sticking
plaster and taped it over the raw parts, put his legs on and tried again.
It was a little better, but then the whole stump was so stiff and sore that
it was hard to tell which part hurt most. That evening a nurse put some
of her cold cream on the raw patches and it was very soothing.

In the morning a car drove him back to Roehampton.

'I thought you'd be back about this time,' Dessoutter said. 'Let's have
a look at those stumps.' He, Tulitt and Walker spent about two hours
adjusting the sockets of the legs.

'Remember it's darned hard for you to tell yet whether there's anything
wrong with the fit,' Dessoutter observed. 'They'll feel awful for a while
anyway, like false teeth when you first put them in. Later, you'll know
anything not fitting in a moment.'

Bader went back to Uxbridge to try again, but they seemed no better.
For two days he stumbled about, continually falling, curtly refusing any
help and getting up unaided to lurch and fall again. Mostly he fell
forward, sometimes backwards, two or three times sideways, sometimes
on hard floors, often on the grass. As he did not fall on the stairs where
he had a banister to cling to the others kept suggesting he use a stick but
he refused tersely. From the parallel bars at prep. school and the years
of rugger he had no fear of falling and that was the big thing that helped.
If he had worried about falling he would probably have been beaten.

Hour after hour he doggedly kept at it when other men would have
given up to rest or despair. Moving the stiff, chafing and aching stumps
was continual torment but he made himself keep on doing so, his face
running with sweat that poured off all over him, soaking his underclothes
and, unfortunately, the stump socks too, so that they lost their woolly
softness and began chafing again, rubbing the skin off in new spots. The
good-humoured barracking that had greeted his first efforts died away
as people became aware that they were watching a man battling to do
something that had never been done successfully before, with only his
guts to help him and a crippled life ahead if he failed. It was something
that could not be laughed off.

Refusing to accept that it was impossible kept him going. He insisted
that he *knew* he could learn to manage the legs with practice. In a way
he was like a man trying to run before he could walk because he would
not stop trying and the right stump was not strong enough to take the
punishment. The more he forced himself to walk the more it hurt, tending
to become a vicious circle and making it even more difficult. Now and
then he *had* to rest a little because the stump would not hold him, and
then he tried again.

Soon, stumps plastered like a quilt, the car took him to Roehampton again where Dessoutter found that the right thigh seemed to have shrunk. In due course, he said, they would rivet the metal a little tighter, and meanwhile he slipped a second stump sock over it. That felt better, and then Dessoutter found a hard muscle developing at the back of the thigh and with a little hammer Tulitt tapped out an almost imperceptible indentation in the metal to accommodate it. To reduce sweat and chafing Dessoutter suggested keeping both stumps well powdered. Then Walker laquered the leather socket of the left leg so that the sides would not hold perspiration. Bader found it fascinating to watch their ingenious approach to each new problem.

But the main problem, the sheer clumsiness, they could not help. Dessoutter, who had noticed the new grimness in Douglas, said: 'Look, in this business I've seen that only people who've actually lost a leg can know the shock of awkwardness when they first try an artificial one; it's just a thing they have to work on till they develop a new skill. Most of them take months to learn. Some never do. In a way it's like a chap starting to play tennis from scratch and having to work up to Wimbledon standard. Chaps who lose one leg have still got a good one to rest and hop on and an ankle and toe to give them spring when they're walking. You haven't, so you've just got more to learn. And it's still harder for you because there's no one with no legs to teach you. There aren't any text books either.'

Back at Uxbridge he kept trying but it seemed impossible to acquire balance and natural movement, and still he kept falling. Gradually he found the right stump did not ache so much, as the flabby muscles hardened with use and the chaffing came under control, but that eased only the pain; the legs were as unwieldy as ever, yielding no fraction to practice and bringing growing disillusionment and anguish as he woke from the dreaming expectations of normality and cricket. Mentally, it was the worst time since the accident. His nature, in any case rejected defeat and now the menacing implications produced obsession to master the legs. The others learned not to try and help him up or steady him as he lurched, realising it was a battle that he himself had to fight. Besides, trying to help only produced rebuffs. He wanted passionately to be independent as much as he wanted to be mobile. It goaded him to think of having to ask help in the simple, physical things of life and he shrank from the idea that people in due course would politely prefer to avoid him as being a nuisance.

He began dreaming about his legs again, not as at Greenlands, about having his real ones back, but something more wickedly subtle. In these new dreams he had his artificial legs – he could see them and they had the nerveless artificial feel – but he was using them easily like his real ones, running around exuberantly, leaping up and down stairs and even, on one bitter-sweet occasion, kicking a football. Waking up was not pleasant.

And then, about ten days after he got his legs, he detected the first hint of automatic control. It was a little like a man learning a strange language that sounds like gibberish until one day he catches a phrase and understands it. As though some barrier had been removed, he began walking a little more easily and after that the improvement was rapid. In five days he was lurching about without having to concentrate so hard either on movement or balance; some automatic instinct seemed to have taken over part of the work. It was not easy, far from it; it was still hard work, but not intolerably hard. He still fell, but not so often. The stumps still chafed, but not badly, and they did not ache or twinge any more. The legs still felt uncomfortable when he strapped them on[1] but after a few minutes he became a little more used to them, though the harness remained just plain, bloody uncomfortable. Best of all was the change in the mental climate as hope, a little qualified, came back. It was strengthened when he went all through one day without falling and also learned to turn by spinning on his right heel.

He telephoned the garage at Kenley and asked them to drive his car over (the doctors gave him permission to have it – good occupational therapy, they said).

'Off to the Pantiles?' Streatfeild asked, and he nodded.

'Ah, well, jolly good luck to you. I kept telling you you'd be all right but all you did was be ruddy rude. There's only one thing you've got to learn now and that's to change your socks now and then. It's getting a bit noticeable already.'

'Why should I?' Bader grinned. 'I haven't even taken my shoes off for two weeks.'

'Please yourself,' said Streatfeild; 'but I can just imagine people some day muttering to each other, "Don't go too near Bader, he's still wearing those same purple socks he had on at Uxbridge twenty years ago".'

Changing into his best clothes that morning while waiting for the car, Bader did take his shoes off and was amazed to see that his socks had practically no feet on them. No only the heels and toes were worn away but almost the whole of each foot as well. He realised it must be because there was friction now on each side of the sock where before there had been soft, yielding skin on one side. Changing his socks, he hobbled out and got a thrill as he saw the familiar old MG with the red wings swing through the gate.

'Cor, I 'ad a time driving it over,' the mechanic said. 'Kept putting my

---

[1] As another man pulls on his shoes and laces them up, Bader pulls on his legs and buckles and laces them up.

foot on the brake to change gear and then treading on the clutch to stop. Be careful with it, sir.'

'You seem to have made it all right.'

'Yes, sir,' the mechanic said. 'In the end I crossed me legs and drove that way.'

Bader heaved himself into the seat behind the wheel. His feet seemed to fit easily enough over the pedals. He pressed the clutch down with the right leg – it was purely a thigh movement with no feeling in the leg or foot at all but he *could* feel the pressure of the clutch against his thigh with enough sensitivity to control it and let it up slowly. He tried the left foot on brake and accelerator and found there was enough feeling in the shin to switch the foot from one to the other. That was strictly a knee movement, but the whole thing seemed to be easier than he had expected. He felt no tendency to use the accelerator with the right leg because it felt obviously too remote, in the way that a man who had lost his right arm would not try to steer with the missing arm. He started up and drove slowly round the asphalt parade ground: no trouble in keeping an even pressure on the accelerator and no tendency to do the wrong thing. For a quarter of an hour he drove in figure eights, stopping, starting and reversing, and was highly gratified. It was almost literally driving a car by the seat of his pants and rather a good augury for the time he started flying again. Doubts were vanishing fast. Now he knew he could go anywhere he liked at any time and was even more mobile than people who had only their legs and no car. Altogether a most prepossessing day. With his old confidence he said to Streatfeild: 'Like falling off a log. Now we're off.'

'God be with you,' Streatfeild said: 'I suppose they'll bring you back without a head this time.'

He steered out of the gates and drove in a sunny mood and at a cautious speed to Kingston Police Station where he lurched with care up to a uniformed man behind a desk and said: 'I'd like to take a disabled driver's test, please.'

'Certainly sir,' said the constable.

'It's just that I've got no legs, but I can handle the car perfectly well.'

He might have been remarking that it was a nice day for all the reaction he got; one would have thought that legless men popped in for driving tests every day. Soon a man in civilian clothes came out and got into the car with him. Bader drove away from the kerb explaining the transposed pedals, but the man did not seem interested. After a couple of hundred yards he said: 'Stop and reverse across the road, will you, please?'

Bader stopped, looked behind to see if everything was clear and reversed as directed.

'Glad to see you look behind first,' the man said. 'Last chap didn't do that. If you'd like to drive me back to the station you can fill out the form and we'll give you your ticket.'

It was as easy as that.

Blithely he set off for the Pantiles and pulled into the gravelled apron about quarter to four. This time as he got out and lurched to the usual table hardly anyone looked except the girl. Out of the corner of one eye he saw her over by the serving hatch, staring, but he kept looking straight ahead concentrating on appearing casual about his metamorphosis. She came across to the table looking very bright and he switched on the glowing grin. With a little less reserve than usual she remarked that he had not been there for some time and he was delighted that she was too discreet to mention the legs, though he had been quite sure that she wouldn't. But it made everything so natural, as though there were nothing at all remarkable about his walking. He chatted before he ordered and chatted again when she brought the tea, and again when she brought his bill. He paid her, got up, stumped over to the car, praying that he would not fall, turned round – she was still watching – and gave her an enormous wink. As he drove away he wondered what her name was.

Now with the car and able to walk, even if still precariously, life took on a new savour and he drove out every day to sample it. Most days he arrived at the Pantiles for tea and the friendship with the girl progressed quietly and decorously with no particular move on either side. He still had to find out where he stood in regard to life.

Patricia wrote from the ship in Madeira, just a brief note to say that she was due back in a fortnight and hoping he was getting along well. That was something more to sort out.

Kendall, the Warden of St Edward's School, had been writing to him constantly and encouragingly ever since the accident and Bader wrote to let him know how successful the new legs were. Back came a suggestion from the Warden: Why not play in the Old Boys' cricket match in a few weeks?

Just that little touch gave Bader a thrill and he wrote back a joyful acceptance.

Several times in this period he went to the Stoops at Hartley Wintney and once stayed the night, scaring the life out of a maid in the morning by bouncing down the stairs on his rump and hands because for some small unremembered errand he could not be bothered to put his legs on. They were still uncomfortable, especially the wretched shoulder straps that seemed to tie him up so that he felt hobbled. Now and then the stumps still chafed or hurt in other ways, but he was able to control those things with powder and sticking plaster. Yet, all the time he was becoming more sure of them, though he still fell from time to time. Audrey Stoop said one day, 'Honestly, Douglas, no one would know that you haven't got your own legs.'

'Oh, don't be silly,' he said. 'Anyone would know.' But, absurdly pleased, he got down on his knees and turned a somersault on the lawn. 'I've been dying to do that,' he beamed.

From time to time the Stoops introduced him to other visitors who were never told, at least till later, that he had no legs, and they were therefore quite natural with him, regarding him only as a young man with a bad limp. Natural reactions like that were good for him; he was already aware of a subtle, constrained atmosphere with some strangers who already knew. They took him one night to a nearby party where someone started playing a gramophone and couples began dancing. Bader, aflame with a new challenge, had to try. He asked a girl to dance; she smiled and got up, and as they started he caught his toe and fell, luckily not dragging her down with him, but as he got clumsily to his feet she said tartly: 'You're drunk,' and left him. Later she was horrified when she found out, but she need not have worried because the incident did not trouble Bader, who was too practical to have any pity for himself.

At Hartley Wintney he met a young flying officer who had had an accident which left him with a stiff knee so that he could not fly any more. Bader picked up his own right leg and waggled the knee. 'There you are,' he said. 'Have it off, old boy. Have it off.' It became his standard joke to anyone with a sore leg.

The Stoops had a testy old wire-haired fox-terrier called Worry who was half-deaf and jealous of his little privileges such as lying in the same spot every night under the dinner-table. Bader was dining with them one night when he moved his legs under the table too near Worry and jerked them away again as a menacing growl came up. Then he remembered and put them back in the objected place. The dog growled again and suddenly snapped at his ankle, bit on the metal and recoiled from under the tablecloth with the hair along his back bristling with shock.

About the middle of June he suggested some sick-leave, and O'Connell, the young doctor who was looking after him, said it was a good idea. He'd better take a couple of months and get really used to life outside again. Rather than go all the way home to Yorkshire straight away Bader said he would go to Kenley for a couple of weeks so that if anything more went wrong with the legs he would be within easy reach of Roehampton.

With nostalgic eagerness for the familiar faces and atmosphere he drove himself to Kenley and walked into a deserted mess, full only of empty memory. A waiter he did not recognise said that most of the pilots were away on an air-firing course at Sutton Bridge. Then Harry Day, who was waiting for a posting overseas, walked in and saved the moment. 'Hey, hey,' Day said cheerfully. 'What've we got here. Good lord, you look like a drunken sailor.' Then the mess sergeant came along beaming with pleasure and said he could have his old room back.

He felt a queer moment of pleasure when he looked again at the spartan bed, the lino, rug, chair and the bookshelves. It was even his old batman who answered the bell, and said warmly: 'Why Mr Bader, sir, it's good to see you back.'

Bader shook his hand. 'It's good to *be* back,' he said. 'I'm staying for a while. Have you still got my kit here?'

'Yes, sir,' said the batman. 'All safely in store. I'll go and bring it straight up.'

Soon he was back with the trunks and Bader rested in the chair while the batman began hanging up the clothes and stowing shirts and things in drawers. There was an awkward moment when, delving into a trunk, he pulled out a pair of rugger boots; their eyes met for a moment and the batman put the boots back in the trunk. A little later Bader said: 'Bring up my cricket-bag, will you?'

Next afternoon was very hot and Day suggested he join his family for a swim – Day had a lovely home with a handsome, blue-tiled swimming-pool on a Surrey hill near Kenley. That raised a new problem. He also had three children.

Bader asked awkwardly: 'Will the youngsters mind if they – er – see me?'

'Good lord, no,' Day said. 'They'll probably be fascinated.'

While the others changed in the house Bader walked the hundred yards across the lawns to the pool, took his legs off and changed under a tree, then rump-walked to the edge of the pool and lay on the grass waiting. When the children came down – girls of eight and three and a boy of six – he was feeling uncomfortably self-conscious but the youngsters, apparently well briefed, did not seem to notice anything unusual.

'Slip in over the side,' Day said, 'and I'll stand by in case you're top-heavy and turn upside down.'

'Hell, no,' he said. 'I'm going in off the springboard.'

At the deep end the springboard jutted over the water from a platform on stilts about eight feet high. He rump-walked to it and hauled himself up the short ladder with his hands (his arms were getting very strong now) holding his weight between hauls with the right stump on the rungs. Then he swung to the end of the springboard, stood on his hands and dived in. Spouting water and grinning, he surfaced (right way up), finding himself more buoyant in the water without his legs, though swimming seemed more tiring because he could not kick to help himself along and, instead of being top-heavy, his rump tended to sag in the water instead of trailing in the normal flat position. But they were details; just being in the water felt glorious.

Having tea on the grass afterwards the children's curiosity overcame their briefing and they stared frankly and with great interest at the stumps, but so innocently and naturally that he was not in the least embarrassed. All afternoon they alternately swam and lay in the hot sun which was good to feel on his bare and pallid skin after the months indoors.

Round about seven the family went back to change and Douglas dressed on the lawn. As soon as he started walking back to the house he felt the shoulder straps chafing his shoulders and realised with annoyance that he was sunburned. By the time he reached the house they were beginning to hurt. He was up against a new problem. Even sitting down at dinner the straps chafed and irritated, and by the time he got back to his room in the mess he was glad indeed to take them off.

In the morning when he got up the shoulders were red and very tender. He strapped the legs on but as soon as he stood up the straps bit into his shoulders like hot bread-knives scraping on the nerves and he sat down hurriedly, wincing, and slipped them off with relief, swearing with frustration. From a little thing like that he was helpless again, unable even to get to the dining-room for breakfast unless he submitted to the unthinkable indignity of the rump-walk in public. More than ever he loathed the shoulder straps.

In desperation he unbuckled them from the belly-belt hoping he might be able to struggle out cautiously without them. After pulling the belt fairly tight, he eased himself up from the bed and gingerly took a few steps; to his amazement and delight the legs felt better than ever before and just as secure. For several minutes he stumped about the room, an odd sight in creaking legs, vest and underpants, and everything he did felt better. After that he tossed the shoulder straps into a corner, dressed and stumped out to breakfast. (He never wore the shoulder straps again.)

Patricia was due back and he rang her home. The butler said yes, she had returned and went to find her, but came back soon to say she was not in. 'Ask her to ring me, would you?' Bader said.

No call came in the next three days, but on the fourth morning a letter arrived from her. It was only about four lines and the line that mattered was, 'I don't think it's any good us going on any longer . . .' It was the first time that he felt he did not belong, was not exactly a wallflower, or a leper, but a man apart. Years later he told me it bounced off his back. It didn't. In an unguarded moment it brought him facing a stark and ugly possibility that he had refused to admit into his controlled thoughts, though it had always haunted the background. The girl herself did not mean a great deal to him but bitterly he felt that she might at least have made some other excuse than hinting so badly that the trouble was that he had lost his legs. That letter rubbing it in loosened some of the roots of his robust but none-too-firmly planted confidence. Outwardly he was as breezy as ever when pilots came back from air firing but in private he had hours of encroaching doubt which, in the end, only made him more stubbornly set on making no major concessions to life and requiring the same important things as anyone else. Several times he went to the

Pantiles and the fact that the girl was so clearly glad to see him, accepting him as he was, strengthened his morale.

A pleasant note came to him from the Under Secretary of State for Air, Sir Philip Sassoon, inviting him for a week-end at his house near Lympne. Clearly it would be not only a pleasant week-end but a chance to find out where he stood for his future in the Air Force: once at Cranwell he had briefly met Sassoon and everyone in the RAF seemed to like and admire him for his hard-working helpfulness. Sassoon even suggested that he bring a young man from the squadron with him as companion so he drove down in the MG with Peter Ross, a thickset, lively young pilot officer with whom he had become friendly.

Sassoon was a millionaire and his house was a mellow old mansion set among cypress trees on a slope beside Lympne Aerodrome where 601 Auxiliary Squadron was busy flying Hawker Demon two-seater fighters on its annual summer camp.

The Saturday afternoon they spent lying beside the swimming pool with the Demons taking off and noisily climbing just over the pool and the tree-tops. As one of them roared over Bader said wistfully: 'By gosh, I wish I were up there again.' He turned to his host and added: 'You know, sir, I'm quite sure I could fly perfectly well now. It'd be easier than driving a car – not so much footwork.'

'Well, they've got an Avro 504 on the aerodrome,' Sassoon said. 'Would you like to have a shot at it?'

'I'd *love* to,' Bader said, exhilarated and hardly believing, and Sassoon promised to arrange it. Bader spent the rest of the afternoon in nervous hopes that Sassoon would not forget, but at dinner that night Sassoon said: 'I've had a word with the CO of 601. The Avro will be ready for you in the morning, and Ross can go with you in the other cockpit.' They were the most melodious and exciting words he had ever heard.

CHAPTER EIGHT

In the morning it felt wonderful just to be putting on overalls, helmet and goggles again and to be walking up to a well-remembered Avro.

'Take it as long as you like,' Norman, the CO of 601 said. 'All I ask is bring it back in one piece.'

Getting into the cockpit was not the trouble he thought it might be. He put his foot into the slot at the side of the rear cockpit and Ross gave him a heave up. Then, clutching the leather-padded rim of the cockpit with his left hand it was simple to grab his right calf and swing it over into the seat. He eased himself down, delighting instantly in the old, familiar smell of an Avro cockpit, the blend of castor oil, dope, leather and metal that rolled the months back more subtly and potently than any other sense. Sitting in the familiar seat, eyeing instruments and crash-pad and taking the stick in his hands, sent a flush of enchantment through him. He set each foot on the rudder-bar and pushed each end in turn – it was easy; nerveless in the foot but sensitive in the shin and right thigh. He'd literally be flying by the seat of his pants.

Ross climbed into the front and shortly his voice came through the earphones: 'Shall I start her up from here, Douglas?'

'No,' he said; 'just turn on your switches and take your hands off. Leave everything alone. I'll do it.'

The Huck starter backed up and turned the propeller; the warmed-up engine caught smoothly and throatily and the aeroplane was quivering with life. He ran up to test magnetos, set the cheese-cutter trim in neutral, waved the chocks away and taxied carefully downwind, jabbing the rudder and finding it easy to steer. Turning at the hedge he saw the grass stretching down to Romney Marsh, pushed the throttle forward and the engine let out a deep, hearty bellow. She started rolling, and as the tail came up and she yawed with the torque he prodded automatically at the rudder and she straightened, gathering speed. Pure joy flooded him at that moment; he knew already he was completely at home. At about 55 mph he let her come gently off the grass, climbed a little, turned and circled the aerodrome and then steered for Kenley. The old touch was back and as she cruised over the familiar fields he was sublimely happy. A circuit over Kenley and then he was slanting in to land. This was the acid test.

She swayed and dipped docilely as he nursed her with delicate and quick little movements of stick and rudder so easily that he did not notice how simple and automatic it was to hold her straight. Quite unconscious of the legs he flattened, held back, back, back, and then she touched gently on three points. On the landing run he was conscious of his legs again but held her straight with ease and turned and taxied to the tarmac apron in front of the squadron's hangar, full of satisfaction. Ross turned his head back from the front cockpit. 'Not bad,' he grinned. 'Not bad at all. I couldn't do much better myself.'

He helped Douglas out, guiding his left foot into the slot because the wooden foot could not feel it. A lanky figure sauntered across the tarmac to them. 'Hey, hey,' said Harry Day. 'Peter been giving you a taste of the air again?'

'No, he hasn't,' Bader grinned. 'I was just giving him a lesson.'

'*You* were,' Day said. 'Well, I might have known it was you from that ruddy awful landing.'

After an extremely cheery lunch in the mess Bader flew Ross in the Avro back to Lympne and made another neat landing. That afternoon he was happier than he could remember. At the house Sassoon asked how he had got on and he said: 'Absolutely fine, sir. Honestly, no different at all to flying with my old legs.' Later he added carefully: 'I've got to have a medical board, sir, to see if I can fly again. I was rather hoping you might let them know in advance that I actually have flown again and that it's perfectly simple with these legs.'

Sassoon said: 'You let me know before you go for your board and I'll see to it.'

That was all he needed. The clincher! All worries fell away in that moment. He'd be back on the squadron flying again as though nothing had happened with the full life he wanted so badly stretching out in front of him. In that faith a glow suffused every part of him.

After that wonderful week-end he drove to St Edward's with his cricket-bag for the Old Boys' match. The Warden and the masters were amazed to see how mobile he was and, changing into flannels, he felt on top of the world. The Old Boys batted first and Bader went in third wicket down with a man by the square leg umpire to run for him. As soon as he had the bat in his hand taking block at the crease he felt natural, but when the first ball came down, pitched a shade too full on the off, and he tried lunging out to drive it he suddenly felt hobbled and helpless, and the ball flashed by the wicket-keeper. The same thing happened next ball; it was as bad as having the ankles tied together. He knew then that his old habit of jumping down the pitch was finished: he would have to wait for the ball and swing cautiously from the shoulders, and even then it had to be a limited swing or he would over-balance. He could block them all right, but that was only negative. Still, the eye was as keen as ever and shortly he broke his duck by glancing one to leg. It was easier to pull balls than stroke them out to the off. He got another single, then a two, and cheering broke out round the ground as he pulled a fast one to the leg boundary. Shortly he did the same again and had scored 18 before he flicked one on the off into the wicket-keeper's gloves. Walking back, he was cheered to the pavilion.

So far, highly gratifying, but when he went to field in slips he was useless unless a ball came high into his hands; he just could not get down to stop a grounded ball in time and if he tried too hard he only fell over. In the outfield it would be worse because he could not throw without falling over. Then his stumps began aching from the constant standing in one spot. He refused to give up but by the time the side came off the field he was exhausted and felt unhappily that he could only be a passenger in any side. It was not a defeat for the legs that day, but neither was it a victory; it left him with a mildly depressed feeling that he would rather not play seriously again, partly because the contrast with the old days would be hurtful and partly because he felt he could not pull his weight on any team.

Later that week he drove home to Sprotborough and relaxed for several weeks in peace, irked only towards the end of the period by an itch to be active again and doing something about the future. His mother asked him one day what his plans were, and he answered: 'I'm going to stay on in the Air Force, Mother. I'll be flying again and everything will be fine.'

'I thought you might have had enough of flying now.'

'Good gosh, no,' he said. 'I've had my crash now. I won't have any more.' In fact, at that time he did have an illogical faith (later destroyed) that he had had his issue of crashes: a little like an artilleryman's theory that a shell never lands in the same place as another. Besides, he pointed out tactlessly, if he crashed again like the last time it would not matter because he had no more legs to lose.

Back at Kenley a telegram arrived telling him to report for his medical board and he drove down to the Central Medical Establishment in Kingsway, filled with confidence and delighted that things were getting under way again. He went the rounds of the doctors who examined his eyes, whispered at the other side of the room to test his ears, looked up his nose and down his throat, listened to his heart and chest and tapped him here and there. One of them absentmindedly took up a ruler to tap his knees for reflexes and then dropped it with a foolish laugh. 'Sorry, old boy, I forgot. We'll take your reflexes as read.' The doctor who took his blood pressure looked up and mused, 'That's interesting. Your blood pressure's down; quite normal now.' He decided it must be because the lack of legs reduced the distance that the blood had to be pumped and added: 'You'll probably be less inclined to black out in steep turns and dives too, because you've got less extremities for the blood to sink into.' Then, with a grin: 'Something to be said for losing your legs after all.'

The senior doctor, a wing commander, glanced over the findings, and said: 'Well, you seem to be in pretty good shape so we're passing you out as A2H, which means restricted flying at home. I'm afraid you won't be able to go solo with that, but we'll recommend you for a posting to the Central Flying School at Wittering and see what the flying boys think of you.'

Bader accepted the finding equably. He knew he would have no trouble with the flying boys, and while waiting for a posting went back to Uxbridge (the depot, not the hospital, this time) and did normal duties, taking parades, acting as orderly officer and so on. It made staying on in the Air Force seem so natural. Several times he went to Roehampton for more adjustments to the legs and also kept driving over to the Pantiles for tea as often as he could, though he still did not know the girl's name and, affected by dormant self-doubt, hesitated to make any overt move.

Yet he felt the friendship was ripening very agreeably so that it came as a shock one day when she mentioned that she was leaving the Pantiles soon and going back to live with her parents in London.

It disturbed him more than he thought it would. Time he did something about it. Also it irritated him because with any other girl, waitress or lady, he could have turned on the bold banter at the drop of a hat and had her giggling and likely it in no time. Yet he did not think of her as a waitress (though it was normal for regular officers in England of the 1930s to consider such questions seriously).

Then the posting arrived, ordering him to the glowing new horizon at the Central Flying School, but his pleasure was tempered by the knowledge that Wittering was far away. One last time he drove to the Pantiles resolved to do something about it and said to the girl when she arrived:

'I'm going away too.'

'Oh,' she said, sounding politely interested but not ostensibly crushed.

'Going up north to Wittering to start flying again.' He tried to be offhand about it, but she clearly guessed its importance because she smiled with pleasure and said: 'Oh, you'll like that, won't you? I *am* glad.'

This was the moment. He said, trying to sound casual again:

'I was wondering if you'd care to come out with me one night in London if I can get down.'

'That would be nice. I'd love to,' she said, sounding neither too eager nor too cool, but observing the rules for young women impeccably.

(What the devil was her name?)

He said blandly: 'Would you give me your address and telephone number in London?'

The girl, knowing quite clearly what he was thinking, printed on the back of a tea ticket:

> Thelma Edwards,
> 12, Avonmore Mansions,
> Kensington, W14.

'Oh, thanks awfully,' he said, relieved. 'My name's Douglas Bader.'

(She had known that for weeks. Three of her cousins[1] were Air Force officers and she had asked them a lot of questions about the interesting young man who had lost his legs. Bader did not discover that till later, when he also found that her father had been a wing commander, that her step-father was a colonel and that the girl had been a young woman of leisure until her beloved pet dog had died and she had gone to stay with a grandmother at Windlesham and taken the Pantiles job to get her mind off grief about the dog.)

---

[1] The Donaldson brothers, who all rose to senior rank and won eight decorations between them (each won a DSO). Teddy Donaldson also broke the world speed record after the war in a Meteor.

For a while he was too joyfully occupied at Wittering to get up to London. His very arrival there on a flying course filled him with thrilling content. First they gave him dual in an Avro 504 and he was so obviously competent that on the third morning his instructor took him up in a two-seater Bulldog. When they landed the instructor said, apparently in ignorance of the doctor's ruling. 'Nothing at all wrong with you, old boy. You might as well take her up by yourself after lunch.'

After four years in the Service Bader did not volunteer the information that he was not allowed to go solo, but went smugly into lunch where, by the sheerest chance, the station doctor observed with appalling clarity in the hearing of the instructor: 'I hear you're doing frightfully well, old boy. You must be *very* fed up at the doctors not allowing you to go solo.'

What made him more furious than ever was that Freddie West, who had lost a leg above the knee winning a VC in the war, was at Wittering doing a refresher course and flying solo every day. And what was more – he walked with a stick.

As consolation the instructor promised him a week-end's leave and he wrote to Thelma saying that he would be in London on duty during the week-end. Would she care to go out with him to the Café de Paris on Saturday night? A decorous note came back accepting and asking if he would care to call for tea beforehand. The flat, she pointed out, was under the name of Addison, her step-father's name.

On the Saturday morning he set out early in the MG with boiled shirt and his tails in a little case. Avonmore Mansions, he found, was six storeys high and the name Addison was under the heading: '6th Floor.' There was no lift. Carrying his case, he dot-and-carried up the stairs, twelve flights, ninety-six steps. He counted them and arrived at the top breathless and heart pumping. As he rang the bell he wondered what it was going to be like. He didn't give a damn if she *was* a waitress, but he was annoyed at being breathless. Might make him seem nervous. He wasn't nervous. Hell, no. Ridiculous thought.

The door opened and a uniformed maid showed him into a pleasantly furnished sitting-room where the girl, looking very fetching in a green dress, rose from the sofa. He'd never seen her without the waitress overall on before. She introduced him to her mother, who looked young and agreeable, and a tall, lean man, her step-father, Lieutenant-Colonel Addison. The girl leaned over the tea things and asked, with a tiny smile: 'Cream or plain?' and after that he felt very much at home.

Later, feeling debonair in tails for the first time since the crash, he took her to the Café de Paris in a taxi. The dinner was good, the girl was utterly charming, and sitting at the little table for two with his legs tucked safely away beneath, the music lilting away in a straight, pre-war rhythm, stimulated a mood of glowing zest. On the spur of the moment he leaned over, and said: 'Would you like to dance?'

Just for a moment she looked uncertain and then she smiled and nodded.

He got up and lurched round to help her up. He hadn't meant to dance at all: the idea had just slipped out but there was no drawing back and, suddenly reckless, he thought: 'Dammit, if I can walk all right, I can certainly walk clutching a girl.'

'I didn't know you danced too,' she said appreciatively as they reached the floor.

'Oh, it's quite easy,' he said airily. 'If I trip I hang on to the girl.'

He took her in his arms, waited a moment for the beat of the music and then hopefully lurched off.

It *was* quite easy – if not especially graceful. He held her a little away to give him space for kicking the right leg forward and for a while he was really only walking in approximate time to the music, steering rounds the bends still in a walk, but it was so uncomplicated that it was almost an anti-climax. Emboldened he tried a mildly fancy turn and it came off. He tried another one and stumbled but instantly she was unobtrusively steadying him and they danced on. 'You seem very good at supporting men,' he grinned.

Now and then his right knee tapped her left knee cap as he jerked the leg forward, but she soon learned to move her own leg a little more smartly than usual. After a couple of numbers they were moving round the floor quite impressively until suddenly he collided with her and she came to a dead stop, her face tight with pain.

'What's the matter?' he asked anxiously. 'Are you all right?'

'Yes,' she said, torn by apology; 'but you're standing on my left foot.'

He jumped off in horror, torn by apology himself, and they danced on. Soon the music changed to a waltz. He had a stab at it but very nearly tripped taking her with him, on the first half-step. 'Sorry,' he said. 'Afraid I can't cope with this one. Let's go and sit down.'

They went off the floor arm-in-arm and as he dot-and-carried up the two shallow steps to their table his other hand missed the banister and he overbalanced backwards, landing heavily on the floor and nearly bringing her down with him. People turned round and stared down their noses as if he were drunk.

She helped him up and they got to the table where he grinned to cover up his inward mortification – he had never fallen in front of her before. She leaned across and put her hand on his arm. 'You know, I think you're really amazing,' she said. It was the first time she had ever even obliquely referred to the loss of his legs and she did it so warmly and naturally that it really endeared her to him.

They danced several more times after that and he blissfully ignored the fact that his legs were aching and that patches on the stumps were rubbing raw. About 2 am he took her home, bade her a decorous good-

good-night and drove off very pleased with himself in the MG to the RAF Club where he had to tape the chafed patches on his stumps before he went to bed. On the Sunday he took her for a drive in the MG and unobtrusively she managed to convey to him that she genuinely admired the way he drove and got around on his legs. Driving back to Wittering that night he was sure he had found the girl he wanted.

Next week-end he drove to London again and took her to the Ace of Spades roadhouse near the Kingston By-pass. They danced again and on the way back he stopped the car and kissed her. (She had been wondering when he was going to do that.) To his delight, after an appropriate time, she kissed him back.

On the Sunday he drove her to the Stoops' and Audrey Stoop, who approved very much, invited both of them down for the following week-end.

That week at Wittering he was doing aerobatics again in a Bulldog as well as ever he had, though still irked by the compulsory presence of the instructor in the back cockpit. Once or twice he assuaged this affront to his dignity by brashly criticising the instructor's own aerobatics and giving him a few tips, though the instructor got his own back a day or so later when a gust caught the aircraft in a cross-wind precautionary landing and the Bulldog swung in an incipient ground-loop till the instructor quickly corrected with his own foot on the rudder bar. He make a few ribald comments, but Bader's flying was so invariably immaculate that resumption of full flying duties seemed 'in the bag.' On the strength of that he traded in his MG for a later model that week, though it took the last penny out of his bank account.

On the Saturday he drove Thelma down to the Stoops' and, when he kissed her good-night at Avonmore Mansions on the Sunday evening, he knew he was in love with her and that she was at least extremely fond of him. He floated back towards Wittering in the usual bliss of a smitten young man, unconscious of a scene that concerned him deeply in the Addisons' flat.

Thelma's mother said guardedly to her: 'You and Douglas are becoming quite a twosome. Is it serious?'

'Yes, it is rather,' Thelma said. 'You like him, don't you?'

'Yes, I do,' her mother said. 'He's charming. But how could you marry a man with no legs? Have you thought of that? you must be very sure.'

'I'm already sure. Without his legs I still like him much more than anyone else.'

'You might have to be a sort of nurse to him,' Mrs Addison warned.

'Not,' said Thelma confidently, 'with Douglas.'

She had no qualms at all about a future with him and though, as an unusually attractive girl, there were also in the offing a naval officer, an army officer and a young stockbroker, they seemed stodgy and even pompous compared to the zest and sparkle of the legless one.

The Chief Flying Instructor sent for Bader and said: 'Look, you're wasting your time up here. There's no point in your mucking about not able to go solo.'

'That's what I was sent here to find out, sir.' Bader said. 'Once I'm passed by you the medical board can decide on my flying category.'

'All right,' said the CFI 'I'll write and tell 'em.'

The answer came back surprisingly quickly – a call for Bader to appear for another medical. He drove to London savouring the moment that evening when he would see Thelma and tell her he was going back to a squadron. In the Kingsway building the round rotund warrant officer receptionist who had seen so many accident cases come up for medical check, welcomed him. 'Hallo, sir. Back again. Just a moment, sir, and I'll get your file.'

He was back with it shortly, saying: 'You don't have to see the doctor after all, sir. Only the wing commander.'

Good, Bader thought. Only a formality. He went into the wing commander's office and the man with the detached professional air behind the desk said: 'Ah, Bader, nice to see you again. Sit down, will you?'

He sat, waiting equably for the good news. The wing commander cleared his throat and glanced at some papers on his desk. Clearing his throat again he said: 'I've just been reading what the Central Flying School says about you. They say you can fly pretty well.'

Bader waited politely.

'Unfortunately,' the wing commander went on, 'we can't pass you fit for flying because there's nothing in King's Regulations which covers your case.'

CHAPTER NINE

For a moment it didn't sink in, and then a cold feeling slowly spread through him. He sat in stunned silence for a few more moments and then found his voice: 'But of course there's nothing in King's Regulations, sir. That's why I was sent to CFS. To see if I *could* fly. They were the only ones who could give a ruling. I mean . . . doesn't that fit the case?'

The wing commander cleared his throat again. 'I'm sorry. I'm very sorry indeed, but I'm afraid not. We've thought about it a lot, and I'm afraid there's nothing we can do about it.'

Forgetting discipline, Bader flared angrily: 'Well, why the hell did you send me there to be tested?'

Embarrassed, the wing commander said apologetically: 'Well, you were very keen to have a shot and I'm just terribly sorry it turned out like this.'

It was then it occurred to Bader that the whole question had probably been decided before he went to Wittering. They had expected him to fail at the flying test – let him see he can't fly and then he won't mind. Now they were embarrassed by it. A little longer he argued the point, but it was obvious that the decision was official, probably made at high level, and he had been in the RAF long enough to know that trying to reverse official decisions was like kicking at a wall of blubber. One could never even track down their source.[1]

Too sick with disappointment and anger to argue any longer, he pushed himself to his feet said stiffly. 'Thank you very much, sir,' and stumped out. Dimly he realised that it was probably not the doctor's fault and they had probably meant well in sending him to Wittering. But that did not help. As he passed the warrant officer he said. 'The bastards have failed me,' and walked out.

Tight-lipped he drove to Avonmore Mansions, walked up the ninety-six steps again and found Thelma sewing in the sitting-room. Surprised and pleased, she asked what had brought him from Wittering, and he told her, barely controlling his anger. She listened quietly and asked: 'What's the situation now?'

'I haven't the slightest idea,' he said moodily. 'I suppose they'll offer me a ground job.'

'Well, you'll still have a career in the RAF,' she said consolingly, and he burst out violently:

'I'm damned if I'd take the job. I'd rather leave.'

She talked to him for a couple of hours before he promised to wait a while and see what happened. A week later – it was November now – he was posted to Duxford, a fighter station some forty miles north of London in Cambridgeshire, where he found 19 Squadron flying Bulldogs, some instructors training the Cambridge University Air Squadron, and a precise, immaculate wing commander in charge of the Station, who said: 'Glad to have you here, Bader. You're taking over the motor transport section.'

The job was simple enough: not much more than sitting in a little office all day drinking tea, signing chits and giving orders about lorries.

[1] Some time later he discovered that while he was at Wittering an article had appeared in a Sunday paper asking rather querulously about the waste of taxpayers' money in giving a flying course to a man without legs. It also pointed out how unfair it was to mothers whose sons might have to fly with this man. Presumably people who saw it were too tactful to show it to him at the time. Whether it had any bearing on the RAF's decision he never discovered.

He knew several of the squadron pilots and he thought it would not be difficult to talk them into giving him some flying. Officially he was still classed as 'General Duties,' the flying branch, and stubbornly he felt there might still be a chance of getting an airborne job – how, he didn't know. They asked if he would like to be reclassified 'Administrative' or 'Equipment,' and he said no. Vaguely unhappy, he soon knew that he could never stay in the RAF doing a ground job because his unhappiness came from watching others flying.

He became friendly with Joe Cox, one of the instructors training the Cambridge undergraduates, and one December day when the wing commander was away Cox took him up in an Armstrong Whitworth Atlas, an Army co-operation biplane. Cox let his passenger do most of the flying and was impressed. Several times after that when the coast was clear they went up together, and after Cox's reports the other pilots were indignant that bureaucracy limited Bader to flying on the sly.

They were discussing it in the mess one night when Cox said: 'Look, come out and watch Douglas do a tarmac landing to-morrow.' (Tarmac landings consisted of coming in so slowly and with such fine judgment that the aircraft touched down on the short tarmac apron and stopped before running on to the grass. They were not officially approved of and therefore popular.)

Next morning at eleven o'clock the pilots watching by the hangar saw the Atlas waffle down with Cox's arms ostentatiously held high out of the back cockpit to demonstrate that Bader was doing the flying. At the critical moment as the Atlas touched neatly on the tarmac the wing commander walked round the side of the hangar, saw the performance, and guessed grimly from the instructor's upheld arms that he was allowing a pupil to do a tarmac landing. As Cox climbed down his grin faded to see the wing commander standing next to him like an outraged schoolmaster. The wing commander opened his mouth to speak, and then Bader pushed up his goggles in the front cockpit and was recognised. The senior man said coldly:

'Was that you flying this aircraft, Bader?'

'Yes, sir.'

'But you're not allowed to fly!'

'No, sir.'

The wing commander turned to Cox. 'Don't you know Bader isn't allowed to fly, Cox?'

Bader cut in. 'No, sir,' he lied. 'Flying Officer Cox had no idea. I should have told him, I know.'

The wing commander said grimly: 'Well, Cox, if you didn't know before, you know now. Bader is not to fly again.' He turned to Bader. 'I shall decide later what action to take about you.'

Apparently he was sporting enough to forget it because Bader heard

no more and the weeks passed tediously. Cox suggested they might fly
again but Bader vetoed the idea for Cox's sake. The only diverting
incident was the time four of his lorries in convoy collided nose to tail on
a wet road when the front one had to brake sharply. Bader's report
exonerated the drivers and blamed the RAF for fitting all the lorries
with solid rubber tyres that skidded easily. The wing commander told
him tersely that it was not his job to tell the Air Force what they should
do with their lorries, and he saluted and withdrew, thinking there was
one further recommendation he would like to make about the lorries to
his seniors.

One week-end on leave Adrian Stoop took him and Thelma to see the
Harlequins play Richmond at Twickenham. Bader was very excited
until the match started, and then in the first couple of minutes as a scrum
triggered off a Harlequin wing movement that ended in a try, he suddenly
became quiet and did not open his mouth for the rest of the match. Stoop
knew that he had made a mistake and that it would be an even worse
mistake to suggest that they leave. In that hour Bader felt more bitterly
than ever before the loss of his legs. All his old friends were playing and
it really hurt. Driving back to the house they talked of other things, and
later that evening he told Thelma that he would never go and see another
rugger match. (Nor did he.)

Towards the end of April he was sent for by Squadron Leader
Sanderson, CO of 19 Squadron and acting station commander in the
senior man's absence. Sanderson had been adjutant at Kenley before
Bader lost his legs, and when the young man walked into his office and
saluted, the good-natured Sanderson said: 'Douglas, this is the worst
thing I've ever had to do in the Air Force. I've just received a letter from
Air Ministry . . . here, you'd better read it yourself.' He passed the letter
across. Bader took it and read:

> *Subject: Flying Officer D. R. S. Bader.*
>
> (1) *The Air Council regrets that in consequence of the results of this
> officer's final medical board he can no longer be employed in the
> General Duties Branch of the Royal Air Force.*
>
> (2) *It is suggested therefore that this officer revert to the retired list
> on the grounds of ill health.*
>
> (3) *A further communication will be sent in respect of the date of his
> retirement and details concerning his retired pay and disability pension.*

Sanderson said: 'I'm terribly sorry, Douglas.'

'That's all right, sir,' he said, and after a while he saluted and stumped
out. There did not seem anything else to say. In a way he had been
expecting it but it was still a shock and left him with an odd numbed
feeling. Shortly it began to seep through that he would soon be unem-

ployed, possessing no skill that he could profitably use and mobile only so long as he could afford to buy petrol for the MG Yet they were giving him a pension – that was quite decent of them – though he knew it would not be much, especially for a man used to pleasant things.

He drove down to see Thelma and told her.

'But you could still stay in on the ground, couldn't you?' she asked.

He said bluntly: 'I suppose I could, but I won't. It's no good being in the Air Force unless you're of it, and as far as I'm concerned you're not of it unless you're flying.'

'Do you have any idea as to what you'd like to do?'

'Frankly,' he said, 'no.'

He took her out to dinner at the Indian Restaurant in Swallow Street, just off Piccadilly, and they sat close together over curry. After a silence he said obliquely: 'I'm not much of a proposition for anyone, you know. No legs. No job. No money.'

'Don't worry,' she said. 'We'll make out. I could always make a few pennies at the Pantiles.'

There was not much more said than that. No blunt question. No blunt answer. Just a delicate understanding that sent him back to Duxford quietly happy, knowing he was not alone.

Shortly another letter came from Air Ministry, impersonal but not unkind, granting him £100 a year total disability pension and £99 10s. a year retired pay. That was not too bad in those days – at least for someone content to exist quietly. Bader wasn't.

For a fortnight he was clearing up the ends of his Air Force life, handing over his job to another officer and packing his civilian clothes: the latter part was easy – he had only one blue suit, a sports jacket and some grey flannels. His uniforms and cricketing kit he gave to Joe Cox. One day he visited the Officers' Employment Bureau at Air Ministry. The Bureau's task was to find jobs for Short Service Officers when they had finished their five years' commission. A brisk, cheerful man asked him what he would like to do and he answered: 'I really have no idea.'

'Would you like to go abroad?'

'Not very much. I wouldn't be any good in the tropics with these legs anyway. It's no good when they start to sweat.'

The man said at last: 'Well, leave it to me and I'll have a look round and let you know if anything turns up.'

Getting his clearances brought one last-minute hitch: six lorries were missing and the transport sergeant who knew all details was away on leave.

'I can't sign your clearance,' said a worried adjutant. 'These lorries are worth £6,000 and if they aren't found you'll have to pay a proportion, you know.'

'It'll be a damn' small proportion and you'll have to take it out of my

end of the month pay,' Bader said, not caring greatly. 'I've only got
forty-five bob at the moment.'

Then the sergeant came back and they traced the lorries to a repair
depot.

The last few days were trying. Suddenly tired of the whole business,
he wanted only to get the final agony over and be away to face what he
had to face. Then there was only one more signature to get; and that
night he took his last uniform off for the last time and handed it to Joe
Cox with no visible sign of emotion. In the morning he dressed in his
sports coat and flannels, looked over the Rooms to Let column in the
Daily Telegraph and marked a few likely ones with a pencil, then
dumped his two suitcases in the MG and about ten o'clock drove to
station headquarters for the final moment of separation. It was quite
undramatic. He said to the adjutant: 'Here are my clearances, sir. Would
you put your mark at the bottom, please?'

The adjutant signed and said: 'Well, there you are, old boy. All clear.'

In that moment he had left the Air Force. His mind deliberately
dulled, cushioned by expectation, he said: 'Thank you very much, sir,'
and walked out.

He drove straight past the guard-room out of the gates and turned left
on the road to London; even in that moment feeling no pang, only a
numbness. It was some minutes before he began to think again, and it
occurred to him first that now he had no home. In the Air Force he could
have gone to any officers' mess in the country and been welcomed and
given a room. Now they were all closed to him, and all he had was a
copy of the *Telegraph* with some pencil marks. He began to realise what
a warm shelter the Air Force had been, and drove thinking: 'I can't go
back there. I can't go back there.' Shortly he tried to make himself accept
that there was nothing behind him that would ever come back, but his
mind kept reminding him that neither was there anything in front.

One of the places ticked in the *Telegraph* was 86 Boundary Road, St
John's Wood, roughly on the way to Avonmore Mansions. Turning into
Boundary Road, he liked its plane trees in fresh spring leaf, pulled up
outside a house, a typical, three-storeyed solid affair, and range the bell.
An attractive blonde woman opened the door. Yes, Miss Markham said,
she had a room for a guinea a week with breakfast, and he followed her
up the stairs. She saw his dot-and-carry movement: 'Oh, you've hurt
your leg?'

'Well, no,' he said. 'I haven't got any legs actually.'

After an embarrassed pause she said: 'Oh, I'm so sorry.'

'That's all right. I don't mind a bit.'

She said she was sorry the room was two floors up and he said he
didn't mind that a bit either.

He liked the look of the room immediately; it was nicely kept and furnished, with a divan bed and good wash-basin, and the window looked out over the plane trees: rather pleasanter than the usual officer's room on a station.

She said apologetically: 'I'm afraid it's a little small.'

'I like them small,' he said. 'I can reach everything more easily.'

He took it on the spot and brought his two suitcases up: their contents, the month's pay in his pocket and the car outside were all he had in the world. After paying Miss Markham for a week in advance he drove off to see Thelma and took her out to the Ace of Spades.

'Well,' she said, over inexpensive bacon and eggs, 'how do you feel about things now?'

'Not too bad,' he said. 'I'll find my feet.'

The following week brought him for the first time in his life a proper taste, a real mouthful, of the unsheltered world where there were few rules and fewer privileges and you scrambled with all the others for your share. It was a cold awakening, facing a future which was the equivalent of facing nothing. This was the neo-post-depression period when the jobs-required columns were full of appeals for permission to sell vacuum cleaners and he was too fresh with past dignity to be bothered with that sort of thing. And yet, for the likes of him, there was no opening in the miniscule jobs-vacant column.

On the Monday at the Officers' Employment Bureau the cheerful man said: 'Got a few feelers out, old boy, but nothing in sight yet. I'll let you know if I hear anything.'

On the Tuesday he drove all over London, but not looking for a job; just driving. On the Wednesday he did the same, not accepting yet the drop in status and the need to scramble. Mixed with this was an attitude, inchoate but stubborn, that he was not going to drop his standards. As at school he had disliked maths and declined to do them until forced to, so now he disliked looking for a job and declined to exert himself in the search until circumstances pressed. It was essentially an English attitude, somewhat head-in-the-sand, slightly snob, and rather deceptive. So far the challenge had not yet stirred. On the Thursday he drove Thelma down to the Pantiles for cream tea. The place had charm for them both. On the Friday he called for her again and she brought out a Thermos of tea and a packet of sandwiches. 'We might as well get used to things,' she said. 'If you won't watch the pennies, I will.'

On the Saturday he began to feel he was in a puzzling vacuum. He wanted to do something but there was nothing to do, nothing to catch hold of, and it began to disturb him.

He went back on the Monday to the Officers' Employment Bureau, where the man was still cheerful but devoid of prospects.

After that a man in the RAF Club suggested he might try journalism and gave him a note of introduction to the assistant editor of a London morning paper. Bader took it along to the paper and found the assistant editor was a slightly overdressed man with sharp features and a brisk manner. Without excessive enthusiasm the man asked: 'What made you think you'd like to work on newspapers?'

'I really haven't the faintest idea,' he answered, 'but I've got to get a job and as I know sport pretty well I thought I might be able to do something along those lines.'

The editor explained that they already had special sporting correspondents and most of them were international names. He thought for a while: 'What about special contacts? D'you know a lot of society people who could give you gossip stuff?'

'Hell, no,' Bader said fastidiously, and lost interest in newspapers. Going out, he thought with satisfaction that at least the man had no idea he had no legs.

In the mornings now, without especially admitting it to himself, he took to looking at the jobs-vacant column in the *Telegraph* but nothing attracted him there. Then a letter came from the Officers' Employment Bureau suggesting he go along to see the staff managers of Unilevers and the Asiatic Petroleum Co. He went to Unilevers first and they told him about soap and its by-products, and offered him a job starting at £200 a year in London before going out to West Africa. He explained that his legs would bar him from the tropics. They said that might not matter, though it might limit his career with them.

Then the petroleum company, where a scholarly, elderly man like a university don also suggested a job that would mean going to the tropics for promotion. Depressed, he explained about his legs. The scholarly man thought for a while. 'We've got a little aviation section growing up here,' he said. 'They might have a vacancy. Would that interest you?'

At the word 'aviation' Bader was extremely interested.

The man took him along to the office of the aviation department, where the manager said magically, yes, he could do with a smart young man. It would be a job in the office helping sell aviation spirit to airlines and governments. Bader began almost literally praying they would take him on. He really wanted the job. Then they took him to the home staff manager, who sized him up in a chat for a while and then said abruptly: 'Well, we'll pay you £200 a year and start on Monday. How's that?'

Bader said cagily: 'I'd like to think about it, sir.'

All the way down the corridor the aviation manager kept saying: 'Of course you'd be foolish, you know, Bader, if you don't take the job. It's a wonderful chance.'

Though he was jumping with delight inside, Bader would say neither yes nor no. He was damned if he was going to look like making a dirty dive for a job in commerce.

He drove immediately to tell Thelma he was now employed, and they went to the Ace of Spades, where, over a more expensive curry, he said with unromantic and irritating masculine directness: 'I suppose we can start thinking about getting married now.'

She looked at him in the odd, half-smiling tolerant way that was coming naturally to her. 'How much do you think we'll need?' she asked.

'Oh, I don't know,' he said. 'I suppose at least £500 a year.'

That seemed reasonable enough. They were only twenty-three, and with his job and pension he now had £399 10s. a year. 'I'll make damn' sure the pay from the job goes up smartly,' he said, rather cockily, and they settled down to an engrossing discussion about cost of flats and food and engagement rings. Thelma suggested with exquisite tact that he should forget about an engagement ring for a while and have a secret engagement to preserve domestic content at her home. Bader knew that though her parents liked him they would justifiably worry about the idea of her marrying him. Thelma knew Douglas didn't have a bean to buy an engagement ring with.

In the morning he rang the aviation manager and said he would report for work on Monday. He was very happy that morning: being engaged to Thelma and having a job had lifted him suddenly out of the vacuum, and already he was feeling eager for Monday.

When the day came he put on his blue suit and drove hatless to his new office just off Bishopsgate in the City of London. (He had thought about buying a bowler hat but the symbolism revolted him.) The manager showed him to a desk with a green top and swivel chair backed against another desk. All told there were eight desks and eight pink and shaven young men. One showed him on a map where all the petroleum installations were, and he listened politely and largely uncomprehendingly while others explained what the organisation did. Then they gave him a mass of documents to read about aviation spirit, prices, marketing and so on, and at the end he was little wiser. 'Take it quietly,' the manager said. 'You'll pick it up in due course.' He lunched in the staff canteen, drank tea at four o'clock and drove to see Thelma at 5.30.

'Well, darling,' she asked, 'how was it? Tell me all about it.'

'Actually,' he said, 'I don't rightly know, but they seem a good bunch of chaps.'

After a couple of weeks he gradually got the hang of things, and was concerned mainly with prices and delivery of aviation spirit and oils to Australia. It was remote and dull, a tenuous, vicarious and somewhat hollow association with flying.

In the third week a senior young man gave him his first specific job to do, handing him a letter from a branch in Australia and saying: 'Look, old boy, write them back and say so and so and thus and thus.' For the first time Bader pressed the buzzer on his desk and a girl came in from the typists pool, sat by his desk with her notebook and pencil poised and waited. And waited. And waited.

For the first time Bader was completely tongue-tied with a girl. After a considerable silence he said: 'Ah ... Dear Sir.'

'To whom shall I address this?' asked the girl.

'Oh ... ah ...' He looked at the address on the letter and gave it confidently to her. Another long silence. At last he said: 'Ah ... Dear Sir.' The girl waited, pencil still poised, and slowly, word by agonised word, the letter took shape, a whole paragraph long.

Later the girl came back with the typed letter and he took it from her with what he hoped was convincing composure. As he read it he could not quite remember what he had said but thought a little smugly that it was rather clearly put, and sent it to the senior man for signing.

Soon the man came over with the letter. 'Look,' he said, 'this is a bit abrupt, you know.'

Bader turned on the luminous smile. 'I'm so sorry. What have I done wrong?'

'Well, it's a bit like a telegram,' the man said. 'You want to wrap it up a bit to the chaps out there, you know: make it a bit longer and use expressions like "We would suggest' and "Perhaps you have already considered." '

Bader said: 'I'm awfully sorry, but I've been used to writing letters in the Air Force so chaps would understand what you were saying.'

Distinctly ruffled, the man said: 'Well, you'll have to get used to different ways here. You'd better do it again.'

Bader pressed the buzzer again, and when the girl came in they struggled together over it for half an hour. The finished article was a full page long and reading it over he thought he had buried the meaning rather well.

'That's the stuff,' said the senior man. 'Just the sort of thing we want.'

As the months rolled slowly by he sank gently into the rut of the job. For a while it was painless enough and he thought he had found the secret of it – never commit yourself; never be forced into a position where you have to make a clear decision; always leave yourself with a let-out. It began to irk him.

One September week-end he drove Thelma to Sprotborough and was delighted that his mother liked her from the start. So did Bill Hobbs, the vicar, and later that week the young man and the girl begn thinking about getting married in a few months if he got his Christmas rise in pay. They could just marry on his present income of a little over £7 10s. a week, but there were two barriers. First, he had to run a car and use it extensively, which was expensive. Standing in tube trains crowded at peak hours was not recommended for a legless man who stubbornly refused to use a stick and just as stubbornly insisted on giving up his seat to any woman, young or old. In that latter habit lay the clue to the second barrier. He lived determined to make no concessions to the loss of his legs but to carry on with touchy pride on the same basis as anyone else. No one must help him because he declined to admit even to himself that he ever needed help. It was the hard way and the only way not just to overcome the handicap but to rub it off the slate. Associated with this principle was a resolve, growing into an obsession, that he would not drop his standards. He was a Cranwell man, still an officer on the retired list; so by God he'd live as an officer like all the others who had been his friends and equals. Ostensibly he might be apart from them but spiritually he was still with them and of them. That was not so much snobbishness as a rigid, foolhardy and admirable refusal to accept any fraction of defeat. On his present income he felt he could not support Thelma in marriage as he should. Therefore, he would wait till he could. She suggested gently that she would go out and work, even at the Pantiles, but that he firmly vetoed and she did not press the point, sensing that for him a wife who worked carried the bitter seeds of partial defeat.

There were other practical considerations. He had, for instance, just £2 in the bank. And what, for example, would happen if the car were damaged? It was only insured 'third party' because the companies seemed to look dourly on Air Force officers with fast sports cars, especially when they had no legs. However warily they viewed the car, Bader cherished it not only for its usefulness but for its symbolism as fitting for a vital young man who loved flying. On the Saturday morning when he hosed and washed it carefully to take Thelma to the Stoops' he was wondering if they dared marry if the rise did not come through.

Soon he forgot that in the joy of driving along the Great West Road at his usual 70 mph, Thelma as usual enduring the speed tolerantly because she trusted his driving. Passing the spot where London Airport is now, a large Humber pulled out ahead on the other side to pass a lorry, and Douglas eased his foot on to the brake to give it time to swing in again. The brakes had not the slightest effect (brake-drums full of water from the hose washing). Suddenly alert to danger, he tried to swing in, but another lorry was parked ahead on the left and the little MG darted at uncontrollable speed for the narrow gap left between the lorry and Humber on one side and the lorry on the other, all unfortunately abreast at the same moment. The gap was not wide enough.

CHAPTER TEN

Even as fright alarmed the mind the MG's offside front wheel sliced along the Humber's running-board as they came together at about 100 mph. In a screeching flash the front wheel had gone, the door by Bader's elbow vanished, the rear wheel tore off and the MG lurched crazily on to its brake drums and screeched along the bitumen. By some luck it ran straight, slowing up on the drums, and then it was motionless and the noise had gone. Thelma relaxed her grip on the seat as Douglas said 'I'm sorry, darling,' and she had enough wisdom and calm left not to rebuke him at the moment. He got out, surprised to see that his door and two wheels were gone, and realised that he was extremely lucky.

The Humber had pulled in to the other side of the road, apparently all right, about 200 yards away, and in it an admiral's wife was shaken by shock but otherwise unhurt. Two daughters comforted her, and the third daughter, a forthright young woman who had been driving, got out and began striding towards the MG. Oddly enough she was an acquaintance of Thelma's, being a neighbour of her grandmother at Windlesham. She arrived and said stormily to Bader: 'Were you the lunatic driving this car?'

'Yes,' he said, 'but I should prefer you not to be rude because I shall only be rude back.'

The two bristled at each other and then the daughter recognised Thelma sitting on the bank of the road. 'Hallo, Thelma,' she said, 'were you in this?'

'Hallo, Maisie,' Thelma said. 'Yes, I was.' She thought it not exactly the moment to introduce Douglas as her fiancé. The moment was odd and confused. A big chauffeur-driven car pulled up and a large businessman got out and entered the conversation with a statement that the young man had driven past him a couple of miles back going like a maniac. He growled angrily: 'It's not safe for a man's wife and children to be on the roads these days.'

'Well, they shouldn't be on the roads,' Bader said truculently. 'They ought to be on the blasted pavement.'

The businessman made it clear that he would be delighted to give evidence for the admiral's daughter. Everyone exchanged names and addresses. The businessman drove off and the daughter went back to the Humber, which was crumpled along one side but still able to drive away.

A man brought along one of the MG wheels he had found in a field a hundred yards away. They could not find the other wheel (it took a garage man two hours the following day to do that). An agreeable young man gave them a lift back to London, and on the way Bader rang a friend who had a garage and asked him to collect the MG. The affair was going to be expensive and he thought wryly that he didn't have a leg to stand on. Well, one thing: it gave him the answer to the marriage question. No!

For the next three weeks he travelled to work by tube or by bus, standing, which was misery and brought it forcibly home to show how much he depended on the car. It was even awkward going to see Thelma, and by the time he reached Avonmore Mansions the ninety-six stairs seemed higher than before and endless. It was a new reminder of what it meant to lose one's legs.

The bill for the Humber came in – £10 (an insurance company paid the rest). Then the MG was ready and he went to collect it. They gave him the bill at the same time – £68. The friend said sympathetically that it was as low as he could make, but he could pay it off at £1 a week or what he could manage. He drove it to Avonmore Mansions and took Thelma to the Ace of Spades for dinner (this time back to scrambled eggs and bacon). He began to feel a little better there at their usual table in the olde worlde barn atmosphere with a tinkling piano, tiny dance floor, and coloured lights round a swimming pool through the window. They danced, and as they came off the floor the paino struck into 'Stormy Weather.'

'Very apt,' Thelma said dryly. 'How long do you think it will take to pay it all off?'

He said that if he got his rise he might be in the clear by next June.

Thelma said comfortingly: 'Never mind, darling. It'll give us good practice for saving for a wedding.'

He thought gloomily in silence for a while and then burst out impulsively: 'Look, why don't we get married anyway now?'

'What would we live on?' asked the practical Thelma.

'We won't starve,' he said eagerly. 'Look, we aren't going to change toward each other, so we might as well be married as not.'

Thelma suggested that there might be a little reluctance from her parents.

'Why tell them?' Douglas asked. 'Why tell anyone?'

'Well, darling, even in this day and age you can't live together and just not tell people you're married.'

'We can't afford to live together,' he said, 'so no one'll have to know. If we get married at least we'll have some object in life.'

They discussed it, oblivious to the piano, and Thelma began to like the idea. After a while she said: 'All right, darling. Let's do it. When?'

'Next Saturday,' he said. 'Sooner the better. I'll hop in and get a licence.'

At Hampstead Registry Office he said to the clerk without preamble: 'I want to get married next Saturday.'

The clerk said yes, that would be all right. He could do it with a special licence for twenty-five guineas.'

'Good grief,' Bader said. 'I haven't got twenty-five shillings.'

The clerk said that then he would have to wait three weeks and it would cost only thirty shillings. Bader found he actually had just over £2 and settled for that. With a new idea he went back to the office, and with hardly any wheedling and without telling them he was getting married, got a fortnight's holiday to start in three weeks. Back at Avonmore Mansions that evening, when the others were out of the room he whispered to Thelma: 'Zero hour October 5.'

'Oh lord,' Thelma said, after a pause, 'I haven't got any clothes.'

He told her about the honeymoon.

'Oh, my gosh,' she said, 'what am I going to tell the parents, going away with you?'

That was another problem. The solution was quite fortuitous. They happened to meet Thelma's uncle just back from a holiday at Porthleven in Cornwall, where he had stayed at a most respectable guest-house.

'I've got some leave coming up,' Bader said artlessly. 'D'you think I'd like it there?'

'You'd love it,' Uncle said. 'So would Thelma. Why don't you both go down for a while?'

With that recommendation it was easy.

In the next two weeks Thelma spent her Pantiles savings on some new clothes.

On Wednesday, 4 October, Douglas got the next day off from the office for 'urgent private business.'

At 10.30 on the Thursday morning Mrs Addison went out shopping, and Thelma rang Douglas and got into her new dress. By eleven Douglas had arrived and they were off to Hampstead.

In a drab, lino-floored office a strange man muttered from a book and at last looked up and said in almost the same monotone: 'Well, congratulations, Mr and Mrs Bader.' Something obviously had to be done about the witness, who was a bored-looking clerk dragged in for the occasion from a next-door office. It was almost the last straw for Douglas, who had had to calculate his honeymoon budget to the last penny.

Driving off in the MG, both were shaken by the unemotional nature of the ceremony, and neither felt really married, though neither said so. Douglas merely observed after a quiet spell:

'We'll have that done again in a church next time,' and Thelma agreed feelingly.

They lunched at a hotel on the Eastbourne Road and Douglas ordered a bottle of champagne. It was the first time he had really had a drink in his life, and as the glow spread through each they began at last to feel happily married. He drove her back to London, dropped her at Avonmore Mansions, and she took the wedding ring off and put it in her purse before she went home. A few hours later he called at the flat for dinner as though he had just come from the office.

That night they announced their engagement to the family, promising, slightly tongue in cheek and with bare technical truth, that they would not be arranging a wedding for some time until he could support her comfortably. Everyone seemed quite happy about that; in fact, Mrs Addison no longer noticed that he had no legs. After he had gone to Boundary Road that night she brought out an old diamond ring and gave it to Thelma, saying: 'Look, darling, I don't suppose Douglas has many pennies to buy a ring, but this old one of Granny's has some nice diamonds and he could probably get them re-set.'

On the Saturday morning *The Times* announced the engagement and the happy couple drove off towards Porthleven for their honeymoon.

It rained all the way down and nearly all the fortnight they spent in the grey, Cornish stone house where the upright and unsuspecting landlord woke each in their separate rooms at eight o'clock every morning with a cup of tea. With each other and a sense of humour they enjoyed it, driving off with a picnic lunch every day round the sodden countryside, and it was even vastly funny when the seagulls choked on pieces of the landlady's adamantine rock cakes and bashed the pieces with their beaks against even harder rocks to break them up into swallowable size.

On the last Sunday they drove back to London to start married life. He left her at Avonmore Mansions and went back to Boundary Road. Thereafter he saw her nearly every evening, either having dinner at Avonmore Mansions or taking her out for scrambled eggs to the Ace of Spades. On Christmas Eve the manager said to Douglas: 'We're very satisfied with your work, Bader, and I'm happy to tell you that we are rising your salary by £50 a year.'

It helped in paying the car bills, but as winter dragged on he began to feel bogged down in a morass, increasingly frustrated by the dull and undemanding job and the virtual and indefinite separation from Thelma. The job offered no challenge and as he was barred from going overseas offered few prospects either except interminable, safe dreariness, bound to debt and a desk as one of the eight pink and shaven 'bog rats,' as they called themselves. There was not even a game he could turn to for relief. His legs still troubled him: he could never walk far without weariness and chafing, and sometimes he had to go back to Roehampton for adjustments. Always he was conscious of the legs, their discomfort and

limitations and the pain they often caused, though he never complained
about them, even when he fell, which was not often now.

Thelma was the one bright spot. She was soothing and undemanding,
knowing instinctively how to cope with his moods which were a form of
rebellion against circumstances. Often the moods led him into extravagance to relieve the drabness and also to maintain the standards he was
bent upon. Maintaining those was like hanging on to a lifebelt in the
morass. It was hard to save. Sometimes he spent as much as £4 in a
week-end, yet any resistance at those times would have driven him to
further excesses. She never nagged him but always waited quietly till his
own conscience stirred and then unobtrusively steered him in the right
direction and encouraged him to relax and carry on. He could hardly
have married a more suitable girl. She was utterly unselfish.

One day she lured him into going to a fortune-teller, getting him, after
his first grumbles, to treat it as a joke. He went into a dark and dingy
room and shortly a wrinkled old woman shuffled in, took his palm and
surprised him by saying that he was destined to have trouble with his
feet and legs. She added: 'There is a period of difficulty in front of you,
but you will be a great deal happier in due course. You will become
famous and be decorated by your King.' Then she made him sign her
book which she kept for people who were going to be famous. In it she
showed him the name of David Beatty, who had signed as a sub-lieutenant
in 1904 and laughed when she told him he was going to be a famous
admiral. Despite himself, Bader was a little intrigued because he knew
she had not seen him limp in. Then he forgot all about it.

About that time 'Derick was killed in an accident in South Africa. The
Bader family seemed to be out of luck.

On a spring Saturday at Hartley Wintney, Adrian Stoop and Tinny
Dean, a Harlequins and England scrum-half, were going to play golf at
a local nine-hole course and suggested that Douglas and Thelma go and
see them hit off. Perhaps Douglas could walk a couple of holes with
them. After they drove off Douglas said he would potter about the fairway
until they returned, so Stoop handed him a seven iron and a ball and
suggested he potter about with them. When Stoop and Dean had gone
on he dropped the ball on the grass and took a swing at it, but the club
missed the ball by inches and he overbalanced and fell flat on his back.
He got up and tried again and the same thing happened. The same thing
happened the third time and the fourth time. He tried changing his stance
and his swing, and the same thing happened. Luckily the turf was soft
and painless. He got a stubborn feeling that he *must* hit the ball and
keep his balance before he gave it up.

Again and again he fell until about the twelfth attempt the club hit the
ball with a sweet click and, lying on his back a moment later, he could
still see it in parabolic flight. Something about that click was very

satisfying. He tried again, missed and fell over. He kept falling over and missing every time until, on about the twenty-fifth shot, he hit it for the second time (or rather, topped it) and fell over again. In the thirties he hit it twice more, one of them another exciting click, but still fell as before. After he had fallen about forty times Thelma said persuasively; 'Now come on, I think you've had enough.'

Next day he tried the seven iron again on the Stoops' lawn, this time with Stoop coaching. Several times he hit the ball but still he kept falling over. It was remarkable how precarious the balance was as soon as the swing of shoulders and arms took his weight a fraction over the straddle of his feet. There was no instinct or agility to correct. He had fallen about twenty times again when he tried a shorter and slower swing, hit the ball and just kept his balance. As he looked up with a triumphant grin Thelma said: 'Good, now you'll be satisfied.'

'Not on your life,' he said, got the ball back and kept on trying. Shortly he hit it without falling again, and did it several times more after that.

The following week-end he tried again at the Stoops', until nine times out of ten he was hitting the ball and not falling. It had started off as a determination to do it once and now it was something more, part obsession to be able to do it every time and part pleasure from the feel and the sound of the click when he hit it cleanly and saw it arc away. Stoop said: 'You're getting the bug, Douglas. Be careful, there's no cure for it.'

Next week-end he improved still more, his brain absorbing the instinctive reflexes needed to keep his balance and thus freeing him to concentrate on hitting the ball. A couple of week-ends later Tinny Dean took him over to the golf course and handed him a three-wood on the first tee. Acutely aware of the concentrated eyes of the usual first-tee onlookers, he desperately wanted to hit the ball, stay on his feet and not let them know he had no legs. 'Don't worry,' Dean assured him. 'Everyone misses on the first tee.'

With taut concentration he braced his feet wide apart, took a slow swing and connected. Stumbling, he still kept his feet and saw the ball flight about a hundred yards, fading with a little slice.

'That was a hell of a good shot,' said Dean.

'It was a hell of a fluke,' muttered Bader, vastly satisfied.

He walked down the fairway with Dean, borrowed a couple of clubs and more or less hacked his way to the green, though he did not finish the hole. He hit off the next tee without any strange prying eyes, and then Dean went ahead to do his round, leaving him a couple of clubs to practise with up and down the fairway. Later he returned to the clubhouse, stumps chafed and aching and glowing with satisfaction and perspiration.

All that week Bader found he was looking forward with longing to the week-end's golf practice. Dean took him to the North Hants course at

Fleet and he struggled round the first two holes, falling over only once, then staying to practise on the third fairway. Already the muscles of the stumps were developing and he learned the trick of smearing zinc ointment on spots that were likely to chafe, then powdering and taping them. He was hitting drives consistently over a hundred yards, sending them farther and farther as he developed more instinctive balance and could put more effort into the swing.

The odd thing was that though he sometimes mis-hit, his good shots sailed dead straight, probably for the simple reason that where normal men tried to 'press' with wild and sloppy swings, Bader *had* to keep perfect balance and control – or fall over. Where other men overbalancing could grab at the ground with toes, or steady themselves with ankle muscles or two knees, Bader had to keep his head still and down, without excessive body sway. It made his strokes look a little stiff, but they were clean-cut and even and had behind them the strength of shoulders, arms and wrists that had been strong before and had developed more since he had lost his legs. Then again, he had the born athlete's coordination of eye, mind and muscle and fanatical tenacity. He had always shone at games and it was an irritant to his ego to feel like a novice, even compared to plump lady battlers of the 'Good shot, Gladys,' school.

He and Thelma went two or three more times to North Hants and it was like a window opening on a new world. They met a lot of people there, and now, as well as the joy of hitting a ball, there was the pleasure of a new social life with fellow addicts. After a month he got to the stage of doing three or four holes every Saturday and Sunday, feeling stronger and hitting the ball longer each new week-end. On anything except very even ground he still had to worry about keeping his balance and therefore often mis-hit, but now and then he did a hole in four or five, and one day coming off the course with Thelma after practice he said: 'You know, this could be a game I might play on level terms with anyone.'

The club secretary suggested he might become a member for a year at nominal rates to see how he got on, and he joined with delight. Then he started wondering how he could afford to buy clubs.

'My dear chap,' Dean said, 'spring along to the Railway Lost Property Office. You can pick 'em up there for a song.'

He did so and bought six good steel-shafted clubs for 7s. 6d. each and a light bag. Thelma became an enthusiastic caddy and never stopped encouraging him. Already she could see he had a new and absorbing interest in life.

Towards the end of August he was playing six holes at a time. In early September he played nine holes for the first time, though towards the end as he got tired and erratic he gave up counting. The following week he did twelve holes. The legs did not ache or chafe so much now and he found himself less and less tired. His drives now were reaching out nearly 200 yards (though not always in the right direction), and he got some satisfaction from the astonishment and admiration of the first-tee spectators.

It was at the beginning of October – nearly the first wedding anniversary – that he played his first straight eighteen holes. Back at the clubhouse, delighted, he said: 'You know I feel so fresh I could do another nine.'

'No, you don't,' Thelma said. 'You come and have some tea.'

He resolved after that to play eighteen holes every time, and at the end of November he broke 100 for the first time. One would have thought he had won the Irish Sweep. Next week-end he played twenty-seven holes in one day, and then in December he played eighteen holes one morning and eighteen in the afternoon, returning to the clubhouse utterly exhausted, with the chafed stumps hurting him, sweat pouring off, but grinning all over his face. Even on cold days the sweat ran off him, evidence of the tremendous effort that he had to exert in getting round. That was the only outward sign that told people how hard he had to work at the normally simple process of walking. He felt now that he was a golf slave for life and that delighted Thelma, who was no golf widow but carried his clubs for him on every round.

There was one further complication about playing golf with artificial legs: the feet had a little fore and aft movement but no lateral 'give' at all, so that when he straddled his legs to play a shot the ankles were quite stiff and he stood uncomfortably on the inside of each shoe. He lamented on this defect at Roehampton, and the ingenious craftsmen there designed and fitted a kind of universal joint in the ankles, allowing lateral 'give' against rubber pads, so that he could stand with legs apart and feet flat on the ground. It felt instantly better the first time he tried it, until at the fourteenth hole his right foot fell off. Luckily he had thought of that possibility and brought a spare pair of legs in the car, so he had only to lie beside the green until Thelma came back with another leg. At Roehampton they redesigned the joint and the new model gave no trouble thereafter.

That Christmas he got a rise of £25 a year. He was out of debt now and it brought his total income to £475 a year, so that they could really start saving for a second wedding. Yet by this time the passionless decorum of the office was reducing him to restive desperation and he began talking fretfully about throwing it up and trying to get something less stultifying. Leaving the job would certainly mean postponing the church marriage again, but Thelma was patient and unselfish about that. Her attitude was that if he were not happy and they married 'officially' he would have no chance then of leaving the company and would be unhappier than ever. Still, the only other jobs that seemed available were the revolting hawking of vacuum cleaners which would be defeat.

Several times he spoke to friends who might know of other jobs, but they all advised him depressingly to stay with the company where the future was safe, if unspectacular. If he had had his own legs still he would probably have resigned, married Thelma again publicly and battled for a new career, but psychologically the loss of legs forced him into unnatural caution because no lowering of present standards could be tolerated. He heard there was a vacancy in the company for aviation manager in Cairo. The lucky man would have a little aeroplane to fly around in and he fairly raced in to ask about it. 'My dear chap,' said a London executive, 'they'll never let you fly. Your future is in the London office.'

One morning (this was 1935) he opened the *Telegraph* and saw a headline: 'Royal Air Force To Be Expanded.' Under it was a speech by Mr Baldwin announcing that Britain's frontier was on the Rhine and that Britain must re-arm to keep pace with Germany.

A bigger Air Force meant they would need more pilots!

All morning he thought about it, and after lunch he dropped his work and wrote to Air Marshal Sir Frederick Bowhill, now Air Member for Personnel, who had been his AOC when he crashed.

An answer came back in a few days, sympathetic and understanding. Sir Frederick said that if it were left to him he would have Bader back in the Service, but there was no chance of persuading others to agree.

Golf was the opiate that made life bearable after that. By late summer he was good enough to start playing competition, his scores ranging between 90 and 110, with a handicap of 18. A few weeks later he won a silver jam spoon in a bogey competition and they dropped his handicap to 16. Now he could hit drives consistently 200 yards, often down the middle, and was sometimes getting into the high eighties.

By some miracle they had still been able to keep the secret of their marriage. Living apart was a thing one got used to – after all, husbands and wives in the Services were often separated for years. Usually they managed to be together the whole of each week-end, either staying at some pub not far from Fleet (which was the usual reason for his week-end extravagance) or staying with Thelma's grandmother at Windlesham. They preferred a pub when they could afford it because at Windlesham they had to keep pretending they were only engaged.

As well as golf, North Hants had several tennis courts near the clubhouse, and one day in summer Tinny Dean suggested: 'Come and have a shot, Douglas.' Bader did not need much persuading, though he had to play in heavy crêpe-soled golf shoes because his artificial feet needed a thick heel under them (tennis shoes would have toppled him backwards).

He partnered Dean in doubles and found it surprisingly and refreshingly easy after the tremendous labour learning to play golf. He was limited in his movements, of course, and out of practice as he had not held a racket for years, but the balance he had learned in swinging a golf club also worked at tennis. Once or twice he tripped and fell through trying to move faster than his lurching walk allowed, but as usual, falling was only a detail. When a ball came within reach he was very accurate, with a smashing forehand drive, yet, as with cricket, he felt he could not pull his weight properly. In doubles he could only get to a ball that came reasonably within reach and his partner had to do a tremendous amount of running. He tried singles but that was unsatisfying because his opponent always had to hit the ball back at him and he hated the idea of people playing down to him.

Still, it was another successful activity and he played often until he was able to enter for tournaments. One day at Fleet he played seventy-two games on end in a tournament, partnered by a Cambridge golf blue, Horton Row, who ran himself almost down to his knees going for the ones just outside Douglas's reach, spurred on by the breezy whiplash of the Bader tongue in full cry.

The main reason he liked tennis was that he could play with Thelma, though golf remained the first love. His fame reached the ears of the urbane and witty Henry Longhurst, author, golfing journalist and addict, who came down to Fleet to play with him. A former captain of Cambridge, Longhurst, who had been rubbing shoulders with the world's greatest golfers for some time and seen just about everything possible to see in golf, was astounded at the first tee when Bader hit a screaming drive. No mean performer himself, being a scratch man, Longhurst was most impressed that day as Bader finished with a card of 81. They played often after that and Longhurst soon learned that Bader did not like being helped up when he fell, though he was prepared to accept a tug up a hill or a shoulder coming down. Usually they played thirty-six holes a day, and even if his legs were raw after the first eighteen, Bader would never call off the second round unless his partner made the first suggestion. On the coldest winter days, with icy winds blowing, Longhurst, rugged up in sweaters and blowing on his hands, used to marvel at him playing in a thin, short-sleeve shirt, still sweating freely, impervious to the cold.

Longhurst began to notice that Bader always hit good second shots on the fifth hole, where the fairway sloped gently up to the green. He mentioned this and Bader said he had noticed the same thing, and thought it was because the uphill stance gave better resistance to his left side against the impact of the club-head hitting the ball and following through. Longhurst thought it was the fact that the uphill lie made it easier to get squarely behind the ball, but they both agreed that it would be a terribly clever thing to do to take half an inch off one leg so that he could get the same effect even on level ground. 'Wish I could do the same,' Longhurst said.

At Roehampton when Bader went along to get the leg shortened,

Dessoutter looked dubious and said that one short leg might lead to curvature of the spine, but Bader said golf was much more important than that and so the deed was done on the set of legs he used for golf. Next week-end he felt the benefit immediately, being able to punch the ball farther and more consistently on level ground than before. He told Longhurst that it worked, and Longhurst wrote a marvelling article in London's *Evening Standard* about the man who had taken half an inch off his left leg to play golf with a permanent uphill lie.

Bader saw it and rang Longhurst in great dudgeon. 'You goat,' he said, 'I had it taken off the right leg, not the left one.'

'Good God,' said Longhurst, 'you've taken it off the wrong leg.'

They started arguing about it and have been arguing ever since, though the reason has long since vanished, because Bader had the leg restored a year or two later when his golf had improved permanently.

At Christmas he got a rise of £30 a year, bringing total income to £505, the mark he had been aiming at, and they began saving more conscientiously, planning to be married again as soon as they had £100. By May they were nearly half-way there, when driving back from Hartley Wintney one Sunday he noticed a knock in the engine. It got progressively worse and soon he had to pull into a garage, where a mechanic diagnosed a broken crankshaft.

For a week Bader travelled by bus and tube again. Then the repaired car was ready. He collected the bill at the same time – £30. When he drove away a loud and unpleasant grating came from the back. Smashed crown wheel and bevel! That brought another bill!

Eventually, driving it back to London with Thelma, they came to an accident at the top of the hill by Virginia Water, where two cars had collided and he stopped to see if he could help. Before he could get out a motor-cycle combination pelted over the top of the hill, swerved to avoid the damaged cars, and the sidecar rammed the MG head on. In the jolt Thelma's face jerked against the ignition key, cutting her nose badly, and the front of the car was stove in, but neither Douglas nor the motor-cyclist was hurt and there was no one in the sidecar. Ambulance men bandaged Thelma's face, which was streaming blood, and he took her back to London in a taxi. She was more or less all right in a day or two, apart from a black eye, but Bader was without the car for nearly a month. Luckily the motor-cyclist's insurance covered most of the damage, but it still left Douglas with some £15 to pay taxis, doctors and incidentals. The savings were wiped out and so were any chances of setting up home together for another six months.

Then in August (with another friend in the car this time) he was approaching a rise near Rugby at about 70 mph when the driver of a large Rolls Royce in front waved him on. As he pulled out to pass, a car came over the rise. He braked and pulled in sharply behind the Rolls, but the Rolls was braking, too, and the MG rammed its rump very hard. Geoffrey Darlington, the passenger, copied Thelma, cutting his face on the ignition key and getting a cut nose and brow and a black eye. Everyone got out of the cars and all were remarkably polite about the affair, but that did not help a great deal towards paying the bill of £30 for the MG. Thelma was haunted for weeks by the guilty note in her fiancé's voice when he rang up and confessed: 'Darling, I've busted the car again.'

At Christmas he got a rise of £35 and said. 'Come hell or high water we're going to get officially married this year.'

CHAPTER ELEVEN

By March he was out of debt again and the money began to mount in the bank. Prodded by Thelma's common sense he was beginning to realise that however much he hated his job it was not so much the job's fault as his own antipathy to that sort of life. The petroleum company was the great Shell organisation and it was Thelma who pointed out to him that if he did get another job it would be the same sort of life as in the Shell Company and probably not as good a job. He faced it, reluctantly but with resignation.

It was Thelma's idea, too, that they should get married again on 5 October, fourth anniversary of the uninspiring Hampstead ceremony. She found a flat in a new block going up in West Kensington and at the end of September the fluctuating bank account was drained again, this time to pay for the furniture.

Only one mild hitch happened at the last moment: at a wedding rehearsal at Avonmore Mansions on the evening of 4 October he bent to kneel in the prescribed way and tipped flat on his face. Everyone laughed amiably: he tried again and tipped forward once more, realising then for the first time since he had lost his legs that he could no longer kneel on both knees because the wooden feet would not bend and enable him to sit on his heels. It was a great joke until he said: 'What the hell do I do to-morrow?' Geoffrey Darlington, who was to be best man, said he would buttonhole the vicar beforehand and get permission to stand.

Next morning they were re-married, standing, in St Mary Abbott's Church, Kensington, Douglas looking very dapper in cutaway coat and sponge-bag trousers, and Thelma weakening at the last moment and uttering the word 'obey' which she had vowed she would not do. All the relatives and friends were so warmly happy to see the couple at last married after so many difficulties. Neither 'bride' nor 'groom' disturbed their sentimental illusions (which have endured to the present day).

Afterwards at Avonmore Mansions the champagne flowed freely and for the first time in his life Douglas joined the others at the trough. As was his nature, he tackled it with rather more zeal than other men, and after seeing him sink the second tumbler, Mrs Addison said: 'Douglas, that *is* intoxicating you know.'

Beaming, his eyes more electrically alive than ever, he boomed: 'Yes, isn't it wonderful,' adjusted a woman guest's hat over her startled eyes and grasped another tumblerful. Colonel Addison counted five tumblers all told, and was amazed that a man could absorb so much and still stay on his feet, especially artificial ones. Later, Douglas lurched unassisted to the car with Thelma and drove off for a second honeymoon in Cornwall.

At Farnborough they stopped to break the news of the wedding to friends in the Royal Tank Corps mess, where they were refuelled with champagne and sped on their journey. He cannot remember seeing another car on the road till they reached their hotel at the Lizard (neither wished to sample again the Porthleven rock cakes).

He woke in the morning issuing low moans, with the leaden pulsing head of the first and last hangover of his life, and for two days he was unusually tractable. Four years earlier no one had guessed they were on a honeymoon, but this time everyone knew because there had been a photograph in the *Daily Mirror* of them walking out of the church at the wedding with the caption 'This Man Has Courage,' and a local shop had hung it up in the window. It was exasperating to sense that everyone was smirking tenderly at them as honeymooners when they were really a veteran married couple. Back in London after a fortnight it was glorious to be able to walk into their own flat and shut the door on the world.

Settled in their own home, Thelma soon noticed that his depressed moods which had sometimes gone on for days were becoming rare and brief. Besides, his golf handicap was down to nine and he had started playing squash at the Lensbury Club, a pleasant recreation spot for Shell Company staff near Teddington. She was a little worried about his playing squash; he put so much energy into it that sometimes he came back with eyes sunk in dark sockets from sheer fatigue. His partners had a gentleman's agreement to try and return the ball just out of reach and Bader lunged furiously about the court, taking some terrible tumbles and with legs thumping and creaking on the protesting floor. Rivets often popped out of the legs under this treatment, and one day the knee bolt of the right leg snapped and, as he fell, the right shin and foot, complete with sock and shoe, shot across the court.

Hitler had never meant much to him until Munich; it was then he realised there was going to be a war and that war was his chance. He wrote to Air Ministry asking for a refresher flying course so that he could be ready when war came, and a polite note came back saying that the doctors still thought that the legs made him a permanent accident risk. Would he consider an administrative job? He wrote back: No.

About April, 1939, when Hitler was marching into the rest of Czechoslovakia, Geoffrey Stephenson was posted to Air Ministry. Stephenson was friendly with the personal staff officer to the new Air Member for Personnel, Air Marshal Sir Charles Portal, and soon, by arrangement under the 'Old Chums Act,' Bader wrote to Portal asking the same old question. He got what looked at first like the same old answer: 'I am afraid that during peace time it is not possible for me to permit you to enter a flying class of the reserve.' And then he came to the last exciting sentence: 'But you can rest assured that if war came we would almost certainly be only too glad of your services in a flying capacity after a short time if the doctors agreed.'

It was not perhaps the accepted thing to do, but part of him began almost praying for war. Thelma, full of dread both at the idea of war and of Douglas trying to fly in it without legs, tried miserably to get him to give up the dream, but he would not listen. She tried to calm herself by thinking that they would never take him. Colonel Addison suggested that he would never get past the people in Whitehall and Douglas answered fiercely: 'Well, by God, I'll sit on their doorsteps till I do get in.'

The day after Hitler marched into Poland he sent Thelma away to join her parents in the country for a few days in case masses of bombers came over when the whistle went. (The family had recently taken over half a bungalow attached to the Pantiles.) He had to force her to go because she had a feeling of impending doom which was not soothed by his eager satisfaction of the turn of events. Next morning, washing up his breakfast things, he heard Chamberlain's tragic voice announcing war. He left the washing up, sat down and wrote to Portal's secretary again.

On the Monday the Shell Company began evacuating some offices to the Lensbury Club, and Bader's boss told him that he would be based there on the list of indispensable workers debarred from call-up.

Bader immediately said: 'Would you mind taking my name off that list, sir. I'm not really indispensable and I'm trying to get back into the RAF. I don't want to risk my pitch being queered.'

'They'll never let you fly,' the executive said.

'I'm still going to try, so please whip my name off the list.'

'My dear chap, you don't have to do that. No one's going to give *you* a white feather.'

Angry at that, Bader pressed the point and shortly his name was removed from the list.

Down at the Lensbury Club he began telephoning and writing peremptory notes to Stephenson and another friend at Air Ministry, Hutchinson, to get things moving for him, but weeks passed and he got restless and even more tersely demanding. Then, early in October, a telegram arrived: 'Please attend Air Ministry Adastral House Kingsway for selection board Thursday 10.30. Bring this telegram with you.'

Eagerly on the Thursday he found the right room. A dozen other men were waiting and he thought they all looked rather old for flying. A corporal called his name and he followed into an inner office where, to his surprise, he came face to face with Air Vice-Marshal Halahan, his old commandant at Cranwell. Halahan got up from his desk and shook hands. 'Good to see you, Douglas. What sort of job would you like?'

It almost took his breath away.

'General Duties,[1] of course, sir.'

Halahan said: 'Oh!' and looked dubious. 'I'm very sorry but I'm only dealing with ground jobs here.'

His stomach sagged a little. 'It's only a flying job I want, sir. I'm not interested in anything on the ground.'

Halahan looked at him steadily and silently for some five seconds and then, apparently making up his mind, stretched out, took a piece of paper and began writing on it. No words were said. He finished, blotted it, sealed it in an envelope and handed it across.

'Take that across to the medical people,' he said, 'and good luck.'

They shook hands again and Bader stumped out. Dying to know what was in the letter he felt strung up with fearful hope. The feeling mounted as he crossed Kingsway and went up in the lift to the bitterly remembered medical unit. Guarding the sanctum was the same stout and kindly Cerebus who had seen so many men broken from crashes come in and try to talk their way back to A1B – full flying category. The warrant officer recognised him:

''Ullo, sir. I thought you'd be along. What's it this time?'

'Same again,' Bader said. 'I think they might pass me this time.'

'Not A1B, sir. Never.'

'We'll see. Would you please give this to the wing commander.' He handed over the letter from Halahan.

After a while the warrant officer came back and got out a new file for him. 'Come along, sir,' he said. 'We'll get you done as quickly as possible.'

Bader always remembered the sequence of events after that. He wrote them down:

'I didn't know any of the doctors this time, but everything went

[1] Flying.

perfectly except for the chap with the rubber hammer who tests your reflexes by knocking you on the knee and seeing how quickly your foot and shin jerk. I'd been stripped except for my trousers, and he said: "Just pull your trouser leg up and cross your knees." I said "I can't and it's no good." I explained the position and we both had a good laugh. He had a look at them while I walked and professionally was very interested. He tested my reflexes by hammering the inside of my elbows instead. Seemed much the same.

'I visited the various rooms in turn; eyes, ears, nose and throat; blood pressure, heart and lungs – never a shadow of doubt. I asked the last doctor, "Am I all right for flying?" and he gave me a short laugh as though I had been joking. Finally, my file was complete and the wing commander sent for me. He also was a different chap, slightly bald but with quite a pleasant face. I sat down. I could see he was looking at my file as though he were thinking, not reading. Then he looked up and said: "Apart from your legs you're a hundred per cent." He pushed a bit of paper across to me, and said: "Have you seen this?" It was Halahan's note. I said: "No, sir." I looked at it and as far as I remember it read:

' "I have known this officer since he was a cadet at Cranwell under my command. He's the type we want. If he is fit, apart from his legs, I suggest you give him A1B category and leave it to the Central Flying School to assess his flying capabilities."

'I handed the note back without a word. I looked at him. I had the feeling of being tremendously alert at a terribly important cross-road. I think I stopped breathing. I remembered 1932 – the same scene, different circumstances, different man behind the desk saying there was nothing in King's Regulations to let me through. The silence seemed to go on. I don't know whether it was a second or ten seconds. I had the feeling the doctor wanted to look away, but I was not going to let him. I was looking directly at him, willing him to think my way. He said, "I agree with Air Vice Marshal Halahan. We're giving you A1B and it's up to the flying chaps. I'll recommend they give you a test at CFS." '

It was too big to show emotion. He felt a serenity pervading him, turning into a glow like a man who feels his fourth whisky flooding him with soft fire. His face hardly changed, except that he took a deep breath, said correctly: 'Thank you very much, sir,' and walked out, feeling that the wasted years were cancelled and he was picking up life again from the moment he had crashed, back on a par with the chosen few.

In that mood he drove to the Pantiles. The fact that a war had opened the gate never crossed his mind; personal content was too deep to bother about externals that could not be changed. As he walked in the doorway the family was listening to a gramophone, the tea things still on the table. Thelma switched off the music and said: 'Hallo, what are you doing here? Lost your job?'

'No,' he said. 'I'm getting my old one back.'

It was her turn to feel that the moment was too big to show emotion, though, as a matter of fact, ever since he had known her she had always retired into a studied restraint in moments of crisis. The deeper the feeling the less she allowed it to show and the most she said this time was, miserably: 'I suppose you'll be very happy now.'

Back at the Lensbury Club a few days passed with no more word from the RAF and he became intolerably impatient. It was not that he wanted to burst straight into action because there was no fighting except far off in Poland. He just wanted to get back into the RAF, into an aeroplane and get the feel of the life back again, especially now that there was a purpose in it. He took to ringing Stephenson and Hutchinson in the old peremptory way, bullying them to make someone do something immediately. All the latent vigour banked up for years was bursting out. On 14 October a telegram came from the Central Flying School at Upavon, 'Suggest report for test 18 October.' He drove down next morning.

It was over seven years since he had flown – he was bound to be rusty – but only on the way down did the insidious, disturbing thought cross his mind that he might fail the test. He tried to put the thought out of his mind but it would not go.

It was odd at first walking into the grey stone mess in flannels and sports coat while everyone else walked about confidently in uniform. He felt awkward and out of place until he came across Joe Cox there, and also the thickset amusing Rupert Leigh whom he had last known as a junior cadet at Cranwell.

'You're my meat,' Leigh said menacingly. 'I am the maestro of the refresher flight and I give you your test. I know you will behave courteously towards me.'

That demolished the insidious fear. Under 'The Old Chums Act' it was in the bag unless he made some unthinkable blunder.

After lunch Leigh took him out to a Harvard advanced trainer on the undulating grass field. This was going to be different from the old Bulldog: the Harvard was a sturdy monoplane, its cockpit crammed with a hundred instruments and knobs compared to the twenty odd in the Bulldog. It had all the modern things he had never encountered before, flaps, constant speed propeller, retractable undercarriage and brakes. Brakes! To his horror, when he got into the cockpit he saw that the Harvard had foot-brakes and they were a physical impossibility for him to manipulate sensitively as well as the rudder pedals. Leigh soothed his truculent lament:

'Forget about the brakes. I'll work them. You won't have to worry about them after to-day because the Harvard's the only aircraft in the Service that hasn't got a hand-brake on the stick.'

Leigh explained the cockpit, climbed into the back seat and started up. 'I'll do a circuit first,' he said, 'and then you have a stab.'

He took the Harvard off with a surging, satisfying bellow and explained what he was doing all the way round. After landing he taxied back to the downwind perimeter and said: 'Right. She's yours.'

Bader was too busy to feel that This Was The Moment. He went through the cockpit drill, turned into wind and opened the throttle, and as she went away with a roar and picked up her tail there was no swing. Soon she lifted, docile in his hands, and he remembered to change pitch as she climbed. Just for a minute or two it felt a little strange, but as he flew round for a quarter of an hour the 'feel' came back, dispersing the last wisp of unease and filling him with joy. With Leigh's voice jogging his mind about pitch, undercarriage and flaps he turned in to land. She was heavier than he realised and he undershot but tickled her over the fence with a bit of engine and flattened, easing back and back till he cut the throttle, held her off and then cut her tail down as she settled. She touched smoothly and ran without swinging. Surprised that she was so easy to fly, he took her off again and spent an hour doing two more landings and then climbing for a roll and a loop before landing again, exultant.

When they taxied in and got out Leigh's first words were, 'Well, it's damn' silly asking me if you can fly. However, I'll humour them and write recommending that you be re-admitted to the fold and posted here for a full refresher course.'

He went back to the Lensbury with warm content that changed to growing impatience, and as the days and then the weeks passed without word he started pestering Stephenson and Hutchinson again.

The news came, and saddened him, that Harry Day, his old flight commander, was missing from a semi-suicidal daylight reconnaissance over Germany.[1]

Towards the end of November an Air Ministry envelope arrived. He ripped it open and there it was in detached official language: they would take him back, not on the Volunteer Reserve but as a regular officer re-employed in his former rank and seniority (which meant higher pay). His retired pay would cease but his hundred per cent disability pension would continue. (That was a droll touch – hundred per cent fit and hundred per cent disabled.) If the terms were acceptable would he kindly state when he was prepared to report to CFS for duty. That day was a

---

[1] Day was later reported a prisoner-of-war.

Friday. He wrote back, naming Sunday, rang his tailor to demand a new uniform within a week, and left his desk for the last time.

That gave him a final day with Thelma at the Pantiles and he could not disguise his glee until, on the Sunday when he had put his bag in the MG and was ready to go, Thelma, for the first time since he had known her, gave way, and the tears began trickling down her face as she stood by the car. Then she turned and ran into the house. He drove away greatly sobered, and the mood stayed until he turned in past the guardroom at Upavon: at that moment he felt back in the Air Force again.

In the morning he drew flying kit, which was deeply satisfying. Along with the new log-book, helmet, goggles, Sidcot flying-suit, and other things, the quarter-master corporal pushed a pair of handsome black flying-boots across the counter and Bader pushed them back, saying: 'No, thanks, Corporal. You can keep these. I don't get cold feet.'

'But you've *got* to have them, sir,' said the Corporal, puzzled, so he took them to give to Thelma.

At the refresher flight he reported to Leigh with a smart 'Good-morning, sir,' and they both started laughing because Leigh, who had been his junior, was now a squadron leader and Bader was still only a flying officer, one of the most senior flying officers in the RAF. After lunch another old friend, Christopher Clarkson, took him up in an Avro Tutor for his first flight as an active officer since the crash. Clarkson handled her for the first 'circuit and bump' and then let Bader have the controls. The Tutor was an aeroplane he knew – a biplane: none of this variable pitch propeller nonsense or flaps or retractable undercarriage. A sensible aeroplane! His first landing was workmanlike and his second a neat three-pointer. As he turned downwind again Clarkson hauled himself out of the cockpit and said: 'She's all yours, chum.'

'This, then, was the moment. At last I was alone with an aeroplane, 27 November, 1939 – almost exactly eight years after my crash.

'I turned Tutor K3242 into wind and took off. I remember the afternoon as clearly as to-day. It was 3.30, a grey sky with clouds at 1,500 feet and a south-west wind. A number of aeroplanes were flying around. I went a little way from the crowd . . .'

Shortly the telephone rang in Rupert Leigh's office and Leigh picked it up and heard the cold voice of Wing Commander Pringle, the chief flying instructor: 'Leigh! I have just landed. On my way down I passed a Tutor upside down in the circuit area at 600 feet.'

Leigh froze with foreboding.

The frigid voice continued: 'I *know* who it was. Be good enough to ask him not to break *all* the flying regulations straight away.'

When Bader landed and taxied in he found Leigh beside him, saying: 'Don't do it. Please don't do it.'

'Do what?'

Leigh told him what had happened but Bader could not very well explain to him that on his first solo flight he *had* to turn the aeroplane upside down at forbidden height. At the time he did not know himself that it had any connection with his last flight in the Bulldog.

> *'I had a new flying log-book then. I look at it to-day and read:*
> *1939. November 27*
> *Tutor K3242. Self.   F/Lt. Clarkson.   25 minutes.*
> *Tutor K3242. Self   ———   25 minutes.*
> *These are the two entries and I recall exactly the feeling of the schoolboy looking at the notice-board and seeing his name in the team for Saturday.'*

After that flight and after meeting some of the others in the mess he did not feel so strange even in his civilian clothes. Many of them were former Short Service officers of about his own age, recalled to do refresher courses like himself, or an instructor's course. Just for a day or so he felt like an old boy back at school as a pupil with his former class-mates as masters and then, just in the way he had got the feeling of flying, so he slipped easily into the old atmosphere again. The last touch was when his uniform arrived and then he was really back at home, belonging as much as anyone else, more deeply content than he could remember.

He flew the Tutor several times more, sometimes under the hood[1] learning to use the new-fangled blind-flying gyro instruments. Then he took her up at night which had a tonic effect on him, making him feel completely alone, master of it all with the blacked-out land quiescent below, lit palely by moonlight. The only awkward thing that remained now was the possibility of being forced, some time, to bale out. Landing by parachute is the equivalent of jumping off a 12-ft wall, and coming down on the right leg would probably be like landing on a rigid steel post that would split his pelvis horribly. He decided to worry about that if and when the moment came.

On 4 December for the first time he flew a modern, operational aircraft, the Fairey 'Battle,' a single-engined, two-seater day bomber. She was heavy to handle, approaching obsolescence and not approved for pupil aerobatics (though after a couple of days he was quietly looping and rolling her away from the aerodrome and prying eyes at 7,000 ft). He preferred a lighter aircraft, but being put on to the Battle did not bother him; he knew he was going on to fighters. No one had said so, but

---

[1] A canvas hood which was pulled over the pupil's head so he could not see outside the cockpit but had to fly on instruments. The instructor was always in the other cockpit at these times to take over in case of trouble.

it was obvious – with his legs it would have to be a single-engined aircraft carrying only a pilot.

On the Battle he quickly mastered the modern gadgets and never looked like committing the classic boob of landing with undercarriage up or trying to take off with propeller in coarse pitch.[1] Upavon boasted a single Hurricane and a single Spitfire: he was burning to fly them, but so were thirty others, and he had to practise on other types first.

Like most of the others, he did not think a great deal about the war. There was not much, in fact, to think about in that respect: in Poland the fighting had ended in tragedy and the enemy seemed locked behind the Maginot Line as approaching winter called its own temporary truce.

A letter reached him from Air Ministry dated 8 December, and with a great red stamp 'SECRET' on it. 'Sir,' it said, 'I am commanded to inform you that a state of great emergency has arisen . . .' It went on to inform him that he was posted to Upavon some weeks previously and enclosed a rail warrant. It was another endearing little touch that the Air Force had not changed.

Time continued to slide by with flying every day and comradeship in the mess at night, often developing into exuberant impromptu parties which revived the old spirit he had missed so much, though still he never took anything stronger than orange squash. Not in the least did he mind others drinking, but for himself, his attitude was, 'If I can't be cheerful without a drink I'm not much good.' In fact, he was tremendously cheerful, in his element day and night. Thelma came down to stay with Joe Cox and his wife for a week and found Douglas happier than she had ever seen him. After that she did not mind him being back in the Air Force so much, though the thought of the future still terrified her.

One night at a mess party an army officer guest from a nearby unit buttonholed him, and said: 'Hallo, chum, didn't you used to grind my face in the mud at inter-school rugger?'

'You look familiar,' Bader said, and then recognised David Niven, the actor.

Winter froze hard that year. He got out of the MG at the mess steps one night and instantly slipped and fell on the icy ground. He got up and slipped over again, soon finding it impossible to keep his balance on the slippery ground. At last there was no help for it: he was forced to crawl his way to the steps on hands and knees and then crawl up them, fortunately just as two brother officers came out and said: 'Good grief, look at Bader! Bottled as a coot.' Everyone pulled his leg about being a secret drinker and his grinning amusement changed to annoyance in the morning when he found the ice still on the ground so that he was

[1] Almost guaranteed to cause an accident. The aeroplane runs fast but not quite fast enough to lift off the ground.

marooned in the mess unable to walk about outside like the others. Joe Cox got a brainwave and suggested he put his socks *over* his shoes instead of inside them: he tried it and found he could walk on ice quite easily.

Early in the new year he began flying the Miles Master, the recognised last step before going on to Spitfires and Hurricanes. Then, a couple of weeks later, he got his chance at the Hurricane. Just getting into the solitary cockpit roused his blood. Another old Cranwell friend, 'Connie' Constantine, pointed out the 'taps.' It was common in those days to feel a little qualm before one's first flight in a Hurricane or Spitfire as there could be no trial 'circuit and bump' with an instructor. Bader felt only deep peace as he taxied out alone. It was such a satisfying aircraft for an individualist. He opened the throttle slowly, corrected a slight drift to port as the tail came up and then he was in the air. From the start he felt a part of the Hurricane: she was the most responsive aircraft he had yet flown and after twenty minutes feeling her out he made a smooth landing. On his next flight in her he tried aerobatics; she felt better than ever and he began to fall in love with the aeroplane. Several times more he flew her but never got a chance at Upavon to fly the lone Spitfire because George Stainforth, a former Schneider Trophy pilot and speed record holder, passed out in it through oxygen shortage at about 23,000 feet. Not far from the ground he came to, pointing straight down at 500 mph and reefing her out, just in time, strained the wings.

At the end of January Joe Cox said to him: 'Well, *we're* happy about your flying if you are. You might as well crack off to a squadron.'

Bader immediately rang Geoffrey Stephenson, who had deftly eased himself out of Air Ministry and was now commanding 19 Squadron at, of all places, Duxford, where Bader thought he had said good-bye to the Air Force for ever. The squadron had Spitfires and Stephenson set about getting him an immediate posting to it. It did not matter that he had not flown Spitfires: the main thing was to get to a squadron, particularly one whose commander would not be dismayed at having a pilot with no legs.

Before he went on end-of-course leave he saw the reports on his flying. Rupert Leigh wrote:

'This officer is an exceptionally good pilot . . . he is very keen and should be ideally suited . . . to single-seater fighters.'

Cox's report said: 'I entirely agree with the above remarks. When flying with this officer it is quite impossible to even imagine that he has two artificial legs. He is full of confidence and possesses excellent judgment and air sense. His general flying (including aerobatics) is very smooth and accurate. I have never met a more enthusiastic pilot. He lives for flying.'

As OC Refresher Squadron, Stainforth noted: 'I am in full agreement with this report,' and then in Bader's log-book under the heading 'Ability as a pilot,' he wrote: 'Exceptional.'

On February 3 Bader drove to the Pantiles for his leave and the next four days were not cheerful. Thelma, unable to mask her feelings as well as usual, was worrying about him, and he was restless day and night wanting to get on with it because he'd feel *really* back in the Air Force again when he got to a squadron. A telegram ended the waiting: 'Posted 19 Squadron, Duxford, w.e.f. February 7.' The date was already February 7. Thelma, the stoic again, packed his kit and within two hours he was on his way in the MG, feeling happier than he could remember.

CHAPTER TWELVE

Duxford was different. About teatime he drove in past the guardroom which he had so poignantly left behind in 1933, but now it was a different guardroom, new and bigger. The mess, too, was new and bigger – not so intimate – but the main change lay in the faces there; they all looked about twenty-one. Yet so they had been in 1933 too; Bader, sitting alone in the ante-room, became sharply aware that he would be thirty in exactly a fortnight and that it was he who had changed most. Geoffrey Stephenson was away for a couple of days and he felt out of it all, unable to retrieve the spirit of the dream.

His only cheerful moment in the mess that evening was meeting again Tubby Mermagen. Years ago he had known Mermagen as a pilot officer, but Mermagen now commanded the other squadron at Duxford, No. 222, which flew Blenheims. It was fun to talk over old times, but when he took off his legs to go to bed he felt again a comparatively elderly flying officer.

It would be all right as soon as he got into a Spitfire; but in the morning the pilots flew off to do convoy patrols from an advanced base and no serviceable Spitfire was left. He flew a Magister instead. The same thing happened next day. Then Stephenson came back and Bader greeted him with a glad cry. Next morning he climbed into a Spitfire and a boy of twenty showed him the cockpit. Above the throttle quadrant were the switches of a TR2 radio set. Bader had not used radio in the air yet. The boy prattled on about R/T procedure, making it sound so complicated that Bader impatiently cut him short and said he'd do without it this trip – just concentrate on the flying. She started easily and he took off without any nerves, feeling instantly that she was extremely sensitive fore and aft. The long, mullet-head cowling that housed the Merlin engine made for restricted vision, but he rapidly got the feel of her and liked the way she handled like a highly-strung thorough-bred. On the downwind leg he started his drill for landing and found he could not move the undercart selector lever into the 'down' position. No tugs, pushes or fiddlings would budge it.[1] Disconcerting! Only one thing to do – 'ring up' and get advice. He switched on the radio and like many of the ill-tuned early models it crackled and popped and buzzed, so that he could not hear a word from the control tower. That was more disconcerting! He tried with the undercart selector lever again and after some time fiddling with this and the pump handle finally got things working and the two green lights winked reassuringly as the wheels locked down. After that the landing was an anti-climax, but neat.

Old emotions were stirring. In this élite of beardless youth he had more seniority than anyone, twice as many flying hours as most and was years older. Long ago he had been the golden boy of such a squadron and now he was the new boy – the 'sprog.' Like a tide in him rose the need to prove himself equal to the young pilots who could play rugger and wore their uniforms with such blithe assurance. Not for a moment did he admit there was anything he could not do as well as they (apart from rugger, which he accepted), but there are other impulses in the mind than those of the conscious.

The old challenge. A new struggle.

That was part of it. There was also an old-fashioned zeal to get his teeth into the enemy, though there seemed few prospects of fighting in sight. Duxford was on the southern frontier of 12 Group which was charged with the air defence of England's vital industrial Midland from a line just north of London. Even the boys in 11 Group guarding London and the Channel were bored.

On February 13 his flight commander, an unblooded veteran of twenty-five, led him aloft for his first formation flying in a Spitfire, and Bader, by God, was going to show him – and anyone else who cared to see. Like the old days in Gamecocks, he tucked his wing in about three feet behind his leader's and stuck there, rocklike, through the whole flight. It takes quick hands and rapt concentration to do that; you watch your leader, not where you're going. Coming in to land the flight commander dipped low beside a wooden hut. Some instinct made Bader look ahead for a second and at the last moment under the Spitfire's nose he saw the hut and that he could not miss it. Shoving on throttle he yanked back on the stick and the fighter reared up, squashing, engine blaring, and the tail smashed into the inverted-V wooden roof, and

---

[1] The young lad of twenty had omitted to tell him that the undercarriage always hung on the withdrawal pins and a couple of pumps removed the weight of the wheels and allowed the selector freedom to travel into the 'down' position.

ploughed through, losing the tail wheel. The rocking fighter was still flying and he steadied her, brought her round again and landed her on the naked rump of the tail, inevitably tearing the metal some more.

The flight commander came across laughing, and said: 'I'm awfully sorry, ol' boy. Most extraordinary thing – d'you know not long ago I landed a chap in a tree just the same way.'

He never forgot the blunt details which Bader told him about his character in the next few minutes.

At dawn a few days later the new pilot made his first operational flight – a convoy patrol. After take-off, according to the drill, he turned the ring of his gun button from 'safe' to 'fire' and that was a good moment, the first time he had ever done it on business. It was exciting to feel there were eight loaded machine-guns in the wings, cocked to obey a thumb on the button. This was war and he had come a long way for it, his life usefully dedicated in a cause for which an Englishman may feel deep and private emotion. In that cause he flew among the vanguard, armed, strong and as fleet as any.

For an hour and a half they flew over a dozen tiny ships crawling over the grey water of the East Coast and saw nothing else in the sky at all. Before landing the gun button went back to 'safe,' and that was that.

Most days they spent practising the three officially approved methods of attacking bombers, known as 'Fighter Command Attack No. 1, No. 2, and No. 3.' In 'Attack No. 1,' for instance, the fighters swung into line astern behind the leader and followed him in an orderly line up to the bomber, took a quick shot when their turn came in the queue and swung gracefully away after the leader again, presenting their bellies predictably to the enemy gunner. Long ago the theoreticians at Fighter Command had decided that modern aircraft, especially fighters, were too fast for the dog-fight tactics of World War I. Bader, his head full of McCudden, Bishop and Ball, thought that was all nonsense and that the three official attacks were likewise absurd.

'There's only one damn' way to do it,' he growled to Stephenson, '. . . that's for everyone to pile in together from each side as close to the Hun as they can and let him have the lot. Why use only eight guns at a time when you can use sixteen or twenty-four from different angles.'

Stephenson and the others argued: 'But you don't *know*, do you? *No* one knows.'

'The boys in the last war knew,' he said, 'and the basic idea is the same now. Anyhow,' he added, 'they'd damn' well soon find out if they tried the Fighter Command attacks, but they probably wouldn't get back to report it.' When he got an idea into his head he wouldn't budge.

'No Hun bomber's going to stooge along in a straight line and let a line of chaps queue up behind and squirt at him one after the other,' he said. 'He'd jink all over the place. In any case, it won't be one; it'll be a lot of bombers sticking together in tight formation to concentrate the fire of their back guns. Why the devil d'you think our bombers have got power-operated turrets?'

Probably after the first pass or two the bomber pack could be split up, he considered. There'd be single bombers around then, but the fighters would be split up too and there'd be dog-fights all over the sky, every man for himself.

'The chap who'll control the battle will still be the chap who's got the height and sun, same as the last war,' he said. 'That old slogan of Ball, Bishop and McCudden, "Beware of the Hun in the sun," wasn't just a funny rhyme. Those boys learned from experience. We haven't got the experience yet, so I'll back their ideas till I find out.'

Some of the other pilots ragged him about being pre-war vintage and old-fashioned (especially on his thirtieth birthday), and Stephenson soothed him, saying in reasonable tones: 'You might be right, Douglas, but we've got to keep on doing what we're told until we find out for ourselves.'

So Flying Officer Bader kept dourly and sometimes profanely following his leader in dummy attacks on Wellington bombers which stooged obligingly in a straight line and never fired back. In those circumstances it was easy enough, until one day, diving in line astern on a hedge-hopping Wellington, one eye on his leader and the other eye on the Wellington, Douglas ploughed into a tree-top at about 250 mph and the Spitfire shot out the other side in a shower of broken branches with one aileron torn and bent. She was controllable, but veering to the right with one wing low and he had a busy and awkward ten minutes nursing her down to firm ground again without further damage.

Stormily he said to Stephenson: 'That silly clot led me into a tree.'

'Well,' said Stephenson affably, '*you're* the silly clot. It's up to you to see where you're going. He can't fly the aeroplane for you.'

With Churchillian grunts, Bader lurched off, convinced for all time of the superior virtues of individual attacks and dog-fights, as against unwieldy processions. At the very least, he thought, if they had to line up in these damn'-fool processions they ought to have good leaders. After that he began to watch carefully where he was led and a few days later, returning late from a convoy patrol in bad weather, noted with disgust that the leader had lost his way. It was dusk, with low cloud – a bad time to fly aimlessly. Bader, who had been map reading and knew exactly where they were, pulled across in front waggling his wings, turned the formation on to course and led them back to Duxford. That evening, in the privacy of his quarters with Stephenson, he said: 'Look, I don't feel happy flying behind some of these young chaps. I'm more experienced and older, although I've not so many hours on Spitfires. Don't forget what we were taught in the old days in 23 Squadron that bad leading always causes trouble. I've had it twice now in a short time and I'm sick of it. I prefer to be killed in action, not on active service. Isn't it about time . . .'

The name of F/O Bader went up on the squadron readiness board next day as leader of a section of three.

He handled his section with confident pride on convoy and lightship patrols, practice battle climbs and even, conscientiously, in the official Fighter Command follow-my-leader attacks (though on the ground later he still scathingly condemned them).

It was the 'phoney war' period, and Thelma, still at the Pantiles, was soothed by it, getting used to the idea of Douglas flying on a squadron – he had not told her about hitting the hut roof and the tree. To him none of this time was dull; he was flying and leading – that was enough for the time being. The fighting was bound to come in the end and as long as he was sure of that he did not mind, even though they did not yet have either armour plate behind the cockpits or self-sealing petrol tanks.

He flew over Cranwell one day and a wave of sentimental affection flooded his mind as he looked down. As he circled it the place seemed to take on a personality and he genuinely felt it was looking up at him, and saying: 'I trained you for this and I trained you well. Don't forget what I taught you.'

Tubby Mermagen's 222 Squadron at Duxford was changing its Blenheims for Spitfires and some of the crews were being posted away. In the mess one night Mermagen buttonholed Bader and casually said: 'I want a new flight commander. I don't want to do the dirty on Geoffrey, but if he's agreeable, would you come?'

Beaming, Bader remarked with vigour that he would be delighted.

'Good show,' said Mermagen. 'I'll talk to Geoffrey and then fix it with the AOC.'[1]

Convoy patrol next day had a new savour. Barring accidents Air Vice Marshal Leigh-Mallory was almost sure to approve. In the morning Bader led his section over to the advanced base at Horsham to await convoy patrol orders, and they had been on the ground only about five minutes, sipping at cups of tea, when the operations phone rang and the orderly who answered it shouted an urgent order to 'scramble' (take off immediately) to cover a convoy. An unidentified aircraft had been plotted near it. Bader put his tea down and lurched as fast as he could after the other running pilots to his Spitfire. Unidentified aircraft! Perhaps at last!

Quickly he clipped his straps and pressed the starter button; the still-hot engine fired instantly and he was still winding his trimming-wheel as the plane went booming across the grass. The other two Spitfires

[1] Air Officer Commanding.

were shooting past him, pulling away, and he sensed vaguely at first, then with sudden certainty, that his aircraft was lagging. A quick glance at the boost gauge; the needle was quivering on 6½ lb – maximum power. She must be all right; but she was still bumping over the grass, curiously sluggish, running at a low stone wall on the far side of the field. The fence was rushing nearer, but still she stuck to the ground. He hauled desperately on the stick and the nose pulled up as she lurched off at an unnatural angle, not climbing. His right hand snapped down to the undercart lever but almost in the same moment the wheels hit the stone wall and ripped away. At nearly 80 mph the little fighter slewed and dipped a wingtip into a ploughed field beyond; the nose smacked down, the tail kicked – she nearly cartwheeled – the tail slapped down again and she slithered and bumped on her belly with a rending noise across the soft earth.

As years ago in the Bulldog memory fled from the jolted mind. She jerked to a stop in a cloud of flying dirt and the perspex hood of the cockpit snapped forward and hit him on the back of the head, maddening him, though other emotions were momentarily frozen. The brain started working again and began wondering what had happened as he sat there with everything so suddenly quiet he could hear the silence and the hot metal of the engine tinkling as it cooled. Automatically his hand went out and cut the switches and then he was motionless again apart from the eyes wandering round the cockpit looking for the answer. It stared back at him – the black knob of the propeller lever on the throttle quadrant poking accusingly at him, still in the coarse pitch position.

His stomach turned. Oh, hell, not that classic boob! He couldn't have! But he had. Angrily he banged the knob in.

Apart from the aggravating crack on the head he himself seemed to be undamaged and he hauled himself out of the cockpit, noticing sardonically how much easier it was to get out of a Spitfire when it was on its belly. Stepping over the hole in the wall which he had knocked down he started walking back across the aerodrome just as the ambulance and fire-truck appeared. Men jumped out and ran up and when they asked whether he was all right and what had happened, he only grunted surlily: 'Coarse pitch.' They drove him back to the operations hut with his helmet and parachute; another Spitfire was parked there and he stumped over to it, climbed in, started up, waspishly pushed the propeller into fine pitch and took off to join the other two aircraft.

Over the convoy he found them sedately orbiting and circled with them for an hour and a half without seeing any sign of the unidentified plane. By the time he landed at Duxford he had a splitting headache. Geoffrey Stephenson said wonderingly: 'Why the hell did you go and do a silly thing like that, taking off in coarse pitch?'

'Because I forgot to put it into fine, you stupid clot,' Bader snarled, and stumped off towards his room. He must have hurt himself somewhere – he could hardly walk. In his room he undressed to lie down and when he took his trousers off realised why he had been walking so shakily: the shins of both artificial legs were smashed in – deep dents that made both legs bend forward like bows. They must have been jammed under the rudder pedals in the crash. He hadn't felt a thing. Sitting on the edge of the bed gazing at them, it occurred to him what would have happened if he had not lost his real legs. Not hard to imagine: both broken and probably the bones splintered. He'd probably have been on the operating table now with a doctor shaking his head over them. Perhaps reaching for the knife and the saw to take them off.

He unstrapped them and took them off himself, feeling more amused. Strapping on his spare pair he went to the door and bellowed for his batman, and when the man came running, handed him the damaged legs.

'Here,' he said, 'pack these up in a box. They'll have to go back to the makers.'

Satisfied at the look on the batman's face, he went back and lay on the bed to soothe his aches and pains. A minute later something else occurred to him and he uttered an extremely strong word.

Neither Leigh-Mallory nor any other AOC was likely to make a flight commander of any prune stupid enough to take off in coarse pitch. He uttered several more uncouth words.

Days passed and no word came from Leigh-Mallory. Then the AOC visited Duxford on a routine inspection and sent for him. Bader walked in, saluted and stood to attention. The thickset square-faced man behind the desk regarded him sombrely.

'Bader,' he said, 'Squadron Leader Mermagen wants you as a flight commander.'

Bader's face stayed expressionless, but inside he was suddenly alert, like the time he had waited for the doctor to speak at the medical board months ago. Leigh-Mallory seemed to be thinking and the silence dragged. Bader had a wild frail hope that he had not heard of the Spitfire.

'I see you took off in coarse pitch the other day and broke a Spitfire,' Leigh-Mallory said.

(Hell!)

'Yes, sir.'

'That was very silly, wasn't it?'

Another silence, very sheepish. Leigh-Mallory was looking at a piece of paper which Bader recognised as his accident report.

'I'm glad to see you've made no attempt to excuse yourself,' Leigh-Mallory remarked in quite a reasonable voice.

'There wasn't any excuse, sir.'

'No, there's no excuse for that sort of thing,' said the AOC. A pause. 'Anyway, you're going to 222 Squadron as a flight commander.'

There were prompt results of Bader's promotion to flight lieutenant. He brought Thelma from the Pantiles to stay at a pub just outside Duxford.

He lost the awkward feeling of being an Old Boy returned to school to pass his exams again.

He told the pilots in his flight that the Fighter Command attacks were no damn' good except as training for flying discipline.

Thelma's landlady at the Duxford pub was a formidable woman known locally as 'The Sea Lion' because of a tendency to a straggling black moustache. She dominated everyone and Thelma was getting a little restive until Douglas gave The Sea Lion the benefit of his overwhelming personality, fixing her with his glittering eyes and speaking a few forceful words. The Sea Lion and he became great friends after that and Thelma was happy.

Even in the shadowed times Bader's presence had tended to command a room and now, once more with responsibility and leadership, he spoke with unmistakable authority; not the bombast of a weaker man trying to assert himself but a compelling aura of will-power and confidence. Like the time he became captain of rugger at school he ran his flight with an enveloping gusto. For some days he led his pilots into the air to do the official Fighter Command attacks. In turn he sent each pilot up as a target aircraft, telling him to turn round in the cockpit and watch each fighter in the approved procession pop up one by one and break away in the same direction, presenting his belly for a sitting shot.

When they came down he said: 'Now, you can see what's liable to happen to you.' Then he took them up for his own style of fighting, leading two or three at a time, darting down out of the sun on each side of a target plane and breaking sharply away forwards and underneath. After that came hours of dog-fight practice interspersed with routine operations like convoy patrols, which were always dull. He led his men also in a lot of formation aerobatics as the best way to teach them complete control of their aircraft. On his own he tested his nerve and skill with illegal low aerobatics, though the Duxford wing commander at one stage said ineffectively: 'I *wish* you wouldn't do that. You had such a *terrible* accident last time.'

Some of the pilots were getting restive. The war had been going for eight months and none of them had even seen a German aircraft. It was a little better on the several days they flew up to Sutton Bridge for air firing, the first time Bader had fired his guns since he had shot part of his propeller away in the Gamecock. They no longer dived at white targets on the water but at a drogue towed by another aeroplane and that

was much more thrilling. Eight. guns, and no interrupter gear to go
wrong! A firm prod with the thumb on the button and the Spitfire
quivered as the guns roared out in a tearing rattle.

Early in May a new squadron arrived at Duxford, No. 66. Its
commanding officer, pint of beer in hand, cheerfully hailed Bader in the
mess.

'Ha,' he said; 'fiddled my way out of Training Command.'

It was Rupert Leigh. Odd how the old Cranwell chums were getting
together ± Stephenson, Leigh and Bader.

After a week even Leigh was bored with training and convoy patrols.

On May 10 he drove over to pick Thelma up at the pub and drive her
back for lunch at the mess with Douglas (who was on readiness).[1]
Climbing into the car, Thelma commented: 'You look very gay this
morning, Rupert.'

Leigh said excitedly: 'Haven't you heard? The war's started.'

'What war? Another one?'

Gleefully Leigh said: 'No. The balloon's gone up. Jerries are on the
move.'

He started telling her about Hitler's attack on France and the Low
Countries, and she listened and said quietly: 'I suppose you'll all be very
happy now.'

In the mess Douglas waved to her from a crowd of jubilant pilots,
stumped over, put his arm round her and hugged. 'Good show, darling,
isn't it?' he exulted. 'Good show. Now we can get at them.' He was
nearly on fire with joy..

She said unenthusiastically: 'I suppose it had to start some time.'

They all thought it would soon be over.

Yet nothing seemed to happen at Duxford except the same old stuff,
practice flying and convoy patrols. The only diverting incident was when
Bader was booked for speeding in the MG through Stevenage. Most of
the pilots began complaining that the war would be over before they got
their chance. They really thought that. The papers and the radio were
full of the confused battle in France, but with the blindness of a small,
select and dedicated circle the pilots almost ignored the ground fighting
and enviously read about the Hurricanes tangling with the Luftwaffe in
France. Like hunting dogs they strained at the leash, too excited to worry
that the quarry might have sharp teeth. The war was an heroic sport
spiced with danger and they were still on the sidelines. Some of them
began talking about transferring to Hurricanes . . . and then as the days
passed the news changed and they were quieter, beginning to understand.

---

[1] On duty by his aircraft to take off at a moment's notice.

May 22 ended the hiatus but not agreeably. A staff car careered up to dispersals, pulled up with a jerk and Mermagen jumped out yelling: 'Squadron's posted to Kirton-in-Lindsay. Everyone ready to leave by 1500 hours.'

After a few stunned moments people started to move.

'Where's Kirton-in-Lindsay?' a young P/O asked Douglas as they scrambled into the flight truck.

'Up north, near Grimsby,' Douglas said.

'Oh, Gawd!' said the P/O. The battle lay the other way.

By three-thirty, after busy hours, the eighteen Spitfires were taking off for Kirton while the ground crews were still packing the lorries to go by road. No one seemed to know what the move was all about, and it was next morning before they found out.

Convoy patrols.

Day after day it was the same, lolling in the sunshine at dispersals while the battle raged across the Channel, waiting for a call that would send them stooging aimlessly in an empty sky over a few small ships. They did not feel heroic. In France the armies were being thrust back into unprepared positions.

On the afternoon of the 27th a lorry pulled up at A Flight dispersal and a flight sergeant jumped down and said to Bader: 'We've got some armour plate for your aircraft, sir.'

Everyone clustered round curiously. Men manhandled the plates of flat steel over to the planes and the pilots helped screw them firmly behind the bucket seats. They had never seen armour plate before and were highly pleased – not so much because of the protection (which seemed so academic), but because it made them feel in a way that they too, were almost 'operational.' Bader went early as usual to bed.

In darkness he came up out of sleep. A hand was shaking his shoulder and a voice saying: 'Wake up, sir. Wake up!' The light clicked on and he blinked and scowled at the batman who stood there.

'Squadron's got to take off for Martlesham at 4 am, sir,' said the batman. 'It's three o'clock now.'

'What the hell for?'

'Dunno, sir, but they said it was very urgent.'

Still half-asleep and irritable he reached out and strapped on his legs, then thumped the other pilots awake. Mermagen arrived, and said: 'I don't know what it's about but we're heading south and not taking any kit. Must be a flap about something.'

CHAPTER THIRTEEN

Dawn glowed in the east as the squadron shook themselves into formation in the still air, and half an hour later they were landing in sections through feathers of waist-high mist on Martlesham Aerodrome, near Felixstowe, on the East Coast. Another squadron of Spitfires had already arrived, their pilots sipping mugs of tea in a group nearby. Bader strolled over and asked 'the form' from a slim, handsome flight lieutenant, elegant in white overalls and with a silver name-bracelet round his wrist.

'Haven't got a clue,' said the debonair young man, who had aquiline features like a matador, a thin black moustache and a long, exciting scar down the side of his face, the type of young blade, Bader thought, who would make a young girl think of darkened corridors and turning door handles. His name was Bob Tuck.[1]

Mermagen bustled over and said almost casually: 'Patrol Dunkirk, chaps, 12,000 feet. Take-off as soon as we're refuelled.'

'What the hell!' Bader said. 'What's happening over there?'

Mermagen shrugged. 'Haven't the slightest idea. Something about evacuating, I think.'

One of the pilots said in an injured voice: 'I must say it's damned early to go junketing over there. I haven't even seen a paper yet.'

It seems odd now that the word Dunkirk did not mean a thing then. The Army had laid a screen of secrecy over the plans for the evacuation and people did not realise that the beaches were filling with exhausted men, least of all the fighter pilots from the north who had not seen the war yet. At least they were going across the water to the edge of France – that was something – but the transposition from peace to war is often cushioned and unreal. They did not quite grasp the idea that they might run into German planes over Dunkirk: and, in fact, that day they didn't.

Mermagen led them off in four neat vics of three; they climbed steadily and about 9,000 feet vanished into a layer of fluffy white cloud that stretched beyond the horizon. At 10,000 feet they popped like porpoises out of the cloud and levelled off at 12,000, still in tidy formation . . . unblooded. A Messerschmitt coming up behind could have shot the whole lot down. Far ahead Bader saw a strange black plume floating hugely

---

[1] A few months later Tuck was famous as a wing commander with a DSO, three DFCs and thirty German planes to his credit.

through the limitless froth they were riding over. Mermagen's voice crackled over the radio: 'That looks like it. That smoke. Must be burning oil tanks.' For a long time they circled the smoke and ranged over the cloud. Mermagen wanted to dive below the cloud but the controller had said 12,000 feet and such orders (in their inexperience) were orders. They saw nothing else in the sky, and after an hour and a half Mermagen led them away. Under the cloud blood was staining the sand as the Stukas dive-bombed and the Messerschmitt 109s and 110s strafed.

On the way back 222 Squadron was told by radio to land at Manston, and after that were told to fly to Duxford, and at Duxford were ordered off again for Hornchurch, a fighter base just north of the Thames and a dozen miles east of London. 'Typical shambles,' they grumbled, blasé about the war. At Hornchurch they gazed, startled, and then with mild derision at pilots of other squadrons walking around with pistols tucked in their flying boots and as often as not with beard stubble. The others had been flying over France for several days and were quiet and preoccupied. Still the impact did not strike the 222 pilots, who considered the pistols and beard stubble as 'line-shooting.'

At 3.30 a.m. Bader was shaken awake again.

'Take-off at 4.30, sir,' said the batman.

It was getting beyond a joke.

Unbroken cloud lay over the land at about 4,000 feet, but this day they flew at 3,000. Skirting the North Foreland to pass Dover on the right, he looked down on the grey seas with amazement. Out from the Thames estuary, from Dover and the bays little boats were swarming, slowly converging, heading south-east till they stretched across the sea in a straggling line, trailing feathers of foam, yachts and tugs, launches, ferries, coasters, lifeboats, paddle steamers, here and there a destroyer or a cruiser. It was unbelievable. 'God,' he thought, 'it's like the Great West Road on a Bank Holiday.' Far ahead the black smoke rolled thickly up from the edge of Dunkirk, where the oil tanks lay, and all the way in between the swarm of little boats streamed white tails across the water. Hundreds of them.

Mermagen led them across the dirty sand by Gravelines and swung along the beaches towards Dunkirk. At first the men in the distance looked like a wide stain of ants teeming over a flat nest and then, as the planes swept nearer, like flies, thousands and thousands stuck together, packing the sand. No holiday beach was ever like that, but this was no holiday and Bader began to understand that this was war. In the green shallows crawled the vanguard of the little boats, and black lines that were the heads of men threaded the water towards them.

A voice on the R/T said: 'Aircraft ahead.' Bader saw them in the same moment, about twelve of them, about three miles ahead and a little to the right. He wondered who they were . . . not Spitfires or Hurricanes, and a surprised voice said in his earphones: 'Christ, they're 110s!'

A shock sparkled through him. They were coming head-on and in seconds he could see the twin-engines and twin fins. The Messerschmitts veered sharply left, climbing for the cloud . . . must be carrying bombs, avoiding a fight. Mermagen in front pulled up his nose and cartridge cases streamed out of his wings as he fired. But he was a long way out of normal range.

One of the 110s suddenly streamed black smoke, dipped out of the formation and went straight down, flaming. She hit and blew up behind Dunkirk. The other Germans had vanished into the cloud and the sky was clear again. It stayed clear for the rest of the patrol, and when they landed back at Hornchurch everyone clustered round Mermagen excitedly.

'Well I must say,' Mermagen said, 'I was *most* surprised when that thing fell down.'

'I must say,' said Bader, 'so were the rest of us.'

But it had been the real thing – if only a taste.

Next morning out of bed at 3.30 again for Dunkirk, and this time not a sign of enemy aircraft, only the ants on the beach and the little boats nosing bravely into the shore. So it was the next day, except that the town was burning and guns flashing round the perimeter. Dunkirk was beginning to mean something. Other squadrons excitedly reported running into packs of Messerschmitts and Stukas, and the bloody fights they had with them. Bader listened intently and with impatience.

Again in the morning up at 3.15, and from the cockpit at 3,000 feet he could no longer see the canals that threaded through the flaming town – smoke brooded heavily and drifted across the stone breakwaters of the harbour. But no German planes. They came and bombed and killed just after the squadron had turned for home. The afternoon was even more frustrating. He led his flight once more over Dunkirk, and after half an hour the engine started misfiring, shaking the plane horribly. For the first time on a battle flight he had to turn back early, and landed in a temper about the war that was raging and always eluded him. A letter awaited, bidding him to answer the charge of speeding at Stevenage. He wrote and asked if they would defer the case for a few days.

In the morning he felt dog-tired when the batman woke him at the same time. Same routine. An odd haze stretched like a ribbon towards London from Dunkirk, and even in the cockpit at 3,000 feet he smelt burning oil and knew what the haze was. Down below the same brave little boats streamed over the water. Dunkirk ahead . . . and over Dunkirk, about three miles away, a gaggle of swift-growing dots. He knew what they were instantly. The 110s wheeled inland without dropping their bombs, but the sky was empty of cloud and the Spitfires leapt after them, blaring on full throttle. No time for thinking, but as he turned his reflector sight on and the gun button to 'fire,' he knew he was going to shoot. A glance back through the perspex; the straining Spitfires were stringing out in a ragged line and up to the left four grey shapes were diving at them – Messerchmitt 109s, the first he had seen. From the beam they flicked across in front like darting sharks, winking orange flashes in the noses as they fired.

He rammed stick and rudder over and the Spitfire wheeled after them. A 109 shot up in front; his thumb jabbed the firing button and the guns in the wings squirted with a shocking noise. The 109 seemed to be filling his windscreen. A puff of white spurted just behind its cockpit as though someone had used a giant Flit-gun. The puff was chopped off . . . for a moment nothing . . . then a spurt of orange flame mushroomed round the cockpit and flared back like a blow-torch. The 109 rolled drunkenly, showing her belly, and in the same moment he saw the black cross on its side. It was true. They did have black crosses. Suddenly it was real and the 109 was falling away and behind, flaming.

Exultation welled sharply up, a fiery thrill running through him as he swung back towards the squadron – but the squadron had gone; not a plane in sight except the plunging torch on the end of the ribbon of black smoke running down the sky behind.

Turning back towards Dunkirk, he did see a plane. From nowhere it seemed a 110 was tumbling down half a mile in front. Incongruously the twin tail was snapped off but still hung to the plane by the control cables, spinning madly like a chimney cowl. Wide-eyed he watched the broken plane erupt into the ground below.

The heady joy of the kill flooded back as he slid out over the water towards England. A glow of fulfilment. Blood runs hotly at the kill when a pilot wins back his life in primitive combat. He had fought a plane and shot at it, impersonally, not seeing the man, and longed to get back and tell everyone, but when he taxied in the joy died. Two of the others were missing.

That afternoon, thirsting for more, he flew back to Dunkirk with the squadron, and on the fringe of the little boats off the breakwater saw a shadow diving on a destroyer. Another shock – black crosses on the wings as a Heinkel 111 swept over the funnels. A white core of water erupted just behind the destroyer and her stern kicked up, the screws foaming out of the water. He was peeling off after the Heinkel, which was swinging back to the coast. Little flashes came from the bomber's glasshouse, and Bader pressed his own gun button and the flashes stopped. Good! Killed the gunner! The Heinkel steep-turned sharply inside him. As he pulled up to swing in again two more Spitfires were closing on the bomber, already a mile away. Amazing how fast everything went. No chance of catching them in time. He looked for the rest of the squadron, but they, too, had vanished.

There was the destroyer though, and he banked over to see if they were all right. They seemed to be; they were flashing at him, and then he saw tiny black spots darting past and knew where the flashes came from. A multiple pom-pom. The Navy took no chances in those days. Bader shot away in the other direction. It was, he thought, rather rude of the Navy.

The squadron stayed at Hornchurch. Morning after morning up at 3.15 for the dawn patrol, and other patrols, but always it was the other squadrons that found the enemy, which was infuriating. All Bader saw were the rearguards on the beaches, embattled and dwindling, and it was not pleasant. When not flying the squadron sat all day by their planes, till nearly 11 pm when the last light went. Geoffrey Stephenson was missing. They said he had tried a copybook Fighter Command attack No. 2 on a Stuka and the single rear gun had stopped his engine, forcing him down, streaming glycol, in enemy territory.

On June 4, the Prime Minister ordered a last patrol and Bader flew on it. The beach by Dunkirk was empty and the crumbling town lay inert under the smoke. Out of the harbour tacked a single yacht with a little white sail; it must have been the last boat out of Dunkirk and they circled it protectively till low petrol forced them home.[1]

Dunkirk was over and Bader, suddenly exhausted, slept nearly twenty-four hours, waking to find a grim new mood lying over England. You could see what the pilots were thinking by their faces – if it was fighting they wanted they were going to get it. Sobering, but not too daunting. Unreasonably, the country refused to see that it was beaten. Bader went a stage further, refusing to believe that he would, therefore, probably be killed. The possibility, or either the theory, lay in his mind but he ignored it and like a dried pea it never took root. Having tasted blood, he thought only of flying, fighting and tactics, things he had wanted so long that nothing else mattered, and the thought never obtruded consciously that no one now could think of him with pity or as second to a man who could run. He lived for the coming fight, Britain's, as well as his own.

A letter came from the court in Stevenage saying 'Guilty' and fining him £2 10s. Furious, he sent a cheque and a stiff note regretting his inability to attend as he had had to go to Dunkirk.

On a week-end pass he drove down to Thelma, who had gone back to the Pantiles. He had to tell her Geoffrey Stephenson was missing, and after that they did not talk about the war.

[1] He always wondered what happened to that little boat.

The fight seemed a long time coming and the days were unexciting with training – formation, dummy attacks, night flying. The squadron moved north again to Kirton-in-Lindsay and Thelma stayed at the Pantiles. At least for the time being, she thought, nothing was likely to happen to Douglas.

Towards midnight on June 13, Bader was 12,000 feet over the Humber looking for an unidentified aircraft that had been tracked in from Germany. Peering out of the little cockpit he could see nothing but a few pale stars and knew there was little chance of seeing anything else. The Spitfire, with its tiny perspex hood and long nose, was not good for night flying, and seeking a raider in the dark was like being blindfolded and chasing a rabbit in the woods. But then there were no other defences.

'Red One, Red One,' the controller's voice said, 'weather closing in. Return to base immediately.'

He swung steeply down towards the blacked-out land, but the rain cloud moved in faster. On a homing course he was only a few hundred feet up, and right over the airfield before, dimly, he picked up the flarepath suffused through a veil of rain, and swung tightly round it to keep it in sight through the rain-filmed perspex. He floated past the first flare ... too high. The second flashed behind ... and then the third before he touched on the downhill runway. The tail was not down and he knew he had misjudged. Stick hard back in his stomach but still the tail stayed up and the flares flashed by. In the same moment he knew he was going to overshoot and that it was too late to open up and take off again; then the tail was down and the brakes were on as hard as he dared.

In front there were no more flares ... only blackness. An agony of waiting, and then a tearing crash as the plane jolted, slid her belly over the low wall of an aircraft pen, sheering the undercart off, and jarred to a stop. Bricks were suddenly raining down on the metal, and the mind for a moment was a blank. No fear, no shock. He just sat there as he had twice before.

Then he said one short, unprintable word.

A car screeched along the perimeter grass. He took off his helmet and heard the rain pattering on the wings. Tubby Mermagen loomed out of the darkness.

'Douglas,' he called anxiously, 'are you all right?'

'No,' Bader growled. 'I'm bloody furious.'

'Serves you right,' Mermagen said, relieved. 'That was a ruddy awful approach.'

In the morning Mermagen greeted him with a sly grin and a significant remark: 'Well, Douglas, we're losing you.'

Bader stared, remembering last night's accident, and thought with a chill of being grounded.

'Where?' he demanded. 'Idon't want to leave.'

'It's all right,' Mermagen said soothingly. 'You're getting a squadron.'

Bader stared again.

'It's not a joke,' Mermagen grinned. 'Or perhaps it is. Anyway, L.M. wants to see you.'

The surge of incredulous joy was cut off a moment later when it occurred to Bader that Leigh-Mallory could not possibly have heard of the latest accident.

He drove to 12 Group Headquarters at Hucknall and stood once more before the AOC. Without preamble Leigh-Mallory said: 'I've been hearing of your work as a flight commander. I'm giving you a squadron, No. 242.'

(Better get it over!)

Bader said: 'Yes, sir. . . . Sir, there's one thing I should tell you. . . . I broke a Spitfire last night. Overshot landing.'

Leigh-Mallory said mildly: 'Well, that happens sometimes, you know.'

Wearing his hair shirt to the last, Bader went on: 'Sir, the point is that last time you promoted me to flight commander, I'd also just broken one.'

Leigh-Mallory looked grave, then grinned. 'Don't worry,' he said. 'Your new squadron has Hurricanes.'

Brisk again, the AOC went on: '242 are a Canadian squadron, the only one in the RAF. Nearly all the pilots are Canadians and they're a tough bunch. They're just back from France, where they got pretty badly mauled and lost quite a few aircraft. They were messed around quite a bit; it wasn't their fault and now they're fed up. Frankly morale is low. They need a bit of decent organisation and some firm handling; someone who can talk tough and I think you're the chap to do it. We may need every fighter squadron we've got on the top line soon. The Luftwaffe seems to be gathering across the Channel.'

The squadron was at Coltishall, near Norwich, Leigh-Mallory said, and Squadron Leader Bader was to take over as from that moment. He stood up, shook Bader's hand, and said: 'Good luck in your first command.'

Squadron Leader Bader! Or at least Acting Squadron Leader! How unemotional the interview had been and how deep the content it stirred. Eight weeks ago he had been a flying officer! It hardly even occurred to him that he had caught up with his contemporaries; he was longing to flex his muscles in his first command.

By evening he had driven a hundred miles back to Kirton, packed his kit, telephoned Thelma and was steering the MG towards Coltishall. Low cloud hung over the sky and he felt his way in darkness. About 11 pm a policeman outside Norwich told him how to get to the aerodrome. Five minutes later he was lost. He saw a man on the road and asked the way but the man did not know. Then he saw a woman and she, fearful of his intentions, fled when he spoke. Not a signpost anywhere (all taken down in case of invasion). He found another man who said suspiciously: 'How do I know who you are? You might be a spy. I dunno where the aerodrome is.' An hour later, content dissipated, he came to a barbed wire barrier across the road and behind it, in the light of a red lamp, stood an RAF sentry. At last! Pleasantly conscious of dignity he said: 'I am the new commanding officer of 242 Squadron,' and waited for the barrier to rise.

The sentry did not move. Stolidly he said: 'Can I have the password, sir?'

'How the hell do I know the password?' exploded the new commanding officer. 'I've never been here before.'

'Sorry, sir, but I can't let you through without the password.'

The new squadron commander simmered by the barrier for another twenty minutes until the guardroom phone located the duty officer, who ruled that he was admissable.

Almost the first man he saw at breakfast in the morning was Rupert Leigh. 66 Squadron, apparently, was now also stationed at Coltishall. Shaking his head on hearing of the promotion, Leigh said: 'Now you won't have to call me "sir" any more. Not that you ever *did*, but it'll be a comfort for you to go on being rude with a clear conscience.'

After breakfast the 'station master' at Coltishall, the pipe-smoking, phlegmatic Wing Commander Beisiegel,[1] told Bader about his new squadron, and was not comforting. The ground crews were about half English, three or four of the pilots were English and the rest were Canadians. Wild Canadians, the least tractable young officers he had ever seen, and most allergic to commanding officers! God knows what they would think when they heard that the new CO had no legs. Already unrest had affected the whole squadron. They needed someone pretty strong and active to discipline them.

It occurred to Bader that he was still wearing only the two rings of the flight lieutenant round his sleeve; he had not yet had time to get the third, thin ring sewn in between, and that would make him look very much a new boy.

'If you don't mind, sir,' he said, 'I'll drive into Norwich and get the extra braid sewn on before I make my entrance.'

He went off in the MG and while he was away the news of his arrival reached the squadron. One of the pilots encountered Bernard West, the squadron 'plumber' (engineer officer) and said: 'Have you seen the new CO?'

---

[1] Known far and wide, naturally, as 'Bike.'

'No, I haven't.' West was greatly interested and a little wary. 'What's this one like?'

'Bit unusual,' the pilot said cryptically. 'I don't suppose we'll be seeing much of him. He's got no legs.'

West, a warrant officer of twenty years' service who had seen most things in the Air Force, gaped and groaned.

CHAPTER FOURTEEN

When Bader got back the pilots were all down at the dispersals, on readiness. He had a long talk about them with his new adjutant, Flight Lieutenant Peter Macdonald, an industrious, imperturbable man who had been an MP for fourteen years and still managed to sandwich his parliamentary duties in between trying to pull the squadron together. At last Bader said: 'Well, let's go down and meet these chaps.'

'A Flight' dispersal was a wooden hut on the edge of the airfield, and he pushed the door open and stumped in unheralded, followed by Macdonald. From his lurching walk they knew who he was. A dozen pairs of eyes surveyed him coolly from chairs and the iron beds where pilots slept at night for dawn readiness. He had had a vague idea that they would stand up respectfully; that was the usual thing. But no one got up; no one even seemed to move except that a couple rolled over on the cots to see him more clearly. Even the hands stayed in the pockets and the room was silent. Watchful. The duel seemed to last a long time.

At last he said, not aggressively but firmly: 'Who is in charge here?'

No one answered.

'Well, who's the senior?'

Again no one answered, though the eyes turned and looked at each other inquiringly.

'Isn't anyone in charge?'

A large dark young man said: 'I guess not.'

Bader eyed them a little longer, anger flaring under his collar. But it was not the moment to get tough. He turned abruptly and went out.

In 'B Flight' dispersal the unresponsive eyes again stared silently.

'Who is in charge here?' he asked.

After a while a thick-set young man with wiry hair and a face that looked as though it had been roughly chipped out of granite rose slowly out of a chair and said in a strong Canadian accent: 'I guess I am.'

He wore only the single ring of flying officer braid round his sleeve.

'Isn't there a flight commander?'

'There's one somewhere but he isn't here,' said the young man.

'What's your name?'

'Turner.' And then, after a distinct pause, 'Sir.'

Bader surveyed again the watchful eyes and again turned and walked out. A dozen yards from the door a Hurricane crouched with the hump-backed, bow-legged look of all Hurricanes. He headed for it and pulled himself up on the wing. A parachute, helmet and goggles already lay in the cockpit and he lifted his leg over the side, hauled himself in and pulled on the helmet. If they thought the new CO was a cripple there was one damn' good way to make them think again. He started up, pointed the Hurricane's snout across the field and opened up.

Right over the airfield for half an hour non-stop he tumbled the Hurricane round the sky, doing the old fluent routines of Hendon, one aerobatic merging into another, without pauses to gain height again, two or three loops in a row, rolls off the top, rolls, stall turns, finishing up with a Gamecock specialty in which he pulled up in a loop, flick-rolled into a spin at the top, pulled out of the spin and completed the loop. When he dropped her on to the grass and taxied in all the pilots were standing outside the hut watching, but he climbed out unaided, did not even look at them, got into his car, drove off to his office in a hangar and sent for Bernard West.

He liked the solid, north-country look of West as soon as the veteran warrant officer walked in and saluted.

'What's our equipment state?' he asked.

'Eighteen Hurricanes, sir,' West said. 'They're all new.'

'Good. I want good serviceability on them.'

'I'll keep them flying as long as I can, sir,' West said, 'but that won't be for long. We have no spares and no tools. I'm scrounging what I can, but if you do any operations they'll all be grounded in no time.'

'What d'you mean, no spares or tools?' Bader demanded.

West explained that they had all been lost in France. Only one of the fitters had brought his own personal tools back in his kitbag. The rest seemed to have brought back only cigarettes. He sounded angry.

Bader, looking grim, asked: 'Have you requisitioned for a new issue?'

West said yes, he had. The indent forms and vouchers and all the duplicates made a pile six inches high, but the station stores officer said they had to go through the normal channels in their turn. West considered that the channels were well clogged.

'Well,' said the new commanding officer grimly, 'we'll ruddy well unclog them.'

In the morning he called all the pilots to his office and they stood there bunched and shuffling in front of his desk while he, this time, eyed them

REACH FOR THE SKY

coolly and silently, noting the rumpled uniforms, the preference for roll-neck sweaters instead of shirts and ties, the long hair and general untidy air. At last he spoke:

'Look here . . . it is *not* smart to walk about looking like mechanics who haven't washed the grease off their hands. I want this to be a good squadron and you're a scruffy-looking lot. A good squadron *looks* smart. Just for a start I don't want to see any more flying boots or roll-neck sweaters in the mess. You will wear shoes, and shirts and ties. Is that perfectly clear?'

It was a mistake.

Turner said unemotionally in a deep, slow Canadian voice:

'Most of us don't have any shoes or shirts or ties except what we're wearing.'

'What d'you mean?' – aggressively.

'We lost everything we had in France.' Evenly, with just a trace of cynicism, Turner went on to explain the chaos of the running fight, how they had apparently been deserted by authority, separated from their ground staff, shunted from one place to another, welcome nowhere, till it had been every man for himself, each pilot servicing his own aircraft, scrounging his own food, and sleeping under his own wing; then searching for enough petrol to take off and fight as they were forced back from one landing ground to another. Seven had been killed, two wounded and one had had a nervous breakdown – nearly fifty per cent pilot casualties. The commanding officer had been missing most of the time, but had managed to get his Hurricane back to the South of England. When the end had come the rest had flown themselves back across the Channel and been sent to Coltishall. Since then things had not greatly improved and they were drifting, without steerage way. It was not a heartening story but there was no self-pity, only a kind of restrained anger.

When he had finished Bader said: 'I'm sorry. I apologise for my remarks.' A brief silence. 'Have you claimed an allowance for loss of kit?'

Apparently they had, and it was assumed, with another tinge of cynicism, that the claim was drifting quietly along one of the proper channels.

'Right,' Douglas said. 'To-morrow the whole lot of you go into Norwich, to the tailors. Order what you want. I'll guarantee that it's paid. OK?'

A shuffle of assent.

'Meantime, for to-night, beg or borrow shoes and shirts from someone. I've got some shirts and you can borrow all I've got. OK?'

'That's fine, sir,' said Turner, who seemed to be spokesman by common consent.

'Right! Now . . .' (briskly) 'relax and take it easy. What fighting have you had and how did you get on?'

The next half-hour was a lively discussion on various aspects of the trade, and afterwards Bader interviewed each pilot in turn, finding, with one or two exceptions, that he liked them very much. Suddenly, they were keen and cooperative, though one pilot, an Englishman, seemed unhappy and thought he would be more suited to Training Command. After talking to him for a while Bader burst out angrily: 'The trouble about you is you don't want to fight. I'll have you posted off this squadron in twenty-four hours.' The remaining flight commander he also summed up swiftly as unsuitable, and as soon as he was alone telephoned Group and asked them to send him the best two flight commanders they could find. For one of them, he suggested Eric Ball, of 19 Squadron. Group said that would be fine, and for the second chap they recommended a young man called Powell-Sheddon.

'What's he like?' asked Bader.

'Stutters a bit,' said Group, 'but he's a very good type.'

'Stutters! Stutters!' the phone vibrated in Group's ear. 'That's no damn' good to me. What's going to happen over the radio in a fight?'

'I should have thought he'd be just the chap for you.' Group sounded slightly injured. 'It's not a bad stutter and he's good leader material . . . ex-Cranwell.'

'Cranwell,' boomed Bader. 'Just the chap. Send him along.'

When he put the phone down he sent for West again, and West marched in to find the new CO, pipe clenched in his teeth like Pop-Eye, leaning thoughtfully back in his chair with his right leg stuck up on his desk. Bader grabbed the trouser leg and dropped the leg with a thud on the floor, leaned forward on his elbows, fixed West with a flinty eye and said: 'Mr West, I want you to tell me what's been going on in this squadron.'

Just for a moment West hesitated before he said: 'D'you want the truth, sir?'

'That's *just* what I want.'

'Well, sir . . .' and West explained, confirming all that Turner had said and adding some extra facets. He added that he himself had been going to ask for a transfer before the new commanding officer arrived. Already between the two men was the indefinable bond that comes from mutual respect and long service in the same cause. Otherwise West would never have added:

'If I may say so, sir, I think the first thing you need are two new flight commanders.'

'Already got 'em,' Bader said. 'They're on the way. Now, any more word about your spares and tools?'

West said no, there wasn't.

Three minutes later the stores officer, working serenely on vouchers in his kingdom of shelves, saw two square hands descend palm down on his desk. He looked up into a pair of glowing eyes. Politely enough, Acting Squadron Leader Bader asked about the tools for his squadron, and the stores officer, shrugging at the masses of paper work, explained that he was nearly snowed under. Coltishall was a new station and there were masses of things to be acquired for the stores . . . blankets, soap, boots . . . The depots only supplied them in their own good time and only if they got all the copies and the correct forms.

'I literally haven't got enough staff to type out the forms,' he said frankly.

'To hell with your forms and your blankets and your blasted toilet paper,' Bader said wrathfully. 'I want my spares and tools and I want 'em damn' soon.'

The discussion raged for some time and was not agreeable to either party. Bader went to Wing Commander Beisiegel and explained that until he got tools and spares and the pilots trained under new flight commanders there was no point in regarding the squadron as operational. This was not happily received.

After lunch he began leading the pilots up in twos for formation, and was pleased to see that they knew how to handle their Hurricanes, though their formation (by his standards) was rather ragged. Though they had done more fighting than he had, he had already decided to train them for future fighting according to his own ideas. That night in the mess all of them were reasonably neat in shoes and shirts and ties, and he turned his sparkling charm on them. Soon the ice was broken and his pilots clustered round, laughing and talking, taking swigs at their beer and getting to know him while he, orange squash in hand, was further summing them up. His breeziness was like a shot in the arm to them, and towards the end of the evening one of the pilots put down his empty pint-pot and said: 'Hell, sir, we were really scared you were going to be a passenger or another goddam figurehead.' The evening progressed with great hilarity.

By the second morning there was already a feeling of direction about the squadron. People were neater and earlier and everyone seemed to be busy. For the first hour or two the new CO was appearing everywhere, at dispersals, in the maintenance hangar, the radio hut, instrument section, armoury. By ten o'clock he was leading sections of Hurricanes into the air again, and this time his voice came snapping crisply over the R/T when any aircraft lagged or waffled a few feet out of position. Later in the dispersals hut he parked his rump on the end of a bed, lit his pipe and called them around.

'That formation was better,' he said. 'Next time I want it better still. It's the best training for co-ordinated flying and air discipline.' Then he gave them his first talk on the ideas of fighter tactics which he had been expounding at 19 and 222 Squadrons. 'I haven't been able to test them properly yet,' he said, 'and you chaps have seen more fighting than I have, but I'm certain Bishop and McCudden and the others were right.' He emphasised other refinements of battle too: never follow an enemy down, never straggle, aim steadily with plenty of deflection, and a host of others, finding an intent and intelligent audience.

In the afternoon Eric Ball and George Powell-Sheddon arrived. Both were English. Ball was lean and firm-jawed with a little moustache above good, smiling teeth. Already he had something to remember the war by – a scar furrowed through the fair curly hair where a 109 bullet had 'creased' him at Dunkirk. Powell-Sheddon was shorter and was solidly built. Almost thirty, he was going slightly bald and was a steadfast type with thoughtful eyes. Both, Bader felt, had the 'good school' background which he valued and would lead with authority. Not that he thought for a moment any the less of the Canadians. Englishmen do not require a 'colonial' to have been to a 'good' school, but respect him for other virtues (and because a 'colonial' does not give a damn whether he has been to the right school or not). He would have been happy to promote a Canadian as flight commander, but none yet had enough leadership experience and he had old-fashioned ideas about that, though they became flexible ideas, not confined to Cranwell or the old school tie.

Ball took over A Flight and Powell-Sheddon B Flight, and that afternoon both were leading their pilots in formation. Within a couple of days there was a perceptible impression of the whole squadron clicking into position as a team.

Bader kept trying to get the tools and spares, bickering daily with the stores officer. Many words were spoken but no equipment materialised. About the seventh day he sent for West and asked if there was any more word about the tools and spares.

'No, sir,' West said. 'The stores chaps started quoting AP 830,[1] volume 1, paragraph something or other; some regulation that says you have to wait three months before you can start the procedure for hastening new tools.'

'They say *that* now, do they?' grated the CO. Shortly after he stamped across to the station commander and said: 'Look, sir, the boys are fit for anything now, but we still haven't got our tools and spares. As the equipment chaps don't seem inclined to do anything about it I've sent this signal to Group.' He handed across a slip of paper and Beisiegel read the curt message with mounting distress:

'242 *Squadron now operational as regards pilots but non-operational repeat non-operational as regards equipment.*'

[1] Equipment Regulations for the RAF.

'Good God,' the wing commander was appalled. 'Why the devil didn't you show it to me first?'

After a heated scene there, Bader went back to his office and showed it to West, whose eyes widened as he read. He wondered discreetly whether the station commander would pass such a blunt signal. Bader said that the station commander *had* been a little perturbed, especially when he heard that the message had already gone.

With masterly understatement, West observed: 'It's . . . a bit unusual, sir.'

'I'll take the kicks,' the CO said. 'Is there anything you'd like to take back about our need for tools and spares?'

'No, sir.'

'Good.'

'There'll be an awful shindig at Group, sir,' West suggested.

'There'll be an awful shindig from Fighter Command, too,' said Bader. 'I've sent a copy there as well.'

West broke a few moments of pregnant silence:

'Well, sir, we'll either be getting our tools or a new CO.'

The upheaval was immediate. Bader was playing snooker in the mess with his pilots that night when an orderly announced he was wanted on the phone. He picked it up and the voice of a squadron leader (equipment) at Fighter Command Headquarters said coldly:

'Squadron Leader Bader, what is the meaning of this extraordinary signal you sent to-day?'

'It means exactly what it says,' bluntly. 'We haven't got any tools or spares and I'm going to keep this squadron non-operational till I get them.'

'But you *must* have *some* tools there surely.'

'About two spanners and a screwdriver.'

The voice observed with severity that these were difficult times and tools and spares were short. He was having a gruelling time organising things, and surely a resourceful squadron commander could borrow things and make do till his requirements could be satisfied. Moreover, there was a proper procedure for obtaining new equipment and if everyone ignored such procedure and did what Squadron Leader Bader had done there would be frightful chaos.

'I've carried out the correct procedure and nothing has happened,' Bader snapped.

'I'm quite sure you can operate with what you've got.'

'Look, don't you tell *me* what I can do. I'll tell *you* what I want and until I get it this squadron stays non-operational.'

'You don't seem to care what trouble you cause,' snapped the equipment officer. 'Well I can tell *you* that signal of yours is going to bring you trouble. The Commander-in-Chief is furious about it.'

He nearly had the receiver slammed down his ear.

In the morning a little communications aeroplane landed on the airfield and Leigh-Mallory got out.

'I just dropped in to see how you were getting on,' he said to Bader and did not mention the other matter till he had half finished his inspection of the squadron. They were leaving dispersals for the maintenance hangar when he said non-committally: 'Your non-operational signal caused a mild sensation at Group. What's it all about?'

Bader told him of everything that had been done. Leigh-Mallory himself inspected the miserable little collection of tools they had been able to borrow and had a few words alone with Warrant Officer West. Afterwards he sent for Bader again and said:

'Well, you've stuck your neck out but I can see why. I'm afraid you're going to be sent for by the Commander-in-Chief about that signal and you can tell him what you've told me. Don't take it too much to heart – his bark is much worse than his bite.'

The summons came a day later. Bader flew down to Hendon and drove from there to Bentley Priory, the fine old house at Stanmore that was Fighter Command Headquarters. Waiting to be ushered in to the C.-in-C., he did not regret what he had done but was acutely conscious that he was only an acting squadron leader. A corporal appeared and said: 'He'll see you now, sir.'

CHAPTER FIFTEEN

Behind a tidy desk sat the austere Air Chief Marshal Sir Hugh Dowding, eyes pale and cold under tufty eyebrows and lips pursed in the craggy face. Known as 'Stuffy' because he could be very stuffy, he gazed unwinking and said baldly: 'What's all this about equipment and that signal of yours, Bader?'

Bader explained that he had done everything he could to get tools and spares, and then decided he would have to do something extra because if the Germans attacked, his squadron would soon be unable to get off the ground. Without a word Dowding passed a typewritten report over and Bader saw it was from the equipment officer – an account of the phone conversation. He glanced over it and said:

'I did have an acrimonious conversation with an equipment officer, sir, but it was between two officers of equal rank. He tried to shake me by saying you were furious about my signal and that annoyed me.'

'Oh, he said I was furious, did he?' Dowding pressed his buzzer.

In a minute the equipment squadron leader came in. His eyes flickered at Bader, whose eyes flickered back.

'Did you say I was furious about the signal from 242 Squadron?' Dowding asked.

'Yes, sir,' said the squadron leader. 'I knew you would be very angry about such a signal.'

Dowding said coldly: 'I will not have any officer taking my name in vain or predicting my emotions. Your job is – or was – to help the squadrons in the field. You will be off this headquarters in twenty-four hours.'

After the equipment officer went out Dowding seemed to relax. He pressed another buzzer and shortly a grey-haired air vice marshall walked in – 'Daddy' Nichol, who looked after all equipment for Fighter Command. He listened to Bader repeating his story and then took him by the arm, and said cheerfully: 'All right. Now you come with me and we'll fix this up.'

At Coltishall the following day Beisiegel held an inquiry into the affair of 242 Squadron's equipment, and next morning, even before the Coltishall stores officer, too, had finished clearing his desk for his successor, the lorries were rolling past the guardroom and up to the maintenance hangar where West, with brisk good humour, supervised his fitters unloading crates of spare wheels, spurk plugs, oleo legs, spanners, files, piston rings and about 400 other assorted bits and pieces. By evening, after the last lorry had gone, West was surrounded by piles of boxes.

'Have you got enough, Mr West?' Bader asked.

'Enough?' declaimed West. 'I've got enough here for ten squadrons, sir. What I want now is somewhere to stow it.'

'That's your problem,' the CO said. 'I'm leaving the aircraft side to you now while I get busy with the pilots. This is going to be the best squadron in the command if it kills me.'

He drove to his office and sent a signal to Group, with a copy to Fighter Command:

'242 *Squadron now fully operational.*'

As a matter of fact, the pilots already thought they were the best squadron in Fighter Command, a distinct change from their opinions of a few days before. Now the Hurricanes were hardly ever out of the air, ranging over Norfolk in formation and cloud flying, climbing on practice interceptions, diving on air firing and tangling in mock dog-fights. Even when they were on the ground there was always something to do, generally listening to the CO expounding with the fervour of an evangelist the finer points of air fighting. He was a dogmatist preaching dogma of a bygone day and because he believed so ardently, they believed too. He made every pilot lead a formation in dummy attacks and barked at him like an exuberant mastiff if the pilot did anything 'clottish.' It was learn by practice, by example, by seeing for yourself, and more practice. As long as one tried, his bark, one felt, was worse than his bite, and they all tried because one also felt that if he *did* bite the wound would be nigh on fatal.

Once he tried to loop the whole squadron in line astern, but only the first four got over the top and the rest stalled and spun off. The CO did not mind; they had tried. Even in the mess they tried, taking a perceptible interest in their appearance.

The first time he did dawn readiness with a section he slept as usual with the rostered pilots on the iron cots in the dispersals hut, taking his legs off and parking them beside the cot, complete with shoes, socks and trousers on them.[1] It was the first time they had seen him with his legs off and surreptitiously they eyed them, fascinated, in a slight hush. No one, of course, made any remark but it was uncanny to see that the man who was so vital and energetic actually *did* have artificial legs. The legend was true.

A squadron in war is a sensitive body. The men who fly find glory and die young. The men on the ground live long with little acclaim but their work is endlessly exacting, and if they fumble once a pilot is likely to die. There must be mutual respect and trust, and it is the commander who must inspire this delicate balance. (I was once on a fighter squadron when a new, weak commander arrived, and in days the close-knit comradeship and teamwork frayed and split into aimless isolation and lack of confidence. It added up to low morale and happened fast.) Within a fortnight 242 Squadron was a cohesive unit, trusting in and loyal to the new CO, and therefore loyal to their corporate selves. They knew just what they had to do, and why, and when, and it all made sense, and they knew the CO would be loyal to them.

Bader, in fact, looked on his squadron with a fierce possessiveness. ('I felt they were *mine*, all the pilots and troops. I used to get furious if anyone said anything about them or did anything to them, and I arranged with the Norwich police[2] that they never put my chaps on a charge in a civil court, but sent the charge to me to deal with. I was tough with them myself, but always closed the ranks if anyone else tried to interfere.

---

[1] In this way Bader could dress ready for action before the others could put on their shoes and socks.
[2] With the urbane help of Peter Macdonald, MP.

I suppose I was unreasonable in my attitude about the squadron, but it was an obsession with me and I would not brook interference.')

Often he worked the ground crews like beavers for long hours to keep the Hurricanes flying and in return defended them aggressively from the station commander, who was a stickler for rectitude according to the book. Bader and Rupert Leigh often marched together into the wing commander's office to assert their points of view. All three were Cranwell men and among them was a strictly unofficial tradition that if junior and senior officer took off their hats they could argue with more freedom than discipline normally allowed. Hatless they had some crisp debates, especially when some of the men were a little late back from leave or careless about the blackouts in the huts.

Now when the 242 pilots went out in the evenings to absorb beer it became a habit to go in a homogeneous group with the teetotal CO, who did not mind how many pints they sank so long as they were fit in the morning. He brought Thelma up to a house in Coltishall and her presence helped ensure that the evenings were decorous enough, though not excessively so. A favourite game was 'The Muffin Man,' where a man has to balance a pint of beer on his head and turn around, singing and bobbing his knees, without spilling the beer. With his legs Bader could not play it but Smith, a young Canadian flying officer, taught him to sing 'Little Angeline' and he became crazy about the song.

Command had now sublimated the last traces of the frustrated years. He lived for his squadron and expected all his men to do likewise. The somewhat swashbuckling figure with the lurching walk was liable to appear anywhere on the squadron at any time, a masterful and undisputed head of the family seeing that his house was in order. As Stan Turner, of the granite-chipped face said to West: 'Legs or no legs, I've never seen such a goddam mobile fireball as that guy.'

The muscular Turner himself was not a mild man, having a large capacity for beer and a penchant for firing off a large revolver in public. The wing commander had suggested to Douglas: 'You ought to get rid of that chap Turner. He's too wild.'

But Bader saw eye-to-eye with Turner, who was a first-class pilot, and fearless and decisive. Turner stayed; in fact, Bader made him a section leader and found that responsibility curbed his wildness.

Leigh-Mallory had been shrewd when he sent Bader to command 242. The Canadians lived with an informal and sometimes noisy vigour, respecting a rule or custom only for its usefulness and never for its age or its index number in a book of regulations. They respected the same qualities in Bader and understood the contradictions in him when his own exuberance clashed with his sense of discipline. Bader's sense of discipline was deep-rooted when it was a matter of obeying an order from Bader, or from anyone whom he respected; it was less predictable in some other circumstances. Often he was bullying with his tongue but his victims had forgiven and forgotten in five minutes, knowing that he likewise would have forgotten.

Already he had his eye on several of the pilots as future section leaders, in particular Hugh Tamblyn, of the firm jaw, steady eye and dry good humour. The handsome Tamblyn had an air of utter reliability about him, and so did Noel Stansfeld, of the fair, curly hair and good looks, and Laurie Cryderman, who was tall and slight with crinkly hair and a cheerful charm. Two years before Cryderman had been leading a jazz band and was still only about twenty-four. Norrie Hart was a different type, shorter, firm-faced, quick of wit and speech delivered in a hard, dry accent. On the side of his Hurricane he had painted a chamber-pot with swastikas falling into it. John Latta was again different, with a drawly voice, a dark, slight young man who occasionally showed the dourness of Scottish forebears. Ben Brown was very handsome, very brave and a very bad shot. Neil Campbell was even more handsome. Bob Grassick was compact and blithely imperturbable.

All the Canadians seemed fearless and none more so than Willie McKnight, a flinty-eyed little dead-shot of twenty from Calgary, who had already knocked down several German aircraft in the shambles over France. Under the tender lips he was a tough little man with a DFC and a weakness for soft music; he had a large collection of Bing Crosby records and played them endlessly in the mess in the evenings, being greatly irritated when Cryderman sang over the top of the velvety Crosby.

Apart from Bader and the two flight commanders, the only other English pilot on the squadron was Denis Crowley-Milling, a sturdy blond pilot officer who looked about seventeen but was, in fact, twenty-one. Then there was also Roy Bush, a steady-eyed New Zealander, yet apart from accents no one noticed nationality any more; they were too busy training as a team, and life under the new CO was stimulating, though no fighting seemed in sight. One never saw a German aircraft. Once in a blue moon a lone raider might flirt round the coast in cloud and they said there were masses of them gathering in France, but unless Hitler tried an invasion it looked as though the war had bogged down. Pity, in a way.

But always in the background echoed Churchill's recent words:

'The battle of France is over. I expect that the battle of Britain is about to begin. Upon that battle depends the survival of Christian civilisation. Let us therefore brace ourselves to our duty and so bear ourselves that if the British Commonwealth and Empire last for a thousand years men will say – this was their finest hour.'

On July 11 a sudden blanket of cloud sagged over Coltishall and streamed all morning, grounding the squadron. Bader was dozing in a chair in dispersals when the telephone rang and Operations said they had a plot of a suspicious aircraft flying down the coast from the north. Could they get a section off? Bader grabbed the phone, and said: 'No, we can't get a section off. The cloud's right on the deck, and I won't send my pilots up in weather like this. It's impossible.'

'Isn't there any chance? It's heading for Cromer and we're pretty sure it's enemy.' Ops sounded anxious.

Oh, the temptation!

'All right, I'll have a go myself.' He dropped the phone and sloshed out through the rain to his Hurricane.

It was almost an instrument take-off through rain that drifted in a veil across the field, and within seconds the cloud closed clammily round him. He called up Ops for a course to intercept, but water had leaked into the radio and no sound came back. Climbing on instruments there was not much point in going on unless he broke soon into the clear. The needle was pointing at just over 1000 feet when abruptly he came out of the cloud like shooting into a new world, and down below saw the coast. More cloud hung close overhead and without word from Ops there was little chance of seeing anything in the broken sky, but he swung north towards Cromer, more to clear his conscience than anything else. Finding an enemy over England was about as likely as finding a burglar in one's room.

Far ahead a dot appeared in the sky and began to grow larger, approaching very fast with the combined speeds, a little higher, just under the cloud. It could not be an enemy, unless a very rash one, or semi-blind, as it was flying straight on towards him. With a queer and abrupt shock he saw the thin body had twin fins. A Dornier!

Heart thudding, he wheeled up towards it as the Dornier slid by above a couple of hundred yards away and the Hurricane was already standing on a wing-tip when the Dornier saw it and lifted for the cloud. Pin-pricks of light flickered from the rear gun and then Bader was lining up the luminous bead of his reflector sight. He jabbed his thumb on the gun button in a long burst, then fired again. The rear-gunner stopped and then the Dornier fled into the cloud and the Hurricane lunged after it, still firing. He saw nothing but milky mist and ranged furiously about the cloud, but it was a limitless yielding ocean and after a while he knew it was no good, dropped out below and hedge-hopped back to base, muttering unprintable things. At dispersals, in a temper, he rang Ops and told them what had happened, then flopped back in his chair in no mood for dozing.

Five minutes later the phone rang again.

'You know that Dornier,' Ops said, excited and triumphant. 'Well, an Observer Corps chap saw it dive out of the cloud and go straight into the sea. You got him!'

That night in the mess they had a party, but Bader still stuck to orange squash. Any further stimulus he needed he found in the fact that he had got the squadron's first enemy bomber in weather which was too bad for him to let the other pilots fly. Now, he thought, he really *had* proved himself to the boys.

But then, he always thought he had to go on proving himself. It was never conscious. The exterior was always masterful but underneath hid the little demon born in him, aggravated in his childhood and again when he lost his legs. He just had to be better than anyone to find the deepest and unconsidered assurance. Such demons never stay content for long, but must be pacified with more evidence. Great men have them, though the demon himself does not make the greatness; he is only the spur for the other qualities of the mind, the body and the spirit.

Outwardly he exuded so much confidence that it was catching. Even Thelma had caught it now; he looked so virile and competent in everything that it did not seem real that he could be killed. The pilots had certainly caught it. Such a leader is precious to a squadron because pilots are young and human and often frightened under the carefree surface. The shrinking mind keeps saying: 'It can't happen to me,' but logic also says it can and it is good to be buttressed by invincible example.

Now the squadron had eighteen Hurricanes and three more young men came to bring the pilots up to twenty-one. Oddly enough they were naval types lent by the Admiralty because the RAF, short of pilots, was manning the ramparts for the battle. One of them, Midshipman Patterson, was about nineteen, still with the fuzz of youth on his cheeks, and the others were a year or two older, Sub-Lieutenants Dickie Cork and Jimmie Gardner. Cork was a rugged, laughing six-footer and Bader often put him in his own section, the third man being the hawk-eyed little Willie McKnight.

On August 8, off the Isle of Wight, sixty Stukas dived out of the sun on a convoy. Two hours later a hundred more attacked the same convoy. Fighters swarmed up from Tangmere and other fields and dived on the enemy. Aircraft spun smoking into the sea and two ships went down in flame and smoke. In the afternoon 130 German aircraft savagely bombed a convoy off Bournemouth. The storm had burst and in the great crook of hostile airfields off south and east England, Goering had 4000 aircraft. Fighter Command's squadrons in the front line had 500 pilots and aircraft and there were not many reserves.

The Stukas swept in again and bombs crashed down on Portland and Weymouth and convoys off the Thames Estuary and Harwich. Goering was going for the vulnerable ships and testing the strength of the air opposition. Then eleven waves of two hundred bombers attacked Dover. Portsmouth was next, and then Portsmouth again, and now the enemy was sending over 400 aircraft in one day. The fighters of 11 Group around London and to the south tore into them and the Luftwaffe had lost over 200 planes. Across the Channel RAF bombers were attacking the gathering invasion barges.

The defences were stronger than Goering had thought. He had to cripple the RAF by mid-September – Hitler planned to launch twenty-five divisions to land between Folkestone and Worthing on 21 September. On August 15 the bombs came down on the fighter fields of south-east England – Dover, Deal, Hawkinge, Lympne, Middle Wallop, Kenley and Biggin Hill. Next day nearly six hundred bombers raided the fighter fields at Kenley, Croydon, Biggin Hill, Manston, West Malling, Northolt and Tangmere, and scores of aeroplanes, German and British, went down blazing.

Bader and 242 Squadron saw none of this, though every day they waited 'at readiness' by the Hurricanes. It was 11 Group's battle and 12 Group was held back to cover England's industrial heart north of London. Burning for the fight, Bader rang Leigh-Mallory and pleaded to be embroiled but Leigh-Mallory told him: 'We can't put all our eggs in one basket, Bader. You've got to hang on and wait. No doubt the enemy would be delighted to draw our fighter cover away from the Midlands. In any case, I can't send you in until 11 Group calls for you.'

It was hard waiting.

There came another lull and England, shocked by the bombing, waited. Goering, shaken by his losses, was reconsidering. And then the weather closed in.

Bader was not in dispersals the day the controller scrambled a section to cover a convoy when thick and heavy rain cloud almost on the ground had stopped flying. Young Patterson was in that section and did not return. Someone on the convoy reported seeing a Hurricane dive out of control from the cloud into the sea and Bader, almost berserk, drove over to the controller and for ten minutes the bull-like voice flayed the man for sending out his pilots in impossible weather. One would have thought it was a father who had lost one of his sons.

Next day (it was 21 August) the weather was better and Bader, bringing a section back over the airfield from a practice flight, had just broken them away by R/T to land when he heard a voice saying: 'Rusty Red Leader calling. Rusty Red section airborne.'

And then the controller: 'Hallo, Rusty Red Leader. Bandit angels seven over Yarmouth. Vector one-one-zero.'[1]

Yarmouth lay fifteen miles to the south-east and Rusty was the call

---

[1] Enemy aircraft 7,000 feet over Yarmouth. Steer 110 degrees magnetic to intercept.

sign of Rupert Leigh's 66 Squadron. As soon as it had registered, Bader's throttle was wide open as he streaked for Yarmouth.

He came to the coast north of the town but saw nothing else in the air. Rusty section had not arrived yet. A layer of strato-cumulus cloud covered the sky at about 8,000 feet. Might be something above that! He lifted his nose and bored into the cloud; twenty seconds later he lifted out of the grey foam into brilliant sunshine and there unbelievably in front of his eyes flew a Dornier 17 with a glistening pale-blue belly. She was about 700 feet above, going from left to right only a couple of hundred yards in front. As he wheeled up, the Dornier spotted him and dived for the cloud, but Bader was between the cloud and the enemy.

Closing fast, he fired, seeing the tracer flick out. The rear gunner was firing. He was nearly straight behind now and something came suddenly away from the Dornier like a little chain with weights on,[1] and then it had whipped past under him. He had his thumb on the button in a long burst when the Dornier slid into the cloud and he followed, still hosing bullets into the greyness.

Suddenly he shot into the clear beneath. No Dornier. He circled under the white ceiling, breathing hard, eyes above the oxygen mask darting everywhere, but still no Dornier. In a rage he turned back to base.

The lull ended on August 24. That evening 110 German fighters and bombers moved towards London, but were intercepted over Maidstone and fled. Next day they were bombing Portsmouth and Southampton, savagely attacked by defending fighters. Then it was Dover, Folkestone, the Thames Estuary and Kent. Time and again the great formations ploughed steadily across the Channel and clashed bloodily with the spearheads of 11 Group. But 11 Group's losses were heavy too; they fought in squadrons, twelve aircraft against fifty or a hundred or two hundred because there were not enough squadrons and some had to be held in reserve. Air Vice Marshal Park, the AOC, never knew where the next attack was coming from, or when. The plot of a hundred plus on the board now might be a feint, to draw all his fighters up so that when they had to land to refuel and re-arm the main attack could sweep in unopposed.

Day after day while the fights raged Bader alternately sulked and stormed in the dispersal hut at Coltishall, where he and the pilots sat restlessly at readiness like pining maidens waiting for the phone call that never came. Ops ignored them and it was intolerable to Bader that others should be plunging into the fire of battle (not to mention honour) while he was held impotently on the ground. It hardly occurred to him that he might be killed up there, and he kept railing at the stupidity of keeping

---

[1] A new weapon which the Germans threw out of bombers. The 'weights' were grenades, to explode on contact with a fighter. They were not effective.

them on the ground while outnumbered squadrons had to engage a massed enemy. Blunt and dogmatic, he snapped at anyone who questioned him. Training had wrapped a cloak of correctness round the ebullient spirit, but now the spirit was bursting the seams again. So might a tribal warrior, sniffing the battle, shed the veneer of the mission school.

Some of the 242 Squadron 'erks'[1] had been careless about the blackout in their huts again and the station commander, worried about the bombing of aerodromes, decided to make an example and ordered them to carry their bedding over to the hangar and sleep there. Bader was furious that anyone should punish his hard-working men without consulting him. He stumped into Beisiegel's room, saluted, took off his hat and sent it spinning across the room, sat on the edge of the wing commander's desk, tapped his pipe out noisily on his metal knee, leaned across glaring, and said: 'I think you're a—!'

Beisiegel, slightly empurpled, recovered his phlegm, and said, half philosopher·and half martyr:

'D'you know, I thought you'd come and say that.'

On that basis the debate waxed vigorously until Bader exploded: 'All right. If the erks have to go and sleep in the hangar, the officers will too – the whole damn' lot of us.'

The erks and the officers continued to sleep in their own quarters. Beisiegel, in fact, was beginning to admire the revitalised squadron.

The intelligence officer buttonholed Bader in the mess, and said: 'You know that Dornier you pooped off at the other day?'

'That—!'

'I thought you might like to know,' said the IO. 'They've fished a couple of bodies out of the sea off Yarmouth. Their log-books show they were in a Dornier on the day in question and their watches had stopped just after the time you said you shot. Obviously you got him. It all clicks.'

It was pleasant to be credited with a kill that one had not even claimed.

Thelma, anxious about the renewed and savage air fighting, tried to curb his eagerness, suggesting that there would be plenty of battles to come and he was not immortal.

'Don't be damn' silly, darling,' said her husband. 'I've got armour plate behind me, tin legs underneath and an engine in front. How the hell can they get me?'

It was hard to argue with him.

On the morning of August 30 the phone rang in dispersals and Ops said: '242 Squadron take off immediately for Duxford!'

Duxford lay south – not far from London – towards the battle.

Bader grabbed the phone and demanded: 'What's happening?'

[1] Aircraftmen.

Ops said they didn't know, but a bit of a battle was going on down south and 242 Squadron might have to do readiness near the scene, just in case. Whooping wildly, the pilots were running for the Hurricanes. Bader, ablaze, bellowing to rouse the ground crews, moved as fast as his legs would go to his Hurricane parked only five yards away from the door. He was the first man strapped in and within two minutes was leading them off in an impatient, thundering stream.

Half-way to Duxford the controller's voice came coolly over the R/T ordering them back to Coltishall immediately.

Irritated, they flew back to base and Bader harangued Ops over the phone. An hour later Ops ordered them off to Duxford again, and this time there was no recall. By 10 am the Hurricanes stood scattered round a corner of the familiar Duxford field and Bader and his men waited in a restless knot nearby. And waited. From Ops they heard that the Luftwaffe was storming over southern England in waves, but still 11 Group sent out no call. Lunch-time came – and went. They had sandwiches and coffee by the aircraft. Bader sat by the phone in the dispersal hut, cold pipe clenched between his teeth, seething. At a quarter to five the phone rang and he grabbed it.

Ops said crisply: '242 Squadron scramble! Angels fifteen. North Weald.'

He slammed the phone down and was outside the door, yelling.

CHAPTER SIXTEEN

As the wheels, still spinning, folded into the wings and the rest of the pack thundered behind, he flicked the R/T switch. 'Laycock Red Leader calling Steersman. Am airborne.'

A cool and measured voice answered: 'Hallo, Laycock Red Leader. Steersman answering. Vector one-nine-zero. Buster.[1] Seventy plus bandits approaching North Weald.' He recognised the voice of Wing Commander Woodhall, Duxford Station Commander.

Behind him the squadron slid into battle stations, four vics line astern, and climbed steeply south through haze. Holding a map on his thigh, he saw that 190 degrees led over North Weald fighter station. The sun hung in the orb of sky over the starboard wing and he knew what he would

[1] Full throttle.

do if he were the German leader: come in from the sun! From the south-west.

This was no damn' good. He wanted to be up-sun himself. Disregarding controller's words, he swung thirty degrees west. Might miss the enemy! One usually obeyed a controller.

Hell, he'd made up his mind the way he thought was right, and now the brain was cool and clear, and only the blood ran hot. Soon, please God, the guns too. At 9,000 feet he was boring steeply up over the haze in steady air, eyes probing to the left, seeing nothing.

'B-b-blue Leader calling Laycock Leader. Th-th-three aircraft three o'clock below.' Powell-Sheddon's voice.

Over the rim of the cockpit he saw three dots well to the beam. They might be anything.

'Blue section investigate.' He did not bother to identify himself. They knew his voice.

Powell-Sheddon peeled off to starboard, followed by his two satellites. Nine left, against seventy plus.

South-west of North Weald a glint, then another, and in seconds a mass of little dots grew there; too many to be British. The skin tingled all over as the blood pulsed and in the same moment he shoved his throttle forward and called tersely: 'Enemy aircraft ten o'clock level.' Young Crowley-Milling on his right noticed that his voice was harsh and vibrant. The Hurricanes were suddenly bellowing.

Now the dots looked like a swarm of bees droning steadily north-east for North Weald, stepped up from a vanguard at 12,000 feet. The bombers were in tidy lines of four and six abreast, and he was counting the lines: fourteen lines – and above and behind them about thirty more aeroplanes that looked like 110 fighters. Above them still more. Over a hundred. The Hurricanes were above the main swarm now, swinging down on them from the south-west out of the sun, a good spot to start a fight if the 110s had not been above. The main swarm were Dorniers. Must go for them. Too bad about the Messerschmitts above. Have to risk them. He called:

'Green section take on the top lot.'

Christie led his vic of three up and away to the right.

Bader again: 'Red and yellow sections, line astern, line astern.' From a thousand feet above he dived on the swarm of seventy followed by the last five Hurricanes, and now among the Dorniers saw more 110 fighters. A gust of rage shook him. 'The bastards – flying over here like that. It's *our* sky.' On the spur of the moment a demonic compulsion took him to dive right into the middle of that smug formation and break it up. He aimed his nose into the middle.

Black crosses! Glinting perspex! Wings that spread and grew hugely, filling the windscreen. He was on them and suddenly the drilled lines burst in mad turns left and right out of the sights, out of the way. He swept under and up swinging right. A ripple was running through the great herd, and then it was splitting, scattering. Glimpse of Willie McKnight hunting left, Crowley-Milling lunging ahead, and three 110s wheeling in front. The last was too slow. Just behind, he thumbed the button and almost instantly, as the bullets squirted, pieces flew off the 110. Fire blossomed at the wing roots, spurting into long flames as it heeled over.

The blood was fired too, nerve and muscle taut and the roused brain racing like an engine in the capsule of the cockpit which bore him through the torrent. Above to the right another 110 was slowly curling out of a stall-turn and he reefed his nose up after it, closing fast. A hundred yards behind, he fired for three seconds; the 110 rocked fore and aft, and he fired again. Pieces flew off the wing near the starboard engine. Flames suddenly burst along the starboard wing and the 110 was going down blazing.

Full of the fire of the kill, he looked for others and exultation chilled; in the little mirror above his eyes a 110 poked its nose above the rudder, slanting in. He steep-turned hard and over his shoulder saw the 110 heeling after, white streaks of tracer flicking from its nose past his tail. The Hurricane turned faster and the 110 dived and vanished under his wing. Bader spiralled steeply after, saw the 110 well below, streaking east, and dived and chased it, but the 110 was going for home like a bat out of hell and it was hopeless. He was startled to see that he was down to 6,000 feet, sweating and dry-mouthed, breathing hard as though he had just run in a race. He pulled steeply up, back to the fight, but the fight was over. The sky that had been so full was empty and he wondered again – as all fighter pilots wondered – that a mass of raging aircraft could vanish in seconds. Plumes of smoke were rising from the distant fields. The pyres of victory. All German, he hoped, with joy, and with a sudden stab that some might be his own men. Climbing back to 12,000 feet, he called Duxford and was told 'Pancake at base.'

A lone Hurricane appeared on the left, and he ruddered towards it, formating alongside till he saw the big scythe, dripping blood, painted on its side. Willie McKnight! Grinning under his oxygen mask, he raised two fingers to indicate that he had got a couple. McKnight nodded vigorously and then three of his fingers were spread above the cockpit rim. Three! Round the field Hurricanes were coming in. Hard to see how many. He swept down to the grass and Woodhall, the station commander, was standing beside the Hurricane when he climbed out. 'Did you get among 'em?'

The old exuberance bubbled up as he told the story. All the Hurricanes were back, the pilots coming in from dispersals hanging on the sides of the flight-trucks, cheering and yelling to each other. 'Did you get one?'

Drunk on high spirits they babbled out their versions and bit by bit the battle was pieced together: a Dornier had crashed into a greenhouse, another into a field full of derelict cars, a 110 had dived into a reservoir, another Dornier exploded into a ploughed field. Two to Bader, three to McKnight; Turner got one, Crowley-Milling had shot the belly out of a Heinkel, Ball had one . . . several others. They totted up the score – twelve confirmed and several more damaged. The rest had dived and fled home. Not a single bullet hole in any of the Hurricanes.

And not a bomb on North Weald.

Later Bader explained to Woodhall why he had disobeyed his R/T instructions. 'From all the combat reports I've seen the Huns seem to be using the sun. After all, they always did. In the mornings they've usually come in from the south-east with the sun behind them, and in the afternoons they swing round to the west or south-west and come out of the sun again.'

He expounded his views with the usual vigour.

'It's no good trying to protect North Weald or other targets over the top of them. In the morning they must be protected from way down south-east and in the afternoon from south-west. We've got to catch them before they get to their target, not when they've got there and are dropping their bombs. If the controller will tell us where they are in time – direction and height – we'll sort out the tactics in the air, get up-sun ourselves and beat hell out of them before they can bomb.'

'I'm with you,' Woodhall said. 'I think you're dead right. It certainly worked to-day and from now on I'll be on the other end of the radio every time you're up, so don't worry. I'll tell you your patrol line and then keep telling you where the Jerries are so you can use your own judgment.' He added grimly: 'We may be sticking our necks out a bit.'

'Someone's got to,' Bader said. 'No one knows much about this game yet and we've got to learn.'

'Nelson put his telescope to his blind eye and got away with it,' Woodhall observed. 'They'll like you if you get away with it too, but they won't if you don't.'

'Trust the Jerries,' Bader said grimly. 'They'll use the same tricks every time.'

From the start he had the comfort of feeling able to talk frankly to Woodhall. The two had plenty in common, though Woodhall was older, a World War I veteran, grey-haired and stocky with a lined and leathery face. A monocle gleamed in one eye but he was no stuffed shirt, being known as a 'character' who could turn a glassy blind eye to the book of rules at the right time. That afternoon his voice had come over the R/T as clear as a bell, with unruffled poise.

Bader led the squadron back to Coltishall in tight formation at 200 feet, turning in his cockpit to make rude and hilarious two-finger gestures at everyone.

Leigh-Mallory flew over that evening full of congratulations and Bader took his chance to broach a new idea: 'As a matter of fact, sir, if we'd had more aircraft we could have knocked down a lot more. Other squadrons in the group have been standing by like us. Would it be possible for us all to take off together?'

'How would you handle them in the air?' Leigh-Mallory sounded interested.

'It'd be easy to lead, say, three squadrons,' Bader said. 'I haven't worked it out, sir, but surely the whole object of flying in formation is to get a number of aeroplanes in the same place together. If I'd had three squadrons this afternoon it would have been just as easy to get them to the enemy, and we'd have been three times more powerful. That's all you want, sir. Get as many as possible into the fight together. Once it starts there's nothing more the leader can do.'

'I think the thing is to dive into these bomber formations and break them up, and the quicker the better. Then it'll be a free-for-all, and the fighters will have the advantage of eight guns against an isolated gun or two.'

'Sounds splendid,' Leigh-Mallory said.

'I think it would save our casualties too,' Bader went on. 'One squadron against a formation of a hundred or more is pretty sticky. We were lucky to-day because we were above and up-sun.'

Leigh-Mallory said he would think about it.

Next day 242 Squadron, flushed with success, were scrambled three times to patrol North London again, but each time was an anti-climax – no trace of the enemy. It seemed 242 were only sent up at lunch-time or tea-time to give 11 Group a spell when no German aircraft were about. It was frustrating but in the evening Bader felt better when Leigh-Mallory phoned and said:

'To-morrow I want you to try this large formation scheme of yours. We've got 19 and 310 Squadrons at Duxford. Take your chaps there and see how you get on leading the whole three squadrons.'

With great warmth for Leigh-Mallory's decisive ways, Bader spent three days practising take-offs with the three squadrons and leading them in the air. 19 Squadron flew the faster Spitfires so he had them flying above and behind as top cover with the 310 Hurricanes staggered behind 242 on the same level. In those three days he also led 242 on several more patrols round North London, but again saw no trace of the enemy. Exasperating!

Once Powell-Sheddon thought he saw something. They heard his voice on the R/T – 'Th-th-thousands on the left!'

A silence as the eyes darted across, and then a cold and scornful voice: 'Barrage balloons, you clot!'

Farther south the Luftwaffe was still smashing at southern England and 11 Group seemed to be hogging the battle. Intolerable! Bader said so repeatedly.

On one abortive patrol a plot came on the board just as the wing had to turn back short of petrol. It was maddening. Far below he saw a lone squadron climbing hard to intercept the plot, and hoped very hard that they could get height in time and that there were not too many enemy.

At Group's request he wrote a report on how to break up an enemy formation. 'They can be dispersed by shock tactics of the leading section fighters diving into their midst as close as possible . . . risk of collision is there, but the fact remains that the effect of a near collision makes German pilots take violent evasive action which, of course, immediately breaks up any tight formation. Apart from giving the fighters their chance, it also ruins the enemy's chance of accurate bombing.'

He kept drumming that into the pilots of all three squadrons, and adding: 'Another thing – keep one eye in your mirror the whole time the scrap's on and if you see a Hun in your mirror, break off fast!' By 5 September he had the 'scramble' time down to a little over three minutes in getting his thirty-six fighters off the ground. In the air, skipping formality, it was, 'Hallo, Woodie,' and 'Hallo, Douglas.' Leigh-Mallory flew down to watch them practise, and said: 'All right, Bader. Next time 11 Group calls on you, take your whole team.'

Next day Goering, for the first time, turned the Luftwaffe on London.

Since dawn waves of bombers had been battering through the defences to the city and Bader, on readiness with his squadrons, heard the reports coming through and was stamping with impatience. All day he railed at Group, at Ops and the imperturbable Woodhall, demanding to be let off the leash, but it was not until a quarter to five that Ops rang and electrified him by saying, 'Scramble!'

In the air Woodhall's calm voice: 'Hallo, Douglas. There's some trade heading in over the coast. Orbit North Weald. Angels ten. If they come your way you can go for them.'

They climbed fast and hard, and Bader disobeyed instructions again, going on past 10,000 feet to 15,000 in his eagerness to be well on top of anything they sighted.

Nearing North Weald Woodhall again: 'Hallo, Douglas. Seventy plus crossing the Thames east of London, heading north.'

Far to the south-east a cluster of black dots stained the sky. Somehow they did not look like aircraft but he swung his squadrons towards them. Flak bursts! That meant only one thing. As he searched the sky, McKnight's voice, sharply: 'Bandits, ten o'clock above.'

He caught the glint and in seconds saw the dots. Damn! A good 5,000 feet above. Throttle hard on, he kept climbing and the Hurricane was vibrating and thundering, clawing for height on full power. Soon he saw there were about seventy Dorniers and 110s mixed up. And more glints above – Me 109s. Behind him the squadrons were trailing, unable to keep up; though the Spitfires were faster they did not climb so well. Only Dickie Cork was anywhere near. It was going to be sticky. Attacking in a straggle from below with the 109s on top. No chance to break them up. No time for tactics. He closed fast and the flanks of the Dorniers were darting by. A quick burst, but the Dornier had only flashed across his sights. Turning under the tails of the rear section, streams of tracer were streaking at him from the rear gunners. Cork was with him – then 'Crow' – the others well back. He lifted his nose and a 110 floated in his sights. A quick squirt. He fired again and his eyes caught the yellow spinner of a 109 in his mirror. A second to spare for one more quick burst at the 110 – triumph as smoke streamed from it, and then a horrible jarring shock as cannon shells slammed into the Hurricane and jolted it like a pneumatic drill. Instinctively he broke hard left as fear stabbed him, horrible paralysing fright like an ice-block in the chest. Crashes and chaos and the cockpit suddenly full of reeking smoke. For a moment he was frozen rigid, then thought and movement switched on – he was on fire and going down! His hands shot up, grabbed the twin handles of the cockpit hood and hauled it back. Must get out! Straps first! He yanked the pin of his straps and suddenly the cockpit was clear of smoke – sucked out by the noisy slip-stream. No fire. Must have been only cordite smoke. No panic now. He was all right, but furious at having been frightened he slammed the hood shut and looked back, hunted and sweating. No Messerschmitt behind.

The Hurricane was in a screaming diving turn and he eased her out. A 110 was sliding below and he peeled off in chase. It seemed to move towards him as he overhauled it and fired three sharp bursts. The 110 fell away on one wing, nosed straight down, and seconds later dived into a field by a railway line and exploded.

He became aware that his Hurricane was crabbing awkwardly, left wing dropping, and he had the stick hard starboard to keep her level. With a little shock he saw out on the wing that the left aileron was tattered and hanging almost off and there were holes on the right of the cockpit. His Sidcot flying-suit was gashed across the right hip, spilling chewing-gum out of the pocket. Near thing! For the first time in his life he had known the sickness of fear.

After nursing the aircraft back to Coltishall he taxied straight in to the maintenance hangar and climbed out, yelling brusquely: 'West, I want this aircraft ready again in half an hour.'

West had a quick look at it, and said: 'Sorry, sir, but this job won't be flying again for a couple of days.'

'That's no damn' good, I want it in half an hour.'

West, who understood his CO, said soothingly but doggedly: 'More like a week, I'm afraid sir. Apart from the aileron you've got four bullets that I can see through the petrol tank. You're lucky it's self-sealing, but it still stinks of petrol. Shells've also smashed your turn and bank, rev counter and undercart quadrant. There are probably other things too. Sorry, sir, but I won't let it fly.'

Bader's anger was cut short. Cork was taxi-ing in and got out painfully, eyes screwed up and face bleeding. Shreds were hanging all over his Hurricane and the cockpit was a mess where 109 shells had smashed it. Glass splinters from shattered instruments, reflector sight and windscreen had hit him in the face and eyes. He said he was fine but Bader sent him away in the ambulance. West marked another aircraft as unflyable. Three other damaged Hurricanes landed.

One by one the pilots reported. Turner had got another and had also seen Bader's first 110 burst into flames and crash. McKnight had also got two; Ball, one; Tamblyn, one – and others. Jubilantly they added the score. Eleven confirmed. But the other two squadrons had been so far behind that they had virtually missed the fight.

Young Crowley-Milling and Pilot Officer Benzie were not back. By dusk they were still missing.

Then a phone call from Crowley-Milling, who had been shot up and cut his face crash-landing in Essex. No word from Benzie. He was dead.

In the morning, a little grimmer, 242 flew again to Duxford, but no call came from 11 Group, though the bombers again were storming London. He could visualise those single 11 Group squadrons climbing up under the German packs, vulnerable to the hovering 109s while they tried to get at the bombers. Often they were picked off like pigeons, and for all the shiny stories of success there were also stories of squadrons which had been almost wiped out in a week. They used to post them north to reform then, and bring down a fresh squadron which might also have to be pulled back north for reforming a week later.

After lunch Leigh-Mallory flew in, and Bader said:

'It didn't come off yesterday, sir. We were too slow. If we'd been higher we could really have got among them and the Spitfires could have covered us from the 109s.' Angry that the squadrons were kept so long on the ground, he added: 'RDF[1] get these plots of bombers building up over France. If only we could get off earlier we could be on top and ready for them. Why can't we do that, sir?'

'The Germans might want us to,' Leigh-Mallory suggested. 'If they can decoy our fighters up they can hold back for an hour till the fighters have to go down to refuel again and then send the bombers in.'

---

[1] Radio Direction Finding – soon to be developed into Radar.

'It's worth taking that chance, sir.'

'So it might be,' said Leigh-Mallory; 'but it's 11 Group's decision and they feel they should wait till the Germans start moving in. That doesn't give them much chance to scramble big formations then, but your score yesterday seems to justify the experiment, so carry on with the three squadrons. After all, it was only the first try. We'll try and get you off earlier in future so you can get your height. Let's see what happens then.'

Next morning to readiness at Duxford again with three squadrons for another day of impatient waiting, and about five o'clock Sector Ops reported that RDF was showing a build-up of enemy aircraft over the Pas de Calais.

Bader rang Woodhall. 'For Christ's sake let's get off in time and catch these — on the way in.'

'Keep your hair on, Douglas,' Woodhall said. 'I'm prodding them hard as I can.'

Soon Woodhall rang back. 'Bombers heading in. Scramble fast as you can!'

And then in the air: 'Hallo, Douglas. Looks like they're heading for London. Will you patrol between North Weald and Hornchurch, angels twenty.'

('Will you patrol . . .?' Woodhall left that part open.)

Bader looked at the afternoon sun and thought: I know damn' well they'll swing west and come out of the sun. He forgot North Weald-Hornchurch and climbed his three squadrons south-west over the fringe of London; ignored the 'angels twenty' too, climbing till they were specks at 22,000 feet over the reservoirs at Staines, still climbing.

And then a few miles in front the sky glinted and around the spot like a film coming into focus the dots appeared; two great swarms of them cutting across fast in front, heading for London. About the same height. (Just as well he'd ignored 'North Weald-Hornchurch' . . . and the 'angels' too.) Looked like sixty odd in each bunch. He wheeled to cut them off, still climbing, swinging higher now and between the swarms with the sun behind him and calling 19 Squadron urgently to climb higher and cover their tails. Then to the rest: 'Line astern, line astern. We're going through the middle.'

In the corner of his eye a scatter of fighters darted out of the sun and he thought with a surge of joy that more friendly fighters had arrived: only a few pilots behind saw that they were 109s and wheeled back to fight them off. Diving now on the first swarm he saw they were mixed Dorniers and 110s. A Dornier was slightly in front leading, and he plunged for it, firing almost point-blank for two seconds, then diving past and under, pulled up again, but the leading Dornier was falling over on its back, smoke pouring from both engines. Other bombers above! He kept zooming up like a dolphin, squirting at them, seeing flashes as the armour-piercing incendiary bullets hit. The mind was racing again in the deadly confusion of high-speed battle.

To the side another Dornier was diving, trailing fire and smoke, and a voice shouted in his ears, 'F-f-f-flamer!' Powell-Sheddon had scored. Black twisting bombs were suddenly falling on Bader as the bombers jettisoned over the fields and turned south-east to flee. He steep-turned out of the way of the bombs, seeing that only about twenty of the bombers still clustered in ragged formation, the rest straggling over the sky, hunted by darting fighters.

Half a mile ahead was a Dornier; he chased it and was soon pulling it back. Five hundred yards now. Two Hurricanes suddenly dived in from each side in front of him, converging on the Dornier. Damn! Daylight robbery! Swiftly the two fighters swept together behind the bomber, and he suddenly screamed into his microphone: 'Look out. You're going to collide.' A moment later they did. The left wing of the Hurricane on the right folded and ripped away, and it spun instantly; the other Hurricane, crabbing crazily on, smashed into the Dornier's tail and the air was full of flying fragments. The two broken aircraft wrenched apart and spun, followed by torn pieces twisting and floating down. It was over in seconds.

A big Heinkel was fleeing about a mile away and well below, and he dived in chase. It seemed to be stupid or helpless, making no effort to dodge as he swept nearer – must have been shot up. It filled his windscreen – a beautiful target. As usual he held his fire until almost point-blank he jabbed the button and heard only the mocking hiss of compressed air through the breech-blocks. Out of ammunition! He flamed with outraged fury and swung across the Heinkel's nose, but it took no notice, lumbering wearily in. He slammed round behind it again raging with a crazy impulse to ram it – cut off its rudder with his propeller – and then sense returned and he turned away.

Back at Duxford two of the pilots, Brimble and Bush, said they saw Bader's first Dornier go down in flames and only one of the crew had baled out. Bush had also got one. McKnight had collected a couple more . . . and others too, Eric Ball, Powell-Sheddon, Turner, Tamblyn had scored . . . eleven confirmed to 242 Squadron.

But Sclanders and Lonsdale were missing.

The other two squadrons added a further nine enemy destroyed, but two of 320 Squadron had not returned.

Later Lonsdale phoned. He had been shot down, baled out and landed in a tree in the grounds of a girls' school, hurting his leg, and could not get down because of his leg. Uncomfortably, he had roosted in the branches for half an hour while the girls stood underneath giggling until the local constable came and brought him down a ladder.

Sclanders was dead.

Then Gordon Sinclair, of 310 Squadron, phoned from Caterham on the other side of London. He had been in one of the Hurricanes that collided and had managed to bale out. Bader grabbed the phone. 'How are you, Gordon?'

'Utterly amazed, sir,' Sinclair said. 'D'you know, I lobbed slap in Caterham High Street and I was picking my parachute out of the gutter when a chap walked up, and said: 'Hallo, Gordon, old boy. What are you doing here?' And I'm damned if it wasn't a chap I was at school with.'

The pilot of the other Hurricane, a Czech, did not bale out.

But the mathematics were good – twenty enemy destroyed for the loss of four Hurricanes and two pilots. In September, 1940, only the mathematics mattered.

Still Bader was not satisfied. He flew to 12 Group HQ, at Hucknall, and told Leigh-Mallory: 'Sir, if we'd only had *more* fighters we could have hacked the Huns down in scores.'

'I was going to talk to you about that,' Leigh-Mallory said. 'If I gave you two more squadrons, could you handle them?'

CHAPTER SEVENTEEN

Five squadrons. Sixty plus fighters! Even Bader was startled. He collected himself:

'Yes, sir. When a fight starts we'd break up anyway. I'd have the Spitfires on top to hold off any 109s, and a mass of Hurricanes below with nothing to worry about on their tails could crucify a pack of bombers.'

'I thought of that too,' said Leigh-Mallory.

He seemed to understand so well that Bader took the plunge and told him about disobeying controller's instructions, not to clear himself but with a proselytising zeal, expounding his ideas.

'The formation leaders might make a mistake and miss the enemy altogether,' suggested Leigh-Mallory.

'The controllers are already doing that, sir. They can't help it. RDF is inaccurate about height.'

'You think the advantages outweigh the risks?'

'Yes, sir, I do.' Bader was emphatic.

'So do I,' Leigh-Mallory said. 'I'll put this up to the right people and meantime you might as well carry on with your theory. It seems to work.'

There was more to the conversation than those extracts, of course. It lasted over an hour, and Leigh-Mallory did not accept all that Bader said without reservations, but he recognised the square-jawed man with the glowing eyes and manner as an individualist with a direct approach that impatiently threw out minor details and concentrated on the elementals. With equal zeal he could be abysmally wrong or brilliantly right on any problem. In this battle, where the right answers had to be won by bitter experience, the AOC thought Bader was right. He added that he was also spreading Bader's gospel of breaking up enemy formations by diving into their midst. Bader had done it the first time on the spur of a moment of anger – from that moment was born a new tactical method that was against all the teachings. Leigh-Mallory called 242 the 'disintegration squadron.'

Up before dawn next morning for Duxford. And the morning after. Several more patrols to relieve 11 Group but nothing seen. Everyone complained of boredom but that was only the fashionable, elaborately casual pose. In the past fortnight 231 pilots had been killed or badly wounded, and 495 Hurricanes and Spitfires destroyed or badly damaged (mostly 11 Group). The factories only turned out about a hundred new ones a week. Pilot replacements were also fewer than the losses and many of the new pilots too raw for battle.

Among the survivors fear and tension lay under the surface like taut sinews in a naked body, but always decently covered with understatement: protection against showing emotion, either fear or unseemly elation at being the only instrument between Hitler and the conquest of Britain. Life was a brutal contrast. Off duty they could joke in a pub and sleep between sheets, to wake in the morning to a new world of hunters and hunted, sitting in deck-chairs on the grass, waiting by the aeroplanes with needles in the stomach. Other men who knew they themselves would still be alive at night brought them sandwiches for lunch and coffee, but any moment the phone might go and they would have to drop the cup: half an hour later they might be trapped in a burning aeroplane crashing from 20,000 feet.

Only Bader had no pose. He swashbuckled around as though he were about to step into the ring and knock out Joe Louis with one punch and without even bothering to change. His exuberance, the way he utterly ignored the danger, was contagious and infected every other pilot. Morale was extraordinary. He loved the battle and talked and thought tactics, fascinated by them. Insensitive to fear, he never had what was known as 'the twitch' like the others. For the Germans (hidden in their aeroplanes) he conceived an impersonal hate, but he passionately loathed 'those aeroplanes with the black crosses and swastikas dropping their filthy bombs on *my* country. By the same token I felt a great love for every single English person I met on the ground.'

About this time he designed the squadron emblem – a figure of Hitler being kicked in the breeches by a flying boot labelled 242. West cut a metal template of it and the ground crews painted it on the noses of all the Hurricanes. The ground crews were working devotedly day and night to keep the aircraft flying.

Off duty, Bader did not mind anyone letting off steam violently. Peter Macdonald helped by turning on a champagne party for the pilots one night. Leigh-Mallory came over and entered into the spirit of things by forsaking his dignity and doing a Highland Fling on a mess table. It all ended hilariously with a crowd of young men squirming on the floor in mock scuffle, punctuated by occasional sharp yelps when one of Bader's flying tin legs hit someone in ribs or head. Leigh-Mallory seemed to be on duty all the time; he had· a weakness for cold baths and midnight conferences and was often working till 3 am, usually rising again at 6.30. He had been known to spend twenty-seven hours in the operations room, and then go and talk to pilots on windy tarmacs when they came back from a flight. After that he would probably take them into the mess, stand drinks all round and listen to any complaints or suggestions.

Bader slept in the mess at Coltishall but used to go and see Thelma every evening to let her know he was all right. On September 13 he was having dinner with her at the house in Coltishall when the phone rang for him in the hall. Leigh-Mallory's voice greeted him courteously: 'Oh, hallo, Bader. I wanted to be the first to congratulate you. You've just been awarded the DSO.'

A great glow suffused him, and then in the emotion of the moment he could think of nothing to say until at last he managed an automatic 'Thank you, sir.'

'And another thing,' Leigh-Mallory added a few moments later. The next morning 302 Squadron (Hurricanes) and 611 (Spitfires) would also be flying into Duxford. Would Bader be good enough to include them in his formation, which was now to be called the '12 Group Wing.'

Bader managed to convey that he would be delighted to.

It is good form to be offhand about decorations, but nothing can dim stirring inner pride. One always feels it and no one more fiercely than Bader, who was living so wholly for the fight. And for the consummation of himself. It was too fierce a moment to be offhand about, or even to mention. He sat holding it to himself for an hour before mentioning it quietly to a flight lieutenant known as Poggi, who was also in the house. Poggi went delightedly to Thelma and said: 'Isn't this wonderful about Douglas's DSO.'

Thelma said, 'What are you talking about, Poggi?' then saw Douglas's face and realised something had happened. There was the usual scene of excitement, affection and congratulations, capped by the general laugh when Thelma, eternal woman, said: 'Well I *do* think you might have told *me* first.'

Next morning, September 14, the two extra squadrons as promised flew into Duxford, and twice that day Bader led the armed pack of sixty fighters into the air to patrol North London. They saw no enemy; the Luftwaffe was coiling for the next leap and only one bomber sneaked through the cloud to bomb Buckingham Palace at the cost of its own destruction. Eric Ball's DFC came through, the first decoration Bader had recommended.

In the still, cool, dawn of September 15 the five squadrons of 12 Group Wing stood in groups about Duxford and its satellite field, waiting. Broken cloud scattered thickly over the sky, offering good cover to attackers, and RDF began reporting plots of enemy aircraft rising over the fields of Northern France. In clumps the plots crept across the screens towards England, and soon the shield of 11 Group squadrons round London was savaging them over Kent. Then the first stage was over; burning wrecks littered the fields, the remnants of the bombers, some winged and smoking, were streaming back to France and the Hurricanes and Spitfires, gun-ports whistling where the patches had been shot off, were coming in to refuel and re-load. At the moment RDF showed another wave of bombers heading for London.

Woodhall scrambled the 12 Group Wing five minutes later.

In the air, the measured voice: 'Hallo, Douglas. About forty bandits heading for London. Will you patrol Canterbury-Gravesend.'

'OK, Woodie.'

Canterbury-Gravesend! That was fine. The morning sun still lay in the south-east, and if the bombers were going for London he knew where to look for them. The three Hurricane squadrons climbed steeply in vics line astern with the Spitfires a little to the left, a little above. To the right London lay under the cloud that had thickened. 12,000 feet . . . 16,000 . . . 20,000 . . . they kept climbing high over the cloud. Nearing angels 23 he saw black puffs staining the sky almost straight ahead, and somewhat below and ahead of the flak almost instantly saw the enemy, drilled black flies sliding towards the naked city. About five miles away . . . forty odd . . . JU. 88s and Dorniers.

Swinging right, he nosed down to come in diving. God, it was beautiful, the sun right behind them, the bombers below. He looked for the 109s behind and above and could hardly believe it . . . not a sign. Unescorted bombers. The heart leapt and the blood sang and the mind ran clear and sharp.

High out of a veil of cloud near the sun little grey sharks were darting. He called urgently:

'Sandy, watch those 109s.'

'OK, chum, I can see them.' Sandy Lane, leader of 19 Squadron, was already wheeling the Spitfires up into the fighters.

'Break 'em up,' yelled Bader and swept, firing, through the front rank of the bombers. He pulled up and veered behind a big Dornier turning away left, fired and fired again. A flash burst behind the Dornier's starboard engine, and flame and black smoke spewed from it. Suddenly he was nearly ramming it and broke off. Hell, aircraft of broken formations darting everywhere in the blurred and flashing confusion. In front – 400 yards away – another Dornier seeking cloud cover between the 'cu-nims'; he was catching it rapidly when his eye caught a Spitfire diving steeply above and just ahead. It happened fast. The Spitfire pilot clearly did not see the bomber under the long cowling; he dived straight into the middle of it and the Dornier in a burst of flame split and wrapped its broken wings round the fighter. Tumbling fragments glinted above the crumpled mass as the two aircraft fell in burning embrace.

Sweating, Bader looked for others. A Dornier was spinning down to one side, dragging a plume of flame and smoke, and as he watched a man jumped out of it. His parachute opened instantly – too soon – the canopy spread into the blaze and shrivelled to nothingness in a sheet of flame. The man dropped like a stone, trailing the cords like a tattered banner. Bader was snarling to himself: 'Good show, you rat. Now you've got a little time to think about it and there isn't any answer.'

After that only the miracle again of the empty sky.

Back at Duxford Eric Ball was missing.

They refuelled, re-loaded, and by 11.45 were on readiness again.

A phone call from Eric Ball. His Hurricane had been shot down in flames but he had baled out and would be back.

Two hours later the Wing was scrambled again to patrol North Weald, and Bader led them through a gap in the clouds. At 16,000 feet, flak bursts ahead, and in moments he saw the bombers; about forty of them, some 4,000 feet above the Hurricanes. Damn! Everything risked again because they were scrambled too late. Throttle hard on, the thundering Hurricane had her nose steeply lifted, nearly hanging on her propeller at about 100 mph.

A voice screamed: '109s behind.'

Over his shoulder the yellow spinners were diving on them and he yelled as he steep-turned, 'Break up!' Around him the sky was full of wheeling Hurricanes and 109s. A yellow spinner was sitting behind his tail, and as he yanked harder back on the stick an aeroplane shot by, feet away. Bader hit its slipstream and the Hurricane shuddered, stalled and spun off the turn. He let it spin a few turns to shake off the 109 and came out of it at 5,000 feet. All clear behind.

Far above a lone Dornier was heading for France, and he climbed and chased it a long way, hanging on his propeller nearly at stalling speed again. Near the coast he was just about in range and fired a three-second burst, but the recoil of the guns slowed the floundering Hurricane till she suddenly stalled and spun off again. He pulled out and searched the sky but the enemy had vanished.

Back at Duxford, Powell-Sheddon was missing.

That was the greatest day of the battle. Odd, looking back, that it seemed no different from any other day. None of the pilots thought much about it at the time; it was just another episode in the confused and wearying tension that had so recently and so completely enveloped them. No time to think, only to dress at dawn and sit waiting, hung in a limbo of queasy time, lazy small talk on the outside and taut nerves inside, waiting for the ring of the phone that sent them into battle again. They found, when they pieced that day's battle together, that the 12 Group Wing had fully justified itself, though in the second battle the roles had been reversed – the Spitfires had got among the bombers while the Hurricanes tangled with the 109s. But that was merely a quirk of the battle; the main point was that in the two mass fights that day the pilots of the five squadrons of the Wing claimed 52 enemy destroyed and a further eight probables.[1]

242 Squadron's share was twelve. At least they were consistent – it was usually either eleven or twelve. Cork, his face repaired, had got two Dorniers, one on each trip. Young Crowley-Milling, whose cut face was also nearly healed, had flown again for the first time since he was shot down, and avenged himself by chasing a 109 across Kent and sending it smoking into a field. McKnight, Turner, Bader, Stansfeld, Tamblyn had all scored. Even Powell-Sheddon, who rang up from somewhere near Epping. It had been going so well, he reported dolefully. He had shot a Dornier down and was chasing another when a 109 came out of cloud behind and he had had to bale out in a hurry as the flames spurted round his cockpit; in such a hurry that he had hit the tail plane and dislocated his shoulder. The doctor said he would be out of the battle for some weeks.[2]

Baker went to Turner and said: 'Stan, how d'you feel about taking over B Flight?'

'Swell, sir,' said Turner.

Leigh-Mallory phoned that night:

'Douglas' (using his Christian name for the first time) . . . 'What a wonderful show to-day!' The AOC's rather formal manner had com-

---

[1] The RAF claimed 185 German aircraft destroyed on September 15. After the war Luftwaffe figures said that only 56 had been lost. RAF pilots who fought in the battle flatly and vehemently disbelieve the German total. One might suspect that some of Goebbels's propaganda figures were discreetly promoted to official record status.

[2] Powell-Sheddon later went on to win a DSO and DFC.

pletely melted. 'It's absolutely clear your big formations are paying dividends.'

Bader said: 'Thank you very much, sir, but we had a sticky time on the second trip. They scrambled us too late again and the Germans were a long way above when we spotted them. It was a bad spot to attack if we'd only been one squadron we'd probably have been chopped up by the 109s, but if they'd let us off ten minutes earlier we could have been just in the right spot to cope, and probably got a lot more of them.

'It doesn't make sense, sir' (warming to his theme). 'As soon as they start building up their formations over Calais we should get into the air and go south. *We* should be the ones to attack them first while 11 Group get off and get height.'

'Well, you know I feel somewhat the same as you on this point,' Leigh-Mallory said. 'At the same time don't forget we have to keep reserves available. It's 11 Group's job to make that decision and it isn't easy for them. I rather fancy they had every squadron they could call on committed to-day.'

'Well, sir, reserves or no reserves, they called on us too late to-day.'

'Quite,' said the AOC. 'But the wing score to-day won't go unnoticed – I'll see to that myself – and I fancy it will encourage them to call for you earlier.'

'I hope they do, sir,' Bader answered feelingly – then enthusiastic again: 'D'you know, sir, what I'd really like to do is shoot down a complete raid so that not one of the Huns gets back.'

The AOC laughed. 'Bloodthirsty, aren't you! If you chaps keep on the way you're going you'll probably get your chance.'

The chance came on the 18th.

About 4.30 in the afternoon the five squadrons were scrambled, and over the R/T Woodhall said that forty plus bandits were heading for London from the south-east. Bader led the Wing through a thin layer of cloud at about 21,000 feet and levelled off in the clear at 23,000. Not far below, the soft feather-bed stretched flat and unbroken for miles, perfect backdrop for searching eyes. Nothing else in sight. But the invisible world under the cloud? In a shallow dive he took his fighters down through the thin layer and they cruised under the white ceiling, feeling comfortingly safe. No one could jump them blind through that curtain.

Once again the flak-bursts led them. First Bader saw the black puffs away to the south-east and in moments picked up the bombers. Two little swarms, about forty in all, were flying about 16,000 feet over a bend of the Thames near Gravesend. More British aeroplanes than enemy! It was unbelievable! As the fighters circled to close in behind he saw with fierce joy that they were all bombers – JU. 88s and Dorniers. Not a sign of any 109s. The bombers were 4,000 feet below, just where he would have wanted them. No question of coming out of the sun – the clouds hid the sun. He dived, aiming for the JU. 88s in the front rank of the bombers, and the ravenous pack streamed after him.

A Junkers filled his sights and as he fired from 100 yards astern its port engine gushed smoke and it fell away to the left. Pulling up into the thick of plunging, criss-crossing aeroplanes, he fired briefly at a couple that flashed across his sights and vanished again; then in quick succession nearly collided with two more bombers. A Hurricane screamed towards him at a crazy angle: he yanked the stick over to get out of the way, hit someone's slipstream and his Hurricane shuddered and flicked into a spin. He got her straight and level again after losing about 3,000 feet, and saw above that the split-up bombers had turned for home, hounded by the fighters. To the south-east, lower and away from the ruck, a Dornier was sneaking east and he chased it. No escape for the slower and cumbersome Dornier; he closed for the kill, holding his fire till he was barely fifty yards away, and then jabbed the button.

As the bullets still squirted, the enemy gunner lost his nerve and jumped. His awkward shape swept back out of the glasshouse and his parachute, streaming open at the same moment, hooked and tangled over one of the twin fins on the tail, pulling him up like a whipcrack. As he dangled helplessly on the shrouds the Dornier, obviously out of control, started 'hurdling,' soaring into steep zooms, hanging a moment at the top and then falling into dives, building speed and zooming again. Bader sheered off to one side, watching, amazed and fascinated. Two more men suddenly tumbled out of the glasshouse and the white silk of their parachutes blossomed below. The empty Dornier kept hurdling imaginary obstacles, losing more height, still trailing the wretched gunner. With sudden pity Bader dived and fired at him to put him out of his misery, but as far as he could see, missed. The Dornier fell into a deeper dive and he left it.

For once the sky about was not empty . . . many white flowers of parachutes were floating down. A little man in a strange brown flying suit fell past his Hurricane very fast with only a little remnant of silk left of his parachute. Bader thought whimsically he must be a Gestapo agent who had been sabotaged by the honest airmen.

At dispersals a mob of hilarious pilots clustered round the intelligence officer, most of them claiming victims. Turner was describing how he saw a German's opening parachute caught in the hatch as he jumped out of a burning JU. 88. The rest of the crew were trying to release it. . . . 'I could damn' nearly hear the poor guy on the end howling "For God's sake, don't tear it!" ' They got him free and jumped out themselves just before the 88 went into the sea.

None of them had ever seen so many parachutes. McKnight had seen the gunner trailing on the cords behind Bader's Dornier and could not stop marvelling at it.

Bader summed it up prosaically in his log book: 'London patrol. Contact.' And alongside it a laconic note: 'Wing destroyed 30 plus 6 probables plus 2 damaged. 242 got 11. Personal score: 1 JU. 88, 1 Do. 17. No casualties in squadron or wing.'

In his formal combat report he wrote: 'To every German there seemed to be about three British fighters queueing up for a squirt, a little dangerous from the collision point of view but a most satisfactory state of affairs.'

That time he rang Leigh-Mallory himself, described the fight like a fisherman telling his favourite story and mourned about the few that had got away.

The point was widely noted that it paid to scramble 12 Group Wing in good time. Peter Macdonald had had a hand in that. In the House of Commons one day he had spoken earnestly with the Under-Secretary of State for Air, who had suggested he see the Prime Minister. Macdonald had an hour and a half with Churchill, who was gruff at first, but then thawed, and the next day began sending for various group commanders.

Goering started to chop and change his tactics more, sometimes sending over squads of 109s in advance of the bombers to draw the fighters up and exhaust their petrol (something like the decoy idea that Leigh-Mallory had mentioned to Bader earlier). It was the beginning of the end of the daylight bombing, but no one knew that yet as the aura of ruthless power still clung to the Germans. At best it seemed a lull.

Bombers still occasionally battered through the defences to London, but the spearhead on that target was blunted: more and more they went for Kent, for the Estuary towns and, in particular, Southampton, all on the south-east fringes of England and away from the 12 Group area.

Once or twice nearly every day, especially at lunch or tea-time, the wing was scrambled to patrol an arc round London, and Bader had a new grievance – they never ran into the enemy any more. His personal score was eleven confirmed, but that only whetted his zest rather than satiated it. Besides, some others had twenty or more!

He was famous now, which would have been good for placating the little demon inside him if he had not been too busy to notice the publicity much. To stress 'team spirit' the RAF did not name its 'aces,' but every time there was some new epic about a fighter pilot with no legs, the Press knew well enough who it was. Bader himself lived in the little world of the Wing, the battle and the tactics. He was aware of the high morale of his pilots but hardly realised how much of it was due to himself: they looked on him as a super-man and would have followed him into the middle of a thousand 109s. He obviously knew what he was doing in the air better than anyone else, and there was a fire about him so much more than breezy confidence. He was a kind of machine genius of the new aerial art with an iron will exalted by the moment.

Every time the wing took off, the masterful voice started firing comments over the R/T with such assurance that pilots could not help feeling confident. His remarks, by design or accident, so often took the nervous sting out of the business ahead. On August 20, for instance, a lanky, nineteen-year-old boy called Cockie Dundas flew with the wing for the first time. Exactly a month earlier Dundas had been with 616 Squadron at Kenley; they were waiting at readiness for an evening visit from Winston Churchill when they had been scrambled and run into a flock of 109s over Kent. It was Dundas's first fight and a 109 had 'jumped' him, shot his controls to bits and put bullets in his engine and glycol tank. Smoke and glycol fumes filled the cockpit and he could not get his hood open. He spun out of control from 12,000 feet till finally he was able to jettison the hood and baled out at 800 feet, breaking his collar-bone at the same time. Now only two of the old pilots were left in the squadron, and Dundas, still shaken, shoulder still weak, was going back for more. They were scrambled in a great hurry and, being young and human, he had 'the twitch,' dry mouth, butterflies in the stomach, and thumping heart. Then in his ears as they climbed that odd, legless leader's voice:

'Hey, Woodie, I'm supposed to be playing squash with Peters in an hour's time. Ring him up, will you, and tell him I won't be back till later.'

(Dear God. Legless! Playing squash!)

Woodhall's voice: 'Never mind that now, Douglas. Vector one-nine-zero. Orbit North Weald. Angels twenty.'

'Oh, go on, Woodie. Ring him up now.'

'Haven't got time, Douglas. There's a plot on the board heading for the coast.'

'Well, can't you make time? You're sitting in front of a row of phones. Pick up one and ring the chap.'

'All right. All right,' said the philosophical Woodhall. 'For the sake of peace and quiet I will. Now would you mind getting on with the war.'

Dundas flew on with lifted heart, like all the others.

Another squadron intercepted the plot on the board, and the wing landed an hour later and was released from readiness. Bader played squash and flew off to see Leigh-Mallory at Hucknall. Dundas thought that evening he would never have the twitch flying behind Bader again. (He was wrong . . . but that came later.)

Some of the credit for the confidence also belonged to Woodhall. It is hard to say how much these absurd conversations were designed as confidence builders and how much was instinctive. Bader himself is not sure, though later he realised their value and used the technique a lot.

Even then it remained at least as much unconscious as conscious. It was just part of him.

On September 24 a DFC came through for Dickie Cork and Bader was as pleased as Cork, not only because he had recommended it but because it was, as far as he knew, the only DFC every awarded to a 'Nautic' (the equivalent Naval decoration is the DSC – Distinguished Service Cross). Cutting across the Navy's bows with a DFC for Cork was a 'jolly good giggle.' He never stopped trying to lure Cork from the customs of the Navy and inject RAF lore and outlook into him. That, too, was a 'good frolic.' He had Cork to the point now where he had naval buttons on the starboard side of his tunic, but down the port side, reading from top to bottom, an RAF button, a Polish Air Force button (which was silver in colour, not even gilded), an RCAF button and a Czech button.

The abortive patrols went on till September 27. About noon that day the wing was scrambled to patrol North London. Woodhall said 'Angels fifteen.' Bader knew that instruction came from 11 Group and climbed to 23,000 feet.

Woodhall on the air again: 'There's a plot of thirty plus south-east of the Estuary. They don't seem to be coming in.'

Bader led his pack over Canterbury. Nothing in sight. He carried on round Dover, headed west for Dungeness and swung back. Woodhall kept talking about bandits cruising about the south-east. Clumps of cloud littered the air below like papers blowing about a windswept park. Otherwise the sky was empty. Woodhall called again: 'All right, Douglas, I think the lunch shift is over. You might as well come back.'

'Just a minute, Woodie,' Bader said. 'I'll do one more swing round.'

Turning back from Dungeness, his eye caught glints well below at about 17,000 feet, and soon he could make out an untidy gaggle of about thirty 109s milling round Dover.

CHAPTER EIGHTEEN

'OK, chaps,' he called. 'Take this quietly. Don't attack till I tell you.' Rather like a huntsman who has sighted shy game, he began stalking them, turning the wing south over the sea so that they could dive out of the high sun. The 109s were so scattered it would have to be a shambles, every man for himself. Still the Germans weaved in a ragged undisciplined tangle like unwary rabbits at play. He yelled: 'Right. Break up and attack!' and was diving steeply, turning in behind a 109. At the same speed it seemed to hang motionless in his sights. A two-second squirt and a pencil of white smoke trailed from it – abruptly the smoke gushed into a cloud spewing past its tail and the little fighter rolled slowly on its back, nose dropping until it plummeted vertically, scoring a long white scar through the clouds to the fields of Kent.

Another 109 crossed in front, rolled swifly on its back and dived. Bader peeled off after him, but the 109 was faster and began to pull away. From four hundred yards Bader fired a forlorn long-range burst and a jet of smoke spurted from the 109. It seemed to be slowing. Bader fired again and again, seeing flashes of bullet strikes.

Something dark spurted from the 109 and a black shadow seemed to slap him nervelessly across the face. He felt nothing; only the eyes sensed it and then saw that his windscreen and hood were stained to black opaqueness by the enemy's oil that the slipstream was tearing in thin reluctant streaks across the glass. Dimly through it he saw the 109 veering aside and turned after it, seeing, amazed, that the Messerschmitt's propeller was slowing. The 109 was coming tail-first at him: he yanked the throttle back and the enemy floated close in front, the perfect shot. He jabbed the gun-button and heard the pssst of compressed air that hissed through empty breech-blocks. Hell! Out of bullets again.

He swore. The 109s propeller spun in shaky spasms and then it stopped dead, one blade held up like a stiff finger. They were over the sea at 10,000 feet, and the 109, still smoking, was gliding quietly down into the Channel. That was the last he saw of it.

The wing got twelve in that fight, half of them to 242 Squadron. One Spitfire and two Hurricanes did not come back, and one of them was Homer, of 242, who had already won a DFC on bombers and was having his first fight in Hurricanes.

Bader hated losing pilots, taking it, illogically, as some sort of reflection on himself. He felt that every man was under *his* care. None of his emotions were half-hearted and under the aggressive exterior lay impulsive sentiment that could be deeply stirred. Yet the impact of a loss was always cushioned by the hope of a phone call. No call came from Homer, who was dead, but there was no time for grief. By tea-time the wing was patrolling London again. No incident, but waiting for the squadron at Coltishall that evening was an Air Ministry signal announcing the joyous news in prosaic official terms that Turner and Stansfeld were awarded DFCs and Willie McKnight a bar to his DFC.

Leigh-Mallory phoned from Hucknall in what was becoming a sort of victory tradition and they had a long discussion about tactics. Bader said that the Hurricanes flew soggily at 23,000 feet. What about the new Hurricane II's?

Leigh-Mallory said: 'Anything you want, I'll try my best to get for you, but 11 Group has priority for equipment.'

From that day the tide of the battle clearly ebbed. Now the bombers rarely appeared, but in their place came packs of 109's darting for London and other targets with small bombs hanging on makeshift bomb-racks under their slim bellies. They came over fast and very high, dodging through cloud banks, and as autumn came the cloud clustered thicker and thicker. Compared to the sound and fury of a few weeks earlier, the new attacks were forlorn: they so often bombed blindly and the number of bombs was not much more than a trickle. The RAF changed its tactics too. At 25,000 feet the Hurricanes found it harder than ever to catch the fleet 109's and the burden fell on the Spitfires, which were scrambled early now so that they were up there, waiting, when the 109's came. Not many Messerschmitts broke through the screen of Spitfires, and now in London, when the sirens wailed, people no longer bothered to stream out of the buildings into the cellars and shelters. It was the same in other cities. After the alarm sirens there was still a lot of noise, but now it was not the crashing symphony of bombs but the cracking of anti-aircraft guns. Apart from those one would not have known that the Luftwaffe was over except for the fantastic pattern of vapour trails high overhead where the fighters, sightless to the upturned faces, fought it out.

For another couple of weeks the 12 Group Wing kept assembling each day at Duxford and patrolling London, usually twice a day, always vainly now, still keyed up but with the tension easing like air leaking out of a bladder as the Luftwaffe faded from the scene. Even the 109 sneak raiders were dwindling and not till the second week in October did Bader get near one. Leading the wing over the Estuary, his radio died and he fiddled with it but it stayed mute, and at last angrily he slid the cockpit lid open, dropped back, signalled by hand to Eric Ball to take over the wing, and then peeled off for base. It was nearly dusk and as he dropped to about 7,000 feet near North Weald the land lay obscured under thick haze, with a low sun dazzling the eyes. Suddenly his radio popped and crackled to life again, and a few seconds later he heard Woodhall: 'Douglas, are you receiving me? Are you receiving me, Douglas? Enemy fighters attacking North Weald with bombs. Do you hear? Do you hear, Douglas? Please acknowledge.'

He called back: 'Already there, Woodie' (which startled Woodhall considerably). 'I'm alone, so tell the others.'

At that moment a 109 shot out of the haze, climbing almost vertically and levelled off about four hundred yards in front, flying straight and level ahead. He was obviously not looking behind, and Bader, slamming the throttle on, practically licked his lips. It was a real squadron leader's shot, a piece of cake on a golden platter. He was overhauling the unwary

109 when another Hurricane shot out of the haze in front like a jack-in-the-box and levelled off about 100 yards behind the 109 – right in Bader's path. Before he had time to be irritated the leading Hurricane fired one brisk burst; a great flash sparked on the cockpit of the 109, the perspex hood flew off and it turned on its back, and the pilot fell out as it dropped into its last dive. Bader flew up alongside the other Hurricane and recognised an old friend, 'Butch' Barton. Barton turned and must have guessed what had happened because he lifted two rude fingers over the side of the cockpit.

The theatrical Goering provided no good 'curtain' for the daylight battles. The Luftwaffe came in like a lion and went out like a lamb, accompanied by a few hesitant and diminishing squeaks from the muted brass. So slowly did it taper that for a while the awakening people on the ground did not fully realise the significance of what was happening. The Germans had been the slaves of time; they had to break Fighter Command to invade Britain before winter and they had failed. On October 12 Hitler postponed the invasion till the following spring. Some people in England still waited for the next assaults, and the fact that Hitler, the invincible, had suffered his first (and resounding) defeat did not make its full impact until Winston Churchill's phrase 'The Battle of Britain' took firmer root along with those other famous words: 'Never in the field of human conflict has so much been owed by so many to so few.' Then the country rejoiced, but Fighter Command had lost 915 aircraft and 733 pilots killed or wounded.

Bader, perhaps alone, felt some sorrow that the brawling was over. The Duxford wing had shot down 152 enemy for the loss of thirty pilots and rather more aircraft. But now the dawn rendezvous of his five squadrons had petered out and the days were more predictable – back to normal readiness at Coltishall.

Among England's crumbled ruins other people were getting back to normal too – even the bureaucrats were catching up with their papers. A letter came to Sub-Lieutenant Cork from the Admiralty, pointing out with a great number of formal words that the DFC was not awarded to naval officers and that Mr Cork would therefore unstitch the ribbon of his DFC and have the DSC sewn in its place.

'By God, no you don't, Corkie,' growled Bader. 'The King has given you that DFC and only the King can take it away from you – not my ruddy Lords of the Admiralty. When the King sends you another letter to say you've got to wear the DSC instead of the DFC, then you can take it down. Not before. That's an order.'

Now there was time for a little spit and polish and congratulations. 242 Squadron flew to Duxford again to be inspected and thanked by the Secretary of State for Air, Sir Archibald Sinclair. Bader made a point of introducing Cork and explaining about the medal trouble. Sir Archibald grinned and said: 'I absolutely agree, Bader. Of course he must keep wearing the DFC. I won't let them change it.' He leaned closer confidingly: 'These Admiralty people are a bit funny, you know . . . sea complex and all that.' He nodded meaningly.

Convoy patrols again! Life was dull. A few 109s still poked their yellow spinners over Kent, but they were reserved for the Spitfires. Bader felt aggrieved, though occasionally he persuaded Leigh-Mallory to let him take the Squadron down over the Estuary. No luck, though.

Now the worst crisis seemed over, the Lords of the Admiralty reclaimed Cork and Gardner and sent them to fly in Cornwall. The squadron farewelled them sadly. More pilots and aircraft came to fill the gaps of the dead, and the fire of the great days was dying. There were compensations. As ever when Mars leaves his arms on the field for home, other welcoming arms await with gratitude in the fire-warmed homes and pubs. Coltishall loved them. They were 'our squadron,' and if one or two parents had qualms, their daughters did not share them.

At The Bell, 242's favourite pub in Norwich, they were grieved to find that the landlord, a special friend, was in bed in a plaster casing. An incendiary had fallen on the pub and he had climbed on to the burning roof to fight it, had fallen through and broken his back. *En masse* the pilots stripped off his pyjama jacket and wrote messages and signed their names on the plaster.

One day a strange aircraft blipped on the radar screen off Harwich, but Bader was not on readiness at the time. A section took off and the handsome Neil Campbell found it, a Dornier, thirty miles to sea. They heard him over the R/T as he yelled that he was attacking, but that was the last they heard. The rear-gunner must have got him because he did not come back. Later the sea washed his body ashore.

A DFC came through for John Latta.

Against the last, petulant stabs of the 109's Bader led his wing on one last flight: an emaciated wing of his own squadron and No. 19. Climbing over the Estuary, a lone startled shout came from Willie McKnight, and then a pack of 109s was spitting through them out of the sun. Only McKnight was quick enough to fire; he caught one as it darted in front and the 109 did not lift its nose like the others but went tumbling down the sky like a broken thing that had lost the grace of flight. Two Hurricanes were spinning down, too, one of them smoking. Later a phone call from one pilot, who had steadied his torn Hurricane and crash-landed. The other, Norrie Hart, was dead.

As autumn gusts whirled the last yellowed leaves across the aerodrome, the embattled nation realised that not even a madman could invade now. In a sturdy people danger deferred is more a stimulant than a cancer, and within the rampart of the sea confidence grew with the defences. For some time Thelma had been losing her fear for Douglas, and now inside her was an odd feeling that he was invincible. Quite illogical. Quite firm. In her pride lay no regret that he was back in the Air Force. Still, she was a practical young woman and therefore glad that the fighting was finished for a while.

Then the bombers struck again. At night!

CHAPTER NINETEEN

Out of the black sky they rained bombs on London, the docks, the city, and the huddled houses around. Unable to invade, Hitler tried to destroy the will to resist. The nights glowed with acres of flame but the glow was never high enough to betray the bombers, and apart from anti-aircraft guns the people had almost no defences. Balloons were too low. Some Spitfires and Hurricanes went up, but it was like playing blind man's buff. They had no radar in aeroplanes then. Luck was the main chance and they found little of that. The bombers switched to Bristol, Liverpool, Hull . . . back to London.

242 Squadron was by-passed, the impotent patrols going to other squadrons, and his helplessness incensed Bader almost as much as the pity of the smoking ruins. In the daylight battle his feeling had been fierce but his emotion against Germans largely impersonal. He had been hot-blooded in the fight and the bombers were ordered pawns. He might have been born a German himself. . . . But the night bombing was different.

The phone rang in the mess one evening and the night controller from Duxford asked urgently: 'How many of your chaps can night-fly Hurricanes?'

'Three,' Bader answered. 'Myself, Ball and Turner.'

'Get 'em into the air as soon as you can,' ordered the controller. 'The Hun's going for Coventry.'

A full moon shone in a cloudless sky as he climbed hard to 18,000 feet over Coventry and was emotionally shaken at the sea of flame below.

For an hour he swung grimly round the city, but a full moon was not enough and the bombers flitted unseen in the high darkness. Short of petrol, he turned back and could just see the flarepath 12,000 feet below when the engine suddenly coughed and then stopped dead.

Trying to force-land a fighter at night 'deadstick' is too dangerous even to be sport. For a moment he was tempted to bale out, but the challenge of it caught him and he decided to try and land it. With the propeller windmilling, he dropped his nose and glided silently down in a series of S-turns, keeping his eye on the flarepath. They were lonely moments that picked at the nerves, but he straightened out finally for the last approach, dropped his wheels and did not even have to sideslip off the last few feet. She settled neatly and a lorry towed him in. The whole affair was a wretched anti-climax, except for one thing: he had begun to hate Germans more personally.

242 Squadron were changing their aeroplanes, becoming the second squadron to get Hurricane Mark II's, which had more power, were faster, could climb higher and all had the new and better VHF radio. Now in the routine of unexciting readiness Bader sometimes swashbuckled about, jabbing his thumb nostalgically on an imaginary gun-button with an accompanying 'raspberry' to signify the rattling guns. He took up squash again, clanking sweatily about the court and mortifying Crowley-Milling by beating him, though in fairness 'Crow' scrupulously obeyed the convention of putting the ball barely within a reasonable distance. Bader fell noisily often but always rose and 'pressed on.' At a cinema in Norwich he tripped in the aisle one night and dented his right kneecap so that the leg hung crookedly. He merely dragged himself to the nearest seat, called an usherette to bring him a screwdriver from the projection room, pulled up his trouser leg, made a few adjustments and was mobile again.

Leigh-Mallory rang one day and said: 'Douglas, we're having a figher conference at Air Ministry to thrash out all we've learned from the recent daylight battles. I want you to come with me.'

On the day, he went to London and met Leigh-Mallory, who said: 'I don't know whether I can get you in. It's rather high-level stuff, but I'm going to try because you're the only chap who's led the really big formations.'

At the Air Ministry building in King Charles Street, next to Downing Street, Bader followed the bulky figure into a quiet, carpeted conference room and felt a twinge of alarm when he saw the braided sleeves round the long table. Not a man below air vice-marshal. He recognised most of them: at the head the Chief of the Air Staff, Sir Charles Portal, 'Stuffy' Dowding looking more craggy than ever, Keith Park, Sholto Douglas, John Slessor, Philip Joubert de la Ferté. And himself, a squadron leader. No other fighter pilots. Leigh-Mallory said to Portal: 'I've brought Squadron Leader Bader along, sir.' Portal nodded courteously.

Bader sat quietly, hands in lap, when the discussion started on the size of fighter formations and the idea of going to attack the enemy at the source when he was building up his formations over the Pas de Calais.

Park pointed out very reasonably that if he sent squadrons over the Pas de Calais the Germans would quickly change their tactics, send up a bogus 'build-up' (probably of fighters) to draw the British fighters and then send off the real bombers, who would have a clear run while the British fighters were heavily engaged away from the targets they were to defend and short of petrol and ammunition. As for big formations – in a crisis 11 Group had no time to put up great wings of aircraft.

Leigh-Mallory said that the work of the Duxford wing showed that big formations paid handsomely if it were at all possible to organise them. He understood the difficulty of scrambling big formations in a hurry close to the enemy, but it could be done at a distance when the enemy build-up was first detected. That was the time to scramble a big formation at Duxford, for instance, which could then climb fast and dive into the German formations as they came in over the coast. Then the southern squadrons, which had taken off later, could set about the broken-up enemy.

Sholto Douglas cut in: 'I'd like to hear what Squadron Leader Bader has to say about leading big formations.'

The eyes were looking at him and he felt suddenly vulnerable. He pulled himself to his feet. Portal said: 'You can stay seated if you like, Bader,' and he cleared his throat and said: 'No thank you, sir, I'm quite all right.' Pet ideas were tumbling through his head, jostling each other into confusion. Dowding seemed to be looking at him severely . . . but Stuffy always looked like that. His mind cleared as it focused on a new thought – 'Whether I leave this room as a flight lieutenant or not . . . I've got to put the figher pilot's point of view . . . it probably hasn't happened like this before.' . . . It all flashed across his mind very fast. He said clearly, looking at Portal:

'We've been learning, sir, exactly what you gentlemen learned in the last war' (that was a crafty start) . . . 'Firstly, that the chap who's got the height controls the battle, especially if he comes out of the sun; secondly, that the chap who fires very close is the chap who knocks them down; thirdly, and most important, it is much more economical to put up a hundred aircraft against a hundred than twelve against a hundred.

'I know we can't always put equal numbers against the Germans because their air force is bigger than ours – if necessary we'll fight one against a thousand – but surely we can manage to put sixty aircraft against a couple of hundred instead of only one squadron of twelve.'

He went on to develop his theories, and as he warmed to them he forgot self-consciousness and the voice grew more confident, more commanding. He delivered himself of a good, terse homily to the effect that the chap in the air, not the controller, should decide when, where and how to meet the enemy. 'In fact,' he added, 'it might be a good idea to have the sun plotted on the operations board.'[1] Making the most of his chance, he covered every point he could think of, all the things he had discussed with Leigh-Mallory, and then suddenly ran dry – finished. There was an awkward silence. He sat down abruptly. He must have said too much: everyone was non-committal as the discussion continued. Some seemed to favour big wings, others did not. It went on for another hour and a half before it broke up, and even then Bader felt that nothing definite had been decided.

A week later he received a letter marked 'Secret.' It said that Air Council had decided that wherever there were two squadrons on one aerodrome they were to practise battle flying as a wing and be proficient as soon as possible. There followed details about recommended wing tactics – it was the stuff that Bader himself had found out and reported.

Fighter Command leadership was reshuffled. Dowding went, which upset Bader (and many others) deeply, and Sholto Douglas took over as C.-in-C. Park went to a new post and Leigh-Mallory took command of 11 Group. To Bader's joy, he immediately arranged that 242 squadron should go to 11 Group too, posting them to Martlesham, near Felixstowe.

For a while Bader was busy with the flurry of moving. He found a billet for Thelma in Martlesham village and sent Crow with the Humber shooting brake to drive her down; war or no war, Thelma was a woman and had tied up many odd little bundles without which she would not move. Martlesham brought back memories of the first time he had taken off for Dunkirk. How much had happened since then! And was still happening. The night skies over England were louder now with the rumbling of bombers dropping hideous loads. The scientists were working to fit radar into aeroplanes, and meantime the RAF was nearly helpless. The fighters went up and roamed, and now and then they caught a bomber, but not often, and the news reports spoke more confidently than the men in private behind them.

242 Squadron still had no part in it. Bader flew convoy patrols with them but felt better the day a phone call came from 11 Group. 'I wanted to be the first to congratulate you again,' said Leigh-Mallory. 'You've just been awarded the DFC. I'm afraid it's long overdue.'

That time he made a point of telling Thelma first. She sewed the diagonally striped ribbon on his tunic after the DSO, and his exuberant exterior was awkward with the effort of hiding his pride when the others saw it. He could – and did – brag about things like squash and golf (often with his tongue in his cheek), but a decoration was different. Outside the heart one deprecated them. Privately he was gratified that they had given him the DSO before the DFC – the DSO was for

[1] Later adopted.

leadership and using his head for the common weal, the 'team stuff' as against the solo effort. That was a smack in the eye for the little demon.

A DFC also came through for Hugh Tamblyn.

Dickie Cork flew in one day for a Christmas visit and was delighted to see his old CO's new ribbon. Bader was *not* delighted to observe that Cork's only ribbon was now the Distinguished Service Cross.

'Corkie,' he bellowed, 'where the hell is your DFC? You turncoat! Didn't I give you an order?'

'Yes, sir,' said Cork, 'but it's a sad story.'

One day on Bath Station, he said, an admiral's eyes had suddenly focused on his DFC ribbon.

'Young man, what's that?' barked the admiral crustily.

Cork explained.

'Distinguished Flying Cross? What's that?' snorted the sea dog (who knew perfectly well).

Rigidly at attention, Cork had explained the circumstances.

The admiral leaned closer to peer at the hybrid ribbon, and his eyes lit upon the silver of the Polish Air Force button, then travelled, bulging slightly, up and down the row, the RAF button, the RCAF and the Czech Air Force buttons.

'There was an unparalleled scene, sir,' Cork said feelingly. 'You see, I've got new buttons too.'

(Corkie grew up fast after that. Flying off the carrier *Indomitable* in a Malta convoy, he shot down six enemy in one day and was a lieutenant-commander with a DSO as well when he was killed flying in Ceylon in 1944.)

On 1 January Bader neatly ruled off the year's flying in his logbook and under the line wrote:

> '*So ends 1940. Since have had 242 Squadron (June) we have destroyed 67 enemy aircraft confirmed for the loss of five pilots killed in action and one killed diving out of cloud. The squadron has been awarded 1 DSO and 9 DFCs.*'

Leigh-Mallory sent for him one day and at his Uxbridge headquarters said: 'I suppose life seems pretty dull lately.'

'Yes, sir.'

'What do you think about going over to France and giving them a smarten-up?'

Bader was glowing again.

'We thought we might send a few bombers over with a pack of fighters,' the AOC went on. 'You're experienced in that sort of thing so I thought you might like to be in it.'

The Operation Order labelled 'First Offensive Sweep' came to Bader soon after in an envelope marked 'Secret.' Three Hurricane squadrons would escort six Blenheims to bomb suspected German ammunition dumps in the Forêt de Guisne near the Pas de Calais. From the Luftwaffe's bitter lesson the RAF already knew that it did not pay to send swarms of bombers with a trickle of fighters. They had to find a new balance. It does not sound ambitious now, but then it was the first real probe into the unknown enemy and it was 'offensive' – taking the fight to the enemy instead of waiting for him to come back. Much better for everyone's morale (except German).

On January 10 Bader, full of hopes for a fight, led 242 Squadron off and over North Weald joined two more Hurricane squadrons led by Wing Commander Victor Beamish. When Bader was thirteen Beamish had been one of the god-like athletic cadets at Cranwell who had inspired him. Now 38, the blocky, square-jawed Beamish had fought like a tiger in the Battle of Britain, even after Park had limited his battle flights to two a day on the grounds that, 'I have to be able to talk to my station commanders *sometimes*.' (Later Beamish was the man who spotted the *Scharnhorst* and *Gneisenau* leaving Brest.)

Over Hornchurch they tagged on to the Blenheims and flew out across the Channel. 242 Squadron was top cover at about 17,000 feet, and Bader felt bold and buccaneering. They nipped over the coast near Calais; France looked peaceful, lying softly under snow. In seconds they were over the Forêt de Guisne, only a couple of miles inland. Seconds later it was virtually over and they were darting out again. No time to look for bomb bursts; the wary eyes roamed the sky looking for 109s but none appeared. In the last moments before they crossed the coast the surprised Germans woke up and black puffs of flak stained the cold, crystal air. Odd to see the flak. It was a new enemy. In the Battle of Britain the bursts had been friendly pointers.

Then they were over the sea, and then they were landing at Martlesham. It was an anti-climax.

The next days were not so mild. Leigh-Mallory had another idea he called 'Rhubarbs' – sending a pair of fighters darting across the Channel whenever layer cloud hung low over the land, to shoot at anything German aground or aloft. If they got into trouble they could climb and hide in the clouds. Some 11 Group squadrons had already tried them, and two days after the sweep Bader got his chance. He took Turner with him and conditions were perfect, a layer of ten-tenths cloud at about 800 feet.

They did not get as far as France. Just off the beach between Calais and Dunkirk, Bader spotted two trails of foam on the water, nosed down to look and saw they were German E-boats. Without a second's thought, he dived; the Germans must have thought they were friendly and been shocked when the bullets raked the first boat. At the last moment they

started to fire, and Bader had a swift glimpse of two of the crew jumping
overboard before he had swept past and was raking the second boat. He
pulled up into the cloud, followed by Turner, then swept down again for
another firing run. After that the bullets were gone and they flew back
in high spirits.

At Martlesham when they told the story everyone wanted to jump into
the Hurricanes and try the same lark. They could not *all* go, said Group,
sounding slightly pained, so Bader fired off McKnight and Brown
together, then a little later, Latta and Cryderman.

Brown was back an hour later. He and McKnight had been having
a good time straffing a German battalion in a field near Calais, he said,
when half a dozen 109s had 'bounced' them and things had been pretty
busy for several minutes until he had got back into the clouds.

McKnight did not return, which shattered everyone.

Then Cryderman landed, looking shaken after a running fight with
Messerschmitts.

Latta did not return.

A week later Bader was leading Cryderman and Edmond in dull,
protective circles round a cruiser and submarine heading north up the
coast when the controller sent them haring east into the North Sea for
a 'suspected bandit.' A few minutes later Bader saw a JU. 88 about a
thousand feet above. Unseen by the German, he pulled steeply up and
fired and a moment later the belly flapped open like a trap-door and half
a dozen black bombs poured out. They just missed him as he wrenched
the Hurricane over on a wingtip and recovered to see the JU. 88 a mile
away, smoking from the port engine, vanish into a little cloud about the
size of a man's hand.

Edmond leapt over the cloud and Cryderman dived underneath;
unimaginatively the German went straight through and came out the
other side, where Cryderman squirted into his starboard engine, which
also started trailing a white stream. As the German turned away Edmond
darted in and the same engine gushed black and orange smoke. Bader
raced up to cut it off, fired, and both engines now were spewing black
smoke. Edmond was in next as his explosive bullets hit, the 88 sparked
all over with flashes like a pin-table machine. Bader was going in again
but Cryderman cut in front with another burst. Douglas tried again but
Edmond was darting in and, struck by a new emotion, Bader wheeled
out to one side like a paternal old lion watching his two cubs eagerly
trying to bring down their first meat. Itching for another burst, he stayed
out of the way while the bullets of the other two kept clawing at the
stubborn 88, which dragged the smoke of its wounds along its trail but
would not fall.

At last Edmond's angry voice on the R/T said that he was out of
ammunition. The smoke from the engines was thinning now but the 88

was flying in a peculiar way, hurdling like a car on a switchback railway. Cryderman went in; the 88 lit with flashes again but flew on, and Cryderman announced that his guns were empty. Amazed at the punishment the German had taken, Bader made a final pass and aimed at the cockpit; bits flew off it but the 88 flew on. Now the smoke had almost vanished. He thought in exasperation that the enemy would never go down when thick orange smoke poured out of the port wing. In a few moments tongues of flame licked through the smoke and slowly the 88 dropped her nose into a steepening dive till she went vertically into the sea in a welter of foam.

A few months ago it was so much part of the day to shoot down an enemy; now there were columns in the papers and people rang up from all over the place with congratulations.

For a while the days drifted; they were busy but it was routine. Occasionally when the clouds were thick they tried a few 'rhubarbs' but saw nothing. With up to four flights a day, Bader's logbook shows the routine: 'Formation practice,' 'Convoy patrol,' 'Trying to find Huns' (that was a 'rhubarb'), 'Dusk and night landings,' 'Formation practice,' 'Engine test,' 'High flying,' 'Looking for Huns,' 'Testing rudder bias,' and so on. Then they hit a bad patch. It started on February 8, a cold day with ice cloud, when Laurie Cryderman sheered off from a convoy patrol to intercept a plotted 'bandit.' They heard him call half an hour later that his engine had cut. He was 600 feet up, far at sea, and never came back.

Only days later Ben Brown, pulling sharply out of a steep dive low down, spun off a high-speed stall into the ground.

With McKnight and Latta it made four dead in a very brief time and seemed so cruel and pointless after they had come so well through the battle. In flying death often seems to come in cycles.

Then Ian Smith, who had taught Douglas 'Little Angeline,' went out on a convoy patrol and did not come back.

Crowley-Milling caught a JU. 88 over the North Sea, and as he dived to attack his bullet-proof windscreen was smashed into a whitely opaque and splintered shield as a cannon shell hit it; he could not see to aim but went on chasing and firing until the 88 vanished into cloud. Crowley-Milling got back.

Then the steadfast, charming Hugh Tamblyn fought an intruder approaching a convoy. An hour or two later a ship found him floating in his Mae West, but he was dead.

Sergeant Brimble was posted to Malta and killed on the way.

Seven in a matter of weeks! At that rate a pilot could expect to live about three months. A squadron of twenty pilots would lose eighty a year, and there seemed no end to the war.

Early in March Leigh-Mallory sent for Bader. 'We're working out ideas to carry the attack across to France in the summer,' he said. 'Fighter sweeps, like that other one you did, but probably more ambitious. To do it we're building up our "wing" system and one of the items on that programme is to appoint wing commanders on certain stations to organise and lead the wings there.

'You,' he went on, 'are to be one of those wing commanders. Should be right down your alley. You'll probably be going to Tangmere.'

There are times when words sound like music. In Army terms, wing-commander meant a rise from lieutenant to lieutenant-colonel in a year. And Tangmere was in 11 Group – on the south coast, just across from France.

When L.-M. had disposed of the congratulations, Bader said: 'Will I be able to take 242 Squadron with me, sir?'

'Afraid not,' Leigh-Mallory regretted. 'You'll already have three squadrons there. All Spitfires.'

Bader suggested awkwardly that in that case he wasn't sure he wanted to be a wing commander.

Leigh-Mallory said firmly: 'You'll do what you're told' . . . and then, because he knew his man: 'Look at it this way. If you take 242 you won't be able to help favouring them a bit. I know you and how you regard them.'

All he could do then was wait for the posting.

242 Squadron was not pleased. The whole squadron, from the lowest 'erk' up, revolved round the CO as a tight and exclusive team that had been firmly knit even before the bloody comradeship of the battle. The greatest leaders in the field always have 'colour' . . . a certain bravura. Bader certainly had it.

Still waiting, he drove with 242 to Debden to meet the King and Queen, and in the mess ante-room before the presentation, Turner jabbed his pipe into Leigh-Mallory's chest and said: 'Look here, sir, you can't go and post our CO away because we won't work for anyone else.'

It was enough to make an English officer's blood run cold.

'Turner,' Bader bawled, 'stop prodding the AOC with your pipe!'

Leigh-Mallory did not seem to mind at all.

On March 18 the bitter-sweet blow fell. A new man, 'Treacle' Treacy, arrived to take over, and Thelma sewed the wind commander braid on Douglas's sleeves. The only man he was able to take with him from 242 was Stokoe, his conscientious and devoted batman.

CHAPTER TWENTY

Tangmere, not far from Southampton, was a pre-war station built for two squadrons. Now three Spitfire squadrons, 145, 610, and 616, and a Beaufighter squadron lived there and the Spitfires were to fly as the wing. He was pleased about 616 because they had been in 12 Group Wing and knew his ways. All the Spitfires were Mark II's, still with eight machine-guns but a little better than the Battle of Britain types.

He arrived on the morning of the 19th, stowed his bags in a room in the station commander's house near the mess, and in half an hour was flying a Spitfire to get the feel again. Two hours later he was leading two of the squadrons over the Channel, having a 'snoop' towards the French coast and trying wing formation. The squadrons had not flown as a wing before and in the next two weeks he trained them hard.

Unlike his early days with 242, there was no need to win their confidence. He was famous now, the RAF's first wing leader, and men and officers jumped to obey his brisk bellows. Most of the pilots (average age about twenty-two) had fought non-stop through the Battle of Britain and he saw that several, especially the leaders, were showing clear signs of overstrain. His impulsive, warm-hearted side became full of love for them, in a way rather like a vet with a hurt animal, and he felt he wanted to say to them: 'Don't you worry, chaps. We'll get you right.' He saw Leigh-Mallory and explained that some of the boys should have a rest. Could he have some good replacements and also have Stan Turner promoted to squadron leader to command 145 Squadron?

'By all means,' said Leigh-Mallory courteously. 'I'm glad you've asked for Turner because he's getting a bit of a nuisance, objecting to fly with anyone else.'

Turner arrived a couple of days later with bad news. Treacy had been leading a 242 formation in a sharp turn when the man behind had collided with him. Bits of the smashed aeroplanes hit a third Hurricane and all three went into the sea, killing Treacy, Edmond and Lang. (The squadron was taken over then by Whitney Straight, pre-war racing motorist who had won an MC in Norway and is now deputy chairman of BOAC.)

As 616 had the least battle experience, Bader attached himself to them and thereafter always flew at their head, leading the wing. It could have been uncomfortable for Billy Burton, ex-Cranwell Sword of Honour and

CO of 616, but he and Bader got along well, though Burton (later DSO and DFC), short, eager and somewhat precise, was constantly appalled by Bader's uninhibited comments. Like Bader, he nearly always had a pipe in his mouth, and sometimes in the privacy of the pilots' room he would take it out and say: 'D'you know what the wingco called me this morning? He called me a —' He used to repeat these things in a voice of wonder as though they could not really have happened, and then break into a puzzled laugh.

Domineering, dogmatic and breezy, Bader saw everything in blacks and whites, never in doubtful greys, and in this new phase of welding an experimental wing together and evolving new tactics to carry the fight to the enemy he made decisions crisply and on the spot with a confidence that would have been dangerous in someone else. He startled Tangmere, whose men first regarded him as a noted curiosity, then were impressed and then, as at 242, became devoted (apart from a few, ruffled by his blunt toughness, who resented him. He left no one unmoved: they either half worshipped or detested him, and the little minority of the latter grumbled in their own wilderness). Fired by his new mission, he was far removed from the frustrated man of the peace. As the wing knit together he got the itch to fight again, but Leigh-Mallory would not let him cross to the French coast, so he took the wing 'snooping' as near as a flexible interpretation of orders would let him, though they never saw a German aircraft.

They only heard them – at night. Tangmere had two long white runways, and on a moon-lit night raiders picked them out miles away, sometimes as a landmark and sometimes as a target. German bombers were over England every clear night, and now and then a low-flying enemy roared in the darkness over Tangmere and everyone hunched their shoulders and winced as the bombs crashed down, rattling the hangars and smashing windows. No one had been killed for some time, but some aeroplanes had been destroyed and it was not comfortable. Gangs of civilian workmen were camouflaging the runways by spraying them with green paint – or were supposed to be: they managed to do about fifty yards a week, working with the lethargy that many pilots noticed on aerodromes. It did not help to know that they were being paid more than the pilots, and Bader longed to have them under RAF discipline.

At this time Woodhall, newly promoted to Group Captain, arrived at Tangmere to command the station and also to act as controller. Leigh-Mallory wanted his old team together again for the work ahead (and for a while Bader shared quarters near the mess with Woodhall). Other wings were training now at stations like Biggin Hill and Kenley under new wind commanders like 'Sailor' Malan, who was top-scoring RAF pilot. To be more easily recognised in the air during wing-flying, Bader had his initials 'DB' painted on the side of his Spitfire, which prompted Woodhall to christen him 'Dogsbody.' He called him that in the mess and in the air, over the R/T, and the name stuck till it became Bader's official call-sign. He did not mind; it rather amused him.

Woodhall and Bader both plagued the workers on the runways to get a move on but it was like talking to a collection of deaf mutes; they sprayed a few more yards in the next week, and it looked as though next moon period Tangmere was going to catch it again (the workmen lived some miles from the airfield). Woodhall rang the Works Department, but the local officials seemed helpless and he could not locate any Olympian official who might have influence.

An ear-splitting crash woke Bader one night, and outside he heard shouts and saw flickering lights. Strapping his legs on, he crossed to the window and saw that a bomb had fallen on a corner of the mess, which was burning. Overhead came a sudden roar and rattle of machine-guns as the raider dived back to strafe the fire. As Bader stumbled out to it the fire-truck arrived and soon got it under control. Strangely, no one inside had been hurt; they had hurled themselves out of the windows into the nearest cover, and the hero of the night was the Roman Catholic padre who, tin hat firmly planted on his head, had walked into the burning mess looking for injured. The story went round that you could hear the German bullets pinging off his tin hat while all the brave fighter boys lay quaking in the air-raid ditches.

But it was the last straw. Bader sent his old golfing friend, Henry Longhurst, an invitation to visit Tangmere. It was just before Longhurst himself went into the Army; he was still a journalist and knew a story when he saw one.

The following week-end a caustic article appeared in the *Sunday Express* about squadrons on a 'certain RAF airfield' being endangered by the sloth of men engaged to camouflage runways.

It was serious for an officer to cut red tape binding the normal channels and tip off the Press about dirty official linen. Outraged officials demanded to know from the newspaper who had let the cat out of the bag, but the *Sunday Express* urbanely declined to say. At last the official asked: 'Was it someone on an aerodrome near Oxford?'

Longhurst said craftily: 'Oh, is it going on there too?'

The official hurriedly rang off. But eventually two and two were put together and the Under-Secretary of State for Air paid a visit to Tangmere, lunched amicably with Bader and Woodhall, and over coffee said, quite politely:

'Look, actually the reason I've come down here is to give you chaps a rocket over that article in the *Sunday Express*. The Air Ministry doesn't take a good view of it.'

Bader, hackles rising, said: 'Well, sir, you can take the rocket back to Air Ministry and tell 'em what they can do with it. Those runways have been glistening in the moonlight for months now, drawing German bombers like flies, so I asked Longhurst down here myself and damn' well told him to write it up.'

The Under-Secretary looked startled at the truculent scorn for a high-level reprimand.

Woodhall put in: 'And I absolutely agree with Bader. I knew Longhurst was coming down that week-end and I also asked him to have a look at the runways. I feel exactly the same as Bader about it.'

Said the Under-Secretary resignedly, as though he were washing his hands like Pontius Pilate: 'Well I was told to deliver the rocket and I've done it.' He seemed glad to get it over.

The camouflaging of the runways was completed in a week, but by that time Bader had moved his aircraft to satellite fields nearby – 610 and 616 to West Hampnett and 145 to Merston. He was also doing some reshuffling in his wing, getting Crowley-Milling and Ian Arthur from 242 Squadron as flight commanders in 610 and 145. Ken Holden, a big Yorkshire flight lieutenant in 616, was promoted to command 610 Squadron. The ruddy-faced Holden was about Bader's age, some years older than the other pilots, a resourceful and rather droll 'old sweat,' fond of adopting a Yorkshire accent and saying to his pilots: 'Now coom on all you lads; trouble with you is you've got no expeerience. Ah'm older than thee.'

Bader also found a house for himself and Thelma five miles from the mess, a pleasant little white place with a garden called the Bay House. Thelma came down with her baggage and bundles and her sister Jill, and was utterly delighted with it, the first house she had ever had. It became a social centre for some of Bader's pilots in the evenings, where everyone relaxed in a different atmosphere, though Douglas usually slept at the mess to keep in touch.

Still the tactical fanatic, he had begun to feel most dissatisfied with the vics of three which had been standard squadron formation for so long. A hangover from peacetime, they were clumsy to deploy in battle, and after a lot of thought he evolved a new basic unit, two aircraft abreast so that each pilot's eyes covered his comrade's tail and cut out the need for weaving. He began experimenting, building his wind round these small sections arranged in various patterns.

As his own Number Two he often picked the gangling 'Cocky' Dundas, who had been so cheered by his voice during a Battle of Britain take-off. He thought that Dundas, still in 616, still only twenty, was a likely lad, and also had his eye on another 616 pilot officer, Johnny Johnson, a muscular effervescent youngster, a 'press-on' type, somewhat wild and in need of discipline but possessing a hawk-eyed talent for the game and no visible fear.[1]

The Luftwaffe's terrifying night raids were easing off a little and the war seemed to be static, though all 11 Group knew it was only a lull and wondered what it was going to be like on the other side. In mid-April Leigh-Mallory called Bader to HQ at Uxbridge, and there he found Malan, Harry Broadhurst, Beamish, Kellett and other leaders. They went into a plain room, sat on folding chairs round a table, and Leigh-Mallory, standing at the head of the table, said quietly:

'Gentlemen, we have stopped licking our wounds. We are now going over to the offensive. Last year our fighting was desperate. Now we're entitled to be cocky.'

He talked a long time about tactics; the idea, briefly, being to send a few bombers over the Channel surrounded by hordes of fighters, and force the Germans to come up and fight.

On the morning of April 17 a screed about a yard long came over the Tangmere operations teleprinter headed 'Secret. Operations Order. Circus No. 1.' There followed a lot of details under headings like 'Target,' 'Bomber Force,' 'Rendezvous,' 'Escort .Wing,' 'Cover Wing,' 'Target Support Wing,' 'Rear Wing,' with heights and speeds and map references.

That afternoon about 100 Spitfires escorted twelve Blenheims to bomb Cherbourg. Bader led his wing of thirty-six and did not see a single enemy. Far away a few puffs of German flak stained the sky, and then they were on the way home again. Leigh-Mallory said later: 'We're just poking the bear in his pit, gentlemen. You'll get some reaction in due course.'

Over the next couple of weeks they did several more trips to Cherbourg, expecting any moment to be 'jumped' by hordes of 109s, but never meeting one. Yet north-west France was said to be a hornet's nest that might swarm any day, an Unknown that must be invaded with more sense than Goering had shown. Rhubarbs were discouraged – two or four aircraft venturing across alone looked too close to suicide.

On the night of May 7 a spontaneous party developed in the mess (as it often did) with pilots talking shop and sky-larking well into the night. Bader was surrounded as usual by his pilots (he always enjoyed that), sipping orangeade while they nuzzled cans of beer, and after a while Cocky Dundas said:

'Sir, let's have two of the new sections side by side – four aircraft line abreast so everyone can cover everyone else's tail and everyone can get an occasional squirt in.'

---

[1] Bader's judgment and teaching seem to have been good. Two years later Turner, Crowley-Milling, Johnson and Dundas were all wing commanders with DSOs and DFCs. At twenty-three Dundas became the youngest group captain in the RAF, and Johnson was top-scorer at the end of the war with thirty-eight confirmed and a string of probables.

The wing commander said it sounded fine. Everyone chattered about the new idea for a long time, working out, for instance, how to handle it in the air when 'jumped' by enemy fighters. They decided that the 'form' was for the two on the left at the critical moment to scream round in a full circle to the left and for the pair on the right to do likewise to the right, thus joining up again on the tails (it was hoped) of the foiled enemy. The debate lasted a long time.

In the morning Dundas came down to breakfast feeling not so gay as usual. His skull throbbed and the dry mouth had a taste of sump oil as his head nodded gently over a sausage, regretting that he had not gone to bed earlier. Bader stumped in and sat at the same table full of rude and ostentatios health. He boomed as he sat down: 'That was a damn' good idea of yours last night, Cocky, about fours flying abreast.'

Dundas smiled wanly and murmured: 'Oh, thank you very much, sir. I'm glad you liked it.'

'Damn' good,' repeated Bader. 'I've been thinking it over. We'll try it to-day.'

Dundas thought without enthusiasm that he did not feel like practice flying.

'Just you and me and a couple of others,' Bader went on cheerfully. 'We'll duck over to France and see if we can get some Huns to jump us.'

For a moment it did not sink in, and then Dundas had a moment of lurching horror. He looked to see if Bader were joking. But he wasn't; he was turning to Woodhouse of 610 Squadron down the table and saying: 'Paddy, get yourself a number two and come with us.'

They took off at 11 am, Bader, Dundas (wondering why he hadn't kept his mouth shut the previous night) Woodhouse and a Sergeant Mains, and swept down the Channel at 25,000 feet between Dover and Calais in a slightly curving line abreast, as though one were looking at the nails of four fingers spread out; Dundas on the left, Bader fifty yards on his right and slightly in front, a hundred yards to Woodhouse level, and fifty yards again to Mains, slightly behind. Thus they flaunted themselves up and down off Calais for half an hour, seeing nothing. Dundas was thinking with longing that in a couple of minutes they would be turning on course for home again when above, five miles behind, slightly to the right and a thousand feet above, he saw five 109s turning on course after them. He called urgently: 'Hallo, Dogsbody. Five 109s five o'clock above.'

Bader's voice came delightedly: 'Oh, good. I can see 'em, Cocky. I've got 'em.' He throttled back a little and the Messerschmitts came up fast. Bader was keeping up a running commentary. . . . 'Oh, this is just what we wanted. Wonderful, isn't it?'

Dundas refrained from answering. The 109s were boring in. Bader was going on exultantly: 'Keep your eyes on 'em but don't break till I tell you. Let 'em come in. Let 'em come in. Don't break' . . . He was beside himself with enthusiasm. 'Don't break yet. I'll tell you when . . .'

The 109's were slanting in for the kill when he snapped 'Break now!' and abruptly four Spitfires spun round on their wingtips, Bader and Dundas fanning left, and Woodhouse and Mains right.

In one of the tightest turns Dundas could remember, Bader's tail-wheel bobbed above his windscreen, but his vision kept greying out as the mounting 'g' kept loading his lanky, sagging frame, forcing the blood from the brain. He'd heard some theory that Bader could turn sharper than anyone because he'd lost his legs and the blood could not sink that far. Better straighten a bit or ease the turn and see where the Huns were. Must be nearly round the circle. He eased pressure on the stick, and as sight returned the Spitfire flinched and shuddered under crashing explosions as cannon shells slammed into her. Sickeningly, he remembered the last time.

Bader, reefing his machine out of the turn, saw the leading 109 darting just in front, fired in the same moment, saw the flash of bullet strikes and the 109 keel over out of sight, shovelling out black smoke. He heard Dundas, tense and edgy, in his earphones: 'Dogsbody, I've been hit.' (They had actually turned inside the two rearmost 109s, which had opened fire as the last two Spitfires straightened. Sergeant Mains was also hit.)

With cannon shells in the wing roots and glycol pipes, Dundas was peeling off gushing white smoke. Bader nosed down after him to give cover, but the 109s had vanished and only one other Spitfire was in sight. With height to play with and some power still in the engine, Dundas nursed his aircraft back over the coast to Hawkinge Aerodrome, where it cut suddenly when he was too high to land properly and unable to go round again. Rather desperately he gingerly pushed his nose, wheels up, at about 150 mph on to the grass to try and break the speed, and she bounced and thumped rendingly, just missing a collection of brand-new Spitfires on 91 Squadron's dispersal. Shaken, he climbed out and was met by a furious 91 Squadron CO demanding to know what the hell he thought he was doing.

Woodhouse got back to Tangmere all right, and Mains, tail damaged, but unhurt, landed at another field.

Holden flew a Magister two-seater to Hawkinge and took Dundas back to Tangmere, where Bader, seeing he was all right, boomed: 'You're a silly clot, Cocky. What the hell did you go and do that for? Anyway, I'm damn' glad to see you're back all right.' Then, suddenly enthusiastic again: 'I think I know what the trouble is. Instead of breaking outwards we should have all broken in one circle, all the same way, so we stick together and don't lose sight of the enemy. All it wants is some practice. We'll try again soon.'

After that the desolate Dundas, oddly, was not so shaken; he felt it was just an incident in the search for knowledge and was proud to be on such terms with the CO Bader tried it again with another section the next day, but this time over Tangmere, with a friendly section of 616 Spitfires doing the attacking. Breaking the same way, he found that the 'finger four' line abreast was ideal; flexible and good for both defence and attack. Inside a week the 'finger four' became the backbone of the wing (and was later copied by other wings and used extensively throughout the war).

He tried it on Channel snoops and 'circuses' to Cherbourg and Le Havre (they were not sent deeper than the coast at this trial stage), but had no chance to test it in action because the Messerschmitts stayed away, though at this time the wing had its first casualties. Coming back from France, 145 Squadron broke off over Tangmere to land in sections, and flight commander, Pip Stevens, and Flying Officer Owen collided and crashed, locked together, just off the airfield. Both were killed.

Now and then over the French coast they began to see three or four Messerschmitts flirting well outside the fringes of the gaggle, obviously waiting for stragglers or trying to lure a section away, but Bader declined to snap at decoys; he wanted bigger game. So did Leigh-Mallory. Then the Hornchurch wing reported that a couple of Messerschmitts floating above had turned on their backs and dived through them firing. No one was hit but it was better than being ignored.

A couple of days later the Tangmere wing was returning from a snoop when Johnny Johnson's voice, high-pitched and excited, shouted: 'Look out! Huns!' Every pilot thought it was a warning about a 109 on his tail, and the formation split like a lot of startled rabbits while a lone Messerschmitt dived through the middle spitting cannon shells, hitting no one, and vanished. When they landed, Bader tore a stinging strip off Johnson and lectured the wing on the importance of proper warnings. Enemy aircraft *must* be reported as to location and height and not (looking scathingly at the squirming Johnson) as 'Look out! Huns!' Otherwise there would be a shambles.

In June the Germans startled the world by marching on Russia and it became imperative to force Hitler into diverting more fighters back to France. Leigh-Mallory thought that the Blenheims with a ton of bombs were too light to force the issue, so he pestered Bomber Command till they reluctantly let him have some four-engined Stirlings which, on the short haul to France, could carry nearly six tons of bombs each. He packed about 200 Spitfires round them and sent them across the coast to an inland target, and with the swarm of darting fighters about them

Bader thought it looked like a great bee-hive. He said so at the Group conference later, and thereafter it was known as the 'Bee-hive.'

Leigh-Mallory sent the swarm inland again to blast the rail yards at Lille, an important junction for the Germans. Agents reported that the French rushed into the streets, cheering and waving towels. Then the Bee-hive went and wiped out a Messerschmitt repair factory at Albert.

Ah, this was better. The Germans were stung. A Staffel of 109s savaged the Biggin Wing and some of each side were shot down. Bader went off later to the usual wing leaders' confab. with the AOC, and landed back storming: 'Malan got two to-day and his boys got a few more. It's damn' well time we found some.'

Leigh-Mallory's tactics began to pay: Goering was pulling fighter squadrons out of Russia. Over France now they were coming up in packs of thirty and forty. Oberstleutnant (lieutenant-colonel) Galland, Germany's most distinguished fighter leader, was reported in St. Omer with a full *Geschwader*[1] of 109s. The RAF estimated that their fighters were knocking down three Germans to every two Spitfires lost and that was profitable. Rarely was a bomber lost, and then only to flak. One bomber straggling with two engines burning was brought back safely to Manston with about a hundred Spitfires packed protectively round it.

On 21 June the Bee-hive went to St. Omer, and the Tangmere Wing flew in ahead to de-louse. Several 109s darted overhead, twisting back and forth waiting for a chance to strike at a straggler. Bader watched them intently. The Bee-hive came and bombed and left, and the Tangmere Wing was following across the coast when out of the sun two 109s dived in a port-quarter attack on Bader's section of four. He yelled 'Break left!' wheeling fast.

The Germans must have been raw because they broke left, too, and Bader, turning faster than anyone, saw the belly of a 109 poised on its side fifty yards in front and fired. Bits splintered off the Messerschmitt and it pulled drunkenly up, stalled and spun.

Back at Tangmere, he marked an asterisk in his logbook with satisfaction and sat down to write his first combat report for some time. At the end he added: 'I claim this as destroyed because (*a*) I *know* it was, (*b*) F/O Marples saw a 109 spinning down at the same time and place, (*c*) F/O Matchack of 145 saw a 109 dive into the sea, and (*d*) I am sure this 109 was mine.'

After that things warmed up. Next day he led his wing with the Bee-hive to Hazebrouck, the day after to Béthune in the morning and to Béthune again in the afternoon; next day to Béthune again and the day after that to Commines. His romantic side was stirred to be flying fighters over towns with the names he had read in the books by McCudden,

[1] Group.

Bishop, Ball and company of the first war . . . Douai, Arras, Hazebrouck, Béthune.

Next morning to Béthune again at 26,000 feet, and this time he took a new sergeant pilot as his No. 2 to show him the ropes (not many leaders did that – they liked experienced No. 2's to guard their tails). Crossing the coast, packs of four or six Messerschmitts roamed about like scavengers, darting in now and then, and sheering off when challenged, pecking at the formations and trying to wing the outriders. Fed up with the nibbling, Bader dived 616 on six 109s about 500 feet below, and as they scattered he got a shot at one. Then the sergeant fired a long-range burst. Bader chased and caught it with another burst, seeing bullet strikes but no smoke or visible damage, yet suddenly a paracute blossomed as the pilot jumped and floated into the sea five miles off Gravelines. Bader thought scornfully he must have been frightened into jumping.

After lunch they were off again, this time to St Omer, where perceptibly more Germans than before were waiting in the same scavenging packs. Eyes warily watched them behind, to the left and also below, then they were all round, moving dangerously into the sun. Someone yelled a warning as a pack lunged, and Bader sharply broke the wing for independent battle – it was the only way – and in seconds the sky was a milling whirlpool. He caught a trailing 109 at close range and it puffed orange and black smoke as it fell into a steep vertical dive. More 109s were diving on him. He got in a short head-on burst at one that flashed past, and as the battling aircraft sorted themselves out he joined up with Ken Holden's squadron, squirted at one more vagrant enemy, and came home bathed in sweat and exhilarated.

Two more asterisks in the logbook, and a score of two and a half destroyed in a week, plus some damaged. Things were getting better. From then on they averaged a sweep[1] a day, except when the weather was bad. Losses were comparatively low, but slowly mounted and an infinity of war stretched ahead. It was easier not to think of that – just to live for the present, but that was not easy either. It was worst when you woke before dawn, but in the air it was all right because the eyes and the mind were busy.

Bader was still immune from nerves, a rollicking figure in black flying suit and blue and white polka-dot silk scarf, stuffing his pipe into his pocket when he hoisted himself into the cockpit. In the air they assembled over 'Diamond' (code name for Beachy Head) and set course for France, seeing far below the wash of air-sea rescue launches speeding out from the ports to take station where they might pick up the lucky ones who

---

[1] A 'sweep' was nominally a raid without bombers but soon all the mass sorties into France, including the 'circuses' (with bombers) were known as sweeps.

were shot down alive into 'the drink' on the way back. Disconcerting but also comforting.

Always it was Bader leading 616 in a loose mass of three 'finger fours,' climbing to about 20,000 feet. A couple of thousand feet above, behind and to the right, Holden led 610, and far above them, perhaps climbing to 30,000, stretched right across the sky in a long crescent, Stan Turner covered them with 145, usually keeping up-sun. Often he lifted briefly into the floor of the vapour trail layer, then eased down just under it again and flew on at that level so that he and his squadron showed no trail but any aircraft above would immediately betray themselves by tails of white vapour. Sometimes the wing sallied into France alone, and sometimes they joined the Bee-hive round the bombers.

On the way across no one broke radio silence till they were nearly over the French coast where the Germans could see them. Then it was usually Bader:

'OK, Green Line Bus.[1] Pull your corks out. You OK, Ken?'

'OK, D. B. In position.' (Holden).

'You OK, Stan? Where the hell are you? I can't see you.'

'OK, D. B. Keep your cork in. I'm here.'

'Hallo, Woodie, any trade in sight?'

'Hallo, Dogsbody. Beetle[2] answering. Seems to be a strong reaction building up over the Big Wood![3] About thirty or forty plus gaining altitude to the east of the objective. I am watching them. That's all for now.'

And Bader:

'Did you get that, Ken?'

'OK.'

'Did you get that, Stan?'

Turner was more inclined to colour his answer, having a habit of saying in a quavering falsetto, like a startled chambermaid: 'Oh dear! Oh dear! How terrifying. How simply terrifying,' followed by a wild sound that was half laugh, half neigh.

As they crossed the coast by the 'Golf Course,'[4] Bader chatted amiably:

'That eighteenth green could do with mowing, Ken, couldn't it?' (From 20,000 feet the greens on Le Touquet golf course were the size of pinheads.)

After remarks like that the tension eased and Woodhall knew exactly where they were; then Bader's voice lost its flippant tone and thereafter was crisp.

Woodhall's voice was unchanging, deep bass and clear, calmly

---

[1] Code name for Tangmere Wing.
[2] Tangmere Ops call-sign. Woodhall occasionally used it instead of his own name.
[3] Code for St Omer.
[4] Code for Le Touquet.

matter-of-fact, sounding somehow as though he were beside you in the cockpit like a reassuring coach. The blend with Bader meant real leadership.

Soon Woodhall again: 'Hallo, Dogsbody. The 109s over the Big Wood are climbing south. Looks as though they might be trying to come in down-sun on your right flank.'

'OK, Woody.'

A few minutes silence and then:

'Hallo, Dogsbody. If you look about three o'clock above I think you'll see what you're looking for.'

It was uncanny how accurate he was. Usually in a few moments someone saw them sliding into sun-ambush, looking against the sky like a stream of silver fish darting in a ragged straggle through a pool. They broke into small packs to come in from many angles, and Bader had his eyes everywhere, assessing, manoeuvring the wing, warning, detaching sections, reorganising, picking the moment to lunge and start the roaring, whirling frenzy.

It used to go like this (taken from the actual radio log of a quiet day early in the season before the battle became savage):

'Fifty plus near two o'clock.'

'I haven't got 'em, Johnny. What are they doing?'

'OK, D. B. No immediate panic. They're going across us. I'm watching 'em.'

'OK, O.K., I see 'em.'

(Silence for a while.)

Then:

'Aircraft behind.'

'Aircraft three o'clock.'

'Aircraft below.'

'Turning right Bus Company.'

'109s overhead.'

'OK, I see 'em.'

'Aircraft behind. Muck in, everybody.' (Bader).

'Tell me when to break. I can't see the bastards.'

'Six bastards behind us.'

'I can see 'em in my mirror.'

'Two aircraft below.'

Then some Messerschmitts must have attacked:

'Break right.'

'He nearly had you, Cocky.'

'Four right above.'

'Right on top of you.'

'Get organised.'

'I'm — if I can.'

'Four behind and above.'

'OK I'm looking after you.'

'Look behind.'

'It's only me. Don't get the wind up.'

'All right, you —!'

'Don't — about. We'll have some collisions in a minute.' (Apparently re-forming after an attack.)

'They're hell-cat boys.' (Probably a Canadian.)

'Your R/T sounds bloody awful.'

'Is mine OK?'

'Just like a lily.'

That covered ten minutes when few German fighters made contact and no one was hurt on either side. It sounds garbled and disjointed, telling none of the visual drama and conveying little of the profane urgency of the voices.

Inside the blast walls of the Tangmere Ops Room a loudspeaker purring with static clicked and spoke the metallic words of the pilots. Sitting at the radiophone, Woodhall had plenty to do, and so did the 'Beauty Chorus,' the team of WAAF's pushing the pawns of the radar plots across the Ops table with long-handled paddles.

CHAPTER TWENTY-ONE

Now the Messerschmitts were ever more numerous and bolder, every day savaging the flanks. More and more often Bader broke the wing to go for them, and for frantic minutes the sky was full of snarling, twisting, spitting aeroplanes. Several of the wwing scored 'kills' and three Spitfires did not come back.

The Messerschmitts – quite rightly – never stayed long to mix it with the more manoeuvrable Spitfires as they could never hold their own in a round-about tail chase. Despite British propaganda, the 109s were slightly faster and their proper tactics were to dive, shoot and break off. Sometimes they pulled up again and sometimes they half-rolled on to their backs and dived steeply out of the fight in the reverse direction. Any Spitfire on its own after a fight was under standing orders to join up with the nearest friendly fighters so there would be at least two in line abreast to watch each other's tail. It was jungle law up there and the devil took the odd man out.

Coming back over the Channel one day, Dundas was startled to see

Bader, flying alongside, flip back his cockpit top, unclip his oxygen mask, stuff his stub pipe in his mouth, strike a match (apparently holding the stick between his good knee and tin knee), light up and sit there like Pop-Eye puffing wisps of smoke that the slipstream snatched away. Dundas longed to light a cigarette himself, but desire was tempered by realisation that no normal man lit a naked flame in a Spitfire cockpit. Bader looked across, caught Dundas's wide eyes, beamed and made a rude gesture.

After that he always puffed his pipe in the cockpit on the way back, and pilots flying alongside used to sheer off, half in joke, half in earnest, in case Spitfire DB blew up. But it never did, adding to the growing and inspiring myth that Bader was bomb-proof, bullet-proof and fire-proof.

With virtually daily trips now, someone dubbed the wing 'The Bader Bus Service. The Prompt and Regular Service. Return Tickets Only.' That tickled everyone's fancy, and some of the pilots painted it on the side of their cowlings. It felt good to be one of the Tangmere Wing. Almost every night he took a few of his boys (and sometimes their girl friends) back to the Bay House, where Thelma and Jill made sandwiches and they sat yarning and quaffing beer. It began to be known affectionately as the 'Bag House,' which Thelma tolerated with her usual imperturbability.

Any new pilots he nursed carefully, yarning to them about tactics, air discipline (e.g. strict radio silence at the right times) and putting them in the middle of the pack for their first few trips. Once in mid-Channel on the way out a new boy in 145 called: 'Hallo, Red Leader. Yellow Two calling. I can't turn my oxygen on.'

A brooding silence followed.

The voice plaintively again: 'Hallo, Red Leader. Can you hear me? I can't turn on my oxygen.'

Then Turner's Canadian voice, ferociously sarcastic:

'What the hell do you want me to do? Get out and turn it on for you? *Go home!*'

No one made that mistake again.

On 2 July they went to Lille, and Bader dived 616 on fifteen 109s. He fired at one from almost dead behind, and as its hood flew off and the pilot jumped, another 109 plunged past and collected a burst. Smoke and oil spurted and he went down vertically. Bader left him and pulled up, obeying the dictum that it is suicide to follow an enemy down. Coming back over the Channel, he dived on another enemy, and as he started firing the 109 rolled on its back like lightning and streaked back into France. Bader was getting fed up with 109s diving out of a fight like that (though he respected the correctness of their tactics), and when he got back to claim one destroyed and one probable, he added as a flippant afterthought: 'and the third one I claim as frightened.'

He hoped for a bite from Intelligence at Group but they maintained a dignified silence. Instead he got a phone call from Leigh-Mallory, who said: 'Douglas, I hear you got another 109 to-day.'

'Yes, sir.'

'Well,' Leigh-Mallory went on in his deceptively pompous voice, 'you've got something else too – a bar to your DSO.'

Down at dispersals next day when he was congratulated, Bader said awkwardly: 'All this blasted chest cabbage doesn't matter a damn. It's what the wing does that really counts.' He meant it, too, and the pilots were surprised at the self-consciousness that lay under the boisterous exterior.

Coming away from Lille a couple of days later, little schools of Messerschmitts began pecking at them again. Bader fired at three but they half rolled and dived away. Two more dashed in and Bader shot one in the stomach from 100 yards. Explosive bullets must have slugged into the tank behind the cockpit because it blew a fiery jet like a blow-torch and fell out of the sky, dragging a plume of black smoke.

Remembering the three that got away, he claimed one destroyed and 'three frightened,' and this time got a bite from Group. A puzzled message arrived asking what he meant and he sent a signal back explaining. Group answered stiffly that they were not amused (though everyone else thought it was a 'good giggle').

It takes an odd genius to handle a wing in the lightning of battle where it is so easy to become confused or excited or tempted by a decoy. There was a day a 109 flew in front and just below them, and Bader called: 'That — looks too obvious. Look up-sun, everyone, and see if you can see anything.' No one could and at last Bader said: 'Come on, Cocky. Let's take a pot. The rest stay up.'

As he led Dundas down, the 109 half-rolled and dived, presumably transmitting, because seconds later his friends came out of the sun. Holden's squadron intercepted some and the rest came down on 616, which swung back into them. Turner's men plunged from above and the fight was on. Separated and set on by four 109s, Dundas fought them alone for five minutes, twisting and gyrating, unable to shake them off, until finally he took the last chance . . . stick hard back and hard rudder to flick into a spin. He let her go for 12,000 feet, came out at 5,000, dived for the coast, dodged several 109s, flashed over an airfield, squirted at a 109 coming in to land, and was chased by others for miles, seeing glowing little balls darting past his wingtip as they fired. Not till mid-Channel did he shake them off and landed with empty tanks, a dry mouth and sweaty brow.

Bader hailed him: 'You stupid goat, Cocky. Serves you damn' well right. Teach you not to get stuck out on your own.'

A day or two later after a brisk 'shambles,' Bader found himself isolated and called Holden:

'Hallo, Ken. I'm on my own. Can you join me?'

'OK, D. B. What's your position?'

'About fifteen miles north of Big Wood.'

'Good show. I'm in the same area at 25,000 feet. What are your angels?'

'8,000.'

In his broadest Yorkshire, Holden said: 'Eee, we'll be a bit conspicuous down there.'

He heard Bader's domineering rasp:

'To hell with that. You come on down here.'

A pregnant silence, and then Holden:

'Nay . . . you coom oop here.'

Dreadful words came over the R/T, but Holden, grinning behind his mask, was already on his way down, and they all came home together.

After a while, to the regret of the Beauty Chorus, Woodhall disconnected the loud-speaker in the Ops Room, feeling that some of the battle comments were too ripe even for the most sophisticated WAAFs. ('They laugh, you know,' he said, 'but dammit I get so embarrassed.') Bader was not exactly the least of the R/T offenders, but whenever his buccaneering presence lurched into the Ops Room there was a lot of primping, giggling and rolling of eyes.

On 9 July, near Mazingarbe, he sent a 109 down streaming glycol and black smoke, and noted the flash on the ground where it presumably exploded. Another 109 lunged at him, and he turned quickly and got in a burst as it broke off. His combat report said:

'A glycol stream started. I did not follow him down and claimed a damaged. Several others were frightened and I claim one badly frightened, who did the quickest half-roll and dive I've ever seen when I fired at him.'

No further bite from Group about the 'frightened.' They only allowed victories when the enemy was seen by witnesses in flames, or seen to crash, or the crew baled out.

Over Chocques next day he dived 616 on twenty Messerschmitts. More 109s swung in from one side and ran into Holden's squadron, then Turner's men came plunging down and the welkin shook to the roaring, swelling thunder of the dogfight. Bader sent one down shedding bits and pieces, pulled up behind another and fired into its belly. Under its cockpit burst a flash of flame, and suddenly the whole aeroplane blossomed with red fire as the tanks blew up and it fell like a torch. July was turning out a wonderful month. In eight days he had four destroyed, two probables and two damaged, but it only whetted his appetite.

For two days the weather was bad and he took Holden to a nearby golf links, arranging first that if it cleared over France and a 'show' was 'on', they would fire Very lights from the airfield. Holden would then run to the car parked by the first tee, drive across the course, pick up Bader and have them both back at the airfield in ten minutes. Bader spent most of his time on the links watching for a Very light, on edge in case something happened and he missed it. He had led the wing on every sweep so far and obviously intended to keep on doing so. But he had little time to relax at golf; even when the wing was not flying, they were on stand-by or readiness in flying kit from dawn to dusk, waiting for a 'show' or waiting in case the Luftwaffe attacked England again. There were no days off for the nerves to relax.

For Bader there was paper work, too, in his office, but he gave it little courtesy. Holden was with him one day when a flight-sergeant came in and dumped a pile of files in his 'in' tray. Bader growled: 'What the hell's this, Flight Sergeant?'

'Files for your attention, sir.'

'I'll give 'em attention all right.' He picked them up and threw the lot in his waste-paper basket.

He had time to write to a small boy, however. Norman Rowley, aged seven, had had both legs amputated after being run over by a bus in a Yorkshire mining village, and Bader wrote to tell him he would be all right and could be a pilot if he tried hard. (It helped the boy more than anything. He was proud to be Bader's friend.)

In some ways Bader overdid the personal leadership, leaving no one trained to follow him. He could not always lead the wing, and it was obvious what a gap his going would leave. But that did not seem in the realm of reality, and people were recognising now that he had more genius for fighter leadership than anyone else alive.

When there were no sweeps (rarely) he still liked to throw his Spitfire round the sky. His solid frame and square jaw would block Holden's doorway.

'Ken! Aerobatics!'

'OK, sir. I'll be with you in a minute.'

'What's the matter, you clot?' (rasping). 'Don't you want to come?'

'Yes, sir, but I've got to finish this readiness roster.'

'Damn that! You come with me!'

For the next hour Holden, Turner and Burton (press-ganged in the same way) would be careering round the sky following Bader in formation loops, rolls, stall-turns and the rest of the repertoire. It was forbidden to do them over the aerodrome, but Bader as often as not ignored that. Coming out of a formation loop one day, he saw other Spitfires doing the same thing over the airfield and snapped into his R/T: 'Dogsbody calling. Stop messing about over the airfield.'

Later, after he had reprimanded the offenders, Holden observed: 'That was a bit tough, sir. Hardly fair to bawl 'em out when you do the same thing yourself.'

With a deep laugh Bader said: 'Ah, that's a very different thing, Ken.'

But that was only cheerful bombast, not to be taken seriously. What he usually told aerobatic offenders was: 'Don't do it. I lost my legs doing it and more experienced chaps than you have killed themselves doing it. If you're going to be killed let it be an enemy bullet, not bad flying. I know – you're thinking you've seen me do it. Well, when you're wing commanders you can do it too. Until then stick to the regulation height.'

Aerobatics after battle was the worst offence. He had never forgotten a World War I picture in a hangar at Cranwell, 'The Last Loop,' showing a tail breaking off at the top of a loop after battle damage. He himself never in his life did one of the so-called 'victory rolls' and threatened to 'crucify' anyone else who did, adding: 'Next time I'll have you posted.'

In all important things he was meticulous. One heard muted criticism that he was too much of a 'one-man-band,' but all dynamic leaders get that. At least, ninety per cent of the feeling was devoted adulation. Even at dusk when they came off readiness, Bader had seldom had enough and kept pestering Tom Pike, CO of the night-fighter squadron, to take him up in a Beaufighter chasing night bombers, his excuse being: 'I'd love to see one of these things come down in flames. It'd look so much better at night.' But Pike could never take him because there was no room in the aircraft. An unusual friendship had sprung up between the two; they were such different types. Pike was tall and lean with a sensitive face and quiet manner. After he had knocked down several German bombers they had christened this gentle and modest man 'Killer.'

On 12 July, over Hazebrouck, Bader took 616 down on fifteen 109s, shot at one and saw a flash on its cockpit as he swept past, then fired head-on at another and saw pieces fly off as it swerved under him. A few seconds later he shot at a third, which spurted black smoke and glycol and wrenched into a violent dive. Then he chased a fourth through a cloud and fired from right behind. An orange, blow-torch flame squirted behind its cockpit and it fell blazing all over. One destroyed and three damaged, but he only put one asterisk in his logbook, no longer bothering to record 'damaged.'

A couple of days later, coming back with Dundas and Johnson, he streaked after a lone 109 below. Seeing him coming, the 109 dived and then climbed, and Bader, trying to cut him off, pulled up so sharply that he blacked out, hunched in the cockpit like an old man carrying a great weight, seeing nothing till he eased the stick forward and the grey film lifted. Then he still saw nothing – the 109 had vanished.

Back at Tangmere, when he landed Dundas and Johnson came charging over and Dundas said: 'By God, sir, that was good shooting.'

'What the hell are you talking about?' Bader grunted suspiciously, wary of sarcasm.

'Well,' Dundas said, 'you must have been 400 yards away when that Hun baled out.'

'What!' (incredulously). 'I never even fired.'

None of them had fired. The patches were still over the gun-ports in the wings. Yet the German *had* baled out. Bader lurched over to get a combat report form and wrote it down quickly: 'Claimed – one Me. 109 destroyed. Frightened. Confirmed. Seen by two pilots.'

Group maintained a stony silence, in marked contrast to the mirth at Tangmere.

The wing was re-equipping with Spitfire Vbs instead of the II's. The Vb was faster, could climb higher and had a 20 mm. cannon planted outboard in each wing. Everyone was excited about them except Bader, who developed a sudden, dogmatic aversion, deciding that cannons were no good because they would tempt a pilot to shoot from too far away instead of getting up close. This time, for once, he was wrong, but nothing would budge him; he was like a choleric colonel barking out obstinately and luridly at Holden, Turner, Dundas, Johnson, Crowley-Milling and anyone else who dared oppose machine-guns. At Group conferences he grunted his vigorous views to Sailor Malan, Leigh-Mallory and even the C.-in-C. Sholto Douglas, but orders still said the wing had to fly Vbs.

As they arrived in ones and twos he gave them first to Turner's top-cover squadron, where their better performance was most needed. Then Holden's team got them, and lastly 616, with whom he led the wing. Stubbornly he himself refused to fly one. Allotting them in this order was ideally correct. A formation leader should fly the slowest aircraft because he sets the pace and people behind must be able to keep up without wasting fuel on constant high power. Not all wing leaders did that, though Bader would have done it the way he did even had he approved of cannon. Finally he got a Va – with machine-guns.

Bad weather set in again and the pilots had time off to relax in surrounding towns. Bader always went with a group round him, demanding the presence of Holden, Turner, Dundas, Johnson, Crowley-Milling and others, even when they did not want to go. He hated being alone and liked to be the genial centre of a little Court Circle, ignoring their feelings in that respect. Not that they usually minded, being under the influence of his personality.

There was an evening dancing with Thelma at Sherry's in Brighton when the other dancers recognised him and queued up for his autograph.

He loved it and no one minded that either, because he did not try to hide it but was like a small boy having a whale of a good time. In those moments the loss of his legs must have meant nothing at all. (It never seemed to worry girls either. His masculinity and audacity drew them in giggling clumps which Thelma eyed with a tolerant smile.)

Rugged mess parties known as 'aerobatics' sometimes developed let off steam. After one of them a group captain had his arm in a sling for days and others bore the marks of combat. There was a lot of 'de-bagging,' fire-extinguishers were sprayed over the room and buckets of water thrown. At one party Cocky Dundas was drinking champagne out of a large water jug when the jug was dropped in a scuffle, and a scrum formed over the broken glass with Billy Burton underneath shouting 'On, on, on!'

After another party a certain visiting wing commander whose name has already been mentioned wrote to the mess: 'Wing Commander — desires to tender his sincere apologies for the usual black put up on the night of the 5th and 6th. He wishes to thank his many friends and admirers for the tender inquiries and floral tributes, and hopes by now you will have recovered from the shocking hangover from which, if there is a God above, you must undoubtedly have suffered.'

And underneath: 'Delete last sentence where applicable.'

(A Cranwell man too!)

After the war Tom Pike, risen to Air Vice Marshal and Assistant Chief of the Air Staff, said this of Bader at the time: 'I think he almost eliminated fear from his pilots. His semi-humorous, bloodthirsty outlook was exactly what is wanted in war and their morale soared. He was a tremendous tonic.'

And the shrewd Holden, looking back: 'I've never known a braver man. He was mad about getting at the Hun and couldn't talk about anything else. He was like a dynamo with terrific morale and a strange power over his men so that they all caught his spirit. After every show he got all the chaps together to yarn about it, though he didn't like people chipping in or putting him in second place. He could be pretty testy with his authority. He always had his own ideas and would take no opposition. It was just as well most of his ideas were sound. Now and then he got a wrong idea and nothing would shake him until he found out himself it was wrong, and then he'd suddenly switch right round the other way.'

Everyone felt he was invincible, and that this power shielded those who flew with him. Thelma now literally *knew* that the enemy would never get him. Every time he came back from a sweep he swooped low over the Bay House to let her know he was safely back, but she had come to regard this more as an affectionate salute than a reassurance.

Some of the Messerschmitts had shrewdly taken to setting about the Bee-hive as it came home over the French coast when the fighters were short of petrol. It was suggested that a fresh wing should go out to meet the homing Bee-hive, and over the Channel on 19 July the Tangmere Wing came down like wolves on an unsuspecting pack of 109s. Bader's first burst sent a 109 spinning down in a sea of flame. His second shot pieces off another, and as the Messerschmitts split up in alarm his bullets flashed on the fuselage of a third. In seconds the fight was over, half a dozen Messerschmitts were going down and the rest hurrying back into France.

On 23 July, when the weather prevented any sweep, he took Billy Burton on a 'rhubarb,' and near Dunkirk saw a Spitfire hurtling out of France, chased by a 109. He squirted into the Messerschmitt's belly and it cart-wheeled into the sea with a great splash.

The next weeks were frustrating. Under pressure, Bader at last tried a Vb, the last in his wing to do so, and only then because the Va was away for a check-up. He grumbled about it mightily because he got into the thick of a lot of fights, but never seemed able to knock anything down now, though Johnson, 'Crow,' Dundas, and the others kept scoring. He swore one day that his shells from each cannon passed each side of a 109 because he had gone up too close.[1]

He had done more sweeps now than anyone else in Fighter Command and still jealously insisted on leading the wing on every raid, urged by the inner devil, driving himself to the limit and driving others to keep pace.

In seven days he did ten sweeps – enough to knock out the strongest man, still more one who had to get around on two artificial legs. Now he was the last of the original wing leaders still operating – the rest were either dead or screened for a rest.

Peter Macdonald arrived at Tangmere on posting, and was disturbed to note that the skin round Bader's deep-set eyes was dark with fatigue. He and Woodhall began telling him that he must take a rest but Bader refused tersely. At last, at the end of July, Leigh-Mallory said to him:

'You'd better have a spell off operations, Douglas. You can't go on like this indefinitely.'

'Not yet, sir,' Bader said. 'I'm quite fit and I'd rather carry on, sir.'

He was so mulish that the AOC at last grudgingly said: 'Well, I'll let you go till September. Then you're coming off.'

Thelma was increasingly worried about him but he would not listen to her, either. The *Daily Mirror* columnist Cassandra wrote that Bader had done enough, was too valuable to lose and should be taken off operations. He read it angrily.

He was not fighting on to build up a personal string of kills, though

---

[1] Later he realised that he had been quite wrong in his dogmatic preference for machine guns.

at this time he was fifth on the list of top-scoring RAF pilots. He had 20½ enemy aircraft confirmed destroyed but, like other leading fighter pilots, his actual score was probably greater. In his logbook he had nearly thirty asterisks – the ones he himself was fairly sure he had got, though he never displayed them. Malan and Tuck had nearly thirty official victories each but Bader was not jealous, though he would have loved to have caught them. The wing was the thing and the battle an intoxicant that answered his search for a purpose and fulfilment.

No luck early in August. On the 4th he noted in his logbook: 'High escort. Dull.' Next day to Lille power station noted tersely: 'Damn' good bombing. Blew 'em to hell.'

On 8 August Peter Macdonald cornered him in the mess. 'I'm going to insist you take a few days off,' he said. 'I'm taking you and Thelma up to Scotland for a week and you can relax with some golf at St Andrews.'

After an argument, Bader said: 'I'll think about it,' and that evening Macdonald forced the issue by ringing St Andrews and booking rooms for the three of them from the 11th. That, he thought, would settle it.

Next day everything went wrong from the start.

TWENTY-TWO

First there was a tangle on take-off and the top-cover squadron went astray. Climbing over the Channel, the others could see no sign of it, and Bader would not break radio silence to call them. Then, half-way across, his air-speed indicator broke, the needle sliding back to an inscrutable zero, which meant trouble timing his rendezvous with the Bee-hive over Lille, and after that a difficult landing at Tangmere, not knowing in the critical approach how near the aeroplane was to a stall. Time to worry about that later: more urgent things loomed. It looked a good day for a fight, patches of layer cloud at about 4,000 feet but a clear vaulting sky above with a high sun to veil the venom of attack. He climbed the squadrons to 28/30,000 feet so that they, not the Germans, would have the height and the sun.

The job that day was to go for German fighters where they found them, and they found them as they crossed the French coast, just south of Le Touquet – dead ahead and about 2,000 feet below a dozen Messerschmitts were climbing the same way, spread in 'finger fours' abreast (which they seemed to have copied lately). None of them seemed to be looking behind. They were sitters.

Bader said tersely into his mask: 'Dogsbody attacking. Plenty for all. Take 'em as they come. Ken, stay up and cover us,' and plunged down at the leading four, Dundas, Johnson and West beside him and rest hounding behind. The Germans still climbed placidly ahead, and steeply in the dive he knew it was the perfect 'bounce.' Picking the second from the left, he closed startlingly fast; the 109 seemed to slam slantwise at him and, trying to lift the nose to aim, he knew suddenly he had badly misjudged. Too fast! No time! He was going to ram, and in the last moment brutally jerked stick and rudder so that the Spitfire careened and flashed past into the depths below, seeing nothing of the carnage among the enemy as the other Spitfires fired and pulled back up.

Angrily he flattened again about 24,000 feet, travelling fast, watching alertly behind and finding he was alone. Better climb up fast again to join the rest: deadly to be alone in this dangerous sky. He was suddenly surprised to see six more Messerschmitts ahead, splayed abreast in three parallel pairs line astern, noses pointing the other way. More sitters! He knew he should pull up and leave them; repeatedly he'd drummed it into his pilots never to try things on their own. But the temptation! They looked irresistible. A glance behind again. All clear. Greed swept discretion aside and he sneaked up behind the middle pair. None of them noticed. From a hundred yards he squirted at the trailing one and a thin blade of flame licked out behind it. Abruptly a flame flared like a huge match being struck and the aeroplane fell on one wing and dropped on fire all over. The other Germans flew placidly on. They must have been blind.

He aimed at the leader 150 yards in front and gave him a three-second burst. Bits flew off it and then it gushed volumes of white smoke as its nose dropped. The two fighters on the left were turning towards him, and crazily elated as though he had just pulled off a smash and grab raid, he wheeled violently right to break off, seeing the two on that side still flying ahead and that he would pass between them. In sheer bravado he held course to do so.

Something hit him. He felt the impact but the mind was curiously numb and could not assess it. No noise but something was holding his aeroplane by the tail, pulling it out of his hands and slewing it round. It lurched suddenly and then was pointing straight down, the cockpit floating with dust that had come up from the bottom. He pulled back on the stick but it fell inertly into his stomach like a broken neck. The aeroplane was diving in a steep spiral and confusedly he looked behind to see if anything were following.

First he was surprised, and then terrifyingly shocked to see that the whole of the Spitfire behind the cockpit was missing: fuselage, tail, fin

– all gone. Sheared off, he thought vaguely. The second 109 must have run into him and sliced it off with its propeller.

He knew it had happened but hoped desperately and foolishly that he was wrong. Only the little radio mast struck up just behind his head. A corner of his brain saw that the altimeter was unwinding fast from 24,000 feet.

Thoughts crowded in. How stupid to be nice and warm in the closed cockpit and have to start getting out. The floundering mind sought a grip and sharply a gush of panic spurted.

'Christ! Get out!'

'Wait! No oxygen up here!'

Get out! Get out!

Won't be able to soon! Must be doing over 400 already.

He tore his helmet and mask off and yanked the little rubber ball over his head – the hood ripped away and screaming noise battered at him. Out came the harness pin and he gripped the cockpit rim to lever himself up, wondering if he could get out without thrust from the helpless legs. He struggled madly to get his head above the windscreen and suddenly felt he was being sucked out as the tearing wind caught him.

Top half out. He was out! No, something had him by the leg holding him. (The rigid foot of the right leg hooked fast in some vise in the cockpit.) Then the nightmare took his exposed body and beat him and screamed and roared in his ears as the broken fighter dragging him by the leg plunged down and spun and battered him and the wind clawed at his flesh and the cringing sightless eyeballs. It went on and on into confusion, on and on, timeless, witless and helpless, with a little core of thought deep under the blind head fighting for life in the wilderness. It said he had had a hand gripping the D-ring of the parachute and mustn't take it off, must grip it because the wind wouldn't let him get it back again, and he mustn't pull it or the wind would split his parachute because they must be doing 500 miles an hour. On and on . . . till the steel and leather snapped.

He was floating, in peace. The noise and buffeting had stopped. Floating upwards? He thought it is so quiet I must have a rest. I would like to go to sleep.

In a flash the brain cleared and he knew and pulled the D-ring, hearing a crack as the parachute opened. Then he was actually floating. High above the sky was still blue, and right at his feet lay a veil of cloud. He sank into it. That was the cloud at 4,000 feet. Cutting it fine! In seconds he dropped easily under it and saw the earth, green and dappled, where the sun struck through. Something flapped in his face and he saw it was his right trouser leg, split along the seam. High in the split gleamed indecently the white skin of his stump.

The right leg had gone.

How lucky, he thought, to lose one's legs and have detachable ones. Otherwise he would have died a few seconds ago. He looked, but saw no burning wreck below – probably not enough left to burn.

Lucky, too, not to be landing on the rigid metal leg like a post that would have split his loins. Odd it should happen like that. How convienient. But only half a leg was left to land on – he did not think of that.

He heard engine noises and turned in the harness. A Messerschmitt was flying straight at him, but the pilot did not shoot. He turned and roared by fifty yards away.

Grass and cornfields were lifting gently to meet him, stooks of corn and fences. A vivid picture, not quite static, moving. Two peasants in blue smocks leaned against a gate looking up and he felt absurdly self-conscious. A woman carrying a pail in each hand stopped in a lane and stared up, frozen like a still. He thought – I must look comic with only one leg.

The earth that was so remote suddenly rose fiercely. Hell! I'm landing on a gate! He fiddled with the shrouds to spill air and slip sideways and, still fumbling, hit, feeling nothing except vaguely some ribs buckle when a knee hit his chest as consciousness snapped.

Three German soldiers in grey uniforms were bending over him, taking off his harness and Mae West. No one spoke that he remembered. They picked him up and carried him to a car in a lane feeling nothing, neither pain nor thought, only a dazed quiescence. The car moved off and he saw fields through the windows but did not think of anything. After timeless miles there were houses and the car rumbled over the *pavé*, through the arch of a gateway to a grey stone building. The Germans lifted him out and carried him through a door up some steps and along a corridor . . . he smelt the familiar hospital smell . . . into a bare, aseptic room, and then they were laying him on a padded casualty table. Old memories stirred. A thinnish man in a white coat and rimless glasses walked up and looked down at him. A girl in nurse's uniform hovered behind.

The doctor frowned at the empty trouser leg, pulled the torn cloth aside and stared in amazement, then looked at Bader's face and at the wings and medal ribbons on his tunic. Puzzled he said: 'You have lost your leg.'

Bader spoke for the first time since the enemy had hit him. 'Yes, it came off as I was getting out of my aeroplane.'

The doctor looked at the stump again, trying to equate a one-legged man with a fighter pilot. 'Ach, so!' he said. 'It is an old injury,' and joked mildly. 'You seem to have lost both your legs – your real one and your artificial one.'

Bader thought: God, you haven't seen anything yet. He waited with a grim and passive curiosity for the real joke.

'You have cut your throat,' the doctor said. He put his hand up and was surprised to feel a large gash under his chin, sticky with blood. It did not hurt.

The doctor peered at it, then stuck his fingers between the teeth and felt round the floor of the mouth. Light-headed, Bader felt a sudden horror that the cut might have gone right through. For some absurd reason that mattered terribly. But apparently it was all right.

'I must sew this up,' the doctor murmured. He jabbed a syringe near the gash and the area went numb. No one spoke while he stitched the lips of the gash.

'Now we must have your trousers off and see your leg,' he said.

Bader thought: This is going to be good, and raised his rump a little as the doctor unbuttoned the trousers and eased them down over the hips. The doctor froze, staring transfixed at the leather and metal that encased the stump of the left leg. There was a silence.

At last he noisily sucked in a breath, and said 'Ach!' He looked once more at Bader, back at the two stumps and again at Bader, and said in a voice of sober discovery: 'We have heard about you.'

Bader grunted vaguely.

'Are you all right?' asked the doctor.

'Fine,' he said tiredly. 'Whereabouts are we?'

'This is a hospital,' said the doctor. 'St Omer.'

St Omer!

'That's funny,' Bader said. 'My father is buried here somewhere.'

The doctor must have thought his mind was wandering. Two grey-uniformed orderlies came and picked him up, carried him up two flights of stairs into a narrow room and dumped him like a sack of potatoes, though not roughly, on a white hospital bed. They took his clothes and left leg off, wrapped him in a sort of white nightshirt, pulled the bedclothes over him, stood the left leg, still clipped to the broken waistband, against the wall, and left him there.

He lay motionless, aching all over, feeling as though he had been through a mangle, his head singing like a kettle. Every time he stirred a piercing pain stabbed into the ribs under his heart, cutting like a knife. Reaction drained him and he knew only utter exhaustion and hurting all over the body, so that for a while he did not think of England or the wing or of captivity, nor even of Thelma.

A nurse came and held his head while she ladled some spoonfuls of soup into his mouth. She went. His mind slowly cleared and a thought came into focus: 'I hope the boys saw me bale out and tell Thelma.'

Dusk gathered slowly in the room and he dozed fitfully. Some time later he woke in darkness wondering where he was. Then he knew and sank into misery, black, deep and full of awareness. He remembered he was to go dancing with Thelma that night and longed to see her, feeling lonely and helpless without legs among enemies. There was the golf, too, at St Andrews. For the first time in his life he looked back over his shoulder, rejecting the present and trying to hold on to the past, but the clock would not go back and the night moved slowly on.

No one had seen him go down. He had vanished after the first dive and did not answer when they called him. In the air they had been chilled by the absence of the familiar rasping banter. Back at Tangmere there was stunned disbelief when he did not return. They watched the sky and the clock until they knew he could have no petrol left, and a gloomy hush seemed to fall over the place.

Pike said to Woodhall: 'You'd better tell his wife,' and Woodhall stalled, saying: 'No, give him time. He may have landed somewhere else with his R/T u/s. He'll turn up.'

But John Hunt, a shy young Intelligence officer, thought Thelma had been told and drove over to cheer her up with a horoscope that a local woman had cast of Douglas, saying that he was in for a dreary time but had a magnificent career after that. He thought it would help her to think that Douglas might be a prisoner.

She was in a deck-chair in the sun, and only when she said: 'Hallo, John. Come for tea?' he realised that she did not know. Somehow, in an agony of embarrassment, he talked of irrelevant things, trying to find an unbrutal way of breaking it, when a car drew up and Woodhall got out and walked straight up to them. Without preamble he said: 'I'm afraid I've got some bad news for you, Thelma. Douglas did not come back from the morning sortie.'

Thelma stood dumbly.

Woodhall went on: 'We should get some news soon. I shouldn't worry too much. He's indestructible . . . probably a prisoner.'

Too numb to ask what had happened, she stood very pale and said: 'Thank you, Woody.' Woodhall was saying something else and after a while she became aware that he had gone and that Jill was there. Hunt thrust a piece of paper into her hand and said: 'This might be a comfort, Thelma. Read it later.' Then he was gone. Jill was saying: 'Darling, you *know* he'll pop up again. They can't get him.' But Thelma had believed he was invincible and now the whole illusion had burst. She would not cry. A fortnight ago a young wife had cried for days when her husband in the wing had been shot down and Thelma stubbornly would not repeat the exhibition. As always with strong emotions, she covered them up.

Later Dundas came with flowers in one hand and a bottle of sherry in the other. He had been out twice alone that afternoon over the Channel as far as France looking for Bader's yellow rubber dinghy till Woodhall had ordered him back. He looked tired and felt guilty because he had not seen Douglas go down. He and Jill got Thelma to take a little sherry but she brought it up again. Stokoe, Douglas's batman, brought in some soup with tears rolling down his face.

Later, in bed when they left her, the tears came and she lay awake all night thinking: If they got Douglas, what chance have the other boys got? They haven't any chance. A thought rose and obsessed her all night: How can I warn them? How can I make them understand they will all be killed now?

In the morning the reporters came.

Dawn brought new strength to Bader. In the light he saw many things more clearly; knew where he was and what it meant and accepted it unwistfully. First things first and to hell with the rest. He must get legs and must get word to Thelma.

The door opened and in came two young Luftwaffe pilots, dark young men in tight short tunics pinned with badges, shapely breeches and black riding boots.

'Hallo,' brightly said the leader, who was Count von Someone-or-other. 'How are you?' His English was good.

'All right, thanks.'

Bader was fairly monosyllabic but the Germans chatted amiably. Would he like some books? They'd just come over from St Omer airfield to yarn as one pilot to another. Spitfires were jolly good aeroplanes.

'Yes,' Bader said. 'So are yours.'

After a while the Count said politely: 'I understand you have no legs?' He was looking at the foreshortened form under the bedclothes.

'That's right.'

They asked what it was like flying without legs. An elderly administrative officer came in and listened, looked at the left leg leaning against the wall and observed heavily: 'Of course it would never be allowed in Germany.'

Later they left and the next visitor was a baldheaded Luftwaffe engineering officer, who asked more boring questions about legs. Bader cut him short: 'Look, can you radio England and ask them to send me another leg?' He did not know how they would do it, but if they did Thelma would know he was alive.

The German thought it a good idea.

'And while you're about it,' Bader followed up, 'could you send someone to look at the wreckage of my aeroplane. The other leg might still be in it.'

The German promised to do what he could.

A nurse brought in a basin of water. She was German and not talkative, making signs that he was to wash himself. He did so, moving painfully, and when he got to his legs was shocked to find a great dark swelling high up on his right stump. It looked as big as a cricket ball and was terribly sore. For ten years since the agony at Greenlands Hospital he had flinched at the thought of anything going wrong with his stumps, and now it loomed large and ugly in his mind.

Later, yesterday's doctor came in, looking precise behind the rimless glasses. Bader showed him the swelling, and the doctor looked grave and prodded it. After a while he said hesitantly: 'We will have to cut this.'

Bader burst out, 'By God, you don't,' panicky at the thought of an experimental knife. They argued violently about it till the doctor grudgingly agreed to leave it for a while.

A dark, plump girl came in, put a tray on his bed, smiled and went out. He realised he was hungry till he tasted the bowl of potato water-soup, two thin slices of black bread smeared with margarine and the cup of tepid ersatz coffee. It left a sour taste in his mouth.

Later it was the doctor again, with orderlies. 'We are going to put you in another room,' he said. 'With friends.'

Friends?

The orderlies carried him along a corridor into a larger room with five beds and dumped him on one of them. A fresh-faced young man in another bed said cheerfully in an American accent: 'Hallo, sir. Welcome. My name's Bill Hall. Eagle Squadron. We heard you were here.' He had a cradle over one leg which was in traction, the foot pulled by a weight on a rope. His kneecap had been shot off. In the next bed was a Pole with a burnt face, and beyond him Willie, a young Londoner who had been shot through the mouth. All Spitfire pilots. They chatted cheerfully till well after dusk. Willie and the Pole had been trying to think of some way of escaping, but the Germans had taken their clothes and they had only the nightshirts, which made it rather hopeless.

Bader asked: 'Isn't there any way out of here?'

'Yes,' Willie answered a little bitterly. 'Soon as you can stagger they whip you off to Germany.' Apparently he and the Pole were due to go at any moment.

'If you had clothes,' Bader persisted, 'how would you get out?'

'Out the bloody window on a rope,' Willie said. 'The gates are always open and no guards on them.' He jerked his head at the door of the room. 'They put the guards outside that door.'

'Hwo would you get a rope?'

Willie said there were French girls working in the hospital who might smuggle one in.

Bader slipped off to sleep thinking grimly about that, but he slept well and in the morning did not feel so stiff and sore.

The plump girl came in early with more black bread and acorn coffee, and Bill Hall introduced her to Bader as Lucille, a local French girl. He tried to joke with her but she barely understood his schoolboy French, though she coloured nicely and smiled at him again. She did not say anything: a German guard stood in the doorway.

The doctor came in to see his stump but the swelling was visibly less, which was an enormous relief. In his blunt way Bader told the doctor that the food was 'bloody awful,' and the doctor bridled. Bader waved a piece of black bread in his face and they had a shouting match till the doctor stormed out. Lucille came back with lunch – more potato water and black bread.

Later a tall, smart Luftwaffe officer of about forty came in. He wore the red tabs of the Flak, clicked his heels, saluted Bader and said: 'Herr Ving Commander, ve haf found your leg.' Like a star making his entrance, a jack-booted soldier marched through the door and jerked magnificently to attention by the bed, holding one arm stiffly out. Hanging from it was the missing right leg, covered in mud, the broken piece of leather belt still hanging from it. Bader delighted, said, 'I say, thanks,' then saw that the foot still ludicrously clad in sock and shoe stuck up almost parallel to the shin.

'Hell, it's been smashed.'

'Not so badly as your aeroplane,' said the officer. 'Ve found it in the area of the other pieces.'

The soldier took two smart paces forward, clicked to a halt again, and Bader took the leg. He unpeeled the sock and saw, as he feared, that the instep had been stove in.

'I say,' he said, turning on the charm, 'd'you think your chaps at the aerodrome could repair this for me?'

The officer pondered. 'Perhaps,' he said. 'Ve vill take it and see.' After a mutual exchange of compliments the officer clicked his heels, saluted, swung smartly and disappeared.

Next it was a new girl, fair-haired and with glasses, carrying a tray. She was Hélène, and everyone goggled to see that she carried real tea on the tray and some greyish-white bread. Apparently the shouting match had been worth while.

In the morning the swelling on the stump had deflated with amazing speed and that was a great relief.

Later the officer with the red tabs marched crisply in, saluted, and as he said 'Herr Ving Commander, ve haf brought back your leg,' the jackbooted stooge made another dramatic entrance behind and came to a crashing halt by the bed, not flicking an eyelid, holding out a rigid arm with the leg suspended from it: a transformed leg, cleaned and polished and with the foot pointing firmly where a foot should be. Bader took it and saw they had done an amazing job on it; the body belt was beautifully repaired with a new section of intricately-worked, good quality leather and all the little straps that went with it. The dent in the shin had been carefully hammered out, so that apart from a patch bare of paint it looked normal. A dent in the knee had been hammered out, and even the rubbers correctly set in the ankle so there was resilient movement in the foot.

'It is OK?' the officer asked anxiously.

Bader, impressed and rather touched, said: 'It's really magnificent. It is very good of you to have done this. Will you please thank the men who did it very much indeed.'

He strapped both legs on, eased off the bed, feeling unsteady for a moment, and went stumping round the room, a ludicrous figure in nightshirt with the shoe-clad metal legs underneath. Without a stump sock (lost in the parachute descent), the right leg felt strange, and it gave forth loud clanks and thumps as he swung it. The others looked on fascinated. Beaming with pleasure, the Germans finally left. Bader lurched over to window and looked thoughtfully at the ground three floors and forty feet below. To the left of the grass courtyard he could see the open gates, unguarded.

They became aware of a drone that began to swell and fade and swell again. The Pole and Willie joined him at the window, and high above they saw the twisting, pale scribble of vapour trails against blue sky; obviously a sweep and some 109's were having a shambles over St Omer. Tensely they watched but the battling aircraft were too high to see. Shortly a parachute floated down. A German, he hoped, and hoped there were more coming down without parachutes. He looked up at the contrails, at the parachute and down at the courtyard and the gates, his mind a fierce maelstrom.

A Luftwaffe Feldwebel came in and told Willie and the Pole to be ready to leave for Germany after lunch. He would bring their clothes later.

When he had gone Willie, depressed, said: 'Once they get you behind the wire you haven't got much chance.' Bader began worrying that it would be his turn next. He *must* stay in France as long as possible.

Lucille came in with soup and bread for lunch. The guard looked morosely in the doorway, and then turned back into the corridor. Bader whispered to the Pole: 'Ask her if she can help me get out or put me in touch with friends outside.'

In a low voice the Pole started talking to Lucille in fluent French. She darted a look at Douglas and whispered an answer to the Pole. They went on talking in fast, urgent whispers, each with an eye watching the door. Bader listened eagerly but the words were too fast. They heard the guard's boots clump in the corridor, and Lucille, with a quick, nervous smile at Douglas, went out.

The Pole came across and sat on his bed. 'She says you're "*bien connu*" and she admires you tremendously and will help if she can, but she can't get a rope because the Germans would guess how you got it. She doesn't know whether she can get clothes, but she has a day off next Sunday and will go to a village down the line called Aire, or something. She says there are "*agents Anglais*" there.'

English agents? It sounded too good. But she was going to try, and hope welled strongly. Sunday! This was only Wednesday. Hell, they mustn't take him. The uncertainty of fear gnawed. Better try and act weak from now on.

They took Willie and the Pole that afternoon. Now he had to rely on his schoolboy French.

In the morning Lucille came in with the usual bread and acorn coffee. The sentry lounged in the doorway. She put the tray on Bader's bed, leaning over so that her plump body hid him from the sentry. He grinned a cheerful '*Bon jour*' at her as she squeezed his hand and then the grin nearly slipped as he felt her pressing a piece of paper into his palm. He closed his fingers round it and slid the clenched fist under the bedclothes. It was very quick. She said nothing, but her mouth lifted in a pale smile as she went out of the room. The door closed behind the sentry.

TWENTY-THREE

Half under the clothes, Bader unfolded the paper and read, written in French in a clear, child-like hand: '*My son will be waiting outside the hospital gates every night from midnight until 2 am. He will be smoking a cigarette. We wish to help a friend of France.*'

It was signed 'J. Hiècque.'

Bill Hall looked curiously across the top of his suspended leg and asked: 'What's that?'

'Oh, just a message of good cheer.' Bader spoke casually, tingling inside with excitement. He tucked the note in the breast pocket of the nightshirt and stuffed a handkerchief on top. It was red hot. Somehow he must get rid of it. Destroy it. He knew that the person who bravely signed a name to it was liable to death. Lucille, too.

Now how the hell to get out of the hospital? And he *must* get his clothes back! Couldn't walk round the town in a white nighshirt. (And Bill Hall had said there was a curfew at ten o'clock.) Pretend he was walking in his sleep! With tin legs sticking out under his nightshirt! Silly thoughts chased their tails in his head. *Must* get clothes and *must* destroy the note.

He had his pipe and matches.

Reaching out, he picked up his tin legs from the wall, lifted his nightshirt, strapped them on and walked out of the door. The sentry stood in his way. He pointed to the lavatory and the sentry nodded.

Inside the lavatory he closed the door, struck a match and burnt the note, holding it by one corner till it was all wrinkled and charred, then dropped the ashes into the pan and flushed it.

Walking back up the corridor, the sentry gaped at him all the way and he knew angrily and self-consciously how ridiculous he looked in the nightshirt with the legs underneath. It was then that the idea struck him. It was a chance.

When the doctor came in later to inspect the stump again, Bader said in a voice of sweet reason: 'Look, I've got my legs back now but I just can't walk around in them with this nightshirt on. It's terribly embarrassing.' He explained about the gaping sentry. 'I'm sure you'll understand,' he went on winningly. 'I must have some clothes to wear. Even in bed this nightshirt's a damn' nuisance. It gets tangled up in my stumps.'

The doctor looked professionally thoughtful and then smiled. 'Oh, well, I suppose it is all right in your case. I will have your clothes brought to you.'

Quite a moment! God, how easy.

Half an hour later a German nurse came in with his clothes, put them in a neat pile beside his bed, smiled briefly at him and went out.

Hall said wryly: 'I wouldn't mind losing this damn' leg of mine just to get my pants back. I feel so stupid in this nightshirt.'

How to get out of hospital! He lay there fiercely thinking about it. It was the last problem. The toughest! No good trying to walk down the corridors and stairs. The guards were on at midnight and all night. They'd frogmarch him back and he'd lose his clothes again, too. He walked over to the window and stood looking down into the courtyard. Perhaps Lucille's *'agents Anglais'* could help.

He was still there when the immaculate young count, the fighter pilot with the Knight's Cross, came in with his comrade. 'Ha,' he said, 'it is good to see you on your legs again. Look, we haf brought you two bottles of champagne. Will you come and drink them with us?'

They took him down a flight of stairs to the doctor's room, but the doctor was not there, just the three of them. The first cork popped. It was the first time he had drunk champagne since his second wedding to Thelma, and it developed into a cheerful little party.

The Count had obviously shot down some British aircraft but was too polite to mention that or to ask how many Bader had shot down. In fact, neither he nor his comrade asked any dangerous questions, but both chatted gaily about their own tactics and aeroplanes. The Count said they always sat in their cockpits at readiness – he always read a book. Bader liked them both; they were 'types' after his own heart and he would have liked to have had them in his wing. What a damn' silly war it was.

'Soon you may haf three legs,' the Count said. 'With the permission of Reichsmarshal Goering, the Luftwaffe has radioed to England on international waveband. They offer to give a British aeroplane unrestricted passage to fly your leg. We have given them a height and a course and a time to drop it over St Omer.' He shrugged, looking philosophical. 'They have not answered. I think they will.'

Bader gave a rich belly-chuckle. 'I bet they drop it with bombs,' he said. 'They don't need any unrestricted passage.'

The Count grinned amiably and raised his glass. 'We will be ready,' he promised. 'Let us hope the next leg will not be shot down.'

There was another thing he said. The Oberstleutnant Galland, who commanded at their airfield, Wissant, near St Omer, sent his compliments to Oberstleutnant Bader and would like him to come and have tea with them.

'We do not try to get information from you,' he added quite sincerely. 'He would like to meet you. We are comrades, as you say, on the wrong sides.'

Bader was intrigued. It would be churlish to refuse, and in any case he would love to meet Galland (probably they had already met in the air). It brought a breath of the chivalry lost from modern war. And it was a chance to spy out the country, to see the other side, life on an enemy fighter station, to weigh it up and compare it. Might get back home with a 109!

'I'd be delighted to come,' he said.

'Good,' beamed the Count. 'A car will come for you.'

Agreeably they finished the second bottle.

The car came bearing the bald little engineering officer, who sat by him all the fifteen miles to Wissant. It was a sunny day and it felt good to be out. They drew up in front of an attractive country farmhouse of red brick. German officers stood outside – it was the officers' mess. As Bader got out a good-looking man about his own age, dark-haired and with a little moustache, stepped forward. He had burn marks round the eyes and a lot of medals on his tunic. The Knight's Cross with Oak Leaves and Swords – almost Germany's highest decoration – hung round his neck. He put out his hand and said 'Galland.'

Bader put out his own hand. 'Oh, how d'you do. My name is Douglas Bader.' Galland did not speak English, and the engineering officer interpreted. A lot of others stepped forward in turn, clicking their heels as they were introduced. Galland led him off, trailed by the others, down a garden path lined with shrubs. Quiet and pleasant, Galland said: 'I am glad to see you are all right and getting about again. How did you get on bailing out?'

'Don't remember much about it.'

'One never does,' Galland said. 'One of your pilots shot me down the other day and I had to jump out. I landed very hard. It must be unpleasant landing with only one leg.'

Bader asked: 'Is that when you burnt your eyes?' and Galland nodded.

He led the way into a long, low arbour, and Bader was surprised to see it filled with an elaborate model railway on a big raised platform. Galland pressed a button and little trains whirred past little stations, rattling over points, past signals, through tunnels and model cuttings. Eyes sparkling, Galland turned to Bader, looking like a small boy having fun. The interpreter said: 'This is the Herr Oberstleutnant's favourite place when he is not flying. It is a replica of Reichsmarshal Goering's railway, but of course the Reichsmarshal's is much bigger.'

After playing a little while with that, Galland led him and the others several hundred yards along hedge-lined paths, through a copse of trees to the low, three-sided blast walls of an aircraft pen. In it stood an Me. 109.

Bader looked at it fascinated, and Galland made a polite gesture for him to climb in. He surprised them by the way he hauled himself on to the wing-root, grabbed his right leg and swung it into the cockpit and climbed in unaided. As he cast a glinting professional eye over the cockpit lay-out Galland leaned in and pointed things out. Mad thoughts about starting up and slamming the throttle on for a reckless take-off surged through Bader's mind.[1]

Lifting his head, he could see no signs of the aerodrome. He turned to the interpreter. 'Would you ask the Herr Oberstleutnant if I can take off and try a little trip in this thing?'

Galland chuckled and answered. The interpreter grinned at Bader. 'He says that if you do he'll be taking off right after you.'

'All right,' Bader said, looking a little too eagerly at Galland. 'Let's have a go.'

Galland chuckled again and said that he was off duty at the moment.

As he stepped out of the 109, Bader looked across country and saw the sea. Far beyond he thought he could glimpse the white cliffs of Dover and for a moment felt quite sick. It brought it all home to him. And the future. England could be no more than forty miles away. Longingly he thought if only they'd leave him for a moment he could get off with the 109 and be back in the mess for tea.

[1] After the war Galland sent Bader a snapshot of the scene, and only then did he discover that a German officer beside the cockpit had been pointing a heavy pistol at him all the time he sat there.

They had tea in the farmhouse mess, waiters in white coats bringing sandwiches and real English tea (probably captured). It could have been an RAF mess except that all the other uniforms were wrong. The atmosphere was wrong too, which was understandable. Everyone smiled, exuding goodwill, but it was a little strained and formal and the talk was stilted. With Galland there no one seemed to speak much. No one tried to pump him for information. The little interpreter told him that the day he was shot down the Luftwaffe had got twenty-six Spitfires for no loss, which was such obvious nonsense that it put Bader in a very cheerful mood, because it confirmed RAF views on extravagant German claims.[1] He himself had got two that day, and possibly three, counting the mysterious man who had hit him.[2]

Later they showed him some camera-gun films – a Blenheim which did not seem to be shot down, a Spitfire which shovelled out black smoke and obviously *was* shot down, and then an odd film of a 109 strafing a British ship and 'sinking' it. The last few frames showed the half-submerged ship, but it was all too obviously a different ship.

Galland gave him a tin of English tobacco, and when he took him out to the car said: 'It has been good to meet you. I'm afraid you will find it different in prison camp, but if there is ever anything I can do, please let me know.'

He smiled warmly, shook hands, clicked his heels and bowed. At a discreet distance behind, everyone else clicked heels and bowed. Bader got in the car with the little engineer and they drove back to the hospital. He would have liked to have had Galland in his wing. Rumour said he had over seventy victories, but of course he had been fighting in the Spanish Civil War and in Poland too.

The engineer officer took him back up to the ward, shook hands, clicked his heels and bowed himself out. More black bread stood by his bed. Lucille had evidently been in with 'dinner.' After his tea with Galland he regarded it distastefully.

'How'd you get on?' Bill Hall asked.

'Fine,' he said. 'Jolly fine. They're a good bunch. Got some loot too.' He held up the tobacco.

A comatose form lay in the bed by the window and the room stank disagreeably of ether. Bader looked across. 'Who's that?'

'New boy came in while you were out,' Hall said. 'Sergeant pilot. Shot down yesterday. They've just taken his arm off. He's still under the dope.'

The door opened and a German soldier wearing a coal-scuttle helmet came in. It was the first of the fabled helmets that Bader had seen. The

---

[1] In the Western Desert in 1942 the German 'ace,' Marseille, claimed personally to have shot down sixteen British aircraft in one day. That day the Desert Air Force lost two aeroplanes.
[2] Much later Bader found that his wing had got eight that day for two lost.

soldier, who must have been awaiting his return, saluted and said in atrocious English: 'Herr Ving Commander, to-morrow morning at eight o'clock you vill be pleased to be ready because you go to Chermany.'

The words seemed to hit Bader right in the stomach. The German clicked his heels, saluted and clumped out. He sat on his bed, stunned. Then, with deep feeling, uttered an eloquent word.

Hall murmured: 'Tough luck, sir. Looks like you've had it.'

Bader roused and said crisply: 'Well, I've got to get out to-night, that's all.'

He lurched over to the window and pushed it open. It seemed a long way down, and immediately below were flagstones. After the parachute affair he did not feel like jumping. He turned back and scowled round the room, austere with its board floor and five prim beds.

My God! Sheets! Knotted sheets!

One learned something from school!

Each bed had an undersheet and a double, bag-type sheet stuffed in the Continental style. He stumbled over to his bed and ripped the sheets from under the blanket. Need a damn' sight more than that! He clumped noisily to the two empty beds and stripped them the same way. With a sudden idea he began ripping the bag sheets along the seams to get two out of each one. The tearing seemed to scream a warning to the Germans.

'Make a noise,' he hissed to Hall, and Hall started on a monologue in a loud American voice, talking nonsense, saying anything that came into his head and laughing loud and humourlessly. Both were acutely conscious of the guard just outside the door. Once they heard the rasp of a boot on the boards and then a couple of clumps. Bader looked up like an animal. Then a creak as the guard sat in the wicker-chair out there.

'Know anything about knots?' Bader whispered to Hall.

'Not a sausage.'

He started knotting the corners together in an unskilled double 'granny' with three hitches, jerking tightly to make them fast and hoping they would stay so when the test came.

'What about the curfew?' Hall asked.

He said: '— the curfew!'

The knots took up a lot of length, and when he had finished the 'rope' was clearly not long enough.

'Here, take mine,' Hall said.

Gently he eased the sheet from under Hall and took off the top one. When he had added them the rope still did not look long enough.

'You'll be up the creek if you're left hanging,' Hall warned. 'Won't be able to climb back and won't be able to drop without bisecting yourself.'

Bader went over to the bed of the sergeant pilot, who was breathing stertorously under the ether. Gently working the sheet from under him, he said: 'This is frightful, but I've just got to.'

'He won't mind,' reassured Hall. 'I'll tell him when he wakes up.'

Soon he had fifteen sheets knotted together, littered around the room, and prayed that no one would come in. He pushed the sergeant pilot's bed to the window, wincing at the noise, knotted one end of the rope round the leg and stuffed the rest under the bed (it still looked pretty obvious). Then he straightened the white blankets on all the beds and climbed back into his own, sweating, heart thumping, praying that darkness would come before the guard.

Time dragged dreadfully while dusk slowly gathered in the room. He and Hall tried to talk in low tones, but his mind kept jumping away from the words. It was not quite dark when the door handle rattled, the door opened and a German soldier struck his head in and looked round. Bader could not breathe. The guard muttered '*Gut Nacht*,' and the door closed behind him.

Three hours to go. As long as no nurse came to see the sergeant pilot!

That evening Thelma, who had eaten nothing for three days, braced herself and asked Stan Turner: 'Well, what do you really think?'

Turner said with simple directness: 'You'll have to face it. We should have heard something by this. I guess he's had it.'

In London the Luftwaffe's radio message had arrived saying that a spare leg could be flown across in a Lysander communications aircraft. Spitfires could escort it part of the way and then Messerschmitts would take over. The Lysander could land at St Omer, hand over the leg and then it could take off again.

From Leigh-Mallory and Sholto Douglas the reaction was prompt, definite and identical. No free passage or German escort (with its lump of propaganda plum cake for Goebbels). They would send the spare leg in a Blenheim on a normal bombing raid.

Dundas, Johnny Johnson and Crowley-Milling had gone across to the Bay House to do what they could for Thelma. She sat quietly, a sphinx-like stoic, and only roused when the phone rang. It was Woodhall for her. The others could only hear her saying: Yes . . . yes . . . yes . . . yes, Woody.' She said 'Thank you very much, Woody,' hung up and came back to the room. In the silence she sat down and lit a cigarette, trembling a little. Then she blew out smoke and said quietly: 'D. B.'s a prisoner.' Shouts of jubilation filled the room but she hardly heard, feeling sick with astonishment and delight and with emotions ploughing over her.

Weary aeons of time seemed to have passed before a clock somewhere in the darkness of St Omer chimed midnight. The night was breathlessly still. He eased on to the edge of the bed, vainly trying to stop the creaks, and strapped his legs on. Then his clothes. Praying that the guard was asleep in his chair, he took a step towards the window; the boards creaked and the right leg squeaked and thumped with a terrifying noise. Hall started coughing to cover it up as, unable to tiptoe, he stumbled blindly across the floor. One or the other was bound to wake the guard. At the window he quietly pushed it open and leaned out, but the night was coal black and he could not see the ground. Picking up the sheet rope, he lowered it out, hoping desperately that it was long enough, but could not tell if it reached the ground. It must have roused the sergeant pilot: coming out of the twilight of ether, the boy was groaning.

Hall whispered: 'We'll have a nurse here in a moment.'

Holding the rope, Bader leaned his chest on the window-sill and tried to winkle his legs out sideways. They seemed fantastically clumsy, more than ever before, huge, disjointed and swollen. Uncontrollable. Sweating, he took a hand off the rope to grab his right shin and bend the knee. Then somehow he was through, legs dangling, hands clutching the rope on the sill. The terrible pain pierced his ribs again, making him gasp.

Hall whispered: 'Good luck!' It sounded like a pistol shot.

He hissed: 'Shut up.' And then, 'Thanks.' Then he started easing himself down.

It was simple. The legs rasping against the wall were useless, but the arms that had developed such muscles since the long-ago crash at Reading took his weight easily. He lowered himself, hand under hand, under sure control. Holding the sheets was no trouble and the knots were holding – so far. In a few seconds he came to a window and knew it was the room where he had drunk champagne with the Luftwaffe. He was horrified to feel that it was open, but inside it was dark and he eased his rump on to the ledge for a breather, hoping the doctor was not sleeping inside. Sitting there, breathing quietly, he looked down but still could not see the ground or whether the rope reached it. (Only later he realised he should have counted the knots.) Too late to go back now; he eased himself off the ledge and went on down.

Very gently his feet touched the flagstones and he was standing, dimly seeing that yards of sheet seemed to be lying on the ground.

'Piece of cake,' he thought, and moved a couple of yards on to the grass, cursing the noise from his legs. Warily he steered across the grass towards where the gates should be, having no plan, only hoping the mysterious Frenchman would be there.

Something loomed darker even than the night. The gates! Good show. Then a shock – they were closed. He got his fingers in a crack between and one gate opened easily a foot. He squeezed through on to the cobbled *pavé* of the road and instantly, immediately opposite, saw the glowing end of a cigarette. He stumped diagonally across the road and the cigarette moved, converging on him. It came to his side with a dark shadow behind it that whispered urgently 'Dooglass!' in a strong French accent.

'*Oui*,' he said, and the shape took his right arm and they moved off along the *pavé*. The town was like a tomb in which his legs were making an unholy clatter, echoing into the darkness. He could not see, but the silent shape seemed to know by instinct. A pressure on the arm and they turned right and stumbled on.

The Frenchman began muttering to him: '*C'est bon. C'est magnifique. Ah, les sales Boches.*'

After a while Bader thought how funny it was, walking through the curfew in enemy-occupied St Omer arm-in-arm with a stranger he would not even recognise by day. He began to giggle. The Frenchman said 'Ssh! Ssh!' but that only made him giggle more. He tried to stop but couldn't, and the more he tried the more he giggled as the strained nerves took control. The Frenchman started to giggle and then it was so grotesque, the two of them giggling and clattering down the street, that it grew into loud laughter mingled with the terror inside him that the Germans would hear. Slowly the pent-up emotion washed away and the laughter subsided into suppressed sniggers that he was at last able to stop.

They walked on – and on – and on. Five minutes, ten – twenty. His right stump without the stump-sock began to chafe. Thirty minutes . . . it was sore and starting to hurt. On and on they walked. He was limping badly and the Frenchman made soothing noises that sounded in inflection like 'Not far now' in French. Forty minutes must have passed. The steel leg had rubbed the skin off his groin and every step was searing agony. Stumbling and exhausted, he had both arms hanging on to the Frenchman's shoulders. At last the man took his arms round his neck, picked him up, dangling on his back, and staggered along. In a hundred yards or so he stopped and put him down, breathing in a rasping way. Bader leaned against a stone wall and the man pushed open a gate in the wall beside him.

He led the way and Bader stumbled after him up a garden path. A doorway showed ahead, framing soft light, and then he was in a little, low-ceilinged room with flowered wallpaper, and a tin oil-lamp on the table. An old man and a woman in a black shawl got up from the chairs and the woman put her arms round him and kissed him. She was over sixty, Madame Hiècque, plump and with a lined, patient face. Her husband, spare and stooping, brushed his cheeks with a wisp of grey moustache. Fleetingly he saw his guide, remembering mostly the lamp-light sheen on the glossy peak of a cap drawn low over the face and the glint of smiling teeth. The young man shook his hand and was off out the door.

The old woman said gently: *'Vous êtes fatigué?'*

Holding on to the table, he said *'Oui'* and she led him with a candle up some cottage stairs into a room with a huge double bed. He flopped on it. She put the candle on the table, smiled and went out. He unstrapped his legs with enormous relief, stripped to his underclothes and slid under the bedclothes into a gloriously soft feather bed, thinking: 'That's foxed the bloody Huns. I'll be seeing Thelma in a couple of days.' Then he was asleep.

A hand on his shoulder woke him about 7 am. The old man was looking down, smiling with tobacco-stained teeth. He left a razor, hot water and towel. Bader freshened up and examined his stump, which was raw and bloodstained, terribly sore. No help for it. Just have to bear the pain. Done it before. He strapped his legs on and went wincingly downstairs. Madame had coffee and bread and jam waiting, and while he ate she planted an old straw hat squarely on her head and went out. Bader sat for a couple of hours in a red plush chair trying to talk to the old man, a stilted, fumbling conversaion of invincible goodwill.

Madame came back in great glee. *'Les Boches,'* it seemed, *'sont très stupides.'* He gathered she had walked to the hospital and stood watching mobs of Germans running around searching the area. Great joke! In halting French he tried to make her understand that his presence was very dangerous to them. If they found him he, himself, would only be put in cells and then sent to prison camp, but the Hiècques were liable to be shot. He should leave them and hide somewhere.

Madame said, *'Non, non, non, non ...'* The Germans would never find him here. That evening her son-in-law, who spoke English, would come and they would discuss things and get him to the Underground. She examined his right stump and produced a pair of long woollen underpants. Cutting one of the legs off, she sewed up the end and there was a perfectly good stump-sock. After she powdered the stump he put the sock on under the leg and felt much better.

At noon the familiar drone came overhead and they took him out into the shelter of the walled back garden. Yearningly he watched the tangled con-trails and saw tiny glints as twisting aircraft caught the sun. Out from the windows of houses all round leaned the women waving mops and towels, and shrilling: *'Vive les Tommies. Vive les Tommies.'* It was moving and delightful. Soon he'd be back up there among the con-trails, thinking differently about the sweeps, knowing what they meant.

At 15,000 feet, just south of St Omer, the Tangmere wing jockeyed round the Blenheim. Crowley-Milling, close escort, saw the bomb-bays open and the long thin box with the spare leg drop out. It looked like a little coffin. A parachute blossomed above it and it floated down, swaying gently, surrounded by the black stains of flak-bursts from the puzzled gunners far below.

The quiet, loyal and gallant Stokoe had asked to be dropped by parachute with it to look after the wing commander in prison, but permission had been refused. He had to content himself in helping Thelma stuff the leg with stump-socks, powder, tobacco and chocolate.

Madame gave Bader cold pork for lunch and went out again to the scene of the crime. She came back hugging herself with delight. Convinced that Bader could not walk far, the Germans had cordoned off an area round the hospital and were running about like ants, searching every house. But nowhere in this area.

He felt like twiddling his thumbs as the afternoon dragged. Madame went out again to see the fun. Sitting in shirt-sleeves in the plush chair, he thought: Roll on that English-speaking chap. About half-past five there came a sudden terrifying banging on the front door and a chill swept him. The old man jumped as though he had been shot, peered furtively through the curtain, turned and whispered 'Les Boches!'

He grabbed Bader's arm and led him towards the back door. Only at the last moment Douglas thought to grab his battledress jacket. Together they stumbled into the garden, moving as fast as the legs would let him. Three yards from the back door, against a wall, stood a rough shed, galvanised iron nailed on posts, covering some baskets, garden tools and straw. The old man pulled the baskets and straw away, laid him on his stomach, cheek pillowed on his hands, against the corner of the wall and piled the straw and baskets on top. Lying there, he heard the old man's footsteps hurrying inside.

There was not long to wait. Within a minute he heard voices and then tramping feet by the back door. He knew the sound of jackboots. A vague kind of twilight filtered through the straw but he could not see anything. The boots clumped along the paved path to the shed. He heard baskets being kicked about. The straw over him started moving with a loud rustle. He lay still, thinking, 'Here we go!'

Miraculously the footsteps retreated, diminishing down the garden path. Elation filled him.

The boots were coming back up the path. Suddenly they clumped again into the shed, then stopped and rasped about a yard from his head. From his heart outwards ice seemed to freeze his nerves.

The baskets were being thrown around, the boots rasped on the paving, and then there was a metallic clang that mystified him. There was a movement in the hay just above and another clang. His eyes, turned sideways, saw a bayonet flash down an inch from his nose and stab through the wrist of his battledress jacket to hit the stone floor. He knew

what the clang was and guessed that the next stroke would go into his
neck or back.

CHAPTER TWENTY-FOUR

It was a lightning decision. He jerked up on his hands, heaving out of
the hay like a monster rising from the sea, straw cascading off his back.
A young German soldier, bayonet poised for the next jab, leapt back in
shock and stared pop-eyed at him, holding rifle and bayonet on guard.
He started yelling hoarsely in German. Boots pounded and three German
soldiers clattered under the iron roof, all armed. They stood round him
in a semi-circle, bayonet tips poised about four feet from him. Slowly he
raised his hands.

A little Stabsfeldwebel (staff sergeant) with a dark, thin moustache
ran up and covered him with a pistol as he stood there feeling like King
Lear, or perhaps an escaped lunatic at bay, with straw in his hair and
all over his battledress.

Looking pleased and quite friendly, the Stabsfeldwebel said in perfect,
unaccented English: 'Ah, Wing Commander, so we have caught you
again.'

'Yes,' said Bader. 'Would you mind asking these soldiers to put their
rifles down. As you can see, I'm unarmed.'

The Stabsfeldwebel rattled off some German, and the soldiers lowered
the rifles.

Still with his hands up, Bader said. 'You speak English very well.'

'Thank you, Wing Commander,' replied the German. 'I lived at
Streatham[1] for eleven years.'

'Did you really,' Bader said. 'I used to live near Croydon myself.'

(It struck him that the conversation was unreal.)

'Ah, I know Croydon well,' the German answered. 'Did you ever go
to the Davis Cinema?'

'Yes. And I used to go to the Locarno at Streatham.'

'Did you?' said the German. 'Many Saturday evenings I have danced
there.'

Bader never forgot a word of that dialogue. The German courteously
invited him to follow, and he stumped out of the shed into the back door
again feeling that the world might well be rid of politicians and that this

[1] London suburb.

was a perfect example of the fact that ordinary people never caused wars. He felt no rancour towards the soldiers who had winkled him out, and as far as he could see they felt no rancour for him. He was thinking it made Hitler and Mussolini look 'pretty bloody stupid' when he saw the old man and woman standing in the room. They looked pale and he stiffly walked past, showing no sign of recognition.

At the front door he nodded his head back and said to the Stabsfeldwebel: 'Those people did not know I was in their garden. I came in last night through that gate in the wall.'

Quite pleasantly the German replied: 'Yes, I understand that.'

By the kerb stood the Germans' car, and as they led him to it the rear door opened and a blonde girl with glasses got out. Rather surprised, he recognised Hélène, from the hospital, and said automatically: 'Hallo, Hélène,' but she walked past him with her eyes down.

They drove him to Headquarters in St Omer, where a German officer questioned him and got no answers. Then into a room where he was surprised and delighted to see the box containing his spare right leg. They explained, smiling, that it had been dropped that afternoon, and took his photograph standing by it. Then, to his annoyance, they refused to give it to him and prodded him instead into an upstairs room. There, for the first time, they really infuriated him; as he sat on a cot an officer and a soldier stood over him with a pistol and a bayonet, and made him take his trousers down and unstrap his legs: then they took the legs away.

He snarled at them, but the officer said stiffly it was orders from above. Two guards stayed and the rest went out, leaving him on the bed helpless, humiliated and seething. All night two men in full battle order, coalscuttle helmets and loaded rifles stood over him. It was hot and he asked for the windows to be opened, but the officer came back and refused, saying that 'orders from above' forbade that too. They were taking no chances!

He lay awake all night as the guards coughed and muttered ceaselessly. It was then he realised that Hélène had betrayed him and that the Germans must know about Madame and the old man, and he grew sick with worrying about what the Germans would do to them and to Lucille. Somehow he could not feel much resentment about Hélène. He supposed they had threatened her.

In Fighter Command Headquarters in England next morning the telephone rang in the office of Sholto Douglas. He picked it up and recognised the voice of Winston Churchill saying: 'Douglas!'

'Yes, sir.'

'I see from the newspapers you've been fraternising with the enemy, dropping a leg to a captured pilot.'

'Well, sir,' Sholto Douglas said, 'you may call it fraternising, but we

managed to shoot down eleven of the enemy for the loss of six or seven of our own, so I hope you might feel it was worth it.'
There was a grunt, and then a click as the phone was hung up.

In St Omer two guards were carrying Bader downstairs to an ambulance on a cradle of their hands, his arms unlovingly round their shoulders. Another carried his legs wrapped in a blanket. He gathered as the ambulance jolted along that they were going to Brussels for a train to Germany. It was the most depressing journey he had ever known, bouncing over the rutted roads and jostled against the wordless Germans while low cloud and pouring rain swept Northern France. He worried about the Hiècques and Lucille and wondered why the Germans looked so square-headed and stupid.
At last Brussels. An officer strutted in front, the two guards carried him and a third brought up the rear with the legs. People turned and stared as they bore him across a square into the railway station. Past embarrassment and humiliation now, he was seething with fury.
Thank God the carriage seats were soft. Sourly he watched the officer put his legs up on the rack. The train jolted off and clicketty-clicked through the rain. Once or twice the officer spoke to him, but in an evil mood he declined to answer. They passed Liège and then, without ceremony, were in Germany. He knew the first gesture he wanted to make. Hoping to get his legs back, he said he wanted to go to the lavatory. No legs! A guard carried him dangling helpless and angry round his neck, and sat him on the seat, then held the doorway open and covered him with a cocked pistol.
Bader snarled at him: 'You stupid clot, how the hell d'you think I can get out of here?'
Guessing his meaning, the guard said woodenly: *'Befehl ist Befehl!'*[1]
That did it! It capped the humiliation, the stupidity, the bombing and killing, the whole misery of the war, and from that moment he loathed the Germans implacably.

High over St Omer four 109s cut Crowley-Milling out of the wing and he roared and twisted all over the sky, no sooner shaking one off his tail than another was on him like a leech. A cannon-slug crashed through the side of his cockpit, sheared through glycol pipes and exploded in the supercharger. White smoke belched round him and the engine started shaking the little fighter like a grinding mill. The radiator needle spun on the clock, and a minute later the engine seized with a last violent spasm. He spun her on her back and pulled the nose straight down. Soon he crashlanded in a cornfield and was trying to set her alight when he

[1] 'Orders are Orders.'

saw Germans running for him half a mile away. Crawling off into the high corn, he tore off his flying overalls and jacket, muddied himself all over and walked south, hiding behind a dung-heap when German lorries went past. That afternoon he walked twenty miles, and at dusk knocked on a farmhouse door. They gave him eggs and a bed, and in the morning the farmer led him away on bicycles. In a couple of days he was hiding in St Omer in the house of a shoemaker called Ditry, who was a leader of the growing Underground.

Ditry told him that Bader was being held in a local hospital and explained his audacious scheme to rescue him; an ambulance with two Frenchmen in Luftwaffe uniforms and a forged authority would drive to the hospital, the disguised Frenchmen would take a stretcher upstairs, put Bader on it and spirit him away. Then they would radio England and hope a Lysander would fly in at night-time to a secret field and take him back home. If caught it would probably mean a firing squad. Would Crowley-Milling like to set off 'underground' to Spain, or stay and help? In his polite, shy way, Crowley-Milling said he would like to stay and help.

Next day word came that the Germans had already taken Bader to Germany, and a fortnight later Crowley-Milling was making the arduous trek over the Pyrenees. There Franco's men caught him and put him in the notorious Miranda Concentration Camp, where he nearly starved to death, then caught typhoid and went blind. Later his sight came back and he was evacuated to England, where he fought on for the rest of the war.

They came to Frankfurt at midnight and carried Bader to a car, which drove for half an hour through a crisp, clear night to Dulag Luft, the reception and interrogation centre for all Air Force prisoners. Two Luftwaffe men carried him into a stone building, down a corridor and dumped him on a wooden bunk in a little cell, stripped his battledress off and locked him in darkness and underclothes.

Tired, he slept well. About eight o'clock in the morning a dapper little man in a grey civilian suit came in, saying brightly: 'Good-morning.' Sonderfuehrer Eberhardt spoke perfect English and was too friendly. He handed Bader a form to fill in, the usual fake form with the red cross at the top that the Germans always used. Bader looked down the headings:

'What base did you fly from?'
'No. of squadron?'
'What type of aeroplane?' and so on.

He scrawled his name, rank and number on it and handed it back.

'If you will fill in the rest,' Eberhardt suggested winningly, 'it will help the Red Cross inform your relatives and forward your letters. Just a formality, you know.'

'That's all you're getting,' Bader said. 'I'm not half-witted. Now if you don't mind, I'd like a bath, a shave and my legs. Then I'd like some breakfast.'

Eberhardt went out, saying he would call the Kommandant.

A tall, slim, good-looking man of about forty-five came in and said smoothly: 'Oh, good-morning, Wing Commander. I am the Kommandant. My name is Rumpel.' He spread his hands sympathetically. 'For you the war is over but we'll try and make you as comfortable as we can. I was a fighter pilot myself in the last war and we Germans want to try and keep alive the last war traditions of comradeship among pilots.'

Bader answered shortly: 'I don't know what you mean. We're enemies and that can't be overlooked.'

'Well, we'll try anyhow,' Rumpel said. 'We're amused at your call sign. It's Dogsbody, isn't it?'

'If you know, why the hell ask me?'

Rumpel probed urbanely on, asking questions about aircraft. 'Of course we know you're having a lot of trouble with the Rolls Royce Vulture engine, aren't you?'

'If you know,' Bader repeated, 'why the hell ask me?'

'We didn't want to fight this war,' Rumpel went on earnestly, 'but the Poles were determined to have Berlin, so we had to deal with them.'

'Eighty million Germans scared of thirty million Poles,' Bader growled acidly. 'Why did you attack Belgium and Holland then?'

'What do these small countries matter?' Rumpel was bland. Bader, amazed, felt he was quite sincere.

'Why did you attack Russia then?' he demanded.

Rumpel spread his hands again. 'We had to have the oil.' He went on persuasively: 'What makes us so sorry ... it seems such a shame ... but we Germans and British never seem to fight on the same side. ... Of course we know you call us Jerries, but ...'

'No, we don't,' Bader snapped. 'We call you Huns!'

The charm fled from Rumpel and he shot up, face cold and rigid, and stalked out.

Bader yelled after him: 'Send me my legs and some tea, damn you.'

He was surprised a few minutes later when a Luftwaffe orderly came in carrying his legs (including the new one, he was delighted to see), some soap and a towel, and took him along to the bathroom. When he got back to his cell he found a tray of English tea with milk and sugar, and some bread, butter and jam.

Usually one did a week or so 'solitary' in a cell being softened up for questioning by mildly unnerving means before going to the adjacent barbed-wire transit cage to await 'purging' to a permanent prison camp. Rumpel must have decided Bader was an improbable prospect because an hour after breakfast they took him out of the cell and thrust him into the cage.

The cage was not inspiring: three drab wooden barrack huts on a patch of trodden earth eighty yards square, fenced by double thickets of barbed wire eight feet high and buttressed at each corner by stilt-legged sentry boxes leaning over the wire with watchful eyes, searchlights and machine-guns. The sight of the gates closing him in that dismal patch was mellowed by the welcome from a few score grounded exiles of his own kind who clustered warmly round, making him feel, if not at home, at least among 'chums.' From the Red Cross store they gave him a toothbrush, razor and some rough aircraftsman's clothes. Then quite a good meal – the cage had plenty of Red Cross parcels.

A big, wavy-haired Fleet Air Arm lieutenant called David Lubbock took him to his room, a wooden box with a dusty floor and double-decker bunks round the walls, each with paper palliasse stuffed with wood shavings and two grey blankets. There he found Pete Gardner, a dark young fighter pilot with eighteen victories, and other kindred spirits, and they gossiped, swapping stories for some time. He felt much better and with a sudden thought asked if they knew of Harry Day, who was a prisoner somewhere.

'Do we not,' said Gardner. 'He was here till a few days ago, but he was naughty and escaped through a tunnel with seventeen others.'

Apparently they had all been caught and sent to a permanent camp somewhere else.

At the mention of escape, Bader was practically on fire, leaning forward with his eyes intense and glowing, wanting to know all about it. Quite a short tunnel, Lubbock said, because the huts were near the wire. They burrowed from under a bed, and the night they went everyone else kicked up a racket to cover the noise.

'If they could do it,' Bader demanded, 'why can't we?'

Lubbock had apparently been thinking the same thing. Pete Gardner, shot down a couple of months ago, four days before his planned wedding, was almost hopping to get home. So were the others in the room.

A day or so later they started carving a hole in the floor under a bunk in an end room of the middle hut, and soon they were burrowing into the dark earth under the hut. With his legs, Bader was no good for the digging: he acted as stooge, watching for Germans outside the window while the others gouged out the dirt and lugged it up in a basin to hide under the hut floor. Like all tunnels, it went slowly, and he bubbled with impatience, obsessed with the idea of getting out and unable to think of other things. His ideas, once he had got out, were sketchy, typical of a new escaper. As usual, he refused to regard his legs as any inevitable barrier. The thing was, get out first and then, he thought vaguely, make for Switzerland ... pinch a car, stow away on a barge or jump a train or something. The goal was infinitely alluring: he'd be back leading his wing, knowing what went on below in France, hitting back at the Germans instead of being humiliated by them. His mere getting back, a legless man, would mock the Germans in the eyes of the world. And perhaps (subconsciously) this unparalleled example would quell the entrenched demon[1] that said he had no legs and helped to drive him on?

Day by day, foot by foot, the tunnel lengthened. After a fortnight, when they thought they were nearly under the wire, Eberhardt came one day into the cage and sought Bader.

'Herr Wing Commander,' he said, 'you must be ready to leave to-morrow morning. You are being taken to Brussels to appear before a court-martial.'

Bader stared at him, astounded, and demanded: 'What the hell am I being court-martialled for?'

'I do not know,' Eberhardt shrugged, 'but you must go.'

Outraged equally by the court-martial and the thought of missing the tunnel, he told the others, but rapidly cooled off when one of them, the Irish Paddy Byrne, gave him a bit of paper with a name and a Brussels address on it.

'Wonderful chance to crack off,' said the crafty Byrne. 'If you can duck the guards and get to these people, they'll hide you and pass you on to the escape chain.'

Gratified, Bader looked forward eagerly to Brussels.

This time in the train they let him keep his legs, but a blond young Sonderfuehrer and two helmeted soldiers never left his side.

In Brussels, towards dark, they put him in a car and drove him through the streets – he hoped towards a ground-floor room in a lonely house. The car turned through a dirty stone arch and soon they were standing in a cold stone hall. Through a heavy barred grille, passages led gloomily away. A gaol!

He said angrily: 'This is a civilian gaol. I'm not staying here.'

'Oh, but you must, Wing Commander,' said the Sonderfuehrer.

'But I damn' well won't.' He was outraged again.

'Oh, please, please. You *must*, Wing Commander, because it would be very embarrassing to me. You must please stay here.' The Sonder-fuehrer looked perturbed.

'I won't. I'm an officer prisoner of war and you can't put me in a criminal prison.' Feeling he was beginning to learn how to handle the Germans, he shouted: 'I demand to see the general in charge of this district.'

On the defensive, the Sonderfuehrer said uncertainly: 'I do not think he is at home.'

---

[1] Not so, I fear. The demon is part of Bader, as indestructible as the rest of him.

It sounded so fatuous that Bader nearly gave the game away by laughing.

'Well, go and get the clot,' he said.

Despairingly, the Sonderfuehrer turned and talked to the stolid Army Feldwebel who seemed to be the gaol reception clerk. He turned back to Bader. 'The Feldwebel says that perhaps if we could take you along and show you your room you might be willing to stay.'

There was not much option really. Sooner or later they would force him, which would be humiliating, and perhaps they would take his legs too. Having had his fun and won some pride back, he grunted: 'All right. I'll come and have a look.'

Stumping at a leisurely pace, he went with them through the barred gate and along the passage, passing cell doors with little peep-holes in them. At one they stopped and pulled the door open. He looked into a tiny white-washed cell so narrow you could touch both walls by putting your arms out. A narrow bed nearly filled one side, and high up was a little barred window.

He snorted: 'I'm damned if I'm going in there!'

'Oh, but *please*, Wing Commander,' begged the Sonderfuehrer. 'You will find it quite comfortable and we will look after you.'

'No!'

'But you *must*. I will be shot if you escape.' He was genuinely distressed and frightened.

Bader eyed him amiably. 'Will you really?'

'We will give you a servant here.' Now he was perspiring.

'What else?'

'We will leave the door open.'

(That didn't mean much – the iron door at the end of the corridor would still be firmly locked.)

'I want a table, too. With a cloth. And some tea.'

'Yes, Wing Commander. Now will you please go in.'

'No. Bring me the servant and table first.'

The Feldwebel went off and after a while came back with a little man in a white coat who carried a small table. Good show, a Belgian, Bader thought.

He stalked into the cell and the servant followed and put down the table. They left the door open and retreated, boots ringing on the stone floor down the corridor.

Alone at last, he moved quickly and shoved the table under the high window, then grabbed the stool, planted it on the table and climbed up till he was standing precariously on the stool. Hands clutching the bars, he tried to pull himself up the extra few inches to see out: he got his eyes up to the bars but the thick wall stuck out beyond the bars and he could not quite see the ground that he was sure was just below. Using all the strength in his thick hands and wrists, he began shaking the bars violently, trying to loosen them.

A respectful cough sounded behind, and he swung and saw the servant standing looking impassively up.

'Vous êtes Belge?' Bader asked eagerly.

'Nein,' said the little man, unwinking. 'Ich bin Deutsch.'[1]

Deflated and with a foolish grin, Bader started climbing down. Impassively the servant helped him, removed the stool, put a tray of tea on the table, nodded a deferential head and glided out on rubber-soled shoes.

After that he found the bed as hard as a plank (which it was), and the night long and sleepless, giving time for discontent.

(Stung by humiliations and the frustration of captivity, Bader was now an unappeasable *enfant terrible*. Until he escaped, that was pride's only defence. Already with Rumpel and the timid Sonderfuehrer he had recaptured some *amour-propre* in scenes that were barely believable, but authentic. One might suppose that the Germans had made allowances and that had he possessed his own legs their tolerance would have frozen. Yet even with his legs, Bader would probably have behaved in much the same way because the demon was spurring him well before the Reading crash. And one doubts whether the Germans themselves would have reacted more firmly, because his pulverising dynamism turned on full flood will daunt any civilised man. The Germans who bowed to rank and force were vulnerable targets ... to a point, of course. But Bader's bull-like thrusts carry sensitive antennae that feel precisely when the goad pricks too deep. Then, tactics somersaulting, he soothes the wound with disarming charm that baffles vengeance. With him it is no good pretending to be ruffled because he infallibly recognises a weak defence and is spurred to crisper aggression. Only when the goad is about to prick the nerve intolerably into frenzy is it suddenly withdrawn.)

About ten in the morning the Sonderfuehrer and guards drove him to a large house and led him into a big room. This was it! At one end was a long table and sitting behind it six solemn officers. Three of them looked like generals (they were). He was not especially perturbed, insulated perhaps by the illogical English arrogance, bred by orderly decades of eminence, which assumed privileges and immunity from illegal international violence.[2]

Sitting on chairs at the other end he noticed the doctor and some soldiers and nurses from the St. Omer hospital. He grinned at them and said a cheerful 'Hallo,' but they only eyed him sourly. A young Luftwaffe

[1] German.
[2] I once saw a noble lord (who snored abominably) throw his Italian captors into uncertain dismay by *demanding* marmalade for breakfast. He was of the Guards and not sensitive to atmosphere.

officer motioned him to a lonely chair in front of the table, saying: 'Will you please sit down?'

'No, I won't,' he answered, conscious that if the officer had told him to stand up he would promptly have sat down.

The judges leaned towards each other and muttered among themselves. A bald, hatchet-faced general in the middle spoke to the Luftwaffe officer who acted as interpreter, and the officer turned to Bader: 'Will you swear to tell the truth?'

'No,' he answered. 'Certainly not.'

The officer looked as though he had not heard properly. 'I beg your pardon,' he said.

'I said certainly not. Go on. Tell the Court.'

The officer turned nervously and spoke to the judges, and the bald general's eyebrows shot up.

The officer turned back. 'The Herr General wishes to know why you will not tell the truth.'

Bader said: 'Well, if you're going to ask me questions about the French I will obviously lie.'

Another muttered conference. The interpreter seemed to have trouble translating the replies politely. He turned again to Bader. 'The Herr General says that the French have already been punished.'

('God,' he thought. 'What have they done to them!')

'What the Herr General wishes to know is whether you think the hospital staff were careless when you escaped?'

It suddenly dawned on Bader that it was not he who was being court-martialled. He said: 'Look, who is being court-martialled here?'

The interpreter looked surprised. 'Why, the hospital staff, of course.'

After that it was easy. He turned on the charm and explained that it was not reasonable to punish the hospital chaps because, of course, they couldn't guess he was going to climb out of the window. They had been very correct, posted a guard at his door and taken all proper precautions in the circumstances. Of course, it was easy to be wise after the event.

He felt he could almost hear the roars of applause from behind.

When he had finished and the Sonderfuehrer took him out, the hospital staff beamed at him. Thereafter the guards never left his side and there was no chance of bolting.

Back at Dulag, the first thing he asked was: 'How's the tunnel getting on?'

Lubbock said it was plodding along quite nicely.

Hands in pockets, Bader was idly leaning in a doorway three days later when a Luftwaffe captain called Muller passed. Bader kept his hands in his pockets and his pipe in his mouth. Muller stopped, turned and said: 'Ving Commander Bader, you should salute me.'

'Why?'

'All prisoners of war should salute German officers.'

Bader said shortly: 'The Geneva Convention says I have to salute enemy officers of equal or senior rank. You're only a captain.'

'I am the Kommandant's representative and you should salute me.'

'I don't salute the Kommandant either,' Bader remarked disagreeably. 'He's only a major.'

'Those are the Kommandant's orders!' (angrily).

'I don't give a damn if they are. They're wrong and I'm damned if I'm going to salute you.'

Half an hour later an orderly came in and told him to be ready to leave Dulag Luft in twenty minutes.

CHAPTER TWENTY-FIVE

For two days he sat glowering on the hard boards of a third-class train that travelled through endless drizzle to Lübeck. Off-loading him there into a farm wagon they trundled him across bleak sandy flats to the lonely, barbed wire compound of Oflag VIB, where they took his finger-prints, watch and signet ring (the last thing he had from his father) and turned him loose among some 400 thin and half-starved British officers behind the wire.

There the real misery started. Lübeck camp received no Red Cross parcels and was ruled by a gaunt, cropped Kommandant who had already achieved fame by saying that the Geneva Convention for the protection of prisoners of war had been drawn up by a lot of old women and he had no intention of observing it.

A few of the inmates were RAF (most were Army), but he knew none of them. The huts were much the same as the ramshackle wooden affairs at Dulag Luft and there seemed nothing to do except talk and think about when the next meal was coming, though that gave little satisfaction when it did arrive. An entire day's food consisted of three slices of black bread with a scrape of margarine, a couple of potatoes and some soup. Now and then there was *Blutwurst* (blood sausage). There were supposed to be other rations but the guards stole them.

One of the guards shot a prisoner in the thigh for picking up a ball over the warning wire[1] and a Feldwebel rushed up to the guard and shook his hand. It was that kind of camp.

Two days after Bader arrived there Lubbock and Pete Gardner walked dolorously in.

'What the hell happened to the tunnel?' Bader demanded.

They looked disgusted and said that just after he had left, a posse of guards had trooped into the cage, gone straight to the trap-door under the bed and wrecked everything with patronising smiles. They even knew who the tunnelers were – hence their arrival.

In the next dreary month Bader adjusted to the new life. Surrendering no fraction of his passion to renew the Tangmere days he wasted little time in crying over spilt milk. As years before he had accepted the loss of his legs so he accepted now the loss of freedom, heartened by the thought this time that there was hope of a cure – escape. He talked about it a lot with men who had been a year or more behind the wire, absorbing what lore they had gathered on the subject and learning that getting out was only half the battle. The other half lay in getting beyond the reach of Germans, and that was the harder half.

Early in October the Germans bundled the whole camp into cattle trucks for transport to a new cage at Warburg, near Cassel, where they were concentrating all British officer prisoners. People were as excited as schoolboys going on holiday. It lifted the tedium and gave hope of better conditions. Also, there were ways of bolting from locked cattle-trucks; that is, ways for the nimble, not for the legless. During the night some of the Air Force officers sawed a hole in the floor of a truck with a jagged knife and during a brief halt several dropped out of it and ran into the darkness. Bader envied them until one man misjudged as the train started and it ran over him, cutting off both legs. He died soon after.

Warburg was a huge cage a quarter of a mile square holding 3,000 men in thirty of the same huts in the same dirt and squalor. But Warburg had Red Cross parcels, enough to give each man a good meal a day as well as the German food, plus chocolate and cigarettes. Print can hardly convey the effect of having real food every day: it killed something that gnawed at the mind as well as the stomach. The compound had a clear patch too where men played rugger and Bader found now that it no longer hurt to watch, unable to play. Unobtrusively the years had softened that blow and he was an eager and vocally critical spectator.

But confinement was a growing ordeal. Others could let off steam tunnelling for escape, by playing rugger or by horseplay or walking mile after mile round the beaten circuit just inside the warning wire. Not

---

[1] Ten yards inside the barbed wire ran the single strand of the warning wire. The No Man's Land in between was 'streng verboten.'

Bader. The stumps had not taken kindly to captivity, having shrunken a little with hunger. They chafed more easily and there was little powder and no Elastoplast. There was no outlet for his brimming vigour. A lot of the time he spent on his bunk with a book in the tiny end room like a cubicle he shared with Lubbock and Gardner, who helped him with his chores.

At last a letter from Thelma. (Mail was very delayed.) She did not say much about the wing, of course, except that he was still badly missed, but she had had a letter from Woodhall which said: 'I am delighted to be able to tell you that Douglas has been awarded a Bar to his DFC. As a matter of fact, the recommendation was in type the day he was posted as missing and so I had to hang on to it until I knew he was safe, and then it was forwarded and awarded.'[1]

(That made him the third man in history to win Bars to both DSO and DFC.)

A letter came too from the little Yorkshire boy, Norman Rowley. 'I am sorry that they take your legs away so that you cannot escape. My mum says she will do that to me, too, if I don't be good and come home at the proper time. I have got one leg now and am getting on all right like you said. One day soon I will get the other one. With love from Norman.'

Warburg had an escape committee headed by a tank major and Bader talked earnestly with them for hours on the subject of getting out, finding, a little grimly, that his legs barred him from most schemes. Unlike others he had little chance of walking out of the gates in disguise; his lurching roll was too familiar. He was game enough to try but not agile enough to succeed in other hare-brained ideas such as scaling ladders over the wires or stowing away, contorted, under a food wagon. Such chances had to go to those with more prospects of success. He could not tunnel, but he could at least crawl through one. The difficulty there was to find a tunnel that surfaced beyond the wire. His name was down for several. Eager syndicates were always digging them and at this time hawk-eyed Germans were always finding and wrecking them.

It was disillusioning, and even worse when the first snow fell and the escape committee had to bank the fires of their activities until next spring. No point wasting good ideas in getting out to be stranded in snow 500 miles from the nearest friendly frontier. One had to be able to sleep out. Bader found it getting harder to damp his unrest.

One outlet still remained— 'Goon-baiting.'[2] He found relief in the sport. With exuberance he tersely provoked all Germans except 'Gremlin

---

[1] Had Bader been killed when he was shot down the Bar to the DFC could not have been awarded. Only VCs. can be awarded posthumously.
[2] To prisoners, Germans were always 'Goons.' It was a satisfying name.

George' the Lageroffizier,[1] who had been a prisoner in the last war and was tolerant and sympathetic because he understood.

His chief butt was Hauptmann Harger, a large, red-faced, red-necked man known as 'Horrible Harger, the— of the Lager,' with whom he had violent brushes which culminated in a day when Bader refused to stand out in the snow for half an hour on *Appell*.[2] Harger found him in his room and angrily ordered him out and in a brief shouting match Bader flatly refused to budge, saying: 'My feet would get cold in the snow. If you want to count me, come to my room and do it.'

Harger shouted: 'You . . . vill . . . go . . . on . . . *Appell*,' drew his pistol and levelled it.

The antennae warned that the time had come and Bader suddenly turned on the glowing goodwill and beamed. 'Well, of *course* I'll go on *Appell* if you really want me to.' He picked up a stool and stumped off to plant it on the snow and sit among his squad, leaving Harger seething.

Bader had found a new game, and on more than one occasion after that he goaded his captors into drawing their pistols and then disarmed them by pricking the strained bladder of their ire with maddening charm and last-minute surrender. It was a crafty technique that left a taste of moral defeat in the man who lost his temper.

Gremlin George was distressed at seeing the legless man sitting in the snow on *Appell*. He said it was not correct or gentlemanly and it humiliated Germany. Thereafter he let Bader stay in his room for *Appell*, which induced the man from time to time to go out and join the others in the snow, where soon he provoked Harger into drawing his pistol again. It was the only way left of fighting back.

Around Christmas time Lubbock and Gardner came to him, and said: 'Look, we've got an idea for escape. Would you like to come with us?'

'What, in winter?'

'Yes. Why not?'

Bader said: 'I'm in.'

Lubbock explained the plot. Just outside the barbed-wire gate was a clothing store hut where occasionally prisoners were taken under guard to draw kit. Gardner, a born lock-breaker, had discovered how to open a spare room in the hut and the idea was for the three of them, together with a Commando captain, Keith Smith, to go on a clothing parade, lock themselves in the empty room till darkness, then climb out of the window, walk up a lighted road past some German huts (hoping no one came out) and then melt into the shadows beyond. Just down the road was Doessel railway station where they could catch a train down into occupied France and contact the Underground. Sounded easy, worked out like that. The

---

[1] Officer in charge of the compound.
[2] Roll call by count.

escape committee had promised them several hundred smuggled marks, maps, a compass and forged passes, and Lubbock (son-in-law of the nutrition expert Lord Boyd-Orr) would bake an escape cake from hoarded food that would keep them going for days.

Everyone said they were mad to try in winter but on January 9, when thin snow carpeted the frosty ground, they marched through the gate with a clothing parade to the hut. Someone started a loud-voiced diversion and under its cover Gardner picked the lock and the four crowded into the room.

Darkness fell early and the wait was long and cold. About eight o'clock they heard a tremendous clatter of tins by the wire, caused by an unruly young flight lieutenant, Peter Tunstall, giving the signal and creating another diversion. All the searchlights obligingly turned towards the noise and Gardner quietly opened the spare room window. Smith, a baldish six-footer, slipped out first and walked up the lighted path, followed by Lubbock and Bader and then Gardner.

Smith reached the shadows but the others were about fifteen yards short when a German soldier ran out of one of the huts in front of them, apparently on his way to the latrine. He looked with shocked surprise at the three walking in British greatcoats and started bellowing for help. Germans came pouring out of huts for yards around and the three were seized by a jabbering crowd. Smith had vanished.

They started hustling the three over to the guardroom, and one of Germans, not realising Bader had artificial legs, thumped him on the toe with a rifle butt to make him hurry. Bader started to laugh and the angry soldier banged harder and harder at his feet with his rifle until one of his comrades explained why it was painless and told him to stop making a fool of himself.

In the guardroom the Hauptmann security officer, a Party member, demanded to know how they had escaped, and Bader said flippantly that they had walked through the wire.

'Did you?' replied the Hauptmann, unamused. 'Well, now you can try walking through the bars because you are going into the cells.'

He went away to make arrangements and came back slightly flushed. Apparently the cells were already full and there was a waiting list. They would have to go back to the compound and await their turn.

Smith was back in five days, having nearly frozen to death in a cattle truck. He, too, had to wait for the cells.

It was about a month before the three were taken across to the wooden cooler[1] for their ten days' solitary. The cells were the usual things, about as wide as one's outstretched arms, but there were books and Red Cross food and prisoners of the rank of major and above were allowed to smoke

[1] Cell block.

(a not untypical German rule). About the seventh night, after the guard had locked up and gone, Bader was lying on his bunk reading when the door opened. He looked up and was startled to see the face of Gardner. 'Hallo,' Gardner grinned, holding up a piece of wire. 'I've found out how to open these damn' doors.'

Delighted, Bader got up and joined him in the corridor, and they unlocked Lubbock's cell. The three of them cautiously explored the place, but no Germans were about and only a couple of flimsy doors lay between them and freedom. Bader suggested they make a break for it then and there, but wiser voices prevailed. Snow still lay on the ground, thawing and slushy, and they had no food, maps, compass or money.

'I know,' said Bader, 'let's finish our time here and wait for the good weather. Then we can all kick that rat Harger in the tail and get sent back. We can smuggle some food and maps in and then make the break.'

Brilliant, they all thought. The 'Goons' would never expect an escape from the cooler and Harger's blood pressure would doubtless spray out of his ears. Cheerfully they went back to their cells.

Three days later they were released and immediately registered the scheme with the escape committee. The date was set for May.

And then, early in April, they got the chance of going out through a tunnel. It had been dug by Air Force men from a hut on the west side of the camp and was well over a hundred feet long. A week or two before, a digger had prodded a stick up at the end and watchers had seen it come up right under the barbed-wire fence. They had dug on a bit more and now with the weather mild everything seemed ready. One night thirty-five would-be escapers collected in the hut, Bader in a tunic roughly re-cut to look like a civilian jacket.

Lubbock said: 'You'll never get through, Douglas. There's a right-angled turn at the bottom of the shaft and it's very small.'

'Well, dammit,' he said, 'I'll take my legs off.'

'Good idea,' enthused Lubbock. 'I'll come after you with your legs.'

A Czech flight lieutenant crawled through to break out the far end and about 11 pm the tense watchers from the hut windows were appalled to see his head poke furtively out of the ground just outside the wire and almost in the middle of the sentry path. He bobbed back in alarm and for a while there was whispering confusion down in the tunnel. Then two other men poked their heads out, saw the sentries' backs were turned, nipped out and hared off into the darkness beyond the lights. Two more followed, then another one.

No more. The sentries were never walking away from each other again that night. Yet, strangely, they did not stumble across the hole until dawn and by that time the rest of the would-be escapers had sneaked back to their own huts.

So it had to be the cooler scheme.

They were getting ready for it when a dismaying kitchen rumour buzzed round the compound that some Air Force officers were being moved to a new camp, Stalag Luft III, at Sagan, between Berlin and Breslau. That evening Germans confirmed it and before anything could be done they were shepherding an enraged Bader and fifty others on to the train. This time they moved them in carriages, under observation, and no one escaped.

Stalag Luft III was a little cage of six huts for officers and another one next door for NCOs, all on barren grey Silesian sand, hedged from the world by spindly pine trees. The aspect did not charm. As they walked in, a lean, rangy figure walked up to Douglas with outstretched hand and the wry, twisted smile he so well remembered.

'Hallo, Douglas,' said Harry Day, more hawk-faced than ever, 'I thought you'd catch up some day.'

Behind him appeared Bob Tuck, still debonair in silk scarf.

Being among old chums helped soothe him a little. The Warburg contingent took over one of the huts and Day and the compound 'Big X,'[1] Jimmy Buckley, came over to talk escape.

Almost before people in the hut had unpacked they had started tunnelling under a stove in the room opposite Bader. Other ambitious tunnels were already under way in the compound, but it was slow work because six inches under the grey topsoil lay bright yellow sand which came up in bucket-loads and was a devil to hide from German eyes. Also, Stabsfeldwebel Glemnitz, the leathery-faced German ferret,[2] was a shrewd man who had microphones buried round the wire so that tunnels had to be about thirty feet deep.

There was nothing Bader could do in the tunnels; he could only 'stooge' outside as a sentry, feeling rather futile. Then Glemnitz found two of the tunnels, including the one in Bader's hut.

His early hopes of getting away were shrinking further, the glorious days of the past receding under the grey present and probable future. Even if he did get out he was beginning to realise how conspicuous he would look; they would only have to take his trousers down to see who he was. He began to get a stiflingly trapped feeling.

Inevitably it inflamed his 'Goon-baiting,' and his scores of admirers, notably the Warburg contingent, followed his example. When German squads strode past singing their marching songs he organised bands to whistle opposition tunes and put them out of step. When Germans found a tunnel and started filling it in he had prisoners gathered round singing 'Heigh-ho, heigh-ho, it's off to work we go.' When the Germans ordered

---

[1] Escape Committees were becoming known as the 'X Organisation' and the leaders were known as 'Big X.' It was for security, not for drama.

[2] Ferrets were the blue-overalled German security guards who ceaselessly snooped round the compounds with torches and probes (for locating tunnels).

all shutters closed at dusk he wanted the camp to tear them all off and throw them into the middle of the compound, and had a violent argument about this with Harry Day, who was in an awkward position. Day himself had a streak of the fiery rebel and would have loved to have torn the shutters off, but he also had the job of keeping the Germans reasonably placated so the prisoners could retain privileges to help escape work. He put a firm foot down about the shutters but there were arguments on both sides (mostly favouring Day).

Camp opinion divided; there were the turbulent rebels devoted to Bader who believed in riling the Germans at every chance and others, some who wanted only peace and some, the wise cool heads, who wanted a judicial amount of Goon-baiting mixed with enough tact and co-operation to ensure peace for escape work.

Bader still desperately wanted to escape. He went to the 'X Committee' with a scheme for a 'blitz' tunnel to be dug in a night by himself, Lubbock and Gardner from a trench near the warning wire.

'How are you going to get away after that?' someone asked.

'The other two can get on each side and help me into the woods,' Bader explained eagerly. 'Then we go across country.'

The Committee turned it down and Bader later growled to Day: 'They say I'm no good for that scheme. It's a lot of —s.'

He went on with the Goon-baiting, backed loyally by many others, and life was a series of uproars. Now and then a German got him chatting in his room and on those occasions Bader was perfectly charming, just to show that he felt no personal grudge. But his pride was touchy. One day he was talking quite pleasantly with his arms folded to the Kommandant, Oberst Von Lindeiner, when the mild Lageroffizier, Hauptmann Pieber, came up, and said 'Wing Commander, you should stand at attention when you speak to the Kommandant.'

Bader turned and snapped: 'When I want you to teach me manners, I'll ask you. Until then, shut up!'

Von Lindeiner was an erect, elderly soldier of the old school, very fair and correct, but, as the baiting campaign worsened, inevitably the reprisals started and the compound lost privileges such as staying outside the huts after dusk, keeping Red Cross tins and others. There was a chance that this might affect escape work, but Bader dogmatically stuck to his view that maximum non-co-operation and baiting were the best ways of exasperating the enemy.

Something had to happen.

Pieber came in one day with Glemnitz and found him by the wire.

'Herr Wing Commander, you are leaving the camp. You must be ready to go in the morning.'

'Oh, am I? Where am I going?' Bader demanded.

Pieber was vague. 'We are taking you somewhere you will be more comfortable – it is not comfortable here' – tartly – 'for anyone.'

Bader grunted. 'Well, I'd rather live in a pigsty with my friends than in a palace alone. I'm not going.'

'The Kommandant says you must go.'

'You take me to the Kommandant.'

'He will see you on the way out to-morrow.'

'No, he damn' well won't. Not unless he drags me out. I'm staying here.'

Glemnitz angrily snapped an order and a guard cocked his rifle and aimed at Bader's chest. Abruptly the atmosphere was electric as the word to fire trembled on the German's lips and Bader knew he had gone too far. This time he would not give way but glared, defiant and stubborn, feeling bitterly he didn't give a damn if they fired. The seconds dragged and then Pieber snapped the tension, telling the guard to lower his rifle. He added: 'We will see about this. You will go.' And stalked out.

That evening the camp buzzed with crisis. There seemed no easy way out. Bader said he was not going and if necessary would jump into the compound firepool, throw his legs out and defy the Germans to get him. Somehow the Germans heard and knew they would be ridiculed floundering about in a pool after a legless man. What could they do? Von Lindeiner was too humane to shoot him in cold blood. In any case, that would lose the Germans far more than dignity throughout the world. They were nonplussed by a man who should have been in a wheel-chair, but even as a disarmed prisoner was an unmanageable and implacable enemy. They even feared that a man of his type might lead a mass rush on the guards.

In the morning you could feel the tension. Hours passed. Nothing happened. Then, towards evening, a company of guards in battle-order marched out of the Kommandantur[1] towards the barbed wire, fifty-seven of them in helmets and webbing, with rifles and fixed bayonets. Striding with them was Von Lindeiner, accompanied by nearly all his officers. Prisoners came running up to mass behind the wire. The Germans crashed to a halt outside. Bader stayed in his room. The new SBO, Group Captain Massey, went to the gate and talked to the Kommandant while an ominous hush hung over the place.

---

[1] German administrative compound.

CHAPTER TWENTY-SIX

Massey went back to Bader. 'There's one thing we might consider,' he said. 'It only needs a spark to start an incident and someone may be shot.'

After that there was only one thing to do. The watchers by the wire saw the legless man come out of his room and stump down the dusty path between the huts. In silence he went up to the gate, passed through and looked around like a man about to call a taxi, then strolled along the ranks of the German squad. 'My God,' someone said behind the wire, 'he's inspecting the bastards.'[1]

Bader grinned at the squad and passed on. Von Lindeiner made an impatient gesture and followed with his officers. The tension burst like a bubble and suddenly there was something ludicrous about the sixty armed and armoured men who had come to quell a lone and legless man. A Feldwebel shouted an order. Fifty-six helmeted soldiers turned left and one fool in the front rank turned right. German faces crimsoned, a howl of laughter burst behind the wire and the squad tramped away tasting the ashes of ridicule.

They put Bader in a train and Glemnitz climbed into the compartment as escort. The prisoner turned on his charm and soon the two were chatting amiably.

He said after a while: 'Look here, you weren't really going to shoot me yesterday, were you, Dimwits?'

'But of course, Wing Commander,' said Glemnitz, who was respected by both sides as a first-class man and soldier.

'You *really* were?'

'Yes, Wing Commander. What else could I do?'

'But for heaven's sake,' Bader exclaimed. 'In England we wouldn't shoot the chap. We'd call a couple of guards and they'd each grab one arm and drag him out.'

'Not in Germany,' Glemnitz said comfortably. 'It would be against an officer's honour to be touched by a soldier. He must be shot.'

Bader put that in the back of his mind for the future, though he

---

[1] From Oliver Philpot's eye-witness account in his excellent 'Stolen Journey.' Philpot was the first of the three to reach safety in the famous 'Wooden Horse' escape.

remembered soldiers at Oflag VIB upsetting officers' honour with rifle butts.

In an hour or so the train stopped at a little halt. Glemnitz motioned him out and they walked a mile along a dusty road to an enormous area of barbed-wire cages. It was Stalag VIIIB – Lamsdorf – where over 20,000 soldiers were imprisoned. Bader was put in a room in Sick Quarters, a hut in a separate cage near the main gate, with another new arrival, John Palmer, a rear-gunner flight lieutenant who needed special treatment for a damaged foot. Palmer was almost a caricature of an English officer, with a cavalry moustache, very blue eyes and a clipped accent.

Through a window a day or so later they watched a party of soldier prisoners march down the road from the big compound and out of the main gate. Bader turned to Duncan, one of the RAMC doctors, and asked where they were going.

'Oh, only a working party,' Duncan said. 'Off to some town a few miles away. There are thousands out on them.'

'Mightn't be too hard to escape from one of those.'

'Hard?' said Duncan. 'It's a piece of cake.'

Bader looked at Palmer and Palmer looked at Bader, who looked again at Duncan.

'Could *we* get on to one of those parties?'

'Not legally,' Duncan said. 'But I know of someone who might help.'

That afternoon he presented three sergeants of the Lamsdorf 'X Committee,' and they started talking escape. First, Bader wanted to know, could he and Palmer get out on a working party?

The leader, eyeing him, said: 'You'll excuse me saying so, sir, but you might look a bit obvious going out. Still, I think we could fix something.'

A blinding thought struck Bader like a revelation. Leaning forward, eyes alight, he asked: 'Sergeant, do these working parties ever go out to aerodromes?'

In his mind was a vision of the map with Sweden only 350 miles away. Stealing an aeroplane was the God-sent answer. Let the Germans take him to one. And then . . . No days of stumbling among the enemy, hopelessly conspicuous, waiting for the end. No trains with police checks or weary miles to walk. No food or language problems. Just sneak in and take off and – oh, the sweet triumph of landing on friendly ground with a piece of expensive loot and asking the Ambassador for a ticket home!

'Sometimes, sir,' said the sergeant. 'I see what you mean. Just leave it to us, sir.'

Three weeks passed. The hospital was comfortable enough but ineffably boring. From the window Bader and Palmer saw many working parties straggle out of the big cage with their guards bound for the outside world. But before the main gate opened they were all stripped and searched in a hut next to the hospital. That was the catch. With his legs he would never pass a search stripped. Moodily he used to watch other prisoners sweeping the road right up to the main gates, and an idea began to dawn. He told the sergeant 'Big X,' who grinned approvingly.

The sergeant arrived one night with two tough-looking sergeant pilots – an Australian, Keith Chisholm, and an Englishman, Hickman (whom Bader had known in the Shell Company in London before the war).

'Now, look, sir,' the army sergeant said, 'there's a light working party going out to an aerodrome near Gleiwitz, up on the German-Polish border. Just the sort of thing you want, simple stuff like cutting grass and so on. If you and Mr Palmer would like to join . . .'

Bader and Palmer said that they would.

The sergeant indicated the two sergeant-pilots. 'These two chaps are going and a Palestinian who is a Polish-Jew and speaks fluent Polish. They're all going to escape into Poland and they've all got false identities. We'll fix you up with the same.'

Two days later he smuggled brooms and army battledress to them and that night Palmer shaved his moustache off.

The morning was warm and sunny, and they lounged on the front step of the hut, trying to look casual and brimming inside with excitement. The working party marched out of the big cage and the escort nudged them into the next door hut to be searched. Bader and Palmer grabbed their brooms, sauntered into the road and started sweeping. One by one the working party emerged from the hut and gathered in a loose knot by the verge. Bader and Palmer swept their way into them. The last man out of the hut dropped his kit which scattered over the ground. He started swearing loudly. The guards looked and laughed. Bader and Palmer handed their brooms to two of the working party, who swept nonchalantly on through the others, back towards the big cage. The swearer gathered up the last of his kit, the guards yelled 'Komm! Komm!' and the party marched up to the main gate. The escort showed passes, an Unteroffizier counted heads, swung open the gates and they walked through, breaking down the pace to a casual amble and clustering round the limping Private Fenton, alias Wing Commander Bader.

Someone took his kitbag and he whispered: 'For God's sake none of you chaps call me "sir." I'm just one of you.'

'Don't worry, mate,' said Chisholm. 'We're already awake-up to that.'

Into a train then at the little wayside halt, and as they rattled and swayed across the country for three hours he hugged the thought that the Germans were taking him to an aeroplane; in fact, were insisting on doing so. There came a sobering thought. It wouldn't take the Germans long to miss him and perhaps they'd put two and two together. He'd have to move fast.

On a blazing hot August afternoon they came to the grimy industrial town of Gleiwitz and started the two-mile uphill walk to the airfield. Within two minutes he was sweating freely and that started his leg chafing. A lanky New Zealand private called Lofty got alongside and helped him along, the others clustering round to hide them from the guards.

The leg was hurting him like that dreadful night in St Omer and Lofty, pouring with sweat himself, was almost lifting and carrying him. Even so Bader was nearly finished when they came to two huts in a tiny barbed-wire cage isolated like a poor relation on the fringe of what looked like a military camp. No signs of an airfield anywhere. Other prisoners came out to greet them as he staggered through the gate, and sagging with fatigue he asked one of them: 'Where's the aerodrome?'

The soldier nodded his head across a rise in the ground. ''Bout a mile over there, mate.'

'What sort of aeroplanes?'

'Gawd knows,' shrugged the soldier. 'They never let us anywhere near the airfield. We never even see it.'

In disappointment, pain and exhaustion he found a room with Palmer, Chisholm and the other two.

An hour later, reviving fast, he said to Palmer: 'We'll go with the other three when they nip off into Poland. If we can find some partisans we might get a wireless message back to England and maybe they'll send an aircraft over one night to pick us up.'

A British sergeant had been in the cage some time as camp leader and he came into Bader's room. 'We won't let the others know who you are, sir,' he said. 'It's safer that way. But it won't be so easy to hide it from the Germans. It's hard manual labour here, moving bricks, digging foundations, filling trucks and things like that.'

Bader knew his limitations well enough. The work would be physically impossible.

'I know,' said the sergeant, with joyful inspiration; 'you can be lavatory man.'

Bader stared at him.

'One chap's allowed to stay behind to clean the latrines and huts,' the sergeant explained. 'You can be him. We'll say you've been shot in the knee and can't walk properly.'

Bader started laughing. How the mighty are fallen. 'All right,' he said.

Chisholm had been walking round spying out the land and came back to report. The wire was only a single fence instead of a double and just outside it at the back of the cage was a field of high corn. There was a wash-house window only a few feet from the wire and it would be easy at night to crawl out of the window and snake through the wire into the corn – except that two guards kept patrolling the cage.

During breakfast next morning the Palestinian went out and started talking to one of the guards through the wire. He came back very excited. 'He is a Pole, that guard,' he said. 'Several of the guard company are Poles, forced into uniform by the Germans. He says they will help us. A Polish guard at night will keep the German guard talking on the other side of the compound while we get out.'

Bader said: 'To-night!'

'No. Not to-night. Two Poles are on guard and it would look suspicious. He is frightened the Germans would shoot them.'

'To-morrow?'

'No. There are two Germans on. But the night after will be a German and a Pole.'

This was Monday. They set the date for Wednesday.

Germans arrived shouting: 'Raus! Raus!' to muster the day's working party and as Bader watched them march out a grinning Cockney corporal thrust a bucket and mop into his hands. ''Ere y'are, Mum,' he said. 'Get cracking.'

He quite enjoyed himself sloshing out the latrines, not caring if he got his feet wet. It did not seem so odd in this camp for the noted wing commander to be washing lavatories – most of the prisoners had been captured at Dunkirk and had never even heard of him. The only thing that bothered him was whether the Germans would follow the trail from Lamsdorf before Wednesday night. Thinking about it only made it worse.

At evening the workers came back and he asked Palmer, who was sweaty and grimy: 'Did you see any aeroplanes?'

'Didn't even see the ruddy aerodrome,' Palmer said disgustedly.

The next day passed quietly enough. Same fears. Same routine. At sunset the Palestinian talked to the Polish guard who was going off duty and learned that the lone Pole who would be 'on' with a German the following night would do what they wanted.

Morning dawned, warm and sunny, perfect weather for escaping, but the day dragged interminably. At last about five-thirty the working party came back and the five rested in their room with the familiar zero-hour feeling fluttering in their stomachs.

At six o'clock boots trampled in the wooden corridor and a German voice shouted: 'Efferybody on parade! Efferybody on parade!'

Cursing, wondering what it was all about, the prisoners got to their feet and slowly shambled out. Raggedly they assembled on the trodden ground by the gate, where a Feldwebel stood watching and as they settled down he opened his mouth and shouted: 'Everybody will take their trousers down.'

The men who did not know burst into incredulous chorus, whistles, catcalls, rude remarks and giggles, but the order seemed to hit Bader in the pit of the stomach. He looked across at the sergeant camp leader who looked back and muttered: 'Hold tight, sir. I'll order the men to refuse.'

'And get yourself shot,' Bader said wryly. 'Thanks, sergeant, but it's no use. They still wouldn't take five minutes to pick me out.'

He swung round but yards of open space separated him from the possible shelter of the hut. No chance of getting there. No escape at all. The mind buzzed furiously and he knew he could not stand the indignity. Heaving himself forward he stumped up to the Feldwebel and said: 'I think I'm the chap you're looking for.'

The Feldwebel stared as though he could not believe it and at that moment a Hauptmann from Lamsdorf and six guards tramped through the gate. The Hauptmann saw Bader, recognised him and his eyes lit up. 'Ah, Ving Commander, I am *delighted* to see you again. Gootness, you *haf* caused troubles.'

He was very friendly, even when he suddenly added: 'Now perhaps Mr Palmer vould come forvard as vell.'

'Good lord,' said Bader. 'Has Johnny Palmer escaped too?'

'No more troubles, please, Ving Commander,' the Hauptmann said tolerantly. 'Otherwise we take you all back to Lamsdorf to check up.'

It struck him instantly that that would wreck the escape plans of the other three.[1] A moment's furious thought. No way out. He turned to the men and called: 'Come on, Johnny. It's all over.'

Palmer shuffled disconsolately out of the ranks, the guards closed round and the two were led away.

The trip back to Lamsdorf was glum, though the Germans were friendly enough right up to the time they prodded them into the Lamsdorf guardroom and the Kommandant came in. Or rather, the Kommandant swept in like a tornado, in a towering anger, a tall, cropped, fine-looking man of about sixty, with cold deep eyes and a tight-lipped mouth that opened and started shouting in German the instant he saw them. He stood in front of them, the tirade pouring out till little flecks of foam flew off his lips. It went on and on, and on, and the interpreter standing beside him had no chance of getting in a word. Palmer still had a cigarette in his mouth and as the Kommandant shouted he drew on it, puffed smoke just past the Kommandant's cheek, turned rudely away to Bader, and said in an extremely British voice: 'D'you know, I haven't the faintest idea what this fellow's saying.'

Bader started to giggle and the Kommandant crimsoned. His voice rose in explosive fury. At last he stopped to draw breath, and the interpreter stepped forward and spoke a stern summary:

'The Kommandant says you have both disgraced the honour of an

---

[1] That night the other three escaped as planned and soon made contact with Polish partisans. Later the Germans caught the Palestinian and Hickman and shot them. Chisholm, after two years of extraordinary adventures fighting with the Poles (including a gallant part in the deadly uprising in Warsaw), got back to England and was awarded the Military Medal.

officer by dressing yourself up as common soldiers and that you have caused a great deal of trouble.'

Bader said: 'Well, will you tell the Kommandant that it's my job to cause him trouble.'

The interpreter was tactless enough to do so and the Kommandant turned a rich red and loosed off another tirade until they thought he was going to have an apoplectic fit. At last he threw his arms in the air and shouted *'Arrestzellen! Arrestzellen!'* then spun round and strode off.

One of the few German words that Bader was familiar with was the expression for arrest cells.

Soon they were in familiar surroundings. An officer pulled open a cell door and Bader peered distastefully in at the familiar interior. With a sudden idea he said: 'Just a minute. I'm not going in there. These are common soldiers' cells. It is most incorrect putting an officer in them.'

The German security officer said politely: 'Ve do not usually haf officer prisoners at Lamsdorf und therefore ve do not haf officers' cells.'

'I can't help that,' Bader said. 'If I'm to have a cell I demand an officer's cell. I understand my honour has already been sufficiently disgraced.'

'Look, Ving Commander,' the German said wearily, 've haf had a lot of troubles vith you and vith the Kommandant. He vas going to take your legs, but I haf talked to him und he has cooled down. If there are more troubles he vill take your legs.'

'I can't help that either. Anyway, I demand a spring bed, not that damned plank.'

'Please go in, Ving Commander, und ve vill deal with it to-morrow.'

'No, I won't. I want a spring bed, I want a table, I want proper food and a proper chair. And while we're on the subject I want a sentence. You haven't sentenced me yet and that is most incorrect. I demand to know how long I'm in here for.'

The German, by some miracle keeping his temper, raised his eyes to the ceiling, muttering: *'Mein Gott!'* He said with resignation: 'Vait here, Ving Commander. I go and get, not, I think, for your sake, the Kommandant, but the second in command.' He strode out and Bader and Palmer waited with the guards.

Soon a dapper, red-faced German major came in and said fluently and heartily: 'I'm sorry about this, Wing Commander, but I'll tell you what we'll do. You can have a spring bed, a chair and a table, proper food and a book to read and I'll send you a servant. A batman. And to-morrow morning we will also sentence you. How's that?'

'Good,' Bader said. 'I'll wait outside the cell till you get them.'

Soon they brought spring mattress, table and chair, and he went in and the cell door locked.

Soon there came a thunderous knocking on it and he yelled: 'Come in.'

He heard the bolts being withdrawn, the door opened and in the frame, filling it, was the rotund figure of a young man with a round, red face and glasses. He was in British battledress and said in a strong Scots accent: 'Guid-after-rnoon, sir. My name is Ross. I've been detailed to look after-r you. I've br-rought you some tea.' He had a great mug of it in his hand.

That night, thinking it over, Bader felt some of his hate slipping. He had to admit that some of the Germans were incredibly decent and reasonable, and had a passable sense of humour.

In the morning he and Palmer were taken before the Kommandant who, cool and correct now, sentenced each to ten days' solitary. Bader again tried the gambit about the incorrectness of putting an officer in a soldiers' cell block and the Kommandant stiffly apologised. He did not have the correct cells so they would have to make do as they were. He hoped, a shade sardonically, that they would be comfortable.

The days in the cell seemed intolerable, and remembering the Battle of Britain and with the old frustration rising in him again like a tide, the hate came back. The only bright factor was Ross, who was loyal, willing and unselfish, bringing tea and gossip and spreading a respectful but companionable cheerfulness.

On the ninth day the cell door opened and the Kommandant appeared. Bader got up from his bunk and they exchanged polite salutes. The Kommandant said: 'I have some good news for you, Wing Commander. To-morrow you go to an *Offizierslager*.'[1]

'Oh.' Bader was interested. 'Whereabouts, Herr Oberst?'

'The Offizierslager IVC at Kolditz.'

Bader knew that one.

'Oh, you mean the *Straflager*?'[2]

The Kommandant looked shocked. '*Nein, nein, Herr Oberstleutnant, Das Sonderlager.*'[3]

Bader started to laugh and then the Kommandant started laughing. Both knew well enough that Kolditz Castle, last stop for the naughty boys, was supposed to be escape proof. The Kommandant went out and Bader stopped laughing.

Next day he made one last effort to delay things by demanding an officer of equal rank as escort, but the Kommandant said curtly that the only such officer available was himself, and he was the one who was *not* going to Kolditz. It was an elderly Hauptmann who got into the train with him and sat silently picking his teeth under cover of his hand. Ross was there too. When Bader had said he was bound for Kolditz, Ross said equably that it would be a nice change for them. Bader said: 'No, Ross.

[1] Officers' Camp.
[2] Punishment Camp.
[3] Special Camp.

Thank you very much, but it's the punishment camp, you know.' Then Ross had argued and argued until Bader had sent a note to the Kommandant who said Ross could go.

The journey was long and dreary and the Hauptmann never seemed to stop picking his teeth. By the time they got to Kolditz it was dark and the station was blacked out. Then, struggling out of the gloom into the road, Bader looked up and got his first glimpse of the future. The fortress towered over the village, seeming to float in floodlight, enchantingly beautiful like a fairy castle. They moved off along a cobbled road which soon rose so steeply that Ross had to put out his hand and pull him along. He was exhausted when they came to the foot of the great wall that reared above, harsh and scarred in the glare of the floodlamps, giving no inch of cover to any would-be escaper. They trod across a drawbridge over a deep moat into the cavern of a stone archway, out of the light. Heavy doors closed behind with a clanking of iron bars and in the gloom a sense of chill pervaded him. Fortress guards, boots ringing on the stone, led them across a courtyard rimmed by stone, through a tunnel, along a cobbled path, through another gloomy archway into a smaller courtyard hemmed inside towering walls deep in the bowels of the castle, through a door, up stone steps. A German flung a door open and Bader looked into a small, stone cell. He thought: 'Oh, God. Is this how we live? Is this the punishment camp?'

CHAPTER TWENTY-SEVEN

As a guard motioned him in, a voice behind hailed: Douglas! There you are!'

He swung round. Geoffrey Stephenson in an old sweater and army trousers was grinning by the steps. An incredibly warming sight. He looked much the same, though not so dapper, and came bounding up the steps. 'Heard you were shot down. Been expecting you. Knew you wouldn't behave.'

They were shaking hands, grinning and talking. As a German started to separate them Bader nodded at the cell. 'Is this how we live here?'

'Good God, no,' Stephenson said. 'You'll be out with us to-morrow.'

He was hustled away and Bader, feeling better and wanting only to lie down, walked docilely into the cell and the door clanged behind.

In the morning they took him out, photographed, finger-printed and searched him, and handed him over to the hovering Stephenson, who took him upstairs into a large and quite pleasant room with a big window overlooking the inner courtyard.

'Your home,' Stephenson announced. 'Hope you like it.'

In many ways it was the best he had known since becoming a prisoner. He shared it with three others, army officers, one of whom he already knew, George Young, who had been SBO at Lübeck. The four single bunks had shelves over them; there were some wicker chairs and even a dirty brown wallpaper hiding the stone walls. The castle had a good supply of Red Cross food and downstairs one could even get a bath, a thing he had not had for over a year.

Stephenson took him on a conducted tour and the rest was not so good. The grim old castle held then eighty British prisoners, 200 French and over a hundred Poles, Dutch and Belgians, and the only communal recreation space was the cobbled inner courtyard, forty yards long and twenty-two yards wide. All round it the walls towered seventy feet so that the cobbles in winter never saw the sun. He looked through a barred window on the castle's outer wall that was seven feet thick and dropped ninety feet to sheer cliff that dropped another hundred feet to a river. The stories about Kolditz being escape proof looked grimly true. Thirty miles south-east of Leipzig, it stood on a rocky peak that jutted into the river so that the only way out was the road up from the village, and to get to that one had to pass through the other half of the castle where the Germans lived. There were more guards than prisoners.

'Used to be a looney-bin before the war,' Stephenson said. 'It's quite a few hundred years old. Built by a chap called Augustus the Strong. We don't know much about him except that he was a pretty good performer. Was supposed to have 365 illegitimate children.'

'Not surprised,' Bader said. 'Not much else to do here. What's it like for escape?'

'Damn' difficult. Everyone's trying like hell but only one or two have ever got out. Tunnels are pretty well out, and you have to be a gymnast to get over the roofs. Best trick is probably to try and walk out in disguise but of course your walk would give you away.'

Within two days Bader had his first brush with the Germans, who then held two *Appells* a day. He told the Lageroffizier, Hauptmann Püpcke, that he was damned if he was going to spend his days lurching up and down the stairs and was so determined that Püpcke finally said he could appear at the window till he was seen and counted. Püpcke was a good-looking elderly six-footer and later became one of the few Germans Bader liked.

He had a long and depressing talk with George Young and a resolute-looking tank captain, Dick Howe, who ran the 'X Committee.' Howe, a brilliant and unselfish escape organiser, pointed out that Kolditz was not like an ordinary camp. Every man was an intractable escape fiend and all sorts of schemes were constantly going on, but even the most acrobatic and the fluent German speakers were having no luck. After that Bader sat back a while to think things out.

Plenty of time for thinking! The days started early with *Appell* and a slice of black bread. Then one could sit and look out of a window, or smoke and read, or sit, or walk round the little courtyard like an animal in a zoo. With escape hopes frustrated again he returned like an addict to his old sport and the repetitive theme of life at Kolditz was punctuated by a sort of a trumpet *obbligato* of Goon-baiting. Bader was not alone in that; he was merely worse than the others. Nearly every man in Kolditz had his record-card marked *'Deutschfeindlich'*[1] and bands of prisoners known flippantly as 'men of spirit' played noisy parts in the orchestrated discords of baiting, with the Maestro Bader making frequent appearances either as conductor or impressario.

Püpcke was not harried much; though alive, he was still regarded as a good German. The main butts were the security officer, a Hauptmann Eggers, and a little major, the second in command, who wore a cloak that gave him a musical comedy look.

For weeks Bader only acknowledged the major's existence by blowing smoke past his cheek when they passed and when the major at last demanded to be saluted Bader pointed out the difference in rank and suggested that if the major liked to wear the Kommandant's uniform into the camp he would salute him.

Often when sufficient sensitive Germans were in the courtyard prisoners in the windows bellowed an aggravating version of the German national anthem: *'Deutschland, Deutschland,* UNTER *alles.'* The taunting voice of Bader was usually identifiable, as it also was when the French started their favourite chorus: *'Où sont les Allemands?'*

A silence till the same voices answered: *'Les Allemands sont dans la merde.'*

'Qu'on les y enfonce?'

'Jusqu'aux oreilles.'

Bader also used to conduct his own leaflet raids, writing uncomplimentary messages in German on sheets of toilet paper and loosing them in a favourite wind from the Castle's outer windows to float down into the village.

Finally, the little major asked him into his office and with a determined smile suggested that life would be easier for everyone if he would be more courteous and set a better example in future. Bader said he did not think it was exactly his job to influence the prisoners to make things easier for the Germans. He enjoyed the heated debate that followed, though the major did not.

[1] Definitely anti-German.

The cheerful but unruly Peter Tunstall had arrived at Kolditz, having at this stage half-achieved his eventual record of six German courts-martial and 360 days in solitary confinement. He and Bader made a natural team. Tunstall had recently discovered an ingenious method of splitting a photograph so that a message could be written on the back, the photograph pasted together again and posted back to England. Bader wrote out a message for Tunstall to transfer to a photograph. It started: 'Message from Wing Commander Bader,' and included all he knew of conditions in Germany, the effects of bombing, the passage of troop trains and so on, and ended: 'The bombing is doing a lot of good. Bomb the bastards to hell.'

Tunstall put it in his wallet and a day or two later the Germans sprang a snap search in several rooms. When they tramped into Tunstall's room the wallet was lying loose by his bunk; he ran to grab it, but too conspicuously, and a German said: 'Give that to me!' Tunstall flung it out of the window but it fell at the feet of Hauptmann Eggers and Eggers walked off with it.

It was all a little disconcerting, but nothing happened for three weeks, and Bader was beginning to think that nothing was going to happen when Eggers shook him awake at six o'clock one morning, saying: 'Get up, Ving Commander. Ve are taking you to Leipzig.'

'What the hell for?' Being woken early did not improve his temper.

'Befehl ist Befehl,' Eggers said cryptically.

He was taken in a car with guards on each side, and it would have been good to be out of the grim old fortress but for the edge of uncertainty in him. In a room in Leipzig he faced a lean, severe German officer behind a desk, and the antennae signalled that it was a moment for wariness. The officer stared at a paper on his desk, then looked up and fixed him with a cold eye.

'I have two charges against you, Wing Commander. The first is that since you have been at Oflag IVC you have incited other officers to disobey and misbehave, and discipline has become very bad.' His voice was impressively icy. 'What do you say to a charge of inciting mutiny?'

'I don't know what you're talking about.'

'Well, now, I have a much more serious charge against you.' A pause. 'The charge of espionage!'

Another silence.

'We have captured a message you were trying to send home with items of military value.'

Leaning forward, Bader could just see on the desk the paper he had given Tunstall. The last line was heavily underscored and he remembered his provocative remark about the bombing.

'Military information!' the German repeated. 'Trying to send that message back is espionage and this will have serious consequences for you. You can be shot for it.'

With sudden inspiration Bader turned on a smile that he did not quite feel and said derisively, 'Don't talk absolute nonsense. Here I am, a British officer, in your custody, where I've been for a long time, in uniform all the time. . . . How can you possibly charge a captured officer in uniform with espionage?'

The point did not seem to have occurred to the German and he looked momentarily uncertain, then returned to the attack. 'Nevertheless, you tried to get information back.'

'I *would* try,' Bader said. 'So would anyone. But it doesn't make me a spy. Here I am. You see me in uniform. You're holding me. How can you possibly charge me as a spy?'

They argued about it for some time until the prisoner became too domineering and the German stood up and snapped: 'That is enough. You must be ready to go to a war court in Berlin on this matter.'

Bader walked out buoyantly enough but on the way back to Kolditz in the car he was not so confident. Half-way back he was stirred by a thought. . . . It would be rather neat to escape and miss the whole unpleasant business.

During the next two days he was seen muttering to Geoffrey Stephenson and Peter Storie-Pugh, a young army lieutenant. Then they discussed the scheme with Dick Howe's escape committee. They would crawl out of an attic window on to the steep roof high over the courtyard and away from the searchlights, scramble somehow up on to the ridge and crawl from there till they could drop into the German part of the castle. Then, skulking through the shadows and climbing over more roofs they would reach a point where the cable of a lightning conductor stretched to the ground a hundred feet below. After sliding down this they would drop by rope forty feet into the dry bed of the moat, climb over a couple of barbed-wire fences and terraces sown with anti-personnel mines and then make for Switzerland. Would the escape committee be good enough to cough up some German marks, forged papers and other details?

'You can't do it,' Howe tried to explain tactfully. 'Two or three teams have had a go at somewhat similar schemes and damn' nearly broken their necks. They were athletes in good training. I'm sorry, but with your legs you just couldn't make it.'

'Absolute tripe,' Bader snorted. 'Of course I could.'

After a turbulent discussion the committee sensibly suggested that they could not cough up the marks and forged papers (which were in short supply).

A few days later Bader was involved with some Poles trying to find a way out of the fortress through the sewer pipes. One of the Poles, Ravinski, lowered himself through a grating into the sewers and snaked through the slimy pipes looking for an outlet. He was back in an hour, reporting that the pipe got narrower and narrower until he could squeeze no farther. However, there were other pipes and he would try again. Ravinski's surveys of the maze lasted several days but each new lead either narrowed or ended in concrete dead-ends, and they knew dolefully that they would find no way out through the sewers.

After that Bader realised the futility of banging his head against a barred window, and under the bravura his practical sense accepted that he was not likely to escape from Kolditz. Though it did not make him any pleasanter to the Germans, he stopped fretting about the Tangmere wing and the fighting. Now it all belonged to another world.

Once he had faced it there were compensations. Swinburne was one; an odd escape for a man of action who seemed such an extrovert, but the dormant crannies of reflection were sensitised by adversity. Thelma, knowing him, had sent volumes of poetry and he read them nearly every day, never tiring of the sardonic Swinburne mocking fate. That was the thing!

> For the glass of the years is brittle wherein we
>   gaze for a span;
> A little soul for a little bears up this corpse
>   which is man.

If a demon disguised as fame was the spur, there was also armour for the flank. And if the past called too hurtfully he found another answer from Robert W. Service:

> Have ever you stood where the silences brood
> And vast the horizons begin.
> At the dawn of the day to behold far away
> The goal you would strive for and win?
> Yet, ah, in the night when you gain to the height
> With the vast pool of heaven star-spawned,
> Afar and agleam like a valley of dream
> Still mocks you a land of beyond.

(Till the day he dies he will remember each word of those pages and more.)

Other things helped too. The prisoners' secret radio had told them of Alamein and Stalingrad and every day it was becoming clearer that the days of wondering if the war would ever end were over.

An army officer wrote in a letter home: 'I had tea to-day with Douglas Bader and came away feeling as though I'd been having cocktails.'

The thought of the Berlin court-martial still gnawed a little but there was nothing he could do about that either except put on a brazen face and keep asking Eggers tauntingly: 'Well, how's the court-martial going, Eggers?' The Hauptmann kept assuring him meaningly that he would hear as soon as the Germans heard. Perhaps the Ving Commander would not be so happy then. Bader privately agreed.

Then came the day that Eggers, bracing himself to an unwelcome task, told him stiffly that the court-martial had been dropped (because the charge was 'frivolous'). Bader, hiding his relief but not his glee, said wickedly: '*Hard* luck, Eggers. Frightfully hard luck!'

Stoolball was another diversion – a rough one; strictly a Kolditz game, devised to let off steam. In the cobble courtyard two teams battled for a football, inhibited only by the flimsiest of rules which forbade actual slaying but approved of temporary throttling – or would have approved had there been such a refinement as a referee. There were no touchlines; one either bounced with dull thuds off the stone walls or was scraped off. Goals were scored by touching a stool with the ball at either end and the goalkeepers sat on the stools, thrusting vigorously with arms and legs till the avalanche of bodies threw them off on to the cobbles. Unable to join the mid-field mêlée Bader was an ardent goalkeeper and many plunging pates recoiled dizzily after contact with his metal legs. Eventually Dick Howe's intelligent but impregnable skull dented his right kneecap. Bader hammered the metal out again, but it kept getting dented, and at last he had to give the game up rather than be left with a permanently broken leg.

He was already having other trouble with his legs and the Germans escorted him to a village workshop for running repairs. As he later wrote to Thelma: 'The leg crisis has passed. A little man has riveted a plate over that crack in the knee. You might tell the chaps who made the leg that I completely dismantled the knee, the brake and the freewheel and greased and reassembled the lot. It is a very well-made job, the freewheel is most ingenious, but I do want another right leg, sweetheart.'

But in London the mould of his right thigh had been destroyed by bombing. The firm of J. E. Hanger and Co. (who now supplied his legs) tried tirelessly all sorts of ingenious methods of making another one (including telegraphed measurements through the Red Cross), but it just could not be done. They were, however, able to get a spare left leg to him through the Red Cross.

Bader began to suffer from the lack of exercise and outlet. It was partly mental. Even others found it bad enough walking round the sloping, uneven cobbles, but to him it was becoming intolerably irksome and bad for the legs. With the SBO's approval he asked the Germans if they would let him out for walks on parole, and after havering for a while the Germans, to their credit, sportingly overlooked his intransigence and agreed, even to letting him take another British officer for company. They did it probably partly out of kindness, certainly out of respect, and possibly because they thought it would make him a little less disconcerting.

As companion he chose Peter Dollar, a ruddy-faced lieutenant-colonel with whom he had become friends,[1] and they signed parole chits and were taken to the castle door where they found a German escort of a Feldwebel with a machine-pistol and two soldiers with rifles.

Bader instantly bridled.

'I've given my parole. I'm damned if I'll be insulted by an armed guard.'

The Germans answered that *Befehl* was *Befehl*, and Bader snapped: 'Well, I refuse to go. Come on, Peter, let's go back inside.'

It was an odd scene that followed. The Germans who went to such trouble to lock everyone in Kolditz then insisted with the strange rigidity of their race that orders said that the Herr Wing Commander was to go for a walk; therefore the Herr Wing Commander must go for a walk. The Herr Wing Commander said he bloody well refused and there was uproar till the tolerant Püpcke arrived and, like Solomon giving judgment, decreed that the escort should leave the machine-pistol and rifles behind. That still left them with pistols in holsters on their belts, but Püpcke explained that they were part of the normal uniform. Would the Herr Wing Commander mind? No, said the wing commander, he wouldn't mind and, honour and *Befehl* both satisfied, he walked. They went down through the village and sauntered for a couple of soothing hours beside pleasant fields, the escort ambling discreetly behind.

After that he went for walks twice a week, usually with Dollar, and mellowed slightly towards the Germans, refraining in good-humoured moments from murmuring *'Deutschland kaput!'* as he passed Eggers and the little major.

The invasion was a relaxing influence too, and when the Allies broke out of the German ring in Normandy even the fervent escape activity at Kolditz eased a little (though not much). The end seemed very near then and prisoners endured a little more stoically the dreary repetition of life that ran on and on like a broken record of a Bach fugue.

Occasionally, however, the needle slipped into another groove and eccentric variations enlivened the theme. Most prisoners had the disturbing experience of seeing men among them slowly crack under the mental strain and start acting oddly. At Kolditz a good-looking young RAF athlete took to playing a guitar in a wash-house with the guitar case on his head. He knocked at Bader's door one day, walked in carrying a bucket of water, came to attention before Bader, saluted, and said politely:

---

[1] They had tastes in common. The Germans had already court-martialled Dollar for insulting them.

'Excuse me, sir, but I don't like the things you've been telling the king about me lately.'

Then he threw the bucket of water in Bader's face, saluted and walked out again.

He was repatriated eventually, along with several others who were sick and maimed.

As Bader's legs had been giving trouble the SBO suggested that he be repatriated too, a suggestion which Douglas emphatically refused, declaring that his legs had not been lost in battle and therefore he was no different as a result of captivity. The SBO, however, put his name on the list when the repatriation commission arrived, and then when the Germans called prisoners from *Appell* to appear before the commission they left out the names of Bader and two very sick men. It was typical of the spirit of Kolditz that all the sick and maimed who were called – including some, like Lord Arundel, who were unlikely to recover – refused to see the commission until the three dropped names were restored.

Eggers called guards and tried to force them to appear, but the sick men stood fast and an ugly scene developed until the Germans gave way. It was pure principle. Bader himself had no intention of being repatriated, but the other two needed it. When called before the doctors and asked how he felt, he answered: 'Absolutely fit, thank you very much.'

'But,' said the chairman, 'your wounds are giving you trouble?'

'Not a bit. They're fine.'

'Are you sure you're all right?' The puzzled doctors had known plenty of prisoners who exaggerated their ills, but never one who did the reverse. One of them seemed to think that Bader should be repatriated on mental grounds, but he finally convinced them he wanted to stay and stick it out with the others. The other two, however, were passed for repatriation.

One day the Fortresses came. There had been a strange disembodied droning and then someone in the courtyard shouted and upturned faces saw the glinting shapes serenely dragging the thin, parallel lines of the con-trails like great rake-strokes across the blue patch over the high walls. Bader shouted: *'Wo ist die Luftwaffe?'*[1] and the rest took it up in chorus because there were no German fighters. It was an emotional moment seeing for the first time the Allied Arms reaching out unchallenged across Germany.

But the armies bogged down on the frontiers of a bravely fighting enemy and as the last leaves fell the prisoners who followed the war more acutely than anyone else guessed miserably that they were in for another winter.

Then the food parcels stopped coming and hunger came back.

[1] 'Where is the Luftwaffe?'

CHAPTER TWENTY-EIGHT

On the twice-weekly walks Bader and Peter Dollar began trading cigarettes with farmers for wheat, barley and eggs (which Dollar put under his peaked cap) to bring back to the communal food stores. It was strictly forbidden by the Germans, but usually a few extra cigarettes were enough to bribe the guards.

Little though it was, the food was such a help that Dollar eventually hung a pillow-case round his neck under his greatcoat, stuffed it with grain and came back looking suspiciously swollen. Everyone else was getting thinner and thinner, but the Germans at the gate never thought to search the rotund Dollar.

On the long walks back from the farms Bader was not able to carry much for a while. He badly wanted to try and carry a pillow-case like Dollar, but impervious as ever to cold he had never worn a greatcoat and the food committee thought it would look suspicious if he suddenly started. It only needed a search at the gate to destroy the whole scheme. Then an ingenious major, Andy Anderson, made him long, thin bags to hang down inside his trousers and he went out armed with those, banking on the fact that the Germans would always expect him to look odd below the waist, anyhow. Twice a week they went out looking gaunt and came back swollen like Michelin tyre advertisements, but the forty or fifty pounds of grain they brought were badly needed. That winter some prisoners lost up to three stones in weight and some had to rest half-way up the stairs.

It was the worst winter of all. For Bader it held some of the joy of accomplishment in bringing back food for his friends, but it took a lot out of him. His stumps were getting emaciated and it was hellish struggling back with the grain bags across the snow and up the slushy, slippery cobbles. As a matter of pride he hid it from the others almost completely, but Dick Howe a couple of times caught him off guard, walking into his room and seeing him lying exhausted on his bunk.

One of the RAF prisoners, Lorne Welch, a gliding expert, conceived the fantastic idea of building a glider and escaping in it by flying from the high castle walls. Two other cronies, Morison and Best, were helping him build it and Bader, as senior RAF officer, was roped in as consultant. They were making a rough wooden frame from bedboards and planned to cover the wings with sheets, sticking the contraption together with glue made from potatoes. As the pieces were made they dispersed them, reckoning that if the Germans found them they would never dream what it was.

To launch the glider they planned to cut holes through all the floors, one under another, and from the roof drop an enormous stone on a rope through these holes to jerk the glider, perched on the battlements, into space. It was to be a two-seater and Bader hoped that he might have a chance of one of the seats. The fact that it would have to be night flying as well (for secrecy) gave the scheme an added flavour. They hoped it would glide 400 yards, though, in fact, it would hardly be likely to travel more than a hundred feet, and that straight down at accumulating speed. (Luckily they were unable to finish it.)

Returning from a food-gathering walk one day, Bader's left foot seemed to disappear as he put it down and he fell forward on his hands. He looked down, surprised, and saw that his leg was broken by the ankle. As he tried to pull the sock down, the whole ankle and foot came away in his hand and he was staggered to see that the metal had corroded right through, apparently from perspiration which had gathered by the bottom of the ankle. There was nothing he could do except drag himself to the side of the road and send a guard back for his spare leg.

Dollar said unsympathetically: 'This'll teach you to change your socks more often.'

The guard came back with the faithful Ross carrying the leg and, unfortunately, a German officer too. As the officer solicitously bent down to help him change the leg it suddenly occurred to Bader that as soon as he took his trousers down the officer would see the full wheat bags underneath. That would be the end of the walks and the end of the extra food. He thought furiously, and then shook his head at the German, and said: 'Nein, nein,' and tried to blush and pretend he was shy. Watched by the startled German, he dragged himself behind some bushes, coyly changed the leg there and the crisis was over.

Spring came at last and with it the Allies pouring across the Rhine. The secret radio followed their progress on the news, and within the old castle grew a tremulous tension of impatience. On April 13 they heard that an American spearhead was only a few miles down the road and that night they went to bed with febrile excitement, knowing that it was nearly over, and yet unable to grasp it. After some hours they slept.

Bader was woken early by a roaring noise. He strapped on his legs and through the window saw Thunderbolts shooting up a nearby target. They went after a while, but soon he heard the sound of engines again and thought it was the Thunderbolts returning until someone yelled: 'Tanks!' Men rushed to the windows of the outer wall and two miles across the river, by a wood, saw gun-flashes and the crawling black beetles of armour. A fascinating and glorious sight! They were here!

The SBO, Willie Todd, appeared in the doorway and called soberly: 'Listen a minute, everybody. The Kommandant has just ordered that we are to evacuate the castle by ten o'clock. He says we're to be marched back behind the German lines.'

There was a stunned and icy silence. No one had dreamed that they would be marched away, though there had been rumours that Hitler was going to hold hostages.

Bader exploded: 'We aren't going to move now.'

'Don't worry,' Todd said. 'I'm going to tell him that, but I want you to be ready for anything if he brings up his Goons to winkle us out with guns.'

They waited tensely while Todd argued with the Kommandant. Apparently an SS Division was going to make a stand behind a nearby ridge; the castle would be in the battleground, and the division commander thought that it and the men inside might impede his defence. Todd threatened that an evacuation would not endear the Kommandant to the Allies and the Kommandant retired to think about this and contact the division commander.

The prisoners were planning to barricade themselves in when the Kommandant sent in a message to say that they could stay at their own risk, provided that no one hung signals out of the windows.

That afternoon the men at the windows saw more flashes and smoke from fires, and shells started screaming over the castle. Bader was watching through the bars with Dollar and Howe when a blinding light flashed in his face with an ear-splitting explosion and he found himself dizzily on his back in the middle of the floor with plaster falling on him and his ears singing like a kettle. In the top corner of the window the stone had crumbled where the shell had exploded. A little later in the Kommandantur, a Feldwebel watching from a window caught a shell in the face and was killed.

No one seemed to know what was happening and at dusk the situation was still confused, though the dogged German guards still stood at their posts and the sentries marched up and down the wired terraces below. Looking at them with admiration, Bader said to Dollar: 'Y'know, even if we tried to escape at this stage they'd still let fly at us.'

That night nearly everyone, paradoxically, was querulous. Some had been in captivity over five years and the last few hours were unnerving. Bader himself had been down now three and a half years.

The castle was nakedly sandwiched in an artillery duel, and all night the shells screamed and whistled over and banged joltingly on each side. At last, towards dawn, it was quieter and a few slept.

Bader came drowsily up from sleep to hear tramping feet in the courtyard and shouting. In an instant he was fully awake and strapped on his legs while others less impeded ran down ahead. He heard shouts coming up and impatiently, with a fast and eager dot-and-carry motion, clumped down after them. In the courtyard, through milling cheering prisoners, he was staggered to see American soldiers, and nearby a line of stolid German guards stepping up one by one to hand over their rifles. He stumped across and joined the laughing noisy mob shaking hands with the Americans who, for once, were quieter than the British but seemed almost as pleased. The noise went on for a few minutes and then it died down.

It was all over. They were free. How confusing and nerveless it was. No one quite seemed to know what to do or feel. The tension had snapped in a moment of joy that had flared like a roman candle, then left them groping in the afterglow.

Püpcke was there. Bader heard a British colonel say to him: 'I want to say that you yourself have behaved very well the whole time we have been here.'

Püpcke gave a little bow. 'Thank you.' And added quietly: 'You know, this is the second time I have seen my country defeated.'

Three American newspaper correspondents appeared and started firing questions at Bader. He was amazed to see that one of them was a girl, a real live girl, with red hair, in battledress, in the courtyard. After a while they said they were going back to First Army Headquarters at Naunberg in a jeep. Would he like to come?

He stuffed a few oddments and his books into a kitbag and then he was in the jeep driving out across the moat, down the cobbled hill and through the village where the white sheets and towels of surrender hung from nearly every window.

They drove fast and he did not feel like talking, but sat and watched the countryside, trying to let it soak in that he was free. But the cherished word had no meaning yet. He was drifting out of Limbo, the mists still round his head, and floating back over the Styx, cut off from the past and rootless in the present, unable to see the home shore, and oddly isolated from the Americans who were riding buoyantly across the everyday currents they knew. Behind he could still hear the guns.

Passing an airfield he recognised Me. 109s, all with broken bellies sagging on the ground. They looked different to the old ones – like tombstones.

'Krauts put grenades in 'em,' one of the Americans said laconically.

They passed an American armoured division moving up, an endless thundering snake of steel that amazed him. In the villages the children waved at the tanks and at him in the jeep. It was unreal.

Around dusk they came to Naunberg, and officers in the school-turned-headquarters greeted him warmly, but they were busy coming and going, doing things, and for all the warmth he felt an odd man out again. Then a British major, a young liaison officer, greeted him and he found a little footing. They dined on army rations and he filled himself gloriously and guiltily. The army bread looked snow-white and tasted sweet, like cake. Feeling better, he asked the major: 'Any Spitfires round here?'

No, the major said, they were all up north with the British forces.

'Can I get to them?' Bader asked. 'I'd like to grab one and get another couple of trips in before this show folds up.'

'Good God, man,' said the shocked major. 'Give it a miss and go home. Haven't you had enough?' He made it clear that it was futile.

Two officers took him through the blacked-out streets to sleep in a private house whose German family had retired quietly behind a blank door at the back. Browsing through the fruitily furnished living-room looking at the bric-à-brac of domestic civilisation, he stopped to look at an antique silver snuff-box.

'Hell, Doug,' one of the others said, 'take it. You don't have to be sorry for these bastards.'

He left it there. The trouble was he *did* feel sorry for them. Now there was nothing to fight, some of the hate seemed to have withered, but he felt it unwise to try and explain it to the others because they were still living in the war and would not understand. Later, he crawled into a feather bed and lay wide awake all night, not disturbed, just thinking, feeling for a grip.

By dawn he had it. Kolditz was a year away and he was in the present, still a trifle insecurely, but looking forward to the future with the old, practical sense that seldom looked back over his shoulder.

They drove him to an airfield where the busy officer clerks said it was forbidden to fly prisoners back yet, so he thumbed a lift with a cheerful young American pilot who said insulting things about bureaucrats and put him in the co-pilot's seat of his pretty little silver Beechcraft bound for Paris. With the rising engine roar, the surge of take-off and the gentle sway as they lifted, a well-remembered thrill tingled his blood.

The Beechcraft skimmed over bombed Coblenz and he looked at the decayed and stained teeth of the ruins with interest but no pleasure, thinking only how stupidly wasteful the war was. They landed on an airstrip in the Versailles woods and he found haven in a house where a dozen warm-hearted American officers offered him champagne to drink to his liberty, but unaccountably liberty did not seem to call for champagne and he drank Coca-Cola instead. Though they were tremendously kind and tactful he still felt awkward in his battledress, which was shabby. He was sitting, talking, when the commanding general tapped his shoulder and said: 'Come on, Doug. I've got your wife on the phone.'

It caught him off balance. He got to the phone and recognised Thelma's voice saying: 'Douglas! Douglas!' Then there was so much to say that

they could not say it for a while. A little later Thelma said: 'When am
. I going to see you?'

'A few days, darling. I'm looking for a Spitfire. I want to have a last
fling before it packs up.'

'Oh, God,' Thelma almost wailed. 'Haven't you had enough yet?'

He talked a long time trying to make her understand, which was
difficult because he did not quite know himself. He just wanted to be in
it again where he knew reassuringly that he belonged.

That night he slept and in the morning they drove him to Paris. At
RAF Headquarters he started telling them about Lucille de Backer and
the Hiècques, but they knew more than he did; the Germans had
sentenced all three to death, an intelligence officer said, but there was a
report that the sentence had been commuted to prison in Germany. They
were trying to trace them and would let him know.

Lucille too! He went out hoping very, very hard that they would all
be found safe – their fate was the only cloud on his liberty. He asked
about old friends on the squadrons and heard that a dismaying number
were dead. But Tubby Mermagen was in France and they got him on
the phone. He was at Rheims, an air commodore, and almost the first
thing Bader said was: 'Can you get me a Spitfire? I want to have another
crack.'

From the other end came a chuckle. 'We thought you'd say that. I
have strict orders from the C.-in-C. that you are not to have his Spitfire
or mine or anyone else's, but I'm to stuff you straight into an aircraft for
London.'

That afternoon Mermagen flew to Paris and did so.

The humble Anson ambled over the fields that used to be Bader's
hunting ground, but he could not recognise anything. Over the Channel
he began looking for England, but half as a stranger, with too many
tumbling emotions for anything so uncomplicated as simple joy. They
crossed the coast at Littlehampton and out to the left he saw Tangmere,
but only dimly through a veil of haze.

At Northolt Aerodrome, just outside London, the RAF gave him
sanctuary while the Great Machine sucked him in again, looking down
his throat, planting stethoscopes on him, giving him clothes, forms to fill
in, questions to answer and fending off clamouring reporters.

On the third morning, with leave for two months, he drove down to
Ascot and Thelma, free at last and for the first time tasting it fully. He
pulled into the drive, walked up the flagged path and as Thelma ran out
of the front door, two reporters stepped from behind a bush saying
cheerfully: 'Got you at last.' And the moment was spoiled.

Next morning he and Thelma fled to a private hotel in a little Devon
village and suddenly he could not face people, think coherently, make
any plans, or even read the letters that came pouring in. The extrovert

surface had cracked off and he was a raw-skinned creature wanting only to retire into an artificial shell of privacy with Thelma while he grew a . new skin to live in a new world. His fame had not died but become a legend and people were clamouring to see him, which made it worse. Some old friends called one day and he climbed out of a window to avoid them.

After three weeks they went back to Ascot where he climbed out of a window again to avoid some visitors. Another time he was trapped in the street by a strange woman who gushed over him with goodwill and bad taste. He stuck it out till she twittered: 'Now tell me ... in all the wonderful things you do without legs, what do you find the most difficult?' Bluntly he answered: 'Drying my bottom after a bath when I have to sit on a stool at the same time,' and walked on, leaving her standing.

One night he *did* enjoy meeting people. Sailor Malan, Bob Tuck, Crowley-Milling, Johnny Johnson and a dozen or so others of the old 1940 team gave him a welcoming-home dinner at the Belfry Club in Belgravia, and that night he felt at ease.

He got his old flying log-book back and entered up his last Tangmere flight of nearly four years before, with the laconic comment: 'Good flight near Béthune. Shot down one 109 F. and collided with another. POW Two 109 Fs destroyed.'

And underneath: 'Total enemy aircraft destroyed – 30.'

That was his own private total which he never mentioned. All successful pilots had such totals, which included those they were sure had been destroyed, but which had been impossible to confirm under the stringent official rules. As it was, under those rules he had 22½ confirmed.

From Paris he learned with joy that the Hiècques and Lucille had been found alive in Germany and were now in an Allied hospital, recovering. He wrote asking to be informed when they returned to St. Omer. News came that the French had sentenced Hélène, who had betrayed him, to twenty years in prison. Still feeling no hate, only vaguely sorry for her, he wrote to the French Government suggesting they cut her sentence to five years and then send her back to live in St Omer.

One day he drove to see Rupert Leigh at the Empire Flying School at Hullavington and Leigh gave him fifteen minutes dual in a Miles Master. Then he climbed into a Spitfire and twirled her round the air for half an hour, knowing with elation in the first minute that the touch was still the same. He landed with some of the old glow back in his eyes and a new confidence, and from that moment began to feel back in the swim again and to come resiliently out of his shell. Within two days he also began scheming for a posting to the Far East to fly fighters against the Japanese. The past might be past, but heady and consummating days might still lie within reach to make up for the life lost in the dead years in Germany. He put out feelers to the right quarters but the people at

Air Ministry, though kind, were not in the least co-operative. He had done quite enough, they said, and in any case the doctors said his stumps would give trouble in the tropics. They might be all right for a fortnight, but the way he sweated with the effort of getting around would soon bring on the rashes and the chafing.

He knew privately that the latter part, at least, was correct and when the usually tolerant Thelma added a stubborn veto to the project he grudgingly shelved the idea.

His old 242 Squadron adjutant rang him at Ascot one night. Now *Sir* Peter Macdonald and still a busy Conservative MP, he said: 'Douglas, it's about the general election. We want you to stand and we've got a very nice safe seat for you at Blackpool.'

'Sorry, Peter,' Bader said; 'but I'm not interested in being a politician.'

Nonsense, Macdonald declared. It was the duty of chaps like him to go into the House.

Getting back to his old form, Bader said pugnaciously: 'Look, I think all politicians are a lot of lousy so-and-so's, and I wouldn't be seen dead in the House.'

Those were the opening shots of a patient campaign to persuade the inflexible to change his mind. He kept saying 'No' with unmistakable vigour, but they persevered until he declaimed with some force: 'Now, look, whenever you want me to be saying yes I'll probably be saying no, and when you want me to say no I'll probably be saying yes, depending on how I feel. I won't be following any party lines. After five years of that no party would put me up for re-election, would they?'

Peace again.

Then in the RAF Club he met Air Commodore Dick Atcherley, the former Schneider Trophy pilot, who said: 'Douglas, I want a man to run the Fighter Leader School at Tangmere. It's a group captain's job. Would you like it?'

He answered with feeling: 'Yes, please.'

Eager for the comfort of harness again, he cancelled the rest of his leave and early in June drove nostalgically to the well-remembered Tangmere. He should have known better. The place looked the same, but that was all that remained of the old days. The tactics were new, the faces were new; above all, the atmosphere was new. It seemed to have turned upside down. Now there was none of the urgency or the inspiration of war, only a team of battle-weary men who wanted to shed the medal ribbons and be civilians again. He tried to revive some of the spirit but there was no spark left in the embers, and it brought only unhappiness, so when he was offered command of the North Weald Fighter Sector he took it.

It brought him control over twelve fighter squadrons spread over six aerodromes, but there was little joy in that either because there was no dynamic purpose any more: he was presiding over their disintegration. The great war machine of the RAF was breaking up as the bolts holding it together were withdrawn and great chunks chopped off and channelled back to civil life. He tried to preserve a hard core, but the best men would not stay because the RAF's future did not look encouraging. It was dispiriting, though at least without the hurt of memories at Tangmere. For miles around he could find no house for Thelma and had to fly disconsolately to see her at week-ends. At least he had his own Spitfire again, and had his old 'D.B.' painted on it.

A letter from Paris told him that Lucille and the Hiècques were back in St Omer and he immediately got into 'D.B.' and flew over there. When he knocked and the door opened, recognition was mutual and there was a tremendously emotional scene, everyone crying and laughing and kissing each other. The Hiècques had not changed as much as he had feared. Madame, a little more wrinkled, was still the same resourceful and compassionate soul, and Monsieur still brushed his cheek with the wisp of moustache. The brave Lucille was thinner and shy, and he could find no way of thanking them properly. The young man who had led him through the dark streets was not there: he had been missing for two years.

In the North Weald Sector one of his squadrons had Meteor jets and as a matter of both desire and duty he flew one. Oddly, the Meteor, which was soon to win the world's speed record at over 600 mph,[1] was the first twin-engined aircraft he had ever flown; also oddly he found that without legs it was easier for him to handle than any other aeroplane because there was no torque and therefore no need to prod the rudder much to correct swing on take-off or in the dive. Comforted by this it occurred to him that when the Far East war moved north to invade Japan the climate would not affect his legs. He was scheming a way of getting out to it when the atom bomb fell and the whole shooting match was over.

For the world, Bader rejoiced as much as anyone; for himself a little less. A tinge of regret itched for a few days but common sense soon dismissed the past, as it had dismissed his legs. Now it was the future that occupied him, like so many others, but he knew his own problem was different to theirs; it could be materially easier if he chose to stay with the RAF, but mentally and physically harder whatever he did. He had enjoyed the glory but you couldn't live on that. Anyway, there was no hurry. Get some of the mess cleared away first and then one could see.

On September 1 he found a letter from Group in his 'In' tray. It said

---

[1] Flown by Thelma's cousin, Teddy Donaldson.

there was to be a victory fly-past over London on September 15 to celebrate peace, and the fifth anniversary of the greatest day in the Battle of Britain. Three hundred aircraft were to take part, with twelve survivors of the battle in the van. Group Captain Bader was to organise the fly-past and lead it.

Stuffy Dowding arrived at North Weald early on the 15th and stood talking to the chosen twelve, looking much the same as five years earlier. The others looked a little different. Crowley-Milling, who had been a pilot officer in the battle, wore wing-commander braid and a DSO and DFC on his chest. So did Stan Turner. So also Bob Tuck and nearly all the others. The atmosphere was different too; they spoke more soberly and hardly mentioned the battle. Bader wound a blue polka-dot scarf round his neck, called: 'Let's go,' picked up his right leg and swung it into 'D.B.'s' cockpit.

Cloud was drooping over London and down in the grey streets the city gathered in stillness, some in tears, watching the cavalcade of three hundred sweep thunderously over the rooftops. Bader hardly saw them – Turner on one side, Crowley-Milling on the other, he was too busy picking his course through the haze. Once, over the city, he remembered the battle and for a moment, nostalgically, wanted to fight it again.

INTERIM EPILOGUE

Now the problem of what to do with life began to concern him urgently. The old dream had come true; the Air Force wanted him back permanently. Though still there was nothing in King's Regulations to cover his case, they offered to wipe out all the wasted years and give him the seniority he would have had if he had never crashed in 1931. He could keep his hundred per cent disability pension, and if he ever crashed badly again he could have another hundred per cent disability pension on top of that. It was more than he had ever dreamed possible – and yet . . . the legs would still not let him serve overseas in the heat, which would limit his experience and therefore his value and promotion. And this strange, post-war Air Force with its sinews cut was different to the dream, holding neither the proud purpose of war nor the old club warmth of 1931. He had achieved the peak and justified himself and the valley on the other side looked barren. Only the distant fields behind were green and he would never see them again except in memory.

The Shell Company wrote pleasantly to him and he dined with his old boss, who was affable and said: 'We've got just the job for you if you'd like to come back.' Douglas, he went on, could have his own aeroplane and fly all round the world on aviation business.

His own aeroplane! Virtually. And what a grand job! A week or two at a time in the tropics would not upset the legs much. It would give him the chance of world travel that otherwise would be lost for ever. They named a salary that was tempting, and said: 'Take your time. No need to make up your mind in a hurry.'

He took four months to think about it, and at the end of February decided. Writing out his resignation from the Air Force, he felt how odd it was that he should choose to turn his back on the old heaven to return to the old hell. Though this time a somewhat transformed hell!

The most heart-warming messages came to him – summed up in a sentence from the Chief of Fighter Command, Sir James Robb. 'All I can say is that you are leaving behind an example which as the years roll by will become a legend.'

In March when the time came to leave he did not feel so badly about it. The job was done and now he knew he would feel a part of the Air Force for the rest of his life. It was on a Saturday after breakfast that he took off his uniform, dressed in civilian clothes, and drove away from North Weald towards Ascot in the MG (a saloon car this time, obtained during his captivity by Thelma, who liked fresh air but in controllable quantities). There was no need to start work yet; officially, he was still on leave from the RAF for three months.

Most of that time he spent working on his golf. Before the war he had never taken a single lesson, partly because he could not afford it and partly because he thought that being without legs would call for a peculiar style so different from normal golf so that a professional could not help. Practising ardently at the Wentworth Golf Club with Archie Compston he soon found he had been wrong, and within three months he had reduced his handicap from nine to four, which is not likely ever to be approached by a legless man again and, in fact, is equalled only by about one golfer in a hundred. Dessoutter once told him he would never walk without a stick. He played Dessoutter, and beat him seven and six. If the little demon became restive in the doldrums of peace it already had something to ponder over. During these months he became increasingly involved in encouraging amputees and cripples. His very existence as much as his bearing and example was a tonic to them.

Late in June he and Thelma moved back to their old flat in Kensington and on the first Monday in July Bader went back to the office for the first time in six and a half years. This time he had an office of his own and the manager tossed him a letter. 'This'll interest you, old boy. We've ordered a Percival Proctor for you. It'll be ready in a couple of weeks.'

He went along to the Ministry of Civil Aviation to get his first private pilot's licence and the clerk when he gave it to him said apologetically, without mentioning the legs: 'Just for the records, sir, would you mind getting us a letter from some competent authority to say you are fully capable of flying.'

A few days later he collected the Proctor, a neat little single-engined cabin monoplane. She was a four-seater, silver with a blue flash down the side, and cruised at 130 mph. He was like a small boy with a new toy. As she was registered 'G-AHWU' (in alphabetical code 'George How Willie Uncle') he christened her 'Willie Uncle.'

In August he started his first trip, accompanied by Lieutenant-General Jimmy Doolittle, a Shell Company vice-president in USA. They were a good pair. Doolittle was another dynamic type, chunky and good-natured, able to be as friendly with office clerks as with directors. A former Schneider Trophy winner (1926), he was America's most noted pilot and had led the famous carrier-borne raid on Tokyo in 1942, one of the bravest feats of the war.

First stop was Oslo, where they had an audience with King Haakon, who was delightfully informal. ('That silly man Quisling came and stayed at the palace here during the war,' he said. 'A very foolish thing to do. The people disliked it intensely.')

In Stockholm a radio announcer asked him what his greatest thrill had been, and Bader said: 'Going round Hoylake golf course in seventy-seven a few weeks ago.'

Then to Copenhagen, The Hague and Paris and receptions in every spot. Doolittle beside him in the Proctor, he flew to Marseilles, Nice and Rome, across the Mediterranean to Tunis, Algiers, Tangier and Casablanca. With only a day or two in each spot and champagne and goodwill flowing all round, the pace began to tell, though Bader never touched the champagne. It was cumulative weariness that caught up with him in Casablanca where he sat next to a French general at a welcome dinner on a very hot night. His head was drooping on his chest as he tried to do his duty, saying: *'Oui mon générale, oui mon générale,'* until he actually fell asleep sitting there, toppling sideways until his forehead squashed into the remains of the fish course on the general's plate. He jerked upright with a *'Pardon, mon générale, je suis un peu malade,'* and they whisked him off to bed where he slept for eleven hours.

Back to London via Lisbon, Madrid and Paris, then off again in the Proctor for West Africa, 'White Man's Grave,' where he could test his legs in the tropics for the first time. Down through Bordeaux, Perpignan, Barcelona, Tangier and Agadir into the steamy heat of Dakar, Lagos, to Leopoldville in the Belgian Congo. Most of the time he flew over jungle that stretched as far as the eye could see and looked like parsley from 7,000 feet, but was quite as dangerous as flying over oceans in a single-engined aircraft. Had the engine failed Bader would have had no chance. Once, in fact, the engine did stop and he was gliding down in a highly disconcerting silence with the propeller windmilling when at about a thousand feet as he was tightening his belt and getting ready to hang on to the crash-pad, the engine suddenly coughed and started again.

Sweat from steamy West African heat soon made the stumps uncomfortable but talcum powder kept the heat rashes under control for three weeks until he was on the way back.

In 1947, on Doolittle's invitation, he went on Shell business to the USA which had 17,000 amputation cases from the war, and visited several veterans' hospitals to help men learn to walk again. He found one who had lost both legs below the knee and was struggling between the kind of low parallel bars that Bader had first seen at Roehampton. Without an introduction he stumped over, and said: 'Why don't you come out from those bars and try walking without 'em?'

Not unnaturally the man growled: 'Who the hell are you?'

'Just a Limey travelling through, but I've lost 'em both too, and I've only got one knee, not two like you.'

'Let's see you walk.'

Bader stumped up and down the room.

'I don't believe you,' the man said.

Bader pulled up his trouser legs and showed him, and the man said: 'Well, goddam.'

He lurched out, and Bader got on one side and helped him to struggle up and down the room. After a while the man was able to take his first couple of steps unaided and his whole manner had changed.

'You figure I'll be able to dance?' he asked.

'Don't see why not. I do.'

'Hell,' the man said. 'I nearly shot myself when I woke up this morning, but I reckon now it's all right again.'

In Chicago Bader read of a small boy of ten who had spilled burning petrol over himself and had both legs cut off below the knee. Douglas, who would do almost anything for children, spent an hour and a half by his bed, showing him that legs did not matter so much. Later the boy's father said worriedly: 'The boy just doesn't realise how serious it is yet.'

Bader said passionately: 'That's the one thing he must *never* realise. You've got to make him feel this is another game he's got to learn, not something that will cripple him. Once you frighten him with it he's beaten.'

That in a nutshell was the Bader philosophy, concerning not only legs but life itself. He spoke to the boy's father for twenty minutes impressing it on him.

In San Francisco he met Harold Russell, the American soldier who had had both hands blown off and been fitted with a pair of mechanical hooks that worked like hands. At that time Russell had just finished his part in the Oscar-winning film, *The Best Years of Our Lives*. Bader found him having dinner with Walter McGonigal, a World War I veteran who had lost both hands and used the same kind of hooks. As Bader lurched in Russell got up with a mouthful of steak and put out his hook to shake hands. Laughing, Bader watched the two of them handling their knives and forks with amazing dexterity. 'Have some coffee,' Russell said, picked up a coffee pot in one hook and a cup and saucer in the other and poured. McGonigal flipped a cigarette out of a packet into his mouth, pulled out a box of matches, picked one out with a hook, struck it and lit his cigarette. It was amazing to watch the two of them enjoying life, unbothered by the hooks, spreading their own bread, stirring their coffee, flicking ash off cigarettes and stubbing them out, all with the hooks.

'I don't know how you do it,' Bader said admiringly.

'Well, I dunno how *you* do it either,' said Russell. 'I'm glad I lost my hands and not my legs.'

In Los Angeles a telegram was waiting. 'Welcome, chum. Ring me at the studios up to six o'clock. David Niven.' He did so, and next day was playing golf with Niven, Clark Gable and James Stewart.

Back in London he took Thelma with him in the Proctor on his next trip, a tour of Scandinavia, and at Tylosand he entered for the Swedish golf championship and delighted everyone by winning his first-round match, then was beaten in the second.

Next journey was down to West Africa again and this time he flew on to Pretoria to meet Field Marshal Smuts, and for a gay reunion with Sailor Malan in Johannesburg, where he also caught malaria and lost two stone in weight in five days. That bout emaciated the stumps so that it was days before he could walk properly again. Later came a trip to the Middle East, Tripoli, Benghazi, Tobruk, Cairo, Cyprus and Athens. In time left over from work he visited several limbless people and the warmth he showed them was in inverse ratio to the pulverising vigour he still turned on tiresome people such as bureaucrats. One day he landed at Tangier, tired after nearly seven hours in the air from Las Palmas, and when he opened his bag in the Customs shed an unshaven official dug grubby hands into it and began pulling the clothes about. Bader grabbed the bag, up-ended it and shook everything out on the table.

'There, you clod,' he said wrathfully. '*Now* look at it!'

The Customs man did not understand English, but the gist was unmistakable. Red-faced, he said in French, his voice rising: 'I have examined the baggage of Englishmen, Americans, Frenchmen, Spaniards, Italians, Greeks, Swedes, Danes . . . and they are all gentlemen except you.'

In the violent debate that followed Bader gave the game away by starting to laugh.

In 1948 he took Thelma with him in the Proctor out to the Far East, and on the way out an Athens newspaper ran his photograph with limbless Greek veterans, referring to him as the 'famous cripple.' Cripple! Servicing his own aircraft in all weathers he flew by way of Turkey, Damascus, Baghdad, Basra, Bahrein, Sharjah, Baluchistan, Karachi, Delhi, Allahabad, Calcutta, Akyab, Rangoon, Merui and Penang to Singapore. From there they went by air to Borneo, Celebes, Java, Bali and New Guinea, covering over 20,000 miles. Only a few years before men with legs had their names blazoned to the world for doing trips like that in single-engined aircraft. In the two months they were away Douglas sweated off many pounds and Thelma put on a stone, earning the new nickname of 'Chubby.' She lost the weight when she got back, but lost only two letters from the nickname, which is now permanently 'Chub.'

Bader was always sorry he could not take the third member of the family on his overseas trips. Shaun was a handsome and intelligent golden retriever and Douglas was utterly devoted to him. He seldom played golf without Shaun loping along beside, and on flights within Britain Shaun usually climbed nonchalantly into the aircraft and flew with him.

In 1949 he took to flying twin-engined aircraft and delivered a Percival Prince to Singapore (taking Thelma again). In 1951 the company thought he should have two engines on his long trips so he changed the Proctor for a twin-engined Miles Gemini which he immediately flew to the Congo.

After a time in London he is off again, sometimes flying himself by Gemini, sometimes delivering a new aircraft to out-of-the-way places, sometimes by airliner. For a man who might be excused for living in a wheel-chair he is fantastically peripatetic, liable to pop up in almost any corner of the globe at any time. Often his golf clubs go with him, and often Thelma too. If you told him to go to Timbuktu he could answer truthfully: 'I've been there.' He has flown forty-seven different types of aircraft now and some fifty or more countries have known memorable and often repeated contact with his exuberance.

Probably no one has done as much for the limbless as Bader's example, which inspires them in a way no doctor can emulate. Tinny Dean, for instance, his old pre-war rugger and golfing partner, had a leg blown off in a Western Desert tank battle and wrote afterwards to Bader, truthfully, that he was not at all concerned about it.

In 1939 a young naval pupil-pilot, Colin Hodgkinson, lost both legs just like Bader in a collision. After Bader's example he was able to talk his way into the RAF and flew Spitfires on operations (later, by a coincidence, being shot down and captured, badly injured, by the Germans, though he never met Bader in prison camp). Hodgkinson, too, plays golf and squash and dances on his artificial legs.

There was Richard Wood, Lord Halifax's son, who had both legs blown off when he trod on a mine in the Western Desert. Oddly enough, he was nursed in hospital by Geoffrey Stephenson's fiancée and after hearing about Bader from her, wrote to Thelma (Douglas was then in prison camp): 'When I woke up from the operation I asked if I would ever be able to walk again and they said, 'Of course, look at Douglas Bader.' Ever since then I have been determined to do whatever he has done and be to others without legs what he has been to me. I should love to meet him sometime and thank him myself. I have just got my legs and started walking.

(Wood's legs are both off above the knees but he walks with only one stick and is also an MP.)

It seldom occurs to me when with Bader that he has no legs, a common experience with those who know him. Bader himself has forgotten the feeling of ever having his own legs, except sometimes, weirdly, when he still gets the phantom feeling of his feet. Some of the nerves and muscles are still in his stumps so that he can wiggle them and feel that he is wiggling his toes. He puts on his legs in the morning as casually as I put on my shoes and this casual acceptance is deceptive. The legs are never entirely comfortable and often are hurting him though he will not confess it. Rarely, in the most intimate circle, there may be a fleeting sign: that is all.

Playing golf with him once in Cornwall he gave no sign of pain but suggested at lunch that the afternoon round might be deferred. I said flippantly: 'You're getting soft,' but when he took his right leg off the thigh was raw and purple all round the top because the metal socket had been dented slightly. It must have hurt wickedly struggling round the course. Next morning a spare leg arrived in a cricket-bag on the train, and with the raw patch taped over, he was playing again. His secret is simple and sounds trite; it is merely that he will not yield.

In 1948 he won the Nineteenth Club's Challenge Cup, playing thirty-six holes (medal) in one day over the hilly Camberley course whose narrow fairways are flanked by thick heather. A full day on that course would tire any man. Bader's off-the-stick card was a 79 and an 82. He was as fit as most athletes of twenty-five, and Rupert Leigh was convinced he would still be playing fly-half for England if he had not lost his legs. At Cranwell they hung an oil painting of him by Cuthbert Orde in the gallery over the main hall, and that stirred him considerably.

He is still a mixture of modesty and ego. In a swashbuckling way he is given to bragging about his golf scores as blatantly as a fisherman describing the one that got away. People who do not know him well have resented that, but they have never heard him brag about important things.

It was not from Bader I learned that he would have played rugby for England, and the research for this book was nearly completed before I discovered by seeing one of his old uniform tunics that as well as two DSOs and two DFCs he also holds the Légion d'Honneur and the Croix de Guerre. They were awarded for his fighting over Dunkirk in 1940 and over Northern France in 1941, but that I had to learn elsewhere too. All Bader would say was that the French Ambassador kissed him on both cheeks after pinning the medals on him.

He rarely, if ever, wears his uniform now. Once he did at a Battle of Britain Day at North Weald in 1949 with other famous pilots. Richard Dimbleby, noted BBC commentator, held a microphone in front of their faces and they spoke a few self-conscious words. A boy of about twelve who could hardly have remembered the battle slipped through the police barrier and walked up to them with an autograph book. He gave it to Dimbleby who signed it and the boy took the book again, innocently turned away from the pilots and walked back to the barrier. The war was really over.

People are too easily deceived by Bader's swashbuckling. Underneath is a generosity easily touched by other people's adversity so that he finds it difficult to walk past a beggar without wanting to help him. He lost a lot of money lending to old associates after the war. Now he prefers to give rather than to lend. He is still as much a man of extremes as ever, blowing hot or cold in enthusiasms, an intensely loyal friend, an uncompromising foe.

I once heard someone suggest that Thelma must have a difficult time with such a man. She doesn't. I have seldom seen a more devoted couple and Thelma is no door-mat. When she decides that enough is enough she waits with unerring timing for the right moment, and then when she sticks her toes in Douglas cannot budge her. Neither is afraid of crashing when they fly in the same aircraft because then they would go together. He will not let her fly without him because, though he does not fear death himself, he cannot bear the thought of those close to him dying. The one thing he fears is loneliness. He has beaten everything else, but that he will never conquer.

I agree with all those who class him as the best fighter leader and tactician of World War II (and one of the best pilots). Also, I know of no other fighter tactician so outstanding in other wars. But his main triumph is not his air fighting: that was only an episode that focused a world's attention on the greater victory he was achieving in showing humanity new horizons of courage, not in war, not only for the limbless, but in life. Sometimes I know he looks back at the war days with nostalgia though not with faint longing. One's life can carry memories without succumbing to them. At times I know he feels lurking regret that his great days are over, not realising that they will never leave him. I do not mean the aura of the past. Bader's war goes on unsung and unceasing to be won anew each day. He has been honoured for courage and skill in the air against the enemy, but no one yet has thought to honour him formally for his continuing fight which profits Man more than his battle deeds. He himself has not considered that as he should; his nature would welcome a more urgent and spectacular battle than the repetitive daily one.

I am no churchman, being unable to imagine God as the rigid Victorian patriarch that some dogmas suggest, but sometimes a vagrant thought intrudes that some hand not of this world may be using Bader as a vessel bearing another lesson for Man in his struggle. Otherwise, it seems odd that the man most fitted to lose his legs and rise above it should do so and reveal the new horizons by means of a war that tested the old ones. Or it may be coincidence, if a long one.

There was the strange intervention of Dingwall, helping him get through school to Cranwell. There was the meeting with Halahan at Air Ministry in 1939 that led to his being accepted for flying again. (That was an odd coincidence – he was summoned by mistake for a ground job.) There was the weird affair of having his right leg ripped away when he baled out. Had the artificial leg not torn away he would have landed on it and very likely been cruelly maimed. And had a real leg been caught he would have been dragged down to death.

How, then, to end this story of a man whose life is not ended. With its meaning? That is a task for Shakespeare:

'There's nothing either good or bad but thinking makes it so.'